W9-CZY-164

THE BEST PLAYS OF 1967-1968

THE BURNS MANTLE YEARBOOK

EDWARD ALBEE

EDITED BY OTIS L. GUERNSEY JR.

Illustrated with photographs and with drawings by HIRSCHFELD

DODD, MEAD & COMPANY
NEW YORK · TORONTO

Library of Congress Catalog Card Number: 20-21432

Printed in the United States of America

EDITOR'S NOTE

IN THIS, the 49th volume of *Best Plays* yearbooks in the series begun by Burns Mantle in the season of 1920-21, we have once again broadened our base of coverage to match the theater's broadening activity. For example, the influence of what for lack of any really satisfactory name is called "off off Broadway"—the informal cafe-and-loft tributary theater in New York City—is becoming stronger and stronger. Off-off-Broadway philosophies and techniques are flowing into the larger streams of production both in America and in Europe, refreshing them and stimulating a reappraisal of theater values. So it was important for *Best Plays* to make the off-off-Broadway scene, where so much was at, in the season of 1967-68. To our usual complete record of professional production on New York stages we have added a list of leading production units in the tributary theater, with details of their most interesting work, compiled by R.J. Schroeder, a critic who explores the alleys of New York theater experimentation and who has reported back to *Best Plays* readers in an article as well as in the listing.

We have added to this volume an expanded section on "The Season in Los Angeles" with an article by Gordon Davidson, artistic director of the Mark Taper Forum, and a summary of highlights by Dale Olson, in line with Los Angeles's increasingly active legitimate theater scene. At the same time we have retained Ella A. Malin's coast-to-coast survey of regional theater programs in "Directory of Professional Regional Theater," introduced by an article by Ruth Fischer, program editor and press representative for The Cleveland Play House, on the regional theater's movement toward "a theater of relevance." This year Miss Malin has included a statistical analysis of the scripts being produced for audiences across America. On the other side of the Atlantic our European Editor, Ossia Trilling, has done his customarily thorough job in listing the major London and Paris productions and reviewing the Continental season in an article. And again Frank Marcus, the British playwright and critic (whose new play, *Mrs. Mouse, Are You Within?* is a West End hit), reviews the London theater year for *Best Plays*. And David Jones, an associate director of the Royal Shakespeare Company, has introduced our Shakespeare and summer festival section with a report from the inside on the achievements and goals of his famous Stratford-upon-Avon troupe.

To the authors of 1967-68's Best Plays, presented in synopsis with liberal quotes to communicate the flavor of the scripts, we are most grateful for keeping the theater itself (and therefore this volume) in good and stimulating form. We owe particular thanks to those playwrights who have chosen to contribute introductions to the synopses, in direct communication with our readers. One of the Best Plays—Neil Simon's *Plaza Suite*—is synopsized in photos to convey the total "look" of 1967-68 Broadway production. A large photo section records the season's acting and production highlights, no small thanks to Friedman-Abeles, Martha Swope and other photographers who cover the theater; and with special thanks to the season's outstanding designers who contributed scenery and costume sketches for reproduction here. Special thanks also to Al Hirschfeld for his drawings which so vividly depict the mood, style and personality of the entire theater season in a few brilliantly informed strokes of the drawing pen.

Obviously, this volume is the work of many hands and talents. It could not exist without the generously willing and expert cooperation of the Broadway and off-Broadway press agents and production staffs, who specialize in cheerful and precise answers to the most irritating questions of detail; nor could it exist without the patient and painstaking assistance of my wife, and her companionship in maintaining an enthusiasm for the theater even while sloshing through the snows of a February night. Among those who made essential contributions to this volume were Jonathan Dodd of Dodd, Mead and Company; Rue Canvin (off-Broadway listings, Shakespeare listings, necrology and publications); Bernard Simon (bus-truck tour information); Ralph Newman of the Drama Book Shop; and Hobe Morrison and *Variety*. To them I extend my sincere thanks for myself and in behalf of the readers of *The Best Plays of 1967-68,* whose enjoyment is both cause and effect of all their fine efforts.

OTIS L. GUERNSEY JR.

June 1, 1968

CONTENTS

Drawings by HIRSCHFELD

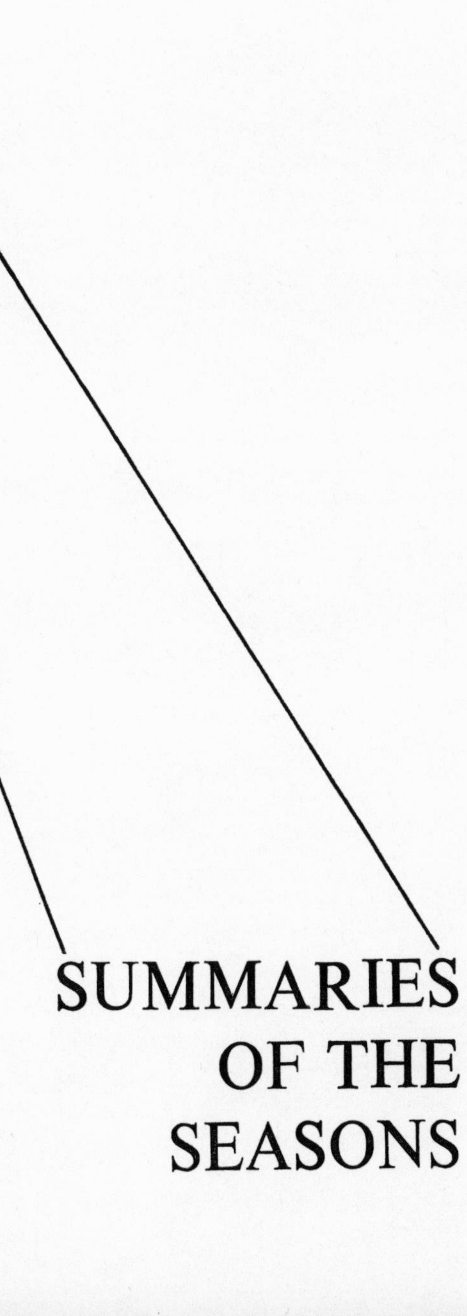

SUMMARIES OF THE SEASONS

○
○
○

THE SEASON IN NEW YORK

BY OTIS L. GUERNSEY JR.

○
○
○

THE NEW YORK theater season of 1967-68 was allergically sensitive to the temper—or, rather *dis*temper—of the times but held few mirrors up to contemporary events. This year of shocking assassinations, when the city, the state, the nation and the world were in an acute phase of sociological and political distress, dramatists were peering almost myopically at the intimate stresses of the human psyche. By far the most popular single subject was sexuality—dramatized or lampooned in all four or five sexes. Intrafamily stresses also came in for a large share of attention. With a few exceptions, shows which edged too close to the factual issues of the day wilted like the wings of Icarus in the sun's rays. The distemper of this era of disillusionment, this age of anxiety, was clearly evident in the blackness of the comedies, the absence of anything like *joy* from the theater's mood; or, to put it the other way, in the fact that "square" theater was out and even the most sorrowful subjects must be twisted into odd, wry shapes before presentation to an audience.

This was not an escapist season by any means. The Broadway musical stage, that traditional refuge of the tired business man, was becalmed and rolling in mediocrity, even in a season in which it might have attracted more audiences than usual, because *everybody* was tired. But if the season was not escapist, neither did it aim for semi-documentation of these times. In its close attention in rich playscripts to father-son relationships; to husband-wife stresses both comic and pathetic; to homosexuality in several phrases, the New York theater both on and off Broadway was going to the root rather than the branch of our discontent for its material.

American playwriting brightened in 1967-68, and its light shone out and around the towering scripts imported from England. The New York Drama Critics Circle and the Pulitzer Prize committee withheld awards for American playwriting; well, that's their hang-up. It's true that the season's very best play, in my opinion, was a British script—*A Day in the Death of Joe Egg* by Peter Nichols—and British work further stimulated the New York season in Tom Stoppard's *Rosencrantz and Guildenstern Are Dead,* Charles Dyer's *Staircase* and John Bowen's *After The Rain.* Right up among these on the 1967-68 Best Plays list, however, were three substantial scripts by veteran American playwrights: *The Price* by Arthur Miller, *I Never Sang for My Fa-*

The 1967-68 Season on Broadway

PLAYS (25)

Dr. Cook's Garden
Johnny No-Trump
Daphne in Cottage D
What Did We Do Wrong?
More Stately Mansions
The Trial of Lee Harvey Oswald
The Ninety-Day Mistress
Something Different
Everything in the Garden
Spofford
How To Be a Jewish Mother
Before You Go
The Prime of Miss Jean Brodie
I NEVER SANG FOR MY FATHER
Avanti!
THE PRICE
PLAZA SUITE
Carry Me Back to Morningside Heights
The Guide
Weekend
The Seven Descents of Myrtle
Mike Downstairs
The Exercise
Happiness Is Just a Little Thing Called a Rolls Royce
The Only Game in Town

SPECIALITIES (6)

Judy Garland at Home at the Palace
Eddie Fisher-Buddy Hackett at the Palace
Marlene Dietrich
By George
Brief Lives
Portrait of a Queen

MUSICALS (10)

Henry, Sweet Henry
Now Now, Dow Jones
The Happy Time
Darling of the Day
Golden Rainbow
Here's Where I Belong
The Education of H*Y*M*A*N K*A*P*L*A*N
George M!
I'm Solomon
Hair

REVUE (1)

Leonard Sillman's New Faces of 1968

REVIVALS (16)

South Pacific
Life With Father
The Tenth Man
The Little Foxes
Lincoln Center Rep:
  Saint Joan
  Tiger at the Gates
  Cyrano de Bergerac
APA-Phoenix:
  The Show-Off
  The Cherry Orchard
Brigadoon
City Center:
  The Pirates of Penzance
  H.M.S. Pinafore
  The Mikado
  The Yeomen of the Guard
  Patience
The King and I

FOREIGN PLAYS IN ENGLISH (17)

Sing Israel Sing (reopening)
The Unknown Soldier and His Wife
Keep It In The Family
Song of the Grasshopper
The Birthday Party
A Minor Adjustment
AFTER THE RAIN
ROSENCRANTZ AND GUILDENSTERN ARE DEAD
There's a Girl in My Soup
Halfway up the Tree
The Promise
APA-Phoenix:
  Pantagleize
  Exit the King
STAIRCASE
A DAY IN THE DEATH OF JOE EGG
Loot
Soldiers

FOREIGN-LANGUAGE PRODUCTIONS (9)

Jewish Theater of Poland:
  Mirele Efros
  Mother Courage
The Grand Music Hall of Israel
Les Ballets Africains
Vienna Burgtheater:
  Professor Bernhardi
  Das Konzert
  Maria Stuart
  Einen Jux Will Er Sich Machen
The Venetian Twins

HOLDOVER SHOWS WHICH BECAME HITS DURING 1967-68

BLACK COMEDY
CABARET
Don't Drink the Water
THE HOMECOMING
I Do! I Do!

Categorized above are all the plays listed in the "Plays Produced on Broadway" section of this volume.
Plays listed in CAPITAL LETTERS have been designated Best Plays of 1967-68.
Plays listed in **bold face type** were classified as hits in *Variety's* annual list of hits and flops published on June 5, 1968.
Plays listed in *italics* were still running on June 1, 1968.

ther by Robert Anderson and *Plaza Suite* by Neil Simon. It's true that plays by Edward Albee, Frank D. Gilroy and Tennessee Williams fell short of their authors' best work, but on the British side so did plays by Harold Pinter and Bill Naughton. The theater is measured by its successes, not its average, and the dynamically creative state of American playwriting, its sheer vitality, was conspicuous in the three off-Broadway scripts on the Best Plays list—*Scuba Duba* by Bruce Jay Friedman, *Your Own Thing* (winner of the Critics Prize for Best Musical) by Donald Driver, Danny Apolinar and Hal Hester and *The Boys in the Band* by Mart Crowley—all professional playwriting debuts. Even in two shows that ranked so near to the top ten as makes almost no difference—*The Prime of Miss Jean Brodie* by Jay Allen and *Hair* by Gerome Ragni, James Rado and Galt MacDermot—American playwriting (in two more professional debuts) shone. Let's try it the other way around, to test it: 1967-68 was a dim year for our dramatists, who produced only *The Price, I Never Sang for My Father, Plaza Suite, Scuba Duba, Your Own Thing, The Boys in the Band, The Prime of Miss Jean Brodie* and *Hair.* Nonsense.

Statistically this season showed manifold improvements over last. There were 84 programs produced on Broadway in 1967-68 (see the one-page summary accompanying this article), as compared with 78 last season, 76 the year before and 81 the year before that. Last season's total was overloaded with revivals; this season the volume of new American work climbed back from its alarming 1966-67 low (19 plays and 8 musicals) to the level of previous seasons—25 new plays and 10 new musicals (compared to 25 and 11 in 1965-66 and 25 and 10 in 1964-65). The total of new foreign plays in English climbed from 10 last year to 17 this year. There were two more specialty shows and two more foreign-language productions. Only the number of revivals declined, from a massive 32 last season to 16 in 1967-68.

Financially, the 1967-68 results were cheering. For the fourth straight year (according to *Variety* estimate) Broadway set a new all-time record total gross well over the $50 million mark at $58,941,849. In addition, the gross from road companies brought the grand total from first-run legitimate theater at more than $104 million, topping the $100 million mark for the first time. (It isn't possible to estimate at close range with any degree of accuracy how much of this is net profit, except to assert that costs and losses did not amount to this much; certainly the year as a whole *was* profitable in at least seven figures.) The phenomenally high Broadway gross was earned by a large number of successful straight plays in combination with the holdover musical blockbusters, but without the usual infusion of new popular musical entertainment. There were no striking new Broadway musicals until *Hair* turned up near season's end.

The number of playing weeks (if 10 shows play 10 weeks, that's 100 playing weeks) in the 1967-68 season was 1,257—fourth highest in Broadway history behind 1,325 in 1947-48, 1,295 in 1965-66 and 1,269 in 1966-67. Notice that the playing-week total in the past three seasons has been exceptionally high (even if attenuating slightly). This indicates not that there are more shows but that the ones we have are running longer, which helps to account for the record grosses when coupled with high ticket prices, particularly on weekends, when the modern theater does most of its business. In 1967-68 the Broadway ticket topped out at $12; next year a $15 top has already been announced for a forthcoming musical.

Financially, when 1967-68 was good it was very, very good, but when it was bad it could be extremely expensive. Musical flops put a multi-million-dollar strain on the Broadway bankroll. David Merrick's *Mata Hari* folded out of town in December to the tune of $500,000 (according to *Variety* estimate), and this was only the beginning. *I'm Solomon* died for $700,000 and *Darling of the Day* fared almost as badly (this would make these two the costliest musical flops ever). *Here's Where I Belong,* which closed after its opening night performance, set a new record for a one-performance Broadway loss: $550,000. *The Education of Hyman Kaplan* lost about $550,000 and *Henry, Sweet Henry* piled up an estimated deficit of $400,000. The total losses on Broadway musical flops measured well over $3,000,000 by May 31.

Esthetically, major honors were divided between newcomers and establishment (if anyone or anything in the theater can be considered established). The year's top script, *A Day in the Death of Joe Egg* (*Joe Egg* for short) was a playwriting debut. So were the three off-Broadway plays on the best list, while *After The Rain* and *Rosencrantz and Guildenstern Are Dead* (*R & G* for short) were the American debuts of their British authors. On the side of experience, Charles Dyer's *Staircase* is his second Best Play. Robert Anderson is making the Best Plays list for the second year in a row, Neil Simon for the third time and Arthur Miller for the *seventh* time (seven straight times with seven original plays beginning with *All My Sons,* not counting one adaptation).

For David Merrick, 1967-68 was a roller coaster ride. His *Mata Hari* folded out of town, and two other Merrick musicals—*How Now, Dow Jones* and *The Happy Time*—limped through the season. Despite these and other annoyances, Merrick finished the season with his richly-deserved reputation as an outstanding showman-impresario not only intact but enhanced. To his list of achievements, Merrick now adds the production of *R & G,* which won both the Critics and Tony awards for the best play of the season. He brought the new Tennessee Williams play to Broadway (with a big publicity boost in the much-publicized quarrel between himself and the author over the title, which was changed from *Kingdom of Earth* to *The Seven Descents of Myrtle*); and the production of a new Tennessee Williams play is the proper business of the art to which Williams has contributed so much. Merrick deserves as much praise for setting it up on Broadway as though it had been a prizewinner. And while he was at it, Merrick also produced the season's biggest hit—and he did it almost without moving from his office chair, in somewhat the same way that Zeus produced Athene full-grown from his own skull. Merrick re-cast his long-run musical *Hello, Dolly!* with Pearl Bailey as Dolly and Cab Calloway as Horace Vandergelder, backed up by an all-Negro cast, and the result was the hottest $9.90 ticket in town for a 5-year-old musical that has already grossed $45,000,000 in America and about $100,-000,000 worldwide. That's showmanship, daddyo. So was the incident in Washington, D.C. on Nov. 4, at one of the tryout performances of Pearl Bailey's *Dolly,* when at the end of the show an enthusiastic couple in the audience was invited to join the cast onstage for a final chorus of the title number—the couple being President of the United States and Mrs. Lyndon Baines Johnson. So was the billing which Merrick arranged for himself in the Playbill for *How Now, Dow Jones.* The note read simply, "DAVID MERRICK (Producer) Mr. Merrick is known as the distinguished producer of *Breakfast at Tiffany's.*" This year he can bill himself as the producer of *Mata Hari,* too. He can remind us of his flops and leave it to others to keep the record of his many distinguished credits.

Another of the season's characteristics was the repeated success of script material from other days. George Kelly's comedy *The Show-Off* (1924) was a Broadway hit in APA-Phoenix Repertory, with Helen Hayes a standout in the mother role. Michel de Ghelderode's *Pantagleize* (1927) was also well received in production by the same troupe. Lillian Hellman's *The Little Foxes* was revived successfully. Shakespeare received a kind of back-handed homage in *R & G,* in the off-Broadway musical *Your Own Thing* (whose book is based on *Twelfth Night*) and a camp *Hamlet* produced by Joseph Papp. The season's most glamorous performance was one that we have enjoyed before in other media: Marlene Dietrich doing her own thing in a one-woman show.

The sharpest disappointment of the 1967-68 season was its inability to come up with a musical blockbuster to match the holdovers from other years: *Hello, Dolly!* (1963-64), *Fiddler on the Roof* (1964-65), *Man of La Mancha* and *Mame* (1965-66) and *Cabaret* (1966-67). The musical *Hair* is a well-deserved hit, of course, but it was borrowed from previous off-Broadway production and came uptown much too late (April 29) to rescue the Broadway season. Among authors who reached Broadway this season but couldn't find an audience for their work were Ira Levin, Henry Denker, Nunnally Johnson (twice), Carl Reiner, Samuel Taylor, Robert Alan Aurthur and Gore Vidal. Among the players who loaned their talent to the season with little or no repayment were Burl Ives, Keir Dullea, Patrick Magee, Maureen O'Sullivan, Alfred Drake, Sandy Dennis, Don Ameche, Eileen Herlie, Barbara Bel Geddes, Vincent Price, Ruth Ford, Robert Reed, Louis Gossett, Paul Rogers, John Forsythe, Dane Clark and Tom Bosley. Michael J. Pollard, who covered himself with glory as C.W. in the brilliant Arthur Penn movie *Bonnie and Clyde,* tried for Broadway but didn't quite reach it in a play called *Leda Had a Little Swan* which closed at its final preview prior to opening night (even though, I am told, it provided a ringing answer to the question "What next?" by supposing that the next generation, the children of the hippies, will make love to animals). Three productions, including one musical, made it to Broadway for only one performance, closing right after opening night.

While not escapist in temper, the 1967-68 theater season offered a dram of consolation in these perplexing times. The constant theatergoer, after his twentieth or thirtieth play about Man as Fortune's Fool, as the last to know or to understand the *force majeur* overwhelming him, could breath a sigh of partial relief: "Well, I'm not paranoid after all, something really *is* out to get me." If the season had any keynote play, it was *R & G,* with two fops being nudged towards death without ever getting the word about what is killing them or why, scarcely even aware that the passionate events of *Hamlet* are taking place around them. The two father plays—*The Price* and *I Never Sang*—sympathized with sons who had made gestures of affection, even major sacrifices, only to discover (the plays concluded) that paternal selfishness and hostility are inevitable. In three plays—*Scuba Duba, Joe Egg* and *Staircase*—the individuals being tortured dramatically or comically were victims of emotional forces beyond their control and sometimes even their perception: despair over a handicapped child (*Joe Egg*), sexual alienation (*Scuba Duba*) and homosexual antagonism (*Staircase*). Neil Simon sent up the whole matter of Man as Victim in a burst of farcical fireworks in the last of three *Plaza Suite* one-acters, in which the father of a bride is thrown into a frenzy when his daughter, on her wedding day, locks herself in the bathroom for no comprehendable reason. On and off Broadway the Fool was the plaything of his Fortune: the boys at the mercy of their neuroses in *The Boys in the Band,* the king kicking and screaming against death in Ionesco's *Exit the King,* the Indian so helpless as to make himself the inevitable target of toughs in Horovitz's *The Indian Wants the Bronx,* Pantagleize ignorant of his own revolution in de Ghelderode's *Pantagleize*—finally, the whole species suffering from the flaws of its violent and authoritarian nature in some all-too-near future century in *After The Rain.*

The theater season displayed two other characteristics which I would like to note before going into a play-by-play report. First and most obviously, in an effort to move closer to their audiences, to penetrate deeper into their minds and hearts, many playwrights have pushed their characters all the way to the apron of the stage to address the audience directly. In these chatty conveyances of confidence (as in *Spofford*), these elucidations of the events of the play (as in *I Never Sang*), these confessions and elaborations of agony (as in *Joe Egg*), it isn't the playwrights themselves who speak directly to the audience, but their characters *in character.* This isn't a case of Shakespeare setting the stage of his "wooden O" with language, it's more like a Greek chorus, the citizens telling you where it's at right now, in Thebes. Rosencrantz and Guildenstern did it from time to time (in *R & G,* not in *Hamlet*). *After The Rain* began with the no-nonsense entrance of a lecturer who stepped to a podium, told the audience to pay attention and delivered a history lesson in which was embedded the gradual discovery that the lecturer is, in reality, the villain and the audience itself the true victim of the play.

So this was a season in which, for one thing, we have had the Greek chorus as both hero and villain. Secondly—and so much less obviously that I offer it as an impression, a cloud no bigger than a playwright's fist which nevertheless shows no sign of going away—the plays of 1967-68, like the people

BARRY NELSON, TAMMY GRIMES AND LEO GENN
IN "THE ONLY GAME IN TOWN"

of 1967-68, were preoccupied with causes and relatively indifferent to consequences. In the theater, this has the effect of eliminating most of the conventional third act; the part that goes into what happens as a *result* of all the stresses that have built up from the first act and burst at the end of the second. Just after the point of decision, of climax, is the point at which, it seems to me, we sometimes drop the whole subject, as though effects were either totally predictable or relatively much less important than causes. *I Never Sang for My Father,* for example (the strongest that comes to mind), is a play in which father and son build up to a big confrontation, whose consequences are described in less than a page of narration as the play ends. If this sample is indeed part of an esthetic development, it is further evidence of the theater's allergic sensitivity to its environment. This is an era in which we seek not so much to punish or reward as to understand; in which we are not often required to accept the full responsibility for our actions; in which we sometimes judge even violence not by its effect but by its causes. Small wonder, in these circumstances, that "Act III: The next morning" seems to be disappearing from the playwriting esthetic.

The playwriting energy of any given moment is like electricity in a wire—you can't tell it's there until you see it light up or move something, or touch it with ungloved hand. The 1967-68 season of American playwriting had juice running through its stage-to-audience circuits in steady amperage and often very high voltage, even though the British playwrights carried off much more than their share of the ultimate "bests" on Broadway. We should take note of comments in two British articles in this very *Best Plays* volume. Summing up the 1967-68 London season, playwright-critic Frank Marcus finds that it was greatly enhanced by the "new-found vitality of the American theater" which sent over its great musicals and its *America Hurrah*. David Jones, associate director of the Royal Shakespeare Company, reporting on his organization, has this to say: "As we look towards the 1968 (autumn) Aldwych season, the dearth of new British writing continues. . . . . It looks as if we may be taking a lead from America for a while now, just as we did in the heyday of Tennessee Williams and Arthur Miller."

With the ascendancy of British playwrights on Broadway, here's a case of the grass growing greener on *both* sides of the electric fence. Never question the logic of this situation, or even the irony; let's just keep our fingers crossed and hope it continues. What more could the theater ask than to have our playwrights writing better than the British, at the same time that the British are writing better than ours? It's David Merrick's Impossible Dream come true.

The Hits

The meaning of the word "hit" as applied to the Broadway theater is exact: a hit is a show that has paid off its production cost. Below are the 1967-68 shows which, according to *Variety's* annual estimate, joined the golden company of Broadway hits by season's end. We add to *Variety's* list one probable hit, a show which is almost certainly destined to pay off (we believe) as it continues its run into the new season. (Parenthetically, the 5 shows listed as "probable hits" in last year's *Best Plays* volume all performed as predicted and achieved hit status.)

There were 13 hits in 1967-68, including the one probable, as compared with 12 in 1966-67. Here they are (titles listed in CAPITAL LETTERS were also Best Plays):

Hits (*Variety* Estimate)

Marlene Dietrich	*The Prime of Miss Jean Brodie*
ROSENCRANTZ AND GUILDENSTERN ARE DEAD	*A DAY IN THE DEATH OF JOE EGG*
There's a Girl in My Soup	*THE PRICE*
The Little Foxes (revival)	*PLAZA SUITE*
More Stately Mansions	*The Seven Descents of Myrtle*
Everything in the Garden	*The Only Game in Town*

Probable Hit

Hair

Some shows are born hits in a blaze of box office popularity. Others are made by movie sales and other special factors. This year's success of the one-woman show whose title says it all—*Marlene Dietrich*—was no fluke of accounting. Miss Dietrich's Broadway debut was one of the year's memorable events, projecting songs and glamor in a style that won her both instant city-wide popularity and a special Tony Award to crown her achievement.

The resounding popular success of the new-play season was Neil Simon's *Plaza Suite,* a triptych of one-acters looking into the lives of three couples occupying in turn a suite at the Plaza Hotel in New York, couples perfectly played by George C. Scott in three different facets of masculine dominance and Maureen Stapleton in three different moods of feminine perseverance. The first couple is middle-aged, married but losing contact. The magic is gone, and they are in trouble—a tired kind of emotional trouble in which each laugh ends in a wrench of despair. The second couple acts out a satire on sex play, as a visiting Hollywood star invites his childhood sweetheart to come in from New Jersey for an afternoon of getting reacquainted. The third couple has a daughter who is getting married today, in about a minute and a half, and she has locked herself in the bathroom and refuses to come out. This last is a farce in which Scott soars to parental fury and plunges into dark wells of humiliation in a hilarious sequence. The program was directed by Mike Nichols, and what more is to be said of Nichols now, after his steady succession of hits on stage and screen? In this season of 1967-68 he has reached a height of celebrity and adulation at which he might be expected to cross a kind of timberline and lose intimate contact with contemporary reality. There's no sign of any such happening in Nichols' work. His insight is unfailing, his touch unerring in any combination of comedy and drama (in the direction of this season's hit revival of Lillian Hellman's *The Little Foxes* as well as in *Plaza Suite*). What more, indeed, is there to be said about Neil Simon? His plays speak louder than any critical praise. He is the Molière of the high-rise era; he knows his contemporaries intimately and he treats them affectionately but never too gently, always living up to our greatest expectations of laughter.

Another hit comedy was British and, like many others this season, amused in its own oblique fashion about the generation gap. Terence Frisby's *There's a Girl in My Soup* made it on Broadway after a long and successful London run. It was comedy frappé, about a middle-aged bachelor gourmet (Gig Young) who prides himself on his prowess with women but meets more than his match in a teen-aged mod (Barbara Ferris) who moves in to keep house with him. She is reconciled, finally, with the boy friend her own age—not a moment too soon for her deflated middle-aged lover.

For once, however, it was the darker shades of theater that dominated the season. The presence on the hit list of Arthur Miller's *The Price* and Tom Stoppard's *Rosencrantz and Guildenstern Are Dead,* as well as Jay Allen's *The Prime of Miss Jean Brodie,* leads inevitably to the conclusion that so-called "serious" theater is not, after all, lying in conspicuous decay like an unburied corpse; in fact, it may not even be dead. True, these are neither classically-formed tragedies nor plays which attack their subjects with the uncompromising gravity of a script like last season's *Hamp.* In them, the comic spirit often makes a jack-in-the-box appearance. Often they borrow, if not the uniform of comedy, at least some of its insignia. But they are plays which can be called serious—on balance.

Miller's *The Price* is the first playscript since the two (*After the Fall* and *Incident at Vichy*) written for the Elia Kazan-Robert Whitehead operation of Lincoln Center Repertory downtown. The celebrated and controversial *After the Fall* contained a scene in which the hero, Quentin, determines to continue his education, even though this self-preoccupation implies a lack of feeling for his father and brother, who need his help at home, in the business, in hard times.

This theme has been expanded to become the whole matter in *The Price,* which dramatizes the results of such a situation, 20 years later. The scene in the new play is the attic of a New York house cluttered with all the furniture from its glory days (a middle-class materialistic fantasy of harp, chiffonier and rowing oar designed by Boris Aronson). Here the brother (Pat Hingle) who stayed to help, now a policeman whose only fortune is his personal honor, has a head-on collision and recrimination with the brother (Arthur Kennedy) who ran out on the whole family problem, continued his training and became a rich and successful doctor. They meet in the attic to sell the jointly-owned furniture to an 80-year-old dealer (a role created by David Burns on the road, then, after Burns' illness, taken over and consummately realized by Harold Gary). The furniture dealer is a grand old comedy character. He is as Tevye might be after coming to America and making money. But the dealer and the furniture are only pawns in the game of guilt played by the brothers as they reproach each other—the one for abandoning their father, the other for a self-pitying pose of moral superiority. In the middle is the policeman's wife (Kate Reid) who never misses a chance to remind her husband how poor they are and what advantages they might have had, were it not for his instinct for self-sacrifice. The interplay is effective, and it is good Miller, which is to say strong, clean-lined, direct and often going deep into emotional complexity. The play concludes that each of us does his own thing for selfish reasons and winds up with whatever life he has bought and paid for (one brother in proud penury, the other in neurotic affluence). Arthur Miller's generation is one which began with the sweet illusion that spirituality was all, materialism nothing. In *Death of a Salesman* Miller let us hear an ominous rumble of truth for our time: that material tensions in this materialistic age can serve as an instrument of tragedy. Miller's *The Price* reverberates with some of the same thunder: in these times no emotion or moral position is entirely free of material influences.

Tom Stoppard's *R & G* was more flippant in manner but equally sharp in its sting. This script won the New York Drama Critics Circle Award and the Tony Award for best play in the American debut of its young British author. The script treats the matter of Hamlet's long-named schoolmates like a photographic blow-up; it takes the scant material from the Shakespeare script and magnifies it a hundred times until Rosencrantz and Guildenstern are seen in all their grainy innocence, with the main part of *Hamlet* only dimly visible around the fringes. While the two are in the foreground wondering who's who and what's what and why they're here at Elsinore, the terrifying events of *Hamlet* take place in the corner of their eyes, uncomprehended, in the deeper shadows of Desmond Heeley's eerily suggestive setting. Thus the theme of Stoppard's play was prototypical of our era: Rosencrantz and Guildenstern in their doublet and hose are stand-ins for Everyman interrupted in a happy-go-lucky course by overwhelming events. Rosencrantz and Guildenstern (who in their ignorance betray Hamlet to Claudius as unfeelingly as Hamlet in his turn betrays them to death) are never going to get the word, but they are surely going to get the axe—that's the heart of the matter. Brian Murray and John Wood in the title roles, and Paul Hecht as the Player King who keeps issuing ironic warnings to the doomed pair, served the material so well that they all received Tony nominations, in an unprecedented citation of three performers in the same play. Noel Craig, too, made his shadowy Hamlet a figure of feral menace, and Derek Goldby's direction played a major part in the success of Tom Stoppard's brilliant Broadway debut.

A choice of the very best play produced professionally in New York during the 1967-68 season would narrow down to a decision between two imported British hits: *R & G* and *A Day in the Death of Joe Egg,* the playwriting debut of its author, Peter Nichols. The critics and the Tony voters gave their deep and flourishing bow to *R & G*. My own choice by a narrow margin of preference is *Joe Egg,* which was billed by its own author in the program as a "comedy" but is much the darker of these two gray playscripts. *Joe Egg* contains many more laughs and is much more harrowing with its examination of a husband and wife in their 30s coping with a child so handicapped that it cannot perform the simplest function for itself and is little better than a vegetable. Like *R & G, Joe Egg* is a play about human beings at the mercy of inexorable fate; but in the latter case the fate is grindingly realistic instead of poetic, so that the sufferers in the grinder react realistically: as their nerve is stretched to the breaking point, they start giving off jokes. The couple in *Joe Egg* is beyond tears, beyond even the metaphor of Rosencrantz and Guildenstern. Their world is so bleak that only jokes will help—and almost all the jokes, the horrid ones as well as the funny ones, have been used up by the time the play begins. Albert Finney played the husband clowning at the end of his rope, and Zena Walker the wife who is barely managing to cling to a straw of hope, in two fine performances. From time to time in the play, husband or wife would come downstage to tell the audience how it really was. The confidences in *Joe Egg* were no less harrowing than the jokes, in a shattering experience of theater.

The Prime of Miss Jean Brodie was another on-balance-serious hit, but here the comic spirit prevailed in scene after scene. This is an American script by Jay Allen, based on Muriel Spark's novel about a Scottish schoolteacher in the 1930s. It had its premiere in London in a widely praised production starring Vanessa Redgrave; then it moved homeward across the Atlantic to Broadway, where Zoe Caldwell played Jean Brodie and won the Tony award for the year's best female performance in a straight play. Miss Brodie is a "character" built out of will, passion and humor, a dedicated Edinburgh girls' school teacher in the "prime" of early middle age. She is a romantic who considers herself and her pupils the *"creme de la creme"* of human society. Miss Brodie encourages them to believe that they are a chosen few, born and destined to appreciate fine poetry, music, art and conversation and at the same time to be excused from ordinary educational discipline and even conventional morality. The male members of the teaching staff make love to Miss Brodie (who returns the favor when she has a mind to), while the female principal of the school is out to "assassinate" her from her beloved teaching job because she is jealous of Miss Brodie's influence on her class. Miss Brodie finally makes a fatal misjudgment: she believes that fascism as manifested in the Spanish Civil War is a romantic, even chivalric movement. And so she is indeed "assassinated" by a favorite pupil who feels that Miss Brodie underestimates her worth and so, impulsively, she bears the tale of Miss Brodie's fascist sympathies to her enemy the principal. Miss Brodie falls from the heaven of her teaching position as doubtless she deserves (in the London version of the play she is a suicide; in the Broadway version she is merely cast adrift). But in the meantime her defiance of the forces of gravity in the excitement of her teaching, the pride and humor of her personality, were a delight of the Broadway season, totally realized in Zoe Caldwell's memorable performance.

Three of our most distinguished American playwrights found something less than instant popular support of their 1967-68 work on Broadway, but made the hit list by virtue of the sale of movie rights to their scripts (which must prove something: either that screen audiences are still less demanding than stage audiences, or they are more celebrity-conscious about authors). In two of these three cases the scripts also represented the common difficulty of drawing definitive boundaries of comedy or drama (none was billed as comedy, none was without humor or poignancy). Frank D. Gilroy's *The Only Game in Town* was one of the season's peak moments of heterosexuality.

Gilroy's tale of a couple of lonely young show business people (Tammy Grimes and Barry Nelson) finding each other in Las Vegas and engaging in an affair which, in spite of their flippancy, solidifies slowly into deep-felt love and inevitable marriage ("The only game in town") was written and presented with comic insight, with sincerity and expertise—a likable play but one which met difficulty in today's rough Broadway waters. *The Only Game in Town* probably has a future in the American theater repertory. Somehow, though, May 1968 on Broadway was the wrong time and the wrong place for its first appearance. The comedy-drama style to which we've become accustomed was better exemplified (though not as well realized) in Edward Albee's *Everything in the Garden,* an adaptation of a Giles Cooper play about suburbanites who find that they can have all the cars, swimming pools, imported vodka, greenhouses and other status symbols—everything in the garden, in fact—if only their wives will bring in the $$$ by working part time as high-priced prostitutes in the big city. That's the kind of black-comedy twist we expect when an earnest subject (in Albee's case, materialism) or emotion is raised in the modern theater: not Romeo and Juliet but Punch and Judy. Contemporary as it was in style, the Albee play finally lost control of its joke (as the suburbanites casually murder one of their number who begins to embarrass them) and became opaquely instead of glossily black in mood.

Of clearly serious intent was the third of the screen-rights hits, *The Seven Descents of Myrtle,* in which our great playwright Tennessee Williams once again put himself to the task of a drama of desire and frustration. In it, Williams ties a fading burlesque actress (Estelle Parsons) in wedlock to a golden-haired mamma's boy (Brian Bedford) who owns a farm worked by his swarthy half-brother (Harry Guardino), the sort of fellow who takes his eyes off a sexy calendar picture only to ogle his brother's neglected bride. *The Seven Descents of Myrtle* is Williams as before—not at his best, but in regular form—yet the whole play seems to teeter on the edge of camp, or we were *expecting* it to cross over into camp like so many other modern plays which raise the subpect of desire and frustration, only to avoid coming to grips with them and copping out into black comedy. Maybe *Seven Descents* doesn't reach us at this time because, although Williams is aiming exactly where he aimed before, we are no longer sitting there. Here too is a script, though, that may have a future in stock and repertory.

Another dramatic work that made the hit list was Eugene O'Neill's *More Stately Mansions,* which brought Ingrid Bergman back to the American stage and confronted her with Colleen Dewhurst in two of the season's vivid performances. The O'Neill script was judged not yet ready for production by its author at the time of his death, but it was prepared for this staging by José Quintero (his eighth O'Neill play) from notes and other indications as to how the playwright intended to proceed. *More Stately Mansions* takes up O'Neill's chronicling of early America where *A Touch of the Poet* left off. Now Sara Melody (daughter of the village tavern-keeper Con Melody) has married Simon Harford of the important big-city Harfords. But all does not

ROBERT MOORE, BARRY NELSON, BEATRICE STRAIGHT AND BARBARA BEL GEDDES IN "EVERYTHING IN THE GARDEN"

work out happily ever after; Sara (Colleen Dewhurst) has won Simon's (Arthur Hill) hand but must fight for his loyalty and even his love against Simon's unyielding mother (Ingrid Bergman). The struggle between the two women is larger than life, a struggle of goddesses. As a whole, this was a murky drama which nevertheless had its moments depicting these Junos in conflict.

Broadway waited until the 11th hour of the 1967-68 season to find anything like a musical blockbuster of the kind which has been its mainstay in this decade—and even then it borrowed from its kid brother. *Hair* originated off Broadway as the first production of Joseph Papp's New York Shakespeare Festival Public Theater, and it didn't move uptown to Broadway until late April (after a stop-off as a special attraction at the night club known as Cheetah). *Hair* was an explosion of musical theater, a rock 'n' roll 'n' rebellious entertainment with a loud, irresistable score by Galt MacDermot; a now-generation book and lyrics by Gerome Ragni and James Rado (who also played leading roles), directed with acute sensibility by Gerald Freedman off Broadway and with wild excitement by Tom O'Horgan on Broadway. It touched and delighted audiences downtown and shocked and delighted audiences uptown. On Broadway it was a bigger, louder presentation which seems surely destined to become the only solid musical hit of the season.

There must come a moment in the life of an up-tight adolescent (I imagine from reading the *Village Voice* faithfully) at which he decides to freak out of the cliches and unreasonable hangups of the "real" adult world; a moment when he decides to join those of his generation, sometimes called "hippies", who are unreachable any longer by any persuasion or appeal except love and soul-brotherhood. This moment of determination to do one's own thing, this act of confirmation of the rebellious spirit, is the moment that *Hair* captures, prolongs and splinters into its dozens of jagged comments on sex, drugs, military service, money, religion, etc., etc. The libretto about a hippie's decision whether to accept or resist being drafted into the Vietnam war had pathetic and chilling overtones downtown; uptown it was camped out of any earnest meaning. For example, the young man's arguments with his parents in the original version were instances of blindfolded people groping for each other across the generation gap; in the Broadway version it was low comedy, with each parent played by three performers of mixed sexes. This loss of narrative focus isn't much of a problem in the all-out, high-volume, hyperthyroid Broadway *Hair,* whose whole impact is far less than that of its insolent parts—parts like Sally Eaton singing of carbon monoxide and sulphur dioxide in "Air", and of love in a ballad whose tenderest regret is that the boy she loves isn't the father of the unborn child she is carrying; parts like Shelley Plimpton's teeny-bopper love song, "Frank Mills"; parts like Ragni's positively acrobatic performance in every defiant, bushy-haired (the title *Hair* is a salute to the shaggy trademark of modern youth) moment of the show. And speaking of defiant moments, *Hair's* first-act curtain number was a be-in with a tangle of bodies choreographed to end in a heap under a gauzy blanket—except for a group of the performers, both boys and girls, who stand for a beat or two fully lit and facing the audience stark naked in a "shock of recognition" moment that rendered Robert Anderson's outlandish suggestion of an actor naked onstage in last season's *You Know I Can't Hear You When the Water's Running* totally and finally done, a *fait accompli,* obsolete. Oddly enough, this radical development was added to the Broadway version; it didn't take place off Broadway (and I am told that the number of actors and actresses in this tableau varied from one performance to another—each did it only when and if he felt like doing it). But off Broadway and on, with or without gimmicks, *Hair* was a detonation of a musical that shook up its audience and made them hear the hippie's cries of joy in living ("I got life, mother!") and of anger ("——you, Margaret Mead!") at any sign of generalization or conformity.

Those were the hits and probable hits of the 1967-68 Broadway season.

Their subject matter was on the dark side, immersing us deep in the agony of parents of a vegetable child; in the wanton murders of two uncomprehending young men; in the unnegotiable resentment of brothers; in the destruction of a glorious personality; in the clash between wife and mother. Our only hit musical harped on two of our most pressing social problems—alienated youth and the Vietnam war. Our funniest comedy began on a haunting note with a loss of communication between a husband and wife; another laughed through clenched teeth at suburban avarice, and only one splashed about happily in a foamy environment of sex and nonsense. To borrow a Jerry Herman punch line that must be almost two decades old by now but gains in meaning with each passing year, "Oh, what a lovely theatrical season we've had!"

Of course it was only a couple of years ago that we were all viewing with alarm the absence of so-called "serious" theater works, the scarcity even of temper in the comedies and musicals. This year the playwrights led the adventurous theatergoer into a terra incognita of strange new shapes like *Joe Egg, R & G* and *Hair*. It was a challenging and exciting season, as the theater once again began to cultivate its black tulip in rich, dark blooms.

New on Broadway

In the theater, as elsewhere on this planet, immediate popularity is only one of many forms of success and gratification. The ultimate insignia of New York professional theater achievement (we insist) is selection as a Best Play in this volume. Such selection is made with the script itself the primary consideration, for the reason (as we have stated in previous volumes) that the script is the very spirit of the theater, the soul in its physical body. The script is not only the quintessence of the present, it is most of what endures into the future.

So the Best Plays are the best scripts. As little weight as humanly possible is given to comparative production values (such as a brilliant performance). The choice is made without any regard whatever to a play's type—musical, comedy or drama—for its origin on or off Broadway, or for its popularity at the box office or lack of same.

The Best Plays of 1967-68 were the following, listed in the order in which they opened (an asterisk * with the performance number signifies the play was still running on June 1, 1968):

After The Rain
(64 perfs.)
Scuba Duba
(off Broadway; 265* perfs.)
Rosencrantz and Guildenstern, etc.
(hit; 262* perfs.)

Staircase
(61 perfs.)
Your Own Thing
(off Broadway; 158* perfs.)
I Never Sang for My Father
(124 perfs.)

A Day in the Death of Joe Egg
(hit; 137* perfs.)
The Price
(hit; 131* perfs.)
Plaza Suite
(hit; 123* perfs.)
The Boys in the Band
(off Broadway; 53* perfs.)

This list of Best Plays, like the hit list, is dominated by earnest efforts (whether they be called "drama", "comedy" or what you will) to stir us up, to make us feel something very like terror or despair. *R & G, Joe Egg* and *The Price,* described in the section on hits, are joined on the Best list by two dramatic works—*After The Rain,* the American theater debut of its British author, John Bowen, and *I Never Sang for My Father* by Robert Anderson, his second Best Play in two consecutive New York seasons and the third in his career as a playwright.

After The Rain is a fantasy that edges oh, so craftily into its dark conclusions about human beings surviving a second Flood "two hundred years after The Rain of 1969." It begins as a "lecture" with the theater audience as the lecture audience. Its "actors" are prisoners who have committed some breach or other of the laws two centuries hence (they are kin to *Marat/Sade's* performing inmates). As part of their rehabilitation program, they have been hypnotized and trained to play the roles of survivors on a raft in the Flood, acting out the illustration of the Lecturer's "historical" account. A handful of men and women survived (the play-within-the-play demonstrates) under the ruthless leadership of an egotistical, authoritarian, lower-middle-class accountant who set himself up first as dictator, then as god. Alec McCowen is domineering and detestable as the god Arthur, nasal and small-minded in his authority, a contrast to Paul Sparer as the donnish Lecturer, who directs the "actors" as he unfolds the tale. We find, at last (after Arthur is killed in a revolt by his companions) that the principles laid down by Arthur—symbolic of man at his worst—are those which govern the new "free" society two centuries later. Like *Marat/Sade, After The Rain* exists on many levels. Its characters represent ourselves, today (on the raft); ourselves viewed with dimming acquaintanceship centuries later (the raft events as history); hypnotized prisoners of the future waiting to play ourselves; and finally (in the case of the Arthur character) a man of the future who manages to throw off the hypnotic veil and, awake, hates what he has become. Vivian Matalon's staging of this intertwined material was impeccable, at times ballet-like. *After The Rain* is a mind-expanding script which for some inscrutable reason didn't find a large audience on Broadway (though it was a hit in London and Paris). I confidently predict that it will find a niche in future production by those who dare greatly in order to achieve much.

The father-son relationship, touched on in Arthur Miller's *The Price,* was the whole matter of Robert Anderson's *I Never Sang for My Father,* about a 40-year-old son trying to establish an affectionate relationship with his aging father and—despite a deeply sincere effort—failing. Where Miller's father-figure was only a clinging memory, Anderson's is frustrating his son, not in memory, but right there on the stage. As played by Alan Webb in one of the season's best performances, he touches the heart at one moment as he tries to concentrate on choosing a coffin for his wife's funeral; at the next moment, he becomes a detestable, wiry little bundle of senile ego, unknowable, unreachable, unloveable. After many failures to build a bridge to his father, the son (Hal Holbrook) gives up, and that's that; that's the point of the play. The consequences, if any, are not explored. This is a generation-gap drama, not in a contemporary but in a universal sense: neither son nor parent, so widely separated by time and yet so closely bound by family kinship, is able to forget himself and suppress his own convictions and feelings long enough to project understanding toward the other—or, if this happens occasionally, it never happens to son and parent at the same moment, so that the instant of perfect understanding and love never happens. *I Never Sang for My Father* was first written as a movie (see Anderson's report on its production history in the "Best Plays" section of this volume), and on the stage it retained a fluidity in action and design. Scenes and locales flowed into each other under Alan Schneider's direction, with settings symbolized by light projections within Jo Mielziner's triple-arched set. For example, the coffin showroom was represented by rectangles of light projected onto the stage floor, in a scene which was visually as well as emotionally haunting. *I Never Sang for My Father* was not only a powerful experience of theater, it was also a triumph of American playwriting combined with Broadway stagecraft.

It would be appropriate at this point to move smoothly into a run-down of other serious matters raised on Broadway in 1967-68, except that in the modern theater is becoming harder and harder to draw meaningful lines between "comedy" and "drama." This season 17 shows were billed by their authors in the program as "comedies"—one of them was *Joe Egg*. And a leading newspaper, commenting on the renaissance of "serious" theater, made a list of 8 noteworthy "dramas"—one of them was *Joe Egg*. So what's in a name? New nerves are tingling in the theater of today; the old skin that established the boundary between flesh and air, between comedy and drama, is sloughing away. This is an era, in the theater as in the streets, of laughter born of tears; tears born of laughter.

This was especially true of the two Best Plays about homosexuality, a subject which our theater explored more thoroughly than ever before this season. One of them, *Staircase,* by the British actor-playwright Charles Dyer, was a haunting two-character study of a couple of middle-aged "hair stylists" joined in a love-hate alliance against loneliness and despair. They have nothing but each other, and that is not much (they keep observing in joke after cruel joke at the expense of their own ludicrous physical and personality characteristics). One of them, Harry, is physically awkward, the butt of several of nature's pranks, generally passive and easygoing except that he wishes he had been born an effective male. The other, Charles, is wiry, nervous, taunting, emotionally unstable—he has been capable both of marriage and of a recent public display of transvestitism while drunk that is going to land him in court. Both are lonely (but Harry is lonelier than Charles, a slow,

pathetic figure as portrayed by Milo O'Shea in the year's top straight-play performance). Both are frightened (but Charles, volatile, an easy prey to remorse, is more frightened than Harry). Often they make fun of each other simply to reassure themselves that the other one is really *there,* that neither is alone in the hostile world. As in *Joe Egg,* however, there is a notable lack of joy in the laughter as these two misfits joke past the cemetery where lies buried all their masculine pride. Their neurosis has destroyed everything except their continuing ability to feel and suffer. Unbeautiful as the subject of *Staircase* may sound, it is beautiful in its insight and sympathy.

This section of the report on "The Season in New York" is concerned with Broadway production, but it is appropriate at this point for reasons of comparison to take up another Best Play about homosexuality, the off-Broadway *The Boys in the Band* by Mart Crowley. Where *Staircase* was concerned primarily with the patients in an emotional study of two victims, *The Boys in the Band* was focused on the disease itself. In this script (its author's first professionally-produced play), six devout homosexuals are giving a birthday party for a seventh, attended in addition by a male prostitute and one "straight" guest who arrives uninvited. In each character the neurosis takes a different form, varying from a pipe-smoking Ivy League schoolteacher (Laurence Luckinbill) to a barelegged, camping interior decorator (played in full color but without offense by Cliff Gorman) who tells the others "I've known what I was since I was four years old." The host at the party (Kenneth Nelson) is 30-ish, high-strung, warped by a doting mother but somewhat ashamed of his homosexuality, taking out his hang-ups in attacks on the others. The birthday boy is a pockmarked ex-figure skater (Leonard Frey) with no inhibitions whatever. The guests include a soft-spoken Negro, (Reuben Greene) two young men in blue jeans, one aggressive (Keith Prentice) and one a diffident observer, mother-spoiled (Frederick Combs). With Peter White as the shocked "square" (who just may not be quite as sharp-cornered as he believes himself to be) and Robert La Tourneaux as a cowboy-costumed male version of a dumb female prostitute, these are the manifestations of neurosis which the playwright and his director, Robert Moore, combined with great skill into a harrowing stage portrait of the neurosis itself. In doing so, *The Boys in the Band* gave no offense to taste or decency. Like last season's *Fortune and Men's Eyes* about homosexuality in prison, the first act tends toward comedy; but then in the second act when the script must reveal the tension underneath the warp, there is an onslaught of bitterness leading to hysteria. Yet there was no emotion, no sympathy evoked by the second-act tears that had not already been evoked in the first-act laughter; that has been a weakness of the theater's treatment of this theme so far in the 1960s. Nevertheless it was handled with admirable sensitivity and skill in *The Boys in the Band* by actors, director and playwright, as it was in *Staircase,* a couple of plays that turned the lights on in a dark corner of human experience.

Among new American plays on Broadway, it's safe to say that the short-lived *The Trial of Lee Harvey Oswald* was a work of serious dramatic intention (but minor accomplishment) which imagined that President Ken-

nedy's assassin was alive and on trial for his crime. In the first act, "witnesses" present much of the real, available evidence against Oswald, and in the second Oswald himself takes the stand to plead that he was the tool of a conspiracy. The season offered one minor melodrama—Ira Levin's *Dr. Cook's Garden*—with Burl Ives as a Vermont small-town doctor improving the breed by killing out all the undesirable human beings in his practise. Mary Mercier's *Johnny No-Trump* was a drama of a young man contending with father images. It was withdrawn from production after only one performance and a mixed press with strong enthusiasm on the pro side. I am told by its producer Richard Barr that he will bring it back to Broadway in a planned schedule of Theater 1969 repertory next season. On the borderline of drama was Stephen Levi's *Daphne in Cottage D,* with Sandy Dennis and William Daniels in a two-character exploration of emotional distress starting out as a bright, bantering drinking party and ending up as a mutual confession of betrayal and guilt. R.K. Narayan's novel *The Guide* was dramatized by the late Harvey Breit and Patricia Reinhart, with its Indian setting and story of a con man who persuades a village he's a saint, then comes to believe in his own beatitude as he tries to relieve a drought. George Panetta was also writing about a kind of saint in *Mike Downstairs:* a resident of Manhattan's Little Italy doing his earnest best to assist his neighbors through the tensions of modern life and, finally, killed for his pains (but Panetta has labeled this play a comedy). Actors' hangups were the subject of Lewis John Carlino's *The Exercise,* a two-character situation in which an actor and actress practise their art by "improvising" impressions of their own emotional disturbances.

Surveying the list of new foreign plays on Broadway in 1967-68, one finds drama—historical drama—in Rolf Hochhuth's *Soldiers* translated from the original German by Robert D. MacDonald. Like Hochhuth's *The Deputy* (which presented Pope Pius XII as soft in his opposition to the Nazi policy of genocide), *Soldiers* was another creaking machine of a play designed to spread guilt as widely as possible. The time of the play is 1943; Stalin is England's most effective ally, holding most of the Nazi army at bay, so that Russian cooperation is Winston Churchill's first priority. Churchill is seen as condoning (if not actually arranging) the death of his friend General Sikorski because of Sikorski's embarrassing insistence on the recognition of Polish territorial rights at Stalin's expense. Churchill is also represented as adopting a policy of cruel and immoral mass bombing of German civilian population centers, in lieu of a second front on the Continent. An uncannily believable and sustained portrayal of Winston Churchill by John Colicos was hypnotically interesting; the actor created, not a replica, but a strong impression of the great man. As for the message of the play, it is suspect; Hochhuth is the sort of writer who has used the words "Hiroshima" and "Auschwitz" in the same sentence as though they have the same moral implications. The bombing of cities (Hochhuth insinuates in *Soldiers*) is a war crime committed by all in equal guilt, but unpunishable because not outlawed by the Geneva Convention. The script had been booked for production by Laurence Olivier and Kenneth Tynan at England's National Theater but was opposed

by the Lord Chamberlain and then brought over here for production by Tynan, Herman Shumlin (who produced Hochhuth's *The Deputy*) and others. Looking upon it as a purported documentary, it seems only a little more foolish to ban than to sponsor its Teutonic sophistries.

Also on the dramatic side, Eugene Ionesco's *Exit the King* was produced on Broadway in an American premiere by APA-Phoenix. It is a paranoid and absurdist nightmare, a fantastic but relentless account of the death of a king who is not pushed but ticked slowly toward his end through an hour and a half of protest against time's inexorable movement toward decay and oblivion. A young second wife consoles Berenger; but his first wife, played with metallic precision by Eva Le Gallienne, is first among those who insist that Berenger's time has come and that he must get on with it and die without making a fuss. This weird experience of theater was enhanced by Rouben Ter-Arutunian's setting—a strange, brown, geometrical Nowhere which transformed itself at the moment of Berenger's death into a Nowhere wrapped in Saran. A new Russian play by Aleksei Arbuzov dealt with a universal theme —the love triangle—in a grave manner, setting up a "design for living" with two youths and a girl who meet as souls lost in the rubble of the siege of Leningrad in World War II. The three maintain their ties through the years, and the girl marries both of the men in turn. This Russian script was not without a sparkle of the comic spirit, and it was so irridescently well-acted by Eileen Atkins, Ian McKellen and Ian McShane that it deserved a larger share of the Broadway audience than it was able to attract.

There's no use pretending as I pass from a report on *The Promise* to a thought about Peter Ustinov's *The Unknown Soldier and His Wife* that I am crossing some well-marked border between drama and comedy. But if there is a border—a lightening of the mood, an alleviation in the terrain—it is here. The characters in *The Unknown Soldier* were hurting badly as they dragged themselves off to war time after time through the ages, killing the Unknown Soldier and widowing his wife again and again for the many causes of history. But always the woes consoled themselves in irony and sarcasm, in a show directed briskly by John Dexter as a black farce. Other foreign comedies of the year shared the general characteristic of being strong in the bass; there was no great abundance of joy. Michel de Ghelderode's *Pantagleize* made its New York debut in an APA-Phoenix production spread across the stage in symbolic revolutionary action by John Houseman and Ellis Rabb. Pantagleize (played by Rabb) is a nonentity whose only offense is that he feels happy one morning and comments that it is a nice day, thus unwittingly giving the signal for the start of a revolution that is destined to destroy him (what else?). De Ghelderode's 1930s play didn't seem all that relevant to the 1960s, but it was full of colorful incidents expertly performed. The late George Orton's black comedy prototype *Loot* exported a few laughs with its juggling of a corpse in order to hide stolen cash in the coffin, but the best part of this show was the performing by George Rose as an inept and crooked Scotland Yard man and Carole Shelley as a murderous nurse. An-

KENNETH CRANHAM, CAROLE SHELLEY, LIAM REDMOND, GEORGE ROSE AND JAMES HUNTER IN "LOOT"

other British comedy, Bill Naughton's *Keep It In The Family,* can be added to the list of the season's father plays. With the locale changed to Boston for American audiences, it worked the theme of the domineering parent who finally goes too far, so that his family rises in revolt. Still another British comedy was Harold Pinter's *The Birthday Party,* about a slovenly young man visited in his boarding house by two strangers who at first throw him a party which ends on a note of horror, then, next morning, spruce him up and cart him away to some strange and probably gruesome destiny. *The Birthday Party* was written by Pinter before his magnificent *The Homecoming* which was last season's best on Broadway. Coming after it in production here, *The Birthday Party* seemed shallow and unfulfilled, merely an experimental step on the way to the masterpiece, though it was well served in the acting of James Patterson as the young boarder, Ruth White as the confused boarding-house keeper, Ed Flanders as the sinister visitor, and the rest of the cast. Other foreign comedic efforts, less than satisfactory, were *Song of the Grasshopper,* a Spanish comedy about a romantic loafer (played by Alfred Drake), and *A Minor Adjustment,* a Canadian sex comedy about a father's effort to tame his rebellious son by arranging for his seduction.

Peter Ustinov's *Halfway up the Tree* (his second script of the season, a British comedy which had its world premiere in New York shortly before its London premiere) and Henry Denker's *What Did We Do Wrong?* both were cheerful plays about harried fathers who decide if they can't lick their hippie kids they're going to join them and out-hip them. The British version was colored with the wit and style of Ustinov's older-generation brand of verbal comedy, as a British general (Anthony Quayle), a ramrod of a man, returns home from duty in the Empire to find his unmarried daughter pregnant and his son a hippie dropout. Instead of losing his cool, the general takes guitar lessons, grows a beard and goes outside to live in a tree. Paul Ford is the harried American parent in Denker's version, a suburbanite saddled with a bossy wife and a dropout son—so of course he stages his own rebellion and becomes a hippie. The gags were broader in the Denker version, but the aim was the same in a trans-Atlantic playwriting coincidence.

With an exception or two like Ustinov's script, the season's foreign comedies were hedged with attitudes that were rueful, enigmatic or black; not so American comedies, which in several cases aimed for the "laff riot" kind of effect. The most effective of these was Carl Reiner's *Something Different,* a wildly improbable tale of a one-play playwright (Bob Dishy) trying to repeat his success by recreating within his suburban affluence the atmosphere of his mom's battered kitchen, in which he wrote his one hit. Reiner directed his own play (and the lead would have been right for him had he wished to play it), which was the season's most interesting loser. It had the best sight gag (twin boys, one white and one black) and some of the funniest gags, but it was a situation comedy that started somewhere and went nowhere. It left you wishing that Carl Reiner would write another play soon; it was a stylistic achievement that did credit to Reiner and to the Alan King group of producers who brought it to Broadway.

Herman Shumlin's *Spofford* was another light-hearted show, about a retired chicken farmer whose rustic domain is under invasion by expanding suburbia. Spofford makes it his business to observe closely and take mental notes on the strange new breed of beautiful people who are making a Westport of his Arcadia, while one of *them* is wooing his granddaughter. Portrayed in full Yankee acerbity by Melvin Douglas in one of the year's top performances, he confides his findings and conclusions directly and frequently to the audience in a play constructed as a long comedy monologue with occasional sketches. Pert Kelton was cool and sensible as a widow with a nature so warm that not even a locked sacroiliac can wipe the smile from her face. Miss Kelton and Douglas staged a middle-aged courtship which was not only the most ingratiating part of *Spofford* but also one of the major delights of the season.

The subject of sex was an American comedy favorite in the season of 1967-68. It appeared in both boy-meets-girl and boy-meets-boy form in Samuel Taylor's *Avanti!* about an American square and a British mod in a Rome hotel suite, egged on by an Italian fixer (played with great relish by Keith Baxter) who is waiting for either one of them to get lonely. Sex came around again in J.J. Coyle's *The Ninety-Day Mistress,* about a girl who shrinks from lasting attachments and so places a time limit on her affairs; and again in Lawrence Holofcener's *Before You Go,* in which a would-be actress comes into the Greenwich Village apartment of a would-be sculptor to get out of a thunderstorm and stays to make love. Among other comedy subjects was the matter of *How To Be a Jewish Mother,* a series of sketches sprinkled with songs with a two-character cast of Molly Picon in the title role and Godfrey Cambridge as a lot of other characters. American racial stress was treated comically by Robert Alan Aurthur in *Carry Me Back to Morningside Heights* (which opened and closed before the Columbia tumult and had no connection with it), staged by none other than Sidney Poitier in his first outing as a director, in which a starry-eyed Jewish youth indentures himself to a Negro law student (Louis Gossett) as a slave, to try to atone in small part for historical injustice; and by Gore Vidal in *Weekend,* mixed with politics, in a comedy about a Presidential candidate whose son brings home a Negro mistress (played with energy and charm by Carol Cole, Nat King Cole's daughter, in a promising Broadway debut), in order to embarrass his father—who promptly turns the whole situation into a political asset. Finally, in comedy, the war between a forcefully ambitious wife and a shy husband was treated farcically in *Happiness Is Just a Little Thing Called a Rolls Royce* which lasted for only one performance but may be remembered as one of the first plays in which a character sets out rather casually to get high on marijuana.

There were no hits as of May 31 among the Broadway season's haircut musicals. But winner or not, *How Now, Dow Jones* took a pleasantly high-spirited view of the stock market, enjoying the occasional bright blaze of a Carolyn Leigh lyric or a sudden George Abbott sight gag. Also profiting from an agile leading performance by Anthony Roberts as a young man on the way up in Wall Street, and from a standout supporting performance by Hiram Sherman as a tycoon who has already arrived and means to stay, *How Now, Dow Jones* had its enjoyable moments—and indeed, that's the most that could be said for the entire 1967-68 Broadway musical season until *Hair* came along. Among these momentary rewards was Alice Playten's schoolgirl villainess in *Henry, Sweet Henry,* about well-bred teen-agers adventuring in New York's streets (based on *The World of Henry Orient*). There was Robert Goulet's strong performance of a footloose French Canadian photographer coming home to visit his family (including David Wayne as his spry old dad) in *The Happy Time,* which also was distinguished by Gower Champion's choreography and by the use of color slides and movie footage as part of Peter Wexler's settings, a step forward in the scenic art. There was Patricia Routledge's star turn as a widow being courted by mail by a famous artist in *Darling of the Day* (based on Arnold Bennett's *Buried Alive*). There was the splashy Las Vegas opening number, plus excellent vocals by Steve Lawrence and Eydie Gorme and a promising supporting stint by young Scott Jacoby, in *Golden Rainbow,* the musical based on Arnold Schulman's play

A Hole in the Head. There was Tom Bosley as an immigrant grabbing life with both hands in *The Education of H*Y*M*A*N K*A*P*L*A*N* based on the Leo Rosten stories. There was incomparable Joel Grey putting out a high-voltage portrayal of George M. Cohan, strutting and singing a wide repertory of Cohan numbers in *George M!* based on the musical star's life and works. There were Rouben Ter-Arutunian's exotic part-Eastern, part art nouveau settings for the lavish but ill-fated *I'm Solomon,* and in the season's single Broadway revue, *Leonard Sillman's New Faces of 1968,* there were moments of musical and satirical freshness. This was Sillman's 11th show under the title which he has made famous. These with *Here's Where I Belong* (the musical based on John Steinbeck's *East of Eden*), which lasted for only one performance, made up the musical scene on Broadway in 1967-68. It was a dark mass like the void of chaos itself, lit here and there by the starlight sparkle of individual contributions.

The season's 1967-68 specialties included, in addition to Marlene Dietrich, Judy Garland in her third solo-show appearance at the Palace, and Eddie Fisher and Buddy Hackett in a two-man show at the same theater. George Bernard Shaw was portrayed by Max Adrian in *By George,* devised by Michael Voysey from Shaw's writings. Roy Dotrice impersonated an aged and gossipy John Aubrey, the 17th century biographer, in *Brief Lives,* adapted by Patrick Garland from Aubrey's writings about the famous personages of his era, and displaying a setting designed as a jam and clutter of museum pieces of the period by Julia Trevelyan Oman. Finally on the list of specialties there was *Portrait of a Queen,* a biography of Queen Victoria assembled from her diaries and letters and from those of contemporaries who helped illuminate her reign. Dorothy Tutin played Victoria from girlhood to widowhood with a graceful and winning sincerity, and James Cossins contributed a remarkable vignette of Gladstone.

Among the foreign-language visitors to Broadway were The Jewish State Theater of Poland with stately Ida Kaminska as Brecht's Mother Courage; The Grand Music Hall of Israel, one of whose performers, Geula Gill, was nominated for a Tony Award; The Vienna Burgtheater impressing all comers with expert ensemble performances of a German repertory which included *Einen Jux Will Er Sich Machen* (He Wants To Have a Good Time), the comedy which formed a basis for Thornton Wilder's *The Matchmaker,* upon which *Hello, Dolly!* was based; and, visiting Broadway for the second straight season, the colorful and sometimes topless *Les Ballets Africains* from the Republic of Guinea. Finally, Broadway received a visit from The Theater of Genoa doing Goldoni's *The Venetian Twins.* Its hopelessly involved mistaken-identity plot was played with joyous caperings and harlequinades, with frequent asides to the audience in English and without insisting on making Goldoni's ironic point about the flexibility of ethics. Alberto Lionello in the dual role of the twins—one a bravo and one a craven—communicated as heartily as any silent-screen comic. His encounter with himself at the town privy as the twins "meet" for the first and only time is a memorable comedy routine.

Throughout these considerations of the hits and new offerings on Broadway in 1967-68 we have mentioned outstanding contributions by individual artists. The theater isn't an average or a statistic, it is the projection of the individual writer, designer and performer's inspiration. However a season may look to anyone as a whole, it was a great year for any artist who made a great individual contribution. It remains to list a *Best Plays* selection of the very best 1967-68 work of the New York theater season. In the category of so-called "supporting" performers, clear distinctions cannot be made on the basis of official billing, in which an actor's contract may call for him to be listed as a star ahead of the play's title, or an "also-starring" star, or not as a star at all regardless of the size of his role. These matters of billing are technicalities which tend to blur the real distinction between a "leading" and a "supporting" performance. In the Tony Awards balloting (which follows billing), for example, Brian Murray and John Wood, who played the leads in *R & G,* and James Patterson, who played the lead in *The Birthday Party,* were considered "supporting" players because they didn't have star billing. And Harold Gary as Gregory Solomon the furniture dealer in *The Price* was considered a "leading" player because he *did* receive star billing.

Not in *Best Plays,* thank you. Here we will ignore technicalities of billing, as we did in last year's volume. For the purposes of consideration in the *Best Plays* list of bests, the acting is divided into "primary" and "secondary" roles—a primary role being one which carries a major responsibility for the play; *one which might some day cause a star to inspire a revival just to appear in that role.* All others, be they as vivid as Mercutio, are classed as secondary in our list. Here are the bests of 1967-68:

Plays

BEST PLAY: *A Day in the Death of Joe Egg* by Peter Nichols
ACTOR IN A PRIMARY ROLE: Milo O'Shea as Harry C. Leeds in *Staircase*
ACTRESS IN A PRIMARY ROLE: Zoe Caldwell as Jean Brodie in *The Prime of Miss Jean Brodie*
ACTOR IN A SECONDARY ROLE: Paul Hecht as The Player in *Rosencrantz and Guildenstern Are Dead*
ACTRESS IN A SECONDARY ROLE: Pert Kelton as Mrs. Punck in *Spofford*
DIRECTOR: Mike Nichols for *Plaza Suite* and *The Little Foxes*
SCENERY: Desmond Heeley for *Rosencrantz and Guildenstern Are Dead*
COSTUMES: Jane Greenwood for *More Stately Mansions* and *The Prime of Miss Jean Brodie*

Musicals

BEST MUSICAL: *Your Own Thing* by Donald Driver, Hal Hester and Danny Apolinar

ACTOR IN A PRIMARY ROLE: Robert Goulet as Jacques Bonnard in *The Happy Time*
ACTRESS IN A PRIMARY ROLE: Leland Palmer as Viola in *Your Own Thing*
ACTOR IN A SECONDARY ROLE: Hiram Sherman as Wingate in *How Now, Dow Jones*
ACTRESS IN A SECONDARY ROLE: Sally Eaton as Jeannie in *Hair*
DIRECTOR: Gerald Freedman (off Broadway) and Tom O'Horgan (on Broadway) for *Hair*
SCENERY: Peter Wexler and Gower Champion for *The Happy Time*
COSTUMES: Theoni V. Aldredge (off Broadway) and Nancy Potts (on Broadway) for *Hair*
CHOREOGRAPHY: Joe Layton for *George M!*
SCORE: Hal Hester and Danny Apolinar for *Your Own Thing*

As I look over this list of bests, I cannot help noticing how large is the number of foreign artists who were tops in their categories. This shouldn't be accepted as any sign of weakness in the American theater, because in almost every case the final choice was a very narrow one with many American contenders. Close to Milo O'Shea for best-actor honors was George C. Scott (*Plaza Suite* and *The Little Foxes*); to Zoe Caldwell was Maureen Stapleton (*Plaza Suite*) and Helen Hayes (*The Show-Off*); to Paul Hecht was Harold Gary (*The Price*); to Desmond Heeley was Jo Mielziner (*I Never Sang for My Father* and *The Prime of Miss Jean Brodie*) and Boris Aronson (*The Price*). And the reverse is true—close to Pert Kelton was Carole Shelley in *Loct;* to Mike Nichols was Derek Goldby (*R & G* and *Loot*) and Vivian Matalon (*After the Rain*); to Leland Palmer was Patricia Routledge (*Darling of the Day*). There was plenty of distinction on both sides and all around.

Revivals

Last year's spate of 32 revivals eased off to a merely handsome total of 16 in 1967-68. The surprise success of the revival season was George Kelly's *The Show-Off* as produced in repertory by APA-Phoenix. The surprise was not so much that there proved to be a strong comedic kick left in this 1924 script about a well-meaning braggart—that has been proven before in stage and TV revivals. The surprise was in the shift of the play's emphasis in this production from show-off Aubrey Piper (the starring role played by Lee Tracy off Broadway and Jackie Gleason on TV) to his foil, Mrs. Fisher, his skeptical and outspoken mother-in-law played in this APA version by none other than Helen Hayes. Under Stephen Porter's direction the old script was re-focussed around Miss Hayes's detailed and engaging performance.

APA did for *The Show-Off* this season what it did for *You Can't Take It With You* two seasons ago; instead of kidding it or exploiting it they shed new light on it and stood it up straight in all its enduring comic glory. APA-Phoenix rounded out its 1967-68 Broadway visit at the Lyceum with an unremarkable staging of *The Cherry Orchard,* but the troupe had already won more than enough applause for the Kelly play and the two fascinating European plays—*Pantagleize* and *Exit the King*—dealt with in a previous section of this report. APA-Phoenix has grown into an American repertory unit of such stature that it no longer leans on its scripts but enhances them, informs them, lights them with ideas of acting, staging and design.

Another outstanding 1967-68 revival was the staging of Lillian Hellman's *The Little Foxes* as a guest production at the Vivian Beaumont Theater in Lincoln Center. The wounds inflicted by the greedy, materialistic Hubbard family as they scrape at the world and each other seem as painful as ever in Miss Hellman's powerful script, produced by Saint-Subber as an all-star presentation (most notably with George C. Scott as Ben Hubbard, Anne Bancroft as Regina, Margaret Leighton as Birdie and E.G. Marshall as Oscar), directed with perfect control and clarity by Mike Nichols and designed in deliberate ostentation by Patricia Zipprodt. Following its limited Lincoln Center engagement the production moved to Broadway with some of the stars switching roles, others moving out of and into the cast. The changes didn't matter; this *The Little Foxes* remained a treat as well as a rarity, a revival that became a hit in the full competition of a commercial theater season on Broadway.

The smooth, impressive mounting of the Hellman play at Lincoln Center helped to point up the general fruitlessness of the effort being expended by the Repertory Company of Lincoln Center, in residence at this same Vivian Beaumont Theater. It is learning, yes, but much of its lesson is obsolete. This year the group mounted adequate revivals of Shaw's *Saint Joan,* Anouilh's *Tiger at the Gates* and a new English version by James Forsyth of Rostand's *Cyrano de Bergerac.* Lincoln Center Rep can't be expected to produce on a Saint-Subber all-star scale (though I admired very much Edward Zang's performance as the Dauphin and Michael Annals' costumes for *Saint Joan*). It can't even hope to compare in ensemble virtuosity with such as APA—it isn't ready yet, and comparison would be unfair. Its most pressing problem, it seems to me, is the much more obvious one of a choice of plays. Lincoln Center Rep did not choose to do *The Little Foxes* or *The Show-Off* or any other American play. It relied on standard European scripts, not even new (to New York) like APA's de Ghelderode and Ionesco plays. I suppose it could be argued that the casting of Diana Sands in the title role of *Saint Joan* was an effort to give the play contemporaneous overtones, but they never materialized. Miss Sands realized Shaw's Maid as a symbol for all time and people, in a fine performance in which negritude nevertheless counted for nothing.

Suppose Lincoln Center Rep had mounted three perfect productions of *Saint Joan, Tiger at the Gates* and *Cyrano de Bergerac?* What then would have been accomplished as the 1967-68 result of all the energy that has gone into Lincoln Center's massive act of theatrical parturition, its effort to give

DIANA SANDS AS JOAN IN "SAINT JOAN"

birth to a New York repertory company; this agony of Elia Kazan and Robert Whitehead, of Herbert Blau and Jules Irving and all the Rockefellers wheeling in their appointed courses? The answer would have been: nothing that could not have been done better by Jean-Louis Barrault, Laurence Olivier and the Comédie Française. Until the American actors and directors at the Vivian Beaumont start working on American plays (at least part of the time), they will not proceed one single step along the path that Kazan and Whitehead started to take, and that APA-Phoenix has followed so painstakingly and with such distinction.

It should be noted right here that Lincoln Center Rep deserves applause for its smaller-scale experimental activities in its basement theater, the little Forum. Here were staged new programs by American playwrights, reflecting more credit on the company than anything it has done since Kazan put on two new Arthur Miller plays several seasons ago. Two of these programs were formally presented to the public as off-Broadway shows: Mayo Simon's double bill of one-acters, *Walking to Waldheim* and *Happiness,* and Ron Cowen's full-length *Summertree.* The latter provided the season's most probing reflection on the Vietnam war, in the fanciful context of a young man's thoughts and dreams as he is trying to grow up but is swallowed by the draft and killed in the war. David Birney as the young man, and Philip Sterling as his well-meaning father bogged down in materialistic cliches, were especially effective. The vignettes of *Summertree* cannot be the ultimate goal of a great American repertory company, but they are a more appropriate stop-off along the way than *Tiger at the Gates.*

The Music Theater of Lincoln Center provided a summer production of the Rodgers & Hammerstein masterpiece *South Pacific* under Richard Rodgers' personal supervision, with Giorgio Tozzi as Emile de Becque and Florence Henderson as Ensign Nellie Forbush. Our good New York City Center gave us not only the City Center Gilbert & Sullivan Company in five expert Savoyard programs; not only The City Center Light Opera Company in highly professional re-stagings of *Brigadoon* and *The King and I;* but also The City Center Drama Company in revivals of American straight plays: *Life With Father,* with Dorothy Stickney playing the Vinnie role she created on Broadway, and *The Tenth Man,* both in their first New York professional revivals. As in the cases of *The Show-Off* and *The Little Foxes,* it was a pleasure to note the enduring vigor of these fine American scripts. They are the mined and smelted treasure of the art form, growing in supply season after Broadway season, waiting to be borrowed by anyone with the wit to use them with skill and respect.

Off Broadway

Burdened with rising costs and a creeping hit psychology, the tributary theater known as off Broadway nevertheless was still resisting in 1967-68 the forces influencing it to become a sort of junior Broadway. Hit musicals and comedies were conspicuously present, to be sure, but the air was not yet dangerously polluted with commercialism. Off Broadway was still trying out new forms and subjects, tinkering with the musical theater, probing the nature of man through various avenues of his sexual nature, and in so doing treading paths seldom if ever before trod in the theater. Off Broadway was still a Mecca for the one-act play, the esoteric revival, the facing of existentialist "facts". 1967-68 reached a peak with the musical *Your Own Thing,* which is not only a Best Play and the recipient of the New York Drama Critics Circle award for the year's best musical (the first off-Broadway musical so honored); it also issued a challenge to the whole theater and beyond the theater to the audience with its theme of "Know thyself" (translated into modern language as "Do your own thing"). Its next-to-curtain lines are a keynote for the 1970s:

"Do your own thing
Find your own dream
Dig your own soul
Or dig your own hole
And die."

When we speak of "off Broadway" in the pages of this volume, we are referring to a specific and definable form of New York tributary theater. We are speaking of those non-Broadway shows which (1) had professional Equity casts, (2) offered themselves for review by the critics and (3) planned a reg-

The 1967-68 Season Off Broadway

PLAYS (27)

- Jonah
- The Niggerlovers
- Fragments
- Beyond Desire
- *SCUBA DUBA*
- The Beard
- Where People Gather
- American Place:
  - Father Uxbridge Wants To Marry
  - The Ceremony of Innocence
  - *The Electronic Nigger and Others (Three Plays by Ed Bullins)*
  - Endecott and the Red Cross
- Lincoln Center Forum:
  - Walking to Waldheim and Happiness
  - *Summertree*
- The Peddler and the Dodo Bird
- A Certain Young Man
- *The Indian Wants the Bronx* and *It's Called The Sugar Plum*
- Oh, Say Can You See L.A. and The Other Man
- Saturday Night
- The Bench
- Scarlet Lullaby
- Two Camps by Koutoukas
- *Tom Paine*
- Rate of Exchange
- *THE BOYS IN THE BAND*
- The Hawk
- *Muzeeka* and *Red Cross*
- *Collision Course*

SPECIALTIES (4)

- I Must Be Talking to My Friends
- Take It from the Top
- Winnie the Pooh
- I Only Want an Answer

MUSICALS (8)

- Now Is the Time for All Good Men
- Hair
- *Curley McDimple*
- Love and Let Love
- Have I Got One for You
- *YOUR OWN THING*
- Who's Who, Baby?
- *The Believers*

REVUES (4)

- In the Nick of Time
- In Circles
- *Jacques Brel Is Alive and Well and Living in Paris*
- Fun City

REVIVALS (15)

- Arms and the Man
- A Midsummer Night's Dream
- American Savoyards:
  - Patience
  - H.M.S. Pinafore
  - The Gondoliers
  - The Mikado
  - Iolanthe
- Hamlet
- No Exit and The Little Private World of Arthur Fenwick
- Iphigenia in Aulis
- Summer of the 17th Doll
- House of Flowers
- The Victims
- Winter Journey (The Country Girl)
- Private Lives

FOREIGN PLAYS IN ENGLISH (10)

- The Poker Session
- Stephen D
- Public Theater:
  - Ergo
  - The Memorandum
- The Trials of Brother Jero and The Strong Breed
- Negro Ensemble:
  - Song of the Lusitanian Bogey
  - Kongi's Harvest
- Goa
- The Four Seasons
- Carving a Statue

FOREIGN-LANGUAGE PRODUCTIONS (4)

- University of Chile:
  - La Remolienda
  - ITUCH Anthology
- Le Treteau de Paris:
  - Le Tartuffe
  - En Attendant Godot

Categorized above are all the plays listed in the "Plays Produced Off Broadway" section of this volume.

Plays listed in CAPITAL LETTERS have been designated Best Plays of 1967-68.

Plays listed in *italics* were still running June 1, 1968.

ular 8-a-week schedule of public performances (visiting foreign troupes are included without these qualifications, however). That is how we define "off Broadway." The more informal type of tributary theater is also considered in this volume, in a listing and article on "off off Broadway" by R.J. Schroeder.

The off-Broadway season tested high on every important count in 1967-68. There were 72 productions of record, as compared with 69, 66 and 75 in recent seasons. These 72 productions broke down into 27 new American plays, 8 musicals, 10 new foreign plays in English and 4 revues (a total of 49 new works almost equaling last year's high total of 50), plus 15 revivals, 4 specialty shows and 4 foreign-language programs. In 1967-68, as last season, three off-Broadway shows made the Best Plays list in competition with the best that Broadway had to offer: *Scuba Duba, Your Own Thing* and *The Boys in the Band* (and *Hair* came very close). Off Broadway came up with the most trenchant comment on the Vietnam war in *Summertree,* described with Lincoln Center Rep's other productions in the previous section of this report. Off Broadway's high spirits were displayed in the provoking two-character play *The Beard;* in Joseph Papp's oddball *Hamlet;* in Ed Bullins' *The Electronic Nigger and Others*—and most impudently in the bouncing bare-breasted scene in *Scuba Duba.* All this and the Drama Critics prize too? It was a *very* good year.

The critics prizewinner *Your Own Thing* is based on Shakespeare's *Twelfth Night* in the sense that its leads, Viola and Sebastian, are sibling look-alikes (and in our modern age, dress-alikes and haircut-alikes) who are shipwrecked in Illyria, neither knowing that the other has survived the wreck. Here's where *Twelfth Night* ends (except for a few quotes from Shakespeare sprinkled into the script) and the 1960s begin. The duke of *this* Illyria is called Mayor John V. Lindsay, and the twins gravitate into the society of pop rock 'n' roll singers. The joke in the beginning is that no one knows which is the brother and which the sister, which is boy or girl; and the topper is that after a while no one cares (do your own thing!). The book by Donald Driver is salted with asides, some of encouragement and some of moral indignation, while images of John Wayne, Shirley Temple, Queen Elizabeth I, Humphrey Bogart, Everett Dirksen and the Sistine Chapel God Himself are projected onto the scenery. Still photos, movies and comic book balloons are set into the live action wherever they can enlarge a mood or throw a comic curve, in a sort of multi-media show. The lyrics by Hal Hester and Danny Apolinar (who also appears onstage as a member of the rock 'n' roll singing group) are monosyllabic but effective in the context of the heavy rock beat. Leland Palmer as Viola, in love with a boy who thinks *she's* a boy but loves her anyway, was far and away the year's most engaging musical actress. Making sport of Shakespeare's work was a popular gimmick last season. Off Broadway saw a camp revival of *A Midsummer Night's Dream,* Joseph Papp's fun-house *Hamlet* and *another* musical based on *Twelfth Night,* the relatively short-lived *Love and Let Love.* From London, Frank Marcus reports that there were three way-out versions of *As You Like It.* But surely the champ at this game was *Your Own Thing,* a delightful show in an outrageous sort of way (or vice versa).

The other off-Broadway Best Plays were comedies: *The Boys in the Band,* described earlier in this report, and *Scuba Duba,* which was billed in the program by its author, Bruce Jay Friedman as "a tense comedy." Its central character is an immature young American wandering around the salon of his rented French Riviera chateau dressed in a bathrobe, carrying a scythe and generally making an ass of himself because his wife has left him for a black scuba diver. All of it—even the scene in which an old broad bounces through the salon naked to the waist, looking for something to read—is written, directed and acted a few degrees too earnestly for farce. Nor is it black comedy—there is no leer, no exaggeration of evil just for the hell of it. It's the tense comedy of a clown act, with Jerry Orbach as the bewildered and bereft husband getting laughs at his clownish defenses against pain. His only comfort is the girl next door, played by Brenda Smiley, a model who soothes him with anecdotes from her past, all so weird that it's a wonder she could have survived them, let alone talk about them so blithely. *Scuba Duba* is a disquieting work, staged disquietingly by Jacques Levy in perfect style. The joke is on our tense hero three ways: he's a clown when he's trying to control himself, he's a clown when he lets himself go, and in either case he's the goat of a ruthlessly humiliating situation when it turns out that his wife's lover is not a black skin diver at all, but a black poet—the husband's intellectual as well as his romantic superior. Tense comedy indeed—and most skillful variation of the comic art.

Another of off Broadway's wildly tossing crests in 1967-68 was the "tribal love-rock" musical *Hair,* which was the opening production of Joseph Papp's New York Shakespeare Festival Public Theater season downtown in his new theater, the Florence Sutro Anspacher, a handsome, multi-level, arena-stage house converted from the Astor Library. When its limited engagement ended, *Hair* would not fold up and go away. It was taken uptown to the discoteque *Cheetah* and then to Broadway, where as we go to press it is firmly established as the only solid musical hit of the season, and as such was previously described in the section on hits.

The creation of a Broadway hit is remarkable in itself, but Papp's first season indoors yielded far more than that. Each of his three productions following *Hair* was provocative theater, though none could be classed as a total success. His *Hamlet* did not come off, but its spirit of adventure, its boldly demonstrated conviction that any play, even *Hamlet,* can be freshly revealed by imaginative innovation, is exactly the spirit required of any such experimental troupe as this one (and certainly Papp no longer needs to prove that he could put on an exciting Shakespeare revival if he chose to play one straight). The Public Theater's third offering, Jacov Lind's *Ergo,* directed by Gerald Freedman, was a grotesque dissection and magnification of the elements of the German character, in order to trace the roots of Nazism. The final production, Vaclav Havel's *Memorandum,* directed by Papp, was a farcical Czech expose of an inhumanly mechanized society, further dehumanized by an artificial language to be used for business communication, a language no one can master. These were challenging plays for both producer and audience. They were received with general, if not total, appreciation—but what really matters is that here, in a theater partly supported by public funds, the public arts interest was being well and truly served in experimental efforts to expand for the public benefit the theater art as a whole, rather than to play it safe and enhance private reputations. My only quarrel with Papp, Freedman and their interesting troupe would be in the choice of two foreign scripts while our own authors are clamoring to be produced. Let's hope the Public Theater's record improves in this one respect. It could scarcely be bettered in others.

The American Place Theater, too, had a noteworthy season of experimental production with four *American* plays. Their first effort, Frank Gagliano's *Father Uxbridge Wants To Marry,* was a difficult and sometimes obscurely symbolic work describing man as the victim of his own life, in a play about an elevator operator who is to be supplanted by automation and who loses control of his machine at the same time that he is caught up in agonized reminiscence. American Place was more communicative with its second play, Ronald Ribman's *The Ceremony of Innocence,* an account of Ethelred the Unready's efforts to bring peace to his realm in 1013, offered by its author as a parable, or at least a silhouette, of our own time. The third production at American Place was Ed Bullins' *The Electronic Nigger and Others,* a program of one-acters whose third and strongest play, *Clara's Ole Man,* was a grim mood piece about the lower depths of South Philadelphia, peopled by twisted minds in twisted bodies (with a piercingly accurate portrayal of a spastic child by Helen Ellis, and of an overbearing lesbian by Carolyn Y. Cardwell). These plays were experiments leading toward what will surely be a major Bullins play to come. It seems necessary to add, only because of the title, that the author and characters of these plays are Negroes. The title was changed to *Three Plays by Ed Bullins* after the program was moved to the Martinique Theater to continue its run when its American Place booking ended.

Finally, American Place presented Robert Lowell's *Endecott and the Red Cross,* rich in language and symbolism as it dramatizes two Nathaniel Hawthorne stories about the Puritan leader Governor Endecott suppressing his compatriot British colony at Merry Mount in 1630—stamping it out with fire and musket because of its establishment and Church of England character, its hedonistic practises and its policy of selling guns and whisky to the Indians. This play was originally intended to form part of Lowell's historical trilogy *The Old Glory,* which included the one-acters *My Kinsman, Major Molineux* (Boston just before the Revolution) and *Benito Cereno* (events aboard a Spanish slave ship in 1800), produced by American Place on November 1, 1964. *Endecott and the Red Cross* was to have begun the trilogy with its assault of the grim Puritans upon Thomas Morton's cheerful colony of maypole dancers—an example, of course, of still another dichotomy in the American personality even as it was being formed. Kenneth Haigh, as Endecott, gave a strong-chinned portrayal of a flawed hero, in this version rewritten and expanded from the 1964 script. Lowell's characters are set firmly on their feet, but some of his symbolism remains obscure to me. For example, Endecott is presented as a man of some charity who tones down many of the harsher punishments suggested by his colleague, the minister Palfrey, and yet he coldly orders the shooting of an inoffensive dancing bear which acts out its astonished pain and dies, suffering. The act robs Endecott of any identity as a rational human being, and—though it probably has significance which escapes me—distorts all the other values of Lowell's script, which came out finally as an interesting but puzzling play.

The Negro Ensemble Company realized this season the dream of its artistic director, Douglas Turner Ward, its executive director, Robert Hooks, and other members of its staff and acting company to establish a Negro-oriented repertory and training group in New York City. It is true, and cannot quite be shrugged off, that this is a form of segregation, like the all-Negro company of *Hello, Dolly!* (and many liberals urged Merrick to integrate Pearl Bailey's cast as he was planning the production). But I admit that in the case of the Negro Ensemble Company (and *Dolly*) a reasonable man would have to conclude that the end (enlarged Negro employment and opportunity) justifies the means (a segregated company). The occasional casting of a Diana Sands in a leading role, or that token presence in a chorus of countesses in a Court of Versailles number, are too narrow an opportunity for Negro actors. In the summer of 1967, when Frederick O'Neal, president of Equity, claimed that Broadway was under-employing Negroes, Richard Barr, president of the League of New York Theaters, argued that the modern realistic theater reflects society, so that not until society integrates can there logically be more Negro characters, and thus wider employment, in the plays. In that case, it could be said that The Negro Ensemble Company is what's happening until society integrates. 1967-68 was its pilot season as it stretched its new muscles in *Song of the Lusitanian Bogey,* a Peter Weiss drama of protest against the exploitation of Africans in European colonies; in a revival of *Summer of the 17th Doll;* and in a new play by the Nigerian author Wole Soyinka, *Kongi's Harvest,* contrasting the old with the new Africa. Soyinka is 32, British-educated, with experience at the Royal Court Theater in London. His work was introduced to off-Broadway audiences earlier in the season in an independently-produced program of his one-acters *The Trials of Brother Jero* and *The Strong Breed,* both set in Africa, about a false prophet and the ritual sacrifice of a teacher. Soyinka was in jail in Nigeria as a political prisoner at the time his one-acters opened in November, 1967. *Kongi's Harvest* came along in April as his second representation here this season. It was a full-length work including singing and dancing, a challenge for the Negro Ensemble. This group will conclude its first year in June 1968 with a production of Richard Wright's adaptation of *Daddy Goodness.* The company showed steady development through the year, and its choice of plays was adventuresome. It has gone a long way toward a total justification of its means in its very first season.

In other organized off-Broadway activity, Dorothy Raedler's American Savoyards presented still another season of excellent Gilbert & Sullivan revivals. The Bil Baird marionetteers contributed a delightful *Winnie the Pooh.* And there were two distinguished foreign visitors: The Theater Institute of the University of Chile and Le Treteau de Paris.

The organized producing groups help to broaden the base of each off-Broadway season, but usually it's the way-out individual effort that gives the tributary theater its heightened color. Off Broadway as on, sexuality was a popular subject—all sizes and shapes of sexuality in *Scuba Duba, Hair, Your Own Thing, Clara's Ole Man* and *The Boys in the Band.* Michael McClure's *The Beard* was a heterosexual hang-up, a two-character play whose characters were not so much sex partners as sex symbols: Billy the Kid and Jean Harlow caught in a symbolic battle of the sexes in a symbolic eternity, finally resolving their struggle in a symbolic sex act on the stage. An imported script by Arnold Wesker, *The Four Seasons,* was another two-character affair taking place in an abandoned house and making the comment that loss of innocence is linked with loss of meaning in life. There was even a play—*Scarlet Lullaby*—about the reform of a prostitute through her association with an innocent child.

Turning from sex to violence, the latter was the subject of a most sensitively perceptive study in Israel Horovitz's one-acter *The Indian Wants the Bronx.* Here is Man as the prototype Victim, in the person of an East Indian waiting for a bus to the Bronx in the wee small hours of the lonely morning, long after the buses have stopped running. Two young toughs happen by, notice him (he sticks out like a sprained thumb), begin to tease him (he cannot speak English) and finally beat him and reduce him to a state of terror for much the same reason that Mallory climbed Mt. Everest. The Indian was so conspiciously *there,* so conspicuously lost and defenseless, so obvious a victim that he seemed an incomplete image until his torturers happened along to complete the circle. It takes two to make an act of violence, Horovitz seems to be saying, a victim as well as a bully (and in real life there are more torturers than potential victims; one has only to stand on a dark corner and wait, as for a bus).

John Allen considered the subject of revenge and its corrosive effect on the human spirit in *The Other Man,* a compelling one-acter about a Jew who has made his one-time Nazi torturer a prisoner and is now torturing him. This play appeared on an Allen program of one-acters which took its title from the second playlet, *Oh, Say Can You See L.A.,* a way-out satire on modern decadence, with song-and-dance characters. The Irish playwright Hugh Leonard was represented twice off Broadway early in the season, almost back-to-back, with *The Poker Session,* a study of a mental patient after his release from the hospital, and *Stephen D,* an adaptation of James Joyce's autobiographical works about his life from childhood through university years. Jerome Kass, author of *Monopoly* two seasons ago, was present again off Broadway with a full-length play, *Saturday Night* about a Bronx librarian with dreams of grandeur and intellectual eminence (it received Martin Gottfried's vote for best American play in the Critics Circle balloting). Paul Foster created a vivid portrait of a flawed hero in the biographical-historical *Tom Paine.* Some of off Broadway's most interesting work crowded into the end of the season with John Guare's *Muzeeka,* a satiric comment on middle-class values (symbolized by the vapid music dispensed by a taping firm) and the Vietnam war and its TV coverage; and with a program called *Collision Course,* a sampler of 11 playlets on now subjects by such writers as Jean-Claude van Itallie, Lanford Wilson, Terrence McNally, Jules Feiffer and Israel Horovitz.

Musically, off Broadway came up smiling not only with *Your Own Thing* and *Hair,* but also with *Curley McDimple,* a successful Mary Boylan-Robert Dahdah spoof of child stars in general and old Shirley Temple movies in particular. Then there was the musicalization of Gertrude Stein's fragment *In Circles,* a series of tentative beginnings of conversations among articulate young people on a chateau terrace, set to music by Al Carmines and choreographed movement under Lawrence Kornfeld's direction. It was one of those off-Broadway productions which may be described as "interesting". Here and there a Stein image or a Carmines music theme took flight, but for the most part it was a mind-blower, of an experience trying to dig Miss Stein's meaning in such disconnected lines as "Papa blows his noses," "Cut wood" and "A circle is a necessity, we each have our circle." Elsewhere off Broadway, the songs of the Paris-based Belgian composer Jacques Brel were cordially celebrated and presented in the Village Gate cabaret revue *Jacques Brel Is Alive and Well and Living in Paris.*

Among the season's off-Broadway revivals, Euripides's *Iphigenia in Aulis,* not seen here since 1921, was mounted most effectively by Circle in the Square under Michael Cacoyannis's direction, with Irene Papas as Clytemnestra. Its drama of the impending sacrifice of the innocent in order to attain a military goal was an ancient Greek drama with strong modern overtones. Some of the same contemporary echoes were heard in a noteworthy revival of Shaw's *Arms and the Man* under Philip Minor's direction.

Looking back on the off-Broadway season as a whole, I am struck by its energy and drive to express everything in terms of theater. The word "struck" is exactly what I mean—I can't think back over the off-Broadway year without being assaulted in heart and mind by a series of memory images: long-haired, clown-suited Danny Apolinar singing in *Your Own Thing* that nature had not formed him to resemble the prince in the fairy tale, so why should he torture himself pretending to be such a one? . . . . . Jerry Orbach clutching an irrelevant scythe in *Scuba Duba* and striving desperately to find a straw of sense in his sea of nightmarish troubles . . . . . bushy-haired Gerome Ragni trying to love everybody all at once in *Hair* . . . . . Cliff Gorman camping through *The Boys in the Band* . . . . . the sterotyped smile of John Cazale as the East Indian and the bored resignation to violence of Al Pacino and Matthew Cowles as the bullies in *The Indian Wants the Bronx* . . . . . the smirking dominance of Carolyn Y. Cardwell in Ed Bullins' *Clara's Ole Man* . . . . . the bland self-satisfaction of Philip Sterling driving his son into the

Army in *Summertree* . . . . . all right, even "Papa blows his noses." Such moments of truth on the stage stop us short and make us take account. There was a time when off Broadway's 1967-68 images might have shocked a majority of us; but in the last decade our literary and performing arts have led most of us slowly through barriers of tabu, superstition, prejudice, modesty, preconception and other hang-ups, so that now we have been trained to observe what once would have merely blown our minds. It's next to impossible to shock today's off-Broadway audience—at least not with any revelation of human suffering or aspiration. I confess that I was shocked—mind-blown out of any delicate appreciation of the play's values—by the slaughter of the bear in Robert Lowell's play. But strike us the off-Broadway theater can and should—and did in 1967-68; often profoundly and, in the case of its dramatized encouragements to know and be thyself, perhaps even with a lasting effect on the general social attitude and philosophy.

Offstage

Behind the scenes of play production, an important 1967-68 development was the concerted effort by theater and New York City authorities to encourage the building of playhouses into new office structures in the Broadway area. Building code regulations in combination with other factors had made it generally unfeasable to combine theaters with office or apartment space under the same roof, so that in the present construction boom the theater might have found itself pressed for lebensraum by the new anthills in its own yard. Now, with the help of Mayor John V. Lindsay and others concerned with the welfare of New York's legitimate stage, in hearings and discussions with various City powers and agencies, the way has been eased and it was more than likely at press time that 1,600-1,800 seat legitimate playhouses would be included in each of the new office structures on the sites of the Astor Hotel and Capitol Theater. The technicalities of the arrangement are complicated, but what it amounts to is an interpretation of the building code —in the Broadway area only—compatible with theater interests, public interest and safety and of course the profit interest of the builders.

The theater count is one of the art form's vital signs. In recent years the Broadway count has remained fairly steady in the low 30s, with theaters shifting in and out of availability—the Palace in, the Ziegfeld out and so forth. This year the ANTA-Washington Square Theater was lost to Broadway production—but it had been only recently (in 1963) gained. Far more significantly, the Playhouse at press time was booked for the bulldozer to make way for a new office complex whose mentors include Rockefeller interests. The fact that they also have announced their intention to include a new theater in their plans for this site is not entirely reassuring. One veteran theater observer pointed out that new builders tend to think big and are likely to plan large theaters (like the ones designed for the Astor and Capitol buildings) rather than medium-sized ones, like those being demolished. This change in the physical environment could induce esthetic change. No longer will the American theater need actors with large voices and personalities projecting to fill a theater in immediate dramatic or comic contact with the audience. The actor will be projected mechanically through microphones in big productions tailored to fit the bigger houses; or he can reach audiences with a whisper in a tiny 300-seat off-Broadway environment. If the present trend continues, there will be no in-between.

The involvement of the theater and its individual artists in the events and issues of the day was about as usual. In this Presidential election year, the photo of a playwright or an actor standing shoulder to shoulder with the candidate of his choice at a political rally became a commonplace. Involvement in the racial issues took many forms including the establishment of The Negro Ensemble Company and pressure for wider casting of Negro actors. Theater folk staged a benefit at Fillmore East for the Black Panther Party for Self-Defense, with the specific aim of helping to raise bail for Eldridge Cleaver, the writer who was jailed on the West Coast after a clash with police. One playwright caught up in direct action was LeRoi Jones, who was arrested during the Newark, N.J. riots in July, tried in a New Jersey court, found guilty of unlawful possession of weapons and sentenced to three years by a judge who read portions of Jones's poetry aloud in court and indicated that he based the harshness of Jones's punishment partly on the poem—not, we hasten to add, because of the quality of the poetry, but because of its militant views. In a less dramatic development, the New York State Commission for Human Rights held hearings in April to inquire whether the theater's hiring practises are fair to minorities; testimony was offered pro and con. And, in May, Oriental actors picketed the City Center revival of *The King and I,* claiming inadequate representation in this show with Siamese setting and characters.

The issue of whether American playwrights should permit their scripts to be produced in South Africa (in order to fight Apartheid with the box office proceeds), or whether they should withhold permission for performances before South Africa's racially segregated audiences, continued to heat up in 1967-68. Neil Simon had permitted *The Odd Couple* and *Barefoot in the Park* to be done there under the first rationale, but this season he switched to the starve-'em-out-culturally position and withheld permission to perform *Sweet Charity* after "second thoughts" about a country "that denies its *majority* of citizens their basic civil liberties." Paddy Chayefsky too declared his works unavailable for South African production.

And speaking of involvement, 1967-68 saw an unusual instance of bringing a social problem onto the stage itself, not merely as the subject of dramatization but in a sort of happening. The tortures of drug addiction were reenacted in a presentation called *The Concept,* not by actors, but by actual victims of this illness. Ex-addicts described and acted out the agony and some of its methods of cure at Daytop Village, Staten Island, communicating their own experiences directly to the audience with minimum intervention of playwriting. They had a basic program of material to be presented, but many of the details and words were improvised from performance to performance.

In subsidy, the regional and experimental theater continued to benefit from foundation support in five- and six-figure grants. Federal support of the arts administered by the National Foundation on the Arts suffered from a cut in appropriations by Congress, but not before a grant of $200,000 had been made by the National Endowment to the Theater Development Fund. This Fund is the professional stage's best hope for subsidy where it will do the most good, and it is now organized and ready to function during the 1968-69 season. With the abovementioned Federal money and other grants received from the Rockefeller Brothers and Twentieth Century Funds and the Mary Reynolds Babcock Foundation, this Fund will support the occasional, especially deserving but not instantly popular New York show by purchasing blocks of tickets during the earlier weeks of its run, and at the same time helping to develop theater audiences by giving these tickets to students and other selected groups. This would give a deserving show a broader hearing and perhaps even buy it the time to develop an audience and become self-sustaining. The Fund is now organized as follows: president, John E. Booth; executive secretary, Hugh Sothern; play selection, Harold Clurman aided by three other members of the Fund's board of directors who are Booth, Clurman, John F. Wharton (honorary chairman), Stuart W. Little (vice president), Richard R. Davidson (secretary) Stephen Benedict (treasurer), August Heckscher (honorary director), Hume Cronyn, Edward F. Kook, Joseph B. Martinson, Alan Pryce-Jones, James Rowe and Irving Cheskin.

New York theater enjoyed virtual freedom from censorship in 1967-68. City authorities took a long, hard look at *The Beard* and, commendably, decided to leave it alone. The New York *Times* rejected a *The Beard* quote ad full of sexual references (without which reviewers couldn't describe the play), and *The New Yorker* ignored the show in its off-Broadway listings after its critic decided it was "unworthy of review." But in our town there were nothing like the police problems which *The Beard* encountered in San Francisco and Los Angeles, or the Lord Chamberlain problems of *America Hurrah, Soldiers* and Edward Bond's *Early Morning* in London this season.

Union activity during the 1967-68 season included a new three-year contract for stagehands. During its term the top weekly minimum will rise to $204 for department heads, $156 for key men and others. Actors Equity reached a new agreement with the League of off-Broadway Theaters and Producers, by which actors' minimums will rise from $65-$130 a week to $75-$150 a week over a three-year period, with stage managers getting $20 more. Actual amounts in individual cases are based on box office receipts off Broadway, so the contract has a bonus clause written into it to benefit actors performing in playhouses so small that the grosses could never be large even if the play is a long-run hit. After a 44 weeks' run in such a situation, actors will receive $7.50 a week extra. In exchange, Equity agreed that its off-Broadway performers could be signed to run-of-the-play contracts of 9 months' duration.

As the season ended, Broadway was facing a renegotiation of its Equity contract, which expired June 2, 1968. As we were putting this volume to press, a League of New York Theaters proposal was rejected by the Equity membership. Principally at issue were the minimum salary, the employment of chorus members and a difference of opinion over when and how to control the casting of foreign actors in Broadway shows. The latter problem is complicated by fiscal as well as esthetic considerations: actors' salaries in speaking roles are almost invariably negotiated far above the minimum level, and there is always the possibility (some actors believe the inevitability) that British actors will settle for a good deal less pay than their American colleagues in the same roles. In any case, the casting last season of Anthony Quayle in *Galileo* and this season of Margaret Leighton in *The Little Foxes,* and of Eileen Atkins, Ian McKellen and Ian McShane in *The Promise*—all non-British roles—and finally almost in the middle of negotiations of Nicol Williamson to replace George C. Scott in *Plaza Suite*—an American actor in an American role—were red flags to the Equity bull. On Monday, June 17, the actors struck (a relatively painless process for a union most of whose members are out of work anyway at any one time). 19 Broadway shows went dark. David Merrick decided to close *How Now, Dow Jones* and *I Do! I Do!* permanently, and Joseph Cates and Henry Fownes closed *A Day in the Death of Joe Egg* (the three shows had run their course at the box office anyway but might have been kept running for a while, for the benefit of those employed in them). Settlement of the strike was reached in an all-night session June 19 at Gracie Mansion under the watchful eye of Mayor Lindsay. The parties agreed to a minimum wage increase from $130 to $155 over the three-year contract period and an employment arrangement for choristers by which they could not be dismissed after 20 weeks (as they could previously) but need not be replaced if they left voluntarily. Alien performers are never to be hired as replacements for American actors, and all disputes about the employment of aliens are to be resolved by binding arbitration. On the evening of June 20 the lights went back on again at 16 Broadway shows. It was estimated that the strike cost actors $80,000 in salaries and producers $400,000 in gross receipts for the 4 canceled performances.

Among theater critics the year's major development was the slotting of Clive Barnes into the job of daily theater reviewer at the New York *Times.* Walter Kerr voluntarily handed over this daily stint so that he could concentrate on his series of critiques in the paper's Sunday drama section. Barnes became the Lord High Everything Else of the *Times* drama desk as he continued to review dance while he took over the reviewing of Broadway productions and selected off-Broadway, out-of-town and other performing arts events. Also at the *Times,* Arthur Gelb replaced Joseph G. Herzberg as the overlord of the paper's cultural coverage. William H. Glover of the AP was elected president of the New York Drama Critics Circle, succeeding Norman Nadel. Richard Watts Jr. was the playwrights' choice as the "most perceptive" critic of the season by a small plurality in annual poll conducted by *The Dramatists Guild Quarterly.* The prime example of critic-baiting was a thrust and riposte of telegrams between David Merrick and Clive Barnes, following unfavorable Barnes comments on Merrick productions (Merrick: "The honeymoon is over." Barnes: "I didn't know you cared.").

The Legitimate Theater Industry Exploratory Commission lost the services early in the season of John F. Wharton, who resigned as the Commission's consultant-director. Wharton explained in a statement published in *Variety:* "The major factor which prompted my action was a decision by the Commission that hereafter the campaign for ticket reform could best be conducted through other channels." Following Wharton's resignation, the Commission's fact-finding and policy-recommending activities appeared stalled, except for a few reports of experiments with computers in the sale and distribution of tickets.

Institutionally, the Broadway theater made special efforts in 1967-68 to improve transportation for some of its patrons and to promote itself in a glorious display of glamor and kleig lights. The first took the form of a special bus service to and from Broadway from the upper East Side. The cost to the passenger was 30¢ each way, but the service cost far more than that, including the price of advertising it so that theatergoers would be aware of its existence. Columbia Records acted as the sponsor for this bus service and picked up the tab for its deficit—ironically, in a season which produced little excitement on the musical stage. The bus service was a big hit with the East Side theatergoing public, however, and the League hoped to arrange for its continuance.

A second conspicuous effort by the League was the glamorization of the Tony Awards ceremony in which citations for the theater's 1967-68 "bests" were bestowed at the Shubert Theater in an evening of network TV coverage and a galaxy of stars (some of whom like Audrey Hepburn, Jack Benny, Gregory Peck and Groucho Marx hadn't been on a Broadway stage in a long time). The show was a good one, but the Tony Awards themselves were subjected to several technical limitations which robbed them of a portion of their meaning and were the subject of controversy long before the ceremony took place. An arbitrary cut-off date for the nominations in March (in order to schedule a TV show before the summer doldrums) prevented consideration of *George M!, Hair* and other spring shows until the next calendar year —and required the inclusion of several productions from last season. Repertory companies including the APA-Phoenix at the Lyceum on Broadway were excluded by the League's rules, as were *all* off-Broadway productions. Distinction between "leading" and "supporting" players was confused by technicalities of billing.

The only comprehensive way to choose a slate of season's "bests", it seems to me, is with a cutoff date in late May after every show has come in (and the hell with TV scheduling), including for consideration *all* shows, Broadway, off-Broadway and repertory, in New York's professional theater—that theater great and small which employs union card-holding professionals to put on a regular schedule of 8 performances a week open to the critics and the public. That's what the *Best Plays* volume means when it says "best." Until the Tonys accept a similar responsibility they are lacklustre awards no matter how many TV lights and Audrey Hepburn smiles radiate upon them.

Such were the revels of 1967-68—the revels of the New York commercial theater. By any possible measurement, Broadway is still the scene. It's where it's at. Even the names of its major tributaries—off Broadway and off off Broadway—are love-hate relationships with the parent. Their names signify that they are *not* Broadway, they are *removed* from Broadway—but not very far; a measurable distance, not a million light years of heredity, style, technique or even intent.

Broadway is where it's at in deed as well as in name. Its best outgoing playscripts become staples of stock and other activity from coast to coast and pole to pole, even when these scripts didn't make it the first time out on Broadway (c.f. *Tiny Alice, Slow Dance on the Killing Ground, The Lion in Winter,* etc.). Broadway can provide an atmosphere of appreciation for the outstanding incoming works of the world theater, however far out, from *Marat/Sade* to *R & G,* including Ionesco and Pinter at their best. Broadway can assimilate all new forms of theater as they reach a state of operational efficiency (c.f. *The Homecoming, R & G, Hair,* etc.); and although Broadway economics work against experimentation in the early stages of new theater forms, where is a major scene of such experimentation? Around Broadway, near Broadway, of course, and this is no accident. All three of the off-Broadway scripts on this season's Best Plays list were mounted by producers who also have Broadway productions in the works or in being. Broadway is not a mere stagnant receptacle of is tributaries, its tides rise and flow back into the small playhouses in the form of ideas, talent and money, refreshing the experimental activity in its turn.

As for environment, Broadway's continuous insistence on freedom of expression has created in New York a theatrical environment in which almost anything goes that can stand up and walk. It was not in commercially polluted New York that such scripts as Michael McClure's *The Beard* ran into trouble, it was out in the pure Rockefeller and Ford-blessed ether of the hinterlands. Homosexuality came under close study with a new dramatic insight during 1967-68, and the subject was accepted almost as unselfconsciously by Broadway audiences in *Staircase* as it was by off-Broadway audiences in *The Boys in the Band.*

Yes, the New York theater is where it's at in name, in creativity, in freedom of expression and in audience appreciation, and Broadway is both the parent and the child of its time and place. Our musical theater is evolving rapidly, and yet *Hello, Dolly!, Fiddler on the Roof, Man of La Mancha, Cabaret* and *Hair* can play side by side, inviting comparison to the detriment of none, like the beauties in Paris's judgment. Some of these productions are years old, but which is tired, which is obsolete? The answer, of course, is not one of them. Time does not wither nor custom stale this wench of infinite variety, this best effort of the Broadway theater which in good and bad seasons, in old and new forms, is created not only to dazzle but also to light the way; not only to startle but inform, not only to delight but also to last.

THE 1967-68 OFF-OFF-BROADWAY SEASON

By R. J. Schroeder

Editor, *The New Underground Theater* (Bantam Books)

Until this season, no one had quite known what that second "off" in off off Broadway really meant. But 1967-68 habitues of the off-off-Broadway theater found out that it refers to that ancient show biz plea, "Take it off!" This was the season when off off Broadway took it off. And then, in hardly more time than it takes to whip off a bra, onstage nudity titillated the off-Broadway and then the Broadway scenes.

But the almost instantaneously brief and dimly lit exposure that brought Broadway's new musical *Hair* instant notoriety was as innocuous as a maiden's wink when compared to this season's off-off-the-main-stem practises. Ed Wode's *Christmas Turkey* at the Cooper Square Arts Theater was first to arrive at the definitive limit—his ingenue played in the altogether altogether in seated and reclining postures, full-face, as it were, in full stage lighting in an intimate audience-to-stage relationship.

But while Mr. Wode's production was, as I have said, definitive, it only served to express the practical limit to a pervasive trend. Ron Tavel's *Shower* at The Extension featured a heroine who was not only virtually nude, but who played frequently and most courageously in the audience area. When the rapist in Leonard Melfi's *The Shirt* began the rape scene at La Mama, he took everything off except his symbolic shirt. In the Playhouse of the Ridiculous's *Conquest of the Universe,* there were not one but five (count 'em) nudie queens bouncing through the frenetic action. In *Tennis, Anyone?* at the Troupe Repertory Theater Club, the victim of a rape played her post-rape scene in the condition in which the rapist had left her.

Literally dozens of other productions could be named—the situation became such that toward the end of the season the ads in the *Village Voice* began to omit descriptive copy and simply show a title, a theater location and a photograph of the particular form of nudity being featured. The fact that this season's old-fashioned clothed performances included Der Grüne Kakadu's *Salome* and The Extension's *The Breasts of Tiresias* could only be taken as examples of off off Broadway's typical perversity.

From an esthetic point of view, it would seem that this season's nudity derived more from the query, "We're supposed to be the new theater, so what can we do that's new for 1968?" than from any artistic or dramatic necessity. I am not so much imputing motivation as I am reporting on how things turned out. And I am reporting that despite the nudity, less that was new came into fruition in the off off Broadway theater this season than in the last several seasons.

Virtually the only exploration of new boundaries took place at Thresholds and at Theater Genesis. At Thresholds, Donna Carlson and John Parkinson sought to evoke the utmost nuance in such unusual works for the stage as Kenneth Patchen's *Now You See It* and Kankred Dorsts's *Freedom for Clemens,* and in a modern dance and music interpretation for Americans of the spirit of the Noh drama.

At Theater Genesis, the staging of Sam Shepard's *Forensic and the Navigators* and Murray Mednick's pre-commercial version of *The Hawk* extended the limits of non-linear and non-intellectually-mediated drama. *The Hawk* dealt in a beyond-the-rational manner with a dope peddler and his victims—creating a lasting impression of the horror of the interpersonal relationships involved without utilization of story line or characterization or melodramatic build-up in any customary sense.

Ralph Cook's direction of *Forensic and the Navigators* was first emotionally and then physically eerie. As a "hero" found his world less and less acceptable or even probable, the play's audience left the "real" world behind along with the hero, as the room filled with a whitish gas, and then the most ear-piercing rock music of modern times pelted the fog and completed each audience-member's isolation. This was the present writer's single most dramatic theater experience on, off, or off off Broadway this season.

With the exceptions noted, most of off off Broadway went on doing its thing. La Mama, The Playbox, The Anthony Mannino Repertory Club, Playwrights' Workshop, and the Troupe Repertory Theater Club, among others, continued to provide facilities for playwrights or directors who "package" their own shows and then bring their productions to these theaters.

Lucille Lortel's ANTA Matinee Theater Series, the Playhouse of the Ridiculous, The Judson Poets Theater, The Dove Company and The Mannhardt Theater Foundation, Inc. continued to produce some old but mainly new plays, with a high degree of "house" participation and supervision.

And the Classic Stage Company, The Extension, the Roundabout Theater, The Rising Sun Theater, The Theater of the Riverside Church, Der Grüne Kakadu, and Equity Theater continued to produce some new but mainly established plays under house participation and supervision. In the case of the Classic Stage Company, Der Grüne Kakadu and the Roundabout Theater, permanent repertory companies are being built by Christopher Martin, David Gale, and Gene Feist, respectively.

A new kind of theater has been added to New York's off-off-Broadway scene by Isaiah Sheffer and Eric Bentley, who are co-producers and founders of the D.M.Z. (yes, the de-militarized zone) Cabaret. This is a political cabaret theater, intended to offer trenchant social and political commentary in the European rather than in the comparatively bland Upstairs-at-the-Downstairs or Plaza Nine American tradition.

But the Lord giveth and the Lord taketh away. Taken from us this season was, I am sad in reporting, the Caffe Cino. Founded and operated until his own untimely death by Joe Cino, this was the original coffee house theater. No off-off-Broadway house or impressario could lay claim to a greater influence on the recent development of experimental theater in New York, and it is a crowning tragedy that the Caffe Cino's passing should follow so closely upon Joe's.

○
○
○

THE SEASON AROUND THE UNITED STATES

with

A DIRECTORY OF PROFESSIONAL REGIONAL THEATER

○
○
○

INTRODUCTION

By Ruth Fischer

Program editor and press representative for The Cleveland Play House, lecturer in contemporary drama at Case Western Reserve University and author of articles for *The New Republic, The Nation* and *Playbill*

EVEN while some of its members still reeled from the impact of their 1966-67 upheavals, the resident theater moved in positive directions in 1967-68—particularly in the area of community involvement. It was almost as if it tried to cast off the chaotic image of the previous year when its internal battles were chronicled down to the liveliest diatribe, its financial crises were diagnosed down to the most whopping deficit, and its diverse artistic policies (one man's Pinter is another man's Neil Simon) were solemnly graded on an index of esthetics. That picture, although it was a bit out of focus, conveyed dishevelment. Now it was time for the resident * theater to turn to the larger issues of its artists, its audience, and its community.

* Mrs. Fischer offers here the following semantic aside: "K. Elmo Lowe, director of the Cleveland Play House, suggests that once and for all we scrap the term 'regional' theater for the more accurately descriptive 'resident' theater. He contends, along with many colleagues, that 'regional' is a misnomer because it implies an artistic motif related to a theater's location. In support of this argument, he cites the name of the agency for negotiating with Actors Equity: League of *Resident* Theaters." The word "resident" is used by Mrs. Fischer throughout this introduction, but *Best Plays* will continue to use the word "regional" at least for the time being, for the same reason that prompted us to select it in the first place when we began the Directory three volumes

The resident theater showed a discernible maturity this year. There were many productions of untried plays by unknown playwrights, important premieres of plays by established playwrights who elected to bypass Broadway, more performances for students, new sociological approaches to the wooing of mass audiences and improved relationships with boards of directors.

The most significant development was a heightened identification with community problems—especially with racial turbulence, the chief characteristic of our time. This is not to say the resident theater turned itself into a soapbox, a propaganda mill, or a settlement house. It never lost sight of its principal function: to produce plays. If this year's major trend needs a name, call it Theater of Relevance. It operates on or off the stage, in or out of the theater. It can be a production of a socially-oriented play (new or old) that makes a statement, provides insights, or simply pokes fun. It can be a program of workshops for underprivileged children or a mobile unit that moves into the inner city (a euphemism for the Negro ghetto).

Sometimes propinquity plays an important role. When your theater is in a slum area, it's out of the question not to identify with what's happening in the streets. A case in point is The Cleveland Play House. Our two buildings, housing three theaters, are on the fringes of Hough, a section that became a household word after the 1966 riots. In 1967 the Cleveland Summer Arts Festival came into being and provided an immediate framework for community action. The Festival was a beautifully meshed program involving a dozen of the city's leading cultural institutions that presided over workshops and presented 63 theater, concert, opera, and ballet performances—all of them free—in public parks and playgrounds. Along with our theater, participating groups included the prestigious Cleveland Orchestra and Cleveland Museum of Art, and Karamu House, a prominent interracial arts center.

On the first anniversary of the riots some 2,000 adults and children turned out to watch our production of *The Tempest*. This was one of 19 outdoor performances of Shakespeare, and it took place in an abandoned major league baseball stadium. For most members of the audience it was an initiation into the living theater, and they celebrated with unabashed pleasure. After the performance they visited backstage and asked questions ("How can I get to be an actor?") and fingered costumes and false beards. Later they helped dismantle sets and portable stages and loaded them onto waiting vans.

Another Festival project was a 10-week program of theater workshops for children. Charge d'affaires in our theater was Stuart Levin, who was a child actor here 25 years ago, later taught in Watts in Los Angeles, and returned to Cleveland as director of our Youth Theater. Mr. Levin, with 445 summer pupils, was a one-man master sergeant, house physician, and repository for switchblade knives. Many of his charges had no permanent addresses, mov-

---

ago: in several cases of well-established and well-respected theater companies which must be included in any listing of America's regional theater, there are creative contributors—directors, actors, designers—who are *not* resident but are brought in to take part in individual productions of that company in that region.

ing from household to household with friends or relatives, but they were eminently at home in the theater. They took to the stage with a style uniquely their own. One of them, asked to improvise a familiar situation, did a sketch called "How My Daddy Got Drunk and Arrested." Another dramatized "Me and Willie Swiping Things at the A & P". These vignettes were not presented for revelatory kicks, but with the matter-of-factness of a suburban child describing his vacation in Maine.

While the Cleveland Summer Arts Festival didn't profess to solve the complex problem of the slums, it did help relieve the nagging tedium of the ghetto and cool down a potentially hot summer. It was a $528,000 venture subsidized by local businesses, local foundations, and the city of Cleveland. The only federal assistance was a $75,000 grant from the Council of Economic Opportunity earmarked for the employment of teen-agers as ushers and assistants. Howard Whittaker, director of the Cleveland Music School Settlement, was the administrator. As this volume went to press the Festival was scheduled for a 1968 encore in Cleveland, and was being viewed as a model program which other cities might duplicate—involving other resident theaters.

On a more limited basis, other resident theaters had similar programs in 1967. The Seattle Repertory Theater, in its third annual "Theater in the Park" program, staged free performances of *The Merry Wives of Windsor.* In Philadelphia the Theater of the Living Arts embarked on a bold "Theater in the Streets" program. With echoes of medieval troupes traveling the European countryside, the Philadelphia actors went into the city's southwest sector, an area that is predominantly Italian, Polish, and Negro, to perform with the youngsters.

Meanwhile, back on the stage, the Theater of Relevance made new inroads. In Cleveland our sleeper of the year was a relatively unknown play, *The Strong Are Lonely,* written by the Austrian playwright Fritz Hochwalder. Its plot revolves about the exploitation of South American Indians by landowners and businessmen in 18th-century Buenos Aires—a story hardly calculated for box office appeal. In its only other American showing, it had a brief Broadway run in 1953. Everyone connected with the New York production was content to abandon the play to the annals of also-rans—except John Marley, a member of the original cast. Mr. Marley, now a West Coast director and actor, was engaged as guest director for the Cleveland production after he convinced K. Elmo Lowe that "the play is more relevant now than when we did it 14 years ago, because the story has a strong parallel in the new Negro revolution." Its timeliness, he believed, could lend it a new theatrical excitement.

It did. It was an artistic and a box office success. Tony Mastroianni, drama critic for The Cleveland *Press,* wrote: "It hammers home the parallels between 1767 and 1967: the problems of civil rights, the question of violence versus non-violence, the problem of conforming to the status quo." Peter Bellamy of *The Plain Dealer* called it "a meaningful and thrilling play of the intellect." Many members of our acting ensemble felt it was the most significant play in a year of 15 productions (including one pre-season revival) that ranged from *Charley's Aunt* and *Luv* to *The Pinter Plays* and *Waiting for Godot.*

Parenthetically, our experience with *The Strong Are Lonely* would seem to refute a statement Lewis Funke made last February in The New York *Times.* "A failure in New York," he said, "no matter how worthy, usually doesn't have a chance elsewhere in the nation, probably because of the national psychology that seeks out hits."

Having found an apparently successful formula, we decided to try it again. Our 1968-69 schedule lists another one of Mr. Marley's long shots, *The Day of the Lion,* Joel Wyman's play about South African apartheid. Once again Mr. Marley will direct, and the production here will be an American premiere.

The race struggle was a prominent metaphor in many new plays this year, and this inevitably raises the question: Does the commingling of art and sociology dilute the art? Not necessarily. The concept of the theater as a valid social instrument is as old as Aristophanes' lampooning of the Athenian establishment, and as new as LeRoi Jones' lashing out against a society he considers hostile. Of all the arts the theater surely must be the most immediately social. At any given moment in history it can reflect changing events and attitudes with an impact unparalleled in the other arts.

A noteworthy example is *The Great White Hope,* a new play by Howard Sackler that became the success story of the season at the Arena Stage in Washington. A grant from the National Endowment for the Arts subsidized the production. Based loosely on the life of the championship boxer Jack Johnson, it explores the prevailing racial attitudes of Johnson's day and projects them as a backdrop for our own time. Several New York critics reviewed it (this is another growing trend in the resident theater) and their reactions, like those of their Washington colleagues, were generally enthusiastic. *The Great White Hope* subsequently was optioned for Broadway and film productions.

That skyrocketing resident-theater-to-Broadway route, however, is rare for a new play. Barrie Stavis' *Harpers Ferry,* a Civil War drama about John Brown, traveled a more characteristic course. It had its premiere at the Tyrone Guthrie Theater in Minneapolis, but it failed to get the critical approval a new work usually needs in order to get off the ground. Everyone agreed that the mere fact of its production was commendable because it fulfilled the resident theater's noblest function: experimentation. But that convention, however valid, poses a dilemma for many struggling theaters, particularly if a new play is expensive to mount and doesn't have the benefit of subsidy.

Philadelphia's Theater of the Living Arts, already burdened this year by an inherited deficit, took a calculated gamble when it canceled a scheduled production of *Twelfth Night* and substituted Lester Franklin's *A Scaffold for Marionettes—A Myth.* (What a switch!) The new play had a lot going for it. For one thing, its story had a ring of authenticity; it was based historically on the case of a Baltimore socialite who caned to death a Negro waitress, and it demonstrated that truth is grislier than fiction. For another thing, Mr.

Franklin, an ex-convict turned playwright-in-residence, made tantalizing biographical copy. *A Scaffold for Marionettes* was not a howling success. When it closed, its shortcomings were acknowledged, the playwright's promising talent and good intentions were praised, and the Theater for the Living Arts received a pat on the back for its venturesome spirit.

That spirit persisted in many resident theaters this year. The Milwaukee Repertory Theater presented two new plays, *The Head of Hair* by Allen Davis III and *Oh, Pioneers* by Douglas Taylor. They attracted only 15 per cent of the theater's 6,000 subscribers, but an assist from the Rockefeller Foundation cushioned the financial blow.

When does a resident theater hang out its S.R.O. sign for a new play? When it's written by a well-known playwright. The sellout premieres of the season were Edward Albee's *Box-Mao-Box* at the Studio Arena Theater in Buffalo, presented as part of that city's well subsidized Festival of Fine Arts, and Paddy Chayefsky's *The Latent Heterosexual* at the Dallas Theater Center. Both playwrights said they chose to unveil their new works outside New York because they wanted to avoid the Broadway hit-or-flop syndrome. (Most resident theater productions have predetermined runs, whatever their notices.) Mr. Chayefsky declared that "Broadway is finished," which, of course, it isn't. And *The Latent Heterosexual* is scheduled for production by the APA Repertory Company.

From the vantage point of having produced 57 new plays in fifty-two seasons, The Cleveland Play House takes a mellow view of the crazy-quilt pattern of untried works. "All things being equal, we'd rather produce a new script than a Broadway success," K. Elmo Lowe observes. "But unfortunately things are rarely equal. Without actively soliciting them, our theater receives over a hundred manuscripts a season. Only about 5 per cent have merit that we can detect."

Not unlike their Broadway counterparts, most of the first-time playwrights whose works were nurtured here eventually vanished into obscurity. Of course there are those who didn't: Elmer Rice (*Not for Children,* 1936); Maxwell Anderson (*The Eve of St. Mark,* 1942); Tennessee Williams (*You Touched Me,* in collaboration with William Windham, 1943); Maurice Valency (*The Thracian Horses,* 1944); William Wister Haines (*Command Decision,* 1946); and Ben Hecht (*Simone,* 1962).

A broad audience is the best assurance that new works (and just about anything else a theater does) will be sustained, and one of the soundest long-range audience building practises is the student program. Aside from its inestimable educational value, it helps build a new generation of theatergoers. Our annual Play House Shakespeare Festival for students dates back to 1939, and we are, by virtue of having bridged two generations, in a fair position to confirm its effectiveness. One of the most frequent and rewarding comments we hear from our adult audiences is: "I began coming to this theater years ago when I was a student." It is sweet music to our ears.

Resident theaters throughout the country accelerated their student programs in 1967-68. In San Francisco 55,000 young people saw special student performances by the American Conservatory Theater. And here's a new slant on the generation gap: The ACT reports that the production most frequently requested by students was Martin Duberman's *In White America,* while teachers preferred *The Crucible* and *Tartuffe.*

At three resident theaters—the Trinity Square Playhouse in Providence, the Repertory Theater in New Orleans, and the Inner City Repertory Company in Los Angeles—performances for students outnumber regular evening performances. These theaters operate under special grants from the National Council on the Arts and the Department of Health, Education, and Welfare. They present 5 student matinees during the week, free of charge, and 3 weekend performances for adults who pay for their tickets. What is significant is that student performances in these theaters virtually underwrite the adult program. Thus, practically speaking, a subsidized educational program can be a survival kit for the resident company that doesn't yet have a firm foothold in its community.

Audience development, adult style, is a perennial concern in the theater. Last year it was the object of a detailed study by the Theater Communications Group. The TCG is an autonymous Ford Foundation-funded agency for resident theaters. The immediate aim of its study was an analysis of audiences; the long-range goal is to double those audiences in the next 10 years. In its survey the TCG asked: Who goes to the theater, who doesn't, and why? There were occupational investigations (teachers, physicians, and dentists go to the theater; engineers, scientists, and blue collar workers, as a rule, don't). There were sex studies (the average audience is 55 per cent female; still it's a pretty good place for husband hunting, according to a section called "Theater and the Single Girl"). There were investigations to determine audience income levels (overall, the TCG found, "the professional theaters in America are the haunt of society's upper middle class"). On the basis of the study, many theaters are waging campaigns to win over the segments of the population who aren't playgoers. They are using not only the standard promotional techniques, but also what the TCG calls the "creative sociology" of its survey.

But the creative sociology, in the view of some of the resident theater's most articulate practitioners and critics, is in the wrong place. If it is to woo mass audiences, it belongs on the stage. Zelda Fichandler, producing director of the Arena Stage in Washington, addressed a national meeting shortly before the 1967-68 season opened. She commented on the dearth of Negroes and members of the working class in our theaters. "We must attract them with the directness of our work, its abrasion, its physical energy, its source within life itself," she said. "The first consideration for a play is its relevance to the audience for which it is to be performed."

Another outspoken advocate of a socially involved theater is Theodore Hoffman, director of New York University's theater program and former chairman of the TCG advisory board. Mr. Hoffman presented a paper to the TCG at about the same time Mrs. Fichandler voiced her plea. He charged that the resident theater was "still fairly pristine, and the foundations would do well to institute instant sociological examination." He maintained that "the real issues of non-commercial American theater have to do with artistic excellence and social action."

Mr. Hoffman also chided the resident theater's boards of directors as representatives of "the forces of oatmeal art." Some months later he told me he modified that view after meeting with board members at The Cleveland Play House where—oatmeal art or sturdier stuff—artistic policy is a fixed menu and the board traditionally observes a hands-off policy. This may account for the fact that there has been relatively little disharmony here between the board and the administration. (K. Elmo Lowe, when he wants to sound out opinion on his selection of plays, turns to his staff. Their dissension may be frequent and outspoken. This may not be the state of affairs in all theaters; other relationships may be the norm.) It may be that the peaceful coexistence between our board and our administration stems from our firm roots. In general, a board's power seems to vary inversely with the age of the theater. Boards who themselves started theaters are prone to upstage the administration during the critical years of early growth. And where they have veto power over the selection of plays, the trouble index is high. This became apparent during the 1966-67 battles, and today there is a more realistic approach to separation of powers.

If the shaping of artistic policy should be off limits for boards, what, ideally, is their area of activity? This is how Ernest Schier, drama critic for The Philadelphia *Bulletin* defines it: ". . . to maintain continuity, to plan for the future, and to do everything in their power to create an atmosphere in which the theater can flourish." Freely translated: to engage an administrator and provide him with adequate funds—with no strings attached.

Now for an overdue word in defense of boards. The idea has been kicking around for some time, and it came into full play during the *sturm und drang* of 1966-67, that the board of directors is the collective hang-up of the resident theater. The archetypal board member has been represented as a comic invention, a dilettante, the quintessential well-heeled philistine. He has been maligned within an inch of his life, and he hasn't even asked for equal time. At the risk of piety, I'd like to note that the trustees with whom I have worked in a decade have been, by and large, well informed, possessed of sophisticated tastes and—on a pragmatic note—wise to the ways of fund raising. Few are stodgy; indeed, their ranks may even include an occasional *enfant terrible*.

With its boards, with its playwrights and in its community action the resident theater took many forward strides this year—but it has by no means arrived at a millennium. Like families, all theaters (including the one I represent) have their problems. Some of the worthiest theaters are steeped in trouble and their future is precarious. The Long Wharf has languished since Dean Robert Brustein created another professional theater in New Haven at Yale's Graduate School of Drama. The Charles Playhouse, eclipsed in recent years by Theater Company of Boston, Inc., reportedly is in distress. In a radical departure from resident theater policy, the Charles announced that it would not have a permanent company for 1968-69 but would job in actors for each production. Philadelphia's spunky Theater of the Living Arts, in a drastic economy measure, ended its season three weeks before its scheduled closing in April.

What will happen next is anyone's guess, so here are some predictions:

Item: Some of the purist theaters, in their search for some degree of solvency, will move toward eclectic programming. Perhaps they'll heed a statement by Harold Clurman, who can hardly be called an artistic slouch. He said: "The theater's subsidy is stored in a treasury of artistically negligible plays, and without such plays there might be no theater at all."

Item: Many resident companies will establish small, auxiliary theaters where they can perform experimental works with reduced financial risks. This year the Tyrone Guthrie Theater opened its small, informal "The Other Place" for an expanded program of experimentation with minimal box office pressure.

Item: There will be more affiliations between resident theaters and nearby universities. Cooperative arrangements already exist in several cities and they have been mutually beneficial. The professional theater can strengthen the university drama department, and the university can extend to the theater what Tyrone Guthrie calls "a protective umbrella." Furthermore, a campus milieu can provide a note of youth and vigor that many theaters now lack.

Finally, the resident theater is likely to upgrade the social involvement that marked this year because it knows that unless it has a strong sense of identification with its community's problems, it may turn itself into a waxworks museum.

A DIRECTORY OF PROFESSIONAL REGIONAL THEATER

Professional 1967-68 programs and repertory productions by leading resident companies around the United States (excluding Broadway, off Broadway, touring New York shows, summer theaters and festivals) are grouped in alphabetical order of their locations and listed in date order from June 1, 1967 through May 31, 1968. This directory was compiled by Ella A. Malin for *The Best Plays of 1967-68* from information provided by the producing organizations at Miss Malin's request. Figures in parentheses following titles give number of performances. Date given is opening date. Special and experimental productions listed in notes at the end of some of the entries are not included in Miss Malin's statistical summary of the season presented directly below.

Summary

This Directory lists 291 programs of 214 playscripts (including one-acters) produced by 37 groups in 44 theaters. 96 were American playscripts. 23 were world premieres and 15 were American premieres (according to information received). Frequency of production of individual scripts (including one-acters) was as follows:

3 plays received 7 productions *(Charley's Aunt, The Miser, A Delicate Balance)*
1 play received 6 productions *(Luv)*
3 plays received 5 productions *(The Threepenny Opera, The Importance of Being Earnest, The Odd Couple)*
5 plays received 4 productions
8 plays received 3 productions
30 plays received 2 productions
164 plays received 1 production

Listed below are the playwrights who received the greatest number of productions. The first figure is the number of productions; the second figure (in parentheses) is the number of plays produced, including one-acters:

Shakespeare	17 (11)	Williams	7 (4)
Albee	16 (7)	Pirandello	7 (3)
Shaw	13 (8)	Schisgal	7 (3)
Molière	13 (5)	Pinter	5 (4)
Anouilh	10 (5)	O'Neill	4 (2)
Beckett	10 (4)	Chekhov	3 (3)
Brecht	9 (5)	Ionesco	3 (3)
Simon	9 (2)	Odets	3 (3)
Miller	8 (4)	Osborne	3 (3)

ABINGDON, VA.

Barter Theater

FIVE IN THE AFTERNOON (16). By Elizabeth Blake. (World premiere) June 12, 1967. Director, Miranda d'Ancona; scenery and costumes, David Pursley; lighting, John Baker. With Barry Corbin, John Sheffey, Jaime Sanchez, Aurelia Troy.

LUV (19). By Murray Schisgal. June 27, 1967. Director, Robert Brink; scenery, Ralph Swanson; lighting, John Baker; costumes, Elizabeth A. Tullis. With Roger Omar Serbagi, James Murtaugh.

BAREFOOT IN THE PARK (20). By Neil Simon. July 4, 1967. Director, Gordon Greene; scenery, Henry E. Scott III; lighting, John Baker; costumes, Elizabeth A. Tullis. With Anna Stuart, Jack Cowles.

ROMEO AND JULIET (23). By William Shakespeare. April 15, 1968. Director, Robert Brink; scenery, Henry E. Scott III; lighting, John Baker; costumes, Elizabeth A. Tullis. With Jack Cowles, Naomi Robin.

THE THIRTEEN CLOCKS (23). By James Thurber. May 2, 1968. Director, Pierre Olaf; scenery, Henry E. Scott III; lighting, John Baker; costumes, Elizabeth A. Tullis. With Pierre Olaf, Jay Bell.

THE PURSUIT OF HAPPINESS (23). By Armina Marshall and Lawrence Langner. May 28, 1968. Director, Owen Phillips; scenery, Henry E. Scott III; lighting, John Baker; costumes, Elizabeth A. Tullis. With Dortha Duckworth, Robert Foley.

Barter Playhouse

WHO'S AFRAID OF VIRGINIA WOOLF? (32). By Edward Albee. June 27, 1967. Director, Paul Emerson; scenery, Ralph Swanson; lighting, John Baker; costumes, Elizabeth A. Tullis. With Max Jacobs, Margo McElroy.

THE ODD COUPLE (12). By Neil Simon. July 18, 1967. Director, Robert Brink; scenery, Henry E. Scott III; lighting, John Baker; costumes, Elizabeth A. Tullis. With Gordon Greene, Roger Omar Serbagi.

ANN ARBOR, MICH.

Association of Producing Artists (APA-Phoenix) Repertory (in University of Michigan Professional Theater Program)

PANTAGLEIZE (14). By Michel de Ghelderode; translated by George Hauger. September 19, 1967. Directors, John Houseman and Ellis Rabb; scenery and lighting, James Tilton; costumes, Nancy Potts. With Ellis Rabb, Patricia Conolly, Sydney Walker.

YOU CAN'T TAKE IT WITH YOU (3). By Moss Hart and George S. Kaufman. October 3, 1967. Director, Ellis Rabb; scenery, James Tilton; costumes, Nancy Potts. With Rosemary Harris, Dee Victor, Donald Moffat, Clayton Corzatte.

RIGHT YOU ARE (3). By Luigi Pirandello; English version by Eric Bentley. October 6, 1967. Director, Stephen Porter; scenery, James Tilton; costumes, Nancy Potts. With Helen Hayes, Sydney Walker, Donald Moffat, Rosemary Harris.

EXIT THE KING (14). By Eugene Ionesco; translated by Donald Watson. October 10, 1967. Director, Ellis Rabb; scenery, Rouben Ter-Arutunian; lighting, James Tilton; costumes, Nancy Potts. With Richard Easton, Patricia Conolly, Louise Latham, Clayton Corzatte.

THE SHOW-OFF (14). By George Kelly. October 17, 1967. Director, Stephen Porter; scenery and lighting, James Tilton; costumes, Nancy Potts. With Helen Hayes, Clayton Corzatte, Gwyda Donhowe.

ATLANTA

Theater Atlanta

WHO WAS THAT LADY I SAW YOU WITH? (10). By Norman Krasna. October 11, 1967. Director, Jay Broad; scenery, lighting and costumes, David Chapman. With Gordon Greene, George Riddle, Stuart Culpepper, Arlene Nadel.

THE ANDERSONVILLE TRIAL (9). By Saul Levitt. October 18, 1967. Director, Jay Broad; scenery, lighting and costumes, David Chapman, Ronald Bush, Clarence Felder, Jim Garner, Harrison T. Wadsworth.

WHO'S AFRAID OF VIRGINIA WOOLF? (11). By Edward Albee. November 4, 1967. Director, Gary Gage; scenery, lighting and costumes, David Chapman. With Margo McElroy, Stuart Culpepper, Arlene Nadel, Terrell Bennett.

MACBIRD! (34). By Barbara Garson. November 21, 1967. Director, Jay Broad; scenery, lighting and costumes, David Chapman. With Jim Garner, Muriel Moore, Terrell Bennett, Stuart Culpepper.

THE MAD SHOW (10). Book by Larry Siegel and Stan Hart; lyrics by Marshall Barer, Stan Hart, Larry Siegel and Steven Vinaver; music by Mary Rodgers. December 13, 1967. Director, Roger Sullivan; scenery, lighting and costumes, David Chapman; musical director, Donald Tucker. With Fred Chappell, Charles Munro, Arlene Nadel, Judy Schoen.

J.B. (17). By Archibald MacLeish. January 24, 1968. Director, Jay Broad; scenery and lighting, David Chapman; costumes, David

Chapman, David Charles. With Clarence Felder, Margo McElroy, Stuart Culpepper, Ronald Bush.

THE MEMBER OF THE WEDDING (17). By Carson McCullers. February 14, 1968. Director, Jay Broad; scenery and lighting, David Chapman; costumes, David Chapman, David Charles. With Arlene Nadel, Georgia Allen, Lee Blackwell.

LYSISTRATA (12). By Aristophanes; adapted by John Lewin. March 6, 1968. Director, Jay Broad; scenery and lighting, David Chapman; costumes, David Chapman, David Charles. With Muriel Moore, Bebe Forehand, Arlene Nadel, Margo McElroy, Ted Harris.

THE INVESTIGATION (8). By Peter Weiss; English translation by Ulu Grosbard and Jon Swan. April 3, 1968. Director, Clarence Felder; scenery and lighting, David Chapman; costumes, David Chapman, David Charles. With Ronald Bush, Stuart Culpepper, Terrell Bennett.

LEE HARVEY OSWALD: A FAR MEAN STREAK OF INDEPENCE BROUGHT ON BY NEGLECK (9). Director, Jay Broad; scenery and lighting, David Chapman; costumes, David Chapman and David Charles. By Michael Hastings. April 17, 1968. With Terrell Bennett, Muriel Moore, Arlene Nadel.

THE UNKNOWN SOLDIER AND HIS WIFE (6). By Peter Ustinov. May 8, 1968. Director, Jay Broad; scenery and lighting, David Chapman; costumes, David Chapman, David Charles. With Fred Chappell, Sandy McCallum, Ronald Bush, Clarence Felder, Jim Garner.

BALTIMORE

Center Stage

WAITING FOR GODOT (30). By Samuel Beckett. September 29, 1967. Director, Ronald L. Hufham; scenery, Douglas Seale; lighting, Lee Dunholter; costumes, James Edmund Brady. With William McKereghan, Charles Siebert, Bruce M. Kornbluth.

THE MEMBER OF THE WEDDING (30). By Carson McCullers. October 6, 1967. Director, John Olon-Scrymgeour; scenery, Douglas Seale; lighting, Lee Dunholter; costumes, James Edmund Brady. With Beatrice Winde, Judy Mueller.

HAMLET (26). By William Shakespeare. November 24, 1967. Director, Douglas Seale; scenery, Douglas Seale; lighting, Lee Dunholter; costumes, James Edmund Brady. With Charles Siebert, Edd K. Gasper, Mary Sinclair, William McKereghan.

THE DEVIL'S DISCIPLE (34). By George Bernard Shaw. January 12, 1968. Director, Douglas Seale; scenery, Douglas Seale; lighting, Lee Dunholter; costumes, James Edmund Brady. With Edd K. Gasper, Charles Siebert.

AN ENEMY OF THE PEOPLE (26). By Henrik Ibsen; adapted by Arthur Miller. February 16, 1968. Director, Leonardo Cimino; scenery, Douglas Seale; lighting, Lee Dunholter; costumes, James Edmund Brady. With William Newman, William McKereghan, Bruce M. Kornbluth.

THE ROYAL FAMILY (35). By George S. Kaufman and Edna Ferber. March 22, 1968. Director, Douglas Seale; scenery, Douglas Seale; lighting, Lee Dunholter; costumes, James Edmund Brady. With Nicholas Coster, Olive Deering, Marcie Hubert.

ET CETERA '68 (36). April 26, 1968. 17 short plays with the whole acting company. Director, John Olon-Scrymgeour; scenery, John Baker III; lighting, Lee Dunholter; costumes, James Edmund Brady. Program included world premieres: *I Hear America Talking* by Russell Baker, *The Spec* by Peter W. Culman, *Lucky Star* by Jean Doron, *Bitter Dialogue* by F. Garcia Lorca, translated by John Olon-Scrymgeour, *Guru Go Back* by Robert Hivnor, *Memorial Day* by Murray Schisgal, *Photograph* (opera) by Gertrude Stein with music by Richard Skapik. American premiere: *Come and Go,* by Samuel Beckett.

BOSTON

Charles Playhouse

AMERICA HURRAH (39). By Jean-Claude van Itallie. September 28, 1967. Director, Thomas Bissinger; scenery and lighting, Hugh E. Lester; costumes, Cecelia Eller. With Bernard Wurger, Al Pacino, Eda Reiss Merin, Jill Clayburgh, John Seitz.

AWAKE AND SING (39). By Clifford Odets. November 2, 1967. Director, Michael Murray; scenery and costumes, Richard W. Kerry; lighting, Hugh E. Lester. With Will Lee, Eda Reiss Merin, Al Pacino.

THE NINE O'CLOCK MAIL by Howard Sackler and THE MADNESS OF LADY BRIGHT by Lanford Wilson, director, Michael Murray; and DUTCHMAN by LeRoi Jones, director, Ted Kazanoff (39). December 7, 1967. Scenery and lighting, Hugh E. Lester; costumes, Richard W. Kerry. With Jennifer Salt, Bob McDonald, Annette Oliver, Michael Smith, Gerald McConagill, Jill Clayburgh, Jay Fletcher.

ROOM SERVICE (39). By Allen Boretz and John Murray. January 11, 1968. Director, Michael Murray; scenery and costumes, Richard W. Kerry; lighting, Hugh E. Lester. With Paul Harrington, John Seitz, Robert Gaus, Judy McMurdo.

A VIEW FROM THE BRIDGE (55). By Arthur Miller. February 15, 1968. Director, Mitchell Nestor; scenery, Richard W. Kerry; lighting, Bruce Owen; costumes, Jan. With Vincent Gardenia, Ben Hammer, Michael Ebert, Marsha Frank.

WAITING FOR GODOT (39). By Samuel Beckett. April 4, 1968. Director, Arthur Storch; scenery and costumes, Richard W. Kerry; lighting, Bruce Owen. With Danny Meehan, Will Hare.

Theater Company of Boston, Inc.

THE DWARFS by Harold Pinter and THE LOCAL STIGMATIC (American premiere) by Heathcote Williams. November 30, 1967. Director, David Wheeler; scenery, Robert Allen; lighting, Lance Crocker; costumes, Catherine King. With Jon Voight, Paul Benedict, Jeremiah Sullivan, Arthur Merrow, Richard Hughes.

LEFT-HANDED LIBERTY (11). By John Arden. (American premiere) January 3, 1968. Director, David Wheeler; scenery, Robert Allen; lighting, William King; costumes, Catherine King. With Harriet Rogers, Paul Benedict, Theodore Kazanoff.

WHO'S AFRAID OF VIRGINIA WOOLF? (10). By Edward Albee. January 18, 1968. Director, David Wheeler; scenery, Robert Allen; lighting, Lance Crocker. With Josephine Lane, Paul Benedict, Larry Bryggman, Lisa Richards.

STOP, YOU'RE KILLING ME (13). By James Leo Herlihy. (World premiere) February 1, 1968. Director, David Wheeler; scenery, Robert Allen; lighting, Lance Crocker; costumes, Cynthia Pallian. With James Spruill, Susan Channing, Larry Bryggman, Roberta Collinge, Laurie Gould, Dan Goldman, William Young, Gustave Johnson.

THE END OF THE WORLD and THE FUN WAR by Geoffrey Bush, directors, David Wheeler and Timothy Affleck; and THE INNOCENT PARTY by John Hawkes, director, David Wheeler (13). (American premiere) February 15, 1968. Scenery, Robert Allen; lighting, Lance Crocker; costumes, Catherine King and Cynthia Pallian. With Paul Benedict, William Young, James Spruill, Larry Bryggman, Susan Channing, Naomi Thornton, Josephine Lane.

HOGAN'S GOAT (30). By William Alfred. February 29, 1968. Director, Theodore Mann; scenery, Charles Norton; lighting, Lance Crocker; costumes, Cynthia Pallian. With Ralph Waite, Joan Potter, Patricia O'Connell, Michael Currie.

PHAEDRA (22). By Robert Lowell; adapted from the play by Jean Racine. March 28, 1968. Director, David Wheeler; scenery, Robert Allen; lighting, Lance Crocker; costumes, Suzanne O'Hara. With Carolyn Coates, Lisa Richards, Josephine Lane, Larry Bryggman.

THE GREAT FUGUE (14). By F. M. Kimball. (World premiere) April 18, 1968. Director, David Wheeler; scenery, Robert Allen; lighting, Lance Crocker; costumes, Marsha MacDonald. With Carolyn Coates, Charles Siebert, William Cottrell, Lisa Richards.

BUFFALO

Studio Arena Theater

BAREFOOT IN THE PARK (44). By Neil Simon. June 8, 1967. Director, Warren Enters; scenery, Russell Drisch; lighting, David Zierk. With Nancy Cushman, Gene Lindsey, Holly Turner.

BEYOND THE FRINGE (20). By Alan Bennett, Peter Cook, Jonathan Miller, Dudley Moore. July 20, 1967. Director, Donald Cullen; scenery, Peter Jajduk; lighting, David Zierk. With Barrie Baldaro, Stuart Hamilton, Nicholas Simons, Roy Wordsworth.

LUV (31). By Murray Schisgal. August 15, 1967. Director, Allan Leicht; scenery and lighting, Douglas Higgins. With Renee Lippin, Robert Murray, Joe Servello.

THE THREEPENNY OPERA (36). By Bertolt Brecht and Kurt Weill; English adaptation, Marc Blitzstein. September 28, 1967. Director, Tom Gruenewald; scenery and lighting, Eugene Lee; costumes, Jean Blanchette; musical director, Philip Saltz. With Dennis Thatcher, Alice Beardsley, Frank Georgianna, Ann Bailey, Betty Lutes, Laura Stuart.

THE IMAGINARY INVALID (36). By Molière. November 2, 1967. Director, Donald Davis; scenery and lighting, Eugene Lee; costumes, Jean Blanchette. With Joe Servello, Ann Bailey, Vincent Baggetta, Jean Hebborn.

H.M.S. PINAFORE (36). By W. S. Gilbert and Arthur Sullivan. December 7, 1967. Director, Allan Leicht; scenery and lighting, Eugene Lee; costumes, Jean Blanchette; musical director, Stuart Hamilton. With David Rae Smith, Kenneth McMillan, Milton Bailey, Ann Bailey, Sally Birckhead.

ENRICO IV (28). By Luigi Pirandello; English version by Eric Bentley. January 11, 1968. Director, Stephen Porter; scenery and lighting, Eugene Lee; costumes, Jean Blanchette. With Stefan Gierasch, Betty Leighton, John Devlin.

A DELICATE BALANCE (28). By Edward Albee. February 8, 1968. Director, Warren Enters; scenery, Nicholas Russivan; lighting, Eugene Lee; costumes, Jean Blanchette. With Henderson Forsythe, Carolyn Coates, Sada Thompson.

BOX-MAO-BOX (29). By Edward Albee. (World premiere) March 6, 1968. Director, Alan Schneider; scenery and costumes, William Ritman; lighting, David Zierk. With Ruth White, Lucille Patton, Conrad Yama, Jenny Egan, William Needles.

CHARLEY'S AUNT (36). By Brandon Thomas. April 4, 1968. Director, Paxton Whitehead; scenery, Maurice Strike; lighting, David Zierk; costumes, Judith Haugan. With Paxton Whitehead, Bruce Gray, Margaret Gathright, Jean Hebborn.

THE KNACK (38). By Ann Jellicoe. May 9, 1968. Director, Maurice Breslow; scenery and costumes, Maurice Strike; lighting, David Zierk. With John Glover, Bruce Gray, Laurie Kennedy, Paul Vincent.

Studio Arena Theater: Studio Two Productions

QUEEN AND THE REBELS (9). By Ugo Betti; translated by Henry Reed. October 20, 1967. Director, Maurice Breslow; designer, Iain Whitecross. With Mary Jane Abeles, Michael Stein.

ENDGAME (8). By Samuel Beckett. November 17, 1967. Director, Stephen H. Foreman. With John Costopoulos, Frank T. Wells.

BRECHT ON BRECHT (9). By George Tabori, from the works of Bertolt Brecht. Director, Maurice Breslow. With Sheila Browne, Russell Drisch, Michael Stein, Betty Lutes.

CHICAGO

Goodman Memorial Theater

THE MISER (26). By Molière; translated by George Graveley. October 20, 1967. Director, John Reich; scenery, Marc Cohen; lighting, Ed Swift; costumes, D. Hudson Sheffield. With Bramwell Fletcher, Donna Holabird.

THE BALCONY (25). By Jean Genet; translated by Bernard Frechtman. November 24, 1967. Director, Patrick Henry; scenery; James Maronek; lighting, G. E. Naselius; costumes, Uta Olson. With Delphi Lawrence, Jan Lanin.

CAESAR AND CLEOPATRA (25). By George Bernard Shaw. January 12, 1968. Director, Warren Enters; scenery, George Petti; lighting, Jerrold Gorrell; costumes, D. Hudson Sheffield. With Murray Matheson, Carrie Snodgress.

OTHELLO (27). By William Shakespeare. February 16, 1968. Director, Charles McGaw; scenery, James Maronek; lighting, G. E. Naselius; costumes, James Larsen. With James Earl Jones, Len Cariou, Saundra Matthews.

A MAN'S A MAN (26). By Bertolt Brecht; English version, Eric Bentley. March 29, 1968. Director, Joseph Slowik; scenery, James Maronek; lighting, G. E. Naselius; costumes, D. Hudson Sheffield. With Terry Lomax, Helena Carroll.

A FLEA IN HER EAR (25). By Georges Feydeau; English version by John Mortimer. May 3, 1968. Director, Warren Enters; scenery, Marc Cohen; lighting, Jerrold Gorrell; costumes, Virgil C. Johnson. With Hiram Sherman, Donna O'Connor, Diane Hurley, Denis Grimaldi.

CINCINNATI

Playhouse in the Park

THE CAVERN (20). By Jean Anouilh; translated by Lucienne Hill. (American premiere) June 8, 1967. Director, Michael Kahn; scenery, Douglas W. Schmidt; lighting, Joe Pacitti; costumes, Caley Summers. With Irene Dailey, Emery Battis, David Hooks, Anne Murray.

ESCURIAL by Michel de Ghelderode; English version by Lional Abel and THE LESSON by Eugene Ionesco; translated by Donald M. Allen (29). July 6, 1967. Director, David Hooks; scenery and lighting, Joe Pacitti; costumes, Martha Braun. With Emery Battis, David Hooks, Richard Von Hoene, Sky Lilly White, Al Corbin, Lynn Milgrim, Virginia Payne.

UNCLE VANYA (29). By Anton Chekhov; translated by Alex Szogyi. August 3, 1967. Director, Cyril Simon; scenery and costumes, Caley Summers; lighting, Joe Pacitti. With Emery Battis, Charles Cioffi, Anne Murray, Lynn Milgrim.

ANATOL (29). Adapted by Tom Jones from the book *The Affairs of Anatol* by Arthur Schnitzler; translated by Lilly Lessing. August 31, 1967. Directors, David Hooks, Brooks Jones; scenery, Douglas W. Schmidt; lighting, Joe Pacitti; costumes, Caley Summers. With Michael Lipton, David Hooks, Lynn Milgrim, Joan Feldon.

MISALLIANCE (38). By George Bernard Shaw. April 4, 1968. Director, David Hooks; scenery, Douglas W. Schmidt; lighting, Joe Pacitti; costumes, Caley Summers. With Ronold Bishop, Joan White, Bernard McInerney, Lynn Milgrim, Michael Lipton.

ENDGAME (38). By Samuel Beckett. May 9, 1968. Director, Brooks Jones; scenery and lighting, Joe Pacitti; costumes, Martha Braun. With Ronald Bishop, Edward Zang, Bernard McInerney, Susan Willis.

NOTE: Balance of the 1968 Playhouse in the Park season will be: *The Miser,* June 13; *Camino Real,* July 18; *Crime on Goat Island,* August 8; *The Madwoman of Chaillot,* August 29.

CLEVELAND

Cleveland Play House: Euclid-77th Theater

THE INSPECTOR-GENERAL (25). By Nikolai Gogol. September 29, 1967. Director, Richard Oberlin; scenery, Paul Rodgers; lighting, Barbara Leatherman, Douglas Bruce; costumes, Jack Casey. With Maury Cooper, Richard Halverson, June Gibbons.

THE STRONG ARE LONELY (24). By Fritz Hochwalder; adapted by Eva Le Gallienne from the French version by J. Mercure and R. Thieberger. November 3, 1967. Director, John Marley; scenery, Paul Rodgers; costumes, Jack Casey. With Maury Cooper, Mario Siletti, Richard Halverson, Allen Leatherman, Bob Moak.

THE ODD COUPLE (45). By Neil Simon. December 8, 1967. Director, Tom Brennan; scenery, Paul Rodgers; lighting, Dan Szescehowski. With Maury Cooper, Robert Snook, Stuart Levin.

GENERATION (30). By William Goodhart. January 19, 1968. Director, Richard Oberlin; lighting, Dan Szescehowski. With Franklin Cover, Jonathan Bolt, Joan McConocha.

THE GLASS MENAGERIE (18). By Tennessee Williams. March 22, 1968. Director, Robert Snook; scenery and lighting, Paul Rodgers; costumes, Carol Margolis. With Dorothy Paxton, David Snell, Addie Johnson, Jonathan Bolt.

HALFWAY UP THE TREE (25). By Peter Ustinov. April 12, 1968. Director, Mario Siletti; scenery, Paul Rodgers; lighting, Perry Lee; costumes, Carol Margolis. With Maury Cooper, Edith Owen, Peter Bartlett, Gigi Gibson, Elizabeth Lowry.

Cleveland Play House: Francis E. Drury Theater

LUV (25). By Murray Schisgal. October 13, 1967. Director, Henry Butler; scenery, Paul Rodgers; lighting, Klaus Euteneuer. With Richard Oberlin, Jonathan Bolt, Elizabeth Lowry.

MORNING'S AT SEVEN (19). By Paul Osborn. November 17, 1967. Director, Jonathan Bolt; scenery, Paul Rodgers; costumes, Jack Casey. With Helen Watkins, Dorothy Paxton, Richard Oberlin, Edith Owen, Clarence Kavanaugh, Janet Downs.

CHARLEY'S AUNT (35). By Brandon Thomas. December 15, 1967. Director, Mario Siletti; scenery, Paul Rodgers; lighting, Klaus Euteneuer; costumes, Jack Casey. With Peter Bartlett, Robert Thorson, Bob Moak, Gigi Gibson.

THE ROSE TATTOO (30). By Tennessee Williams. February 2, 1968. Director, Mario Siletti; scenery and lighting, Paul Rodgers; costumes, Carol Margolis. With Evie McElroy, David Snell, Myriam Lipari, Robert Thorson.

DEAR LIAR (14). By Jerome Kilty. March 15, 1968. Director, Richard Oberlin; lighting, Klaus Euteneuer; costumes, Carol Margolis. With Edith Owen, Mario Siletti.

THE MERRY WIVES OF WINDSOR (48). By William Shakespeare. March 27, 1968. Director, Richard Oberlin; scenery, Jonathan Bolt; lighting, Klaus Euteneuer; costumes, Carol Margolis. With Robert Snook, Myrna Kaye, Jean Morris, Robert Allman, Evie McElroy, Ronald Parady.

WAITING FOR GODOT (19). By Samuel Beckett. April 19, 1968. Director, Stuart Vaughan; scenery, Paul Rodgers; lighting, Rusty Fitzmartin; costumes, Carol Margolis. With Richard Oberlin, Jonathan Bolt, Mario Siletti, David Snell.

Cleveland Play House—Brooks Theater

THE DUMBWAITER and THE COLLECTION (18). By Harold Pinter. December 22, 1967. Director, Tom Brennan; scenery, Jonathan Bolt; lighting, Perry Lee; costumes, Carol Margolis. With Allen Leatherman, David Snell, Mario Siletti, Jonathan Bolt, Larry Tarrant, Elizabeth Lowry.

DALLAS

Dallas Theater Center: Kalita Humphreys Theater

LUV (10). By Murray Schisgal. June 6, 1967. Director, Ryland Merkey; scenery, Nancy Levinson; lighting, Bob Baca. With Ken Latimer, Fritz Lennon, Jane Milburn.

BAREFOOT IN THE PARK (23). By Neil Simon. June 22, 1967. Director, Preston Jones; scenery, Nancy Levinson; lighting, John Figlmiller. With Ginger Valone, Christopher Hendrie, Anna Paul Rogers, Ryland Merkey.

THE DECLINE AND FALL OF THE ENTIRE WORLD AS SEEN THROUGH THE EYES OF COLE PORTER (21). A revue conceived and assembled by Ben Bagley. August 17, 1967. Director, David Pursley; musical director, Raymond Allen; projection series, Shirley Kaplan; continuity, special vocal arrangements and grand finale, Bud McCreery. With Kaki Dowling, Anna Paul Rogers, David Pursley, Mona Pursley, Randolph Tallman.

TWELFTH NIGHT (29). By William Shakespeare. October 12, 1967. Director, Norman Ayrton; scenery and costumes, Charlote Cole; lighting, Randy Moore. With Robert Rude, Mike Dendy, Anna Paul Marsh-Neame, Preston Jones, Penny Metropulos, Randy Moore, Ryland Merkey.

THE ODD COUPLE (19). By Neil Simon. November 9, 1967. Director, James Nelson Harrell; scenery and lighting, Bob Baca; costumes, Pat Baca. With Matt Tracy, Ken Latimer.

A DELICATE BALANCE (9). By Edward Albee. December 7, 1967. Director, George Webby; scenery, Kathleen Latimer; lighting, Carleton Tanner. With Mary Sue Fridge Jones, Fritz Lennon, Lynn Trammell.

PINOCCHIO (20). By Brian Way, in collaboration with Warren Jenkins. December 21, 1967. Director, Louise Mosley; scenery, Yaichi Aoki; lighting, Randy Moore; costumes, Anne Butler; mime and choreography, Kaki Darling. With Camilla Ritchey, Mary Jean McCullough, Steven Mackenroth, Arthur Jennings Rogers, John Shepherd.

A STREETCAR NAMED DESIRE (21). By Tennessee Williams. January 16, 1968. Director, Ryland Merkey; scenery, Arthur Jensen Rogers; lighting, Bob Baca; costumes, Reta La Force. With Mary Sue Fridge Jones, Keith Rothschild, Jane Milburn Tracy, Preston Jones.

VASCO (12). By Georges Schehade; English version by Bernard Noble. (American premiere) February 17, 1968. Director, Kosta Spaic; scenery, Nancy Levinson; lighting, Bob Baca. With Edward Kirk Herrmann, James Nelson Harrell, Kaki Dowling, Gene Leggett.

THE LATENT HETEROSEXUAL (24). By Paddy Chayefsky. (World premiere) March 18, 1968. Director, Burgess Meredith; scenery, Virgil Beavers; lighting, Matt Tracy. With Zero Mostel, Jules Munshin, Randy Moore, Chris Richard.

CHARLEY'S AUNT (24). By Brandon Thomas. April 18, 1968. Director, Anna Paul Marsh-Neame; scenery, David Pursley; lighting, Don Granbery. With David Pursley, John Figlmiller, Steven Mackenroth, Kaki Dowling, Becky Frazier, Pat Baca, Mike Dendy, Fritz Lennon.

Dallas Theater Center: Down Center Stage

R.U. HUNGRY (SPECIALTY: SHORT ORDERS) (6). By Randy Ford. (American premiere) June 23, 1967. Director, Paul Baker; scenery, Nancy Levinson; lighting, Randy Ford; costumes, Charlote Cole. With Mike Dendy, Judith Davis, Ronald Wilcox, Betty June Lary, Reta La Force.

LOOK BACK IN ANGER (21). By John Osborne. July 6, 1967. Director, Anna Paul Rogers; scenery, Anne Butler; lighting, Leonard T. Wagner. With John Logan, Don Davlin, Charlote Cole, Becky Frazier, Mona Pursley, Ronald Wilcox.

A DELICATE BALANCE (12). By Edward Albee. September 28, 1967. Director, George Webby; scenery, Kathleen Benke; lighting, Carleton Tanner. With Mary Sue Fridge Jones, Fritz Lennon, Lynn Trammell.

SPOON RIVER ANTHOLOGY (12). By Edgar Lee Masters; adapted by Charles Aidman. November 2, 1967. Director, Mike Dendy; scenery, Tina Navarro; lighting, Sally Netzel; music, Naomi Caryl Hirshhorn; lyrics, Charles Aidman. With Judith Davis, Anna Gonyaw, Christopher Hendrie, Tim Green, Anne Butler, Steven Mackenroth.

THE PRIVATE EAR and THE PUBLIC EYE (16). By Peter Shaffer. December 14, 1967. Director, John Logan; scenery, Ella-Mae Brainard; lighting Anna Paul Marsh-Neame. With Edward Kirk Herrmann, Pat Baca, Irene Lewis.

THE KNACK (18). By Ann Jellicoe. February 1, 1968. Director, Preston Jones; scenery, Carleton Tanner; lighting, Don Granbery; costumes, Pat Baca. With Rene Assa, Patricia Chrane; Don Granbery, Johnny McBee.

CHAMBER MUSIC by Arthur Kopit, director, Judith Davis; and THE DAY IT RAINED FOREVER (12) by Ray Bradbury, director, Ken Latimer. March 14, 1968. Scenery and costumes, Anne Butler; lighting, Kathleen Latimer. With Sally Netzel, Pat Baca, Kathleen Latimer, Mike Dendy, James Nelson Harrell.

HARRISBURG, PA.

Arena House Theater

THE THREEPENNY OPERA (13). By Bertolt Brecht and Kurt Weill; English version by Marc Blitzstein. October 1, 1967. Director-designer, Tom Ross Prather; musical director, James Reed Lawlor; musical staging, Darwin Knight. With Dean Santoro, Rose Roffman, Joel Wolfe, Susan Hufford.

THE ODD COUPLE (17). By Neil Simon. October 18, 1967. Director-designer, Tom Ross Prather. With Bruce Hall, Herb Buck.

J.B. (11) By Archibald MacLeish. November 15, 1967. Director-designer, Tom Ross Prather. With Bruce Hall, Stuart Howard, Richard Kuss, Jo Henderson.

LUV (20). By Murray Schisgal. December 31, 1967. Director, Tom Ross Prather; scenery, Marty Taras. With Kate Lewis, Mark Shapiro, Vic Vallaro.

A DELICATE BALANCE (11). By Edward Albee. January 24, 1968. Director-designer, Tom Ross Prather. With Richard Kuss, Alice Scudder, Kate Lewis.

CHARLEY'S AUNT (23). By Brandon Thomas. February 7, 1968. Director, Tom Ross Prather; scenery and lighting, Tom Ross Prather; costumes, Peggy Hobin. With Robert R. Wait, John Frey, Jeanne Rostaing.

BAREFOOT IN THE PARK (11). By Neil Simon. February 28, 1968. Director-designer, Tom Ross Prather. With Robert R. Wait, Jeanne Rostaing.

THE FANTASTICKS (15). Book and Lyrics by Tom Jones; music by Harvey Schmidt. April 4, 1968. Director, Darwin Knight; musical director, Jack Normain Kimmell; designer, Tom Ross Prather. With Dean Santoro, Margaret Frawley, Michael Patton.

THE MOUSETRAP (11). By Agatha Christie. April 24, 1968. Director-designer, Tom Ross Prather. With Robert R. Wait, Dean Santoro.

HARTFORD

The Hartford Stage Company

SKINFLINT OUT WEST (34). By Jacques Cartier; based on *The Miser* by Molière. October 20, 1967. Director, Jacques Cartier; scenery and costumes, John Conklin; lighting, Peter Hunt; choreography, Rudy D'Angona. With Henry Thomas, Marilyn Murphy, Elizabeth Farley, Don Barshay.

A VIEW FROM THE BRIDGE (34). By Arthur Miller. November 24, 1967. Director, Melvin Bernhardt; scenery, John Conklin; lighting, Peter Hunt; costumes, Kate Vachon. With Frank Savino, Karen Ludwig, Rue McClanahan, Peter DeMaio.

HAY FEVER (34). By Noel Coward. December 29, 1967. Director, Jacques Cartier; scenery and costumes, Holmes Easley; lighting, Peter Hunt. With Swoosie Kurtz, Saylor Creswell, Barbara Cason, Julia Curry.

THE HOSTAGE (34). By Brendan Behan. February 2, 1968. Director, Louis Beachner; scenery, Santo Loquasto; lighting, Peter Hunt; costumes, Kate Vachon. With Rue McClanahan, John Leighton, Judith McCauley, Saylor Creswell, Virginia Downing.

ANTIGONE (34). By Sophocles. March 15, 1968. Director, Michael Murray; scenery, lighting and costumes, John Conklin. With Dana Ivey, Judith McCauley, Frank Savino.

THE FIREBUGS (34). By Max Frisch; translated by Mordecai Gorelik. April 19, 1968. Director, Jacques Cartier; scenery, John Conklin; lighting, Peter Junt; costumes, Kate Vachon. With Macon McCalman, Rue McClanahan, Richard Ward, James Preston.

THE THREEPENNY OPERA (34). By Bertolt Brecht and Kurt Weill; English adaptation by Marc Blitzstein. May 24, 1968. Director and lighting, Peter Hunt; scenery and costumes, John Conklin; musical director, Arthur Rubinstein. With Louis Beachner, Rue McClanahan, Judith McCauley, Tom Urich, Katherine Helmond.

HOUSTON

Alley Theater

THE CARETAKER (18). By Harold Pinter. July 18, 1967. Director, Nina Vance; designer, Paul Owen. With Brian Gilmar, John Wylie, Tom Toner.

A DELICATE BALANCE (62). By Edward Albee. October 5, 1967. Director, Louis Criss; designer, Paul Owen. With Jeannette Clift, John Wylie, Bella Jarrett, Lillian Evans.

THE MISER (61). By Molière. November 30, 1967. Director, Louis Criss; designer, Paul Owen. With Tom Toner, Bella Jarrett, John McMurtry, Lillian Evans, Trent Jenkins.

CANDIDA (62). By George Bernard Shaw. January 25, 1968. Director, Louis Criss; designer, Paul Owen. With Bella Jarrett, John McMurtry, William Hardy.

LOS ANGELES

Center Theater Group

THE SORROWS OF FREDERICK (53). By Romulus Linney. (World premiere) June 23, 1967. Director, Albert Marre; scenery and lighting, Ralph Alswang; costumes, Robert Fletcher. With Fritz Weaver, Albert Dekker, Nancy Marchand.

THE MARRIAGE OF MR. MISSISSIPPI (53). By Friedrich Duerrenmatt; translated by Michael Bullock. August 25, 1967. Director, Malcolm Black; scenery, costumes and lighting, Peter Wexler. With Nan Martin, Frank Schofield, Edward Andrews, Jack Albertson.

WHO'S HAPPY NOW? (53). By Oliver Hailey. (World premiere) November 3, 1967. Director, Gordon Davidson; scenery, Archie Sharp; lighting, Michael Devine; costumes, Dorothy Jeakins. With Malcolm Atterbury, Warren Berlinger, Betty Garrett, Warren Oates, Peggy Pope.

THE MISER (69). By Molière; translated by George Graveley. March 15, 1968. Director, Douglas Campbell; scenery, lighting, and costumes, Lewis Brown. With Hume Cronyn, Jessica Tandy, Mariette Hartley, Patrick Horgan.

IN THE MATTER OF J. ROBERT OPPENHEIMER (61). By Heinar Kipphardt; translated by Ruth Speirs. (American premiere) May 24, 1968. Director, Gordon Davidson; scenery, Peter Wexler; lighting, Gilbert V. Hemsley Jr.; costumes, Marianna Elliott. With Joseph Wiseman, Harry Townes, Eduard Franz.

NOTE: This list does not include Center Theater Group's experimental programs in the Monday Night series. Other highlights of the Los Angeles theater season of 1967-68 appear in another section of this volume entitled "The Season in Los Angeles."

LOUISVILLE

Actors Theater of Louisville

ALL THE KING'S MEN (26). By Robert Penn Warren. October 5, 1967. Director, Richard Block; scenery, Brooke Karzen; lighting, Richard Mix; costumes, Lucile Paris. With Grace Chapman, Grant Sheehan, James Woodall.

THE HOSTAGE (27). By Brendan Behan. November 2, 1967. Director, Gerald Harte; scenery, Brooke Karzen; lighting, Richard Mix; costumes, Lucile Paris. With Dale Carter Cooper, Grant Sheehan, Jane Singer, Lenny Baker, Michael Henderson.

THE FIREBUGS (26). By Max Frisch; translated by Mordecai Gorelik. December 7, 1967. Director, Richard Block; scenery, Brooke Karzen; lighting, John Page Blakemore; costumes, Lucile Paris. With Barry Michlin, Lenny Baker, Dan Goldman, Max Howard, Jane Singer.

LONG DAY'S JOURNEY INTO NIGHT (27). By Eugene O'Neill. January 4, 1968. Director, Gerald Harte; scenery, Brooke Karzen; lighting, Richard Mix; costumes, Lucile Paris. With Gerald Harte, Dale Carter

Cooper, Grant Sheehan, Lenny Baker, Jane Singer.

MISALLIANCE (27). By George Bernard Shaw. February 8, 1968. Director, Gordon Phillips; scenery, Brooke Karzen; lighting, Richard Mix; costumes, Lucile Paris. With Reedy Gibbs, Dale Carter Cooper, Lenny Baker.

STRIP-TEASE by Slawomir Mrozek, director, Gerald Harte; and ENDGAME by Samuel Beckett, director, Richard Block (27). March 7, 1968. Scenery, Brooke Karzen; lighting, Richard Mix; costumes, Lucile Paris. With Lenny Baker, Max Howard, Grant Sheehan, Barry Michlin, Gerald Harte, Dale Carter Cooper.

NIGHT OF THE DUNCE (27). By Frank Gagliano. April 4, 1968. Director, William Woodman; scenery, Brooke Karzen; lighting, Richard Mix; costumes, Lucile Paris. With Barry Michlin, Jane Singer, William Hillis, Lenny Baker.

THIEVES' CARNIVAL (27). By Jean Anouilh; translated by Lucienne Hill. May 9, 1968. Director, Richard Block; scenery, Brooke Karzen; lighting, Richard Mix; costumes, Lucile Paris. With Max Howard, Jane Singer, Billy Bradford.

MEMPHIS

Front Street Theater

LUV (25). By Murray Schisgal. September 28, 1967. Director, Charles Maryan; scenery and lighting, Grady Larkins; costumes, Gail Bakkom. With Apollo Dukakis, Madison P. Mason, Victoria Mitchell.

WHO'S AFRAID OF VIRGINIA WOOLF? (24). By Edward Albee. October 26, 1967. Director, Sarah Sanders; scenery and lighting, Grady Larkins; costumes, Gail Bakkom. With Victoria Mitchell, Jerry Hardin.

THE KNACK (25). By Ann Jellicoe. November 23, 1967. Director, Sarah Sanders; scenery and lighting, Grady Larkins; costumes, Gail Bakkom. With Apollo Dukakis, Ray Edelstein, Madison P. Mason, Nancy Dawson.

THE SUBJECT WAS ROSES (25). By Frank D. Gilroy. December 28, 1967. Director, Keith Kennedy; scenery and lighting, Grady Larkins; costumes, Gail Bakkom. With Jerry Hardin, Victoria Mitchell, Ray Edelstein.

TWELFTH NIGHT (25). By William Shakespeare. January 25, 1968. Director, Harvey Landa; scenery, Grady Larkins; lighting, Chuck Hover; costumes, Jim Bakkom. With Gail Oliver, Ray Edelstein, Jerry Hardin, Madison P. Mason.

THE IMAGINARY INVALID (25). By Molière; translated by John Reich. February 22, 1968. Director, Al Barraclough; scenery, Grady Larkins; lighting, Chuck Hover; costumes, Jim Bakkom. With Jerry Hardin, Gail Oliver, Ray Edelstein, Ed Preble.

MILWAUKEE

Milwaukee Repertory Company

OTHELLO (33). By William Shakespeare. October 12, 1967. Director, Robert Benedetti; scenery and costumes, William James Wall; lighting, William Mintzer. With Clayton Corbin, Mark Alaimo, Erika Slezak, Penelope Reed.

A STREETCAR NAMED DESIRE (38). By Tennessee Williams. November 16, 1967. Director, Eugene Lesser; scenery and costumes, William James Wall; lighting, William Mintzer. With Penelope Reed, Michael Fairman, Rhoda B. Carrol, Charles Kimbrough.

AMPHITRYON 38 (26). By Jean Giraudoux; adapted by S. N. Behrman. December 14, 1967. Director, Tunc Yalman; scenery, lighting and costumes, William James Wall; musical score, Michael Hammond. With Charles Kimbrough, Erika Slezak, Michael Fairman, Jeff Chandler.

MARY STUART (26). By Friedrich von Schiller; translated by Sophie Wilkins. January 18, 1968. Director, Eugene Lesser; scenery, William James Wall; lighting, William Mintzer; costumes, Cara S. Shubin. With Penelope Reed, Erika Slezak, Charles Kimbrough, Mark Alaimo.

WAITING FOR GODOT (26). By Samuel Beckett. February 29, 1968. Director, Eugene

Lesser; scenery and costumes, William James Wall; lighting, William Mintzer. With Michael Tucker, Charles Kimbrough, Michael Fairman, Jeff Chandler.

THE BIG KNIFE (26). By Clifford Odets. March 28, 1968. Director, Hy Kalus; scenery, Kenneth W. Mueller; lighting, William Mintzer; costumes, Cara S. Shubin. With Michael Fairman, Rhoda B. Carrol, Frank Borgman, Mark Alaimo.

THE IMPORTANCE OF BEING EARNEST (35). By Oscar Wilde. April 25, 1968. Director, Tunc Yalman; scenery and costumes, William James Wall; lighting, William Mintzer. With Charles Kimbrough, Virginia Payne, Mary Jane Kimbrough, Jeff Chandler, Erika Slezak, Diana Kirkwood, Michael Tucker.

Milwaukee Repertory Company: Theater for Tomorrow Studio Series

THE HEAD OF HAIR (6). By Allen Davis. (World premiere) November 21, 1967. Director, Robert Benedetti; scenery, Robert Benedetti; lighting, William Mintzer; costumes, Cara S. Shubin. With Michael Tucker, Frank Borgman, Jeff Chandler, Erika Slezak.

OH, PIONEERS (9). By Douglas Taylor. (World premiere) February 20, 1968. Director, Tunc Yalman; scenery, Kenneth W. Mueller; lighting, William Mintzer; costumes, William James Wall. With Mary Jane Kimbrough, Erika Slezak, Frank Borgman, Mark Alaimo.

MINNEAPOLIS–ST. PAUL

Minnesota Theater Company: Tyrone Guthrie Theater

THE SHOEMAKER'S HOLIDAY (27). By Thomas Dekker. June 1, 1967. Directors, Douglas Campbell, John Olon-Scrymgeour; scenery, lighting and costumes, Dahl Delu; choreography, Robert Moulton; music, Dominick Argento; additional lyrics, John Olon-Scrymgeour. With Paul Ballantyne, Lee Richardson, Douglas Campbell, Len Cariou, Helen Carey, Grace Keagy, Moira Wylie.

THIEVES' CARNIVAL (27). By Jean Anouilh; English version by Lucienne Hill. June 2, 1967. Director, Stephen Porter; scenery, lighting and costumes, Carolyn Parker; choreography, Robert Moulton; music, Herbert Pilhofer. With Philip Kerr, Patricia Elliott, Lee Richardson, Robin Gammell, Katherine Squire, Paul Ballantyne.

HARPERS FERRY (25). By Barrie Stavis. (World premiere) June 3, 1967. Director, Tyrone Guthrie; scenery, lighting and costumes, Lewis Brown. With Edward Binns, Katherine Squire, Robert Pastene.

THE HOUSE OF ATREUS (29). Adapted by John Lewin from *The Oresteia* of Aeschylus. (World premiere) July 21, 1967. Director, Tyrone Guthrie; scenery, lighting and costumes, Tanya Moiseiwitsch; masks, Carolyn Parker; Furies masks, Dahl Delu; music, Dominick Argento. With Douglas Campbell, Paul Ballantyne, Edward Binns, Lee Richardson, Robin Gammell, Robert Pastene, Len Cariou, Patricia Elliott.

THE VISIT (29). By Friedrich Durrenmatt; translated by Maurice Valency. September 11, 1967. Director, Mel Shapiro; scenery, Dan Snyder; lighting, S. Leonard Auerbach. With Gale Sondergaard, Len Cariou, Edward Binns, Katherine Squire.

Minnesota Theater Company: Crawford Livingston Theater

SHE STOOPS TO CONQUER (32). By Oliver Goldsmith. December 28, 1967. Director, Douglas Campbell; scenery, Robert D. Mitchell; lighting, Richard Borgen; costumes, Carolyn Parker. With Paul Ballantyne; Ann Casson, Patricia Elliott, Joseph Klimowski.

TANGO (36). By Slawomir Mrozek; adapted by John Lewin with Tadeusz Gierymski. December 29, 1967. Director, Edward Payson Call; scenery, Robert D. Mitchell; lighting, S. Leonard Auerbach; costumes, Carolyn Parker. With Ann Casson, John Ramsey, Paul Ballantyne, Robin Gammell, Gale Sondergaard, Lee Richardson, Helen Carey.

ENRICO IV (29). By Luigi Pirandello; English version by Eric Bentley. February 16,

1968. Director, Mel Shapiro; scenery, Robert D. Mitchell; lighting, S. Leonard Auerbach; costumes, Carolyn Parker. With Robert Pastene, Michael Moriarty, Lee Richardson, Gale Sondergaard.

NEW HAVEN

Long Wharf Theater

THE GLASS MENAGERIE (25). By Tennessee Williams. October 20, 1967. Director, Arvin Brown; scenery and lighting, James Gohl; costumes, Rosemary Ingham. With Charles Cioffi, Mildred Dunnock, Joyce Ebert, Joseph Hindy.

THE REHEARSAL (25). By Jean Anouilh. November 17, 1967. Director, Arvin Brown; scenery and lighting, James Gohl; costumes, Rosemary Ingham. With Joyce Ebert, William Swetland, Denise Fergusson, Laurie Kennedy.

THE PLAYBOY OF THE WESTERN WORLD (25). By John Millington Synge. December 15, 1967. Director, Siobhan McKenna; scenery, John Conklin; lighting, Therald Todd; costumes, Alec Sutherland. With Denise Fergusson, Joyce Ebert, Joseph Hindy, Leo Ciceri.

ROOM SERVICE (25). By John Murray and Allen Boretz. January 12, 1968. Director, Jon Jory; scenery, Richard Klein; lighting, Therald Todd; costumes, Rosemary Ingham and Alec Sutherland. With Don Plumly, Dermot McNamara, William Swetland, Joyce Ebert, Kevin Conway.

A WHISTLE IN THE DARK (25). By Thomas Murphy. (American premiere) February 9, 1968. Director, Arvin Brown; scenery and lighting, Virginia Dancy and Elmon Webb; costumes, Alec Sutherland. With William Swetland, Leo Ciceri, Denise Fergusson.

A DOCTOR IN SPITE OF HIMSELF by Molière and THE BALD SOPRANO by Eugene Ionesco (25). March 8, 1968. Director, Jon Jory; scenery and lighting, Therald Todd; costumes, Alec Sutherland. With Joyce Ebert, Roger Omar Serbagi, Denise Fergusson, Ken Jenkins, Garry Mitchell.

TINY ALICE (25). By Edward Albee. April 5, 1968. Director, Michael Youngfellow; scenery, Santo Loquasto; lighting, Ting Barrow; costumes, Margaret Mahoney. With Roland Hewgill, Joyce Ebert, Ken Jenkins, Garry Mitchell, William Swetland.

DON JUAN IN HELL (25). By George Bernard Shaw. May 3, 1968. Director, Arvin Brown; scenery and costumes, Will Steven Armstrong; lighting, Peter Hunt. With Michael McGuire, Denise Fergusson, William Swetland, Ken Jenkins.

NEW ORLEANS

Repertory Theater

THE CRUCIBLE (15). By Arthur Miller. October 20, 1967. Director, Stuart Vaughan; scenery and costumes, Gordon Micunis; lighting, Louise Guthman. With Thomas Coley, Joanna Featherstone, Suzanne Grossmann, Donald Perkins, Barbara McMahon.

A MIDSUMMER NIGHT'S DREAM (15). By William Shakespeare. December 1, 1967. Director, Stuart Vaughan; scenery and costumes, Gordon Micunis; lighting, R. Patrick Mitchell. With Steve Perry, Herbert Nelson, Anne Thompson, Donald Perkins, Jenneth Webster, Stuart Vaughan, Nina Polan.

SAINT JOAN (15). By George Bernard Shaw. January 19, 1968. Director, Stuart Vaughan; scenery, costumes and projections, Gordon Micunis; lighting, R. Patrick Mitchell. With Suzanne Grossmann, Donald Perkins, Herbert Nelson, Stuart Vaughan, Peter Stuart.

TARTUFFE (15). By Molière; adapted and translated by Richard Wilbur. March 8, 1968. Director, Stuart Vaughan; scenery and costumes, Gordon Micunis; lighting, R. Patrick Mitchell. With Dillon Evans, Herbert Nelson, Barbara McMahon, Donald Perkins.

OKLAHOMA CITY, OKLA.

The Mummers Theater

THE MEMBER OF THE WEDDING (30). By Carson McCullers. October 26, 1967. Director, Mack Scism; scenery and lighting, Bill Dallas; costumes, Jean McFaddin. With Gertrude Jeannette, Anne Ault, Maxwell Glanville.

NIGHT OF THE DUNCE (30). By Frank Gagliano. November 23, 1967. Director, Mack Scism; scenery and lighting, Bill Dallas; costumes, Jean McFaddin. With Louise Speed, Bill Henderson, Jack Hammett.

LIFE WITH MOTHER (45). By Howard Lindsay and Russel Crouse. December 21, 1967. Director, Jack Jones; scenery and lighting, Bill Dallas; costumes, Jean McFaddin. With Hannah Stone, Jack Jones, Bill Henderson.

THREE SISTERS (38). By Anton Chekhov; translated by Anya Lachman and Mack Scism. February 1, 1968. Director, Mack Scism; scenery and lighting, Bill Dallas; costumes, Jean McFaddin. With David Manning, Laura Esterman, Leslie Keltz, Gene Gross.

ARMS AND THE MAN (38). By George Bernard Shaw. March 7, 1968. Director, Jean McFaddin; scenery and lighting, Bill Dallas; costumes, Katherine Hammett. With Anne Ault, John Wylie, Jack Davidson.

RIGHT YOU ARE (30). By Luigi Pirandello. April 11, 1968. Director, Mack Scism; scenery and lighting, Bill Dallas; costumes, Jean McFaddin. With John Wylie, Eleanor Caughron, Jack Davidson.

STRANGE BEDFELLOWS (46). By Florence Ryerson and Colin Clements. May 9, 1968. Director, Jean McFaddin; scenery and lighting, Bill Dallas; costumes, Helen Wilkinson, Jean McFaddin. With Jerry Allred, John Wylie, Louise Speed, Katherine Hammett.

PHILADELPHIA

Theater of the Living Arts

THE ENTERTAINER (30). By John Osborne. November 1, 1967. Director, Art Wolff; scenery, Douglas W. Schmidt; lighting, William Eggleston; costumes, William French; music, John Addison; choreography, Rhoda Levine; musical director, Manford Abrahamson. With Harris Yulin, Ann Whiteside, Ludi Claire, James Valentine.

THE CARETAKER (36). By Harold Pinter. November 15, 1967. Director, Charles Maryan; scenery, Marsha L. Eck; lighting, William Eggleston; costumes, William French. With Dylan Green, Ronald Roston, David Margulies.

THE IMPORTANCE OF BEING EARNEST (30). By Oscar Wilde. December 6, 1967. Director, Art Wolff; scenery, Marsha L. Eck; lighting, William Eggleston; costumes, William French. With Michael McGuire, Pamela Simpson, Ann Whiteside, James Valentine, Gloria Maddox.

A SCAFFOLD FOR MARIONETTES (30). By C. Lester Franklin. January 31, 1968. Directors, Mark Epstein, Art Wolff; scenery, David Mitchell; lighting, William Eggleston; costumes, Melly Eigsti. With David Congdon; Micki Grant, Brendan Hanlon, Betty Liveright.

THE REHEARSAL (30). By Jean Anouilh; translated by Lucienne Hill. February 21, 1968. Director, Sarah Sanders; scenery and costumes, Fred Voelpl; lighting, William Eggleston. With Nicholas Pryor, Harris Yulin, Ann Whiteside, Janis Young.

PITTSBURGH

Pittsburgh Playhouse: Hamlet Street Theater

ONCE UPON A MATTRESS (48). Book by Jay Thompson, Marshall Barer, Dean Fuller; music by Mary Rodgers; lyrics by Marshall Barer. September 23, 1967. Director, Robert Baker; choreographer and musical director, George Bunt; scenery and costumes, Kurt

Wilhelm; lighting, Patricia Simmons. With Helen Raub, John Towey, William Malloy, Judy Knaiz.

BORN YESTERDAY (36). By Garson Kanin and Ruth Gordon. November 23, 1967. Director, Robert Baker; scenery, Conrad Penrod; lighting, William Lindstrom; costumes, Kurt Wilhelm. With Kathy Barr, Art Kassul, Donald Fenwick.

THE SUBJECT WAS ROSES (33). By Frank D. Gilroy. January 27, 1968. Director, M. Lee Miller; scenery, Conrad Penrod; lighting, Pat Simons; costumes, Kurt Wilhelm. With Gerald Richards, Scottie MacGregor, Harvey Keitel.

A DELICATE BALANCE (30). By Edward Albee. February 28, 1968. Director, Ronald Satlof; scenery, Conrad Penrod; lighting, William Lindstrom; costumes, Kurt Wilhelm. With Scottie MacGregor, James Noble, Barbara Cason.

THE ODD COUPLE (48). By Neil Simon. April 3, 1968. Director, Word Baker; scenery, Conrad Penrod; lighting, Pat Simmons; costumes, Kurt Wilhelm. With Robert Alda, MacIntyre Dixon.

Pittsburgh Playhouse: Craft Avenue Theater

THE TAVERN (20). By George M. Cohan. September 30, 1967. Director, William Woodman; scenery, William Ritman; lighting, Gilbert V. Hemsley Jr.; costumes, Kurt Wilhelm. With William Hansen, Harold Scott, Gretchen Oehler, Larry Bryggman, Irwin Atkins.

AFTER THE FALL (44). By Arthur Miller. October 14, 1967. Director, Hal J. Todd; scenery, William Ritman; lighting, Gilbert V. Hemsley Jr.; costumes, Kurt Wilhelm. With Stephen Pearlman, Gretchen Oehler.

HENRY IV, PART 1 (31). By William Shakespeare. November 18, 1967. Director, Ronald Satlof; scenery, William Ritman; lighting, Gilbert V. Hemsley Jr.; costumes, Kurt Wilhelm. With Wil Albert, Howard Witt, Henry Oliver, Irene Bunde.

ARMS AND THE MAN (31). By George Bernard Shaw. December 16, 1967. Director, Jon Jory; scenery, William Ritman; lighting, Gilbert V. Hemsley Jr.; costumes, Kurt Wilhelm. With Lee Ann Fahey, Howard Witt, Irwin Atkin.

RASHOMON (15). By Fay and Michael Kanin; based on stories by Ryunosuke Akutagawa. January 20, 1968. Director, William Pappas; scenery, William Ritman; lighting, Gilbert V. Hemsley Jr.; costumes, Kurt Wilhelm. With Stephen Pearlman, Irene Bunde, Harold Scott.

THREE MEN ON A HORSE (34). By John Cecil Holm and George Abbott. February 17, 1968. Director, Robert Baker; scenery, William Ritman; lighting, Gilbert V. Hemsley Jr.; costumes, Kurt Wilhelm. With Max Gulack, Jack Axelrod, Stephen Pearlman, Wil Albert.

GALILEO (20). By Bertolt Brecht; English version by Charles Laughton. April 17, 1968. Director, Ronald Satlof; lighting, Gilbert V. Hemsley Jr.; costumes, Kurt Wilhelm. With Max Gulack, John Towey, Doris Hackney, Irwin Atkins.

PRINCETON, N.J.

McCarter Theater

THE DEVIL'S DISCIPLE (7). By George Bernard Shaw. October 7, 1967. Director, Basil Langton; scenery, Walter K. Sloan; lighting, Clyde Blakeley and John C. Schenck; costumes, Marney Welmers. With Mary Doyle, Suzanna Love, George Hearn, David Byrd.

TWELFTH NIGHT (7). By William Shakespeare. October 13, 1967. Director, Jon Jory; scenery, Walter K. Sloan; lighting, Clyde Blakeley and John C. Schenck; costumes, Marney Welmers. With George Hearn, Ronald Steelman, Jake Dengel, David Byrd, Anne Gee Byrd, Susan Babel.

ENRICO IV (7). By Luigi Pirandello. November 3, 1967. Director, Arthur Lithgow; scenery, Walter K. Sloan; lighting, Clyde Blakeley and John C. Schenck; costumes, Marney Welmers. With Susan Babel, Pamela Hawthorn; George Hearn.

THREE ONE-ACT PLAYS (6). November 16, 1967. *The Words upon the Window Pane* by W. B. Yeats; director, Arthur Lithgow.

With Will Hicks, Timothy Jerome, Mary Doyle. *It Should Happen to a Dog* by Wolf Mankowitz; director, Pamela Hawthorn. With Jake Dengel, George Hearn. *The Second Shepherd's Pageant,* Wakefield Mystery Cycle; director, Byran Hull. With K. Lype O'Dell, Ronald Steelman, Philip Piro, Yusef Bulos. All plays: scenery, Walter K. Sloan; lighting, Clyde Blakeley, John C. Schenck.

THE MERCHANT OF VENICE (7). By William Shakespeare. January 5, 1968. Director, Arthur Lithgow; scenery and lighting, Clyde Blakeley; costumes, Charles Blackburn. With Rudy Caringi, K. Lype O'Dell, Ann Gee Byrd, Susan Babel.

THE CRUCIBLE (8). By Arthur Miller. January 19, 1968. Director, Ken Costigan; scenery, Walter K. Sloan, Clyde Blakeley; lighting, John C. Schenck; costumes, Charles Blackburn. With George Hearn, Mary Doyle, Jake Dengel, Susan Babel.

THE BEGGAR'S OPERA (8). By John Gay. February 2, 1968. Director, Jon Jory; scenery, Robert Edmonds; lighting, Clyde Blakeley; costumes, Charles Blackburn; musical director, Paul Alan Levi. With Timothy Jerome, George Hearn, Anne Gee Byrd, Susan Kaslow, Judith Lane, Jake Dengel, James Tripp.

THE TRAGICAL HISTORY OF DOCTOR FAUSTUS (6). By Christopher Marlowe. March 2, 1968. Director, Ken Costigan; scenery, Robert Edmonds; lighting, Clyde Blakeley; costumes, Charles Blackburn. With George Hearn, Arthur Lithgow, Rudy Caringi, Judith Lane.

THE MARRIAGE OF FIGARO (7). By Beaumarchais. April 5, 1968. Director, Robert Moss; scenery, Robert Edmonds; lighting, Clyde Blakeley; musical arrangements, Timothy Jerome; choreography, Susan Babel. With James Tripp, Susan Kaslow, Bryan Hull, K. Lype O'Dell, Jane Cronin.

PROVIDENCE

The Trinity Square Repertory Company

THE THREEPENNY OPERA (28). Book and lyrics by Bertolt Brecht; music by Kurt Weill; English adaptation by Marc Blitzstein. October 5, 1967. Director, Adrian Hall; scenery, Eugene Lee; lighting, Roger Morgan; costumes, John Lehmeyer; music director, Richard Cumming. With Katherine Helmond, Richard Kneeland, Robert Van Hooton, Leta Anderson.

JULIUS CAESAR (16). By William Shakespeare. November 16, 1967. Director, Adrian Hall; scenery, Kert F. Lundell; lighting, Roger Morgan; costumes, John Lehmeyer. With Clinton Anderson, William Cain, Richard Kneeland, Barbara Orson.

THE IMPORTANCE OF BEING EARNEST (16). By Oscar Wilde. December 28, 1967. Director, Henry Butler; scenery, Eugene Lee; lighting, Roger Morgan; costumes, John Lehmeyer. With William Cain, Richard Kneeland, Joan White, Katherine Helmond, June Emery.

YEARS OF THE LOCUST (22). By Norman Holland. (World premiere) February 8, 1968. Director, Adrian Hall; scenery, Eugene Lee; lighting, Roger Morgan; costumes, John Lehmeyer. With Richard Kneeland, Peter Gerety, Robert Colonna, Marguerite Lenert.

AN ENEMY OF THE PEOPLE (16). By Henrik Ibsen; adapted by Arthur Miller. March 21, 1968. Director, Adrian Hall; scenery, Eugene Lee; lighting, Roger Morgan; costumes, John Lehmeyer. With William Cain, Ed Hall, Barbara Orson, Andra Akers.

PHAEDRA (22). By Jean-Baptiste Racine; English version by Robert Lowell. April 25, 1968. Director, Adrian Hall; scenery, Eugene Lee; lighting, Roger Morgan; costumes, John Lehmeyer. With Katherine Helmond, Marguerite H. Lenert; Peter Gerety.

ROCHESTER, MICH.

John Fernald Company

THE IMPORTANCE OF BEING EARNEST (28). By Oscar Wilde. October 5, 1967. Director, Eric Berry; scenery and lighting, Frank Masi; costumes, Elizabeth Penn. With Curt Dawson, George Guidall, Leora Dana, Barbara Caruso.

JOHN GABRIEL BORKMAN (31). By Henrik Ibsen; English version by John Fernald and Jenny Laird, in collaboration with Johan Fillinger. November 10, 1967. Director, Johan Fillinger; scenery and lighting, Frank Masi; costumes, Elizabeth Penn. With

Eric Berry, Herbert Foster, Leora Dana, Jenny Laird.

CHARLEY'S AUNT (31). By Brandon Thomas. December 15, 1967. Director, John Fernald; scenery and lighting, Frank Masi; costumes, Elizabeth Penn. With Neil Hunt, Lorna Lewis, Eric Berry.

AND PEOPLE ALL AROUND (28). By George Sklar; music and lyrics by Booker T. Bradshaw, Jr. January 18, 1968. Directors, John Broome, George Guidall; scenery and lighting, Frank Masi; costumes, Elizabeth Penn. With Booker T. Bradshaw Jr., Beverly Atkinson, Otho Burr, Pam Guest, Lorna Lewis, Henry Thomas.

KING LEAR (27). By William Shakespeare. February 23, 1968. Director, John Fernald; scenery and lighting, Frank Masi; costumes, Elizabeth Penn. With Eric Berry, Jill Tanner, Barbara Caruso, Lorna Lewis, Joshua Bryant, Booker T. Bradshaw, Jr., George Guidall.

NO EXIT by Jean-Paul Sartre, adapted by Paul Bowles; and THE FIREBUGS by Max Frisch, translated by Mordecai Gorelik. (27). March 29, 1968. Director, Milo Sperber; scenery and lighting, Frank Masi; costumes, Elizabeth Penn. With Joshua Bryant, Otho Burr, Jill Tanner, Barbara Caruso, Colin Pinney, Victor Holchak, Betty Sinclair.

THE SEAGULL (27). By Anton Chekhov; translated by J. P. Davis. May 3, 1968. Director, John Fernald; scenery and lighting, Frank Masi; costumes, Elizabeth Penn. With Jenny Laird, George Guidall, Lans Traverse, Curt Dawson.

ST. LOUIS

Repertory Theater of Loretto-Hilton Center

THE CAUCASIAN CHALK CIRCLE (16). By Bertolt Brecht; English version by Eric Bentley. November 3, 1967. Director, Philip Minor; scenery, Raymond Jens Klausen; lighting, Peter Sargent; costumes, Vita. With Joy Mills, Louis Basile.

THE TIME OF YOUR LIFE (16). By William Saroyan. November 4, 1967. Director, James Bernardi; scenery, Raymond Jens Klausen; lighting, Peter Sargent; costumes, Vita. With Jane Lowry, Robert Murch.

THE MISER (16). By Molière. November 29, 1967. Director, Michael Flanagan; scenery, Raymond Jens Klausen; lighting, Peter Sargent; costumes, Vita. With J. Robert Dietz, James Scott, Joy Mills.

THE MERCHANT OF VENICE (16). By William Shakespeare. February 2, 1968. Director, Michael Flanagan; scenery, Grady Larkins; lighting, Peter Sargent; costumes, Vita. With Chet London, Philip Minor, Carol Keefe.

SIX CHARACTERS IN SEARCH OF AN AUTHOR (16). By Luigi Pirandello; English translation by Paul Avila Mayer. February 3, 1968. Director, J. Robert Dietz; scenery, Grady Larkins; lighting, Peter Sargent; costumes, Vita. With Bernie Passeltiner, Virginia Payne, Joy Mills, Doris Diener.

MISALLIANCE (16). By George Bernard Shaw. February 28, 1968. Director, Philip Minor; scenery, Grady Larkins; lighting, Peter Sargent; costumes, Vita. With George Addis, Marion Clarke, Robert Murch.

ST. PAUL (See Minneapolis-St. Paul)

SAN FRANCISCO

NOTE: ACT presented a 40-week repertory at the Geary and Marines' Memorial Theaters from October 31, 1967 through May 31, 1968 and continuing into July, 1968. Number of performances of each play has been omitted from this list, since the total count was not available as of press time.

American Conservatory Theater (ACT): Geary Theater

TWELFTH NIGHT by William Shakespeare. October 31, 1967. Director, William Ball; scenery, Stuart Wurtzel; lighting, John McLain; costumes, Lewis Brown. With DeAnn Mears/Ellen Geer, Paul Shenar, Carol Jenkins/Deborah Sussel, Ray Reinhardt/Harry

Frazier, Mark Bramhall/Mark Schell, Ken Ruta/Patrick Tovatt.

DEAR LIAR by Jerome Kilty. November 3, 1967. Director, Jerome Kilty; scenery, Stuart Wurtzel; lighting, John McLain; costumes, Walter Watson. With Jerome Kilty/Robert Gerringer, Barbara Colby/Patricia Falkenhain.

UNDER MILK WOOD by Dylan Thomas. November 21, 1967. Director, William Ball; scenery, Stuart Wurtzel; lighting, John McLain; costumes, David Toser. With Larry Ferguson, Scott Hylands, Gil Turner, Ellen Geer, Dana Larson, Izetta Smith.

TARTUFFE by Molière; English version by Richard Wilbur. December 3, 1967. Director, William Ball; scenery, Stuart Wurtzel; lighting, John McLain; costumes, Jane Greenwood. With Rene Auberjonois, Ramon Bieri, Judith Mihalyi, DeAnn Mears.

THIEVES' CARNIVAL by Jean Anouilh; English version by Lucienne Hill. December 20, 1967. Director, Jerome Kilty; scenery, Stuart Wurtzel; lighting, John McLain; costumes, Marianna Elliott. With Ruth Kobart, Harry Frazier, Charlene Polite, Kate Hawley.

TINY ALICE by Edward Albee. January 16, 1968. Director, William Ball; scenery, Stuart Wurtzel; lighting, John McLain; masks, Robert Joyce. With Paul Shenar, DeAnn Mears, Ray Reinhardt, Scott Hylands, Harry Frazier.

OUR TOWN by Thornton Wilder. January 25, 1968. Director, Edward Hastings; scenery, Stuart Wurtzel; lighting, John McLain; costumes, Patrizia Von Brandenstein. With Robert Gerringer, Ellen Geer, Mark Bramhall, Ray Reinhardt, Jay Doyle, Carol Teitel, Josephine Nichols.

THE CRUCIBLE by Arthur Miller. February 8, 1968. Director, Allen Fletcher; scenery, Stuart Wurtzel; lighting, John McLain. With Ramon Bieri, Angela Paton, Jay Doyle, Josephine Nichols.

THE MISANTHROPE by Molière; English version by Richard Wilbur. March 28, 1968. Director, David William; scenery, Stuart Wurtzel; lighting, John McLain. With Barry MacGregor, John Schuck, Michael Learned, Kitty Winn.

HAMLET (Part 1: *Elsinore*) by William Shakespeare. April, 1968. Director, William Ball; scenery, Stuart Wurtzel; lighting, John McLain. With Paul Shenar, Ray Reinhardt, Angela Paton, Izetta Smith.

ACT: Marines' Memorial Theater

ALBEE ACTS by Edward Albee. November 14, 1967. *The American Dream,* director, William Ball; scenery, Stuart Wurtzel; lighting, John McLain. With Ruth Kobart, Harry Frazier, Jay Doyle, Scott Hylands. *The Zoo Story,* director, Richard A. Dysart; scenery, Stuart Wurtzel; lighting, John McLain; costumes, Walter Watson. With Scott Hylands/Paul Shenar, Robert Goldsby/Barry MacGregor.

TWO FOR THE SEESAW by William Gibson. November 16, 1967. Director, Byron Ringland; scenery, Stuart Wurtzel; lighting, John McLain; costumes, Walter Watson. With Ramon Bieri, Barbara Colby.

LONG DAY'S JOURNEY INTO NIGHT by Eugene O'Neill. November 19, 1967. Director, Byron Ringland; scenery, Stuart Wurtzel; lighting, John McLain; costumes, Walter Watson. With Angela Paton, Ramon Bieri, Patrick Tovatt, David Grimm.

ENDGAME by Samuel Beckett. November 26, 1967. Director, Edward Payson Call; scenery, Stuart Wurtzel; lighting, John McLain; costumes, David Toser. With Ken Ruta/Barry Kraft, Rene Auberjonois/Michael Lerner, Dion Chesse/Robert Feero, Enid Kent/Mary Ellen Ray.

CHARLEY'S AUNT by Brandon Thomas. December 19, 1967. Director, Edward Hastings; scenery, Stuart Wurtzel; lighting, Allan Melad; costumes, William French. With Rene Auberjonois, Scott Hylands.

IN WHITE AMERICA by Martin Duberman. January 10, 1968. With John Schuck, Ann Weldon, Marguerite Ray, Lynne Arden, Gil Turner.

DON'T SHOOT MABLE IT'S YOUR HUSBAND by Jerome Kilty. (World premiere) February 7, 1968. Director, Jerome Kilty; scenery, Stuart Wurtzel; lighting, John McLain. With Barbara Colby, Barry MacGregor, Mark Bramhall.

AN EVENING'S FROST by Donald Hall. February 17, 1968. Director, Marcella Cisney;

scenery, Stuart Wurtzel; lighting, John McLain. With Will Geer, Peter Donat, DeAnn Mears, William Paterson.

A DELICATE BALANCE by Edward Albee. March 23, 1968. Director, Edward Hastings; scenery, Stuart Wurtzel; lighting, John McLain. With Josephine Nichols, Robert Gerringer, Patricia Falkenhain, Ellen Geer.

SEATTLE

Seattle Repertory Theater

HENRY IV, PART 1 (29). By William Shakespeare. November 1, 1967. Director, Allen Fletcher; scenery, Robert E. Darling; lighting, David F. Segal; costumes, Allan Granstrom; music, Conrad Susa. With Josef Sommer, Richard Kavanaugh, Patrick Hines, Pearl Castle, Archie Smith.

THE REHEARSAL (29). By Jean Anouilh; English version by Pamela Hansford Johnson and Kitty Black. November 8, 1967. Director, Byron Ringland; scenery, Robert E. Darling; lighting, David F. Segal; costumes, Allan Granstrom. With Pauline Flanagan, Kay Doubleday, Jacqueline Coslow, Patrick Gorman, George Vogel.

YOU CAN'T TAKE IT WITH YOU (35). By Moss Hart and George S. Kaufman. December 13, 1967. Director, Allen Fletcher; scenery, S. Todd Muffatti; lighting, David F. Segal; costumes, Allan Granstrom. With Maureen Quinn, Archie Smith, Chris Ditmars, Richard Kavanaugh, Kay Doubleday.

THE RIVALS (26). By Richard Brinsley Sheridan. January 24, 1968. Director, Allen Fletcher; scenery, John Conklin; lighting, David F. Segal; costumes, Allan Granstrom; music, Kenneth W. Benshoof. With Margaret Hamilton, Jacqueline Coslow, Kay Doubleday, George Vogel, Archie Smith, Patrick Hines.

THE FATHER (29). By August Strindberg; Translated by Arvid Paulson. February 7, 1968. Director, Pirie MacDonald; scenery, John Conklin; lighting, David F. Segal; costumes, Allan Granstrom. With Josef Sommer, Pauline Flanagan, Jonathan Farwell, Margaret Hamilton.

THE THREEPENNY OPERA (28). By Bertolt Brecht and Kurt Weill; English version by Marc Blitzstein. March 13, 1968. Director, Allen Fletcher; scenery, Robert E. Darling; lighting, Roger Morgan; costumes, Allan Granstrom. With Jonathan Farwell, Patrick Hines, Maureen Quinn, Myrna Walker, Eve Roberts, Olivia Cole.

SRT Off Center Theater

THE DEATH OF BESSIE SMITH and THE AMERICAN DREAM (10). By Edward Albee. November 10, 1967. Director, Allen Fletcher; scenery, S. Todd Muffatti; lighting, David F. Segal; costumes, Jack Smith. With Patrick Hines, Eve Roberts, Jason Bernard, Stanley Anderson, Pearl Castle, Richard Kavanaugh.

U.S.A. (8). By Paul Shyre and John Dos Passos; based on the novels of John Dos Passos. November 24, 1967. Director, George Vogel; scenery, James P. Bertholf; lighting, David F. Segal; costumes, Allan Granstrom. With Jacqueline Coslow, Kay Doubleday, Jonathan Farwell, Pauline Flanagan, John Gilbert, Patrick Gorman.

LITTLE MURDERS (8). By Jules Feiffer. December 15, 1967. Director, Hal J. Todd; scenery, William Raoul; lighting, Phil Schermer; costumes, Jack Smith. With Pearl Castle, Kent Bishop, George Vogel, Patricia Hamilton, Jeffery Craggs.

CHRISTOPHER (8). By Clarence Morley. (American premiere) January 26, 1968. Director, scenery and effects, James P. Bertholf; costumes, Jack Smith; film sequence, Lawrence Robbin. With John Odegard, Jonathan Farwell, Jeffery Craggs, Elane Hellmuth, Maureen Quinn.

KRAPP'S LAST TAPE by Samuel Beckett, INFANCY and CHILDHOOD by Thornton Wilder (8). February 9, 1968. Director, Patrick Hines; scenery, S. Todd Muffatti; lighting, James P. Bertholf; costumes, Jack Smith. With Jason Bernard, Mendy McLean, Jacqueline Coslow, Stanley Anderson, Olivia Cole, Richard Kavanaugh.

BRECHT ON BRECHT (10). By George Tabori, from the works of Bertolt Brecht. March 15, 1968. Director, Archie Smith; scenery, S. Todd Muffatti; lighting, Dan Goodwin; costumes, Jack Smith. With Stanley Anderson, Jacqueline Coslow, Kay Doubleday, John Gilbert, Robert Loper.

SPRINGFIELD, MASS.

The Springfield Theater Company

THE COUNTRY WIFE (21). By William Wycherley. November 16, 1967. Director, James Cromwell; scenery and costumes, Judith Haugan; lighting, Ronald W. Wallace. With Susan McArthur, William Needles, Ruth Nelson.

CHARLEY'S AUNT (21). By Brandon Thomas. December 14, 1967. Director, William Needles; scenery, Judith Haugan; lighting, Ronald W. Wallace. With Gregory Abels, Janet Kapral, John Cromwell.

CANDIDA (21). By George Bernard Shaw. January 11, 1968. Director, Michael Youngfellow; scenery and costumes, Judith Haugan; lighting, Ronald W. Wallace. With Ellen Darrell Tovatt, Gregory Abels, Leonard Hicks.

THE ENTERTAINER (21). By John Osborne. February 8, 1968. Director, James Cromwell; scenery, Judith Haugan; lighting, Ronald W. Wallace; costumes, Michael Eagan; choreography, Buck Heller; musical director, Stephen E. Hays. With Donald Davis, Janet Kapral, Ruth Nelson.

THE KNACK (21). By Ann Jellicoe. March 7, 1968. Director, Donald Davis; scenery, Richard Montfort Cary; lighting, Ronald W. Wallace; costumes, Corinna Taylor. With Kevin Bryan Conway, John Glover, Gregory Abels, Janet Kapral.

LONG DAY'S JOURNEY INTO NIGHT (21). By Eugene O'Neill. April 4, 1968. Director, James Cromwell; scenery, Judith Haugan; lighting, Ronald W. Wallace. With Donald Davis, Ruth Nelson, Ron Leibman, Gregory Abels.

STANFORD

Stanford Repertory Theater

THE CAVERN (14). By Jean Anouilh; translated by Lucienne Hill. November 29, 1967. Director, Sirin Devrim; scenery, Warren Travis; lighting, Derek Hunt; costumes, Douglas A. Russell. With Gerald Hiken, Sirin Devrim, Stephen D. Newman, Paul E. Richards.

CANDAULES, COMMISSIONER (19). By Daniel C. Gerould. (West Coast premiere) January 10, 1968. Director, William Sharp; scenery, James Lyon; lighting, Steven A. Maze; costumes, Carol Rountree. With Sheldon Feldner, N. R. Davidson, Elizabeth Huddle, Sergei Tschernisch.

COCK-A-DOODLE DANDY (9). By Sean O'Casey. March 6, 1968. Director, Charles Olsen; scenery, Richard L. Hay; lighting, Nancy Tenbroeck; costumes, Warren Travis. With N. R. Davidson, Ruth Hunt, Gerald Hiken, Paul E. Richards, Reba Waters.

THE INSPECTOR-GENERAL (14). By Nikolai Gogol; translated by Andrew MacAndrew. April 24, 1968. Director, Douglas Johnson; scenery, Jerome Marcel; lighting, Larry Davidson; costumes, Douglas Russell. With Joseph Medalis, Paul E. Richards, Gerald Hiken, Sirin Devrim.

SYRACUSE, N.Y.

Syracuse Repertory Theater

THE MISER (15). By Molière; English version by Kirk Denmark. February 29, 1968. Director, Walt Witcover; scenery, Otto Theuer; lighting, Robert Willard; costumes, Ruth Frank. With G. F. Reidenbaugh, Richard Fancy, Adale O'Brien.

HAMLET (13). By William Shakespeare. March 7, 1968. Director-adapter, Rex Henriot; scenery, Otto Theuer; lighting, Robert Willard; costumes, Ruth Frank. With Roger Robinson, James Callahan, Zoaunne Henriot, Michael McGuire.

THE HOSTAGE (9). By Brendan Behan. March 28, 1968. Director, G. F. Reidenbaugh; scenery, Leonard Dryansky; lighting, Robert Willard; costumes, Ruth Frank. With James Callahan, Zoaunne Henriot, Gary Gage, Gerard Moses, Shirley Ann Fener.

THE QUEEN AND THE REBELS (9). By Ugo Betti; translated by Henry Reed. April 4, 1968. Director, Rex Henriot; scenery, Otto Theuer; lighting, Robert Willard; costumes, Ruth Frank. With James Callahan, Roger Robinson, Zoaunne Henriot.

THE PLAY'S THE THING (9). By Ferenc Molnar; adapted by P.G. Wodehouse. April 25, 1968. Director, Rex Henriot; scenery, Otto Theuer; lighting, Robert Willard; costumes, Ruth Frank. With Don Phelps, Gerard Moses, Adale O'Brien, James Callahan, Gary Gage.

WALTHAM, MASS.

Brandeis University: Spingold Theater

SCHWEYK IN THE SECOND WORLD WAR (11). By Bertolt Brecht; translated by Peter Sander. November 1, 1967. Director, Peter Sander; scenery, William Fregosi; lighting, David Sackeroff; costumes, Susan Dubiner; musical director, Arthur Finstein; music, Hanns Eisler. With Morris Carnovsky, David S. Howard, Matt Conley, Charles W. Moore.

COLOMBE (10). By Jean Anouilh; adapted by Louis Kronenberger. December 6, 1967. Director, Howard Bay; scenery, Richard Keshishian; lighting, Robert Swanson; costumes, Doug Marmee. With Terry Lumley, Vanya Franck, Howland Chamberlain.

THE IMPORTANCE OF BEING EARNEST (9). By Oscar Wilde. February 7, 1968. Director, Charles Werner Moore; scenery, Anthony Sabatino; lighting, Wayne Chouinard, Candy Land; costumes, Cletus Anderson. With Peter Lempert, James Sims, Vanya Franck.

PARADISE LOST (9). By Clifford Odets. March 27, 1968. Director, Morris Carnovsky; scenery, Susan Dubiner; lighting, Christopher Idoine; costumes, Marla Nedelman. With Vanya Franck, Matt Conley, David S. Howard.

FIRE (9). By John Roc. (World premiere) May 1, 1968. Director, Charles Werner Moore; scenery, Christopher Idoine; lighting, Reuben Goldberg; costumes, Barbara Cox. With David S. Howard, Mervyn Williams, Matt Conley, Vanya Franck.

NOTE: New plays presented in the Laurie Premiere Theater were *Sunday* by Joseph Scott, *Mom-Art* by Donald H. Julian, *Satsuma Incident* by Arsene Davignon, *Funeral Games* by Stan Thomas, *The Cruelest Month* by Henry C. Timm, *Playsongs* by Joseph Scott and *The Mentor* by Daniel Estow.

WASHINGTON, D.C.

Washington Theater Club

LUV (26). By Murray Schisgal. August 10, 1967. Director, Davey Marlin-Jones; scenery, Alton Miller; lighting, William Eggleston; costumes, Terry Munger. With Joan Porter, Ralph Strait, Raymond Thorne.

MY SWEET CHARLIE (33). By David Westheimer. October 12, 1967. Director, Davey Marlin-Jones; scenery and costumes, James Parker; lighting, William Eggleston. With Damon Brazwell, John Hillerman, Sue Lawless, Ralph Strait.

EH? (40). By Henry Livings. November 23, 1967. Director, Davey Marlin-Jones; scenery, James Parker; lighting, William Eggleston; costumes, Terry Munger. With Bob Spencer, Bryan Clark, Ginger Gerlach, Ralph Strait.

NO MAN'S LAND (33). By John Wilson. (World premiere) January 4, 1968. Director, Davey Marlin-Jones; scenery and costumes, James Parker; lighting, William Eggleston. With John Hillerman, Bob Spencer.

CALIGULA (40). By Albert Camus; translated by Justin O'Brien. February 15, 1968. Director, Davey Marlin-Jones; scenery and costumes, James Parker; lighting, William Eggleston. With John Hillerman, Damon Brazwell, Joan Matthiessen.

FIVE EVENINGS (40). By Aleksandr Volodin; translated by Ariadne Nicolaeff. (American premiere) March 28, 1968. Director, Davey Marlin-Jones; scenery and costumes, James Parker; lighting, William Eggleston. With Ralph Strait, Ann Chodoff.

THE BASEMENT by Murray Schisgal, directed by Herb Sufrin; and GREEN JULIA

(American premiere) by Paul Ableman, directed by Davey Marlin-Jones. May 9, 1968. Scenery and costumes, James Parker; lighting, William Eggleston. With John Hillerman, Bob Spencer, Ann Chodoff, Ralph Strait, Bryan Clark.

Arena Stage

MAJOR BARBARA (40). By George Bernard Shaw. September 26, 1967. Director, Edwin Sherin; scenery, Robin Wagner; lighting, William Eggleston; costumes, Marjorie Slaiman. With Jane Alexander, Eugene R. Wood, James Kenny, George Ebeling.

POOR BITOS (30). By Jean Anouilh; translated by Lucienne Hill. September 27, 1967. Director, Harold Stone, scenery, Robin Wagner; lighting, William Eggleston; costumes, Leigh Rand. With Richard Venture, Richard McKenzie, Richard Bauer, Anna Shaler, Jane Alexander.

THE GREAT WHITE HOPE (34). By Howard Sackler. (World premiere) December 12, 1967. Director, Edwin Sherin; scenery, Douglas W. Schmidt; lighting, William Eggleston; costumes, Marjorie Slaiman; music and sound, Charles Gross. With James Earl Jones, Norma Donaldson, Jane Alexander, Lou Gilbert, Jimmy Pelham.

THE BLOOD KNOT (7). By Athol Fugard. January 16, 1968. Director, Gladys Vaughan; scenery, Nicholas Russiyan; lighting, William Eggleston; costumes, Julia Gillett. With James Earl Jones, Robert Foxworth.

THE TENTH MAN (34). By Paddy Chayefsky. February 13, 1968. Director, Donald Moreland; scenery, Ming Cho Lee; lighting, William Eggleston; costumes, Marjorie Slaiman. With Anna Shaler, George Ebeling, Barton Heyman, Max Wright, Lou Gilbert, Ned Beatty.

ROOM SERVICE (34). By John Murray and Allen Boretz. February 14, 1968. Director, Donald Moreland; scenery, Ming Cho Lee; lighting, William Eggleston; costumes, Marjorie Slaiman. With Lou Gilbert, Robert Foxworth, Richard Venture, Jane Alexander, Max Wright.

THE ICEMAN COMETH (35). By Eugene O'Neill. March 26, 1968. Director, Edwin Sherin; scenery, Ming Cho Lee; lighting, William Eggleston; costumes, Marjorie Slaiman. With Richard McKenzie, James Kenny, Tana Hicken, Eugene R. Wood, Richard Venture.

National Repertory Theater: Ford's Theater

JOHN BROWN'S BODY (33). By Stephen Vincent Benet. February 12, 1968. Director, Jack Sydow; scenery, William Pitkin; lighting, Tharon Musser. With G. Wood, Ellen Holly, Paula Bauersmith, Geoffrey Garland.

THE COMEDY OF ERRORS (35). By William Shakespeare. February 26, 1968. Director, G. Wood; scenery, William Pitkin; lighting, Tharon Musser; costumes, Jane Greenwood. With Terence Scammell, Paul Massie, Paula Bauersmith, Edith Meiser, Geoffrey Garland, Patricia Guinan, Anne Draper.

SHE STOOPS TO CONQUER (35). By Oliver Goldsmith. March 26, 1968. Director, James D. Waring; scenery, William Pitkin; lighting, Tharon Musser; costumes, Alvin Colt, Jane Greenwood. With Sylvia Sidney, G. Wood, Geoffrey Garland, Susan Sullivan.

○
○
○

THE SEASON IN LOS ANGELES

○
○
○

A BEGINNING FOR CENTER THEATER GROUP

By Gordon Davidson

Artistic director, Mark Taper Forum, Los Angeles

The Mark Taper Forum has its very foundations in a special and exciting physical environment, which offers many unique possibilities for interaction between theater artist and audience. That environment is the intimate open stage embraced on three sides by an audience of no more than 750. It is a theater which can utilize the most advanced techniques of film and television projection and still remain a simple platform for an actor's communication of a playwright's ideas unencumbered by gadgets and machinery.

This small theater's larger environment is that of a handsome cultural center with all its attractive advantages and its inevitable institutional inhibitions. The fact that three playhouses (additionally a 2,100 seat theater and a 3,200 seat concert hall) exist in one setting—that audiences can assemble to hear and witness programs of opera, symphony, dance and drama—promotes significant focus of attention in the battle for the individual's leisure time and entertainment dollar. The reality, pressure and responsibility of living and working in a publicly-owned (Los Angeles County) facility are enormous. Political sensitivity to the righteous wrath of taxpayer pressure is immediate and disconcerting, but freedom of artistic expression is essential to any creative endeavor. Ultimately the answer to our theater's work lies in the community's realization that we cannot be all things to all people. Furthermore, it will be realized in our acceptance of the idea that "the theater," and our small theater particularly, is not a mass art; that quantity is not a measure either of excellence as an art form, or impact and influence as a projection of and reflection of the society in which it functions.

Buildings by themselves are no answer to an artistic director's problems: often they create more obstacles than they solve, for in many instances the containing cart has come before the creative horse. The theater building represents a path by which a journey can begin. It is a tool and not the creative end itself.

It is my belief, however, that physical structures (environment) help shape personality—in this case, of the theater—and have a great influence on both actor and audience. The Globe Theater did not inspire Shapespeare, but the Elizabethan audience attending a performance of *Hamlet* or *Twelfth Night* was at one with both the material and the form of presentation. The religious experience of the Greeks assembling in the Theater of Dionysius to watch the sun actually rise at the moment it was required in *Agamemnon* is one of the earliest examples of a society and a theater and an artist being of one mind. Perhaps this is no longer possible in our fragmented mod world. Perhaps the closest we can come to this sense of being at one with our lives and the reflection of our lives through art is a "be-in" or a "freak-out." I have hopes to the contrary.

Creating an audience is the first requirement of a new and vital theater life, and this already has been handsomely met in Los Angeles. There is indeed an audience hungry for good, provocative entertainment (our subscription audience numbers close to 30,000) and with this capability of filling this new theater, half the battle has been at least joined, if not won.

The key factor in this audience, however, is not its size but its sense of continuity. Over half the subscription audience is known to have attended anywhere from 30 to 50 productions of the Theater Group, both when it was associated with UCLA Extension and also at the Music Center. This continuity has helped create or recreate theatergoers as differentiated from playgoers or star gazers. This known profile permits Center Theater Group to build upon a common theatergoing experience as it strikes off in new experimental directions. This knowledge of an audience is becoming more common to the regional theaters throughout this country and is unheard of in the Broadway theater, in which each producer starts from scratch every time he presents a play.

One of the dangers of a subscription audience—especially as it exists in a cultural center—is the danger of middle-class homogeneity. We have taken steps to encourage students, culturally disadvantaged minority groups, city and county employees and others to attend previews and regular performances at special prices.

Our sense of continuity can be furthered by the development of an acting ensemble. By the end of our third year (1968) I hope to have worked with enough talented and interested actors who will, all conditions being favorable, form the nucleus of such a company. The key to this ensemble will be the development of the most exciting young actors we can find. We've already begun through the use of a journeyman program, a training program tied in with the universities in the community and special projects such as a new playwrights program utilizing a company concept. I will always want to make it possible for the serious mature actor to work at the Mark Taper Forum without having to make any significant sacrifices. But living in Hollywood, the difficulty always is that you can't have it both ways, and some sacrifices must be made. The frustrations and disappointments are enormous. The impossibility for long-range planning because of movie and television obligations and seduction is heartbreaking. It will be a long time before actors, agents and movie producers regard the theater not as diversion but as a necessary creative partner in the growth of artists. Perhaps then Los Angeles will be more like London, where, instead of actors taking time off from movies to do a play, the reverse is true—one takes time from the stage to do film. The enthusiasm and the sense of commitment that most of the actors who worked for us in the last two seasons displayed gives one the courage to move ahead.

I feel we've only begun to explore the possibilities of the Mark Taper Forum from the point of view of the use of the theater, the esthetics of a thrust stage and the kind of acting, writing and directing that can happen in that theater. The programming of the first two seasons had to do with just such an exploration. I think we've begun to find actors who can create both a sense of intimate reality as well as considerable style, but we haven't integrated this concept enough in our work. One goal is to try to solve the problem of continued growth and exploration in a play and in actors once a production opens to public performance, and then to extend that growth from play to play. The rehearsal period is only one small part in the development of an artistic concept. Continuity of a pool of actors over a period of years will begin to develop a meaningful way of working. While we're exploring these areas our audiences are being asked to open themselves up to a new kind of adventure not all of which is totally satisfying. I'm constantly asked why we don't do "happier" plays. The happiness or unhappiness of a play is not as important to me as the degree to which the audience is engaged in an evening of emotional and intellectual stimulation. Most heartening of all were the turn-away crowds we developed for the New Theater for Now program. In a series of Monday night events we produced the new works of sixteen playwrights and this year we expect to increase that number. This proved to me that there is a portion of our audience which is enthusiastically venturesome and willing to take some chances.

I firmly believe that the thrust and force of our operation in the Mark Taper Forum is in the area of new work—not just because it happens to excite and stimulate our audiences, but because I have a tremendous sense of obligation to the writing talent in this country to provide them with a responsible and highly professional atmosphere in which they can create. It's a large responsibility, and inescapable. To that end, this coming year there will be an expanded New Theater for Now program. We have not even begun to scratch the surface, in our community or in the nation. Not every play, especially not every good play we get, can be produced, but in some manner—informal reading, staged reading, modest productions—more plays must and will get done in the mornings, afternoons, or evenings throughout the year. I told a recent Monday night audience that the New Theater program was dedicated to the idea that there shall never be a dark night at the Forum. The audience shouted, "Hear! Hear!" It was thrilling.

Writers must come to know that there is both a place and a person (or persons) who will encourage them to tackle important contemporary themes rooted in our community and speaking to our problems as well as to the world at large. We will be fulfilling the most important function of this new theater if we honor our obligation to these writers. By stimulating new work, by heightening the sense of participation of the audience and by evolving a style of acting and production that can cope with the varied repertory today's audiences demand, we have set our sights on important goals.

Center Theater Group's activities in the Mark Taper Forum also have an obligation to the artistic company—the actors, designers, directors, composers and administrators—to provide both training and development. It must create in a community, which is freeway-flung and sun-lulled, a chance to rub creative shoulders with one another, for no theater can exist in a vacuum and no artist can communicate without a sense of his own place in a community of creative people. The essence of acting is establishing living ties between people. It is a ceremonial act of self-discovery, and one of the problems we must face is that the conflict of contemporary theater lies in its disavowal of identity. Today's playwrights have a great desire and need to express the paradox, the contradiction, the incompleteness of experience. We must find new ways to rekindle the spark of what Harold Clurman calls the "true theater" which is "not entertainment as titillation, but entertainment (yes!) as the engagement of the heart, mind, soul and senses . . . The theater in its every dimension must be judged on the basis of what is being expressed and how well. Since human expression is all-encompassing and since the character of stage expression is immediate, I hope to see a theater ever more relevant to the entire human situation of our day. That is the way it may best move toward truth, achieve the universal. But the universal reveals itself only with time. The more deeply engaged we are in voicing and demonstrating the truth we perceive in our world, the more we approximate the purposes of art."

I have always believed theater to be a total art form wherein every element must be in place and all of it related somehow to life. Once created, this type of total theater must then find its own special identity, its own statement and sense of timeliness. The Forum provides a unique and challenging opportunity to create just such a theater. Its very name—Forum—suggests a sharing of ideas, a spirited dialogue existing between audience and artist. Out of this comes provocative thought, perception, and—ultimately—the excitement of mutual expression.

Highlights of the Season in Los Angeles

By Dale Olson

Nowhere in the last year has there been so marked a growth in theater activity, particularly in the energetic development of new material, as in Los Angeles. Here we have seen new works by such playwrights as Paddy Chayefsky, William Inge, Calder Willingham, Jerome Chodorov, Philip Abbott, Ray Bradbury, N. Richard Nash and John Kander and Fred Ebb—all in one year—and an abundance of interesting material from a battery of promising new writers, some of whom give evidence of real scope and power. Significantly, the city's audiences, which too have grown appreciably, have begun to take a new kind of pride in the new work and are supporting new plays with vigor and enthusiasm.

Perhaps the most striking examples of the healthy new activity were seen in the programs of Center Theater Group's New Theater for Now series, under the splendid direction of Edward Parone, and the Actors Studio West-UCLA Committee on Fine Arts' series entitled Plays in Progress, supervised by Jack Garfein and Lyle Dye Jr. Two of the New Theater for Now presentations have been produced in New York City: John Guare's impressive *Muzeeka* and a collection of brief theatrical tidbits collectively entitled *Collision Course*. A second season is under way, made possible by a $200,000 Rockefeller grant. Four new plays have already been selected by CTG's Play Reading committee.

The Actors Studio series, like CTG's aimed to aid the playwright, produced William Inge's *Don't Go Gentle,* now preparing for a Broadway bow, as well as Calder Willingham's first play in several years, *How Tall is Toscanini?* and Lonny Chapman's *Echoes*. But its most exciting contribution was Harvey Perr's *The Adventures of Jack and Max,* which also was Lee Grant's impressive debut as a director. With this play, admittedly unfinished, Perr shows real promise.

Within its full-scale production season, CTG presented two additional new plays in Romulus Linney's massive *The Sorrows of Frederick* and Oliver Hailey's most impressive *Who's Happy Now?,* by far the strongest new entry of the season.

More than 200 professional productions appeared in Los Angeles between June 1, 1967 and May 31, 1968—not all of the same quality, of course. The first American staging of Eugene O'Neill's massive *More Stately Mansions* failed to live up to the late great playwright's earlier material or to the glamor of its star, Ingrid Bergman, although it certainly did provide a bright galaxy for the local theater. Similarly, James Doolittle's presentation of Chayefsky's *The Latent Heterosexual,* in its first all-professional production, proved to be exciting only in its view of an exciting performer (Zero Mostel). The big, costly rock version of *Othello* entitled *Catch My Soul* was splendid in its visual concept but otherwise inept; the lavish Edwin Lester production of *Dumas and Son* lived up to Lester's reputation for super production values but turned out to be very dull; and the only mildly entertaining musical, *The Happy Time,* satisfied our theatergoers only because of their pride in seeing it first, prior to Broadway.

These were minor disappointments that still left a tinge of pleasure in their wake. Not so the first season of the Inner City Repertory Company, the organization founded with government funds and a lofty ambition to bring theater education to high school youths. Artistic differences hampered the opening production, a totally ill-conceived *Tartuffe*. With *The Seagull* it appeared the company was to be on its feet; it was followed by a finely-developed production of *Slow Dance on the Killing Ground* but then lost all sense of direction in a sloppy, senseless production of *A Midsummer Night's Dream,* an attempt at modernizing Shakespeare.

Another blow to the community came with the loss of free Shakespeare in the park. The two-year program had made strong public impact with Diana Sands and Robert Lansing in *Antony and Cleopatra* and a fine rendering of *The Two Gentlemen of Verona* supervised by Ira Cirker, but it ran aground in political interference and appears to have run its limit. Even the efforts of critics and organizations like the Council for Professional Theater have been unable to resurrect the project in time for this summer.

The year's most significant work is listed below, in the order of quality in this writer's opinion. Such non-plays as *The Beard* are included, not for their artistic contribution but because they stirred interest. Not listed in entirety is the consistently important work of such smaller organizations as Roy Schallert's excellent New Playwrights Theater; Paul Kent's consistently fine Melrose Theater Workshop; the East-West Players, the Stage Society, State Repertory Company, Theater West, Repertory Unlimited, the superb Los Angeles Repertory Company, Adrienne Marden's Players Production Company, Theater Now and Theater 40. Nor are the successful touring companies mentioned, although one must note that APA-Phoenix first introduced its productions of *Pantagleize, Exit the King* and *The Show-Off* to Los Angeles prior to New York acclaim. It has been an impressive and important season that augurs well for the future of Los Angeles theater.

OUTSTANDING PERFORMANCES

ZERO MOSTEL
as John Morley in
The Latent Heterosexual

JOANNE LINVILLE
as Fanny Cruickshank in
The Adventures of Jack and Max

COLLEEN DEWHURST
as Sara in
More Stately Mansions

PAUL WINFIELD
as The Gentleman Caller in
The Glass Menagerie

DIANA SANDS
as Cleopatra in
Antony and Cleopatra

LUANA ANDERS
as The Girl in
Echoes

DAVID HURST
as Count Bodo Von Ubelohe-Zabernsee in
The Marriage of Mr. Mississippi

BETTY GARRETT
as Mary in
Who's Happy Now?

MIKE RUPERT
as Bibi Bonnard in
The Happy Time

JOAN TOMPKINS
as various characters in
John Brown's Body

HUME CRONYN
as Harpagon in
The Miser

FRITZ WEAVER
as Frederick the Great in
The Sorrows of Frederick

NANCY MARCHAND
as Elizabeth Christine in
The Sorrows of Frederick

LORETTA LEVERSEE
as Lula Roca in
Hey You, Light Man

RICHARD ROAT
as MacBird in
MacBird!

OUTSTANDING DIRECTORS

EDWARD PARONE
New Theater For Now series

DOUGLAS CAMPBELL
The Miser

BURGESS MEREDITH
The Latent Heterosexual

OUTSTANDING SCENE DESIGNERS

WILL STEVEN ARMSTRONG	STEPHEN HENDRICKSON	OLIVER SMITH
Catch My Soul	*Tartuffe, The Seagull*	*Dumas and Son*

OUTSTANDING NEW PLAYS

WHO'S HAPPY NOW?* by Oliver Hailey. A lad's process of growing up in a Texas town includes clashes with his father. Directed by Gordon Davidson. With Malcolm Atterbury, Warren Berlinger, Betty Garrett, Warren Oates, Peggy Pope. Mark Taper Forum.

MUZEEKA by John Guare. A comment on the inanities of modern society. Directed by Edward Parone. With Philip Proctor, Caroline McWilliams, Sheree North, Lou Frizzell, Philip Austin, Lucian Baker, John Rose, Gary Haynes. Mark Taper Forum.

THE ADVENTURES OF JACK AND MAX by Harvey Perr. A look into the wasted lives of a family of non-adventurers. Directed by Lee Grant. With Charles Aidman, V. Baker, Anthony Costello, Joseph Feury, Steven Gravers, Clint Kimbrough, Maria Lennard, Joanne Linville, Ike Williams, Ellie Wood Walker, Helene Winston. Schoenberg Hall, UCLA.

THE LATENT HETEROSEXUAL by Paddy Chayefsky. A man changes into a corporation to avoid income tax and destroys himself. Directed by Burgess Meredith. With Zero Mostel, Jules Munshin, Alvin Epstein, Gwyda Donhowe, Alan Oppenheimer, Ben Baker, Jerry Mann, Paul Winfield. Huntington Hartford Theater.

HOW TALL IS TOSCANINI? by Calder Willingham. A study of the lack of personal communication. Directed by Jack Garfein. With Michael Strong, Diane Shalet. Schoenberg Hall, UCLA.

THE SORROWS OF FREDERICK * by Romulus Linney. The bold and tragic life of Frederick the Great of Prussia. Directed by Albert Marre. With Fritz Weaver, Albert Dekker, Nancy Marchand, Milly McMickle, Frederick Tozere, Robert Fletcher, Ed Zimmermann, Paul Stevens, Thayer David, George Coulouris.

THE HAPPY TIME musical with book by N. Richard Nash, music and lyrics by John Kander and Fred Ebb, based on the play by Samuel A. Taylor and the book by Robert L. Fontaine. Directed by Gower Champion. With Robert Goulet, Jeanne Arnold, George S. Irving, Mike Rupert, Charles Durning, Kim Freund, Julane Stites, Connie Simmons, June Squibb, David Wayne. Ahmanson Theater.

DON'T GO GENTLE by William Inge. A reaffirmation of human worth and self-respect in the face of failings demonstrative of human weakness. Directed by Jack Garfein. With Jon Lormer, Steve Franken, Clint Kimbrough, Don Keefer, Gerald O'Loughlin, Martine Bartlett. Schoenberg Hall, UCLA.

MORE STATELY MANSIONS by Eugene O'Neill. A chapter in O'Neill's study of a tragic American family. Directed by José Quintero. With Ingrid Bergman, Arthur Hill, Colleen Dewhurst, Helen Craig, Barry Macollum, Vincent Dowling. Ahmanson Theater.

MISS PERKINS by Ronald Collier. Dramatization of theories about sexual abnormalities and degenerated lives. Directed by Don Conreaux. With Lorri Scott, Arland Schubert. New Playwrights Theater.

THE WEB AND THE ROCK by Philip Abbott, from the novel by Thomas Wolfe. Directed by Philip Abbott. With Dolores Sutton, Peter Jason, Walter Coy, Anthony Dillon, Peggy Doyle, Olive Dunbar. Actors Theater.

CATCH MY SOUL musical with book by Ray Pohlman based on Shakespeare, conceived and directed by Jack Good. A rock version of *Othello*. With William Marshall, Jerry Lee Lewis, Julienne Marie, Gerrianne Raphael, William Jordan, Gloria Jones. The Frank Walker Singers, The Blossoms. Ahmanson Theater.

ECHOES by Lonny Chapman. A dramatic allegory of the stages of life. Directed by Lonny Chapman. With Roscoe Lee Browne, Robert Porter, Janet MacLachlan, Luana Anders, Martin Landau, Barbara Bain, Madeleine Sherwood. Schoenberg Hall, UCLA.

DUMAS AND SON musical with book by

* These and other major 1967-68 productions of Center Theater Group at the Mark Taper Forum are listed in the Los Angeles section of the "Directory of Professional Regional Theater" in this volume.

Pearl Bailey as Mrs. Dolly Gallagher Levi in *Hello, Dolly!*

Zoe Caldwell as Jean Brodie in *The Prime of Miss Jean Brodie*

Milo O'Shea as Harry C. Leeds in *Staircase* (FAR RIGHT)

Helen Hayes as Mrs. Fisher in *The Show-Off* (FAR LEFT)

Hiram Sherman as Wingate in *How Now, Dow Jones*

Melvyn Douglas as Spofford and Pert Kelton as Mrs. Punck (FAR RIGHT) in *Spofford*

Jerry Orbach as Harold Wonder in *Scuba Duba* (FAR LEFT)

Alan Webb as Tom Garrison in *I Never Sang for My Father*

Robert Goulet as Jacques Bonnard in *The Happy Time*

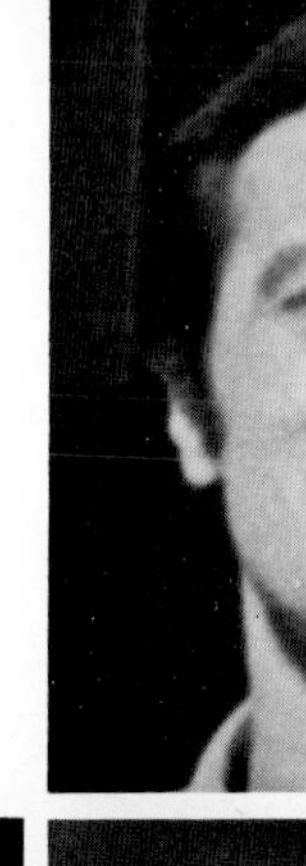

Leland Palmer as Viola in *Your Own Thing* (FAR RIGHT)

Sally Eaton as Jeannie in *Hair* (FAR LEFT)

Paul Hecht as The Player in *Rosencrantz and Guildenstern Are Dead*

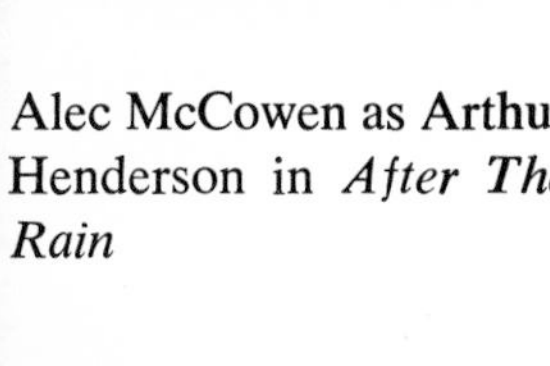

Alec McCowen as Arthur Henderson in *After The Rain*

Albert Finney as Bri in *A Day in the Death of Joe Egg* (FAR RIGHT)

George C. Scott (FAR LEFT) Roy Hubley and Maureen Stapleton as Karen Nash in *Plaza Suite*

Above, Elizabeth Hubbard and John Carson *(in background)* as friends visiting Zena Walker and Albert Finney in a scene from Peter Nichols' *A Day in the Death of Joe Egg*

THE PRICE—Above, Kate Reid with Pat Hingle and Arthur Kennedy as two brothers quarreling in Arthur Miller's play. *Below,* a Boris Aronson sketch for his design of the setting, an attic cluttered with furniture

I NEVER SANG FOR MY FATHER—Jo Mielziner's drawing for his triple-arched design in Robert Anderson's play shows *(above)* the railroad station scene. *Below,* the restaurant scene with mother (Lillian Gish), waitress (Sloan Shelton), father (Alan Webb) and son (Hal Holbrook)

Eli Wallach as Charlie and Milo O'Shea as Harry in Charles Dyer's *Staircase*.

John Wood (Guildenstern), Noel Craig (Hamlet) and Brian Murray (Rosencrantz) in a scene at Elsinore in Tom Stoppard's *Rosencrantz and Guildenstern Are Dead*

R & G DESIGNS—*Above,* three of Desmond Heeley's costume sketches for *Hamlet* characters in Stoppard's play

Below, still more liberties were taken with *Hamlet* by Joseph Papp off Broadway. Pictured in this scene are James J. Sloyan as "Guilderstone", Martin Sheen as Hamlet and Merwin Goldsmith as "Rossencraft" at the Public Theater downtown

Above, Gretchen Corbett, John Colenback, Nancy Marchand, Alec McCowen and Maureen Pryor in John Bowen's *After The Rain*

Gig Young and Barbara Ferris in *There's a Girl in My Soup,* British comedy by Terence Frisby

THE LITTLE FOXES—Left, George C. Scott as Ben, E. G. Marshall as Oscar and Anne Bancroft as Regina in the revival of Lillian Hellman's play at the Vivian Beaumont. *Below,* the same production moved to Broadway with new leading players: E. G. Marshall as Ben and Margaret Leighton as Regina

THE PRIME OF MISS JEAN BRODIE—Above, Diana Davila, Kathryn Baumann, Catherine Burns and Amy Taubin as students with their teacher Miss Brodie (Zoe Caldwell) in the picnic scene of Jay Allen's play. *Left,* Jane Greenwood's design for Miss Brodie's costume in this scene

Left, Colleen Dewhurst as wife, Ingrid Bergman as mother and Arthur Hill as husband and son in Eugene O'Neill's *More Stately Mansions*

BROADWAY IN AN ANTIC DISPOSITION—*Right,* Melvyn Douglas and Pert Kelton in a scene from *Spofford,* the comedy by Herman Shumlin. *Below,* a scene from Carl Reiner's *Something Different* with Gabriel Dell, Bob Dishy and the Messrs. Starkman and Battle (thus identified in the cast list) playing twin boys

Above, John Forsythe and Carol Cole in *Weekend,* by Gore Vidal

Above, Barry Nelson and Tammy Grimes in Frank D. Gilroy's *The Only Game in Town*

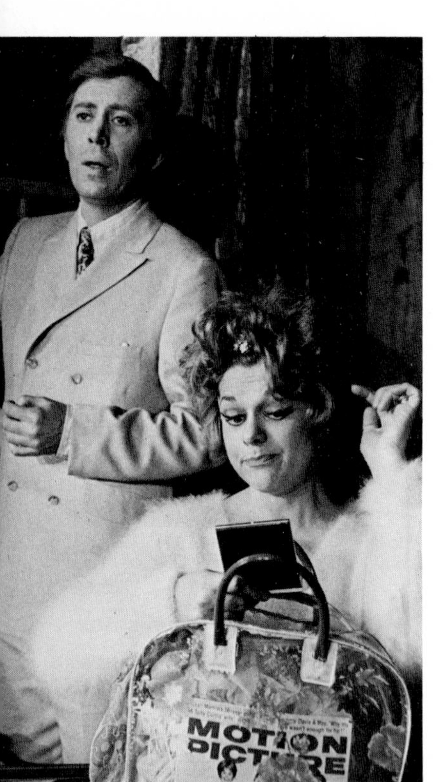

Above, Brian Bedford and Estelle Parsons in Tennessee Williams' *The Seven Descents of Myrtle*

Right, Ian McShane, Ian McKellen and Eileen Atkins in *The Promise*

Above, Anthony Quayle as a general turned hippie in Peter Ustinov's *Halfway up the Tree*

Above, George Rose and Carole Shelley in *Loot*

Above, Dorothy Tutin as Queen Victoria in William Francis's *Portrait of a Queen*

Left, Roy Dotrice as John Aubrey in *Brief Lives*

HAIR DOWNTOWN — *Left,* Walker Daniels and Gerome Ragni in the original off-Broadway production

HAIR UPTOWN—*Right,* a Nancy Potts costume sketch, and *below,* two of the numbers from the Broadway version

Above, Anthony Roberts with Francesca Smith, Sally DeMay, Lucie Lancaster, Charlotte Jones and Fran Stevens in the "Step to the Rear" number from *How Now, Dow Jones*

Below, Joel Grey as George M. Cohan in the "Give My Regards to Broadway" number from *George M!*

THE HAPPY TIME: Above, a Gower Champion dance number (The Boys' Ballet). *Left,* a Peter Wexler sketch of his scene design.

Left, Steve Lawrence and Edyie Gorme in *Golden Rainbow*

AT CITY CENTER—*Above,* the musical *The King and I,* with Constance Towers as Anna and Michael Kermoyan as the King. *Right,* Dorothy Stickney as Vinnie and Leon Ames as Father in *Life With Father*

AT LINCOLN CENTER—*Left,* Suzanne Grossmann as Roxanne, Robert Symonds as Cyrano and Dennis Cooney as Christian in *Cyrano de Bergerac* (in a new English version by James Forsyth)

IN APA-PHOENIX REPERTORY

Above, Ellis Rabb (white suit) in *Pantagleize,* with Nicholas Martin, Sydney Walker, Patricia Conolly, Keene Curtis and Nat Simmons. *Right,* Nancy Potts' design for the Generalissimo's costume, same play.

Below left, Richard Easton and Eva Le Gallienne in *Exit the King. Below right,* Helen Hayes and Clayton Corzatte in *The Show-Off*

Rudy Challenger, Jennifer Warren, Jerry Orbach and Cleavon Little in a scene from Bruce Jay Friedman's *Scuba Duba*

Above, Kenneth Nelson, Frederick Combs, Laurence Luckinbill, Leonard Frey (seated, wearing beads), Reuben Greene, Keith Prentice, Cliff Gorman and Robert La Tourneaux in Mart Crowley's *The Boys in the Band*

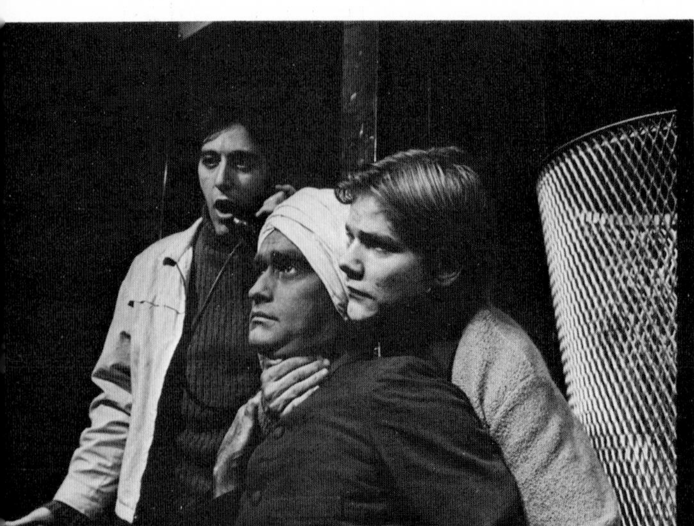

Left, Al Pacino, John Casale and Matthew Cowles in Israel Horovitz' *The Indian Wants the Bronx*

Right, Don Emmons, Joyce Nolen, Hansford Rowe and Helon Blount with Bayn Johnson *(foreground,* title role) in the musical *Curley McDimple*

Below, Leland Palmer as Viola *(foreground)* with Danny Apolinar (co-author of the score), Michael Valenti and John Kuhner as the Apocalypse singing combo in *Your Own Thing,* the New York Drama Critics Circle prize musical

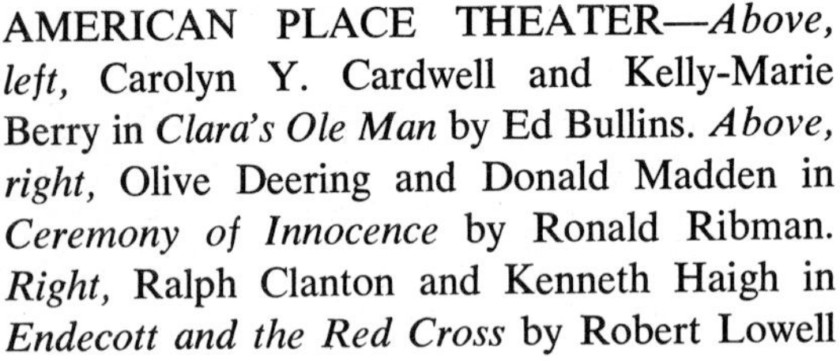

AMERICAN PLACE THEATER—*Above, left,* Carolyn Y. Cardwell and Kelly-Marie Berry in *Clara's Ole Man* by Ed Bullins. *Above, right,* Olive Deering and Donald Madden in *Ceremony of Innocence* by Ronald Ribman. *Right,* Ralph Clanton and Kenneth Haigh in *Endecott and the Red Cross* by Robert Lowell

Left, Irene Papas (in black) as Clytemnestra and Jenny Leigh *(foreground)* as Iphigenia with chorus in *Iphigenia in Aulis*

Above, Jack Hollander and Miriam Lehmann-Haupt in the Public Theater production of Jacov Lind's *Ergo*

Right, Clarice Taylor, Douglas Turner, Frances Foster, Robert Hooks and chorus member in Negro Ensemble's *Kongi's Harvest,* by Wole Soyinka

Left, Billie Dixon and Richard Bright in Michael McClure's *The Beard*

Above, the Pooh marionette in the Bil Baird version of *Winnie the Pooh*

Left, Arlene Rothlein and Al Carmines (composer) in Gertrude Stein's *In Circles*

VISITORS

JEWISH STATE THEATER OF POLAND—*Above,* Ida Kaminska and Dina Fijalowska in Polish-language production of Brecht's *Mother Courage*

VIENNA BURGTHEATER — *Below,* Ernst Deutsch (third from left) with members of the German-language acting ensemble in Schnitzler's *Professor Bernhardi*

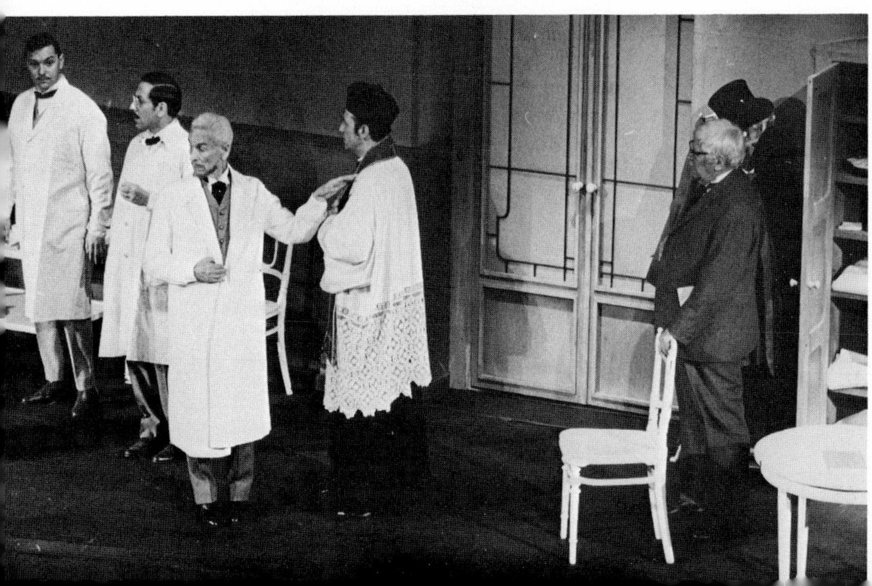

REGIONAL THEATER AROUND THE UNITED STATES

WASHINGTON, D.C.—National Repertory company in *John Brown's Body,* opening bill at newly-refurbished Ford's Theater. George Washington photo between boxes was hung in honor of Lincoln's presence the night he was killed

CLEVELAND—*Below,* A student matinee audience at the Play House applauds *The Glass Menagerie*

BUFFALO—*Above,* world premiere of Edward Albee's *Box-Mao-Box* at Studio Arena Theater, with William Needles, Conrad Yama, Lucille Patton, Jenny Egan

MINNEAPOLIS—*Below,* members of Minnesota Theater Company in *The House of Atreus,* new John Lewin adaptation of Aeschylus

CINCINNATI—*Above,* American premiere of Anouilh's *The Cavern* at Playhouse In The Park, with Irene Dailey, Lynn Milgrim

MILWAUKEE—*Below,* Charles Kimbrough and Michael Tucker (sleeping) in *Waiting for Godot* at Repertory Theater

PITTSBURGH—*Above,* Robert Milton, Arthur Rosenberg, Robert Nellis, Robert Alda and Steve Levycky in *The Odd Couple* at The Playhouse Hamlet St. Theater

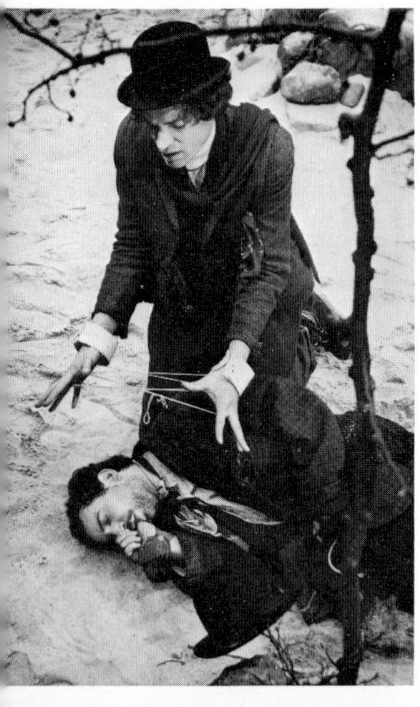

SEATTLE—*Left,* Richard Kavanaugh as Hal and Patrick Hines as Falstaff in *Henry IV, Part 1* at Repertory Theater

PROVIDENCE — *Above,* Richard Kneeland as Oscar Wilde in Trinity Square Repertory Company's world premiere of *Years of the Locust* by Norman Holland

STANFORD — *Above,* Stephen D. Newman and Elizabeth Huddle in *Candaules, Commissioner* at the Repertory Theater

BOSTON—*Right,* Theater Company of Boston's American premiere of Pinter's *The Dwarfs,* with Arthur Merrow, Jeremiah Sullivan, Richard Hughes

SAN FRANCISCO — *Right,* American Conservatory Theater's *Under Milk Wood* with Judith Mihalyi and Deann Mears

LOS ANGELES — Center Theater Group's programs at Mark Taper Forum included *(above)* Oliver Hailey's *Who's Happy Now?* (with Betty Garrett, Peggy Pope, Warren Oates, Warren Berlinger, Malcolm Atterbury); Jessica Tandy and Hume Cronyn *(top left)* in *The Miser;* Nancy Marchand and Fritz Weaver *(below left)* in world premiere of Romulus Linney's *The Sorrows of Frederick*

Jerome Chodorov, music and lyrics by Robert Wright and George Forrest, adapted from Camille Saint-Saens. A story of the great writer and his personal life. Directed by Joseph Anthony. With Inia TeWiata, Frank Porretta, Constance Towers, Edward Everett Horton, Hermione Gingold, Gregory Morton. Dorothy Chandler Pavilion.

AND MISS REARDON DRINKS A LITTLE by Paul Zindel. Serious comedy about wasted lives. Directed by Edward Parone. With Marti Stevens, Marjorie Bennett, Philip Austin, Joan Banks, Gail Kobe, Helen Page Camp. Mark Taper Forum.

THE ANTHEM SPRINTERS by Ray Bradbury. A writer visits Ireland for research and gets caught up in the strange mores of the people. Directed by Charles Rome Smith. With Monte Markham, Garry Walberg, Patrick Sullivan Burke, Fred Villani, Sean Morgan, Michael Bell. Coronet Theater.

WHAT ELSE HAVE YOU GOT IN THE CLOSET? by Laslo Vadnay and Hans Wilhelm. A comedy about an exiled premier of Russia. Directed by Christopher Cary. With Robert Emhardt, Spring Byington, Julie Adams, Christopher Cary, Alan Carney, Curt Lowens. Pasadena Playhouse.

MARTYRS CAN'T GO HOME by Soon Taik Oh. The disillusioning and ultimately tragic involvement of students and a Christian North Korean family in the early months of the Korean War. Directed by Mako. With Soon Taik Oh, Jeanne M. Joe, Pat Li, Yuki Shimoda, Ernest Harada, Alberto Isaac. East-West Players.

OUTSTANDING NEW LOCAL PRODUCTIONS

SLOW DANCE ON THE KILLING GROUND by William Hanley. Directed by Vinnette Carroll. With Diane Shalet, Michael Strong, Glynn Turman. Inner City Repertory Company.

YOU'RE A GOOD MAN CHARLIE BROWN musical based on the comic strip "Peanuts" by Charles M. Schulz, book, music and lyrics by Clark Gesner. Directed by Joseph Hardy. With Gary Burghoff, Judy Kaye, Russ Caldwell, Hal-James Pederson, Nicole Jeffe, Robert Towers. Ivar Theater.

MACBIRD! by Barbara Garson. Directed by Thomas Bissinger. With Richard Roat, Taldo Kenyon, Donna Mantoan, Robert Doqui, Jerome Guardino, William Lucking. Players Ring Gallery.

PHILADELPHIA, HERE I COME! by Brian Friel. Directed by Tom Palmer. With Michael Scanlon, Hal England, John Harding, Iris Korn, J.P. Burns, Brendan Dillon. Stage Society Theater.

LOCK UP YOUR DAUGHTERS musical adapted by Bernard Miles from Henry Fielding's *Rape Upon Rape,* with lyrics by Lionel Bart, music by Laurie Johnson. Directed by Malcolm Black. With Murray Matheson, Holly Harris, Jack Ritschell, Bill Elliott, Kim Davis, Guy Spaull. Pasadena Playhouse.

HEY YOU, LIGHT MAN by Oliver Hailey. Directed by Joel Oliansky. With A. D. Holt, Morgan Sterne, Loretta Leversee, Robert Artz, Helen Page Camp, Bonnie Osoff. Pasadena Playhouse.

COMINGS AND GOINGS; KEEP TIGHTLY CLOSED IN A COOL DRY PLACE by Megan Terry. Directed by Steven Kyle Kent. With Candace Loughlin, Dennis Redfield, Lance Larsen, Paul Rucelli. Company Theater.

THE BEARD by Michael McClure. Directed by Robert Gist. With Alexandra Hay, Richard Bright. Warner Playhouse.

OUTSTANDING REVIVALS

THE SEAGULL by Anton Chekhov. Directed by Alfred Ryder. With Ion Berger, Malachi Throne, Bonnie Bedelia, Hanna Landy, Mitzi Hoag, Arthur Malet. Inner City Repertory Company.

ANTONY AND CLEOPATRA by William Shakespeare. Directed by Michael Kahn. With Diana Sands, Robert Lansing, Dan Travanty, Theo Marcuse, Richard Lupino, Tani Phelps. MacArthur Park.

THE GLASS MENAGERIE by Tennessee Williams. Directed by Lonny Chapman. With Maxine Stuart, Bonnie Bedelia, Larry Kert, Paul Winfield. Inner City Repertory Company.

THE SIGN IN SIDNEY BRUSTEIN'S WINDOW by Lorraine Hansberry. Directed by Paul Kent. With Paul Kent, Ellen Miller, Paul Mantee, Roger Helfand, Sandi Allan, Don Eitner. Melrose Theater-Workshop.

MISALLIANCE by George Bernard Shaw. Directed by Robert Ellenstein. With Anthony Call, James Orr, Susan Howard, Enid Baine, Victor Izay, John Lawrence. Los Angeles Repertory Company.

TWO GENTLEMEN FROM VERONA by William Shakespeare. Directed by Robert Moss. With Michael Stark, Douglas Lambert, Susan Albert, Savannah Bentley, Ginny Gan, Don Parker. Venice Pavilion.

JOHN BROWN'S BODY by Stephen Vincent Benet. Directed by Karl Swenson. With Jerry Douglas, Frederick Hoffman, Arlene Martel, Joan Tompkins. Repertory Unlimited.

THE TROJAN WOMEN by Euripides. Directed by Kay Cousins Johnson. With Joan Tompkins, Mercedes Shirley, Eve McVeagh, Joanna McNeil, Melora Conway, Michael Forest. Theatre 40.

AN ALBEE ALMANAC (*The American Dream, The Sandbox* and *The Zoo Story*) by Edward Albee. Directed by Michael Pataki and Lawrence Brown. With Dave Sheehan, Noel Swann, JoAnne Meredith, Edith DeSantis, George Andre, Marcia Scott. Theater Now.

THE CARETAKER by Harold Pinter. Directed by Sherman Marks. With Ray Stricklyn, Tom Troupe, Richard Bull. Los Angeles Theater Company.

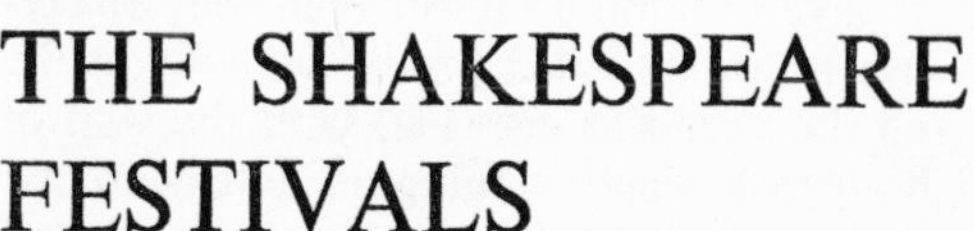

THE SHAKESPEARE FESTIVALS

and Other Summer Repertory

○
○
○

INTRODUCTION

By David Jones

Associate director of the Royal Shakespeare Company,
Stratford-on-Avon, England

IT ALWAYS comes as something of a shock to find out just how high and almost legendary the reputation of the Royal Shakespeare Company is throughout the world. I suppose the working conditions and standards you live with daily become very easily taken for granted. Faced with the admiring envy of the outside world, we tend to list vehemently the frustrations and deficiencies that still exist for us, as for any section of the theatrical world, and to slur over the immense advantages that the Company's organization brings to every area of our work. It's not surprising that we often seem ungrateful and downright spoilt to less privileged and subsidized repertory theaters still at the beginning of the struggle towards a really creative and confident ensemble.

I don't think, though, it's a question of being jaded. Quite simply, we are at the point where success could become dangerous. The basic principles the RSC stands for were not established overnight—they've been gradually tested, explored, and fought for over the past eight years, fought for artistically and fought for financially. That fight guaranteed the Company a continuing vitality and freshness, as it advanced. Now that it's won, we cannot stand still, or rest on that achievement. What looks like dissatisfaction with an ideal state of affairs, is, in fact, a vigilance from all of us against the dangers of complacency, of repetition, of the hardening of creative ideas into deadening rules. A theater like ours must have a style, but a style that is a freedom, not a prison. The history of the Moscow Art Theater and the Comédie Française is warning enough. The original inspiration and drive can so easily settle into a tradition, and in no time at all the museum doors are clanging shut on an Institution. That we intend to avoid.

That warning apart, 1967 could hardly have been a more successful year.

Stratford presented its largest-ever Shakespeare season, running from early April right through into December; the Aldwych (our theater in London) had its best box office season ever and gave London no fewer than four Shakespeare productions. Audience response to an extended provincial tour in the autumn was the strongest to date, and the year was crowned with the visit of *Macbeth* and *All's Well that Ends Well* to Finland, Leningrad and Moscow; and the playing of a six-week date in Los Angeles by *As You Like It* and *The Taming of the Shrew,* these last two productions breaking all records for the Music Center's Ahmanson Theater. In addition, the RSC finished its first Shakespeare film, *A Midsummer Night's Dream,* shot on location at Compton Verney in Warwickshire and due for release later in 1968; and our traveling theater group, Theatergoround, continued to reach a vast new audience in schools and community centers throughout the country.

The beliefs behind our approach to presenting Shakespeare remain constant. Our strength still lies in drawing on the ensemble virtues of a permanent company, and not in building productions around a handful of "guest star" performances. In last year's productions Paul Scofield (Macbeth) and Dorothy Tutin (Rosalind) were the only publicly acknowledged star names in evidence, and both have been closely connected with the company since its inception; for the rest, Ian Richardson (Coriolanus), Janet Suzman (Katherina), Michael Williams (Petruchio and Orlando) and Ian Holm (Romeo) have all progressed to the playing of leading roles through their work within the Company over the years. The move towards an even simpler, less cluttered flexibility of design continued—the ideal, to achieve a visual unity which expresses the central spirit and theme of a play, and allows a maximum fluidity of action. John Bury's pioneer work in this field was strongly reinforced during 1967 by the Company's new associate designers, Christopher Morley *(Shrew* and *The Revenger's Tragedy)* and Timothy O'Brien *(As You Like It, All's Well* and *Romeo and Juliet).*

Our emphasis in rehearsal still lies on Sense (communicating the full content and meaning both of the play and each individual speech within it) rather than on Sound (a surface preoccupation with rhetorical effectiveness, and the "beautiful" speaking of the poetry). But I suspect this is one area where vigilance is particularly necessary, and a development of approach overdue. The intelligence of RSC productions has never been in doubt and shouldn't in any way be sacrificed. But some of last year's productions were too cool, clinical and drily reasonable for their own health, with an original purity of intention hardening into a Puritanism that was both arid and pedantic. I think the next two seasons will see a less ashamed use of the human and the theatrical, and that the poetic values of the plays will be allowed to take flight far more than they have done in the past—the groundwork of understanding is, after all, by now secure.

This shift of emphasis is likely to be necessary in any case, as we move into new areas of the Shakespeare canon. The new intelligence was brought to bear initially on the wit and brightness of the comedies in previous seasons, first in Peter Hall's romantic but youthfully vital productions of *Twelfth*

Night and *A Midsummer Night's Dream,* and then in Clifford Williams's astringent *The Comedy of Errors.* It then transformed the sprawling world of the early histories into a quite remarkably incisive and adult study of the splendors and miseries of political man, in the Wars of the Roses trilogy. The Company's work in these, and then in Shakespeare's maturer histories, remain its greatest triumph, culminating in John Barton's remarkable production of *Henry V,* which uncovered for the first time the full ambiguities of that play in its attitudes to the twin themes of patriotism and war. Secure in the areas of the comedies and the histories, the Company's successes in other directions have been more sporadic and individual. Peter Brook's *King Lear* and Peter Hall's *Hamlet* both achieved an admirable freshness and modernity of interpretation; but both deliberately eschewed the more poetic values of these plays. Certainly no consistent approach to tackling the greater heights of the tragedies has been found—each production tends to be a start from scratch again.

To revert again to the 1967 season, *Macbeth* has to be accounted less than a success, and *Coriolanus,* though respected, did not represent the breakthrough into the world of the Roman plays that was hoped for. More predictably, *As You Like It* and *Shrew* maintained the Company's reputation for clear, forceful, ungimmicky presentation of the comedies; but perhaps the season's most interesting success was Barton's *All's Well* which handled the play's dialogue between grave autumnal wisdom and the follies of youth with such transparent and delighted simplicity that many people felt the play had been moved out of the vaults of the problem comedies for good. Guest director Karolos Koun's *Romeo and Juliet* had a spontaneity and high emotional content that achieved one or two really remarkable performances, though the spine of the production was a little insecure. The other outright winner of the season, along with *All's Well,* was Trevor Nunn's revival of *The Revenger's Tragedy*—a mordant, stylish, scintillatingly vicious presentation of this dark Jacobean piece which continued the policy of reclaiming lesser-known Elizabethan plays, which began with *The Jew of Malta* and will continue next season with *Dr. Faustus.* What is clear is that a great deal of Shakespeare still remains to be colonized. The tragedies, the Roman plays, and, perhaps most interesting of all, the magnificent work of his last period, are what will challenge our abilities for the next few years; and that challenge is bound to move us towards new methods and new approaches as we meet it.

The other cornerstone of our thinking has always been the necessary relationship between Shakespeare and the modern repertory: the belief that actors and directors in their work, and audiences in their response to that work, should experience the modern and the Shakespearean in as close a juxtaposition as possible and allow each to enrich the other. In that way, we hope our interpretation of Shakespeare is immediate and of the present moment, speaking directly to the minds and emotions of a 1960s audience; and our new authors are presented with a classic precision and astringency that is informed by a proper use of tradition. Peter Hall's productions of *Hamlet* and Harold Pinter's *The Homecoming* exemplify these principles in action.

With Shakespeare so much in evidence at the London end in 1967, it looked a good year for really developing this interplay. Unfortunately, the new scripts were just not forthcoming: it's a sad fact that the last British premiere staged by the RSC was my own production of David Mercer's *Belcher's Luck,* back in November 1966. Last year, the best we could muster was Jules Feiffer's *Little Murders,* already seen in New York, and *The Criminals* by Cuban author Jose Triana. Feiffer's play was much more successful here than in New York, but, in my opinion, was softened in its passage across the Atlantic into a rather conventional, near-English comedy about a kooky family, rather than projected as the savage exploration of metropolitan violence that it deserved to be. *The Criminals* was forcefully directed, with a trio of bravura performances, but this did not disguise the rather faded and aggressively portentous nature of the play's attempt to be avant-garde—it was not well supported. What audiences responded to was a respectable revival of *Ghosts* with Peggy Ashcroft as Mrs. Alving, plus an extremely fresh and lively version of *The Relapse* directed by Trevor Nunn, and the Shakespeare productions; new writing was not at the center of our Aldwych work in the way that we want it to be. As we look towards the 1968 Aldwych season, the dearth of new British writing continues. It's significant that the two new plays scheduled for production to date are both American—Arthur Kopit's *Indians,* to be directed by Jack Gelber, and Paddy Chayefsky's *The Latent Heterosexual.* It looks as if we may be taking a lead from America for a while now, just as we did in the heyday of Tennessee Williams and Arthur Miller.

There are, in fact, plenty of problems to busy and occupy our minds and talents as we move on into the next few seasons. Money, as always, is one—the Arts Council subsidy still resolutely treats us as a poor relation of the National Theater, though the number of theaters we maintain, the number of productions we mount, the audiences we play to overall are far larger, and we have an equal international reputation to maintain on far slenderer resources. Another is expansion—we have moved into the field of Shakespearean film production, partly because we believe in it artistically, partly to secure a necessary increase in our income. That means more actors. So do the provincial and foreign tours that audiences increasingly demand and deserve. The expansion is still manageable—just. But we must guard against the time when the limit is passed and a tight, unified company could suddenly become a sprawling, rather incoherent empire.

There are artistic challenges, too—new areas of Shakespeare to be tackled, whole departments of other English classical drama as yet untouched. After all, *The Relapse* was the first Restoration play we'd attempted in eight years. And somehow, we have to get the stream of new English writing flowing again, even if it's by the authoritarian methods of television story editors! The problem here is that the English theater seems to be going into one of its periodic phases of reaction against the literate play and the individual author. Two years ago, documentary theater was all the rage. Now the talk is all of projects—treatments of burning topical issues, where the director lays down an outline which is then realized in rehearsal by the improvization of the actors, and the script is gradually accumulated by a team of dialogue writers. This, of course, was the method used by Peter Brook for *US,* and it certainly has its validity and an immense importance. It is threatening to become all-exclusive, however, and there's far too ready a tendency to throw all "old-fashioned" imaginative authors and their self-created plays on the bonfire in the process. Personally, I think that creative playwrights of stature must be at the center of any healthy theater, and it's only a director of quite exceptional brilliance and breadth of mind that can usurp their function. Playwrights, of course, cannot be made; but a good deal more can be done to find and encourage them than perhaps we are doing at present.

In conclusion, perhaps the most important event of the year: at the end of May 1968, Peter Hall, who created the RSC as we now know it, relinquished the post of managing director, though he will remain closely connected with the RSC as a member of the direction and with particular responsibility for the Company's film activities and for the realization of the plans for our new Barbican Theater in the City of London. The newly-created top post of artistic director of the RSC goes to 28-year-old Trevor Nunn, an associate director of the Company since 1965. Peter Hall's achievement, his vision of what the RSC should be, and his steady translation of that vision into action over the past nine years needs no tribute from me. Trevor Nunn is probably the most exciting and fertile directorial talent to emerge in English theater during the 1960s. He commands tremendous loyalty and respect from the Company and is passionately committed to extending the RSC's reputation for a fresh and questioning approach in all areas of its work. It's an indication of the unity and commitment to a common ideal that has been built up in the Company over the years that the leadership can change hands at this stage, in the secure knowledge that such a change will bring none of the reverberations and halts in progress that previous theater history might lead one to expect.

No, perhaps there's not much danger of the RSC growing moribund after all! There's plenty to be done, and no danger of becoming a museum, if we remember Richard Wilbur's anecdote:

"Edgar Degas purchased once
A fine El Greco, which he kept
Against the wall beside his bed
To hang his pants on while he slept."

Tradition and its masterpieces are not there to be worshipped; they are there to be made use of, to be given an immediate and useful contact with our living, now. You may say that's arrogant and the prerogative of genius only. But if we can keep something of that laughing and responsible irreverence going, our work should stay alive for a while yet.

The Royal Shakespeare Theater. The Royal Shakespeare Company in a repertory of six plays by William Shakespeare, one by Cyril Tourneur and one by Henrik Ibsen. **The Taming of the Shrew** (39). Opened April 5, 1967; directed by Trevor Nunn; design, Christopher Morley; music, Guy Woolfenden; lighting, John Bradley. **Coriolanus** (57). Opened April 12, 1967; directed by John Barton; design, John

Bury, Ann Curtis (costumes), Elizabeth Duffield; music, Guy Woolfenden; lighting, John Bradley. **All's Well that Ends Well** (52). Opened June 1, 1967; directed by John Barton; design, Timothy O'Brien; music, Derek Oldfield; lighting, John Bradley. **As You Like It** (26). Opened June 15, 1967; directed by David Jones; design, Timothy O'Brien; choreography, Sheila Falconer; music, William Mathias; lighting, John Bradley. **Macbeth** (52). Opened August 16, 1967; directed by Peter Hall; design, John Bury (costumes in collaboration with Ann Curtis); music, Guy Woolfenden and Unit Delta Plus Electronic Music; lighting, John Bradley. **Romeo and Juliet** (32). Opened September 13, 1967; directed by Karolos Koun; design, Timothy O'Brien; music, Guy Woolfenden; lighting, David Read; dances, Pauline Grant. **The Revenger's Tragedy** (9). By Cyril Tourneur. Opened May 4, 1967; directed by Trevor Nunn; design, Christopher Morley; music, Guy Woolfenden; choreography, Pauline Grant; lighting, John Bradley. **Ghosts** (3). By Henrik Ibsen; adapted by Denis Cannan from William Archer's translation. Opened December 1, 1967; directed by Alan Bridges; design, Jocelyn Herbert; lighting, David Read. Produced by The Royal Shakespeare Theater in association with the Arts Council of Great Britain at The Royal Shakespeare Theater, Stratford-on-Avon, England. (Repertory closed December 9, 1967)

PERFORMER	"CORIOLANUS"	"ALL'S WELL THAT ENDS WELL"	"MACBETH"	"ROMEO AND JULIET"
Sheila Allen			Lady Macduff	Lady Capulet
John Bell	Nicanor		Lennox	Paris
Mike Billington				Abram
Edward Cicciarelli	Tullus Aufidius	Duke of Florence	Young Siward	
Jeffery Dench	1st Roman Senator		Old Man; Scottish Doctor	Escalus
Peter Gordon			2d Murderer	Gregory
Terence Greenidge				Old Capulet
Phillip Hinton	1st Roman Citizen	Younger Dumain	3d Murderer	Sampson
Ian Hogg	Adrian	Lavache	Seyton	Tybalt
Ian Holm				Romeo
Clare Kelly	Valeria		Witch	Lady Montague
Natalie Kent		Mariana		
Estelle Kohler	Virgilia	Helena		Juliet
Catherine Lacey	Volumnia	Countess Rousillon	Witch	
Robin Langford	Young Marcius		Fleance	
Colin McCormack		1st Suitor	Donalbain	
Brewster Mason	Menenius	Lafeu	Banquo	
Vivien Merchant			Lady Macbeth	
Helen Mirren		Diana		
Richard Moore	2d Servant		1st Murderer	Peter
Daniel Moynihan	1st Aedile	Elder Dumain	Lord; Sergeant	
Patrick O'Connell	Cominius	Morgan	Macduff	
Ian Richardson	Coriolanus	Bertram	Malcolm	
Peter Rocca	Messenger		English Doctor	Friar John
Norman Rodway				Mercutio
Hector Ross	1st Volscian General	Rinaldo	Siward	Montague
Paul Scofield			Macbeth	
Nicholas Selby	Junius Brutus		Ross	Capulet
Sebastian Shaw		King of France	Duncan	Friar Lawrence
Elizabeth Spriggs		Widow	Witch	Nurse
Clive Swift	Sicinius Velutus	Parolles	Porter	
David Weston	Titus Lartius		Menteith	Benvolio

PERFORMER	"THE TAMING OF THE SHREW"	"AS YOU LIKE IT"	"THE REVENGER'S TRAGEDY"	"GHOSTS"
Peggy Ashcroft				Mrs. Alving
Martin Best		Amiens		
Brenda Bruce			The Duchess	
George Cormack	Pedant; Peter	Adam		
Frances de la Tour	Widow; Nicholas	Audrey		
Jeffery Dench			Antonio	
Robert East	Huntsman	Jaques de Boys	Junior; 1st Officer	
Michael Goldie	Tapster	Charles		
Terrence Hardiman	Gremio	Corin	Ambitioso	
Alan Howard		Jaques	Lussurioso	
Michael Jayston				Oswald
John Kane	Biondello; Curtis	Silvius	Supervacuo	
John Kaye		Hymen		
Lila Kaye	Hostess			
Clare Kelly			Gratiana	
Roy Kinnear	Baptista	Touchstone		
Robert Lloyd	Lucentio; Philip	1st Lord		
Seymour Matthews	Bartholomew	Dennis		
Helen Mirren			Castiza	
Natasha Pyne				Regina
Ian Richardson			Vendice	
Norman Rodway			Spurio	
Clifford Rose				Engstrand
Nicholas Selby			The Duke	
Morgan Sheppard	Christopher Sly	Duke Frederick		
Richard Simpson	Vincentio; Tailor	Sir Oliver	Piero; Judge	
Patrick Stewart	Grumio	Duke Senior	Hippolito	
Janet Suzman	Katherina; Officer	Celia		
Charles Thomas	Tranio; Nathaniel	Oliver		
Dorothy Tutin		Rosalind		
David Waller				Pastor Manders
June Watts	Bianca; Joseph	Phebe		
Michael Williams	Petrucio; Officer	Orlando		
Tim Wylton	Hortensio	Le Beau; William		

Others in the 1967 Stratford company: Dallas Adams, David Ashford, Gordon Bennett, Christopher Bond, Philip Box, Geoffrey Browne, Donald Burton, Ray Callaghan, Heather Canning, Ann Constant, Robert Davis, William Eedle, David Evans, Rufus Frampton, Amaryllis Garnett, Tom Georgeson, Don Henderson, Patricia Hope, Sarah Hyde, Oscar James, Richard Kahn, Trevor Kent, David Kincaid, Ben Kingsley, Alton Kumalo, Edward Lyon, James MacGillivray, Gerald McNally, Louis Mahoney, Chris Malcolm, Ursula Mohan, Lynn Moore, David Munrow, Bruce Myers, Stephen Nagy, Peter Nobbs, Derek Oldfield, Matthew O'Sullivan, Roger Lloyd Pack, Gregg Palmer, Robert Pritchard, Roger Rees, Gregory Reid, Gareth Richards, Matthew Roberton, Rainer Schuelein, Katherine Stark, Derek Steen, Michael Tubbs, Ted Valentine, James Vallon, Anna Volska, Edward Watson, Robin Weatherall, Richard Williams, Mark York.

New York Shakespeare Festival. Season of three plays by William Shakespeare. **The Comedy of Errors** (22). Opened June 7, 1967 (Closed July 1, 1967); directed by Gerald Freedman; scenery, Ming Cho Lee; music, John Morris. **King John** (19; 20th rained out in mid-performance). Opened July 5, 1967 (Closed July 29, 1967); directed by Joseph Papp; scenery, Douglas Schmidt; music, David Amram; fights,

James J. Sloyan. **Titus Andronicus** (17). Opened August 2, 1967 (Closed August 26, 1967); directed by Gerald Freedman; scenery, Ming Cho Lee; music and sound score, John Morris; choreographic movement, Joyce Trisler. All plays: lighting, Martin Aronstein; costumes, Theoni V. Aldredge; press, Merle Debuskey. Produced by Joseph Papp in cooperation with the City of New York at the Delacorte Theater, Central Park, New York City.

NOTE: Listing of New York Shakespeare Festival Public Theater's winter season of plays at the Florence Sutro Anspacher Theater appears in the "Plays Produced Off Broadway" section of this volume.

THE COMEDY OF ERRORS

Egeon ....Ralph Drischell
Solinus ....Jonathan Reynolds
Gaoler ....James A. Preston
1st Merchant; Dr. Pinch....Joseph R. Sicari
Antipholus of Syracuse........David Birney
Antipholus of Ephesus..........Joseph Bova
Dromio of Syracuse ....John Call
Dromio of Ephesus ....Charles Durning
Adriana ....Julienne Marie
Luciana ....Elizabeth Eis
Angelo ....Robert Roman
Balthazar ....Jack Hollander
Luce (Nell) ....Zoe Kamitses
2d Merchant ....Albert Quinton
Officer ....Charles Seals
Courtesan ....Shellie Feldman
Emilia ....Eve Collyer
Clockworks ....Steven Shaw, Donald K. Warfield

Others: Mik Cribben, Lydia Fisher, Robert Gold, Phillip Johnson, George McGrath, William Shephard, Gene Whittington.

KING JOHN

King John ....Harris Yulin
Chatillon ....Ralph Drischell
Queen Elinor ....Cavada Humphrey
Lord Bigot ....Stephen Van Benschoten
Philip the Bastard ....Robert Burr
Robert Faulconbridge;
Messenger ....David Clennon
Lady Faulconbridge ....Winifred Mann
James Gurney ....Charles Durning
Philip ....David O'Brien
Arthur, Duke of Britain ......Mark Jenkins
Duke of Austria ....Gregory Sierra
Constance ....Marian Winters
Citizen of Angiers; Melun ....Albert Quinton
French Herald;
Peter of Pomfret ....James A. Preston
English Herald;
Messenger ....Donald K. Warfield
Blanch of Spain ....Elizabeth Eis
Lewis ....David Birney
Earl of Salisbury ....Michael McGuire
Cardinal Pandulph ....Staats Cotsworth
Hubert De Burgh .....Clarence Williams III
Earl of Pembroke ....Stan Dworkin
Executioner ....James Daniel
Messenger to Lewis ......Stephen Coleman
Prince Henry ....Matthew C. Cowles

Others: William Beckwith, Lydia Fisher, Phillip Johnson, Zoe Kamitses, George McGrath, Anthony Lang, Maro Riofrancos, Harold Schwartz, Charles Seal, William Shephard, Gene Whittington, Paul Zimet.

TITUS ANDRONICUS

The Narrator ....Charles Durning
Saturninus ....Robert Stattel
Bassianus ....John LaGioia
Marcus Andronicus ....Clayton Corbin
Titus Andronicus ....Jack Hollander
Lucius ....Jonathan Reynolds
Tamora ....Olympia Dukakis
Chiron ....David Birney
Demetrius ....Raúl Juliá
Alarbus ....George McGrath
Lavinia ....Erin Martin
Mutius ....William Shephard
Quintus ....Donald K. Warfield
Martius ....David Clennon
Aaron ....Moses Gunn
Young Lucius ....Alan Howard
Nurse ....Zoe Kamitses

Others: William Beckwith, Steven Coleman, James Daniel, Lydia Fisher, Taro Ichinose, Phillip Johnson, Ralph Nelson, Harold Schwartz, Charles Seal, Carlos Sille, Terje Thoresen, Steven Van Benschoten.

New York Shakespeare Festival Mobile Theater. Mobile production of a play by Ben Jonson. **Volpone** (45). Opened June 22, 1967 (Closed August 19, 1967); directed by George L. Sherman; scenery, David Mitchell; costumes, Jose Varona;

lighting, Lawrence Metzler; music, David Amram; press, Merle Debuskey. Produced by Joseph Papp on tours of the five boroughs of New York City.

Volpone ....Alexander Panas
Mosca ....Roscoe Lee Browne
Nano ....Roger Hendricks Simon
Castrone ....John McCurry
Androgyno ....C. Leonard Williams
Voltore ....Paul Hecht
Corbaccio ....Fred Warriner
Corvino ....Alfred Leberfeld
Celia ....Marlene Warfield
Bonario ....Saul Fredericks
Lady Wouldbe ....Susan Peters
Drunk ....Robert Einenkel
Beggar ....Catherine Ryan
Streetwalker ....Laura Bendersky
Ultra Fop; Court Clerk .....Darryl Croxton
Fop Boy; Gentleman ....Lawrence Cook
Servant; 2d Judge ....Peter Jacob
Pickpocket; Officer ....Joseph Mydell
Old Man; 3d Judge ....Joseph Cazalet
Gentlemen ....Lisle Wilson, William Gearhart
Ladies ......Mallory Hoover, Sally Lansing
Chief Advocate ....Herb Davis
Commandatore ....Joseph Capone
Officer; Gentleman ....Samual Blue, Jr.

The American Shakespeare Festival. Repertory of three plays by William Shakespeare and one by Jean Anouilh. **A Midsummer Night's Dream** (30). Opened June 17, 1967; directed by Cyril Ritchard; scenery, William and Jean Eckart; costumes, Robert Fletcher; lighting, Tharon Musser; music and songs, Conrad Susa; choreography, Robert Tucker. **The Merchant of Venice** (31). Opened June 20, 1967; directed by Michael Kahn; scenery, Ed Wittstein; costumes, Jose Varona; lighting, Tharon Musser; music, Richard Peaslee; choreography, Robert Tucker. **Macbeth** (23). Opened July 30, 1967; directed by John Houseman; scenery and costumes, Rouben Ter-Arutunian; lighting, Jennifer Tipton; music, John Duffy; fight choreography, Rod Colbin. **Antigone** (26). By Jean Anouilh; translated by Lewis Galantière. Opened June 18, 1967; directed by Jerome Kilty; scenery, Donald Oenslager; costumes, Gordon Micunis; lighting, Tharon Musser; music, John Duffy. All plays: musical director, John Duffy; press, Shirley Herz. Produced by The American Shakespeare Festival Theater and Academy at the Festival Theater, Stratford, Conn. (Repertory closed September 10, 1967).

NOTE: A season of special preview performances for school children opened February 27, 1967, and the performance schedule was *Julius Caesar* 59, *A Midsummer Night's Dream* 25 and *The Merchant of Venice* 9. *Macbeth* received 55 additional post-season student performances September 22, November 11, 1967.

PERFORMER	"A MIDSUMMER NIGHT'S DREAM"	"ANTIGONE"	"THE MERCHANT OF VENICE"	"MACBETH"
Tom Aldredge	Quince	Chorus	Gratiano	Macduff
Barbara Baxley			Portia	
Morris Carnovsky		Creon	Shylock	
Richard Castellano		1st Guard		1st Murderer
John Colicos				Macbeth
John Cunningham	Demetrius		Bassanio	Malcolm
Diana Davila	Hermia			
John Devlin		Messenger	Antonio	Banquo
Jerry Dodge	Puck		Lancelot Gobbo	Porter
Carl Don	Snug; Lion			
Myles Eason	Theseus			
Jane Farnol	Titania	Euridice		
Robert Frink	Wall; Starveling		Balthasar	
Ted Graeber	Lysander		Salarino	Lennox
Ernest Graves				Duncan
Marian Hailey		Ismene	Nerissa	
Fred Jackson			Palatine	Witch

PERFORMER	"A MIDSUMMER NIGHT'S DREAM"	"ANTIGONE"	"THE MERCHANT OF VENICE"	"MACBETH"
Tom Lacy	Snout; Moon		Old Gobbo	
Marilyn McKenna	Hippolyta			
Anthony Mainionis		Haemon	M. LeBon; Guard	Seton
Richard Mathews			Salerio; Duke	Ross
Laura Michaels	Cobweb			
Carrie Nye				Lady Macbeth
Elliot Paul	Guard	Secret Service	Leonardo	
Mylo Quam	Flute; Thisby		Salanio	2d Murderer
Doris Rich		Nurse		
Cyril Ritchard	Bottom; Oberon; Pyramus			
Jack Ryland			Lorenzo	Captain; Angus
Michael Scotlin	Moth			
Rusty Thacker	Mustardseed		Stephano	
Dorothy Tristan	Helena			Lady Macduff
Maria Tucci		Antigone	Jessica	
Ian Tucker	Peaseblossom		Lucentio	Fleance
James Valentine	Philostrate; Egeus		Arragon	

Singers in *Antigone:* Bill MacAdam, Peff Modelski, Michael Scotlin, Ian Tucker. Others in all plays: Tony Bassett, Frank Caltabiano, Linda Caputi, Alan Causey, Ian Crosby, Ronald DiMartile, Robert Fitzsimmons, William Herter, Norman Kingoff, Robert Kya-Hill, Jan La Prada, Michael Liquigli, Luiz Lopez-Cepero, Garry Mitchell, Peff Modelski, William Myers, Peter Norden, Richard Novello, Billy Partello, William Pritz, Charles Stallman, Ian Tucker, Charles Turner, Janyce Wagner, Ricky West, Denise Winston, Bramwell Teuscher, Edward Rudney.

The Stratford Shakespearean Festival Foundation of Canada. Repertory of three plays by William Shakespeare, one by Nikolai Gogol and one by James Reaney. **Richard III** (45). Opened June 12, 1967; directed by John Hirsch; design, Desmond Heeley; music, Stanley Silverman. **The Merry Wives of Windsor** (42). Opened June 14, 1967; directed by David William; design, Brian Jackson; music, Louis Applebaum. **Antony and Cleopatra** (36). Opened July 31, 1967; directed by Michael Langham; design, Tanya Moiseiwitsch; music, Louis Applebaum. **The Government Inspector** (20). By Nikolai Gogol; adapted by Peter Raby. Opened June 13, 1967; directed by Michael Langham; design, Leslie Hurry; music, Raymond Pannell. **Colours in the Dark** (12). By James Reaney. Opened July 25, 1967; directed by John Hirsch; scenery, Eoin Sprott; costumes, Don Lewis; music, Alan Laing. Produced by The Stratford Shakespearean Festival; Shakespeare and Gogol plays at the Festival Theater, Reaney play at the Avon Theater, Stratford, Ontario, Canada. (Repertory closed October 14 1967).

PERFORMER	"RICHARD III"	"THE MERRY WIVES OF WINDSOR"	"ANTONY AND CLEOPATRA"	"THE GOVERNMENT INSPECTOR"
Alan Bates	Richard	Frank Ford		
Bernard Behrens	Tyrell	Evans	Lepidus	Osip
Mervyn Blake	Derby	Host		Zemlyanika
James Blendick	Ratcliff		Mardian	Merchant
David Bolt			Seleucus	
Barbara Bryne	Duchess of York			Locksmith's Wife; Korobkin's Wife
Zoe Caldwell	Lady Ann	Mrs. Page	Cleopatra	
Leatham Carroll	Prince Edward	William Page		
Jane Casson				Avdotya

PERFORMER	"RICHARD III"	"THE MERRY WIVES OF WINDSOR"	"ANTONY AND CLEOPATRA"	"THE GOVERNMENT INSPECTOR"
Eric Christmas	Lord Mayor; 1st Murderer	Shallow	Soothsayer; Peasant	
Leo Ciceri	Buckingham		Agrippa	Lyapkin-Tyapkin
Eric Donkin	Ely; Urswick		Gallus	Bobchinsky
Ann Firbank	Elizabeth		Octavia	Lukich's Wife; Corporal's Widow
Colin Fox	Dorset	Slender		Shpekin
John Gardiner	Archbishop of York; Berkeley; Messenger		Proculeius	Ilich
Jean Gascon		Dr. Caius		
Dawn Greenhalgh			Charmian	
Amelia Hall				Anna
Max Helpmann	Brakenbury; Blunt	Pistol	Menas	
Dominic Hogan	Canterbury; Herbert	Robert		
William Hutt	Clarence		Enobarbus	Khlestakov
Frances Hyland	Margaret	Mrs. Ford		
Peter Jobin	Priest		Varrius	
Joel Kenyon	Lovel		Maecenas	Rastakovsky; Ivanovich
Al Kozlik		Nym	Decretas	Mishka
Marilyn Lightstone			Iras	Lyapkin-Tyapkin's Wife
John Livingston	Duke of York	Robin		
Barry MacGregor	Richmond		Dolabella	Dobchinsky
Roberta Maxwell		Anne Page		Marya
Richard Monette	Messenger	Simple	Eros	
Christopher Newton	Catesby		Pompeius	Khlopov
Blaine Parker	Vaughan; Sheriff			
Briain Petchey	Edward IV		Alexas	
Christopher Plummer			Antony	
Kenneth Pogue	Rivers	George Page	Ventidius	
Leon Pownall	Grey	Bardolph	Scarus	Abdulin
August Schellenberg	Surrey; Keeper	John	Ambassador	
Joseph Shaw		Rugby		Korobkin
Tony van Bridge		Falstaff		Antonovich
Kenneth Welsh	Hastings	Fenton	Octavius	
Jonathan White	Norfolk; Messenger		Thidias	Derzhimorda
Anna Wing		Mistress Quickly		

COLOURS IN THE DARK

Grandfather and others ...... Sandy Webster
Grandmother and others ..... Barbara Bryne
Father and others .... Douglas Rain
Mother and others .... Martha Henry
Son and others .... Heath Lamberts
Daughter and others .... Mary Hitch

Others in all plays: Garnet Brooks, Jane Brooks, David Carroll, Laurie Carroll, Lea Carroll, Peter Cheyne, Patrick Crean, Jack Cunningham, Neil Dainard, Richard Davidson, Jocelyn Drainie, Ronald East, Kathleen Flaherty, Michael Fletcher, David Foster, Roger Gaskell, Lewis Gordon, Muriel Greenspon, Elliot Hayes, Martha Henry, Tim Henry, Terry Judd, Jimmy McGorman, Jack Messinger, Gregory Misener, William Mockridge, Judy Murray, Edward Neigh, Dermot Nolan, Paul Robertson, Bruce Rowe, Elsie Sawchuck, Cedric Smith, Patricia Steenberg, John Turner, Jim Wendland, Peter Young, Jean Yundt.

Great Lakes Shakespeare Festival. Repertory of three plays by William Shakespeare, one by Edmond Rostand and one by George Bernard Shaw. **Romeo and Juliet** (18). Opened July 7, 1967; directed by Lawrence Carra; scenery, Milton Howarth; costumes, Joseph F. Bella; lighting, William Nelson. **Love's Labour's Lost** (14). Opened July 12, 1967; directed by Philip Minor; scenery, Milton Howarth; costumes, Joseph F. Bella; lighting, William Nelson; music, Richard Cumming. **All's Well that Ends Well** (9). Opened August 23, 1967; directed by Lawrence Carra; scenery, Milton Howarth; costumes, Bernadette O'Brien; lighting, David Jager. **Cyrano de Bergerac** (20). By Edmond Rostand; translated by Brian Hooker. Opened July 26, 1967; directed by Lawrence Carra; scenery, Milton Howarth; costumes, Bernadette O'Brien; lighting, David Jager. **Misalliance** (10). By George Bernard Shaw. Opened August 9, 1967; directed by Lawrence Carra; scenery, Milton Howarth; costumes, Bernadette O'Brien; lighting, David Jager. Produced by Great Lakes Shakespeare Festival at the Lakewood, Ohio, Civic Auditorium. (Repertory closed September 16, 1967)

NOTE: The repertory was presented in two post-season weeks of student performances, September 17 to 30, 1967.

PERFORMER	"LOVE'S LABOUR'S LOST"	"ALL'S WELL THAT ENDS WELL"	"ROMEO AND JULIET"	"CYRANO DE BERGERAC"
Peter Blaxill	Holofernes	Younger Dumain	Friar Lawrence	Ragueneau
William Bush	Boyet	Duke of Florence	Capulet	de Guiche
James Cahill	Don Adriano	Parolles	Prince	1st Marquis; Musketeer
Matthew Chait	Longaville	Morgan	Balthasar	Meddler
Thomas Cuff	Moth	2d Soldier	Peter	Cut-Purse
Jack Davidson	Dull	Bertram	Romeo	Ligniere
Gary De LaVigne	Dumaine	Lavarche	Benvolio	de Neuvillette
Patricia Devereaux		Mariana		
Louis Edmonds				Cyrano
Michael Harrah	Marcade	Lord	Paris	Le Bret
Delphi Harrington	French Princess	Helena	Lady Capulet	Lise; Mother Marguerite
Gregg Heschong	Naval Attache			2d Marquis
Mary Hudson	Katharine	Isbel		Orange Girl
Norma Joseph	Maria	Diana	Juliet	Sister Marthe
Gerald Kline	Aide-de-camp	Lord	Abraham; Friar John	Bellerose
Penelope Reed	Jaquenetta	Widow	Lady Montague	Roxane
Jim Scott	Costard	Elder Dumain	Watchman; Gregory	de Valvert
Charles Smith	Sir Nathaniel	Lafeu	Montague	de Castel-Jaloux; Montfleury
Jeremiah Sullivan	Berowne	King of France	Mercutio	Brissaille; Capuchin
George Vafiadis	Ferdinand	Rinaldo	Tybalt	Cuigy
Susan Willis	Rosaline	Countess Rousillon	Nurse	Duenna; Sister Claire

MISALLIANCE

Johnny Tarleton .... Gary De LaVigne
Bentley Summerhays .... Peter Blaxill
Hypatia .... Penelope Reed
Mrs. Tarleton .... Pauline Homi
Lord Summerhays .... William Bush
Tarleton .... Jeremiah Sullivan
Joey Percival .... Jack Davidson
Lina .... Susan Willis
Gunner .... Matthew Chait

Others in all plays: Richard Carra, Valerie Hendy, Eric Heschong, Pamela C. Jager, Albert Morrill, Lee Waldron, Elizabeth Weber.

Asolo Theater Festival. Repertory of four plays, one each by William Shakespeare, Jean Giraudoux, Molière and Mario Fratti. **Romeo and Juliet** (22). Opened July 15, 1967; directed by Robert Strane; dances staged by Carol Lee; swordplay, Eberle Thomas. **The Madwoman of Chaillot** (23). By Jean Giraudoux; adapted by Maurice Valency. Opened July 6, 1967; directed by Eberle Thomas. **Scapin** *(Fourberies de Scapin)* (23). By Molière; translated by Paul Weidner. Opened July 8, 1967; directed by Paul Weidner. **Eleonora Duse** (22). By Mario Fratti, commissioned by the Asolo Theater Festival. Opened July 12, 1967; directed by Richard G. Fallon; scenery, Charles I. Reimer; costumes, Harlan Shaw. All plays except *Duse:* scenery, Ray Perry; costumes, Joy Breckenridge. All plays: lighting, Richard C. Evans; music, Stephen Smith. Produced by Asolo Theater Festival at the Asolo Theater, Sarasota, Florida. (Repertory closed September 9, 1967.)

NOTE: Asolo Theater Festival added a winter schedule from February 16, 1968 to May 11, 1968, with repertory and performances as follows: William Shakespeare's *Henry IV, Part 1* (25), Carlo Goldoni's *Servant of Two Masters* (26), Molière's *Tartuffe* (20), Archibald MacLeish's *JB* (23) and John Osborne's *Look Back in Anger* (18).

PERFORMER	"ROMEO AND JULIET"	"THE MADWOMAN OF CHAILLOT"	"SCAPIN"	"ELEONORA DUSE"
Iris Aikenhead				Duse
David Aldrich	Capulet	Baron; Prospector		Stage Doorman
Ben Bayol	Page	Doorman		Propman
Fred Breckenridge	Friar John; Old Man	Little Man		
Dan Briekjern	Abraham	Juggler		
Robert Britton	Tybalt		Octave	4th Actor
C. David Colson	Romeo	Dr. Jadin; President		2d Actor
Kathy Fleming		Therese		
Susan Goff			Nerine	
Annette Hannon	Lady Montague			Lady in Black
Anthony Heald	Balthasar	Pierre	Leander	
Barbara Hicks		Flower Girl		
Donald C. Hoepner	Peter	Policeman	Geronte	
Polly Holliday	Lady Capulet	Mme. Constance		4th Actress
Margaret Kaler		Irma	Hyacinth	2d Actress
Linda Kampley	Juliet	Gabrielle		1st Actress
Michael P. Keenan	Escalus	Broker; Press Agent	Sylvester	
Linda Kimbrough		Paulette		3d Actress
Macon McCalman	Mercutio	Sergeant	Scapin	
Sandy Moffett		Street Singer		
Charlotte Moore		Aurelia	Zerbinette	5th Actress
Tom O'Hagan	Officer	Professor; Press Agent		
David O. Peterson	Montague	Sewer Man; President	Argante	
Richard Pierce	Servant	Shoelace Peddler		
Peter Saputo	Apothecary; Gregory	Martial		5th Actor
Albert L. Smelko	Paris	Prospector		1st Actor
Robert Strane		President	President	
Eberle Thomas	Friar Lawrence			
Isa Thomas	Nurse	Mme. Josephine		Drama Coach
Bradford Wallace	Benvolio	Ragpicker	Carle	
Paul R. Weidner		Deaf-Mute		3d Actor

Others: Dan Ater, Mimi Beck, William Gable, Drew Katzman, Ben Rogers, Joseph Rosendo, Kenneth Walker, Bob Bernreuter, Ashley McCormack, Morgan Roe Shaw.

San Diego National Shakespeare Festival. Repertory of three plays by William Shakespeare. **Twelfth Night** (42). Opened June 13, 1967; directed by Edward Payson Call; scenery, Peggy Kellner; costumes, John T. Naccarato. **All's Well that Ends Well** (36). Opened June 16, 1967; directed by Macolm Black; scenery and costumes, Peggy Kellner. **Othello** (33). Opened July 13, 1967; directed by Milton Katselas; scenery and costumes, Peggy Kellner. All plays: music and songs composed by Conrad Susa; lighting, Joseph Anthony Rubino. Produced by the Eighteenth San Diego National Shakespeare Festival at the Old Globe Theater, San Diego, California. (Repertory closed September 10, 1967).

PERFORMER	"TWELFTH NIGHT"	"ALL'S WELL THAT ENDS WELL"	"OTHELLO"
George Backman	Orsino	Elder Dumain	
Jacqueline Brookes	Maria	Helena	Emilia
James B. Douglas	Sir Toby Belch	Bertram	
Susan French		Countess Rousillon	
Janice Fuller		Mariana	
Katherine Henryk	Viola	Diana	Bianca
John Holland		King of France	Brabantio
Richard Kavanaugh	Sebastian	Lord	
Joseph Lambie	Valentine; Priest	Servant	Cassio
Robert Lawson	Curio		Lodovico
Joseph Maher	Sir Andrew	Interpreter	Roderigo
Dixie Marquis	Olivia		Desdemona
Charles Napier	Antonio	Duke of Florence	Montano
John Oldham	Sea Captain	Gentleman	1st Senator
Joseph Sommer	Malvolio	Younger Dumain	
Al Wallen	Officer	Rinaldo	2d Senator
Douglas Watson		Parolles	Othello
Donald West	Feste	Lafeu	Duke of Venice
Anthony Zerbe		Lavache	Iago

Others: Robert Anderson, Annette Cammer, Fred Coleman, Tom Corcoran, J.S. DiGioia, Jim Eggleston, Edward Horton, David Lambert, Madelon Lambie, Robert Lawson, Elizabeth Lowry, Biff Manard, Dennia Manuel, Joe Neuhart, Wess Neuhart, Halcyon Oldham, John Oldham, John David Peters, Dave Pleznac, J. Michael Ross, Tim Thomerson, Vince Vitale.

Oregon Shakespearean Festival. Repertory of four plays by William Shakespeare and an 18th century comic opera attributed to Isaac Bickerstaffe. **Pericles** (13). Opened July 22, 1967; directed by Nagle Jackson. **Antony and Cleopatra** (13). Opened July 23, 1967; directed by Jerry Turner. **The Taming of the Shrew** (13). Opened July 24, 1967; directed by Richard D. Risso. **Richard III** (12). Opened July 25, 1967; directed by Hugh C. Evans. **The Maid of the Mill** (6 matinees only). Comic opera by Isaac Bickerstaffe; based on the novel *Pamela* by Samuel Richardson. Opened August 17, 1967; directed by Carl Ritchie; costumes, Jean Schultz Davidson; lighting, Steven A. Maze. All plays: managing director, Angus L. Bowmer; scenery, Clayton Karkosh; music director, W. Bernard Windt; choreography, Shirlee Dodge. All Shakespeare plays: costumes, Jack A. Byers; lighting, Robert Brand. Produced by the Oregon Shakespearean Festival Association, Ashland, Oregon. (Repertory closed September 10, 1967).

PERFORMER	"PERICLES"	"ANTONY AND CLEOPATRA"	"THE TAMING OF THE SHREW"	"RICHARD III"
Joanne Bayless	Marina			
Robert Black	Gentleman			Grey
Karen Sue Boettcher		Iras	Bianca	Clarence's Daughter
George Brown	Fisherman			Dorset
Randall Craig			Huntsman	Oxford
Philip Davidson	Gower	Enobarbus	Sly	Edward IV; Brandon
Ken DeGusta	Pandar	Soothsayer; Seleucus	Pedant	Blunt; 2d Murderer
Tom Donaldson	Pericles	Philo; Agrippa	Petruchio	Richmond
Sherman Dorsey		Menecrates		Ely; Berkeley
Rick Hamilton		Alexas	Grumio	Herbert; Tressel; 1st Murderer
Dan Hays				Lord Mayor
Arnold Hummasti	Cerimon	Mardian	Gremio	Brakenbury
Nagle Jackson		Octavius	Hortensio	
Ann Kinsolving		Cleopatra	Katherina	Lady Anne
Vincent Landro	Boult	Pompey	Tranio	Buckingham
Richard Lincoln	Leonine			Scrivener
Sidney McLain			Tailor	Prince Edward
Tom Martin	Cleon	Maecenas	Biondello	Catesby
Glen Mazen	Antiochus	Antony		Hastings
Joseph G. Medalis	Philemon	Lepidus; Clown	Vincentio	Stanley
Tom Oleniacz	Gentleman	Demetrius; Dollabella	Servant	Norfolk
Patrick Omeirs	Escanes	Canidius; Diomedes		Archbishop of York; Tyrrel
Shirley Patton	Thaisa			
Hal Poe	Simonides	Varrius; Scarus	Baptista	Rivers
Michael Poe				Duke of York
Scott Porter	Lysimachus		Lucentio	Lovel; Surrey
Molly Risso				Elizabeth
Richard D. Risso				Richard
William Roberts		Menas; Proculeius	Lord	Clarence
Timothy Shelton	Fisherman	Messenger	Curtis	
Rosemary Shevlin	Diana	Charmian		
Dennis Sparks		Decretas		Canterbury
Vernon Statler				Keeper
Jay Theodore Sterling			Haberdasher	Urswick
Milton Tarver	Thaliard			Ratcliff
Cindy Kay Veazey	Dionyza	Octavia		Duchess of York
Claudia Wilkens	Bawd		Widow	Margaret
Roald B. Wulff	Helicanus	Thidias	Tapster	Vaughan
Valerie Zellerhoff	Lychorida		Hostess	

THE MAID OF THE MILL

Lord Ainworth ....Richard Lincoln
Sir Harry Sycamore ....Robert Black
Mervin ....Larry Alan Haynes
Fairfield ....Dan Hays
Giles ....George Brown
Ralph ....Jonathan Hardy
Patty ....Joanne Bayless
Fanny ....Karen Sue Boettcher
Lady Sycamore ....Claudia Wilkens
Theodosia ....Theresa Krug
Gypsy Boy ....Sidney McLain
Fortune Teller ....Betsy Sacks Hamilton
Gypsy Violinist ....Patrick Omeirs

Others in all plays: Emily Carpenter, Cathy Christy, Leslie Ann Clumpner, Evelyn C. Davenport, Jennifer Herring, Dick Hooser, Bob Horn, Sandy Logan, Mary Ed Peters, Randall Eugene Stothers, Craig Williams, David Kent Nale, Hank McCormick.

THE SEASON IN LONDON

By Frank Marcus

Author of *The Killing of Sister George* (a Best Play in the 1966-67 volume), of *Mrs. Mouse, Are You Within?* (produced in England this season) and drama critic for *The Sunday Telegraph*

IT IS a pleasure to report that in one sphere at least there has been a totally successful foreign conquest by America. The territory in question is the musical theater of London. Has there ever before been such a massive takeover? At the time of writing, *Fiddler on the Roof* has been joined by *Sweet Charity, Cabaret, Man of La Mancha,* and—less sensationally—the "Peanuts" show, *You're a Good Man Charlie Brown.* Scheduled for the near future are *I Do! I Do!* and *Golden Boy,* with Sammy Davis Jr.

How did these shows survive the Atlantic crossing? Pretty well, on the whole. After a year's run of *Fiddler,* the comedian Alfie Bass replaced the dazzling Topol, and reminded us that Tevye was not an Old Testament prophet but a humble milkman imagined by Sholom Aleichem. In *Sweet Charity,* Juliet Prowse substituted leggy vitality for Gwen Verdon's downtrodden resilience. This show was deemed the most efficient and least pretentious of the imports. *Cabaret,* my own favourite, still has its great moments and its disastrous central flaw: the reduction of the fascinating and subtle brother-and-sister relationship between Isherwood and Sally to that of a banal heterosexual *affaire.* One of our best young actresses, Judi Dench, did her best for the diminished Sally. She had too much intelligence and warmth for the part, turning her into a neurotic dumpling instead of an angular frenetic madcap, but it was still a compelling performance. Barry Dennen had a great success as the Emcee, but could not dispel memories of the unforgettable Joel Grey. We had a Franco-Russian Fraulein Schneider (Lila Kedrova) and an English, strictly non-kosher Schultz. The cabaret scenes were stunning as in New York.

How did London react to this challenge? By declaring artistic bankruptcy. There wasn't even a fight! After several months, I still find it hard to write with moderation about *The Four Musketeers,* at present desecrating the hallowed stage of the Theater Royal, Drury Lane. Reputedly the costliest British musical ever, this witless, tuneless, cluttered-up, amateurish extravaganza would not have survived one preview on Broadway. Carrying feebleness to the point of arrogance, it seems to say "We know it's awful, old boy, but by God it's British!". Trapped in a labyrinthine folly of a setting (designed by Sean Kenny), that amiable buffoon Harry Secombe, playing a Welsh d'Artagnan, deserves sympathy. As if this were not enough, the long-standing idol of the provinces, John Hanson, is delighting coachloads of middle aged ladies with *The Desert Song,* to be followed soon by—can you guess?—*The Student Prince.* So much for swinging London. Oh, yes, there's also a charming revival of *The Boy Friend,* which would have been welcome as an addition to new work, and an Oxford scholar, Prof. Nevill Coghill, has gone back to Chaucer and come up with *Canterbury Tales,* a bawdy romp full of rude words (always acceptable in archaic spelling). This musical is alive—at least, from the waist downwards. Who knows what the next season will bring? *Beowulf,* transposed to Carnaby Street?

I saw only two British musicals of interest, both well away from the West End. At Stratford East, Joan Littlewood produced *The Marie Lloyd Story,* an affectionate chronicle of the turbulent life of the Queen of the Music Halls. The true events of her life, professional acclaim counterpointed by private disaster, read like a librettist's dream. We were spared that cliche ingredient of so many musical biographies: the fight for recognition. Instead, the show began with Marie at 40, at the height of her fame. A victim of prudery and hypocrisy, she fought back heroically, supported by her public. She died in harness. The strength of the show lay in its unsentimental attitude and in the use it made of the lovely old songs. Its weakness—rectifiable, I should have thought—was the insertion of new conventional songs at moments of dramatic climax. Avis Bunnage was a tough and spirited Marie. The other show was even more modestly presented. The repertory theater of the small seaside town of Worthing saw the first performance of *Sit Down, Banna* written and composed by a Guianan, Norman Beaton. This tale of four Negro immigrants living in squalor in London had something to say and said it with verve and a notable lack of self-pity. There were beguiling calypso numbers and a couple of lilting ballads. It was much too long, and some of it was brash, amateurish, and melodramatic. But when considering that it was rehearsed for two weeks—with a cast of 25!—at a cost of an approximate equivalent of a handful of costumes for *The Four Musketeers,* it becomes a heartening and almost miraculous achievement. No West End managements bothered to go and see it. They must be satisfied with things as they are.

The new-found vitality of the American theater impressed in other ways, too. Curiosity had been aroused by reports from Greenwich Village—mine included, I'm proud to admit—about *America Hurrah,* and it burst upon London. The style and cohesion of the performance was appreciated as much as the content—possibly more. The last of the triple bill, the puppet play *Motel,* made a shattering impact, although motel culture has mercifully not yet invaded the British way of life. *America Hurrah* was about to transfer to the West End when, possibly due to pressure from the Lord Chamberlain, the theater owners got cold feet and closed the door. Meanwhile, a bill abolishing the Lord Chamberlain's function as play censor is shortly expected to be passed by the House of Commons. The Open Theater was followed by the more extreme, but less polished, troupe from the Cafe La Mama. Their principal offering was *Futz,* the lamentable tale of a farmer who sleeps with his sow. I hasten to add that it wasn't just her body he wanted—he loved her romantically, too. There were audible intakes of breath from the London audience at the four-letter words and the mimed copulation.

In the realm of straight plays, however, the American contribution was not only less notable but almost nonexistent. After an hysterically funny first half, Jules Feiffer's *Little Murders* declined fatally in the second. Maybe violence just isn't funny to an inhabitant of New York. The ability to laugh at it would be a sign that the fight was won. A new Tennessee Williams play entitled simply *The Two-Character Play* received its premiere at the Hampstead Theater Club, devotedly directed by James Roose Evans. I was almost alone in admiring it—and I admired it enormously. This was a Pirandellian piece about an actor and actress, brother and sister, bound to each other by blood and madness, forcing themselves to enact a play which is their own lives. They have only a hazy idea of the dialogue and they fear the outcome. The play ends. The audience goes home. But the actors are trapped in the theater; the doors have been bolted from the outside. They must act the play again. The only remedy is death. I found this a most moving metaphor for madness, beautifully written and full of insinuating magic. Peter Wyngarde, ravaged and poetic, and Mary Ure, in turn fiery and icy, were outstanding.

And so we come to our home-grown produce. Both The Royal Shakespeare Company and The National Theater had a problematical season. For the RSC, Peter Hall directed a chill, prosaic *Macbeth,* with Paul Scofield and Vivien Merchant. It misfired almost completely. In other ways, too, *Macbeth* lived up to its awesome reputation. Hall resigned as artistic director, in order to devote himself to films; Scofield followed suit shortly after, for undisclosed reasons. The new director is Trevor Nunn, a young man in his 20s. Most of RSC's other offerings were worthy rather than exciting. There was a pedestrian *Ghosts,* with Peggy Ashcroft; a competent *As You Like It,* with Dorothy Tutin; a lively *The Taming of the Shrew;* a warmly-welcomed *All's Well that Ends Well;* a jolly *Under Milk Wood.* Apart from *Little Murders,* the only new play was a grim, intense parable on the Cuban revolution (parricide committed by a brother and two sisters), *The Criminals* by José Triana. It was set in a nursery, in shades of unremitting grey. Much the most enjoyable offering of the RSC was a splendidly stylish and exuberant revival of Vanbrugh's *The Relapse,* with Donald Sinden suggesting the virility, innocence and pathos behind the affectations of Lord Foppington, without losing sight of the fun.

The National Theater, too, had its difficulties. First came the serious illness of its director, Sir Laurence Olivier, now happily recovered; then, a rumpus over Rolf Hochhuth's Churchill play, *Soldiers.* Though the play was backed by Olivier and his literary manager, Kenneth Tynan, the chairman of the board, Lord Chandos, refused point-blank to countenance a production at the National Theater of a work which he considered libelous to the memory of his wartime chief. There were rumours of resignations but, fortunately, calm prevailed. Olivier directed a sensitive, poetic *Three Sisters,* in daringly evocative settings by the Czech Josef Svoboda, with a deeply-felt performance as Masha by Joan Plowright, and a poignantly crushed Vershinin by

Robert Stephens. This was followed by a hair-raising gamble, which succeeded—indeed, triumphed—against all expectations: *As You Like It* with an all-male cast. This was no romp in drag, but an ecstatic magical dream in which asexual figures moved in a synthetic landscape of perspex rocks, trees of tubular glass, and foam-rubber clouds. Clifford Williams (director), Ralph Koltai (designer), and Ronald Pickup (Rosalind) shared the honors. Next, Sir Tyrone Guthrie returned after a long absence with characteristically vivacious productions of *Volpone* and *Tartuffe*. In *Volpone,* he stressed the animal—in particular the avian—derivation of the characters, strutting, squawking, swooping, and spreading their wings, as the evening became somewhat exhausting. *Tartuffe,* given in a skillful version (in rhymed couplets) by Richard Wilbur, was more traditional. Cast against type, Sir John Gielgud was a subtle Orgon, and Joan Plowright simply glowed as the maid, Dorine; but Robert Stephens' Tartuffe, conceived as a young man with a rural accent, was too exaggerated to be convincing. To complete the parade of directorial big guns, Peter Brook made his National Theater debut with *Oedipus,* in the hitherto unperformed text by Nero's tutor Seneca. Stoicism and the gory descriptive narrative inspired Mr. Brook to prepare a modish mixture of Artaud, Grotowski, and the Living Theater. Actors were scattered in the auditorium, humming, hissing, buzzing and generally supplying a tonal background to the rhetorical recitation on stage (there was little action); everyone except Jocasta (Irene Worth) and Oedipus (Gielgud) wore identical sweaters and slacks; the whole thing was given the semblance of an ancient rite. It ended with a Bacchic celebration: a statue of a golden phallus was unveiled; the actors—in glittering costumes and masks—streamed through the auditorium, and a brass band marched up and down the aisles, playing "Yes, We Have No Bananas". The curtain fell on a scene of uninhibited dancing. Comparative sobriety returned to the Old Vic with Brecht's version of Marlowe's *Edward II*. This literary curiosity, directed by Frank Dunlop, treated epic tragedy in the manner of a medieval street ballad, with the emphasis on gore. The actors looked Shakespearean, but spoke in a somewhat flavorless flat idiom. This experiment was only partly successful.

Among the straight plays, too, it was the gambles that paid off. Who could have foreseen that audiences would laugh heartily, but not at all callously, at the plight of a young couple trying to cope with their 10-year-old inert spastic child? This is what Peter Nichols achieved with *A Day in the Death of Joe Egg*. If comedy is defined as the last alternative to despair (Eric Bentley), this was an example of it. Joe Melia and Zena Walker were funny and touching as the stricken couple. There was brilliant writing, too, in *The Restoration of Arnold Middleton,* the first play by the novelist David Storey. Here was another schoolmaster and his wife (John Shepherd and Eileen Atkins). This time the husband was the problem: the play chronicled his cheerfully defiant withdrawal into madness. At one point, he rushed upstairs and raped his mother-in-law! Another play about madness by another novelist was James Kennaway's *Country Dance*. This described the shrinking into conformity of an overfervent relationship between a brother and sister (Edward Fox and Jane Merrow). Altogether, this was the year in which novelists ventured on the stage (the previous crop of writers had nearly all been actors). *Wise Child* by Simon Gray was yet another example. This black farce centered on two criminals on the run, one disguised as the other's mother. Every imaginable perversion was flung at the (by now shock-proof) West End audience. I doubt if this play would have survived but for the presence of Sir Alec Guinness, enjoying himself as the dowdy "Mrs. Artminster", the thief in drag. For my money, the best performance was Gordon Jackson's as a queer, creepy, religious, Scottish landlord (what a mixture!). A much better effort was the double bill by John Bowen (author of *After The Rain*) presented under the title *Little Boxes.* The first, *The Coffee Lace,* was a macabre yet compassionate study of six members of a once-successful vaudeville act, now living in voluntary confinement. The second, *Trevor,* concerned two young lesbians who try to reassure their respectively conventional and progressive parents by hiring an out-of-work actor—the Trevor of the title—to impersonate both the fiance of the one girl and the married lover of the other: a kind of servant of two mistresses. There were hilarious complications and an unexpectedly serious ending, about which I had my doubts. The plays were briskly directed by Philip Grout and extremely well acted. Mention should also be made of John McGrath's taut account of a last night in a death cell, *Bakke's Night of Fame,* in which our best Negro actor, Johnny Sekka, played a non-Negro part, and Tom Stoppard's re-working of an earlier television play, *Enter a Free Man,* which brought a bravura performance from Michael Hordern.*

We also had our share of adaptations of novels. Robert Shaw dramatized his own *The Man in the Glass Booth,* a psychological thriller on the subject of guilt and redemption, derived from the Eichmann case. This was directed by Harold Pinter, and had at its center another dazzling virtuoso display by Donald Pleasence. James Saunders adapted Iris Murdoch's *The Italian Girl,* a characteristic set of sexual permutations fitting together neatly—if that's

* Editor's note (by Ossia Trilling): Modesty prevented the author of this London report, Frank Marcus, from mentioning one of the season's hits: the transfer from the Bristol Old Vic of his own spicy tragi-comedy, in the same vein as his *The Killing of Sister George,* entitled *Mrs. Mouse, Are You Within?,* in which this acknowledged master of female psychology has excelled himself in sensitivity, wit and humanity in the handling of a delicate theme that touches on sex and the color bar. In his capacity as drama critic of *The Sunday Telegraph,* Marcus reviewed his own play in a note at the tag end of his May 19 column as follows: "Lastly, a warning. *Mrs. Mouse, Are You Within?* (Duke of York's Theater), reviewed when it opened in Bristol last month, has arrived in London. What can I say? One is used to slightly dubious entries from the managerial stable of Mr. Michael Codron—*Codron bleu,* as it were—but how could that excellent director Mr. Val May and the charming ladies and gentlemen in the cast get mixed up in this? A play in which a black gets into bed with a white girl—no, *two* white girls; in which a self-confessed Red wins in the end; and last but certainly not least, in which a middle-aged employee of British Rail removes his trousers for the purposes of—er—intimacy? If you have a shred of decency, folks, don't see this show! The author? In my day he'd have been horsewhipped. Nowadays, who can tell: he might be a masochist and actually enjoy the experience."

the right expression—in the end. This one had a somewhat Gothic aura, e.g. a scene in which a nymphomaniac, clad in a nightie, watches worms dancing on the lawn at midnight. Richard Pasco, Timothy West, and Jane Wenham shone in Val May's production. There were two dramatizations of stories by Chekhov: *Beware of the Dog,* with John Neville and Ann Bell, and *The Duel,* with Peter Wyngarde, Michael Bryant, and Nyree Dawn Porter. Neither convinced me that Chekhov had been wrong to write them as stories. The legendary Frederick Rolfe, alias Baron Corvo, made an appearance in Peter Luke's adaptation, *Hadrian the Seventh.* As the rejected failure imagining himself to be Pope, Alec McCowen presented a stunning case history of *folie de grandeur,* with all the pathos that stems from delusion.

It was a poor year for light comedies. The firm of Hugh and Margaret Williams provided an efficient sample, on the subject of wife-swapping, in *The Flip Side,* followed shortly after by a repellent mixture of aging promiscuity and Tory snobbism called *Let's All Go down the Strand.* The dwindling band of admirers of Dame Gladys Cooper, Miss Evelyn Laye and Mr. Williams himself could not be recruited in sufficient numbers to ensure a run. Peter Ustinov's *Halfway up the Tree* was even more depressing. Here was a considerable talent descending to foolish homilies and feeble half-hearted humor. The trouble with this tale of a general returning home to find his children become hippies and, instead of admonishing, joining them, was its total remoteness from contemporary life. There is nothing wrong with fantasy, provided it is used as a vehicle for humor or profundity, or bold flights of fancy, but this was woefully pedestrian and self-indulgent. With Robert Morley as the Billy Bunter-Peter Pan general, *Halfway up the Tree* is enjoying considerable success. It is also sad to record a limp entry from the Littlewood stable, *Mrs. Wilson's Diary.* Described as "an affectionate lampoon", this mixture of political impersonation and schoolboy smut was based on a column in the magazine *Private Eye.* The joke consists of pretending that the Prime Minister's wife is just an ordinary lower-middle-class housewife. To keep up with political events such as Cabinet changes, the show was in a state of constant revision, which made life exciting for the actors. I suppose we ought to be thankful that poor, plodding Mr. Wilson did not engender a *MacBird.* That talented but erratic writer Charles Wood (better known for his screenplays for *The Knack* and *Help!*) had two near-misses with *Fill the Stage with Happy Hours,* a sordid picture of provincial backstage life, and *Dingo,* a searing denunciation of war, set in the North African desert. Brian Friel's *Philadelphia, Here I Come!,* a charming and gentle play, did not survive in the rigorous climate of Shaftesbury Avenue.

Revivals fared unpredictably, as usual. The farces of Frederick Lonsdale, in the shape of *The Last of Mrs. Cheyney* and *Aren't We All?,* came and went. Wilde arrived shakily with *A Woman of No Importance,* but was fortunate to have his reputation rescued by his devoted champions, the management of H.M. Tennent, with a superbly stylish production of *The Importance of Being Earnest.* Isobel Jeans was Lady Bracknell to the manner born, and Dame Flora Robson and Robert Eddison discovered almost ecstatic depths in Miss Prism and the Canon. But the most notable feature of the evening was John Standing's Algernon: a brilliant and engaging comedian, clearly destined for stardom. Robert Chetwyn directed with discernment. The spate of inferior late Shaw has come to a halt. Instead, there was an intelligent, deeply-felt revival (directed by John Clements) of *Heartbreak House.* Mr. Clements himself gave the most distinguished performance of his career as Capt. Shotover, and Irene Worth—surely our greatest actress—was the definitive Mrs. Hushabye: alluringly feminine, limpidly passionate, surpassingly understanding. The only other Shaw was a dramatized version of *The Black Girl in Search of God,* narrated by Dame Edith Evans to celebrate her 80th birthday. A workmanlike *The Cherry Orchard* occasioned a much-admired interpretation of Madame Ranevsky by Lila Kedrova. Galsworthy's *Justice,* with Eric Portman, failed to cash in on the popular television series of *The Forsyte Saga.* Restoration comedy was represented by *Intrigues and Amours,* interestingly adapted from Vanbrugh by Joan Littlewood, and Farquhar's *The Constant Couple.* West End Shakespeare brought an indifferently produced *The Merchant of Venice,* with Sir Ralph Richardson playing Shylock in isolated brilliance. Two productions originating from the National Theater had commercial runs: Noel Coward's *Hay Fever* (with Celia Johnson) and Peter Shaffer's *Black Comedy,* preceded by a new rather stodgy piece, *The White Liars* (American title was *White Lies*). They showed to better advantage at the Old Vic. Marius Goring tried unsuccessfully to exercise Sir Henry Irving's old warhorse, *The Bells.*

Going back 30 years, Dodie Smith's *Dear Octopus* proved surprisingly resilient. There was no mention of Munich in this family saga centered on a golden wedding celebration, but plenty of sharp observation, convincing characterization and skillful manipulation of the large cast. Frith Banbury's unpatronizing approach to the play kept it safely this side of nausea, and the ebullient, indestructible Cicely Courtneidge—with Jack Hulbert at her elbow—led the starry contingent with superb authority.

Going back 60 years, the Royal Court Theater exhumed the neglected plays of D.H. Lawrence. Three of his plays—he wrote eight altogether—were played in repertory: *A Collier's Friday Night, The Daughter-in-Law,* and *The Widowing of Mrs. Holroyd.* The first two had been tried out previously. Here was a challenge to the critic: was Lawrence, the dramatist, worthy of reassessment? The plays were a revelation; this was unquestionably the artistic event of the season. An austerely naturalistic trilogy of life in the Nottinghamshire mining village of Eastwood, one watched with hypnotic fascination the prosaic chores of cooking, washing, ironing and, in the last play, laying out the body of a miner killed in a pit explosion. The action was unhurried, the dialogue minimal, yet these plays generated an electric tension. The air was thick with suppressed passion: the humble cottages were the battlefield on which the war of the sexes was fought to the death. The women were proud, practical and unforgiving; the men wayward, feckless, almost artistic, emerging troll-like from the bowels of the earth, blinded by the light. The devotion and integrity of the young director, Peter Gill, infused the very spirit of Lawrence in his cast. Victor Henry, Michael Coles, and Mark Jones were outstanding among the men; Anne Dyson played a variety of mothers with peasant strength. But to my mind Judy Parfitt's Mrs. Holroyd earned the season's special glory. Tall, pale, gauche and inhibited, she suggested profound depths of feeling with an extreme economy of means. Here is an actress of potential greatness.

Eagerly awaited, John Osborne's new play *Time Present* was mild by his standards. Once again we had a virtual monologue, this time delivered by a thirtyish actress, whose adored father lies dying. The recipient of the torrent of words is a sympathetic lady politician. There is hardly any plot and very little action. She rails against a wide variety of contemporary phenomena, many of them trivial. Many of the critics (themselves under attack from Osborne) found her exceedingly tiresome. I was held by it (just about), largely owing to Jill Bennett's sincere performance.

For thriller addicts, there were three mediocre samples: *The Deadly Game,* based on a macabre joke by Friedrich Duerrenmatt, *Minor Murder,* in which two young girls bound together by unnatural love dispose of one of the girls' mother, and *According to the Evidence,* a conventional courtroom drama.

Most seasons bring a crop of freaks and aberrations which are bad almost beyond belief. Sometimes these works are perpetrated by writers of great talent; occasionally, in a ghastly sort of way, they can be quite enjoyable to watch. Here is my Curiosity Corner for 1967-68: a musical, *Queenie,* about a widowed owner of a pub, wooed by three suitors called Tom, Dick and Harry (I kid you not). This was written in doggerel verse by a Socialist member of the House of Lords. My second choice: David Pinner's *Fanghorn,* directed by Charles Marowitz. This deep-purple farce, school of Orton, had as its leading figure a green-haired lesbian clad in black leather, who is an expert in ritual murder. I saw the second performance and there was not a single curtain call. No. 3: *Staring at the Sun,* in which a young man was helped with his problems by means of spectral intervention by his late fiancee, appearing sporadically in a blue spotlight. No, it was not meant to be funny. There was also *Early Morning,* a new play by Edward Bond, author of the controversial *Saved.* This phantasmagoria involved an affair between Queen Victoria and Florence Nightingale—yes, lesbianism was the color of the year!—and ended with a cannibal feast, set in heaven. Given a Sunday performance at the Royal Court before an invited audience, a repeat performance was canceled, after threatened police prosecution. We were not amused, it seems.

Originality, rather than freakish curiosity, asserted itself in three examples of swinging Barderie: *As You Like It* (the third production this season), imported from Birmingham; *A Midsummer Night's Dream,* with Puck dispensing flower power, imported from the Edinburgh Festival; and *Twelfth Night* in pop art settings and costumes by Patrick Procter, with a delightfully androgynous Viola (Kika Markham) and a Jean Harlow Olivia (Vickery Turner) who had never heard of *The Beard.* A documentary about soccer, *Zigger Zagger,* by a noteworthy young writer called Peter Terson, boasted a cast of 80, chanting, singing, waving scarves and rattles, and throwing streamers of toilet paper, in an authentic re-creation of the popular Saturday afternoon ritual. Unfortunately, the size and volume of the framework overwhelmed and suffocated the strip-cartoon narrative. Directed by Michael Croft for the National Youth Theater—a vigorous amateur organization—this show looked incongruous in the West End and departed quickly. On some nights there were more people on the stage than in the auditorium.

Lastly, let me record with gratitude a Christmas visit with the children to a performance given by the Paper Bag Players. This was the most imaginative and entertaining children's performance I have seen; what's more, the children thought so, too! I need hardly add that the four geniuses who comprised the company came from New York. I hope they'll be back this year. America Hurrah!

Highlights of the London Season

Selected and compiled by Ossia Trilling

OUTSTANDING LONDON PERFORMANCES

PEGGY ASHCROFT
as Mrs. Alving in
Ghosts

PETER WYNGARDE
as Felice in
The Two-Character Play

DONALD SINDEN
as Lord Foppington in
The Relapse

JOAN PLOWRIGHT
as Irina in
Three Sisters

JULIET PROWSE
as Charity in
Sweet Charity

ALEC GUINNESS
as Mrs. Artminster in
Wise Child

RONALD PICKUP
as Rosalind in
As You Like It

DONALD PLEASENCE
as Arthur Goldman in
The Man in the Glass Booth

JOHN GIELGUD
as Orgon in
Tartuffe

JOHN SHEPHERD
as Arnold in
The Restoration of Arnold Middleton

JUDY PARFITT
as Mrs. Holroyd in
The Widowing of Mrs. Holroyd

BARRY DENNEN
as Emcee in
Cabaret

PAUL SCOFIELD
as Macbeth in
Macbeth

IRENE WORTH
as Jocasta in
Oedipus

ALEC MCCOWEN
as Rolfe in
Hadrian the Seventh

OUTSTANDING DIRECTORS

TREVOR NUNN
The Taming of the Shrew

TYRONE GUTHRIE
Volpone

PETER BROOK
Oedipus

OUTSTANDING DESIGNERS

RALPH KOLTAI
Little Murders

BORIS ARONSON
Cabaret

CARL TOMS
Edward II

OUTSTANDING NEW ENGLISH PLAYS

(D)—Playwright's London debut. Figure in parentheses is number of performances; plus sign (+) indicates play was still running on June 1, 1968.

CRIMES OF PASSION (THE RUFFIAN ON THE STAIR and THE ERPINGHAM CAMP) by Joe Orton. A married woman terrorized by a suicidal maniac; a British holiday-camp run on Nazi death-camp lines. With Avril Elgar, Michael Standing, Bernard Gallagher, Ken Wynne. (15)

COUNTRY DANCE by James Kennaway. (D) The obsessions of a spiritually and sexually isolated Scottish laird. With Edward Cox, Jane Merrow. (21)

RAFFERTY'S CHANT by Keith Dewhurst. (D) A jocular conman gulls his greedy victims. With James Grout, Toni Palmer. (58)

THE RESTORATION OF ARNOLD MIDDLETON by David Storey. (D) Cockeyed history teacher's home cares provoke a ghastly crisis, but all ends well. With John Shepherd, Eileen Atkins. (85)

A DAY IN THE DEATH OF JOE EGG by Peter Nichols. (D) The trials of the parents of a helpless spastic child. With Joe Melia, Zena Walker. (148)

FILL THE STAGE WITH HAPPY HOURS by Charles Wood. Transfer of Nottingham production of backstage comedy of humors. With Harry H. Corbett, Sheila Hancock, Faith Brook. (32)

WISE CHILD by Simon Gray. (D) The path of a lag in drag on the run is crossed by three troublemakers. With Alec Guinness, Gordon Jackson, Simon Ward. (126)

DINGO by Charles Wood. Virulent anti-war satire, acted to club audiences only, after Bristol Arts Center private tryout. With Tom Kempinski, Henry Woolf, Leon Lissek. (19)

BAKKE'S NIGHT OF FAME by John McGrath. Adapted from William Butler's *A Danish Gambit* about a man in a condemned cell. With Johnny Sekka, David McKail. (25)

LITTLE BOXES (THE COFFEE LACE and TREVOR) by John Bowen. Two one-acters about self-enclosed and thwarted people. With Sylvia Coleridge, Angela Thorne, David Cook, Maureen Prior, June Jago. (97+)

MRS. MOUSE, ARE YOU WITHIN? by Frank Marcus. The tragi-comic mishaps of two sisters, one pretty, the other plain. With Barbara Leigh Hunt, Angela Down. (19+)

TIME PRESENT by John Osborne. A desperate and witty actress attacks the contemporary scene of superficial success from within. With Jill Bennett, Katherine Blake, Valerie Taylor. (4+)

LIMITED RUNS OF INTERESTING NEW BRITISH PLAYS

THE MIGHTY RESERVOY by Peter Terson. (D) Transfer from Stoke-on-Trent of house-dramatist's allegorical duologue on the meaning of manhood. With Ray McAnally, Tim Preece. (5)

A VIEW TO THE COMMON by James Casey. (D) The hopeless relationships of mental and sexual incompatibles. With Victor Henry, Thelma Ruby. (15)

OGODIVELEFTTHEGASON by Donald Howarth. The figments of an introspective postulant's musings come to life. With Dudley Sutton, Jean Heal, John Phillips. (8)

THE RISING GENERATION by Ann Jellicoe. The monstrous regiment of schoolgirls on the rampage. Written for and acted by a cast of schoolchildren. (1)

THE HAPPY APPLE by Jack Pulman. (D) A capsule history of the human race. With Lance Percival, Pauline Collins. (21)

NATHAN AND TABILETH and OLDENBERG by Barry Bermange. (D) Two short plays: an absurdist view of an aging couple; pride and prejudice in suburbia. With Robert Bernal, Roger Booth, June Jago. (21)

HONEYMOON by Malcolm Quantrill. (D) A married couple make believe. With Caroline Mortimer, Dinsdale Landon, Jean Muir. (20)

FANGHORN by David Pinner. Send-up of sadism, sex and sacrilege. With Glenda Jackson, Peter Bayliss. (4)

THE ROYAL PARDON by John Arden and Margaretta D'Arcy. A fantasy for children of all ages on war and civics. With Brian Osborne, David Leyland. (30)

BACKBONE by Michael Rosen. (D) A student love-affair in defiance of prejudice. With John Shepherd, Faith Brook, Marty Cruikshank, Harry Towb. (14)

ZIGGER ZAGGER by Peter Terson. The hysteria and social envy induced by football mania. With the company of the National Youth Theater. (22)

THE GUY by Walter Lever. (D) The travels of a modern Odysseus. With Gary Files, Leader Hawkins. (11)

ENTER A FREE MAN by Tom Stoppard. Revised version of a 7-year-old comedy (and onetime TV drama) about a Quixotic would-be inventor. With Michael Hordern, Vanessa Forsyth, Megs Jenkins. (44)

EARLY MORNING by Edward Bond. A sleazy satire on Victorian mores, stopped by the censor. With Marianne Faithfull, Moira Redmond, Nigel Hawthorn. (2)

MOONEY AND HIS CARAVANS by Peter Terson. The disappointment of a Midland couple's social ambitions. With Diana Bishop, Barry Evans. (20+)

POPULAR ATTRACTIONS

A MIDSUMMER NIGHT'S DREAM by William Shakespeare. Inaugural production of the 1967 Open Air Theater. With Peter Bayliss, Jill Dixon. (40)

AS YOU LIKE IT by William Shakespeare. Transfer from Birmingham Repertory Theater. With Deborah Stanford, Brian Cox. (70)

THE CONSTANT COUPLE by George Farquhar. New production with incidental music by Benjamin Pearce Higgins. With Robert Hardy, Juliet Harmer, Eileen Beldon. (36)

AS YOU LIKE IT by William Shakespeare. Transfer to Royal Shakespeare Company repertory from Stratford. With Dorothy Tutin, Michael Williams, Roy Kinnear. (23 in repertory)

LET SLEEPING WIVES LIE by Harold Brooke and Kay Bannerman. A Yankee corporation director in a British takeover-bid situation. With Elspet Gray, Derek Farr, Leo Franklyn. (348+)

THE MAN IN THE GLASS BOOTH by Robert Shaw. (D) Harold Pinter's production of Shaw's own adaptation of his novel about an Eichmann-type American Jew. With Donald Pleasence. (151)

THE FLIP SIDE by Hugh and Margaret Williams. Two married couples try changing partners. With Anna Massey, Ronald Lewis. (346+)

THE TAMING OF THE SHREW by William Shakespeare. Trevor Nunn's brilliant Stratford production transferred to Royal Shakespeare Company repertory. With Janet Suzman, Michael Williams, Roy Kinnear. (21 in repertory)

THE FIGHT FOR BARBARA by D.H. Lawrence. Autobiographical drama, preceeded by real-life cuts of those taking part. With Stephen Moore, Adrienne Corri. (48)

THE RELAPSE by Sir John Vanbrugh. Transferred to Royal Shakespeare Company repertory from Stratford. With Donald Sinden, Janet Suzman, Frances de la Tour. (40 in repertory)

MRS. WILSON'S DIARY by Richard Ingrams and John Wells. Littlewoodian satire on present-day political leaders. With Myvanwy Jenn, Bill Wallis, Bob Grant. (263+)

THE MERCHANT OF VENICE by William Shakespeare. New all-star revival. With Ralph Richardson, Angela Thorne, Karin Fernald. (100)

ACCORDING TO THE EVIDENCE by Felicity Douglas and Henry Cecil (with Basil Dawson). Dramatization of Henry Cecil's murder thriller. With Douglas Wilmer, Muriel Pavlow, Naunton Wayne, Michael Gwynne. (260)

A MIDSUMMER NIGHT'S DREAM by William Shakespeare. Frank Dunlop's Pop-Theater production from the Edinburgh Festival. With Jim Dale, Cleo Laine, David Baxter. (38)

AS YOU LIKE IT by William Shakespeare. Clifford Williams' all-male National Theater production based on Jan Kott's theories. With Ronald Pickup, Jeremy Brett, Charles Kay, Robert Stephens. (40+ in repertory)

LET'S ALL GO DOWN THE STRAND by Hugh and Margaret Williams. Too much bubbly and a betrayed wife forgives her errant husband. With Gladys Cooper, Evelyn Laye, Hugh Williams. (371+)

HEARTBREAK HOUSE by George Bernard Shaw. Transfer from the 1967 Chichester Festival. With Irene Worth, John Clements. (116)

NUMBER TEN by Ronald Miller. Dramatization of William Clark's peek into the Prime Minister's sanctum. With Alastair Sim, Dulcie Gray, Michael Denison, John Gregson. (125)

THE HOLLOW CROWN by John Barton. Revival of dramatic history of England. With

Peggy Ashcroft, Derek Godfrey, Donald Sinden. (16 in repertory)

HALFWAY UP THE TREE by Peter Ustinov. Retired General outbeatniks his beatnik children. With Robert Morley, Pinkie Johnstone, Ambrosine Phillpotts. (315+)

THE MARIE LLOYD STORY by Daniel Farson and Harry Moore. Joan Littlewood's final fling with a Theater Workshop musical about the famous music-hall star. With Avis Bunnage, Maxwell Shaw. (32)

A WOMAN OF NO IMPORTANCE by Oscar Wilde, adapted by Paul Dehn. Revival of Wildean comedy with borrowed lines from other Wildeana. With Tony Britton, Phyllis Calvert, James Hayter. (55)

THE BOY FRIEND by Sandy Wilson. Revival of ageless send-up of the 1920's. With Ann Beach, Marion Grimaldi, Jeremy Hawk. (212+)

THE FOUR MUSKETEERS by Michael Pertwee, Laurie Johnson, and Herbert Kretzmer. Crazy musical of old romantic favorite. With Harry Secombe, Stephanie Voss. (205+)

DEAR OCTOPUS by Dodie Smith. Revival of sentimental British 1930's family drama. With Cicely Courtneidge, Jack Hulbert, Richard Todd, Joyce Carey. (214+)

LITTLE WOMEN by Bruce Walker. Holiday-time adaptation of Louisa M. Alcott's book. With Lynn Rainbow, Hannah Watt, Roderick Lovell. (43)

MACBETH by William Shakespeare. Transferred to Royal Shakespeare Company repertory from Stratford and Finnish and Russian tour. With Paul Scofield, Vivien Merchant, Ian Richardson. (40 in repertory)

VOLPONE by Ben Jonson. Tyrone Guthrie's animalistic revival at National Theater. With Colin Blakely, Frank Wylie, Robert Lang, Graham Crowden, Gabrielle Laye. (22+ in repertory)

ALL'S WELL THAT ENDS WELL by William Shakespeare. Transferred to Royal Shakespeare Company repertory from Stratford. With Catherine Lacey, Ian Richardson, Lynn Farleigh. (41 in repertory)

MR. PIM PASSES BY by A.A. Milne. Revival of popular old comedy. With Thorley Walters, Adrienne Corri. (20)

JUSTICE by John Galsworthy. Revival of 58-year-old social drama. With Eric Portman, Barbara Murray, Richard Briers. (45)

TWELFTH NIGHT by William Shakespeare. Jane Howell's modern-dress revival at the Royal Court Theater. With Kika Markham, Jack Shepherd. (31)

THE ITALIAN GIRL by James Saunders and Iris Murdoch. Dramatization (transferred from Bristol Old Vic) of Miss Murdoch's venture into the land where sex rears several ugly heads. With Richard Pasco, Elizabeth Sellars, Jane Wenham, Timothy West, Imogen Hassall. (138+)

AERIAL FOOTBALL and THE BLACK GIRL IN SEARCH OF GOD by George Bernard Shaw, adapted by Basil Ashmore. Dramatized philosophical Shaviana. With Edith Evans, Mona Hammond, Paul Hardwick. (38)

THE IMPORTANCE OF BEING EARNEST by Oscar Wilde. All-star revival of Wilde's best-known comedy. With Isobel Jeans, Daniel Massey, John Standing, Flora Robson, Robert Eddison. (130+)

HAY FEVER by Noel Coward. All-star revival of Coward's comedy. With Celia Johnson, Roland Culver, Prunella Scales. (69)

THE WHITE LIARS and BLACK COMEDY by Peter Shaffer. Double-bill: a clairvoyant takes in a pop singer and vice-versa; the farce of a blown fuse. With Ian McKellen, Dorothy Reynolds, Angela Scoular, Robert Flemyng, Kenn Wynn. (93)

A COLLIER'S FRIDAY NIGHT by D.H. Lawrence. First of a trilogy of plays about Nottingham miners and their families, in a Lawrence season at the Royal Court Theater. With Victor Henry, Anne Dyson. (16 in repertory)

THE DAUGHTER-IN-LAW by D.H. Lawrence. Second in the same trilogy. With Judy Parfitt, Anne Dyson, Victor Henry. (23 in repertory)

THE WIDOWING OF MRS. HOLROYD by D.H. Lawrence. Third in same trilogy. With Judy Parfitt, Michael Coles, Anne Dyson. (25 in repertory)

OPEN ON SUNDAYS by Michael Landy and Ron Pember. Panorama of Jewish fun. With Selma Vaz Dias, Leonard Fenton. (36)

CANTERBURY TALES by Nevil Coghill and Martin Starkie. British musical based on

Chaucer. With Nicky Henson, Kenneth J. Warren, Wilfrid Brambell, Jessie Evans. (82+)

HADRIAN THE SEVENTH by Peter Luke. Transfer from Birmingham Repertory Theater of dramatization of Rolfe's semi-fictional anti-Papist autobiography. With Alec McCowen, Donald Eccles, Margaret Courtenay. (54+)

THE QUEEN'S HIGHLAND SERVANT by William Douglas Home. A new view of Queen Victoria's platonic yen for John Brown. With Pamela Stanley, Archie Duncan. (34+)

THE SLEEPING PRINCE by Terence Rattigan. Revival of popular hit. With Susan Hampshire, George Baker. (29+)

NATIONAL THEATER AT THE OLD VIC. Continuing schedule of repertory. *The Royal Hunt of the Sun* by Peter Shaffer. (6). *Love for Love* by William Congreve (10). *Much Ado About Nothing* by William Shakespeare (20). *A Flea in her Ear* by Feydeau, adapted by John Mortimer (24+). *The Dance of Death* by August Strindberg (27+). *Rosencrantz and Guildenstern Are Dead* by Tom Stoppard (50+)

SOME AMERICAN PLAYS PRODUCED IN LONDON

LITTLE MURDERS by Jules Feiffer. With Derek Godfrey, Brenda Bruce, Barbara Jefford. (44 in repertory)

DUTCHMAN by LeRoi Jones. With Toby Robins, Clavin Lockhart. (13)

MOURNING BECOMES ELECTRA by Eugene O'Neill. With Valerie Sarruf, John Fraser, Judy Campbell. (6)

SANCTICITY by Robert Head. With Gary Files, Tony Cyrus. (6)

AMERICAH HURRAH by Jean-Claude van Itallie. With Open Stage company. (74)

FUTZ by Rochelle Owens (25), CHICAGO by Sam Shepard (13), MELODRAMA PLAY by Sam Shepard (6), TIMES SQUARE by Leonard Melfi (6) in repertory. With the La Mama troupe.

THE OTHERS by Richard Lortz. (D) A whodunit disguised as a ghost story. With Margaret Lockwood, Donald Houston. (53)

SWEET CHARITY (musical) by Neil Simon. With John Keston, Juliet Prowse (succeeded by Gretchen Wyler). (267+)

TOM PAINE by Paul Foster. With the La Mama troupe. (34)

THE HIGH BID by Henry James. With Fenella Fielding, Edward Woodward, Laurence Hardy. (38)

CLIMB THE GREASED POLE by Vincent Longhi. (D) Determined New York atheist longshoreman's running battle with devout Catholic spouse. With Bernard Miles, Libby Morris. (30)

THE TWO-CHARACTER PLAY by Tennessee Williams. Theater of Panic drama of siblings marooned backstage. With Peter Wyngarde, Mary Ure. (24)

YOU'RE A GOOD MAN CHARLIE BROWN (musical) by Clark Gesner. With David Rhys Andersen, Gene Kidwell. (130)

COMPLEXIONS by Jan Quackenbush. (D) A whore spills out her heart. With Muriel Gantry. (53)

CABARET (musical) by Joe Masteroff. With Judi Dench, Barry Dennen, Peter Sallis, Lila Kedrova. (107+)

THE BORDER by Jan Quackenbush. One-acter about an escaping refugee and a border guard. With Maggie Jordan. (24)

COME ON KIDS, LET'S GO TO SLEEP by Benedict Yahya. (D) One-acter about a modern Good Samaritan. With Tony Crerar. (18)

STARING AT THE SUN by Alfred Aitkens. (D) Battle of the generations in New England. With Joan Miller, Andrew Ray, Robert Ayres. (21)

THE OUTCRY by Henry James. With Helen Christie, Kenneth Farrington. (18)

THE DUEL by Jack Holton Dell, adapted from Chekhov's short story. (D) With Peter Wyngarde, Michael Bryant, James Hayter, Nyree Dawn Porter. (22)

HOME FREE! and THE MADNESS OF LADY BRIGHT by Lanford Wilson. With the American Theater Project company. (19)

MAN OF LA MANCHA (musical) by Dale Wasserman. With Keith Michell, Joan Diener. (43+)

I DO! I DO! (musical) by Tom Jones. With Ian Carmichael, Anne Rogers. (16+)

CINDY by Johnny Bradon. With Hy Hazell, Avril Angers, Geraldine Morrow. (5+)

SOME FOREIGN PLAYS PRODUCED IN LONDON

BEWARE OF THE DOG by Gabriel Arout. With John Neville, Ann Bell. (45)

GHOSTS by Henrik Ibsen. With Peggy Ashcroft, John Castle. (53 in repertory)

THREE SISTERS by Anton Chekhov. With Sheila Reid, Joan Plowright, Robert Stephens, Louise Purnell, Derek Jacobi. (51+ in repertory)

CLOPE by Robert Pinget. With Timothy Bateson, Bee Duffel. (12)

CYRANO DE BERGERAC by Edmond Rostand. With David Buck, Christopher Gable, Gabrielle Drake. (46)

SIGN HERE, PLEASE (adapted from THE DAY OFF) by Valentin Katayev. With Peter Bayliss, Moyra Fraser. (28)

THE SCHOOL FOR WIVES by Molière. With Jack Tweddle, Penny Jones. (13)

NATHAN THE WISE by Gottfried Ephraim Lessing. With Maurice Denham, June Ritchie, William Dexter. (43)

PHILADELPHIA, HERE I COME! by Brian Friel. With Patrick Redford, Donal Donnelly. (61)

THE CRIMINALS by José Triana. (D) With Brenda Bruce, Susan Fleetwood, Barrie Ingham. (18 in repertory)

THE PUBLIC PROSECUTOR by Georgi Djagarov, adapted by C.P. Snow and Pamela Hansford-Johnson. With Glyn Owen, Bernard Lloyd. (21)

THE CHERRY ORCHARD by Anton Chekhov. Transfer of 1967 Edingurgh Festival production. With Lila Kedrova, Patrick Wymark, Terry Scully. (53)

BUROCTOPUS and QUOTIDIANS by René Tholy. With Ioan Meredith, Christopher Guinee, Matyelock Gibbs. (16)

MARYA by Isaac Babel. (D) With Diane Cilento, Niall MacGinnis, Elizabeth Bell. (25)

TARTUFFE by Molière, adapted by Richard Wilbur. With John Gielgud, Robert Stephens, Joan Plowright. (35+ in repertory)

THE LAUNDRY by David Guerdon. With Valerie Sarruf, Sandor Eles. (12)

PRECIOUS MOMENTS FROM THE FAMILY ALBUM TO PROVIDE YOU WITH COMFORT IN THE LONG YEARS TO COME by Naftali Yavin. (D) Set pictures of traditional family life in present day society. With Heinz Bernard, Mary Herbert, Judy Liebert. (12)

THE DRAGON by Yevgeni Schwartz. With Victor Henry, Elizabeth Bell, Arthur Lowe. (38)

LECTURE TO AN ACADEMY by Franz Kafka. With Tutte Lemkow. (58+)

THE VERY LONG LIFE OF TOLA MANOILOVICH by Moma Dimic. (D) With Tutte Lemkow. (48)

THE FARCE OF DEATH WHO ALMOST DIED by Michel de Ghelderode, and THE PROPOSAL by Anton Chekhov. With David Leyland, Matyelock Gibbs. (16)

OEDIPUS by Seneca. (D) Peter Brook's Theater of Ritual version. With Irene Worth, John Gielgud, Colin Blakely. (22+ in repertory)

CROSS PURPOSE (LE MALENTENDU) by Albert Camus. With Kate Binchy, Pauline Delaney, Paul Farrell. (23)

WORLD THEATER SEASON, with the Czech Balustrade Theater in *The Clowns* (6), *The Fools* (6), and *Ubu Roi* (4), the Théâtre de France in *Partage du Midi* (8), *Il Faut Passer par les Nuages* (4), and *Le Barbier de Seville* (4), the Rome Stabile Theater in *Naples by Night, Naples by Day* (8), the Dublin Abbey Theater in *The Shaughraum* (16), the Stockholm Royal Dramatic Theater in *Hedda Gabler* (8) and the Bunraku National Theater of Japan in two mixed programs (8 each).

EDWARD II by Brecht, adapted from Marlowe. With John Stride, Robert Lang, Charles Kay, Geraldine McEwan. (12+ in repertory)

IN THE PENAL SETTLEMENT by Franz Kafka. With Stephen Berkoff. (14+)

○
○
○

THE SEASON ELSEWHERE IN EUROPE

By Ossia Trilling

○
○
○

ONCE AGAIN, as I look back on the past year, it is Germany that holds the center of the stage. The eyes of the entire world were focused on the world premiere at the West Berlin Freie Volksbühne on October 9, 1967, of Rolf Hochhuth's second documentary drama, *Soldaten (Soldiers)*. This was the play that had been turned down by the board of the National Theater in London and banned by the British censor (not the last expiring gesture of an institution in its death-throes, as it turned out). Its leading character, the British wartime prime minister, Winston Churchill, was said to have been libeled in it. In fact, the play, even in the shortened version that Hans Schweikart staged in Berlin in Wilfried Minks' suggestive decors, dealt less with the speculation as to whether Churchill had plotted, or connived at a plot, to do away with the Polish premier in exile, Gen. Wladyslaw Sikorski (who was dangerously rocking the Allied boat during a crucial moment of the war against Hitler), than with the author's sincere, though naive, plea to the nations of the world to agree to restrict aerial warfare to combatants. Hochhuth's detractors had forgotten that politics had been staple theatrical fare in the theater of Germany since Schiller. Hochhuth was by no means the only writer in the German language seeking to shake the world's conscience at "man's inhumanity to man".

Like Hochhuth, who is a practising Christian, Peter Weiss, who is not, thinks of himself as a political dramatist. His most recent drama, whose forty-eight word title * can be conveniently shortened to *Vietnam Dialogue,* which is what Harry Buckwitz did in the case of his production of the documentary drama at its world premiere at the Frankfurt City Theater, is not only a rebuke but a call to action. This at least emerges from the final line of the dialogue ("The struggle goes on"). Weiss is troubled by the "credibility gap" between political acts and political deeds, and in this play he seeks to expose Western Hemisphere propaganda about Vietnam. In twenty-two scenes of

* *Discourse over the Previous History and the Long Continuing Freedom Fight in Vietnam as an Example of the Unnecessary Weaponed Battle for the Underdogs Against Those Pressing Them Under as Well as of the Attempt of the United States of America to Destroy the Causes of the Revolution*

retrospective history, he portrays two and a half centuries of duplicity and violence at the expense of an ancient land that has never known freedom from invasion or occupation. Shortly after the Frankfurt premiere, the City Theater of Rostock staged the play by giving it a far more recognizably Marxist interpretation (director: Hans Anselm Perten). Paradoxically, the succeeding version, at the East Berlin Berliner Ensemble was at once less Marxist and more esthetically stylized (director: Ruth Berghaus). It was in West Berlin, too, at the intrepid little Schaubühne am Halleschen Ufer, that Weiss's anti-colonialist satire, *The Song of the Lusitanian Bogey,* received its most esthetically satisfying production (director: Karl Paryla). An earlier play by the same author, a sort of 20th-century Morality, entitled *How Passion Was Driven out of Mr. Mockinpott,* was also first staged in Germany, at the Hanover State Theater. Using the doggerel technique of the knockabout guignol play, it depicts a Chaplinesque figure, bullied and brainwashed by present-day society, still retaining a semblance of cheerful human dignity.

The Kassel State Theater put its own spoke into the political wheel by staging the world premiere of Armand Gatti's *The Passion of General Franco* (in the teeth of protests from Franco Spain and with federal government encouragement), a play that revealed the author's preoccupation with the fate of the victims and not of the upholders of fascism. In East Berlin two productions at the Deutsches Theater tackled the problem of totalitarianism: Rolf Schneider's *Trial at Nuremberg* (director: Wolfgang Heinz) sought to teach that "war crimes are repeatable" by a simple re-staging in miniature of the famous trial of Nazi criminals of 1945; Friedbold Bauer's *Baran* was the poetic tragedy of a Polish slave-laborer in Hitler Germany. A third play, Horst Salomon's *A Layabout* was more of a demonstration of a brilliant director's way with thin material than anything else. Benno Besson, the director in question, capped this rollicking comedy of contemporary East German life with a masterly new production of Molière's *Don Juan* (at the same theater) in which Reimar Joh. Bauer played the title role of a bombastic playboy of the 1960s, and Rolf Ludwig gave the finest performance of his career as the poor, bedraggled devil, Sganarelle, who has to serve a rakish master—not quite a political, but a thoroughgoing contemporary interpretation.

Two modern authors with political plays behind them were Hans Günther Michelsen and Martin Walser. Heinrich Koch staged the former's *Frau L* in Frankfurt: it mingles recollection of things past with things present, as in his previous work, but the political background is nonexistent. In Munich Fritz Kortner added another directorial feather to his cap with Walser's *Chamber War,* a blow below the belt at middle-class hypocrisy, in terms of the sex war, but without any verifiable social or political roots. Herbert Asmodi's *Die and Yet Live,* which Peter Palitzsch staged with pomp and ceremony in Stuttgart, belonged to the same category, though the German version of *MacBird,* at the same theater, presented as a satirical revue with song and dance, pleased the public rather more. Palitzsch, a former Brecht pupil, and newly appointed manager of the drama department at the Stuttgart State Theater, has given it a new and exciting profile and turned it into one of West Germany's most talked-of playhouses. In this he has been helped by the imaginative settings of guest designer Wilfried Minks, those for Babel's *Maria* and Chekhov's *The Cherry Orchard* (guest-director: Peter Zadek) being the most memorable.

Zadek, after winning an enviable reputation in Bremen, went over to free-lance directing, but not before bequeathing to Bremen City Theater a production of *Measure for Measure* (adapted by Martin Sperr) that had all the outrageous marks of an American far-out off-off-Broadway experimental drama. It must have made Shakespeare turn in his grave, though it delighted audiences at various festivals throughout Europe. In it, Mistress Overdone, played by a hysterically falsetto-voiced male, supplants the Duke and sows havoc throughout the land. Sperr disowned it officially, preferring an alliance with more orthodox fare, like his own *Tales of Landshut,* in Munich, with its skilled psychological portrayal of the provincial bourgeoisie—the second member of a trilogy about the social and political remnants of Nazi ideology in the Federal Republic. A similar theme informed Jochen Ziem's second contribution to the West Berlin Schiller Studio Theater's politically-conscious repertory, entitled *News from the Provinces.* Among the highlights at the Schiller were Martin Held's powerfully acted Player in *Rosencrantz and Guildenstern Are Dead,* Kortner's idiosyncratic handling of *The Tempest,* Leonard Steckel's profoundly moving Gregory Solomon in Arthur Miller's *The Price* (on the Schiller's small stage, the Schlosspark), and Rumanian guest director Liviu Ciulei's eye-catching production of *Danton's Death,* in which the crowd was promoted to protagonist.

Zurich was the scene of a theatrical scandal surrounding the world premiere of Max Frisch's *Biography,* an extremely deft translation into dramatic terms of the main preoccupation of the author's novels, that of identity. Shaped like a theatrical rehearsal, in which an Olympian overseer stage manages the events of the drama, the complex relations of a university professor and his wife are played over and over again, since each time the protagonist is given a free choice to change any given moment of his life. Entrusted by Leopold Lindtberg, the theater's manager, to a guest director (Rudolf Noelte), the play became gradually unrecognizable in rehearsal, until Frisch's patience and the director both went. Lindtberg stepped into the breach, making a fine job of an intelligent (though somewhat superficial) intellectual tragicomedy for the times. In Vienna, at the Burgtheater, the self-exiled Austrian dramatist Fritz Hochwalder had his much-discussed Eurovision TV drama about a Nazi war criminal in occupied Holland, entitled *The Command,* staged and acted with that theater's usual and exemplary finesse. Here, too, Ewald Balser impressed with his poetic vision of the second-hand dealer in the Miller play, by contrast with Peter Pasetti's more realistic version in Munich, or again with Mathias Wieman's in Zurich, which failed artistically because a caricature of the comic stage-Jew, all the more so in the ironic light of the actor's well-known quondam pro-Nazi sympathies.

Once again, the German-speaking theater has stolen the year's theatrical thunder and occupied a great part of the space allotted to me. This situation looks like being repeated annually, though the French theater, with its growing number of provincial Arts Centers and Parisian peripheral playhouses, is at last taking itself as seriously as the German. It was in Toulouse that Armand Gatti's passionate plea against the horrors of the Vietnam War *(V for Vietnam)* saw the light of day, before guesting for a month at the Theatre de L'Est Parisien. And even the other guest production at the T.E.P., Aimé Césaire's poetically inspired though over-writtten near-documentary of the martyrdom of Lumumba, entitled *A Spell in the Congo* (director: Jean-Marie Serreau), was first performed at the Venice Festival by the visiting company. Horror, violence, and hatred found their way from the streets onto the stage. The signal for this was given by the Cuban players from Havana in José Triana's *The Criminals,* a play that astonished audiences at the Theater of the Nations and in many corners of Europe, wherever these gifted actors toured, though it confined itself to a narrow family circle and used Freudian rather than Marxist symbols to make its points. The same emotions informed Ariane Mnouchkine's circus-ring production of *A Midsummer Night's Dream,* that clearly took its cue from Jan Kott and peopled the stage with imbecilic monsters. Even if one disagreed with it, it was brilliantly done.

More ritualistic violence in Seneca's *Medea* at the Théâtre de France contrasted nicely with the prettifying sentimentality of Goethe's *The Triumph of Sensibility* on the same stage, both transferred from the Avignon Festival, and each directed in totally disparate idioms by Jorge Lavelli, a tribute to his versatility, if nothing else. Here Barrault revived *Golden Head* as homage to Claudel in his centenary year, just as at the Comédie Française Maurice Escande invited Jean-Marie Serreau to try his hand at *The Hostage,* a difficult play that he successfully enlivened with an electronic display (designer: Claude Lemaire) that was at least calculated to keep Morpheus at bay. The other two main attractions at Barrault's theater were Giorgio De Lullo's carbon-copy production of Pirandello's *The Rules of the Game* (distinguishable from the Italian version only by the Gallicism of the performances), and Edward Albee's *A Delicate Balance,* which lent itself curiously well to the Gallic temperament.

At the Théâtre National Populaire, Brecht's *The Mother* was given a faithfully Brechtian production by guest-director Jacques Rosner (from Planchon's troupe), while Georges Wilson's own performance as an unscrupulous ex-Nazi in Martin Walser's *The Rabbit Race* on the small stage made a perfect foil to Jacques Dufilho, in a strangely haunting performance of the unsexed, simple-minded victim of German Nazism, Alois Gruber. Michael Cacoyannis, in casting two untried newcomers (Robert Benoit and the French Canadian Francine Racette) in the leads of his second guest production at the T.N.P. of *Romeo and Juliet* (decor: Jacques Le Marquet), stacked the cards against himself and in favor of Jean-Pierre Cassel's boisterous Mercutio, who alongside Lise Delamare as the Nurse and Jacques Mauclair as Friar Laurence put the lovers of Verona completely in the shade.

The Boulevard continued to attract its dwindling audiences with catchpenny fare, including masses of revivals, ranging from Feydeau and Labiche to Guitry and Achard. Jean Meyer, having once failed to secure the rights of Henry de Montherlant's *The City Whose Prince Is a Child* for the Comédie Française, now staged it, 16 years later, at his own private theater, with, it must be said, considerable tact, considering the ambivalence of the subject matter: the clash of wills in a Jesuit school, and the unmentionable motives that animate the teachers and their charges. A delicate theme, but hardly as shocking today as, say, Jean Cau's *Les Yeux Crevés,* a title that implies both "plain-faced" and "clueless", and rings the changes on the love-hatred between an elderly homosexual, his wife and their young lodger.

Three new plays in French, two by newcomers, rate a special mention. Jean-Claude Grumberg won the Paris critics' award for his *Tomorrow a Window with a View on the Street,* in which typically apathetic French citizens look out from the seeming security of their apartment windows on the disasters taking place, symbolically, on the boulevard below. René Ehni's *What Are You Doing in November?* is bold enough to mock ineffectual left-wing eggheads and parlor radicals with a rarely-seen, insouciant dramatic eloquence, and a bitter venom not heard on a European stage since *Look Back in Anger.* The third play, premiered at the French-speaking Belgian National Theater in Brussels is Paul Willems' *The City in Sail,* which won the 1966 Marzotto Prize. It is set in Antwerp and is a poetic fantasy about unfulfilled and deceptive dreams.

The 1968 Marzotto Prize was awarded to Natalia Ginsburg's *The Advertisement,* a play not staged publicly during this season, though an earlier play, *The Secretary,* by the same author, aroused some interest. Most of the new plays in Italy appeared too parochial, with the possible exception of Giancarlo Sbragia's *The June Affair,* which dealt with the murder of Matteotti by the *fascisti* and was one of two plays that for the first time put Mussolini on the stage. Franco Zeffirelli's production of *A Delicate Balance* benefited from this director's scenic flair and had a great performance by Sarah Ferrati as Agnes. During this time, the Italian stage welcomed back after too long an absence its onetime matinee idol Vittorio Gassman in an anti-heroic Brechtian *Richard III.* The Bologna City Theater and the Milan Piccolo combined forces to mount a version of *Henry V* in a sports arena, using live TV among its technical aids to understanding—too ambitious an undertaking, as it proved, not least when compared with the precision and effectiveness of Raffaelle Maiello's staging of *Marat/Sade* at the Piccolo. Luigi Squarzina's staging of *The Bacchae* in Genoa and Gianfranco de Bosio's of *The Ruzzante Dialogues* (just before resigning as the Turin City Theater's manager) helped to give a special color to an unusually colorless Italian theater year.

Apart from a stylish double bill (of Molière's *School for Wives* and *Critique of a School for Wives*) at the Royal Dramatic Theater, Ingmar Bergman's farewell to the stage seems to have been meant seriously. It was left to Alf Sjöberg to win the directorial honors in Stockholm with his finest and most perceptive Brechtian production to date, that of the Brecht adaptation of Lenz's *The Tutor,* about an impoverished 18th-century teacher who is humiliated by the gentry who employ him and tempted by fleshly instincts beyond his control, until he is forced to unman himself in self-protection. The revival of *The Dance of Death,* at the same theater, was notable for Gunilla Palmstierna-Weiss's sensitive and largely successful attempt to provide a seemingly naturalistic drama with a virtually abstract setting. But it was not all esthetic experience for its own sake in Sweden, despite the curiously estheticized garb in which the American-born guest director from London, Charles Marowitz, tried to dress his *Hamlet* in Gothenburg. The London anti-Vietnam War play *Us,* was refitted by Geoffrey Reeves, who had worked with Peter Brook on it, for the Royal Dramatic's small stage and even incorporated a TV interview with the first G.I. deserter accorded official political asylum by the Swedish government. The City Theater had a telling production of *Viet Rock* on view. The Royal Theater in Copenhagen staged Klaus Rifbjerg's third drama, entitled *Wax,* a picture of despondent disillusionment with the bourgeois way of life, culminating in a scene of wanton destruction.

Disillusionment is not a privilege of bourgeois writers. East Europeans have much to be angry and despondent about. Yet a new wind of change has been blowing and its effects have been chiefly felt in Czechoslovakia and in Rumania. In Poland, by contrast, what seems to me to be worth recording is not what has been done on the Warsaw stage, so much as what has been undone or not done. I am referring to the ban on Kazimierz Dejmek's production at the National Theater of Mickiewicz's classical drama *Forefathers' Eve,* interpreted by the powers that be as anti-Soviet in part, after running for several weeks unmolested; to the refusal of the same powers to lift the ban on Witkiewicz's anti-totalitarian farce of the 1920s, *Gynbal Wahazar,* though it was rehearsed and ready to open; to the continued ban on Ireneusz Iredynski's latest play *Farewell, Judas,* whose hero is cursed with a traitor's name and fate, and which had to have its world premiere given in Salzburg in Austria, while its author languishes in a Polish jail. I reported last year how Anatoli Efros had been sacked from the Lenin Komsomol Theater in Moscow for not heeding official criticism. He was, however, given the smaller Theater of Drama, on the "Malaya Bronnaya", in its place, and with twelve of his original actors staged a superb new production of Chekhov's *Three Sisters,* which brought the town running to his theater but earned him more official opprobrium (reflected in a prolonged press controversy, which is still continuing as of this writing) from those who accused him of betraying Chekhov, because he had stressed the sadness and futility of the ambiance and not its optimism, in a production that was outstanding for its anti-naturalism. At the Sovremennik, Oleg Yefremov joined in the celebration of the 50th anniversary of the Russian Revolution by completing his revolutionary trilogy with Mikhail Shatrin's much-praised *The Bolsheviks.* Even the veteran directors were able to hold their own: Yuri Zavadsky revived Bill-Belotserkovsky's *Storm,* at the Mossoviet Theater, in a stylized new production without decor, costumes or makeup; at the Vakhtangov, Ruben Simonov staged Leonid Zorin's *Warsaw Melody,* a two-character romance (delicately acted by Yulia Borisova and Mikhail Ulianov) about a Pole and a Russian girl whose love is nipped in the bud in 1947 by an unfeeling Soviet bureaucracy but who meet again 10 years later, married and greatly changed; a touchingly naive entertainment which the company also toured in Western Europe.

That Prague and Bucharest are looking westward today is only half the truth. They have shaken off the ideological and esthetic shackles of that much-abused and misleading term "Socialist Realism", without either forgoing their socialism or their own particular sense of what is real in the theater. The Balustrade Theater of Prague staged Vaclav Havel's latest satirical comedy, *The Increasing Impossibility of Keeping One's Mind on One's Work,* about a man who cannot make up his mind between three women: these are interchangeable, it seems, and the entire action is built on a flexible time-scale and, as in Havel's other works, bureaucratic idiocy is pilloried. Otomar Krejca, manager of the Gate Theater, after putting on a charming composite melodrama comprising two Nestroy farces (as *The Rope with a Single End*), staged Jozef Topol's ceremonially anti-totalitarian *The End of the Carnival* at the Burgtheater in neighboring Vienna with much *éclat.* Jan Grossman, too, was finally allowed, nay, encouraged to go abroad and put on a *Threepenny Opera* in Munich that carried his specific esthetic signature. Directed by him in Josef Svoboda's self-changing decors, Brecht's satire was updated into the field of present-day big business, prostitution and gambling, a milieu that spawned the welfare-state phenomena of the Profumo and similar scandals.

These are only a few of the directors from the East who regularly work in the West. Liviu Ciulei, manager of the Bucharest City Theater, won golden opinions for his work both in Berlin and in Göttingen, and his positive contribution to theater art has been no less marked at home. His *Macbeth* significantly attempted to gain for a difficult tragedy a measure of contemporary acceptability, partly by putting the witches into modern dress and presenting them as camp followers of Macbeth's army, and partly by designing a flexible permanent timbered setting that allows the Shakespearean action to unfold without pause. This set also did service for *Julius Caesar* which a 24-year-old director, Andrei Sherban, lifted out of ancient Rome and set in a timeless, barbaric environment, much to the consternation of the traditionalists. The young directors are setting the tone everywhere in Rumania. Lucian Pentilie's hilarious and fast-moving version of *The Cherry Orchard,* at the same theater, also provoked dissent, but fully answered the play's comedic demands. Dinu Cernescu, taking a leaf out of the Western tradition of the Theater of Cruelty and Panic, staged de Ghelderode's *Escorial* with tremendous passion at the Nottara Theater, where Horia Lovinescu's historical drama *Petru Raresh* offers a blend of political criticism and folklore ritualism. Lucian Penciulescu's epic adaptation, directed by himself with Brechtian subtlety, of Mihail Sadoveanu's famous novel *The Hatchet* at the Little Theater followed on a scarifyingly realistic production of *Tango.* At Radu Beligan's Comedy Theater, social criticism and comedy rub shoulders, notably in the shape of the imaginative productions by David Esrig of Shakespeare, and the anti-bourgeois satire by the octogenarian surrealist dramatist Gheorghe Ciprian, *The Duck's Head,* which was as popular at home as when taken to the Venice Festival.

Highlights of the Paris Season

Selected and compiled by Ossia Trilling

OUTSTANDING PERFORMANCES

Gérard Lartigau
as Camille Chandebise in
A Flea in Her Ear

Louis Seigner
as The Coachman in
The Brisbane Emigrant

Raymond Devos
as Himself in
Extra Muros

Madeleine Renaud
as Agnès in
A Delicate Balance

Simone Valère
as Julia in
A Delicate Balance

Pierre Vaneck
as Henry Higgins in
Pygmalion

Gabriel Cattand
as Guido in
The Rules of the Game

Michel Bouquet
as Stanley in
The Birthday Party

Paul Guers
as L'Abbé de Prats in
The City Whose Prince Is a Boy

Colette Renard
as Irma in
Irma la Douce

Jean-Paul Roussillon
as Mascarille in
The Physician in Spite of Himself

Marie Bell
as Barbara in
Eyes Plucked Out

Françoise Seigner
as Nérine in
The Gambler

Eléonore Hirt
as Pelagia Vlassova in
The Mother

Jacques Dufilho
as Alois Grubel in
The Rabbit Race

OUTSTANDING DIRECTORS

Giorgio De Lullo
The Rules of the Game

Victor Garcia
The Automobile Graveyard

Ariane Mnouchkine
A Midsummer Night's Dream

OUTSTANDING DESIGNERS

Victor Garcia, Michel Launay, Nestor de Arzadu
The Automobile Graveyard

Claude Lemaire
The Hostage

Jacques Le Marquet
The Rabbit Race

OUTSTANDING NEW FRENCH PLAYS

(D)—Playwright's Paris debut

V COMME VIETNAM (V for Vietnam) by Armand Gatti. Anti-Vietnam-War documentary. With the Ensemble of the Grenier de Toulouse.

L'ARME BLANCHE (The White Weapon) by Victor Haim. (D) The pricking conscience of a soldier from a dirty war returning. With Katharina Renn, André Cellier.

UNE SAISON AU CONGO (A Spell in the Congo) by Aimé Césaire. The rise and fall of Patrice Lumumba. With Bachir Touré, Moro Bitty, Jean-Marie Serreau.

LA BUTTE DE SATORY (Satory Hilltop) by Pierre Halet. The tragic fall of Capt. Louis Rossel, supporter of the Paris Commune. With Jean-Pierre Miquel.

LA JOURNÉE D'UNE RÊVEUSE (A Day in a Girl's Dreams) by Copi. (D) A woman relives her past in the space of 24 hours. With Emmanuelle Riva, Gilles Segal, Juliette Villard.

MONSIEUR FUGUE OU LE MAL DE TERRE (Mr. Fugue or Earth-Sickness) by Liliane Atlan. (D) The heroic story of Professor Korczak and the doomed Jewish children. With the Ensemble of the Comédie de St. Etienne.

LA VILLE DONT LE PRINCE EST UN ENFANT (The City Whose Prince Is a Child) by Henry de Montherlant. Drama of buried passions in a Jesuit College. With Paul Guers, Didier Haudepin, Jean Deschamps.

LE CIMETIÈRE DES VOITURES (The Automobile Graveyard) by Fernando Arrabal. This and other Arrabal dramas provide the framework for an evening of Theater of Panic. With Jean-Paul Drouot, Michèle Oppenot.

LE SOLEIL DES EAUX (The Sun of the Waters) by René Char. First performance of a 50-year-old drama of Provençal fishermen, who wreck a sluice to safeguard their livelihoods. With Jean-Claude Giraud, Martine Redon.

DEMAIN UNE FENÊTRE SUR RUE (Tomorrow a Window with a View on the Street) by Jean-Claude Grumberg. (D) Prize-winning first play about bourgeois apathy in a troubled world. With Marcel Cuvelier, Michèle Moretti.

LES TREIZE SOLEILS DE LA RUE SAINT-BLAISE (The Thirteen Suns of the Rue Saint-Blaise) by Armand Gatti. The audience itself, as it were, provides the discussion on local affairs. With Maurice Barrier, Arlette Téphany.

QUE FEREZ-VOUS EN NOVEMBRE? (What Are You Doing in November?) by René Ehni. (D) The hot air spouted by feckless intellectuals and drifting Bohemians. With André Cellier, Isabelle Ehni.

LIMITED RUNS OF INTERESTING NEW FRENCH PLAYS

LES GIRAFES (The Giraffes) by Richard Bohringer. (D) Five youngsters imagine their world peopled by giraffes. With Jacques Zanetti, Stéphane Bony.

LES BOUQUINISTES (The Bookstall Keepers) by Antoine Tudal. (D) Two quayside booksellers discuss an angler's identity. With Roger Trapp, Jean Lescot.

JEUX POUR LE CIEL (Games for Heaven) by Etienne Bor. (D) An unfulfilled woman dreams of happiness. With Florence Biot.

LES ROSENBERG (The Rosenbergs) by Alain Decaux. Documentary seeking to prove the executed American spies innocent. With Silvia Montfort, Bernard Rousselet, François Darbon, Charles Denner.

OPÉRA POUR UN TYRAN (Opera for a Tyrant) by Henri-François Rey. (D) The rise and fall of a modern dictator. With Bernard Noël, François Maistre, Alain Mottet.

LE PAIN SEC (Dry Bread) and AKARA (Akara) by Romain Weingarten. Two short plays: in the first, two men, played by a single actor, accuse each other of murder; in the second, first staged in 1948, a woman denounces the man she loves. With Roger Jacquet, Juliette Villard, Michel Subor.

DES PETITS BONSHOMMES DANS DU PAPIER JOURNAL (Little Paper Cut-Out Dolls) by Jean-Claude Darnal. A voguish cameraman and a cover girl take it out on a puffed-up couple. With Pascale Roberts, Pierre Hatet, Uta Taeger.

YES PEUT-ÊTRE (Yes, Maybe) and LE SHAGA (The Shaga) by Marguerite Duras. Two one-acters, one about an atomized desert, the other about a paralysed Japanese G.I. With Claire Deluca, Marie-Ange Dutheil, René Erouk.

VOLTIGE (Slack-Rope) by Philippe Hériat. A returned pilot, reported missing, catches up on his legend. With Jeanne Colletin, Marcelle Ranson.

LA POUDRE DE L'INTELLIGENCE (The Powder That Makes You Clever) by Kateb Yacine. Satirical treatment of the classical revenge theme in modern terms. With Boudgema Bouhaha, Françoise Rive.

DIALOGUES DES COURTISANES (Courtesan Dialogues) by Dimitri Koliatos. (D) Dramatization of Lucian's *Dialogues* with some present-day allusions. With Arlette Baumann, Claude Lougier.

LA BAYE (The Bay) by Philippe Adrien. (D) Curious encounter of two stereotyped families at a seaboard resort. With Suzanne Flon, Yves Robert.

LE GRAND CÉRÉMONIAL (The Great Ceremonial) by Fernando Arrabal. A typical Arrabalesque exercise in the Theater of Panic. With Michelle Marquais, Marie Hermès, Gérard Desarthe.

POPULAR ATTRACTIONS

LE PAIN DES JULES (The Pimps' Bread) by Ange Bastiani. The rivalry of two procurers for the love of their kept woman. With Pierre Gatineau, Jean Luisi, Evy Cavallero.

LES ESCROCS DE MADAME (Her Crooked Winnings) by Frédéric Valmain and Dominique Nohain. How to make a million, tax-free. With Raymond Bussières, Dominique Nohain.

FRÉDÉRIC by Robert Lamoureux. A nuclear scientist with a phenomenal memory is kidnaped by a foreign power. With the author, Jacqueline Noëlle.

QUARANTE CARATS (40 Carats) by Pierre Barillet and Jean-Pierre Gredy. Can a 40-year-old mother marry a man the same age as her 20-year-old daughter, and what does grandma make of it all? With Jacqueline Gauthier, Philippe Etesse.

INTERDIT AU PUBLIC (No Entry) by Jean Marsan. Up-dated version of 20-year-old backstage drama about Hervé, the actor. With Maria Pacome, Jean Le Poulain.

EXTRA MUROS by Raymond Devos. (D) A dramatist projects his Protean personality into five distinct disguises. With the author, Paul Prébost, Arlette Didier.

COPAINS CLOPANT (Palsie-Walsies) by Christian Kursner. A pop singer's irruption into a group of teenagers affects their fortunes profoundly. With the author, André Bezu, Yvon Dibié, Dominique Prado.

PIC ET PIOCHE (Pick and Mattock) by Raymond Vincy. Musical comedy about a highly original treasure hunt. With Annie Cordy, Darry Cowl (who wrote the music).

SAINT DUPONT by Marcel Mithois. Three failures take their revenge on the women who failed them. With Henri Virlojeux, Yvonne Clech.

L'OEUF (The Egg) by Félicien Marceau. Revival of cynical blackmailing comedy hit. With Jacques Duby, Alain Mottet.

L'ÔTAGE (The Hostage) by Paul Claudel. Centenary revival of the famous Catholic historical drama. With Jacques Toja, Christine Fersen, François Chaumette.

QUOAT-QUOAT by Jacques Audiberti. Revival of 22-year-old romantic drama of a Mexico-bound adventurer. With Colette Bergé, Louis Arbessier.

LES CHEMINS DE FER (The Railroads) by Labiche. Revival of famous old farce. With Jacques Duby, Robert Vattier.

LA PUCE À L'OREILLE (A Flea in Her Ear) by Feydeau. Revival of famous old farce. With Jean-Claude Brialy, Micheline Presle, Gérard Lartigau.

LES SUISSES (The Switzers) by Aristide Bréal. Two Swiss mercenaries find their way home after the French Revolution. With Jacques Fabbri, André Gille.

QUI VOUS SAVEZ (You Know Who) by and with Henri Tisot, and BOUDU SAUVÉ DES EAUX (Boudu Rescued from a Watery Grave) by René Fauchoix. Tisot's impersonation of a famous head of state, followed by a revival of a drama about a troublesome tramp. With Henri Tisot, Micheline Luccioni.

LE GADGET (The Gadget) by Alexandre Rivemale. A secret lethal weapon gives unlimited powers to its possessors. With Jean-Pierre Darras, Amarande, André Thorent.

LE TRUFFATOR (The Con Man) by Jean Canolle. A wily Neapolitan guide gives his tourists a taste of what they really want. With Pierre Fresnay, Yvonne Clech.

L'AMOUR PROPRE (Vanity) by Marc Camoletti. A couple's vanity trips them up all along the line. With Philippe Nicaud, Claude Gensac.

DÉSIRÉ and LE RENARD et LA GRENOUILLE (The Fox and the Frog) by Sacha Guitry. Reival of 40-year-old comedy about a susceptible butler, and a curtain-dropper about a cocotte. With Robert Lamoureux, Marie Daems, Monique Tarbès.

LES YEUX CREVÉS (Eyes Plucked Out) by Jean Cau. Untranslatable punning title alludes to an Oedipal triangular drama and the destruction of a corrupt youth by a decadent couple. With Marie Bell, Jacques Dacqmine, Alain Delon.

CHÂTEAU EN SUÈDE (Castle in Sweden) by Françoise Sagan. Revival of author's hit drama of cardboard passions. With Francine Bergé, Dominique Rozan.

LA SEMAINE DE LUBECK (The Week in Lubeck) by Marc Fontenay. A German trio in the last week of Hitler's war. With Henri Serre, Javotte Lehmann, Nicole Norden.

FIN DE PARTIE (Endgame) by Samuel Beckett. Revival of world-famous 11-year-old black comedy. With Roger Blin, André Julien.

SOME AMERICAN PLAYS PRODUCED IN PARIS

LOVE IN E FLAT by Norman Krasna. With Jacques Fabbri, Geneviève Fontanel.

MYSTERIES AND SMALLER PIECES by and with the Ensemble of the Living Theater.

A DELICATE BALANCE by Edward Albee. With Madeleine Renaud, Claude Dauphin, Simone Valère, Edwige Feuillère.

THE FANTASTICKS musical with book and lyrics by Tom Jones, music by Harvey Schmidt. With Géraldine, Daniel Lambo.

JEU D'ENFANTS (Childs' Play) and SPECTACLE by Carol Bernstein. (D) World première of two one-acters about the American way of life. With François Maistre, Pascale de Boysson.

OUR TOWN by Thornton Wilder. With Douchka, Richard Leduc.

ROOM SERVICE by John Murray and Allen Boretz. With Francis Blanche, Jacques Jouanneau.

DEAR LIAR by Jerome Kilty (in English). With Barbara Sommers, Lee Payant.

CHICAGO by Sam Shepard, and FUNNY HOUSE OF A NEGRO by Adrienne Kennedy. With Dominique Paturel, Jean-Pierre Granval, Toto Bissainthe.

SOME OTHER FOREIGN PLAYS PRODUCED IN PARIS

THEATER OF THE NATIONS SEASON included, in 1967, the Milan Piccolo's production of *The Giants of the Mountain,* the Prague Balustrade Theater's *The Trial,* and the Havana Studio Theater's *The Criminals;* and, in 1968, the Royal Shakespeare Company's *All's Well that Ends Well.*

THE REPULSE by Rafael Alberti. With the Ensemble of the Comédie de la Loire.

THE PROMISE by Aleksei Arbuzov. With Colette Castel, Claude Giraud, Philippe Avron.

ROSENCRANTZ AND GUILDENSTERN ARE DEAD by Tom Stoppard. With Bernard Fresson, Michel Lonsdale.

PYGMALION by George Bernard Shaw. With Pierre Vaneck, Caroline Cellier.

THE TAMING OF THE SHREW by William Shakespeare. With Dora Doll, Pierre Hatet.

HALFWAY UP THE TREE by Peter Ustinov. With Pierre Dux, Eléonore Hirt.

ADDRESS TO AN ACADEMY by Franz Kafka. With Paul Le Person.

THE WAY OF THE WORLD by William Congreve. With Mary Marquet, Claude Titre, Olivier Hussenot, Geneviève Brunet.

A SCENT OF FLOWERS by James Saunders. With Maria Machado, Jean-Marc Tennberg.

THE GHOST SONATA by August Strindberg. With Marcel Cuvelier, Tania Balachova, Gregory Chmara.

KING HUNGER by Leonid Andreyev. World première. With Claude Barey, Danielle Chinsky.

STIENZ by Hans Günter Michelsen. With Pierre Baton, Josine Comellais.

THE BIRTHDAY PARTY by Harold Pinter. With Michel Bouquet, Madeleine Barbulée.

ANTIGONE by Bertolt Brecht. With the Ensemble of the Living Theater.

THE GOVERNMENT INSPECTOR by Nikolai Gogol. With Gilles Guillot, Jean Dasté and the Ensemble of the Comédie de St. Etienne.

ARLECCHINO, SERVITORE DI DUE PADRONI by Goldoni. With the Ensemble of the Milan Piccolo.

HARLEQUIN, SERVANT OF TWO MASTERS, by Goldoni. With the Ensemble of the Compagnie de la Contrescarpe.

STAIRCASE by Charles Dyer. With Paul Meurisse, Daniel Ivernel.

AFTER THE RAIN by John Bowen. With Bernard Noël, Michel de Ré.

THE BRISBANE EMIGRANT by Georges Schéhadé. With Louis Seigner, Claude Winter.

BLACK COMEDY by Peter Shaffer. With Jean-Pierre Cassel, Perrette Pradier, Raymond Gérôme.

ENRICO IV by Luigi Pirandello. With Sacha Pitoëff, Luce Garcia-Ville.

THE RULES OF THE GAME by Luigi Pirandello. With Jean Desailly, Gabriel Cattand, Françoise Brion.

THE MOTHER by Bertolt Brecht. With Eléonore Hirt.

VASA ZHELEZNOVA by Maxim Gorki. With Micheline Genty.

YOU CAN'T BE SURE OF ANYTHING by Luigi Pirandello. With Dominique Vilar, Henri Garcin.

BIEDERMANN AND THE FIREBUGS by Max Frisch. With Jean Parédès, Etienne Bierry, Hélène Sauvaneix.

DESIGN FOR LIVING by Noel Coward. With Jacqueline Ricard, Jacques Clancy.

A MIDSUMMER NIGHT'S DREAM by William Shakespeare. With René Patrignani, Germinal Casado, Urusula Kübler.

THE RABBIT RACE by Martin Walser. With Georges Wilson, Jacques Dufilho.

THE ASTRAKHAN COAT by Pauline Macaulay. With Daniel Emilfork, Françoise Domer.

THE FORENOON OF A LETTERED MAN and LADY MACBETH, adapted by Tania Balachova from Chekhov. With Marc Eyraud, Tania Balachova, Sylvie Joly.

THE SOLDIERS by Jakob Michael Reinhold Lenz. With Melly Tourzoul, Jacques Dubary, Jacques Seiler.

THE TRIUMPH OF SENSIBILITY by Wolfgang von Goethe. With Alain Mottet, Françoise Brion, Philippe Avron.

ROMEO AND JULIET by William Shakespeare. With Robert Benoit, Francine Racette, Lise Delamare.

PUSS IN BOOTS by Ludwig Tieck. With Wolfram Mehring.

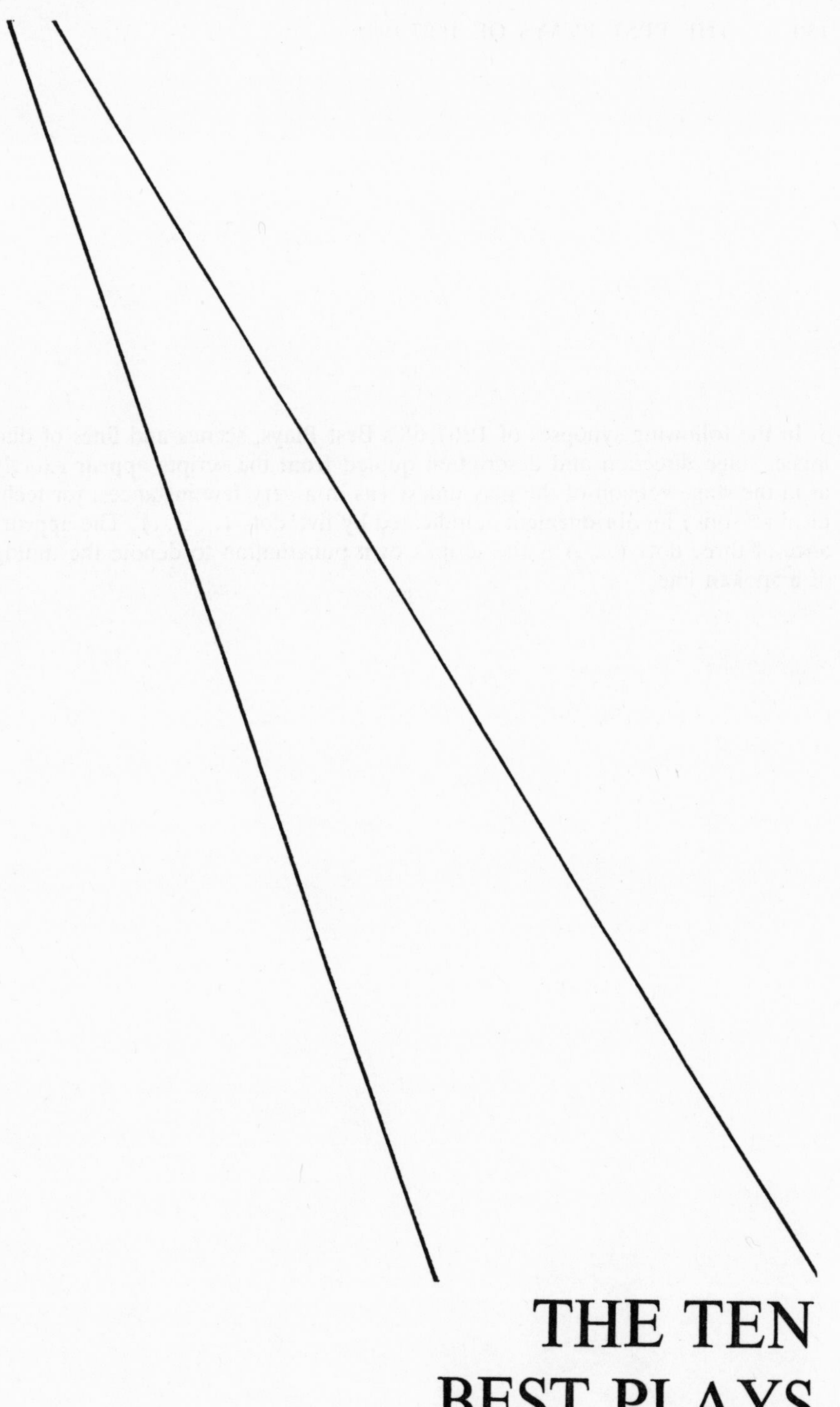

THE TEN BEST PLAYS

In the following synopses of 1967-68's Best Plays, scenes and lines of dialogue, stage direction and description quoted from the scripts appear *exactly* as in the stage version of the play unless (as in a very few instances, for technical reasons) an abridgement is indicated by five dots (. . . . .). The appearance of three dots (. . .) is the script's own punctuation to denote the timing of a spoken line.

AFTER THE RAIN

A Play in Two Acts

BY JOHN BOWEN

Cast and credits appear on page 343

JOHN BOWEN supplied his own biographical note for this Best Plays *volume, in the third person, as follows: "He was born in Calcutta, India, Nov. 5, 1924, and was reared by various relatives in various parts of England. He went back to India in 1940, served in the Indian army during the war and was demobilized in 1947. He obtained a place at Pembroke College, Oxford, but, since Oxford was very crowded after the war, he could not go into residence until October, 1948. He studied Modern History as an undergraduate, graduated and was awarded the Frere Exhibition in Indian Studies by the University, so that he went on to do some postgraduate work at St. Anthony's College. He was in the United States from the fall of 1952 to 1953, partly teaching Freshman English at Ohio State University, partly hitchhiking and partly on a scholarship to the Kenyon School of Letters at the University of Indiana. He returned to Oxford, ran out of money, and took a job as assistant editor to a fortnightly magazine,* The Sketch, *now defunct. He has also worked as an actor, and in advertising. He has written six novels, of which four—*After The Rain, The Center of the Green, The Birdcage *and* A World Elsewhere *have been published in the U.S.A.*

"His first play for the theater, I Love You, Mrs. Patterson, *opened at the St. Martin's Theater, London, in 1964 and ran five weeks in a heat wave.* After The Rain, *a very free adaptation of his novel of the same title, opened at the Hampstead Theater Club in 1966 and transferred to the Duchess Theater in January 1967, with the same cast. It was highly praised both in Lon-*

don and New York, and a French translation has been played at the Théâtre de l'Athenée, Paris, and a German one at the Kammerspiele, Frankfurt. A new double bill of linked plays, Little Boxes, *has opened at the Hampstead Theater Club this year and has also transferred to the Duchess Theater. He has made a selection and translation of some Medieval mystery plays under the title* Fall and Redemption *which he himself directed at the London Academy of Music and Dramatic Art last year, and which he is to direct again for the Pitlochrie Festival Theater next year. He is currently at work on a new play,* The Disorderly Women.

"Bowen has also written dramatic and literary criticism and is a regular contributor to the London Sunday Times and the New York Times Book Review. He is unmarried and lives in South Kensington."

Time: 200 years after the Rain of 1969

Place: A university lecture hall

ACT I

SYNOPSIS: The curtain is up on a stage that is bare except for a very few simple objects. These include eight straight chairs along the back wall, a lectern down right, a chair in each wing and a wooden table holding various props and cards reading "Hold," "Cabin," "Deck" and "Sea," which will be placed at appropriate areas of the stage.

NOTE ON THE OBJECTS AND COSTUMES: Two hundred years after the Rain of 1969 a society has grown, founded by the six survivors of our play. (There may have been other societies from other survivors, but we are not concerned with them.) The clothes and furniture of this society will be based on an imperfect tradition of what life was like in 1969, modified by the fact that this society has had to rediscover a large number of skills.

While the house lights are still on, the Assistants enter and take their places on either side of the stage. The Lecturer enters and places his notes on the lectern. The actors' clothes—and the furniture—are futuristic without being science-fictionish. The Assistants, for example, are wearing some kind of simple uniform, and the Lecturer has on an academic gown. His manner is businesslike.

LECTURER: Lower the lights, please, Mr. Porter, and take the names of any latecomers. I'll see them in punishment room this evening after Discussion.

House lights lowered.

In my first lecture, I tried to give a general review of life before the Rain of 1969. For our reconstruction of that time we have to rely on secondary sources—that is, on the books actually on board the raft on which our forefathers survived. I myself am not convinced of the value as guides to the period either of *Better Sight Without Glasses* or *Goldfinger*. There are many areas of life in 1969 about which we can only speculate. For life on board the raft we have two direct sources. The first is the Book of Arthur, which seems in part to be allegorical. The second is the diary of Alan Armitage. The raft itself was destroyed in the fire of 1998, and we have no picture of it. There seems to have been a central structure consisting of a main saloon, with kitchen and bathroom, a smaller cabin, and a hold beneath. The deck of which we show you only a part ran all round this central structure. The sea we indicate by this lower level of the platform—the area, in fact, into which I have just stepped. . . .

The Lecturer indicates that the stage is going to represent the raft surrounded by its sea. This raft, the Lecturer explains, had been built to advertise Glub Flakes, a breakfast food. It had been captained by one George Hunter (who now comes onstage), a retired army officer who was a misfit in civilian life until employed by Glub to sail the raft around the world living on his huge supply of Glub Flakes and other Glub products stored on board.

After Hunter had begun his journey, rain started falling in a dead calm. It never stopped raining. One night, the raft hit and swamped a fishing boat.

HUNTER: . . . . . Nobody in it but Arthur and Gertrude and Tony and a lot of dead chaps.

LECTURER: So?

HUNTER: Arthur took over.

LECTURER: Sit down now.

Hunter sits at one of the chairs in the back.

These were Arthur Henderson, Gertrude Forbes-Cooper and Anthony Batch. *(To Assistant.)* Henderson, next.

Arthur enters and takes up position, while:

You may be puzzled by the name "Henderson". Our ancestors used the suffix "son" in names just as we do—Cook*son,* Baker*son,* Master*son,* Farmer*son*—but what a "Hender" was, we've not yet been able to discover. *(To Arthur.)* You are Arthur Henderson?

ARTHUR *(slight pause):* Yes.

LECTURER: Yes what?

ARTHUR: I am Arthur Henderson.

LECTURER: Profession?

ARTHUR: Accountant.

LECTURER: Vocation?

ARTHUR: Leader.

LECTURER: Explain.

ARTHUR: When the orders came to move to camps on the high ground, I knew what would happen. Cholera. Rioting. Food running out. I took a few who would follow me, and set out for myself.

LECTURER: You chose badly. Most died.

ARTHUR: I took those who would come. Two lived.

LECTURER: Yes. *(To Assistants.)* Forbes-Cooper and Batch.

Gertrude and Tony enter and join Arthur, while:

ARTHUR: I began with two of the most necessary parts of man's nature. Miss Forbes-Cooper represents the arts. Batch had bodily strength. Intelligence I had myself.

Gertrude Forbes-Cooper is a speech-and-drama schoolteacher in early middle age. Tony is a physical specimen. Gertrude recalls what happened: "The streets filled with water and the people in the basement tried to move upstairs." Luckily, she met Arthur right about then—Arthur, who looks at first glance like an overzealous grocery clerk but gradually reveals in speech and gesture and judgment that there is a good deal of hawk in him.

Gertrude and Tony sit in chairs at the back.

LECTURER *(to Arthur):* What other people did you pick up when you had reached the raft?

ARTHUR: I decided to accept anyone who came, if he were healthy and had some sort of skill. Unfortunately most of those we found were, by that time, no longer healthy. Consequently, they were left to die.

LECTURER *(to Assistants):* The Otterdales now, and Banner.

ARTHUR: The Otterdales were in reasonable health, however. And Banner was clearly an educated man.

Harold Banner—a priest of the Church of England—and Wesley and Muriel Otterdale—a middle-class English couple—enter and explain that they were picked up from a rowboat. Banner was rowing at the time (he once rowed for Oxford) but Wesley wouldn't, believing "the Rain was a punishment. . . . . it was God's will not to row."

The Lecturer orders the four to sit at the back. Arthur hesitates for a moment, then obeys like the other three. The Lecturer summons onstage the final two survivors—Alan Armitage and Sonya Banks, both young and good looking. Like the others, they are directed by the Lecturer to chairs at the back.

The Assistants bring in a board on wheels which is to represent a rubber dinghy tossing in the sea.

Lecturer snaps his fingers. All the performers drop into sleep except Arthur, who remains looking at the Lecturer.

LECTURER: You will sleep. I will snap my fingers once, and you will sleep.

Snaps fingers. A long pause. Snaps fingers again. Arthur's head drops in sleep. Lecturer hesitates a moment, obviously worried, then comes back downstage.

New students may be unfamiliar with our procedure at these lectures. It is most important that there should be no distractions from the hall. Consequently I must ask you not to cough, whisper or indulge in love-play of any kind. Each of these criminals is under deep hypnosis to enable him to be the person he represents to you. Before the Rain, this was called acting, and was used, as we use it, for educational purposes. But if the hypnosis should be broken by distraction, the consequences might be unfortunate. Please remember that, although these people *are* criminals, that is no reason for you to put them at risk, especially since, when this task is over, they will have earned remission and will be permitted to return to normal community duties.

He speaks to the characters.

Wake.

They do so.

Places.

Alan and Sonya enter the boat. Arthur takes his chair to the upstage section, and sits. Gertrude, Muriel, Wesley and Banner take theirs to the Main Saloon. Hunter puts on a pair of oilskins and goes on deck. Tony stays where he is.

Raining.

Hunter turns up his collar and reacts to the rain.

Begin.

Alan and Sonya go through the motions of rowing as though they had been long in the rain (an Assistant pulls their "boat" forward). They sight the raft and hail it. Hunter reports to Arthur that newcomers are approaching, and Arthur sends Hunter ahead of him with a crude spear (handed to him by one of the Assistants).

Arthur forbids Alan and Sonya to come aboard, threatens to set Hunter upon them with his spear. Alan begins to row away, but Arthur decides to question them.

ARTHUR *(calls):* You! Boat people! You need not leave us yet. I wish to interrogate you, if you are prepared to suffer it. How old is the woman?

ALAN: Twenty-three.

ARTHUR: Is she healthy?

ALAN: She's healthy.

ARTHUR: Who are you? Are you husband and wife?

ALAN: No SONYA *(simultaneously):* Yes.

ARTHUR: What?

ALAN: Yes, we are. SONYA: Not exactly.

ARTHUR: It is of no consequence. I suppose we could take the woman anyway. You—what do you do?

Alan is a writer, but to Sonya's astonishment he tells Arthur that he is a cook. It happens that the raft needs a cook, if only to invent new ways of preparing Glub Flakes. The raft also could use the dinghy. Arthur decides to allow Alan and Sonya on board and leaves Hunter to tie up the dinghy. Alan (who assures Sonya he can cook, a little) and Sonya decide to take a chance and throw in their lot with the raft passengers.

Hunter leads the way to the Main Saloon, and behind his back Alan and Sonya kiss passionately. Then the Lecturer orders: "Supper." All but Arthur and Tony take places around the table where Muriel is serving fish—which, hopefully, Alan will know how to cook more tastily in future.

Hunter comments that each member of the group has his or her special tasks. Hunter approves of Arthur's discipline: "When I was here on my own, I got a bit slack actually. Wrong. I see that now." Banner and Gertrude list their tasks, while Wesley offers various religious maxims, punctuated by an odd droning noise.

Arthur is in the small private cabin area upstage. Muriel goes to call him to supper. Banner is saying grace as Arthur enters. Alan makes an irreverent comment, and Arthur rebukes him. Arthur is an agnostic, but he believes in preserving a civilized formality, especially at mealtimes.

ARTHUR: . . . . . I should have preferred a Latin grace, but unfortunately Mr. Banner failed his degree, and cannot remember any.

BANNER: I am a broad Churchman, you know.

ARTHUR: On this raft, Mr. Banner, you will be the sort of churchman *I* decide, and no other. Remember that.

Tony enters the Main Saloon, coming in from the performance of his duty to catch fish. Arthur makes a special point of introducing Tony, the strong man, to Sonya, the dancer. Arthur encourages Tony and Sonya in a plan to convert part of the hold into an exercise area which the two can share. Alan is barely able to register a jealous protest.

The Lecturer interposes his comment that the Book of Arthur is a less reliable guide to the early stages of the voyage (despite its comments on the weather and asterisks possibly denoting "solitary sexual practises") than the Diary of Alan Armitage.

The Lecturer directs Alan and Arthur into conversation about the flood. Wesley Otterdale (Arthur observes) thinks the flood is sent from God. Arthur thinks the flood is the best thing that could have happened.

ARTHUR: Natural selection is responsible for this flood, Mr. Armitage, and by natural selection certain people will survive it. I shall be one of them. So will you, as long as you obey me.

ALAN: Why did natural selection pick us, do you think?

ARTHUR: I can see you are not a serious student of human affairs, Mr. Armitage.

ALAN: So much of my life has been spent in the kitchen.

ARTHUR: I shall explain. Humanity has been increasing at an increasing rate. People have spawned people.

ALAN: Yes. They do that.

ARTHUR: And not only were men increasing their numbers, so that in three generations we should have used up the natural resources of the world, but worse—far worse—the poorer, more brutish sort were increasing faster than the rest. The proportion of morons and near-morons has been a rising curve, Mr. Armitage, because although one can persuade intelligent people to control their numbers, one cannot teach contraception to idiots. Idiots have more and more outnumbered the intelligent and, under a system of democracy, had as much political power. Lunacy! The Rain has wiped that out. Only intelligent people will survive it, and such of the less intelligent as they choose to carry with them.

ALAN: Why carry any?

ARTHUR: For the rough work.

ALAN: What if they refuse?

ARTHUR: They won't refuse. . . . .

Arthur points out that the others—including Alan himself—readily accept survival. Later on, when the waters subside, there will be careful breeding of new human beings. In the meantime, the men and women sleep separated—although, Arthur understands, there may be opportunities, and he doesn't necessarily mean to enforce total chastity aboard the raft.

Arthur is certain the waters *will* subside: "Do you imagine that natural selection intends to replace us by fish?"

In the hold (as Arthur and Alan return to their seats) Sonya and Tony are doing their exercises—he his weight-lifting, she her ballet practise. Tony tells her he used to pose for strong-man photos. He asks to see what her act was like. Sonya shows Tony a syncopated modern dancing beat, then persuades him to try it. (Alan gets up and moves toward the hold.) The beat gets faster and faster, and Sonya and Tony break up, laughing, as Alan enters. Sonya and Tony tell him what they have been doing, and Alan apologizes for interrupting.

The Lecturer observes that Arthur saw in Alan a threat to his leadership. So Arthur set out to cripple Alan with jealousy by throwing Sonya and Tony together—and succeeded in dominating Alan in this way.

In the evening, Wesley is on lookout. Banner and Hunter are playing Battleship in the Main Saloon, watched by Muriel. Tony and Sonya are still in the hold. Arthur is in his cabin, Gertrude in the kitchen. Alan is looking for a copy of *The Naked and the Dead.*

Gertrude enters the saloon, explaining that she has tried and failed to shred a twig for a toothbrush. Arthur, entering right after her, explains that she needs a special kind of wood.

Hunter observes that he, too, might like to do some exercises, but "two's company." Hunter's insinuation angers Alan, who declares that anyone would be welcome to join Sonya and Tony in the hold at any time.

Wesley, Sonya and Tony are called in for a general meeting. Arthur brings up the subject of damp. They will light the stove once a week. They can start with wooden crates in the hold and lean driftwood against the stove to dry and then be burned to dry *other* driftwood, in a perpetual supply of fuel.

All but Alan admire Arthur's idea. Alan thinks it "stupid" to burn the stove only once a week when there's an unlimited supply of driftwood. Arthur bridles at the word "stupid." Alan insists that they ought to discuss the matter further. Gertrude and Muriel move away from Alan to dissociate themselves from his rebellious arguments.

ALAN: Arthur, I'm not opposing you or anything. All I'm saying is that we can quite easily—

ARTHUR: I'm delighted to find that Mr. Armitage considers himself equally able to take decisions. It is a quality of leadership.

Banner also moves.

BANNER *(nervous):* We don't disagree with Arthur here.

HUNTER: By George, no. Better not, eh?

MURIEL: Arthur knows what's good for us.

ARTHUR: A mutineer puts his close friends in danger.

ALAN: Perhaps I was wrong.

ARTHUR: Are you sorry for that?

ALAN: Yes, I am sorry.

ARTHUR: It would be improvident—do you agree?—to burn *all* the wood.

ALAN: It was a very stupid suggestion. I see that now.

ARTHUR: Nevertheless you may feel free to *make* suggestions, Mr. Armitage, I shall decide whether they be stupid or not.

ALAN: Thank you, Arthur.

The others return to their places, and Arthur orders them to go on with Gertrude's evening Study Period. They are studying Shakespeare's *Julius Caesar.* Arthur observes: "Caesar was a great man. He found his vocation, as I have, in middle life." Then he goes to his cabin and leaves the others to their discussion.

They comment on Caesar's murder as a Freudian image of patricide. The suggestion is repugnant to Tony, who points out that Arthur himself is like a father to them all. Banner changes the subject to Antony's funeral oration. Gertrude begins to recite this speech but is interrupted by the Lecturer. Gertrude's feelings are hurt, but she takes her place, seated, with the others while the Lecturer takes up the matter of the storm.

Alan begins to mime the act of fishing.

LECTURER: As I explained in my first lecture, we do not know exactly when the Rain began, because nobody noticed it. They only began to take notice when it did not stop. In its nature, it appeared to have been a calm, settled downpour, with no wind. On June 26th, 1971, when the Rain had continued for approximately two years, this calm was broken.

Alan moves on his chair, as if the raft should be beginning to rock a little. When he notices what is happening, he is surprised. He gets up and begins to go indoors. All look up as Alan goes swiftly through the Main Saloon and into the upstage area.

Alan warns Arthur that the weather is changing. Arthur goes to see for himself, as Wesley begins his droning noise. It is getting darker, and the raft is lurching. Hunter dons oilskins. Arthur asks his advice as to what they should do. Hunter suggests getting the sail down, and Arthur orders Tony to help him. Alan and Wesley are to pull the dinghy in. Again asking Hunter's advice for the next step, Arthur is told they must close all cabin openings tight and ride out the storm.

There is a violent "rocking", during which Tony and Wesley make their way to the deck, and Muriel cuts her lip when Gertrude falls over her.

Before the men can take action, Hunter shouts a warning "Hang on to something! Bloody tidal wave."

The Lecturer interrupts the action to describe "a succession of monstrous waves" followed by a strong wind. As the action resumes, Banner and the women are clinging to the cabin table while the others, including Arthur, are on deck trying to secure the raft. Wesley is droning and declaring, "Oh Lord, we are fit and ready for Thy chastisement"—he does not hang on, and the others try to hold him. Arthur cries out for Alan to pull Wesley back from the edge of the raft, where Wesley seems almost to be welcoming disaster. The force of the waves is great, and Wesley is swept overboard. He lies there, drowned, in the "sea."

"He went mad, I think," Alan observes. Arthur, after giving orders to bring in the dinghy and cut down the sail—and for Banner to start praying—decides "He was expendable."

With waves roaring over them, Arthur, Alan, Hunter and Tony manage to do their work while, in the cabin, Banner prays for the Lord's mercy until he is knocked down by an overturning bookcase. The men come into the cabin and close the portholes, as Arthur gives orders to hold onto the unconscious Banner to keep the storm from flinging him about.

Muriel notices that Wesley is missing.

MURIEL: . . . . . What have you done with my husband?

LECTURER *(gently):* No more now. *(Moves across to the characters.)* No more rain now. Rest now.

Characters quietly go back to their places, watched by the Lecturer. When they are seated:

Sleep now.

Characters' heads drop. Lecturer advances to audience. To assistant:

Revive him.

Assistant revives Wesley, points the way off stage. Wesley goes, moving like an automaton. Lights lowered.

Nobody in this hall has committed a criminal offense, or you would not of course be here. Consequently you may not realize that what you witness is not only a History Lecture, but also a necessary part of the reconditioning of some unhappy people who have committed crimes against the Community. In each case the criminal's offense has a parallel in the historical person he is presenting. Thus your Arthur Henderson has been guilty of persistently individualistic behavior. Your Alan Armitage has a history of petty crime—lack of group effort, psychosomatic asthma, public sarcasm. Both your Captain Hunter and your Sonya Banks have been guilty of private pleasure and irrational enjoyment, leading to the neglect of tasks. Your Gertrude Forbes-Cooper is a persistent liar, your Muriel Otterdale a murderess, your Tony Batch has been either late for or absent from Community Meetings ever since he was old enough to attend them, and your Harold Banner suffers from doubt, leading often to despair. In volunteering to present these characters the criminals concerned are able to act out their own anti-communal tendencies, providing not only instruction for you, but therapy for themselves.

The Lecturer orders the characters to wake, tells them that now the sun is out, the raft is still, the heat-light batteries cannot recharge. He directs them: "Reveal yourselves a little." Gertrude and Banner comply at once.

GERTRUDE: I never married, you know. Nobody lasted long enough for me.

BANNER: I wanted to be of use.

GERTRUDE: Sir Laurence Olivier once told me I was too intense for life. Born for the theater, not for life, he said. But then he had to be polite, because he was turning me down for a part.

Alan joins Tony and Sonya in the hold. He insists on joining them in exercise, stretches out to do pushups. Muriel goes to Arthur's door and waits outside.

Meanwhile, Banner explains to Gertrude how he was recruited into the ministry after attracting the attention of the Moral Rearmament group while he was a rowing blue at Oxford. Banner explains: ". . . . . I was so busy with the Youth Club, and the Suicide Service, and Meals on Wheels, and senior citizens' evenings, I had little time to think about religious questions. And when I did, I discovered that most things could be explained quite simply. All those doubts people used to have in Victorian novels. There was never any need for them, now that any competent biologist can duplicate The Virgin Birth with a darning needle, and people are being raised from the dead every day. In any case, nobody wanted me to believe in God as a person, or in Christ as anything else. Nowadays, Heaven is not a place, you know, but a oneness with God. The individual soul just dissolves into the God soul. Not an easy thing to explain to my parishioners, but I didn't have to, because they never came to church."

Muriel gains access to Arthur's cabin, in order to tell him "I'd always do anything *you* wanted, Arthur. You've only to ask." Arthur thanks her.

In the hold, Alan's attempt to demonstrate physical prowess is an abject failure. He can't even reach ten pushups.

All at once, Hunter, on lookout, shouts "Land ho!" but his land turns out to be an ark (the Lecturer knows only very vaguely what an ark is). When Alan and Arthur board the ark the stench is horrible. The Lecturer describes their encounter with a filth-caked old man, mimed by the Second Assistant. Alan supports him and gives him a drink of water, while the Lecturer recites the old man's dialogue in a flat, matter-of-fact tone.

LECTURER: Dead. All dead.

ARTHUR: Did you have livestock? Cows? Pigs? Chickens even?

LECTURER: All dead. There was no water. And they had fouled their quarters.

ARTHUR: You had better take a look round, Mr. Armitage.

Alan ceases to support the Assistant.

LECTURER: I have drunk blood. Blood. I have drunk blood.

ARTHUR: See if you can find anything that may be of use.

Alan summons his resolution, and goes quickly through the imaginary door to the extreme side of the stage.

LECTURER: Ham . . . Shem . . . Both dead. My wife left me, you know, before the word was fulfilled. Forty days and forty nights, I lost count. She took Japhet and went to her married sister in Manchester. More has occurred that was foretold.

Alan finds some grain which they decide to ferry to the raft in the dinghy. The Lecturer asks Arthur what he means to do with the old man, and Arthur replies: "Oh—kill him, of course."

The ferrying of the grain takes two days. On the second night the ark catches fire. The Second Assistant gives a long scream, which rouses Alan and Muriel from sleep to observe the burning ark. Alan blames Arthur for murdering the old man on the ark and Muriel agrees: "Oh yes. My husband too." She thinks that Arthur arranged for Wesley's death because "Arthur takes what he wants. After all, he has to, hasn't he, if we're to respect him?"

Muriel goes inside, but the Lecturer stops Alan to ask him if he intends to protest. Alan answers "No," explains that it would be as pointless as life itself. It is his opinion that "Much of your life is spent in discomfort, and more in boredom, and most in indifference. All you have to expect is monotony and struggle while you're working, and loneliness and fear in your old age. And what's it all for? You don't really believe that making things, and packing them up, and moving them about, and selling them, and buying them, and consuming them, and making new things to replace them, add up to a reason for living. But you go on—keeping alive, because you're afraid of death. If Arthur knows what he wants, and why he wants it, what can I do?"

Alan should speak of his jealousy to Sonya, the Lecturer advises, and he summons her to join Alan. Alan reminds Sonya of the three weeks when they just drifted in their dinghy, going hungry, singing, making love. Sonya admits that she, too, misses the closeness with Alan and would like to be alone with him—but that is impossible on the raft.

Alan kisses Sonya passionately and tries to persuade Sonya to make love then and there ("I ache for it"). But Sonya feels that sex is not always necessary between two people as close as she and Alan—she wants to talk to him the way she talks to Tony.

Alan picks up the subject of Tony and drives forward with it: does Tony have sex on his mind? No, Sonya replies, she and Tony merely get on well and do exercises together. Sonya believes Alan should trust her, and Alan reminds her that the very first time they met they made love.

ALAN: . . . . . We dived into sex. We pulled it up over our heads, and drowned in it. And you were a bloody sight better than I was. More experienced. But I suppose that's because it was "just sex," eh? Not *that* important.

SONYA: And?

ALAN: If me, why not Tony? If so *soon* with me, so quick with me?

Pause.

SONYA: I think I'll go in now. I've gone off you. Funny!—I came out to tell you something. It's rather important actually. I've been saving it to tell you. Nobody else knows.

ALAN: Not even Tony?

SONYA: I'm pregnant.

Pause.

ALAN: What?

SONYA: I thought you'd be pleased. I was *that* stupid.

ALAN: But I am. I am, love. I am. I am pleased.

SONYA: Are you? Well, that won't last, will it? After all, you don't know whose it is.

She turns her back on him and goes inside. He watches her.

Meanwhile, the Lecturer directs them to the meeting of August 3, and the characters place themselves on deck, as Arthur calls to order the First Meeting of the New Society. He ignores a question from Alan about their ability to survive. The raft's log book will be used to record the minutes (and Arthur proceeds to write in it). Arthur has decided that their New Society needs but one officer, a president who will also be secretary and treasurer. Arthur is nominated, seconded and unanimously elected to this office.

Alan's suggestion that they might also need a deputy president in case something happens to Arthur is waved aside.

ARTHUR: . . . . . Now . . . Rules. As your president, I shall promulgate rules from time to time. Rule One. Doubt can disable us. Any part of the body politic which doubts its survival must be cut out.

ALAN: Ah!

ARTHUR: You spoke?

ALAN: Just breathing.

ARTHUR: Breathe more quietly. Any questions?

ALAN: None.

ARTHUR: Rule Two. While we remain becalmed, we shall cut down on the use of power. No lights will be used. We shall rise with the sun, and retire with it. Furthermore, there will be no cooking. We have been becalmed for two months. We must conserve power. Heat will be used only to distill water.

Their diet of raw fish (the Lecturer explains) weakened them, and the hot sun encouraged self-doubts. Banner has difficulty communicating. Gertrude remembers that she played Antigone when she was young but never lived up to her promise. Tony and Sonya are heard giggling in the hold. Hunter confesses he knew he was "not bright" and was likely to go under. All but Alan agree that Arthur sees things in proportion, Arthur knows what's best for them all.

Alan calls Arthur "A murderer" and continues: "Arthur's our leader, and we depend on him, but he's not a god. He's not above doing foolish and wicked things, you know that. It wouldn't have hurt us to have taken that old man from the ark, but Arthur murdered him."

Gertrude, Banner and Muriel pretend they don't hear this. But Muriel goes to Arthur's cabin to report on all that she has seen and heard. Sonya and Tony are "carrying on" (Muriel tells Arthur), and Arthur approves because this will make it easier for Sonya to accept the fact, later, that all the women will be shared and loved equally by all the men.

Muriel also reports Alan's conversation. Even so, Arthur believes that Alan "does no harm," but he urges Muriel to keep an eye on Sonya—she is concealing something.

Muriel's manner is proprietary, inviting, and Arthur makes love to her—but his mind is still on Alan's remark that he is "not a god."

At the evening meal, Arthur announces that they are in a mythological situation—"A new race will spring, as it were, from our loins." Perhaps their descendants will wish to think of the raft passengers, their forbears, as gods and goddesses.

ARTHUR: What makes a god? Any thinking person will tell you that men make their own. They do so by worship. Whatever you worship is God, whether it be a tree, or the sun, or two sticks, or a bull, or a ring of stones. Simple men worship the things themselves. Complicated men worship the ideas the things express. But ultimately it makes little difference. The behavior—the ritual—is what matters. Interpretations may change, but the ritual endures. Is that not so, Mr. Banner?

BANNER: Very largely, Arthur.

ARTHUR: Very largely?

BANNER: Entirely.

ARTHUR: Good. *(Looks round the table.)* You had better begin by worshiping me. Some of you may feel that I am unworthy. You must conquer that feeling. It will, in any case, die with you, while what is recorded of your behavior will live on as revealed religion. Any questions?

Pause.

ALAN: No questions.

ARTHUR: Then we shall begin our meal. Mr. Banner, please ask a blessing.

Banner looks timidly at Arthur, who gives him an encouraging nod.

BANNER: For what we are about to receive, may Arthur make us truly thankful.

ARTHUR: Quite right. And so I do.

They begin to mime eating. . . . .

The Lecturer explains that still the much-needed wind did not come, and Arthur directed the others to try magic, as befits characters in a myth. They whistle for a wind, they nail money to the mast, they throw money in the sea. Alan finds himself making a jocular reference to Iphigenia and the sacrifice of a child to the gods—then he stops, horrified at his own joke. In the water, a fish strikes at a pound note, and Arthur declares that their gift to the sea has been accepted.

In the distance, they spy what appears to be fog rising under a clear sky. "The edge of the world was held by the ancients to be a place for fogs," remarks Banner. Gertrude and Muriel, frightened, move closer to Arthur.

Now the raft is in the fog, and the Lecturer signals for a high noise on one note, becoming louder and louder. Suddenly, the water is choppy without wind. The water turns brown with weed. The characters are still while the Lecturer tells his listeners: "They had, of course, come to what is indeed a common enough phenomenon at sea—the meeting of two currents, one warm, one cold. All this time they had thought themselves motionless, they had been drifting with one current. Now they had come to the junction, and found mist there, and a great deal of weed, and a high concentration of marine life, most of it in violent activity."

The action continues: the passengers feel the cold as the raft strikes the cold current, and the Assistants hand out blankets all around. Fish jump onto the deck; the noise is growing louder; Muriel and Gertrude admit to being frightened. As Alan, feeling slightly seasick, makes the discovery that the sea water is now cold, Gertrude and Muriel hold Arthur's hands for security. Arthur tries to shake them off but cannot.

The noise—which, the Lecturer says, is the sound of fish screaming—gets louder. A fish comes aboard and strikes Gertrude, who, terrified, grabs Arthur. Muriel, jealous as well as frightened, tries to pull Gertrude away and hugs Arthur, who is trying to pry himself loose from both of them. Sonya puts her hands protectively over her stomach, and the men mill around purposelessly. The raft is a mob scene, nearly out of control, close to panic.

MURIEL *(to Arthur):* You're God! You told us. Make it stop.

GERTRUDE: God. You're God.

MURIEL: God! God! Make it stop.

GERTRUDE: God make it stop.

A pause while the men wait for Arthur to respond. All talk has to be loud above the noise.

ALAN: Go on, Arthur. Make it stop if you're God.

Pause.

ARTHUR: Let go your hands, women. Take your hands from my robe.

The women let go. All watch Arthur. He goes to the edge of the deck area, spreads his blanket like wings from his shoulders and addresses the audience area.

Waters! by virtue of the authority vested in me as God, I command you to stop.

A small pause. Then the noise cuts out.

I will have no more nonsense, waters. I command it.

Pause.

Now, go forth, and feel the waters, Mr. Armitage.

Alan does so.

ALAN: They're warm again.

BANNER: God be praised.

Arthur turns and looks at him.

God Arthur be praised, that is.

ARTHUR: We shall go in now. There is nothing more to do here.

Wearing his blanket like a robe, he walks upstage. The others fall in behind him, making a procession. The procession goes offstage completely.

LECTURER *(steps forward):* Please break for fifteen minutes, and reassemble here.

Goes offstage and the house lights come up to signal the end of the act.

ACT II

The actors (all but Arthur) have taken their places on their chairs. The Assistants have arranged the props for the second act. The Lecturer comes on as the house lights dim.

LECTURER *(to audience):* The miracle by which Arthur proved his godhead was not really a miracle. The raft had passed out of the junction area of the two currents: that is all. But to the people of the raft—and certainly to Arthur himself—it did seem miraculous. Meanwhile the sun shone. A warm wind blew. The days passed. Miss Banks' condition became obvious, and was accepted.

An Assistant ties a bolster to Sonya's stomach to symbolize her pregnancy. She seeks out Tony's company, though she can no longer practise her ballet.

Arthur, in his godliness, remains in seclusion. Banner has become his priest, prepares his food, is the only one in direct communication with him. Alan continues to cook for the others.

Childishly, Muriel bounces a ball against the cabin wall. Banner prepares

Arthur's lunch, dons a surplice and ceremoniously carries the plate to Arthur's upstage area.

Muriel, childlike in speech and directness, comes into the cabin to announce that she has made 31 bounces. She also informs Alan that Hunter has taken to hiding in the toilet for long periods of time, sucking his thumb.

Sonya, on deck, is teaching Tony to sing "Flow Gently Sweet Afton," but Muriel interferes like a naughty child, intruding with another song.

Alan observes to Gertrude that he is a better cook than Banner, so the passengers are eating better than the god. Gertrude rebuffs him: "Harold isn't a cook at all. He's the priest of the god. You are awful, saying that. Harold doesn't cook. He prepares the god's repast. *You* cook."

Banner comes in to report that the god wants some glue, for some inscrutible purpose. There's some in the hold, which Banner himself goes to fetch "otherwise it would only have to be purified." Gertrude and Alan set up the checkerboard on deck. Sonya continues to teach Tony the song, which annoys Alan.

Banner comes on deck to inform the others that they are to make a mask for Arthur with paper soaked in the glue, because Arthur's face is "too terrible for us to see," being the face of a god. This one is to be a smiling mask. He may need a frowning one later.

The Lecturer orders the god brought onstage. Arthur is brought in to his private area upstage by the Assistants. He is masked, with beard protruding. The Assistants help him to stand on a stool. Banner makes the others ready to come into the presence of the god (though Hunter, who has to be pulled from his chair and placed in line, continues his infantile behavior, sucking his thumb). Sonya is feeling the heat. Banner knocks on the door to Arthur's cabin.

BANNER *(calls):* The worshipers approach, God Arthur. All make reverence before thee.

They go in, much crowded together. Banner motions them to kneel. They do so, Gertrude helping Hunter. Great squash and discomfort.

LECTURER *(to audience):* There was some defect in the construction of the mask. It made the god sound as if he had no roof to his mouth. Mr. Banner, as priest of the god, supplied a running translation.

ARTHUR: Hee ha hee ho high.

BANNER: The god tells us we shall see great things.

As Arthur goes on with his gibberish generalities with Banner translating, Sonya complains of the heat there in the stuffy cabin, then keels over in a dead faint. To Muriel's jealous consternation, this is interpreted as a kind of miracle brought on by Sonya's nearness to the god and willed (as Arthur signifies) by the god himself.

Alan carries Sonya out of the Main Saloon, revives her and calms her fears about the forthcoming birth, which is expected imminently. Alan promises Sonya that Muriel will be kept out of the way while the child is being born.

Meanwhile Muriel, not to be outdone, screams and throws a noisy fit. She is stretched out unconscious on the table. Now she has been "possessed" by the god Arthur, just as Sonya was.

BANNER: What really worries me is the possibility that having been possessed, Muriel may bear fruit. . . . . You must see how this undermines my position.

Pause. Broken by Lecturer.

LECTURER *(to audience):* I have used the words "the god" so far because it seems that this is what Arthur sincerely believed himself to be. But it was, as I've said, hot in the holy place, and the air was offensive, and the circumstances uncomfortable. A god would not have minded such matters.

He has walked easily to the cabin area and stands behind Arthur.

But Arthur minded. There was a small, persistent voice inside that spoke to him. It was the voice of his own doubt. As he grew more uncomfortable, the voice became more insistent and more persuasive. I speak now as the voice of Arthur's doubt. *(To Arthur.)* Can it be that you have made an elementary theological error?

ARTHUR: Hee hoh.

LECTURER: Yes, it is hot. And horrid in every way. A god could not be uncomfortable. But you are. Can it be that you are not the god?

ARTHUR *(reacts away):* Hoh. Hoh.

LECTURER: What if the god were only to inhabit you? Then he could, at any time, leave.

Pause.

No man could carry the god within him forever. The god would not wish it.

Pause.

Only for a time. To those found worthy. . . . .

At dinner time sometime later, Banner is preparing the god's dish and Muriel is lording it over the others, especially Gertrude, because Muriel was chosen to be possessed. Gertrude claims that *she* was possessed by Arthur too, before he became a god. The quarrel between the two women descends to loud name-calling and vituperation. As Muriel calls her a bitch, Gertrude declares that she won't be insulted in this way, she has borne too much already in her lonely life: "I've eaten dirt. I've been refused. I've watched my own pupils pretend not to see me in the foyers of theaters. I've been ignored in the street."

With the others watching, the two women attack each other. As they are wrestling, the Lecturer tells Arthur that now is the time for the god to leave him. Arthur gives a long scream. The fight stops and all freeze. The Assistants remove Arthur's mask, then Arthur walks from his private quarters into the saloon area.

ARTHUR: Why are there broken plates upon the floor?

Pause. All look at each other.

BANNER *(timidly):* Thy servants fought amongst themselves.

GERTRUDE *(a little bow):* I'm sorry, God Arthur. The woman provoked me, and I did throw a plate at her.

ARTHUR: I am not the god Arthur. The god Arthur has gone back to heaven. I am his vicar here on earth. *(To Banner.)* So you may remove that surplice, Mr. Banner. I shall be the god's high priest from now on.

Pause.

LECTURER *(to cast):* Evening service.

All but Arthur bring chairs out to the deck area, Hunter as always being guided and helped, and sit in two rows. Arthur watches, waits until they are ready, then takes the ship's log from the table, and comes out to them standing before them as the priest, while:

(To audience) They had a service every evening, out on the deck. It began with a reading from what had once been the ship's log, then became the minutes of the New Society, and was now the Book of Arthur.

ARTHUR *(reads):* There came a great wind over the surface of the waters, and the waters rose up, and the face of the sky was made black by the water, and the voice of the god Arthur was heard in the wind, crying, "Woe! Woe! to the sons of men." Then many of those who were not of the Selected were swallowed up. They and their wives, their children and their beasts, both of the greater and the lesser sort, were swallowed up.

Assistant makes a plopping noise with his mouth. Heads turn.

But over the Selected, the god held the shield of his hand, and all save one—being judged unworthy—were saved by the god.

TONY *(quiet; to Sonya):* What one?

SONYA *(whispers):* Wesley.

The Assistant makes more plopping noises, attracting everyone's attention. At Banner's request, Arthur declares the meeting over, and all proceed to investigate the phenomenon. There are so many shrimp in the water that they look to Hunter like "jolly little brown cobblestones. All over. You could walk to land if you knew where it was."

Among them, the voyagers discover, is a huge creature, a giant squid with black snake-like tentacles. To their alarm, the squid toys with the raft. Arthur has no power over the monster, which soon loses interest in the raft and drifts away. Arthur declares that this was the god paying them a visit in the form of a squid—and the god will come again.

ALAN: It was only a squid. You know that bloody well. Frightening the women! It was a giant squid—that's all.

ARTHUR: The god can take many forms. He can take the form of a man or a squid. But in any form, he is terrible.

ALAN: Oh, for Christ's sake, you don't really believe in all that!

Arthur steps forward and hits him. Then he turns and goes inside to the cabin area, followed by Banner. All the others but Sonya and Tony follow him inside, but sit on their chairs on the back wall. Sonya hesitates, as if to stay with Alan.

No. You go in. I'm in disgrace.

Sonya goes. An Assistant comes to Arthur with a frowning mask.

Bloody madness!

Tony is relaxed, watching the water; the shrimp have gone. But Alan already regrets his outburst. When Banner comes to summon Alan into Arthur's presence, Alan resolves to apologize to Arthur for what he now sees was an act of blasphemy, for which Arthur could exact a fearful punishment.

Alan comes before the frowning-masked Arthur and apologizes for his moment of doubt, promising "Never again." Arthur explains to Alan that the god willed the doubt and also wills the expiation for this error. They must make a sacrifice; they must offer an Iphigenia to the god.

Alan fears that he himself is to be designated as the sacrificial victim. He declares himself unworthy—And Arthur agrees. Alan is somewhat relieved for a moment, then he begins to fear desperately that Arthur will choose Sonya. Arthur speaks of Sonya's advanced pregnancy, of the possibility of making the sacrifice in secret, following Sonya's confinement. Alan pleads that the god will not accept a blemished body, that the others will resent the sacrifice of Sonya when they discover that she is missing.

ARTHUR: We shall take the child.

ALAN: The child?

ARTHUR: An innocent life. Unblemished. For the god.

ALAN: The child?

ARTHUR: Yes.

ALAN: Not . . . ?

ARTHUR: Really, Mr. Armitage, have you been following me at all?

ALAN: You're going to take the child? . . . Oh . . . Oh yes, I had quite the wrong idea. Oh, that's wonderful. The child . . . yes. Yes, you do: you must: that's much better. I was quite wrong. I was very afraid and quite wrong. The child. *(Now it hits him.)* But how can you tell her?

They have anesthetics in the first aid kit, Arthur explains, they will put Sonya out and tell her later that the child died at birth. They will make the sacrifice which the god demands.

Dazed, Alan leaves Arthur's presence and goes out on deck, ignoring Tony. Alan, brooding, sits alone *"crouched in a back-to-the-womb position."*

Sonya rises from her chair and follows Alan on deck. But Alan ignores even her until a small signaling gesture passes between Tony and Sonya, arousing Alan's old jealousy. Tony and Sonya know that Arthur has been harassing Alan. They want to comfort and reassure him, but he snaps at them. Alan demands to know whether Tony believes that Arthur is a god.

Tony informs Alan that he doesn't pay attention to such matters, he just minds his own business and tries to keep out of trouble.

Alan is so rude that Sonya apologizes for Alan's jealousy (this is the first that Tony has heard of it). Nothing they can say will make Alan believe anything but the worst.

TONY *(to Alan):* You stupid bastard. You don't know nothing about it.

Pause.

I can't, if you want to know.

Pause.

It's not that I don't fancy you, Sonn, I do, as a matter of fact.

SONYA: Tony, this is not the time.

TONY: But I just can't; that's all. I don't know why. If it was anyone else, it'd be funny. Laughable. When I was sixteen, the boys used to call me a sex maniac—I wore myself out, like; it wasn't healthy. Then I saw an ad in the papers, Why Be a Ninety-Eight Pound Weakling. I thought doing exercises might take me mind off it, you know what I mean. And after a bit I found I wasn't interested no more. I thought it was the exercise done it. Being tired when I came home from the gym. And then I won all them prizes, and had me picture on the cover of "Health and Strength," and they was all after me—I could take me pick—and then when I did want to, I just couldn't.

SONYA: Tony! Give over, eh?

TONY: I've tried. There was one bird I fancied, she wouldn't believe it. She thought I was queer, and she could cure me, but I'm not.

Pause.

So now you know. She's safe with me. Any bird's safe with me.

Alan is abjectly sorry for his suspicions, his sick jealousy. Alan suggests that the three of them find some means of getting away. He tells Tony and Sonya of Arthur's horrible intention of sacrificing the baby to the god. Alan confesses that Arthur so frightened and confused him that he told Arthur he would agree to let this horror take place.

"You must be bloody mad," Tony comments and takes characteristically simple and direct action: he strides into Arthur's holy-of-holies. Arthur moves to protect himself by assuming the mask of the god, but Tony merely throws the mask aside and confronts Arthur man to man.

An Assistant gives Arthur a wooden knife. Arthur stabs Tony, then runs into the Main Saloon, giving the alarm. Tony isn't badly hurt; he runs after Arthur, warning the others that "This loony wants to kill little kids."

Arthur appeals to Alan for help, but Tony warns them all off. Even Banner declares that this quarrel is for the god himself to settle.

Tony and Arthur circle the table. But suddenly Arthur stops. It must appear as if the actor himself has forgotten his lines, and begun to feel ill. He leaves the fight, and supports himself by first holding, then sitting on the table.

ARTHUR: Sorry. I can't go on.

Cast are surprised. They look at the Lecturer for guidance. They will remain still until their next move is indicated, and will always be looking at the Lecturer wherever he may be.

LECTURER: What?

ARTHUR: I'm sorry. I can't go on. I know what will happen.

LECTURER: You are Arthur. You know only what he knows. You cannot know the future.

ARTHUR: I know what will happen. I was a student here.

Lecturer signs to Assistant who goes offstage.

LECTURER *(gentle):* If you know that, if you can remember that, then you know that you will survive it, and go free afterwards.

ARTHUR: But Arthur will die. Tony will break his neck. And I will feel his death. His pain. And you make this happen. You make this happen. You make me Arthur.

LECTURER: You volunteered.

ARTHUR: Yes, I volunteered for prison too, do you remember? We all volunteer. *(To audience.)* You volunteered to attend this lecture. You volunteered to be students, and those who are not students, volunteer not to be. We volunteer to obey in this community. We—

LECTURER: Stop!

The Assistant has brought the Lecturer a glittering object with which the Lecturer re-hypnotizes Arthur—or tries to. The Lecturer tells Arthur that he is to continue the play, as the god. But Arthur refuses; he is not hypnotized.

ARTHUR: You are the god.

LECTURER: I am Leading Lecturer in the History of the Community; that is all. And you are Arthur Henderson. The god Arthur.

ARTHUR: There are no gods here but you. You are the resurrection and the life. You put us here. You plan out the path we are to travel. But I have free will, and I choose not to die, so you can keep your resurrection.

Arthur continues to challenge the Lecturer: what if he decides to kill Tony in the play and change history? The Lecturer, confident, replies that Arthur is not physically strong enough to kill Tony. The Lecturer warns Arthur: it is only as an actor submitting to the Lecturer's will that he can be "revived" after the character of Arthur Henderson is "killed" in the historical play. If Arthur goes on as his unhypnotized, free-willed self, he may really die.

But Arthur chooses to remain himself, and the fight with Tony resumes. Arthur drops his knife. Tony gets a grip around Arthur's neck and is going to kill him, when the Lecturer stops the action. Arthur is unhypnotized, conscious, but held fast in Tony's grip.

Obviously they won't go on with the scene and really kill the actor (the Lecturer tells the audience), but history remains unchanged.

LECTURER: . . . . . Tony killed Arthur, and with the death of the God they came to land, and our New Society began. I do not wish you to undervalue Arthur Henderson. Those early minutes of the New Society are the source of many of our Community Rules. Our very first Community leader was, in fact, the son whom Muriel Otterdale bore to Arthur after his death. The Community always uses what is good in a man. Next week we shall discuss the Early Settlement, the Period of Chaos, and the evolution of the Community Spirit. Mr. Batch, remain. Places, the rest.

Alan, Sonya, Hunter, Banner and Muriel return to their places. Lecturer goes to where Tony still holds Arthur, using Arthur as a specimen in his talk to the audience.

In the case of this criminal who presented Arthur to you, you have been able to study the effects of advanced individualism, which made him, as we now discover, a bad subject for hypnosis, and has caused technical difficulties during the lecture. However, the Community does not and will not allow waste of any kind. We cure criminals; we do not kill them. This man will be returned to medical care—

ARTHUR: No.

LECTURER *(ignores him):* —and you may be sure that, however long it takes, however intense the treatment, in the end he will walk among us again, a free and obedient member of the Community. *(Starts to cross.)* Mr. Batch—

ARTHUR: Kill the god!

Snaps fingers. Tony breaks his neck. Arthur falls to the floor.

LECTURER: Release him. *(To Tony.)* To your place.

Tony goes to join the rest of the cast. Lecturer crosses to Arthur's body, motioning the Assistants away to their stools. He examines the body, then stands, and shaken, addresses the audience.

The prisoner is dead. I have told you that this was no part of the intention of the lecture. Consequently, it is clear that the man himself chose— *(Catches himself in what he is saying. Turns to the Assistants and gestures to them.)* Remove the prisoners.

Lecturer crosses to lectern as the Assistants rise and start tapping the prisoners and pointing the way out.

BANNER: We have come to land, Muriel.

MURIEL: I wonder how we shall go on there, then.

LECTURER: There will be no questions.

MURIEL: I wonder how we shall go on there, then. I wonder how we shall go on there, then.

LECTURER: You will not discuss what you have seen. The lecture is over.

He exits as the last prisoners are going out. Muriel keeps repeating her speech until the curtain has fallen.

SCUBA DUBA

A Comedy in Two Acts

BY BRUCE JAY FRIEDMAN

Cast and credits appear on page 388

BRUCE JAY FRIEDMAN was born in the Bronx in 1930. His father, whose business was women's apparel, moonlighted as a piano player for silent films, and his aunt was assistant treasurer of the Broadhurst Theater, where young Friedman saw his first Broadway shows. He graduated in 1947 from DeWitt Clinton High School and in 1951 from the University of Missouri, where he was drama critic for the college newspaper. He served two years as a lieutenant in the Air Force and wrote a series of "fables" for the magazine Air Training *until these were suppressed because of their anti-establishment flavor.*

Friedman's first professional publication was the short story Wonderful Golden Rule Days *in* The New Yorker *in 1953. Other short Friedman pieces have appeared in* Playboy, Commentary, Mademoiselle *and other magazines, and they have been published in two collections:* Far From the City of Class *(1963) and* Black Angels *(1966). In 1954 Friedman joined the Magazine Management Company and remained there for 12 years, editing the publications* Man, Male *and* Man's World.

Friedman is the author of two novels, Stern *(1962) and* A Mother's Kisses *(1964), the latter now being adapted into a stage musical. He adapted his own story* 23 Pat O'Brien Movies *for an experimental production at The American Place Theater, but* Scuba Duba *(for which he wrote the first draft while visiting the Riviera in 1965 and which he calls "a tense comedy" on the title page of the script) is his professional playwriting debut. Friedman is married, with three sons, and lives on Long Island.*

Time: The present, summer

Place: A chateau in the south of France

ACT I

SYNOPSIS: It is early evening. Harold Wonder, an American in his 30s, is pacing up and down the high-ceilinged main room of his rented chateau in the south of France. The room, furnished conventionally, is a sieve of openings. Along the right wall are French windows looking onto the house of a near neighbor (Miss Janus). The chateau's main entrance gives into the room, upstage. At left is a stairway leading to the second-floor level of bedroom doors along a balcony. Under the stairs is the door to a storage closet and an entrance to the kitchen.

On this particular evening Harold Wonder is patently upset. He paces nervously. He is dressed in pajamas and dressing gown, though it is nowhere near bedtime. He scarcely seems to notice that he is carrying a large scythe.

Brisk piano music next door causes Harold to open a window and shout out a friendly "Hello!" The music stops; then, in answer to Harold's call, his neighbor, Miss Janus steps in through the French window. She is a shapely young creature dressed in a bikini. Harold and Miss Janus take each other's appearance in stride, playing it cool.

HAROLD: Hey, thanks for dropping in. I'm not allowed to leave, myself. *(Defensively.)* I don't need anyone's permission . . . It's just better if I stay here.

MISS JANUS: I thought you might have a giant bird flying loose around here and called me over to help. Every few months someone does that to me. I seem to give the impression I'd know what to do about people's loose birds.

HAROLD *(distantly):* I wish that's all it was. I wish I could turn the whole thing into a bird problem. *(Coming back.)* I thought you'd look different. I thought you'd be a little, I don't know, a little noisier-looking.

He has been using the scythe to accompany his speech.

Oh, this? I'm sorry. I just picked it up and started carrying it around. Well, I didn't just pick it up. Actually, we had a prowler a few nights ago. My wife opened the shutters and came face to face with him, some kind of Swede she said it was. With a frying pan on his head. *(Snapping out of it.)*

MISS JANUS: Maybe he didn't want to steal anything. Maybe he just wanted to go through your wife's purse. Not to steal anything, but just to see what was in it. I had a Syrian friend once who loved to do that. We had a thing where I'd fill up my purse, pretend to be asleep and then he'd tiptoe in and go through it. I put all kinds of surprises in there for him—birth control pills, religious ornaments, surgical appliances, pictures of other Syrian guys . . .

HAROLD: I don't think he was after any of that. I think he was after much bigger stuff. Look, I'm here with my wife. Except for the slight problem that I'm suddenly not here with my wife. That she decided not to be here.

Gesturing with scythe.

Look, on that prowler I mentioned, I'm actually big enough under these things to take care of any trouble by myself. *(Referring to scythe.)* It's just something I do. Whenever there's trouble I pick up things. A friend of mine and I once started a little fight, just for fun. Before we began I remember unconsciously picking up a chicken. One of those ready-made roasted things. I wasn't going to use it or anything. You can imagine how much good it would do you in a fight. Fly all over the goddamned place. I just seem to need something in my hands.

MISS JANUS: You're probably a very tactile person. I am too.

She gets up and flicks at her bikini bottom.

Miss Janus consults Harold about the fit of her bikini—she has been told that it is too small. Harold, through the mist of his own problems, assures her it fits. Miss Janus tells Harold about her experiences in a Greenwich Village night club frequented by electricians, and how she posed in the nude for their photography. Harold can't help being interested in her story, though he finds it rather peculiar that she would make intimate revelations on such a short acquaintanceship.

Besides, Harold has his own story to tell, his own problem that he'd like to get off his chest. He has been trying to reach Dr. Schoenfeld, a psychiatrist Harold knows and likes, who happens to be visiting Monaco.

While Harold is talking, a life-sized cut-out caricature of Dr. Schoenfeld appears from under the staircase at left.

HAROLD: . . . . . I was fired from a job once. It was a big argument over whether I was allowed to use the executive john. Later I started to make more money than ever—but the idea of being fired was wiping me out. So Dr. Schoenfeld says . . .

DR. SCHOENFELD'S VOICE: You're good at looking up and down, Harold, but you've never once looked at life sideways . . .

HAROLD: . . . I never looked at life sideways. He was suggesting I start looking at my problems out of the corner of my eye. It doesn't sound like much, but I tried it . . . *(Demonstrating.)* You know, there's a hell of a lot going on over there on the sides . . .

Dr. Schoenfeld's cut-out exits.

I have to call him in a little while. Look, I feel much better now, even though that electrician story of yours got me a little nervous. . . . .

Now that they have made friends, Harold assures Miss Janus, she may play the piano as loudly as she chooses. Harold tells her he is a writer, specializing in copy for billboards. A Bennington girl once called his billboard copy "the true urban folk literature of the sixties."

Harold is grateful for Miss Janus's company: ". . . . . you've gotten me through a little piece of the night and that's the whole deal. If I can just make it through to the morning I'll be able to handle things a little better."

They are interrupted by the entrance of Harold's landlady—*"a French woman, slightly past middle age"*—with a potential client, a middle-aged American tourist who might rent the chateau after Harold vacates it.

Miss Janus exits at right, as the Landlady tells the Tourist how many famous people have rented this chateau. Harold suggests it's an awkward time for such a business call. The Tourist, garrulous and vulgar, admires Harold's frankness but angers Harold with blunt comments on such matters as "Chink" cooking. Harold loses his temper and asks the Tourist to leave. The Tourist does so, with the final comment: "I like it here. I think I'll take it. It's French. Got a little of that salesgirl smell to it. . . ."

The Landlady remains behind, satisfied that she has rented the chateau for another month, believing (as she does about everybody) that the vulgar American is a famous actor, maybe Tony Curtis.

The Landlady makes it clear to Harold that she would "open her petals" for him, but Harold confesses that he is a mere wreck, in no condition. He wonders why she didn't answer his call for help—*"Au secours!"*—when he saw the prowler the previous evening, but the Landlady doesn't reply, she merely corrects his French pronunciation. The police were no help to Harold, either.

The Landlady repeats her offer of "a special cure for young men" and then she departs. Left alone, Harold smokes nervously, paces up and down, shouts *"Au secours!"* out of the window. Finally the phone rings. It is a trans-Atlantic call Harold placed to his mother (and a cut-out of her appears as she comes on the line).

Harold tells his mother that everything's fine, France is fine, the children are fine. And mom seems to know without being told, halfway around the world, that Harold is holding something heavy in his hand (mom's intuition makes Harold drop the scythe). Harold is very worried about the cost of the call and can't seem to unburden himself as he wishes to, but mom presses on.

MOTHER'S VOICE: Is your wife at your side—where she belongs?

HAROLD: No, mom, Jean is out. That's what it's all about.

MOTHER: I knew it. I could have predicted the whole thing. Who is she out with, darling?

HAROLD: Mom, I can hardly get it out of my mouth. She's run off with a spade frogman.

MOTHER: What kind of frogman, darling?

HAROLD: A spade. Don't you know what that is? She's run off with a goddamned black scuba diver! . . .

MOTHER: Don't talk that way, Harold. It's not nice.

HAROLD: All right, mom. She's with a dark-skinned phantom of the ocean depths. Is that better? How do you think I feel saying something like that on the phone and you don't think I said it politely enough?

MOTHER *(still calm, although news is sinking in now):* A colored frogman. That's what she needed, a colored frogman. You know why she's doing that, don't you, Harold. Because you didn't do enough for her. None of us did. The whole family didn't strip itself naked enough for her. And what did you give her, Harold. The French Riviera? That isn't a vacation, darling, that's a punishment. Didn't you know that. That's where you take people instead of throwing them into dungeons. You know where I would have taken her, Harold. I WOULD HAVE BROUGHT HER BACK TO THAT GHETTO IN BALTIMORE WHERE YOU FOUND HER ON THE STREETS . . .

HAROLD: Look, now don't go too far. You're not exactly a bargain yourself, you know!

MOTHER: Harold, I think there's something wrong with the connection. You couldn't possibly have said what I just heard you say.

HAROLD: How about that cello player you took me up to see when I was seven years old? You forgot him, eh? And that guy who made those alligator handbags. Never heard of him, eh? Well, I didn't forget them so easy. It didn't exactly do me any good to be in on that stuff, so don't go picking on Jean.

MOTHER: Is that why you called, Harold? You thought your mother needed a little filth thrown in her face. All the way from France.

HAROLD: All right, mom, I'm sorry. I didn't mean to get into that.

MOTHER *(in tears):* That's all right, Harold. I'll just consider that my payment after thirty-six years of being your mother.

HAROLD: I think she's going to stay out the whole night and I'm not sure I can take it. I'm waiting for a call now, I'm all alone here.

Mom offers to come to France to be with her boy, but Harold is anxious to end the conversation. He manages to do so, and mom's cut-out disappears as Harold hangs up the phone.

To relieve his tensions, Harold Wonder goes to the window and shouts "JEANNIE, YOU BASTARD. FRANCE YOU PICKED TO PULL THIS ON ME. NOT IN QUEENS WHERE I HAVE DEFENSES. WHERE I HAVE FRIENDS." Harold hears the piano, but the music stops and Miss Janus enters *"wearing flowered slacks, poor boy sweater, eating from a fruit bowl."*

Harold refuses Miss Janus's offer of fruit (but he loves the sloppy way she eats it) and tells her about his wife and the scuba diver. "Scuba duba duba" keeps reverberating in Harold's head. (A cut-out of a giant ape-man appears for a moment, with the sound of jungle drums; then the drums cease and the cut-out disappears.)

Miss Janus offers to cradle Harold Wonder's head to ease his torment, but no—all Harold wants is her company for awhile.

MISS JANUS: I can stay as long as you like. I was just chateau-sitting for my friend Abby and her new husband. Abby and I were roommates in New York while she was going with him. He's a sculptor named Nero. For three years she couldn't even get him to *talk* about marriage—until two months ago when she had her left breast removed. Suddenly Nero felt responsible as hell, wanted to marry her immediately. She hadn't come out of the ether and he had her in front of a minister. Abby wouldn't let me move out—it was almost as though she felt sorry for me for having both my breasts and having to be single. So I kind of tagged along with them to France. Something's supposed to happen between the three of us. I'm not sure what. It hasn't yet, but it's always in the air. At least once a day someone says "What'll we do tonight?" Then the air gets very tense, I think it would have happened already, but no one knows how to start. Or who's supposed to do what to who. And then there's always Abby's breast to worry about. How are you supposed to work that in?

HAROLD *(abashed):* You walked in here with some collection of stories.

MISS JANUS: Maybe one night Nero will say "Let's go girls" and we'll all take off our clothes. Simple as that.

Harold comments of his wife's lover that he wears his flippers out of water—and looks graceful in them. Miss Janus rambles on in her corrosively innocent fashion: perhaps they are waiting for Abby to die. Nero once made her inhale something from a sponge, but drugs (she has tried them all) have no effect on her except to make her behind itch.

Harold tells Miss Janus that his wife Jean has had three previous lovers—a floor shellacker, a swimming pool cleaner and a garbage collector. (Three men enter, notice each other, lock arms in a comradely manner and exit without a word.) Harold once tried dressing in flashy clothes to attract Jean, but Jean reacted by holding on to the roll of fat around Harold's midriff until Harold had to hit her to make her let go.

Suddenly Harold changes the subject and asks Miss Janus why she doesn't just move out on her two friends. Miss Janus replies with another of her stories, about how she drifted into her first love affair (her father aimed a gun at the boy's head in fun, and she promptly led the boy out to a shed full of old newspapers and magazines, where they made love).

Harold alternates between worrying about his children asleep upstairs, lashing out in anger at his wife and the scuba diver, and reacting to Miss Janus's stories.

Harold would like to run the scythe through the scuba diver's gizzard, except . . . in a way, Harold himself was responsible for throwing the two together. Harold describes to Miss Janus how he and Jean met the diver in Cannes, using a projector and color slides to illustrate his description.

HAROLD: . . . . . What happened is that we met the black bastard in Cannes one afternoon, right after we got here, standing around at one of those sidewalk restaurants, with his flippers on and this black suit and that breathing equipment on his back. Wait a minute.

Goes to get slide machine.

You want to hear one. I even took pictures of the thing.

Sets up slide show, ad libs.

You take away the skin diving stuff and he isn't really that handsome, but he has this smile that shows up now and then. It's as though he has a zipper across his mouth. He kind of unzips that smile and when you see his teeth it kind of puts him in a different league . . . Anyway, all summer long, we'd been hearing about this wonderful loup fish. . . . .

The restaurant had no loup that day, Harold continues, so the skin diver obligingly jumped into the water and came out with one of them on his spear.

HAROLD: . . . . . Well, it really *was* a kind of charming thing to do. I mean the *way* he presented the damned thing. Anyway, we bought him a drink, dinner—he didn't say much except that even as a kid he'd always had these strong lungs. *(Goes to screen, shouts.)* COME ON OUT YOU SONOFABITCH. I'LL TAKE YOU EVEN IF YOU HAVE STRONG LUNGS AND I AM A LITTLE AFRAID OF THAT SPEARGUN.

Climbs down as though nothing had happened.

Calmly, Harold goes on: the diver was a good guy, really, and they sought his company whenever they went to Cannes. In another of his outbursts of rage, Harold tears up a slide, then controls himself. He continues: more and more often his wife Jean insisted on being by herself in the afternoons.

HAROLD: . . . . . and then I get this call earlier tonight. This is it, she says. I'm with him, I'm staying with him and it isn't just for tonight, it's for always, words and music by Irving Berlin. I can go down to the Mediterranean and drain it out cup by cup as far as she's concerned and it's not going to do any good. I'm supposed to stay with the children and maybe she'll call and at a certain point she'll come and get them because she wants them. And she's not kidding, either, this really *is* it. You should have heard her voice. So what am I supposed to do now, ask some spade if I can come visit my kids once in a while? Work my ass off so that she can buy gold flippers for a goddamned spade frogman? What's he gonna do, send my kids to some spade school? A spade underwater school in France somewhere? Now you take the flippers in your right hand . . . What am I supposed to do, start calling up girls now and ask them out on picnics? In the condition I'm in? What do I do, go to Over 28 dances? I mean, what the hell am I supposed to do? I'm shaking like a leaf. How do you feel about men crying?

It's O.K. by Miss Janus, but Harold Wonder's moment of despair passes quickly. At first (he explains to Miss Janus) he tried to ridicule his wife's relationship with the frogman. Then he tried appealing to her by reminding her of all the good times they had together (but in reality they didn't have a strong bond; once he made love to her one-handed, and from then on their sex life went downhill until finally Harold's wife could be excited to love-making only in strange bathrooms in other people's houses).

Finally Harold "hit her with the kids" but this didn't work either because Jean and her lover expect to take care and custody of the children themselves. Harold loves his children (he assures Miss Janus) and often plays a favorite game with them. He shows Miss Janus the game, which is twisting her arms and legs together until she is all tied up in a knot which Harold calls the "Double Reverse Panther Bear Pretzel Twist."

While Miss Janus is cramped in this fashion Harold kisses her, which reminds her of another of her stories. Her only real love was a writer and "What we did, really, was wander through each other like we were the first man and woman."

Harold tries a couple of pushups and knee bends to pass the time, and finally Miss Janus, untangled, suggests that she give him a massage. Miss Janus assures Harold that massage is not, as some people have suggested, a homosexual pleasure (in fact she doubts whether there really is any such thing as a homosexual relation: "Certainly not between two men. Why would they bother? There are so many other things they could be out doing.").

Harold reflects that it might have been worse, he might have lost his wife to a *fag* frogman. Miss Janus massages Harold's knees and momentarily he is distracted by enjoyment. But Harold soon snaps back into his troubles.

He picks up the phone and calls Dr. Schoenfeld in Monaco and describes his problem (as Dr. Schoenfeld's cut-out appears). The doctor tries to soothe Harold with jargon, but Harold pleads with him to come to the chateau, to help him get through the night. Dr. Schoenfeld agrees to come, and is bringing a friend. The cut-out disappears as the phone conversation ends.

Harold conjures up the thought that "right this second, as we sit here, my wife is up on a chandelier with a spade." Miss Janus remarks that Harold seems to like that word and Harold agrees—he likes the word "spade," it has a smooth sound. The Negroes, he thinks, have all the best slang names, whereas "Wop. Kike. See? Nothing." Harold is mixed-up about Negroes (he confesses to Miss Janus). He once went on a freedom march, but instead of concentrating on the speeches he was attracted by a girl and took her behind a tree.

Miss Janus assures Harold that this was the act of a warm, glandular human being. She has come around to thinking that she would like to go to bed with Harold to see what it would be like. But before she can persuade him, the phone rings.

Harold goes to phone, looks back and then takes it near a clothing closet where, standing up, he begins to pull coats over his head for privacy.

HAROLD: Hello Jeannie-and-if-it-is-don't-say-a-word-because-I'm-doing-all-the-talking. Now Jeannie, look, I don't care what's happened. You got a little nervous, it's a foreign country, all right I'm a little shook up, but it's over, I forgive you and you're coming right the hell home where you belong.

We'll take a few trips. Remember we were going to use this as home base and see Barcelona? . . . It is *not* just the beginning! . . . All right then, we'll go to Liverpool. Any place you say . . . I'm the one who *is* facing facts! . . . Jeannie, I'm all alone here. What do you think this has been like for me? . . . A *strain?* . . . You're holed up with a nigger frogman and you call me up and all it is is a little strain . . . Strain? . . . . .

Harold goes to the window and screams his defiance of her lover into the night, then returns to the phone and assures his wife that he can be nice to her—"In my own style . . . I use both hands, too! It was just that one time. I can't explain it."

Harold orders his wife to come home. He deprecates her lover. He threatens to walk out and leave the children alone in the chateau if she doesn't come home within the hour.

HAROLD: . . . . . I mean just come home. Will you just do that. He won't *let* you. *(Out the window.)* YOU WON'T LET HER, YOU FAG BASTARD. I JUST HEARD ABOUT THAT. IT JUST CAME IN OVER THE WIRE. WHAT DO YOU MEAN YOU WON'T LET HER. YOU OPEN THOSE GODDAMNED DOORS OR I'M COMING OVER THERE TO CUT YOUR BALLS OFF. *(To the phone.)* All right, I'm calm . . . I am . . . It's because you can't see me. I'm in complete control of myself.

Thief enters, begins to steal things—Harold doesn't see him. Miss Janus tries to reason with Thief.

(Out the window.) YOU LIKE MY BILLBOARDS, EH. I'LL GIVE YOU BILLBOARDS. I'LL BILLBOARD YOUR ASS WHEN I GET HOLD OF YOU. YOU BLACK SONOFABITCH.

Into the phone at the same time he spots Thief.

Yeah, well he can afford to be a gentleman. I'll show him dignity. I'll show him who's beneath who. Now Jeannie will you just come home. *(Hollering out the window.)* YOU WENT ONE STEP TOO FAR. A LOT OF GUYS MAKE THAT MISTAKE WITH ME. *(Noticing Thief.)* HOLD ON A SECOND. *(Into phone.)* Hold on a second.

Picks up scythe and hurls it through the shutters, then plumps down in a chair, addressing Miss Janus.

She'll be here in twenty minutes flat. Have I steered you wrong once tonight?

Curtain.

ACT II

Shortly afterward, Miss Janus is admiring the speed with which Harold Wonder moved to throw the scythe after the thief. A Gendarme knocks and enters with the Thief in custody. The Gendarme has a chip on his shoulder over the American economy and attitude, and it is almost impossible not to insult him.

The Landlady enters, denying that any unpleasantness took place in her chateau. The Thief protests in his defense that all men are thieves. Harold wants the Thief put in jail, but the Thief, the Gendarme and the Landlady sing "La Marseillaise" in defiance of Harold and exit singing as Dr. Schoenfeld enters with a lot of luggage and a wild, roaring blonde named Cheyenne. Cheyenne confronts Harold and comes right to the point.

CHEYENNE: . . . . . Say, Phillsy told me about your old lady. Never you mind. Soon as she runs out of money that spade'll drop her like a hot pizza.

HAROLD: Good Christ!

DR. SCHOENFELD: Harold, I'd like you to meet Cheyenne. *(Noticing Miss Janus.)* I don't think I've had the pleasure.

MISS JANUS: Hi, Dr. Schoenfeld, I'm Carol Janus.

CHEYENNE: 'Ello, lambchop, how are you?

HAROLD: This is the fancy treatment you thought up. My wife's out screwing the rules committee of SNICK and you had to come running over here with this.

DR. SCHOENFELD: It's just one chapter.

CHEYENNE *(at bookshelves):* Say, you got any books by Bernie Malamud? Once you get started on those urban Jews it's like eating potato chips. If you ask me, you can take C.P. Snow and shove him up your keester.

DR. SCHOENFELD: Cheyenne, please. I have something important to say to Mr. Wonder. . . . .

What Dr. Schoenfeld has to say is, the old sideways advice won't work any longer, he and Harold must intensify their relationship. Harold must give Dr. Schoenfeld something that Harold greatly values, so that Harold will also value and heed the doctor's advice.

Harold exits in search of a valuable object while Cheyenne unburdens herself chattily to Miss Janus: her problem is too many sexual climaxes. Dr. Schoenfeld is trying to train her down to five a night.

Harold comes back with a muffler his mother knitted and presents it to Dr. Schoenfeld. Dr. Schoenfeld tries to help Harold with a story about barley distribution in the army, as an illustration of his advice. But the story's point is so obscure that Harold asks for his scarf back and wrestles for it until he recovers it.

Dr. Schoenfeld resigns himself to try again in the morning. He and Cheyenne go upstairs with the luggage and exit into their assigned bedroom.

Miss Janus tells Harold another of her stories, this one about a timid obscene phone call from a boy at Columbia. Cheyenne reappears on the balcony in her bathrobe in search of the bidet and is directed to the proper door. Miss Janus continues with her story about arranging a rendezvous with the perpetrator of the obscene phone call—a youth whose face was "practically all horn-rimmed glasses." Cheyenne reappears in her underwear, soaked and complaining about the function of the bidet, as she exits through the bedroom door.

Harold remembers that he himself once placed an obscene phone call, saying the word "pelvis" to his teacher. Cheyenne appears *again,* nude from the waist up, and comes downstairs in search of some warm milk for Dr. Schoenfeld. She finds it and returns upstairs, nonchalantly and immodestly, whistling "Winchester Cathedral."

MISS JANUS *(stretching):* You know, it isn't that much . . . we could just sort of drift upstairs too . . .

HAROLD *(getting up):* I don't know how it would be . . . Maybe if you just told me a few more of those stories. Do you have any left? Just feed me a few more and we'll see what happens.

MISS JANUS: All right.

She comes toward him, sits behind him.

Once I was trying on dresses in a store up in Maine. I reached into the size nine rack and there was a little man all covered up inside a two-piece jersey ensemble . . .

Light changes as though many hours have passed. Indication is that it is dawn. Harold is still in his bathrobe, groggy, exhausted. Miss Janus has been going on with her stories, as though she has been telling them endlessly.

. . . a Russian take-out restaurant. Anyway, I was delivering an order of borscht to a customer and I see his pockets are all filled with petitions, bills, proclamations. So I put two and two together and I said, "Listen, just because you're in the House of Representatives doesn't mean I'm staying over tonight." *(Realizes how much time has gone by.)* Oh my God, I locked Nero and Abby out.

Exits. Jean Wonder appears—young, early 30s, attractive, rather forlorn at the moment, and prone to bumping into things.

JEAN: Harold . . . How are you . . .

HAROLD: What do I know . . .

JEAN: How are the kids?

HAROLD: They're fine, under the circumstances. You all right?

Jean has a pain in her arm, and her neck is a little tensed up, but she's going to have to live with it. Nervously, Jean begins to dust the room and Harold makes her stop. Jean accuses Harold of putting on his little-boy face that he uses whenever he wants something.

HAROLD: I never made this face before in my life.

JEAN: Right. I just came in here . . . I was going to get a few things . . .

HAROLD: No things, no things. That's one line I never want to hear. *(In British accent.)* "Dudley, I've come for my things." Anybody gets their things, that's the end of their things. In this house, you get your stuff, hear? And you don't get that either . . . This is some mess . . .

JEAN: I know.

HAROLD: I think this is the worst we ever had.

JEAN: I don't know, Harold. I think when I was pregnant and we couldn't get any heat in the apartment and you had to organize a warmth committee in the building at four in the morning. I think that was worse . . .

HAROLD: No, I think this is worse. I had a lot of people on my side in that one. I had the whole building cheering me on. I'm all alone on this one.

Jean feels disturbed and disconnected in this situation, too, and "at this point I'd settle for just getting through the morning." Harold goes on his knees to beg her to come home. But then he reflects that possibly she may have told her lover his pet name for her—"Pidge"—and once again anger gets the better of him.

HAROLD: . . . . . Drag in that chocolate shithead. I've been waiting for this all night.

JEAN: Harold, could you try to be a little dignified. I can get that style from my father. I don't need it from you. I grew up with that. You know, for a second, I really felt a little something . . . the first time in years . . . and then you have just heaved it right out the window . . .

HAROLD *(peering through window):* Is he out there?

JEAN: Yes, he's out there, Harold. But you can't see him because it's still a little dark and he has all this natural camouflage.

HAROLD *(still looking out):* How come he's afraid to get his black ass in here?

JEAN: He couldn't possibly face you, Harold. Not after what I told him. You see, I told him about your poise. About your quiet dignity. About your finesse in handling difficult situations. He wouldn't come within ten miles of the place . . .

HAROLD: I'm going to be dignified. I'm going to be Dag Hammarskjold. Just get the sonofabitch in here . . .

Elaborately, Jean tries to calm Harold by pointing out that most tourists who have come three thousand miles to enjoy the charming French villages do not stand around in a bathrobe shouting out of windows. She has found, on the outside, that some men actually treat women gently, romantically, even read poetry to them. Out there, she doesn't feel awkward, or trip, or bump into things.

Frogman in full undersea regalia enters casually, speargun in hand. Harold walks through door and doesn't see him.

HAROLD *(shouting):* I dare you to come in here and face me . . . *(Spots Frogman.)* I'm sorry, I got a little confused.

FROGMAN: That's all right, sweetie-baby, it's a tough scene all around. I can tell you got a lot of heart.

HAROLD: Now look, I'm cold, I'm shaky, I've been up all night. I'm not at my best in the morning. It takes me till around noon to hit my stride. To be perfectly frank, I'm a little afraid of colored people. It's a completely irrational thing. Little girls, even old ladies. I have this feeling they were all in the Golden Gloves once . . . You know what I mean?

FROGMAN: Let me give you a little advice, Jim. You sass an old colored lady, she gone lean back and give you the bad eye. She gone work some roots on you, babe, then you really in a shitstorm.

HAROLD: Very cute, very cute. There's just one thing. We happen to be on *my* turf now, you sonofabitch . . .

Second Negro enters, pipe-smoking, intellectual, quite good-looking in an esthetic way. This is Reddington.

REDDINGTON: Hi, Pidge.

HAROLD: Everybody knows Pidge. Who the hell is this.

REDDINGTON: Is everything all right . . . Pidge?

JEAN: I'll just be another minute.

FROGMAN: Hey baby, you made the scene just in time. We all going sit down and have some chitlins.

REDDINGTON: Cool it, Foxtrot.

HAROLD: Oh, now we're getting a little "cool it." How about a little "daddy." A little "dig," a little "daddy." Who is this guy, Jeannie?

JEAN: Harold, this is Ambrose Reddington.

HAROLD: That tells me a lot.

JEAN: Harold, I'm sorry, I really wanted to avoid this. I met Ambrose a few days ago . . . A complete accident. He was very sweet to me and I take full credit for him. Foxtrot is your idea, one hundred per cent. A Harold Wonder special. You like him, you can't live without him. I'll tell you what—pick up the phone, make a reservation and the two of you can go flying down to Rio.

HAROLD: Hilarious.

FROGMAN: Suppose I'll just hop right into my travelin' duds . . .

HAROLD *(threatening):* Don't push me too far, just don't push me too far. *(Recovering.)* Give me a minute to adjust to this. *(Contemplates.)* I can't adjust to this.

Walks toward Reddington. Resuming anger.

I WAS JUST SAYING WE'RE ON MY TURF NOW, YOU SONOFABITCH. YOU'RE NOT AT ANY BLACK MUSLIM CONVENTION.

FROGMAN: Oh, I now see where it's at . . .

HAROLD: Look, I'm sorry to have to use the racial stuff, but you'll just have to overlook it. It gives me a slight edge, but I can assure you it's got nothing to do with my true feelings. If everyone felt the way I did, you'd have clear sailing from here on it . . . WHAT'S IMPORTANT IS THAT I CAN STILL SMELL MY WIFE ON YOU, YOU BASTARD . . .

REDDINGTON: Mr. Wonder, I can see that this is a difficult situation for you, but we certainly ought to be able to deal with it as mature adults.

Reddington has a coughing fit. Harold finds himself fetching and feeding Reddington some cough medicine. But Foxtrot the Frogman continues to jeer at Harold: "That poor old colored man went out there in the bushes and jugged your wife." Harold is almost certainly not going to behave as a mature adult.

The Landlady enters with the Tourist and assumes that the Frogman is Sidney Poitier. The Tourist makes bigoted remarks about Slavs, so Frogman recognizes him as his lawful prey and begins needling. Meanwhile Reddington is attempting to explain to Harold (as a mature adult) that his relationship with Jean started innocently but has become "a powerful attraction."

The Tourist tees off on Italians, then follows the Landlady in an inspection of the chateau. Frogman is still needling. Reddington quotes a few lines of his poetry which has been accepted by the *Partisan Review*. Harold, now professionally as well as emotionally jealous, fights back with verses of his own.

HAROLD: . . . . . Here's a little poetry . . . *(Reciting.)*
Intruders ye be . . . make haste, abandon this place . . .
Or I'll punch that spade in his colored face . . .

REDDINGTON: Don't push me too far, Mister.

HAROLD *(to Reddington):* Push you too far . . . The main thing is I can outwrite you, I can outfight you, I can outthink you . . .

FROGMAN: Yeah, but there's one thing you can't *out* him, babe. That man there is a colored man.

REDDINGTON: Foxtrot . . .

FROGMAN: Yeah, baby.

REDDINGTON: I see no point in turning this into a gutter confrontation.

FROGMAN: Shit, man, I was just holdin' up my Negritude. That man was hittin' up on you, Ambrose.

REDDINGTON: I can take care of myself.

HAROLD: Well, what the hell would you do? I mean say you were in my shoes. Say I was you for a second and you were me . . .

FROGMAN: You askin' an awful lot, babe . . .

HAROLD: No, I'm serious. What the hell am I supposed to do. Let your friend just waltz off with her. Because he's colored. Throw in a few kids. Maybe some General Electric stock I've been saving up. To show I'm not prejudiced. You know this is not an easy position to be in. I'm just trying to hang in there. It's bad enough I'm not allowed to get as angry as I'd like to . . . If I toss in a little racial slur every now and then, you'll just have to put up with it. If you don't like it, you know where the door is.

Harold suddenly grabs a wine bottle and smashes it on a ledge, brandishing the jagged edge on the group, the Negroes in particular.

All right, that's it. There's no more problem because I just solved the whole thing. The first sonofabitch that comes near me is going to get my initials carved in his head.

Everyone freezes as Harold grabs Jean, brandishing jagged bottle with great menace.

I can't go through with the thing.

Flings away bottle. Frogman catches it.

FROGMAN *(to Harold):* You know I like that . . . the way you whipped out that bottle and almost cut your own natural-born ass off. Little more of that, you gonna be ready for 125th Street . . .

Harold admits that he is not at his best. He is confused; beaten. Frogman chases the Tourist off with his speargun. Harold asks for a few moments alone with Jean, and Reddington accedes to his request. The Landlady leaves and Reddington exits.

Frogman remains behind and asks for corn bread, still putting Harold on. Then, for a moment, he drops his pose.

FROGMAN *(straight, no accent, serious):* I was born on a farm in Aiken, South Carolina, one of nine children, six boys and three girls. They called me Billy-boy in those days because no matter what happened, I'd just buck my way through. Once I was driving and I turned a car over, seven times, got out, kept walking to the post office. I stay close to one brother, George, who sees to it that I don't wise off. He says, "Maybe you're great, but let other people find it out. Don't you tell them." I lost my father in a farm accident, and didn't care much about it one way or the other. My mom's still pretty. She won a contest designing hats and my brother told the newspaperman if any of them interviewed her he'd go after them and kill them no matter where they tried to hide. I haven't got tired of the water yet. Nothing much to it. I'll just stick with it, make a few bucks, probably quit, sometime.

HAROLD: What?

Frogman exits.

Boy, what a pleasure to have two seconds of peace in your own home.

JEAN: All right, Harold, what's the great thing that you had to have me all alone to tell me about . . .

Harold promises Jean he will give her anything she wants, if only she will come home. He will act colored (he says, doing a Bill Robinson shuffle) if that's what she wants. But far from persuading Jean, Harold's pleas merely bring on some of her ailments. Harold's words hurt her hip, his ironies threaten her sinuses.

Harold wants to know what it is that Reddington does that is so attractive to Jean.

HAROLD: . . . . . He's a colored guy, he knows stuff, he does stuff, they teach him things. Give me an idea.

JEAN: Oh, God. He doesn't do any *one* thing, Harold. People don't do *one* thing. It's a whole lot of things, if you must know. A whole combination of things.

HAROLD: Well what are they? Can you tell me a few?

JEAN: You're really going about this the wrong way . . .

HAROLD: Tell me just one . . . One thing.

JEAN: I can't.

HAROLD: Will you come on, one lousy thing. What do you have to lose?

JEAN: I can't *do* that.

HAROLD: Jeannie, for crying out loud, the marriage is down the drain, I'm sitting here, I'm a terminal marriage fellow, will you tell me one thing . . .

JEAN: He strokes my ear . . .

HAROLD *(leaping up):* I can't do that? I can't outstroke that sonofabitch twenty times a day? Stroke, stroke . . .

He fights to stroke her ear. She struggles.

JEAN: HAROLD . . .

He wins through.

HAROLD: There. All right, how was it?

JEAN: It was thrilling, Harold. It really turned me on. Can I go now?

Harold hurtles down the wrong track. He clutches Jean in an absurd attempt to make love to her. Jean warns him that they are not in the bathroom now, there are people about. For a few moments Harold persists in frantic attempts at lovemaking, then sees that it is no use and breaks off.

All right—Harold will resign himself to Jean's leaving. He pretends that he has an inner strength that will permit him to endure and enjoy life. He warns Jean that a beautiful young girl has been trying to make love to him.

Harold calls out the window for Miss Janus and she enters informing them that a huge statue has fallen on her friend Nero, but he escaped injury because he was covered with grease and managed to slide out of the way (Nero is on a grease kick just now).

To Harold's disgust, it turns out that Jean is not at all jealous of Miss Janus—in fact the two girls like each other from the start. Jean admires Miss Janus's slacks.

Dr. Schoenfeld and Cheyenne pick this moment to appear with bags packed, on their way out. Dr. Schoenfeld leaves with a parting word of advice to Harold: "It's time you got up on your own two feet and faked your way into the adult community."

Frogman enters and sings a chorus of "Uncle Misery," just to bear out Harold's stereotype vision. Jean ridicules Harold for being a Defender of the Negro, describing how Harold is extremely aggressive while driving a car except toward Negro drivers.

Harold cries out that "I've straightened out plenty of colored guys. I just don't do it in front of you. I've taken on whole moving vans full of them." To prove it, Harold punches Frogman in the jaw and knocks him down. Tourist and Landlady come in to see what's happening, and Harold punches Tourist so that he reels out the door in the Landlady's arms. Reddington comes in and grabs Harold, immobilizing him.

Jean has rushed to the aid of Frogman, who staggers to his feet doing a Joe Louis imitation. Harold realizes that he has made a mess of the situation. The others want no more of it, they are determined to leave. Jean will return later to take away the children.

REDDINGTON: . . . . . You've blown your cool, Mr. Wonder, and you are far from a credit to your race.

HAROLD: Jeannie, please, no doors, okay. No doors. I'm not fooling around any more. You leave now you might as well sign a death certificate for me. Just fill one out and leave it over there on the couch on your way out. Jeannie, I'm about to come out with the worst thing a guy ever said in the whole history of modern recorded statements. The kind of thing that if I knew I was going to be reduced to saying it, I wouldn't have even bothered growing up. Jeannie, I have to have you in the house. And you can do whatever the hell you want. Just so long as you're there. You have to have colored guys, you got 'em. Take them upstairs with you. Close the door, I'll make the goddamned beds for you. You want a trapeze, I'll set that up, too. Anything you want. I just need to have you here awhile. So I can slowly build up my strength. You want to leave then, we have a whole new situation. *(To Negroes.)* Look, what do you guys have to lose. You're coughing your head off; *you* can hardly stand on your feet. Where you going to get a cab at this hour. You go upstairs with her, it's cool, it's comfortable, you got television, you got everything you want . . .

JEAN: Will somebody get me out of here. Right now.

REDDINGTON: Jean.

Jean takes Reddington by the arm.

HAROLD *(to Jean on her way out):* What did I just do. I was trying to be nice to them. Well, what am I supposed to do, throw them out on their ass. Punch them in the mouth . . . I did that already . . .

Jean and two Negroes exit.

(Calling through door.) These people haven't had it that easy, Jeannie. They haven't had any sleigh ride. We tend to forget . . . They've done plenty of suffering . . .

Runs to window now.

JEANNIE . . . Where you going . . . Hey, can't you get your own broads. Wait till I get my hands on you . . . You black bastards . . . What the hell did I do. Did you see me make one wrong move? Did I step out of line once? She'll be back. She just needs a few days in the sun. A different kind of sun. We get crummy sun right here around the house. You sit out there for hours you end up white as a sheet.

MISS JANUS: You know, I think you're right. I think I'm whiter than when I started . . .

HAROLD: What the hell am I supposed to do now. I'm a lonely guy.

Miss Janus has a suggestion. She and her two friends Abby and Nero are going shell-collecting this evening, and she invites Harold to come along. Harold accepts her invitation, he must start his new life at once, and he will be all right this evening, he's sure, if he can just get through until about 3 o'clock in the afternoon.

Miss Janus departs, expecting to see Harold later.

Harold paces back and forth, picks up scythe, looks at it, flings it aside, can't seem to get comfortable. Recreates all activities he's tried—calls, kneebends, etc., everything that's worked for him—all cut off in the middle.

HAROLD *(shouting out window):* JEANNIE . . . I'M GOING OUT WITH BROADS . . . TWO OF THEM . . . WE'RE GOING TO LOOK FOR SHELLS . . . YOU MET ONE, REMEMBER . . . HER FRIEND'S EVEN BETTER LOOKING . . . THERE'S NO COMPARISON. YOU SEE THIS NEW GIRL, YOU FORGET THE OTHER ONE'S ALIVE . . . I'M GOING OUT WITH THE TWO OF THEM . . . AND THIS GREASY GUY . . . HE'S COMING ALONG, TOO . . .

He turns away for an instant, then returns to window as lights dim.

ONCE I GO LOOKING FOR SHELLS, THAT'S THE LAST WORD YOU'LL EVER HEAR FROM ME. IF I FIND OUT I LOVE IT, I'LL THROW YOU RIGHT OUT OF THE HOUSE. RIGHT OUT OF THE HOUSE. YOU HEAR ME JEANNIE!

As the lights go to black.

RIGHT OUT OF THE GODDAM HOUSE.

Curtain.

ROSENCRANTZ AND GUILDENSTERN ARE DEAD

A Play in Three Acts

BY TOM STOPPARD

Cast and credits appear on page 344

TOM STOPPARD was born in 1937 in Zlin, Czechoslovakia, where his original family name was Straussler. When he was 18 months old his father, a physician, moved the family to Singapore, and from that time on Stoppard was brought up within the English-speaking culture. During World War II the doctor sent his wife and son for safety to India, where the boy attended an American school in Darjeeling. His father was killed in Singapore by the invading Japanese. After the war Stoppard, age 9, and his mother (remarried to an English major) moved to England, where Stoppard attended school until he was 17 and then entered upon a writing career, first as a journalist (at Bristol) and then as a free-lance whose credits include several TV and radio plays. Stoppard's first stage play, A Walk on Water, *was produced on British TV in 1963 and on the stage in Hamburg and Vienna in 1964 (and is to be staged in London soon). His first novel,* Lord Malquist and Mr. Moon, *was published last year.*

Stoppard's present play, his first to appear on the London and New York stages, began as a one-act verse burlesque called Rosencrantz and Guildenstern, *written in Berlin on a Ford Foundation grant in 1964. Returning to England, Stoppard began work on a full-length version which emerged as* Rosencrantz and Guildenstern Are Dead, *produced by the Oxford Theater*

Group at the 1966 Edinburgh Festival. A new Stoppard play, The Real Inspector Hound, *is to be produced in London in 1968-'69. Stoppard now lives in London and is married, with one child, a son.*

INTRODUCTION BY THE PLAYWRIGHT

This is a play about Rosencrantz and Guildenstern; that much I'll allow. Writers I have read and admired in varying degrees include Beckett, Kafka and Pirandello; that much I'll admit. For the rest, when people talk to me about this play I feel like a smuggler's dupe confronted by a Customs Officer. I cheerfully declare my responsibility for a play about two specific individuals in a particular situation, and then the fellow starts ransacking my luggage and coming up with all manner of exotic contraband such as the nature of identity, of life, of death, of God, and I have to admit the stuff is there all right but I can't for the life of me remember packing it.

In other words, a play isn't the end product of an idea—the idea is the end product of a play.

—TOM STOPPARD

Time and Place: Within and around the action of Shakespeare's Hamlet

ACT I

SYNOPSIS: Two well-dressed Elizabethan young men are killing time in a place *"without any visible character"* except that it seems to be outdoors, somewhere. The young men are Rosencrantz and Guildenstern, one of them in black doublet and hose and one in brown, one with a full leather money bag and one with a nearly empty one. But they are almost interchangeable and even between themselves unconcerned as to which is which, Guil or Ros, Ros or Guil.

The two young men are matching coins, and they have been doing it for a long time.

> *The run of "heads" is impossible, yet Ros betrays no surprise at all—he feels none. However, he is nice enough to feel a little embarrassed at taking so much money off his friend. Let that be his character note.*
>
> *Guil is well alive to the oddity of it. He is not worried about the money, but he is worried by the implications; aware but not going to panic about it—his character note.*

Guil sits. Ros stands (he does the moving, retrieving coins). Guil spins, Ros studies coin.

ROS: Heads *(He picks it up and puts it in his bag. The process is repeated.)* Heads. *(Again.)* Heads. *(Again.)* Heads. *(Again.)* Heads.

GUIL *(flipping a coin):* There is an art to the building up of suspense.

ROS: Heads.

GUIL *(flipping another):* Though it can be done by luck alone.

ROS: Heads.

GUIL: If that's the word I'm after.

ROS *(raises his head at Guil):* Seventy-nine love.

Guil gets up but has nowhere to go, his attention being directed at his environment or lack of it.

GUIL: A weaker man might be moved to re-examine his faith, if in nothing else at least in the law of probability.

But the coins continue to come up heads, ninety times and more. Guil tries every tricky way of flipping them, but to no avail—still heads. Guil deliberates: there must be a reason for this suspension of the law of averages—time has stopped, or God is doing Ros a favor, or something.

Guil jumps nervously in conversation from a syllogism to a series of prodding questions: What is the first thing Ros remembers? Is Ros happy? What are they going to do now? In rising tension, Guil remembers that a messenger called on them—the memory sends him skittering into verbiage, as though words themselves were a protection against the fearsome dark. Guil expounds on the possibility that they are in the grip of some supernatural force, then rejects this notion.

GUIL: . . . . . We can take it that we are not held within un-, sub- or supernatural forces after all; in all probability, that is. Which is a great relief to me personally.

Small pause.

Which is all very well, except that—a messenger arrived. We had been sent for. Nothing else happened. Ninety-two coins spun consecutively have come down heads ninety-two consecutive times . . . and for the last three minutes on the wind of a windless day I have heard the sound of drums and flute . . .

ROS *(cutting his fingernails):* Another curious scientific phenomenon is the fact that the fingernails grow after death, as does the beard.

GUIL: What?

ROS *(loud):* Beard!

GUIL: But you're not dead.

ROS *(irritated):* I didn't say they *started* to grow after death!

Pause, calmer.

The fingernails also grow before birth, though *not* the beard.

GUIL: *What?*

ROS *(shouts):* Beard! What's the matter with you? *(Reflectively.)* The toenails, on the other hand, never grow at all.

GUIL *(bemused):* The toenails on the other hand never grow at all?

ROS: Do they? It's a funny thing—I cut my fingernails all the time, and every time I think to cut them, they need cutting. Now, for instance. And yet, I never, to the best of my knowledge, cut my toenails. They ought to be curled under my feet by now, but it doesn't happen. I never think about them.

Pause.

Perhaps I cut them absent-mindedly, when I'm thinking of something else.

GUIL *(tensed up by this rambling):* Do you remember the first thing that happened today?

ROS *(promptly):* I woke up, I suppose. *(Triggered.)* Oh—I've got it now—that man, a foreigner, he woke us up—

GUIL: A messenger. . . . .

They remember being sent for. Now, at the behest of that messenger, they are traveling—they don't know exactly why.

ROS *(dramatically):* It was urgent—a matter of extreme urgency, a royal summons, his very words: official business and no questions asked—lights in the stable-yard, saddle up and off headlong and hotfoot across the land, our guides outstripped in breakneck pursuit of our duty! Fearful lest we come too late!!

Small pause.

GUIL: Too late for what?

ROS: How do I know? We haven't got there yet.

GUIL: An awakening, a man standing on his saddle to bang on the shutters, our names shouted in a certain dawn, a message, a summons . . . A new record for heads and tails. We have not been . . . picked out . . . simply to be abandoned . . . set loose to find our own way . . . we are entitled to some direction . . . I would have thought.

Ros declares that he *does* hear music in the distance. Soon band music is heard, as a group of Tragedians approaches.

The Tragedians are six in number, including a small boy (Alfred). Two pull and push a cart piled with props and belongings. There is also a Drummer, a Horn-Player and a Flautist. The spokesman (the Player) has no instrument. He brings up the rear. . . . .

The Player, seeing Ros and Guil, cries "An audience! Don't move!" and proposes that his troupe put on a show.

ROS: Tumblers, are you?

PLAYER: We can give you a tumble if that's your taste, and times being what they are . . . Otherwise, for a jingle of coin we can do you a selection of gory romances, full of fine cadence and corpses, pirated from the Italian;

and it doesn't take much to make a jingle—even a single coin has music in it, should it be gold.

They all flourish and bow, raggedly.

Tragedians, at your command.

ROS: My name is Guildenstern, and this is Rosencrantz.

Guil confers briefly with him.

(Without embarrassment.) I'm sorry—*his* name's Guildenstern, and *I'm* Rosencrantz.

PLAYER: A pleasure. We've played to bigger, of course, but quality counts for something. I recognized you at once—

ROS: And who are we?

PLAYER: —as fellow artists.

ROS: I thought we were gentlemen.

PLAYER: For some of us it is performance, for others patronage. They are two sides of the same coin, or, let us say, being as there are so many of us, the same side of two coins.

For a price, the troupe will offer a very special performance that Ros and Guil may watch as spectators—or as voyeurs—or join in as participants. Ros does not quite understand the Player's proposition, so the Player gives up and makes a move to withdraw. The troupe will continue its wanderings from tavern to court, court to tavern, wherever destiny leads.

GUIL: . . . . . You said something—about getting caught up in the action—

PLAYER: I did!—I did!—You're quicker than your friend . . . *(Confidingly.)* Now for a handful of guilders I happen to have a private and uncut performance of the Rape of the Sabine Women—or rather woman, or rather Alfred— *(Over his shoulder.)* Get your skirt on, Alfred . . .

The Boy starts struggling into a female robe.

. . . and for eight you can participate.

Guil backs, Player follows.

. . . taking either part . . . or both for ten.

Guil tries to turn away.

. . . with encores.

Guil smashes the Player across the face. The Player recoils. Guil stands trembling.

(Resigned and quiet.) Get your skirt off, Alfred . . .

Alfred struggles out of his half-on robe.

GUIL *(shaking with rage and fright):* It didn't have to be *obscene* . . . It could have been—a bird out of season, dropping bright-feathered on my shoulder . . . It could have been something . . . I was *prepared.* But it's this, is it? No enigma, no dignity, nothing classical, portentous, only this—a comic pornographer and a rabble of prostitutes . . .

PLAYER: You should have caught us in better times. We were purists then. On-ward.

The Tragedians make to leave.

Ros has finally understood that they are exhibitionists as well as actors. He is curious and offers them a single coin for a sample of their act, but it is too little—the Player spits at it, angering Ros who hurls the word *"Perverts"* at the troupe.

Guil calmly challenges the Player to flipping coins. The mysterious run of heads continues, and soon Guil has all the Player's money. Guil flips again, but the Player refuses to bet. Then Guil plays a mathematical trick on the Player, who now owes more than he can pay and brings Alfred forward in settlement of the last bet.

Alfred moves down and stands, frightened and small.

GUIL *(gently):* Do you lose often?

ALFRED: Yes, sir.

GUIL: Then what could you have left to lose?

ALFRED: Nothing, sir.

Pause. Guil regards him.

GUIL: Do you like being . . . an actor?

ALFRED: No, sir.

GUIL *(looks around, at the audience):* You and I, Alfred—we could create a dramatic precedent here.

And Alfred, who has been near tears, starts to sniffle.

Come, come, Alfred, this is no way to fill the theaters of Europe.

The Player has moved down, to remonstrate with Alfred. Guil cuts him off again.

(Viciously.) Do you know any good plays?

PLAYER: Plays?

A Greek tragedy, perhaps, in payment of the last bet, Guil suggests. The Player confesses that his troupe knows only love and rhetoric mixed with blood. The Player signals for the troupe to take their places, and they go offstage, pulling their cart. But the Player himself does not budge and insists that he can act his role where he is standing. Ros makes the Player move and finds that he was standing on a coin.

The Player turns and goes. Ros has bent for the coin.

GUIL: Come on.

ROS: I say—that was lucky.

GUIL *(turning):* What?

ROS: It was tails.

He picks up the coin and throws it to Guil who catches it. Simultaneously—a lighting change sufficient to alter the exterior mood into interior, but nothing violent.

And Ophelia screams and runs on in some alarm, holding up her skirts—followed by Hamlet.

Hamlet, with his doublet all unbraced, no hat upon his head, his stockings fouled, ungartered and down-gyved to his ankles, pale as his shirt, his knees knocking each other . . . and with a look so piteous, he takes her by the wrist and holds her hard, then he goes to the length of his arm . . . . . thrice his head waving up and down, he raises a sigh so piteous and profound that it does seem to shatter all his bulk and end his being. That done he lets her go, and with his head over his shoulder turned, he goes out backwards without taking his eyes off her . . . she runs off in the opposite direction.

Guil unfreezes first.

But a flourish—enter Claudius and Gertrude, attended.

CLAUDIUS *(as in Act II, Scene 2 of* Hamlet):

Welcome, dear Rosencrantz . . .

He raises a hand at Guil while Ros bows—Guil bows late and hurriedly.

. . . and Guildenstern.

He raises a hand at Ros while Guil bows to him—Ros is still straightening up from his previous bow and half way up he bows down again. With his head down, he twists to look at Guil, who is on the way up.

Moreover that we did much long to see you,
the need we have to use you did provoke
our hasty sending.
Something have you heard
of Hamlet's transformation. . . . .

Act II, Scene 2 of *Hamlet* continues in exact adherence to the Shakespeare text (with new stage directions added), as Claudius makes his wishes known. Ros and Guil, youthful companions of the ailing Prince Hamlet, have been sent for to cheer him in his melancholia and to find out what is troubling him. They are to glean what afflicts Hamlet and report back to his solicitous mother and stepfather. Gertrude chimes in and pleads for their cooperation.

GERTRUDE:

. . . . . Your visitation shall receive such thanks
as fits a king's remembrance.

ROS:

Both your majesties
might, by the sovereign power you have of us,
put your dread pleasures more into command
than to entreaty.

GUIL:

But we both obey,
and here give up ourselves in the full bent
to lay our service freely at your feet,
to be commanded.

CLAUDIUS:

Thanks, Rosencrantz . . .

Turning to Ros who is caught unprepared while Guil bows.

. . . and gentle Guildenstern.

Turning to Guil who is bent double.

GERTRUDE *(correcting):*

Thanks Guildenstern . . .

Turning to Ros, who bows as Guil checks upward movement to bow too—both bent double, squinting at each other.

. . . and gentle Rosencrantz. . . . .

Act II, Scene 2 of *Hamlet* continues, as Polonius announces the return of the ambassadors from Norway. Polonius also believes he knows the cause of Hamlet's distress. The court characters exit (and the Shakespeare dialogue ends), leaving Ros and Guil alone in this interior setting, a half-seen, dimly-lit arrangement of vaulted, cobwebby arches.

ROS: I want to go home.

GUIL: Don't let them confuse you.

ROS: I'm out of my step here—

GUIL: We'll soon be home and high—dry and home—I'll—

ROS: It's all over my *depth*—

GUIL: —I'll hie you home and—

ROS: —out of my head—

GUIL: —dry you high and—

ROS *(cracking, high):* —over my step over my head body!

Simple realities seem strange to them now, as though they couldn't remember ever having seen a word like "wife" or "house" before and couldn't spell it. One thing is clear: they were summoned and they came. "We've been caught up," Guil decides, they must be careful, follow instructions "till events have played themselves out."

They are to find out what ails Hamlet by "asking the right questions and giving away as little as we can." It's like a game, with a king's reward as the prize. Should they follow after Hamlet? No, they have been placed, they'd better stay where they are and await developments.

ROS: . . . . . I feel like a spectator—an appalling prospect. The only thing that makes it bearable is the irrational belief that somebody interesting will come on in a minute . . .

GUIL: See anyone?

ROS: No. You?

GUIL: No *(At the footlights.)* What a fine persecution—to be kept intrigued without ever quite being enlightened . . .

Pause.

We've had no practise.

ROS: We could play at questions.
GUIL: What good would that do?
ROS: Practise!
GUIL: Statement! One-love.
ROS: Cheating!
GUIL: How?
ROS: I hadn't started yet.
GUIL: Statement. Two-love.
ROS: Are you counting that?
GUIL: What?
ROS: Are you counting that?
GUIL: Foul! No repetitions. Three-love. First game to me . . .
ROS: I'm not going to play if you're going to be like that.
GUIL: Whose serve?
ROS: Hah?
GUIL: Foul! No grunts. Love-one.
ROS: Whose go?
GUIL: Why?
ROS: Why not?
GUIL: What for?
ROS: Foul! No synonyms! One-all.
GUIL: What in God's name is going on?
ROS: Foul! No rhetoric. Two-one.
GUIL: What does it all add up to?
ROS: Can't you guess?
GUIL: Were you addressing me?
ROS: Is there anyone else?
GUIL: Who?
ROS: How would I know?
GUIL: Why do you ask?
ROS: Are you serious?
GUIL: Was that rhetoric?
ROS: No.
GUIL: Statement! Two-all. Game point.
ROS: What's the matter with you today?
GUIL: When?
ROS: What?
GUIL: Are you deaf?
ROS: Am I dead?
GUIL: Yes or no?
ROS: Is there a choice?
GUIL: Is there a God?
ROS: Foul! No non sequiturs, three-two, one game all.
GUIL *(seriously):* What's your name?
ROS: What's yours?
GUIL: I asked you first.

ROS: Statement. One-love.

GUIL: What's your name when you're at home?

ROS: What's yours?

GUIL: When I'm at home?

ROS: Is it different at home?

GUIL: What home?

ROS: Haven't you got one?

GUIL: Why do you ask?

ROS: What are you driving at?

GUIL *(with emphasis):* What's your name?!

ROS: Repetition. Two-love. Match point to me.

GUIL *(seizing him violently):* WHO DO YOU THINK YOU ARE?

ROS: Rhetoric! Game and match!

Pause.

Where's it going to end?

GUIL: That's the question.

ROS: It's *all* questions.

Hamlet crosses the stage reading a book, paying no attention to his onetime friends. He exits, but his momentary presence has added to the confusion of Ros and Guil. There is an aura of mystery, of dangerous tension, around this Hamlet each time he appears. Ros and Guil are to "glean what afflicts him," but they don't know where to start. Indeed, they scarcely know where they are and at times have doubts about *who* they are (but tend to be reassured by shouting their own names out loud).

Hamlet is "not himself"—well, who is he then? And, for that matter, who are Ros and Guil? Guil pretends to be Hamlet so that Ros can question him. Ros establishes the facts: Hamlet's father, the king, died, and Hamlet's uncle "slipped in" to the throne and into marriage with Hamlet's mother, while Hamlet was away in Germany. Finishing off his questioning of Guil as Hamlet, Ros sums up: "Your father, whom you love, dies, you are his heir, you come back to find that hardly was the corpse cold before his young brother popped on to his throne and into his sheets, thereby offending both legal and natural practise. Now exactly why are you behaving in this extraordinary manner?"

It would seem obvious what ails Hamlet, Guil concludes, except all this is known and yet they have been sent for to "glean what afflicts him."

Ros looks to see what Hamlet is doing. The prince is talking to Polonius and soon enters with the old man, mocking him in some of the dialogue of *Hamlet,* Act II, Scene 2. Polonius takes leave of Hamlet and exits.

GUIL *(as in* Hamlet, *Act II, Scene 2; calls upstage to Hamlet):* My honored lord!

ROS: My most dear lord!

Hamlet, centered upstage, turns to them.

HAMLET: My excellent good friends! How dost thou Guildenstern?

Coming downstage with an arm raised to Ros, Guil meanwhile bowing to no greeting. Hamlet corrects himself. Still to Ros.

Ah Rosencrantz!

They laugh good naturedly at the mistake. They all meet midstage, turn upstage to walk, Hamlet in the middle, arm over each shoulder.

Good lads how do ye both?

Blackout. Curtain.

ACT II

The action is a continuation of the previous scene, with the dialogue taken from Act II, Scene 2 of *Hamlet*. Hamlet, Ros and Guil walk up and down talking. The players arrive at Elsinore, and Hamlet welcomes them. To Guil, Hamlet confides: "I am but mad north-north-west; when the wind is southerly I know a hawk from a handsaw."

Polonius enters, and is baited by Hamlet. Polonius recommends the players to Hamlet, who strolls off with the old man leaving Ros and Guil to ponder (as the *Hamlet* dialogue ends) the conversation they have just had with the prince.

Guil thinks they have made some headway in their attempt to "glean what afflicts him," but Ros thinks Hamlet made them look ridiculous.

GUIL: He caught us on the wrong foot once or twice, perhaps, but I thought we gained some ground.

ROS *(simply):* He murdered us.

GUIL: He might have had the edge.

ROS *(roused):* Twenty-seven-three, and you think he might have had the edge? He *murdered* us.

GUIL: What about our evasions?

ROS: Oh, our evasions were lovely. "Were you sent for?" he says. "My lord, we were sent for . . ." I didn't know where to put myself.

GUIL: He had six rhetoricals—

ROS: It was question and answer, all right. Twenty-seven questions he got out in ten minutes, and answered three. I was waiting for you to *delve*. "When is he going to start delving?" I asked myself.

GUIL: —And two repetitions.

ROS: Hardly a leading question between us.

GUIL: We got his *symptoms,* didn't we?

ROS: Half of what he said meant something else, and the other half didn't mean anything at all.

GUIL: Thwarted ambition—a sense of grievance, that's my diagnosis.

ROS: Six rhetorical and two repetition, leaving nineteen of which we answered fifteen. And what did we get in return? He's depressed! . . . Denmark's a prison and he'd rather live in a nutshell; some shadow-play about the nature of ambition, which never got down to cases, and finally one direct question which might have led somewhere, and led in fact to his illuminating claim to tell a hawk from a handsaw.

Pause.

GUIL: When the wind is southerly.

ROS: And when it isn't he can't.

GUIL: He's at the mercy of the elements.

They try to figure out which direction is south, and what time of day it is. They would like to stir up some action, but Guil is convinced that "Wheels have been set in motion, and they have their own pace to which we are . . . condemned." If Ros and Guil take the initiative they will create a shambles.

Guil muses about a Chinese philosopher who dreamed he was a butterfly and thereafter was never sure it wasn't true. Ros shouts "Fire!" to prove the existence of free speech by demonstrating its misuse. Ros spins a coin and then forgets whether it came up heads or tails. They play a guessing game, interrupted by the arrival of Polonius and Hamlet with the Tragedians.

Hamlet requests a performance of the Murder of Gonzago (as per *Hamlet,* Act II, Scene 2), with the addition of a speech which he will supply. As the prince and Polonius drift off, Guil observes to the Player that he has finally caught up. The Player accuses Ros and Guil of walking out on his performance. The Tragedians had begun a roadside rendition of one of their plays, when they discovered to their great disappointment that no one was watching them.

Guil tries to take credit for arranging the performance of the Tragedians at court. But the Player has been to Elsinore before and is more at home than Ros and Guil.

GUIL: We're still finding our feet.

PLAYER: I should concentrate on not losing your heads.

GUIL: Do you speak from knowledge?

PLAYER: Precedent.

GUIL: You've been here before.

PLAYER: And I know which way the wind is blowing.

The Player's grave face does not change. He makes to move off again. Guil for the second time cuts him off.

GUIL: The truth is, we value your company, for want of any other. We have been left so much to our own devices—after awhile one welcomes the uncertainty of being left to other people's.

PLAYER: Uncertainty is the normal state. You're nobody special.

He makes to leave again. Guil loses his cool.

GUIL: But for God's sake what are we supposed to *do*?!

PLAYER: Relax. Respond. That's what people do. You can't go through life questioning your situation at every turn. You know why you're here at least.

GUIL: We only know what we're told, and that's little enough. And for all we know it isn't even true.

PLAYER: For all anyone knows, nothing is. Everything has to be taken on trust; truth is only that which is taken to be true. It's the currency of living. There may be nothing behind it, but it doesn't make any difference so long as it is honored. . . . .

They consider Hamlet's mental state, and they conclude that he may just be "Stark raving sane." Perhaps he is the victim of his love for Ophelia. Once again the Player moves to leave, and he does so even though Guil tries to stop him. Ros calls for someone else to join them, but no one comes.

Ros drifts into thinking about death, about what it would be like to be shut into a box (in which case he would rather be alive than dead, he concludes, because alive there would at least be the chance that someone would come and let him out). "Eternity is a terrible thought," Ros admits. Later he wonders: "Whatever became of the moment when one first knew about death? There must have been one, a moment, in childhood when it first occurred to you that you don't go on forever. It must have been shattering—stamped into one's memory. And yet I can't remember it. It never occurred to me at all. What does one make of that? We must be born with an intuition of mortality. Before we know the words for it, before we know that there are words, out we come, bloodied and squalling with the knowledge that for all the compasses in the world, there's only one direction, and time is its only measure. *(He breaks out.)* They're taking us for granted! Well, I won't stand for it! In future, notice will be taken. *(He wheels again to face into the wings.)* Keep out then! I forbid anyone to enter! *(No one comes.)* That's better . . ."

Claudius, Gertrude, Polonius and Ophelia enter as in *Hamlet,* Act III, Scene 1, and the Shakespeare dialogue begins with Gertrude's question to Ros and Guil: "Did he receive you well?" As in the *Hamlet* scene, Ros reports that the prince was enthusiastic about the arrival of the Tragedians. Ros is instructed to encourage Hamlet's interest in them.

Claudius reveals the plan to observe Ophelia and Hamlet together, then the court characters leave Ros and Guil alone as the *Hamlet* material ends. Ros is disturbed, confused, wants to leave. They can see Hamlet walking up and down (musing "to be or not to be," though his thoughts are unspoken here).

Ophelia enters and encounters Hamlet. Claudius and Polonius spy on this meeting, which unfolds in the Shakespeare dialogue of *Hamlet,* Act III, Scene 1 up to Hamlet and Ophelia's discussion of beauty and honesty; then the court characters drift out of Ros and Guil's earshot and the *Hamlet* dialogue ends.

A female figure comes onstage. It is not Gertrude, but Alfred dressed for the Tragedians' final rehearsal of the Murder of Gonzago. The actors run through the dumb show of the poisoning.

With a scream, Ophelia runs onstage, pursued by Hamlet. The prince exhorts her: "To a nunnery, go." Hamlet and Ophelia exit as Claudius enters explaining to Polonius that he has decided to send Hamlet to England (as in Act III, Scene 1). The court characters exit.

The Player directs his troupe to take positions for the second act, and Guil is surprised that there is more of the play.

GUIL: Wasn't that the end?

PLAYER: Do you call that an ending?—with practically everyone on his feet? My goodness no—over your dead body.

GUIL: How am I supposed to take that?

PLAYER: Lying down. *(He laughs briefly and in a second has never laughed in his life.)* There's a design at work in all art—surely you know that? Events must play themselves out to esthetic, moral and logical conclusion.

GUIL: And what's that, in this case?

PLAYER: It never varies—we aim at the point where everyone who is marked for death dies.

GUIL: Marked?

PLAYER: Between "just deserts" and "tragic irony" we are given quite a lot of scope for our particular talent. Generally speaking, things have gone about as far as they can possibly go when things have got about as bad as they can reasonably get. *(He switches on a smile).*

GUIL: Who decides?

PLAYER *(switching off his smile): Decides?* It is *written.*

He turns away. Guil grabs him and stops him.

(Unflustered.) Now if you're going to be subtle, we'll miss each other in the dark.

The dumb show continues with a passionate scene between the royal lovers. Then the Player takes the part of Hamlet in the closet scene with Gertrude and plays out the murder of Polonius. All the while the Player speaks a narration to Ros and Guil explaining the plot: "Lucianus," the Player King's nephew, confronts his mother and begs her to repent. "The King," the Player continues, "Tormented by guilt—haunted by fear—decides to despatch his nephew to England—and entrusts this undertaking to two smiling accomplices—friends—courtiers—to two spies—."

But when they arrive in England (the narration and the dumb show disclose), a twist of fate arranges that the two so-called "friends," the spies and not the princely nephew, will be executed. The English King orders their deaths.

GUIL *(fear, derision):* Actors! The mechanics of cheap melodrama! That isn't *death! (More quietly.)* You scream and choke and sink to your knees, but it doesn't bring death home to anyone—it doesn't catch them unawares and start the whisper in their skulls that says—"One day you are going to die." *(He straightens up.)* You die so many times; how can you expect them to believe in your death?

PLAYER: On the contrary, it's the only kind they do believe. They're conditioned to it. I had an actor once who was condemned to hang for stealing a sheep—or a lamb, I forget which—so I got permission to have him hanged in the middle of a play—had to change the plot a bit but I thought it would be effective, you know—and you wouldn't believe it, he just *wasn't* convincing! It was impossible to suspend one's disbelief—he did nothing but cry all the time—right out of character—just stood there and cried . . . never again.

In good humor he has already turned back to the mime: the two Spies awaiting execution at the hands of the Player, who takes his dagger out of his belt.

Audiences know what to expect, and that is all that they are prepared to believe in.

To the Spies, as he stabs them with his dagger.

Show!

The Spies die at some length, rather well. The light has begun to go, and it fades as they die, and as Guil speaks.

GUIL: No, no, no . . . you've got it all wrong . . . you can't act death. The *fact* of it is nothing to do with seeing it happen—it's not gasps and blood and falling about—that isn't what makes it death. It's just a man failing to reappear, that's all—now you see him, now you don't, that's the only thing that's real: —an exit, unobtrusive and unannounced, a disappearance gathering weight as it goes on, until, finally, it is heavy with death.

The two Spies lie still. Ros starts to clap, slowly. Blackout.

After a beat of silence, there is a noisy disturbance, as at the end of the play-within-the-play in *Hamlet,* Act III, Scene 2. But when the lights come up in the manner of a sunrise, Ros and Guil are alone onstage lying in the same position as the Spies had been. Guil declares: "As soon as we make a move they'll come pouring in from every side, shouting obscure instructions, confusing us with ridiculous remarks, messing us about from here to breakfast and getting our names wrong."

Indeed, Claudius and Gertrude do enter, disturbed, calling for Guildenstern, explaining (as in *Hamlet,* Act IV, Scene 1) that the prince has killed Polonius, directing Ros and Guil to find Hamlet, calm him, and bring the body into the chapel.

Claudius and Gertrude exit. As Ros and Guil are wondering how to approach Hamlet, the prince drags the body of Polonius on and off stage. They call Hamlet's name, and he re-enters. They ask him (as in Act IV, Scene 2) what he has done with the body. But Hamlet will not be questioned and calls Ros a sponge.

ROS *(as in* Hamlet, *Act IV, Scene 2):* Take you me for a sponge, my lord?

HAMLET: Ay, sir, that soaks up the king's countenance, his rewards, his authorities. But such officers do the king best service in the end. He keeps them, like an ape, in the corner of his jaw, first mouthed, to be last swallowed. When he needs what you have gleaned, it is but squeezing you and, sponge, you shall be dry again.

ROSS: I understand you not, my lord.

HAMLET: I am glad of it: a knavish speech sleeps in a foolish ear.

Hamlet exits as per the end of Act IV, Scene 2. He has deliberately tricked Ros and Guil into a clownish posture, causing them to bow in the wrong direction as Claudius enters behind them.

Claudius wants to know what Ros and Guil have done about the prince (as per Act IV, Scene 3). Ros pretends that Hamlet is under guard, awaiting Claudius' pleasure. Claudius orders Hamlet brought before him, to Ros's consternation. But when Ros calls "Ho! Bring in the lord," things happen as they should—Hamlet is brought in under guard. The situation is saved. The court characters exit as Ros comments, "It was a trying episode while it lasted, but they've done with us now."

But Guil believes this is not the end—they are to escort Hamlet to England. Hamlet enters talking to a soldier (as in *Hamlet,* Act IV, Scene 4), but Ros and Guil continue their own conversation: they will wait and the weather will change, the brown of autumn is already creeping up on them. Faintly they can hear the sound of the Tragedians' band.

Hamlet orders Ros and Guil "Go you a little before" and turns to face upstage, his conversation with the soldier ended. Once again Ros and Guil can see that Hamlet is thinking, but they cannot hear the words of his Act IV, Scene 4 soliloquy.

ROS *(. . . . . makes to leave):* He *said* we can go. Cross my heart.

GUIL: I like to know where I am. Even if I don't know where I am, I like to know *that.* If we go there's no knowing.

ROS: No knowing what?

GUIL: If we'll ever come back.

ROS: We don't want to come back.

GUIL: That may very well be true, but do we want to go?

ROS: We'll be well out of it.

GUIL: I don't know. It's the same sky.

ROS: We've come this far. *(He moves toward exit.)* And besides, anything could happen yet.

He exits. Guil follows slowly. Blackout.

ACT III

It is pitch dark, with soft sea sounds. Ros and Guil are wondering, in the dark, where they are—Ros pinches Guil to make sure they are alive. The sea sounds become louder, with shouted nautical instructions until the conclusion is inescapable even for Ros: "We're on a boat."

A lantern is lit (by Hamlet) so that now rigging and spars are visible. There are three large casks on deck. The sea is rough. Ros investigates upstage while Guil muses.

GUIL: One is free on a boat. For a time. Relatively. . . . . Free to move, speak, extemporize, and yet. We have not been cut loose. Our truancy is defined by one fixed star, and our drift represents merely a slight change of angle to it: we may seize the moment, toss it around while the moments pass, a short dash here, an exploration there, but we are brought round full circle to face again the single immutable fact—that we, Rosencrantz and Guildenstern, bearing a letter from one king to another, are taking Hamlet to England.

By which time, Ros has returned, tiptoeing with great import, teeth clenched for secrecy, gets to Guil, points surreptitiously behind him—and a tight whisper:

ROS: I say—*he's* there!

Indicating Hamlet.

GUIL *(unsurprised):* What's he doing?

ROS: Sleeping.

In some way, Guil observes, Hamlet "has got us now." Everything is done for Hamlet, and Ros and Guil will wind up empty-handed.

To cheer Guil up, Ros offers him a coin guessing game fixed so that Guil will win each time. Then Ros becomes tearful and Guil comforts him. They size up the situation: they are on their way to England, to see the king, with a letter from Denmark that explains everything.

They check to see who has the letter. For a few panicky moments they cannot find it; but Guil has it, safe. Ros doesn't really believe in England. He tries to imagine himself arriving, riding to the palace, meeting the English king, but he cannot, his mind remains a blank.

He wonders whether death is a boat, but Guil reminds him that this cannot be, death is the ultimate in not being, and boats *are*. Ros concludes: "All right! we don't question, we don't doubt. We perform. But a line must be drawn somewhere, and I would like to put it on record that I have no confidence in England."

Ros expresses his doubts by acting out their arrival. He plays the stern English king, sneering at Guil who, optimistically and patiently, explains their errand. Ros, pretending to be the king, implacably skeptical, is carried away by his role.

ROS: You march in here without so much as a by-your-leave and expect me to take in every lunatic you try to pass off with a lot of unsubstantiated—

GUIL: We've got a letter—

Ros snatches it and tears it open.

ROS *(efficiently):* I see . . . I see . . . well, this seems to support your story such as it is—it is an exact command from the King of Denmark, for several different reasons, importing Denmark's health and England's too, that on reading of this letter, without delay, I should have Hamlet's head cut off—!

Guil snatches the letter. Ros, doubletaking, snatches it back. Guil snatches it half back. They read it together, and separate. Pause. They are well downstage looking front.

The sun's going down. It will be dark soon.

GUIL: Do you think so?

ROS: I was just making conversation.

Pause. . . . .

We're his *friends.*

GUIL: How do you know?

ROS: From our young days brought up with him.

GUIL: You've only got their word for it.

ROS: But that's what we depend on.

GUIL: Well, yes, and then again no. *(Airily.)* Let us keep things in proportion. Assume, if you like, that they're going to kill him. Well, he is a man, he is mortal, death comes to us all, etcetera, and consequently he would have died anyway, sooner or later. And then again, what is so terrible about death? As Socrates so philosophically put it, since we don't know what death is, it is illogical to fear it. It might be . . . very nice. Or to look at in another way—we are little men, we don't know the ins and outs of the matter, there are wheels within wheels, etcetera—it would be presumptuous of us to interfere with the designs of fate or even of kings. All in all, I think we'd be well advised to leave well alone.

ROS: But what's the point?

GUIL: Don't apply logic.

ROS: He's done nothing to us.

GUIL: Or justice.

ROS: It's awful.

GUIL: But it could have been worse. I was beginning to think it was. *(And his relief comes out in a laugh.)*

ROS: The position as I see it, then. We, Rosencrantz and Guildenstern, from our young days brought up with him, awakened by a man standing on his saddle, are summoned, and arrive, and are instructed to glean what afflicts him and draw him on to pleasures, such as a play, which unfortunately, as it turns out, is abandoned in some confusion owing to certain nuances outside our appreciation—which, among other causes, results in, among other effects, a high, not to say, homicidal excitement in Hamlet, whom we, in consequence, are escorting, for his own good, to England. Good. We're on top of it now.

In the darkness, Ros and Guil lie down to sleep. Moonlight appears, and with it Hamlet, who steals the letter from unconscious Guil and carries it behind an umbrella, where he reads it by lantern light. After an interval Hamlet returns, replaces a letter on the sleeping Guil, then blows out the lantern and retires.

Dawn comes up. Ros and Guil sit staring, as Hamlet lounges in a deck chair behind them like a passenger on a luxury liner. The sound of the Tragedians' music is heard, then the Player pops out of the middle barrel. The other Tragedians, all but Alfred, emerge from the other two barrels carrying their instruments (a comic impossibility, like the overcrowded car at the circus). Alfred emerges from the Player's barrel.

The Player explains: their play offended Claudius, and they had to flee his wrath. Under questioning by the Player, Ros and Guil admit that they are still at a loss to solve the mystery of Hamlet, with his symptoms of madness and shrewdness and introspection.

Hamlet comes downstage to the footlights, watched by the others. He spits, and the spittle is blown back into his face. He turns back upstage. Ros comments: "Incidents! All we get is incidents! Dear God, is it too much to expect a little sustained action?!"

At this moment, there is a cry of "Pirates!" and panic breaks over the scene, with everyone running for their lives.

Hamlet, in the lead, leaps into the left barrel. The Player leaps into the right barrel. Ros and Guil leap into the middle barrel, all closing the lids after them. The lights dim to nothing while the sound of fighting fades to nothing.

The lights come up. The middle barrel, Ros's and Guil's, is missing. The lid of the right-hand barrel is raised cautiously. The heads of Ros and Guil appear. The lid of the other barrel, Hamlet's, is raised. The head of the Player appears. All catch sight of each other and slam down lids. Pause. Lids raised cautiously.

ROS *(relief):* They've gone. *(He starts to climb out.)* That was close. I've never thought quicker.

They are all three out of the barrels. Guil is wary and nervous. Ros is light-headed. The Player is phlegmatic. They note the missing barrel. Ros looks round.

ROS: Where's—?

PLAYER: Once more, alone—on our own resources.

The Player thinks they are "dead lucky" that Hamlet has gone. Hamlet is "dead as far as we're concerned," Ros comments, and the Player adds, "Or we are as far as he is."

But Guil is disturbed. They need Hamlet, he insists, for their explanation, their release when they get to England. Now it's Guil who doesn't believe in England and Ros who tries to reassure him. Now it's Guil who plays the part of the skeptical English king as Ros hands him the letter of explanation.

GUIL *(snatches it, opens it):* A letter—yes—that's true. That's something . . . a letter . . . *(Reads.)* "As England is Denmark's faithful tributary . . . as love between them like the palm might flourish, etcetera . . . that on the knowing of this contents, without delay of any kind, should those bearers, Rosencrantz and Guildenstern, put to sudden death—"

He double-takes. Ros snatches the letter. Guil snatches it back. Ros snatches it half back. They read it again and look up. The Player gets to his feet and walks over to his barrel and kicks it and shouts into it.

PLAYER: They've gone—it's all over!

One by one the Tragedians emerge, impossibly, from the barrel, and form a casually menacing circle around Ros and Guil.

GUIL *(quietly):* Where we went wrong was getting on a boat.

ROS: They had it in for us, didn't they. Right from the beginning. Who'd have thought that we were that important?

GUIL: Was it all for this? Who are we that so much should converge on our little deaths? *(Strong.)* Who are *we?*

PLAYER: You are Rosencrantz and Guildenstern. That's enough.

GUIL: No, it's not enough. To be told so little . . . to such an end—and still—finally—to be denied an explanation . . .

PLAYER: The bad end unhappily, the good unluckily. That is all.

That is mere play-acting, Guil exclaims, death is a real void with no applause, no getting up afterward. Angry, Guil snatches the dagger from the Player's belt and stabs him, determined that the Player shall share their fate. The Player dies in agony; lies silent for a beat and then rises and dusts himself off as the Tragedians applaud. It was a stage dagger with retractable blade—he had them fooled, and Ros appreciates the performance, calls for more.

The Player signals his troupe to start performing.

Alfred, still in his queen's costume, dies by poison: the Player, with rapier, kills the "King" and duels with a fourth Tragedian, inflicting and receiving a wound. And the light is fading over the deaths which take place upstage.

PLAYER *(dying amid the dying—tragically, romantically):* So there's an end to that—it's commonplace: light goes with life, and in the winter of your years the dark comes early . . .

GUIL *(tired, drained, but an edge of impatience):* No, no, no. . . . not for us, not like that. Dying is not romantic . . . and death is not a game which will soon be over . . . death is not anything . . . death is not. It's the absence of presence, nothing more . . . the endless time of never coming back . . . A gap you can't see, and when the wind blows through it, it makes no sound . . .

The light upstage has gone. Only Guil and Ros are visible. Pause.

ROS: That's it, then. *(No answer—He looks out front.)* The sun's going down, or the earth's coming up, as the fashionable theory has it.

Small pause.

Not that it makes any difference. What was it all about? Where did it begin?

Couldn't we just stay put? I mean no one's going to come in and drag us off. They'll just have to wait. We're still young, fit . . . we've got years . . . we've done nothing wrong. We didn't harm anyone. Did we?

GUIL: I can't remember.

Ros pulls himself together. He looks up, his face in the remaining light.

ROS: All right then. I don't care. I've had enough. To tell you the truth, I'm relieved.

Ros moves into the upstage dark and disappears. Guil does not notice.

GUIL: Our names shouted in a certain dawn . . . a message . . . a summons . . . There must have been a point somewhere at the beginning when we could have said no. But somehow we missed it . . . Rosen . . . Guil . . . *(Gathers himself.)* Well, we'll know better next time. Now you see me—now you . . . *(And disappears from view.)*

Immediately the whole stage is lit up, revealing, upstage, arranged in the approximate positions last held by the dead Tragedians, the tableau of court and corpses which is the last scene of Hamlet. *That is: the King, Queen, Laertes and Hamlet all dead. Horatio holds Hamlet. Fortinbras is there. So are two Ambassadors from England.*

AMBASSADOR *(as in* Hamlet, *Act V, Scene 2):*

The sight is dismal;
and our affairs from England come too late.
The ears are senseless that should give us hearing
to tell him his commandment is fulfilled,
Where should we have our thanks?

HORATIO:

that Rosencrantz and Guildenstern are dead.
Not from his mouth,
Had it the ability of life to thank you:
He never gave commandment for their death.
But since, so jump upon this bloody question,
you from the Polack wars, and you from England,
are here arrived, give order that these bodies
high on a stage be placed to the view;
and let me speak to the yet unknowing world
how these things came about: so shall you hear
of carnal, bloody and unnatural acts,
of accidental judgments, casual slaughters,
of deaths put on by cunning and forced cause,
and, in this upshot, purposes mistook
fallen on the inventors' heads: all this can I
truly deliver.

Music swells. Lights fade. Curtain.

STAIRCASE

A Play in Two Acts

BY CHARLES DYER

Cast and credits appear on page 358

CHARLES DYER was born in Shrewsbury, in England's Shropshire, on July 17, in either 1923 (a close business associate), 1926 (Dyer himself a few years ago) or 1928 (his Who's Who in the Theater *biographical sketch), according to different sources; on this subject Dyer in 1968 stands mute. He was educated at Queen Elizabeth's School, in Barnet. From 1942 to 1947 he served in the RAF as a navigator, during which term of service he wrote his first play,* Clubs Are Sometimes Trumps, *produced in 1948. Following his discharge, he worked in the theater as an actor and director. His* Rattle of a Simple Man *(1961) was produced on Broadway by David Merrick during the 1962-63 season and was named a Best Play of its year.*

Other Dyer plays produced in England have been the following: Who on Earth! *(1948),* Turtle in the Soup *(1951),* The Jovial Parasite *(1954),* Single Ticket Mars *(1955),* Time, Murderer, Please, Poison in Jest *and* Wanted—One Body *(1956),* Prelude to Fury *(1959) and* Gorillas Drink Milk *(1965). Movie audiences have seen him as a performer in* The Loneliness of the Long Distance Runner *(as the mother's boy friend) and they will see his adaptation of his own* Staircase *on the screen, starring Rex Harrison and Richard Burton. Dyer is married and the father of three children.*

Time: The present

Place: A barber's shop in a suburb of London

ACT I

Scene 1

SYNOPSIS: It's Sunday night, and there's no one in the barber shop except the two middle-aged men who operate the place. One of them, Charles Dyer (which also happens to be the name of the author of *Staircase*), is seated in one of the two barber's chairs, a sheet tucked under his chin. The other, Harry Leeds, is shaving Charlie. Harry, wide-hipped and comfortably overweight, is wearing a thick wrapping like a turban on his head, and he is enjoying Handel's "Hallelujah Chorus" coming from a portable record-player.

The shop contains all the usual gadgets and supplies for the practise of "hair styling" for men. The windows to the street are upstage. A door near them at right opens to the hall and staircase going to the upper floors, and gives access to the door leading to the street. The door to the stock room is downstage right.

Harry finishes shaving Charlie, goes to the stock room for a hot towel which he then pats onto Charlie's face. Harry takes off his white coat with "Harry" on the pocket, dons a cardigan and settles himself into the other chair—it is now *his* turn to be served.

Charlie flings off the towel and rises. He is leaner, perhaps more vain, quicker than Harry. Charlie puts on his own white coat with "Charles" on the pocket and proceeds to attend Harry, while commenting that the arrangement of the gas flame in the stock room is dangerous, because each time the door is opened its draught nearly blows the flame out.

The sound of a man's footsteps descending the staircase rivets their attention and starts them laughing and joking. The man calls back upstairs pretending that he has left some typing for Miss Ricard, a tenant (Harry's mother owns the building and the shop).

Harry's and Charlie's sure knowledge of what Miss Ricard and her visitor have been up to brings Harry to comment that ". . . . . I feel that sex . . . all sex could have been better arranged." As Charlie dabs disinfectant on a blackhead near Harry's jaw, Harry elaborates on this notion.

HARRY: I believe half man's trouble's due to Nature's reproductive systems, I do. I firmly believe this, Charlie. Oh, you can scoff. But it should be nicer, cleaner, *prettier*. It shouldn't be so folded up and sort of underneath.

CHARLIE: Juggling us about a bit, aren't you, dear!—And where, pray, should we keep our paraphernalia? On our heads?

HARRY: And why not, *pray?* What's wrong with having, say . . . a couple of antennas. Males. Females. The lot. Nothing different or sniggery. Pleasant smile; raise your hat; shake antennas; good laugh in the bargain.

CHARLIE: O lovely, dear! Lovely! Just what I fancy in the morning—good laugh and shake me antennas.

He returns the bottle to its cupboard. Harry rises and folds up his sheet—throws his towel in the basin.

HARRY: There'd be no shame, I think. I think there'd be a kind of . . . picturesqueness about antennas on folks' heads. *(Lip quivers slightly.)* I shouldn't be as I am if it had been an easy business . . . nice and clean and open.

CHARLIE: Starting our weeping stint, are we? Our weeping stint?

HARRY *(strongly):* No we're not.

CHARLIE: Splendid!

He sits in the chair. Harry brings a small table and chair. He sits beside Charlie and begins manicuring Charlie's nails.

Antennas, she wants! Antennas.

HARRY: Oh, shut your mouth. Keep the draught out.

Charlie continues to mock Harry about his antenna idea, nearly sending Harry into another of his "stints"—a sulk. Charlie himself is in a black mood. He fears he is going to be served by the police with a warrant for an offense he has committed. Charlie is hoping against hope that the warrant will be cancelled, the offense overlooked.

Meanwhile, Harry reminisces happily about the days of his youth, running with his sisters to wet his face in the dew. In contrast, there is precious little romantic rusticity here, where their shop adjoins Brixton Market.

Harry proposes various diversions including TV, but Charlie prefers to spend the evening hanging around the shop—even though, as Harry points out, there's little to do here.

Harry busies himself brewing tea and flagellating himself with words. Last night he dreamed he was naked in public, on an escalator. He stepped back to look at himself and saw, to his horror, "a fat old man, bloated and hanging . . . . . a yellowing sow's ear . . . a curled-at-the-edges *passé* phallic symbol."

Charlie warns Harry to "Walk tall!" in spite of everything; they are all growing old, after all. Harry tells Charlie "But you're still beautiful on the surface." Charlie looks at himself in the mirror, agrees that he has kept himself fairly fit.

Charlie is to meet his daughter Cassy at the station the next day—a 21-year-old daughter Charlie has never seen. He is apprehensive about explaining Harry to his daughter. He remembers his marriage bitterly. Harry reproaches him.

HARRY: . . . Grumbling, because you'd been a father; a privilege denied thousands of us.

CHARLIE: Privilege, was it! Oh, I should rub a dub, dear. What! Nine months of sick mornings, two bitchy weeks in maternity . . . she flung me daffodils in a bedpan; and after an eternity of yowling, on me only silent night—there was a note pinned to the cot. Left me! They left me!

Harry pours the tea.

Even me honeymoon was a . . . a . . . a holocaust: one night of passion and food-poisoning for thirteen. Maggots in the haddock, she claimed.

Harry giggles.

Oh, I was laughing. Yes! What! Lovely—your blushing bride all shivering and turgid in the promenade shelter; hurricanes whipping the shingle . . . couldn't even paddle for a plague of jellyfish.

Harry roars with laughter. He takes Charlie's arm and leads him back to the chair.

HARRY: Come and have your tea, dear.

CHARLIE *(sits):* She had years of allotments, you know. Fifty bob a week, Harry. Fifty bob it was.

HARRY: Must've been a nasty judge.

CHARLIE: Nasty!—he wore a black cap, dear. Divorce Hearing; black cap! *(Nasal voice.)* "Oh, we're in the Theater, are we," he said. Course I was big time in those days, Harry. Played all the Number Ones. Don't think you realize just how big I was.

HARRY: Yes I do.

CHARLIE: Ask Archy Selder. Archy Selder'll tell you.

HARRY: Yes I know.

CHARLIE: Too true! But Theater's a dirty word, see, Harry. Dirty word, it is. "Oh, we're in the Theater, are we," he said, speaking on the verge of a burp. Well, I was young, see. Young, I was. And for a gag . . . a gag, that's all, Harry . . . I said "We?" I said. "What pantomime are you in, then?" I said.

HARRY: You never told me this.

CHARLIE: I didn't? Oh yes, dear. Brought the house down. Oogh, but the judge went puce. Puce, he went. Bats fluttered from his ears. I reckon he doubled me allotment. *And* she got custody of the child. I was *robbed* of my child. Robbed! The most expensive joke *I* ever cracked.

Charlie re-reads the letter announcing that his daughter Cassy is coming to see him. Evidently her mother believes that Charlie can get their daughter a job in TV, which of course he cannot. He's done only one commercial in ten years.

Charlie enters into a devious explanation to Harry about a friend who very obligingly would lend his car for Harry to take his mother for an outing any time (Harry's mother, an arthritic, lives upstairs; Charlie's mother is in an institution where he visits her from time to time). Why doesn't Harry take his mother out tomorrow night? Of course this happens to coincide with Cassy's arrival; and the truth is, Charlie fears to have Cassy meet Harry. He shrinks from having to explain Harry to his daughter.

But Harry sees through Charlie's inept subterfuge and understands that

Charlie is ashamed to have Cassie meet him, "afraid of . . . of . . . of Cassy's accusing finger." He is very angry.

HARRY: *(. . . . . moves here and there, snatching up scissors and combs; throwing them down again):* D'you know, I hope the police clutch on you, dear! Teach you a lesson . . . Twisted sod! . . . By God! Ashamed of his daughter meeting *me.*

CHARLIE *(almost a whisper):* Nothing personal.

Harry plugs in the electric kettle again.

HARRY: Oogh, you're all intertwined, Charlie. One great big tube of non-sequitur.

Harry's turn of spirit gives us a first suspicion that Charlie is not always top dog . . . Charlie is subdued for a while. He "walks" his fingers along the bench . . .

Harry continues his reproaches: "*You* got married; *you* had the daughter. Well, now you've got *me!* . . . . . me! Dirty Harry Leeds, who fed you; taught you a trade when you flopped in the theater." Weakly, Charlie boasts that he will be back on TV soon, in his own series, and move into the Hilton. Harry threatens to throw him out right then and there, but Charlie backs off and calms Harry down.

Harry confesses he would have liked to be married, it would have saved him great embarrassment.

HARRY: . . . . . the filthy questions they asked . . .

CHARLIE: Who asked?

HARRY: . . . "Are you clean, Mr. Leeds?" . . . "D'you live with your mother?" . . . "Who was that young man I saw you with last night?"

CHARLIE: Who's this? Who's this? Eh? Eh?

HARRY: The mothers; parents; when I had that Scout troop.

CHARLIE: Oh.

HARRY: And my face flamed up; always blushed. I could see it coming: they'd stop me in the street. A bit of yack-yack, then slam below the belt: "Are you married?" . . . And they had that raised-eyebrow'd purposeful disinterest . . . "No, I fear not" . . . "Oh-oh-oh-oh, aren't you! . . . Mm, well little Johnny tells us *everything that happens,* Mr. Leeds" . . . And my face like the backside of a gibbon.

CHARLIE: Oh well. Never mind.

He picks up his marzipan roll. Harry refills the teacups.

HARRY: How dare they! How damn dare they!

CHARLIE: You're not tying yourself in knots, for God's sake? It's twenty years ago.

HARRY: It leaves a scar.

Harry tries to boast about once going to a brothel. Charlie angers Harry by reminding him he's heard the brothel story before.

Harry asks Charlie to reflect on his name: Harry C. Leeds. Maybe he doesn't really exist at all.

The doorbell rings, and the sound terrifies Charlie—this might be the arrival of the feared police summons. Charlie peers through the keyhole. Indeed, a policeman is peering back at Charlie.

There is nothing to do but open the door a crack. The policeman passes in an identifying card. Charlie goes out onto the landing and returns with an envelope as the policeman clumps off. Charlie closes the door and opens the envelope—it is the dreaded summons. Charlie, too weak to read it, hands it to Harry.

HARRY *(reads aloud):* "To Charles Dyer, c/o Chez Harry . . ."

CHARLIE: Skip the address, mate.

HARRY: Um . . . "Information has been laid this day by Rychard Lees, Chief Constable . . ."

CHARLIE: Yes, yes. Skip to the meat.

HARRY: Um . . . Oh God! Listen, Charlie: ". . . that you did at the County Borough aforesaid at a private club known as The Adam's Apple behave in a manner likely to cause a serious breach of the peace and did parade in female attire . . ." Oh, God, Charlie!

CHARLIE: Read it, Harry! Read it!

HARRY: ". . . And did importune in a manner calculated to bring . . . depravity . . ."

Charlie sinks into the chair. Harry is himself near to tears.

Oh hell, Charlie. *(Whispers.)* Oh hell.

CHARLIE: Whoosh . . . they've . . . they've really come thundering into Jordan, haven't they! I should rub-a . . . whoosh!

He looks old, tired, frightened.

HARRY: Oh Charlie!

The summons is returnable in ten days—ten more days of fearful suspense after a fortnight of it already. Harry's mood changes to anger at Charlie for behaving as he did at the club. Charlie pleads he was only doing "me old panto act" in the cigarette girl's borrowed jumper, with his pants rolled up—not really drag. An acquaintance—Ed Chrysler—had bet Charlie he wouldn't do his imitation of a lady launching a battleship.

Chrysler is above suspicion, he has a wife and five children—it was all a gag—but it happened that Charlie was sitting on Chrysler's knee when the police came pouring in on someone's complaint of rowdyism. Charlie begs Harry to believe him; it was all just a gag.

HARRY *(nods):* Yes; but . . . but why did they take your name?

CHARLIE: It was this young copper, Harry. You see . . . I was on Ed Chrysler's knee and I pushed me t-t-tongue out and said Yarboo, Arrest me! . . . or something . . . You know what?—*he bloody did!* This young copper. Kept pushing me; p-pushing me, Harry. People watching. Wretched,

Harry . . . it w-was wretched . . . "Aw, come off!" I said "I'm old enough to be your father; your daddy," I said. *"Please,"* I said. *"Please,* son . . . !" *(He drops his voice to a whisper. There are tears in his eyes.)* They were going to put me in the Black M-Maria, Harry . . . If it hadn't been for the Inspector . . . nice elderly man . . . he checked me driving license; sent me home.

He wipes his eyes; blows his nose; then he forces himself into the attack . . .

But, by God, I'll prove 'em wrong! What! "May it please Your Honor! I am an established member of the theatrical profession. Yes!—*profession, sir! And* a married man. Yes sir! Married."

Charlie continues to plead for Harry's belief that he is innocent; he was only joking. He will tell the judge he is a professional female impersonater, he was merely showing off his act.

Suddenly, Charlie realizes he hasn't been on the stage in a long time and will probably have to throw himself on the mercy of the court as a "small-time back street hairdresser." He wasn't impersonating a woman in that TV commercial, so it doesn't support his case.

He is extremely frightened.

Charlie flops at Harry's feet. Harry cradles Charlie in his lap, stroking his head and rocking him backwards and forwards.

HARRY: Don't fret, Charlie. Don't fret. We'll see. We'll—see, Charlie.

CHARLIE: I'm innocent, Harry. Innocent.

HARRY: Oh Charlie—you poor old bugger.

CHARLIE: Yes.

He sits back on his haunches. He tries to smile.

D'you ever see two such frail old twits!

HARRY: But you won't be alone, Charlie: at the trial. I'll come with you.

CHARLIE: You! Come with me? God no, they'd give me ninety years.

Curtain.

Scene 2

Half an hour later, Charlie is slumped red-eyed in his chair as Harry enters from outside, wearing mackintosh and sou'wester. He has gone out in the rain to fetch Charlie some aspirin. What Charlie really wanted was gin, but the pub has closed.

Again Charlie smells gas, as though the flame in the stock room had blown out, but it hasn't, it's O.K. The gas jet, Harry comments, "might be handy in a pinch," but Charlie objects: "That kind of talk's against God."

Harry sets out to make some hot chocolate. Charlie, lacking the gin, is in a quarrelsome mood.

CHARLIE: . . . . . You look like a pregnant hen. Have you seen your hips? Have you? Ever seen 'em?—far to wide for a man . . . Oh yes. A real man has great broad withers which taper to powerful flanks: what one might call the crutch of the matter. And look at you! Hen is too delicate a term . . . Um, pelican! Yes! You're a pregnant pelican, mate.

Charlie has another look at Harry. He points at Harry's bandages. Bit much when you even pad sou-westers with 'em!

HARRY: I feel safer. . . . .

Charlie continues irritable, cautioning Harry against "tail wagging", against seeking affection in return for his attentions. He needles Harry for liking chocolate and cooking. He attacks Harry's mannerism of sniffing and jerking his head to the left each time he brings a forkful of food near his mouth.

Harry accuses Charlie of cutting his toenails in the kitchen, and this begins a shouted, angry catalogue of each other's faults. Charlie even accuses Harry of dragging him down into the barbering profession when he was doing fine on the stage. Harry denies this pityingly. Charlie tries another hostile tack: Harry is gloating because Charlie will be haled into court to meet his lonely fate with everyone including his ex-wife present to witness his humiliation. In his paroxysm of self-torture, Charlie shouts at Harry to go away (not forgetting to remind him that *everybody* has toenails, they are not obscene). But when Harry leaves the shop, Charlie calls him back, afraid to be alone.

Harry resumes brewing his chocolate concoction. Charlie wants to know when Harry's head bandages are coming off; Harry wants to keep them on yet awhile.

As they sip the brew, they remind each other of all the fine plans they once had to spruce up the shop, maybe to start other branches in fashionable neighborhoods.

HARRY: . . . And then me hair falls out! Bluddyell!

They sit shaking their heads. After a pause . . .

CHARLIE: I was telling your mother . . . "Overnight, Mrs. Leeds," I said. "There it was," I said, "on his pillow." Oh, the shock! "Harry," I shouted. "Your hair, mate! Look at your suffering hair. On the pillow!" I should rub a dub. You went white. Did you know you went white and started screaming?

HARRY *(nods):* Like finding me own eyeball. That's the only way I could describe it to someone like you, Charlie who still has hair. Think how you'd feel, finding your eye looking at you and one side of your face all black.

CHARLIE: Urrgh. You sickly sod!—always were a messy talker. No breeding; no culture.

HARRY: I was trying to make you appreciate . . .

CHARLIE: . . . I don't have to appreciate empty eye sockets, mate. It was me wakened you, wasn't it?

HARRY *(nods):* Horrible.

CHARLIE: Thought it was a kitten curled on your pillow. "Where did he get a kitten?" I thought. I was going to stroke it. Stroke it, dear!

Puts out his hand and draws it back.

Oh my God! Well, you always did have a funny head, Harry. I mean, you did, dear; but all hairless! Like a washerwoman's elbow, it was.

HARRY: Can't you shut up! You cruel sod! Call yourself a friend! . . . knowing how I suffer?

CHARLIE *(casts his glance at the ceiling and mutters . . .):* Now for the great martyr stint.

Baldness is a severe affliction (Harry claims) because people are never considerate of the poor victim's feelings. It's not like being one-legged or wall-eyed; with baldness, people are always joking.

Charlie urges Harry to wear his wig, but Harry doesn't like it because "my neck is naked," there is no way of joining the wig to natural hair. Charlie demands that Harry take off the bandages soon, and Harry promises to do it provided that Charlie promises not to make any of his cruel jokes. Harry will convince himself that the customers aren't peering at him in curiosity. He'll face them.

But Charlie reminds him: "You're not stepping into this shop, Harry. A bald hair stylist!" Harry must hide upstairs—how else can they sell those bottles of hair restorer in the stock room?

CHARLIE: Your clipping days are over, dear.

HARRY: I'll die.

CHARLIE: You and your one-legged men with wall eyes! Be polite as you wish, you never find them in the Royal Ballet, do you?

HARRY: I'll swallow the stock room gas. Sniff it till I'm gone.

CHARLIE: I'm asking if you find knock-knee'd men in the Royal Ballet?

HARRY *(shouts):* No. No. No.

CHARLIE: Then there you have it, dear, haven't you. There you have it. So what with me and me magistrates, and you and your peeled head, we'll have a right happy Tonsorium, shan't we!

Harry bursts into tears and flings himself to the ground, sobbing bitterly. Charlie flops into his chair.

I reckon I'll write a pantomime. *(Nods.)* Write a pantomime and call it *Noddy in Hell.*

Curtain.

ACT II

Some hours later, the street lights outside are still shining, but the sun is up. Charlie is sitting on the floor, leaning against the chair. Harry comes in, flicks on the lights, hands Charlie a dressing gown.

Charlie is still irritable; Harry can do or say nothing right. Charlie is still afraid that the judge will throw the book at him.

CHARLIE: . . . . . Young copper; first case. Everyone free from stain except Dirty Charlie. The way that copper'll paint me, I'll have asked him for a kiss in the bargain . . . And I'm innocent, Harry. As God's my witness, I did it for a gag.

HARRY: There's a new law—Consenting Males or something.

CHARLIE: Oh God help us all and Oscar Wilde!—I was on Ed Chrysler's knee: he's as butch as Kong, dear. Been married to half Charing Cross Road. I need no laws. Need no laws.

HARRY: No. No, but I thought . . . you know . . . I mean, won't Ed Chrysler speak for you?

CHARLIE: They hate getting mixed, you see. I've rung, oh yes, I've, um, rung three times; and heard a click! He's living with Sherry Clade. Lovely girl. I was in a show with her.

Chrysler will be called as a witness at the trial, Harry reassures Charlie. Charlie continues edgy as he takes a box of mementos from the shelf. Harry, rejected, retreats into a crossword puzzle; then goes to the shelf for his dictionary and finds a birthday bottle of gin. Charlie, gleeful, seizes it and pours drinks for himself and Harry; downs his and pours another.

Charlie pushes Harry's dictionary aside and shows him a crushed rose from the memento box; a rose which belonged to his mother, now a wizened 90 years old. Charlie dwells on his mother's physical and mental decay. He feels guilty about putting the old lady away in a home, and at the same time he feels that if he hadn't had this expense he might have married again. He tells Harry: "Many a woman I could've had. Many! I'm not like you—with your antennas and scout poles! Hundreds of women I could've had."

Harry gives Charlie some more gin, and Charlie rewards him with further gruesome reminiscence of his mother's nursing home. If things turn out badly at Charlie's court hearing, he may have to miss some visiting days. What will he tell the old lady?

Harry confesses to Charlie that he sometimes wonders what his own mother and sister say about him when they talk together: "Margie'd say, 'He's old enough to've been married.' Then she'd say . . . I can just hear her: 'Mum, d'you think he's . . . he's a . . .' "

Charlie tries to talk about his troubles, but Harry in his aching sensitivity continues his own tale of woe.

HARRY: When I was over at Margie's last year . . .

CHARLIE: Oh, is she back again?

HARRY: No, listen: I had, well, a dreadful experience. I was bouncing their little boy on my knee. Gurgling; chubby. He's about three. And he threw his arms round my neck and pushed his peanut nose in my ear; and, oh Charlie, I couldn't help hugging and squeezing him. "Oh you darling darling thing," I whispered. Then it all happened.

CHARLIE: Happened? What happened?

HARRY: The baby—began screaming. Wouldn't stop. Then Dick ran in—

all diddems and waddems. "What did you do?" he said. "What did you do?" . . . His voice thick and accusing: face all over the front of his head. *(He sighs deeply.)* How can you tell a man with hairs curling over his collar that you only wanted someone to hug; something to love?

Harry would love to have a baby to cherish, but he knows "they wouldn't give a baby to our kind." Charlie accuses Harry of becoming maudlin; children are merely an ungrateful nuisance. He knows.

Charlie rummages through the box of mementos while he remembers how aggressive his mother used to be when she was young and strong. Charlie comes upon a lock of hair: "Good God, it's mine! A lock of me infant's hair. *(Lips quiver.)* Oh-oh H-Harry! Worms're crawling in me stomach and screaming for those dear dead days! *(Slams the box lid.)* Bastard! Bastard! Hate me mother! Always did!"

And now (Charlie continues somewhat remorsefully) he has put his mother away in a back room of a gloomy rest home. He always weeps after every visit to think of leaving his mother in this "resting place of elephants." He considers bringing her home, but Harry will have none of that. They are close to a quarrel, somewhat inflamed by the gin; but the anger dissolves in humor as Charlie shouts "alopecia!" (baldness) repeatedly at Harry, to the tune of the "Hallelujah Chorus."

Charlie has no childhood memories (he confesses to Harry) except one of a little girl at school who stole his pet frog. "I could lend you memories; but you never listen," Harry replies. Harry begins to remember how mixed-up he was as a child (while Charlie's thoughts move on to the forthcoming trial, and how he should look there).

HARRY: . . . . . Unhappy child I was, Charlie. It was all this "Vive la difference!" hoo-hah. I remember, as a lad at the swimming baths . . . the women with their bodies all private, on one side; and the men on another side. A funny business it seemed. I'd look at *my* body; and I'd think there's a woman next door, looking at hers. And I couldn't, you know, get me thoughts untangled.

Charlie is gazing at himself in the mirror.

CHARLIE: I might dye my hair, I think. Make me look less evil at the trial.

HARRY: Life's just two great separate piles. You're supposed to whoop from one to the other; and if God's given you enough bounce, Bob's your uncle. If not—you're right in it! I've tried hard, Charlie. Once I wore long scarves; rubbed me hands when anyone mentioned beer; and bellowed in dark brown if they asked "Are you courting?" Till I was thirty-five I did that; then I started getting headaches . . . Just those two piles; nothing down the middle.

CHARLIE *(still at the mirror):* I have a kindly face in the main. Fairly kindly. They'll surely believe I'd do no messing.

Harry once took his troubles to a parson, but it was no help. Charlie, self-preoccupied, considers taking Cassy to the trial, as a kind of exhibit of his prowess, particularly if Cassy turns out to be beautiful. But this sudden thought passes, leaving Charlie still in despair. Harry tries to comfort him: "If it's any help, Charlie—I'm frightened too." Charlie is genuinely touched by Harry's concern and thanks him—in Charlie's way—with an affectionate insult.

Charlie tries to squeeze his eyes shut, hoping that his problems will disappear—but he opens them again to the same dreadful moment and anxiety. Harry repeats his detestation of the whole system of sex, the clinical as well as emotional details. This reminds Charlie that he may be "Remanded for a medical report" by the court. The thought of such a humiliation devastates Charlie. It might even be in the papers.

Charlie looks small, old and pathetic.

CHARLIE: . . . Charlie Dyer, hair stylist and one-time tragedian of Clapham, was this morning rem-m—

He covers his mouth. Now Harry clears his throat and puts on a businesslike air.

HARRY: I'll leave you alone, Charlie, when . . .

But before Harry can finish his sentence, Charlie moves to him and grabs his arm anxiously.

CHARLIE: . . . No! Guddelpus no! *Not alone.*

HARRY: When Cassy comes, I meant.

CHARLIE: Oh! Oh yes . . . thanks.

HARRY: And be quite honest, Charlie. Above board: tell her the truth; and ask if she'll come to court with you. It's your best bet.

CHARLIE: Yes. Yes, it is. It is. And maybe I could borrow your dragon dressing gown . . . the one you brought from Saigon . . . She may think I'm still a big actor, you understand, Harry.

Charlie asks also to borrow some of Harry's mother's things to spread around his room, so that Cassy will perhaps assume her father is living with an actress. Perversely, Harry resents being pushed off like this, denied, obliterated. He'd like to meet Cassy. She is the one thing about Charlie that is real.

Charlie should try to say things that make Harry feel big (Harry declares), not keep cutting him down all the time. Charlie has no right to feel superior (Harry continues), not even on the grounds that he's "artistic." Charlie has never done anything—and how does he know that Cassy is his child, when it comes to that?

This remark gets to Charlie, and Harry immediately regrets it. Charlie protests that Cassy is certainly his: "Me and the Old Sow were slicing it off for years, boy years!" Harry doesn't believe it.

HARRY *(quietly):* You weren't, Charlie. You weren't.

CHARLIE: You wide-hipped belly-grubber . . .

Charlie's intended blistering volley stops suddenly. The words

choke him. He covers his face; and his voice is low, near to tears.
Did you *have* to bring it up? . . . Couldn't've done without this one . . . W-wouldn't involve me own daughter, I wouldn't: just a quick idea to keep me going.

Raises his face; eyes closed, hands clenched.
If only I'd been certain all those years ago. If only I'd been sure, I might never have . . . Oh, if only it hadn't happened. *(Then ferociously to Harry.)* You! . . . Hope your nipples drop off as well! . . . Dog in the manger?—you've got hyenas. . . . .

Charlie strikes back at Harry with the counterinsinuation that Harry feels inadequate and is trying to bring Charlie down to his level. Harry is hurt by this, but his reaction is a mild one. He merely wonders once again if he, Harry Leeds, is really there. Or is he like Charlie's agent, Archy Selder—nonexistent?

Charlie protests, but Harry goes on.

HARRY: Archy . . . spelled with a Y. Usually it's spelled IE. Isn't it?
Charlie is still and apprehensive. He says nothing. Harry takes a paper from his pocket.
And d'you remember those postcards when you were away? . . . when you used to write about the great play you were starring in; and your co-star Sherry Clade?

CHARLIE: A great voice! Sherry Clade could reach a top C above . . .

HARRY: And your famous impresario D'Arcy Relshe; and the society woman who worshipped you, Sherly Drace? And Chard Seerly and so on . . . ?

CHARLIE: Doing a biography, are you? Biography?

HARRY: I jotted all those names on a paper. I got to thinking, you see. What a funny name, I thought—Chard Seerly; and Archy Selder with a Y; and D'Arcy Relshe!

He rises to face Charlie.
They all spell Charles Dyer. *They're all you,* Charlie! You've never mentioned anyone who isn't an anagram of Charles Dyer.

Charlie sits and swings to face the mirror. Harry tosses the paper in front of him.

CHARLIE *(clears his throat):* Bit dumb if you've only just found out.

HARRY: I've known for years.

CHARLIE: I once started a play, Harry. Never finished it . . . Thought it might be an idea to have everyone's names the same as mine.

HARRY *(nods):* I used to search theatrical papers for mention of the show you were starring in. Two years! And all those postcards!

Charlie was really selling encyclopedias during those two years (he tells Harry). Charlie confesses that after half-writing the play he remembered the anagrams and used them, whenever he needed to invent "a bit of glamor in me background."

Harry persists in believing that Charlie is keeping a secret about those two years, which occurred ten years ago after Harry and Charlie separated for awhile. Charlie was on the road selling encyclopedias and—he admits at last—served some time in jail, thirty days, which will be on his record.

CHARLIE: I did nothing, Harry. It was a pub near this air force base . . . Youngsters marching with their proud chests . . . and I was kipping in this cellar at four bob a night . . . old meths drinkers belching in me ears. And you know I enjoy a bit of comfort . . . I . . . I just asked a lad if I could come back to camp with him.

Harry, his arms crossed, slaps his own shoulders . . . over and again. It is an action of hopelessness. His gaze is to the ceiling.

I never *do* anything, you know that, Harry. God's Truth, I never *do* anything. I just like clean, new people; fresh and young. Like being *near* them.

Now we realize—gradually—that Harry is the stronger of the partnership. It is Charlie who is the weak one.

Harry gets Charlie to admit that his sentence was two years, not thirty days. He becomes angry: "D'you never consider anyone? Never think of *my* shame? . . . staying with you! People pointing at us—at the two weirdies, Harry and Charlie.—*And there's nothing wrong with me*. There's nothing wrong, and I have to suffer the stain because of you. . . . . This finishes us." But Harry is far from finished with Charlie. He takes a piece of paper and writes down a name: Ed Chrysler, another anagram, another fantasy of Charlie's.

Charlie admits there was no Ed Chrysler at the time of his latest arrest. He was drunk, he hardly remembers what happened until they were dragging him out of the club, charging him with masquerading as a woman. Charlie remembers begging the police to let him go; they let him go home, but charged him.

Charlie recalls his marriage: he knows his wife put up with him only in order to get a baby, but still he wishes that the "Old Sow" hadn't kicked him out.

Harry understands—he once let a neighborhood druggist believe that he was a married man, and he enjoyed the role (and Harry has noticed that it is morning; in a matter-of-fact way he goes about picking up and getting the shop ready). The druggist's wife spoiled it all by coming to call, and Harry had to slam the door in her face.

Harry challenges Charlie with another anagram: Harry Leeds also spells Charles Dyer because Harry always signs himself with his middle initial, Harry C. Leeds. Charlie, genuinely upset, backs away from Harry with the comment "I'm getting out before little goblins start running up me arm."

Charlie grabs a suitcase and starts packing, while arguing that if he were going to invent a companion he wouldn't invent Harry, he'd invent someone with black curls.

Charlie wants Harry to stop him from going, but Harry calls his bluff—

shakes hands goodbye and warns Charlie that he can't wipe their 20 years together from his mind just by walking out the door. Harry comments: "Terrible terrible thing—not to be liked; not to be even necessary. If a great big nozzle sucked me into oblivion, there isn't a clock'd stop ticking." Harry sums up their 20-year relationship: his companionship has provided Charlie with "a clothes horse to hang your troubles on," and Harry has taught Charlie a trade which Charlie affects to despise.

HARRY: Yes, I can understand how you've resented my being so ordinary. You'd've swapped a bit of comfort for someone more er, more artistic, I dare say.

CHARLIE: Oh, you've done your best, mate. Done your best.

HARRY: It's not one-sided, Charlie: because I need somebody all my own. And after all, I can't see a "little me" in *you,* Charlie. Can't watch *you* growing up. A shame, it is: we could've walked through the years together. Blame's on both sides, I suppose.

Harry exits into the stock room. After a second, Charlie moves to the stock room door. He calls quietly:

CHARLIE: Harry! . . . Harry? . . . Aren't you going to wait for me then? Aren't you going to keep me room? . . . keep me room warm? . . . Harry? . . . Oh, suit yourself!

There is no reply. Charlie kicks the door and moves to the gin bottle. It is empty.

Dry as a camel's chamber pot!

He tosses the bottle into a waste bin; then looks about him, scratching his neck and licking his lips.

Hair restorer! I'll have a tot of that. *(He shouts at the stock room.)* And maybe I'll die; then you'll be sorry!

He rummages in one of the cupboards and produces a bottle of hair restorer . . . which he pours into the gin bottle.

(Shouts.) I'm having hair restorer! D'you hear!—you ramshackle old queen! . . . *(To himself.)* But he's not. He's nice and ordinary; that's the trouble. *(He clenches his teeth.)* God, I wish I could crack through me hard crust and say straight out "Harry, you're a beautiful old stick, love." . . . Why can't I say it? Why can't I say "Please Harry, keep me room warm for me when I come out of jail?"

He turns to face the stock room door. Firmly he calls . . .

Harry! Harry, will you . . .

But he cannot make his lips finish the sentence. Instead, he puts the bottle to his lips and gulps the hair restorer . . . which he immediately spits into the basin.

Uurrgh! I'll die *next* week, I think.

For awhile he leans on the wash basin, peering at himself in the mirror.

Harry C. Leeds. Harry C. Leeds. Fantastic! . . . I never planned that one! Don't say I'm seeing 'em as well! *(He swings away from the mirror and shouts.)* Of course you're there! I wouldn't invent a shriveled mirage like you, mate! *(To himself.)* Oh no! I'd have someone with black curls and slim hips. Anyway, that's his chair!

He kicks it.

Spectacle case!

He picks up the spectacle case.

Go on! Vanish, you bugger!

He throws it down.

Ha! Of course, he's there. *(Shouts.)* You there, mate! You're horrible and concrete!

He moves to the stock room door; bangs on it.

D'you hear? . . . Harry? . . . Harry!

He tries the door knob. Seemingly it is locked.

Harry, what're you doing?

Bangs on the door.

Damn fool!—locking the door. Harry! You all right, Harry? Harry! . . . Harry, what've you done?

Charlie's shouting and banging becomes frantic. He pushes against the door. It begins to open—slowly, as though something heavy were lying on the other side.

Charlie manages to get the door open against the weight of Harry lying inert on the floor. We hear Charlie break the glass of the stock room window, then he drags Harry into the room and works over him, trying to revive him, begging Harry not to leave him alone.

Harry coughs and sits up. He is perfectly all right. He has just had a minor fainting spell, possibly because of high blood pressure. Charlie cannot comprehend that Harry has *not* attempted suicide; the gas flame is still lit, everything is in order—except for the needlessly broken window.

Charlie sinks to his knees, nearly fainting with relief. Harry now sees that Charlie thought him dead or dying.

HARRY *(kneels beside him):* Bit of a shock, was it?

CHARLIE *(nods):* I thought, um . . . I thought I was on me own, Harry. And um, I think you're . . . *(He tries again.)* I think you're . . . *(And in a whisper.)* a beautiful old stick.

But Harry doesn't hear Charlie's whisper.

HARRY: Pardon? . . . I couldn't hear, Charlie . . .

CHARLIE: Oh belt up, and give me breathing space.

He elbows Harry away.

Harry and Charlie agree that under the circumstances they will close the shop and take the day off. Harry goes into the stock room.

Charlie, alone, declares to God that he will never forget the lesson of this incident, in which he thought for a moment that he had been left alone in the world. He promises God to make Harry diet, "And may Mum drop dead and everyone leave me alone if I don't remember this lesson. *I will. I will.* Please Jesus, make me remember how lonely people are; little cripples and little blind folks. Amen."

Harry re-enters from the stock room: he is wearing a thin, ill-fitting dark wig. Charlie tries to be tactful about it, but Harry sees through Charlie's pretense. Strangely, Harry doesn't feel comfortable with Charlie in this mood of forbearance, telling him: "I'd rather you said one of your cruel thrusts." Slowly Charlie pulls himself together, stares at Harry and obliges.

CHARLIE: Where're you going to keep it at night—in a cage?

HARRY: Yes, that's you! That's my old You. Go on! More. Tell me more.

CHARLIE: Well—it looks like you've spat ink on a hot boiled egg!

But this is too much for Harry . . .

HARRY: Oh, you bastard! You're horrid and vicious.

CHARLIE: You asked me! Asked me!

HARRY: You and your pretty hair! I hope it erupts from your scalp. Erupts and erupts—until the shop's an overgrown church hassock with taps; and you in the middle, clawing for life. Hair in your eyes, through your ears, and up your bloody jumper!

He flops into his chair. Charlie crosses to him.

CHARLIE: You going to wear that when you meet Cassy?

HARRY: Meet her?

CHARLIE: Might as well. Anything for peace.

He walks round Harry, surveying the wig.

Could be worse . . . Pleasantly surprised, I am . . . It sort of grows on you . . . Sorry, Harry.

Charlie considers himself in the mirror. A night has passed, and his chin is shadowed again. We hear creaking on the staircase. They look upwards. Harry rushes to listen; but Charlie just rubs his chin at the mirror, and murmurs:

Ta-ta, sexy!

Now Charlie sighs; sits in his chair. Harry bustles to his record player; puts on "Hallelujah Chorus": then he takes his little bowl, his soap, and begins lathering the brush . . . Curtain.

YOUR OWN THING

A Musical in One Act

BOOK BY DONALD DRIVER

MUSIC AND LYRICS BY HAL HESTER AND DANNY APOLINAR

Suggested by William Shakespeare's Twelfth Night

Cast and credits appear on page 398

DONALD DRIVER (book) was born on the West Coast in Portland, Oregon. He graduated from Pomona College in Southern California and served in the Navy in World War II. He started in show business as a performer, first as a ballet dancer then as a comedy actor, and then branched out into directing and writing. He has staged many productions in theaters across the country and came to Broadway in January, 1967 as director of the American production of Marat/Sade, *for which he was cited in the Tony nominations. He directed* Your Own Thing *himself and later this season he staged* Mike Downstairs *on Broadway.*

Driver has his own firm, Driver Productions Inc., which has produced and written industrial shows for General Motors, Bell Telephone, Westinghouse, Nabisco and others. In collaboration with Richard Rodgers he wrote a stage version of the Rodgers & Hammerstein TV musical Cinderella *which has been produced in stock.* Your Own Thing, *which won the New York Drama Critics Circle award for the season's best musical, is Driver's New York playwriting debut.*

HAL HESTER (co-composer, co-lyricist) was born June 10, 1933 in Paducah, Ky., where he attended the Tilgman High School. Following his gradua-

tion from the Cincinnati Conservatory of Music, where he double-majored in piano and composition, he began writing songs and is now an ASCAP writer with 30 published works including recordings by Nat King Cole, Roy Hamilton and Gloria Lynne. A piano-and-songs act with his collaborator Danny Apolinar (see below) was broken up when Apolinar was drafted into the Army, but for two years Hester was part of another act, a singing trio that appeared at the Blue Angel and the Copacabana.

The score for Your Own Thing *was cited for an ASCAP Popular Award. It is Hester's first work for the theater. Hester's home is in Puerto Rico, where for the past six years he has owned and operated The Sand and Sea Club.*

DANNY APOLINAR (co-composer, co-lyricist) was born in Brooklyn and educated at the High School of Industrial Art and Pratt Institute. He embarked on a career as a commercial artist. His first contact with show business was as a singer with his collaborator, Hal Hester, for Atlantic Records in an act called The Madhattans. They were just about to break in a piano-and-songs act in New Haven when Apolinar was drafted for service in the Army. Later, with the Danny Apolinar Trio, he toured the Playboy Club Circuit and has been featured as solo pianist at Dick Kollmar's Left Bank and Kippy's. Apolinar has appeared on TV shows, but Your Own Thing*—in which he plays the role of Danny in the Apocalypse singing group—is his first experience in the theater both as an author and a performer.*

Time: The present

Place: Manhattan Island, Illyria

SYNOPSIS: The scene is an open acting area (blacked out at the beginning of the play) with a pair of ramps upstage. There are doors left and right downstage, plus upstage exits. The cyclorama and other planes facing the audience are to become screens for the projection of slides and movies which will depict settings, enlarge moods or make comments. Comic-strip balloons or voices recorded on tape will accompany photo inserts of Everett Dirksen, Mayor John V. Lindsay, Queen Elizabeth I, W.C. Fields, Shakespeare, John Wayne, Shirley Temple, Humphrey Bogart and others. *(". . . . . one must keep in mind the fact that film and slide projections, taped and live sound effects . . . . . form a mixed media collage which is the final effect of the script.")*

In the blackout, a loud rock overture begins, then is suddenly cut off.

EVERETT DIRKSEN (SLIDE): If music be the food of love, play on! I can't remember if that's Marlowe or Bacon.

The Shipwreck: The film begins with an explosion aboard ship and continues throughout the scene showing a shipwreck at sea and the ship finally sinking. Accompanying slide projections are stills taken from that movie. . . . .

VOICE OVER: Passengers please don't be alarmed. Please don't panic. The life boats are being lowered. We'll take on women and children as soon as the ship's Xerox and IBM machines are loaded.

During the shipwreck scene the entire company appear as panicked passengers, running about trying to put on life preservers, jump overboard, and generally escape the disaster. Viola and Sebastian (two members of the "Now Generation" who had been a rock duo. They are completely uninhibited and adventuresome . . . . identical in dress and hair style) are finally the last passengers left on board.

SEBASTIAN: Where are you going?
VIOLA: I'm going back to the cabin.
SEBASTIAN: Vi, you can't go back to the cabin!
VIOLA: I've got to save our orchestrations.
SEBASTIAN: Stupid sister, we're sinking.
VIOLA: You don't care if we end up back in Akron, Ohio!
SEBASTIAN: Do you want a singing job at the bottom of the ocean?
VIOLA: Well, it's no farther under than Akron!

Viola insists that they can't afford new orchestrations. Their argument becomes a song: "No One's Perfect, Dear." The Purser enters and looks at Viola and Sebastian and tells Viola: "Don't just stand there fellow, get your sister to the lifeboat!" The Purser exits. Sebastian finally agrees to go below over, calling instructions at him. The Purser re-enters.

PURSER: Come on! Move your ass, mister, we're going fast!

Purser slaps Viola's ass.

Move your ass, lady, we're going fast.

Blackout. Purser and Viola exit. Projections: slides of waterfront buildings in semi-abstract. Lights. Enter Purser and Viola.

VIOLA: What country, friend, is this?
PURSER: This is Illyria, lady.
VIOLA:

And what should I do in Illyria?
My brother, he is in Elysium.
Perchance he is not drowned;
What think you sailor?

PURSER:

It is perchance that you yourself were saved.

VIOLA:

And so perchance may he be.

In Shakespeare's words, the Purser tells Viola that he saw Sebastian bind himself to a floating mast just before the ship sank. The Purser exits before Viola can question him about this island upon which they have been cast up.

VIOLA *(calling after Purser):* Who governs here?

MAYOR LINDSAY (SLIDE): New York is a fun city. Cough, cough.

VIOLA: And what should I do in Illyria?

During the following song the motion picture film shows varying shots of New York City skyline and skyscrapers. The film is at the same time beautiful and impersonal; and in a nutshell capsulizes the exterior shapes of 20th century urban life.

The slide projections which accompany this film are stills of steel and glass structures and change constantly during the song.

VIOLA *(sings):*

So much glass, so much steel,
What's there to care? What's there to feel?
All that glass, all that chrome,
Can I ever call this place home?

Here the air is grey and smoggy
My eyes burn and my head seems groggy
How do the flowers grow
In their sweet little box
In their neat little row.

Here come the men to plant new flowers
The beautiful people must see beautiful flowers
From their beautiful ivory towers.

A slide of God as Michelangelo painted him in the Sistine Chapel and a slide of Buddha appear and "speak" of responsibility for the shipwreck. Buddha appears to hand Viola a card reading "Boy wanted," and she dances off to claim the job. By means of projections, the set is transformed to a background of telephones.

Orson *("A graduate of the beat generation who has become a theatrical agent and whose biggest client is the Apocalypse rock 'n' roll group . . . . . his attempts to emulate the now generation are heartfelt and hopeless. He is a square")* enters left. Olivia *("A very charming, witty and deliciously droll woman of 30 who owns and operates a discotheque. She loves to be surrounded by the young and is dressed in very chic versions of the latest fashion fad")* enters right. They are speaking to each other as though on the telephone, looking off into space.

ORSON: Olivia, I love you.

OLIVIA: You're just stimulated by rejection.

ORSON *(turning to Olivia):* I am not.

OLIVIA *(turning to Orson):* All right, then you're too old for me.

ORSON: I am not; we're the same age.

OLIVIA: That proves it; I like younger men. . . . .

Actually, this is a business call. The Apocalypse, Orson's four-man singing group, are booked into Olivia's discotheque, but one member of the Apocalypse—Disease—has been drafted. Olivia demands her full quota of four singers, or the booking is canceled.

Olivia exits. A slide representing Orson's office is projected onto the set. The Apocalypse enter *("Danny, John and Michael . . . . . wear far-out clothes, long hair and say and do anything that pleases them")*. They kid Orson about his long unrequited romance with Olivia. They even joke about their own urgent need to find a fourth singer, or lose all their bookings. The Apocalypse exit, clowning.

Lights down.

QUEEN ELIZABETH (SLIDE): Why do they need a fourth musician? In my day troubadors sang alone.

HUMPHREY BOGART (SLIDE): We call that folk singing. The government frowns on it.

SISTINE GOD (SLIDE): The old queen's right, Four's not a Biblical number.

QUEEN ELIZABETH (SLIDE): Did I hear that Vatican Manifestation on the ceiling refer to me as the "old queen"?

JOHN WAYNE (SLIDE): It don't matter who they put in the group. I can't tell the boys from the girls anyway.

BOGART (SLIDE): You do have a problem.

Lights up.

ORSON: I can't get through to these guys. God knows I've tried. There's no generation gap with me. I read Ramparts and The East Village Other. I've been to the Electric Circus. I've studied their language. I read that article in McCall's by Lynda Bird. I've studied their music, and everything teen, their every scene. I try every way I can to get through to them with God knows what-not. Even pot. Blahh. It makes you hungry. I gained four pounds on candy bars alone. To them I'm Orson Uptight. Big Square. Nowhere. But I'm not! I'm the personification of all the accumulated knowledge of the beat generation and I try to be it. Why can't they see it. What do I have to do to show I know . . . how to be one of them?

Orson exits. Apocalypse enter during end of Orson's speech.

DANNY *(sings):*

I don't have to show anyone
I want to be one of them;
'Cause deep inside is the feeling of pride
The *me* from which the mighty oaks stem. . . . .

JOHN:

This is a man, look at his clothes
Not your idea of a tough man.

DANNY:

Think what you will, this is no pose
Don't have to pretend I'm a rough man
I'm enough, man.

MICHAEL:

This is a man, look at his eyes
They're expressive

DANNY:

I can feel

JOHN:

This is a man, look at his heart
It's impressive

DANNY:

I am real

ALL:

Why does everybody have to be afraid to be a human being
Why does everybody have to be afraid of other people seeing

DANNY:

Everybody has emotion buried deep inside
When they feel one truthful emotion,
They feel that's what they've got to hide

JOHN:

Me—I'm not afraid to cry
Me—I'm not afraid to die
I'm not afraid to weep when I'm sad
I'm not afraid to laugh when I'm glad
I'm not afraid to know when I'm bad
I'm not afraid to love. . . . .

DANNY:

I'm not the starry eyed boy next door
I'm not the life of the party
I've got to be what I've got to be
I'm me!
I'm not the prince in a fairy tale
I'm not as strong as an oak tree
I like the feeling of feeling free
I'm me!

Viola enters Orson's office and presents her "Boy wanted" card from Buddha, declaring that she's a boy named Charlie. When Orson asks her if she can sing, she claims that she can, and she is immediately auditioned with the Apocalypse, borrowing Michael's tambourine.

While Apocalypse sing "Baby, Baby", Viola, making mistakes, tries to sing along with them, play the tambourine, dance and give a good audition. The impression is more frantic than anything as she tries to copy each of their styles. She wins them over as they end up copying hers.

VIOLA AND APOCALYPSE *(sing):*

Somethin's happenin' makes me want to fly

Baby! Baby! Baby! Baby!
Somethin's happenin' some new kind of high
Baby! Baby! Baby! Baby!
Over and over and over and over and over
And over and over and over
Over and over and over and over and over
And over and oh! . . . . .

ORSON: You're real groovy. You're . . . you know . . . ah . . .

DANNY: Solid?

ORSON: Yea, solid.

JOHN: Jackson!

ORSON: Bug out!

JOHN: You'll learn to cope with the parochial entrenchment of the Victorians.

ORSON: Get out!

The Apocalypse exit. Orson hires "Charlie" to fill the Apocalypse vacancy.

Orson tells "Charlie" (Viola) of his love for Olivia and her rejection of him because he is too "square". Viola reassures him that he is square in just the right, groovy way. With some of Shakespeare's words, Orson persuades Viola to deliver a note to Olivia and put in a good word for him at the same time.

After a blackout, the scene changes to a hospital, where we see that Sebastian has survived the shipwreck. Sebastian thinks that his sister Viola was drowned, however, and he sings a Shakespearean lament:

"Come away, come away death
And in sad cypresses let me be laid.
Fly away, fly away breath:
I am slain by a lost lovely maid. . . . ."

A nurse enters and plops a thermometer in Sebastian's mouth. She mistakes Sebastian for a girl until, giving him a sponge bath, she finds out the truth. The angry nurse tells him he "should be in the Army with a haircut," but Sebastian admits he doesn't take to the idea of being shot. Sebastian gives a tender farewell to the nurse as he leaves the hospital. Looking around, he wonders "What should I do in Illyria?"

Sebastian's environment changes from trees to big-city skyscrapers. Once again the Buddha hand appears and delivers a card reading "Boy wanted."

SEBASTIAN *(sings):*

I've got all of the aces, hear me holler hooray!
Don't you wait up for me, I've got places to see
That would make your eyes pop
I'm on my way to the top.

Sebastian knocks on Orson's door.

ORSON *(taking Buddha card from Sebastian):* This Buddha must be a poor loser, I'm your new agent.

SEBASTIAN: You are?

ORSON: Look, Charlie, the first thing you've got to learn to do is trust me.

SEBASTIAN: Right, right, I will.

ORSON: I've been thinking about that letter to Olivia.

SEBASTIAN: What letter?

ORSON: You got the letter?

SEBASTIAN: No sir.

ORSON: Charlie, didn't my secretary give you a letter?

SEBASTIAN: No, sir.

ORSON: Well, it doesn't matter. I wrote a stronger one. One I know will really get through to her. Here.

Orson has mistaken Sebastian for Viola, of course. They are both "Charlie" to him, one and the same person. Orson gives the second letter to Sebastian with instructions to deliver it to Olivia. After another chorus of "I'm on My Way to the Top," Sebastian goes off on his errand.

Viola enters with the Apocalypse. Olivia joins them and is introduced to the new member of the singing group. Olivia studies Viola, whom she believes to be a beardless youth. The Apocalypse start clowning.

VIOLA: Are you guys always such a bunch of fools?

JOHN: Good sir, I'll bet I can prove you're a fool.

VIOLA: You can?

JOHN: Dexteriously, good sir.

VIOLA: Good fool, make your proof.

MICHAEL: Good sir, why mourn'st thou?

VIOLA: Good fool, for my brother's death.

DANNY: I think his soul is in hell, sir, and black.

VIOLA: I know his soul is in heaven, fool, and white.

JOHN: The more fool, sir, to mourn for your brother's soul, being in heaven and *white*. Think if he were on earth and *black*.

The Apocalypse do a back roll upstage. The action freezes while Olivia muses in Shakespeare's words that "Methinks I feel this youth's perfections." She admits frankly to herself that she admires this beardless "Charlie."

OLIVIA *(sings):*

You can catch cold very fast, well let it be
It can take hold very fast, well let it be
If this happens to me, well let it be
Well let it be

If I've found love very fast, well let it be
And if this love doesn't last, well let it be
If this happens, at least it happens to me
So let it be.

The Apocalypse clown their way offstage. Viola delivers Orson's letter to Olivia, who insists that "Charlie" read it out loud. Orson's letter protests that Olivia ought to prefer him to "those kids you've been hanging around." Viola argues that Orson is not really a square, and that he loves Olivia, but Olivia has eyes at this moment only for "Charlie"—she likes the way Charlie reads. She suggests that Orson send another letter the next day—by boy. Olivia exits.

Viola reports back to Orson, who is encouraged because Olivia asked for another letter.

Meanwhile, Sebastian knocks on Olivia's door. He is bringing the second letter. Olivia (who believes Sebastian and Viola are the same youth) asks him to read aloud again. Sebastian notices that Olivia "made good view of me" while he was reading. He reports back to Orson that Olivia seems so eager, one more letter ought to do the trick.

Now it's Viola's turn to deliver the third letter. This time, Olivia is so interested in "Charlie" that she unzips Viola's shirt. But Viola manages to preserve her masquerade. Olivia asks for more letters.

Viola and Sebastian always just miss each other as they criss-cross on their letter-carrying errands. Olivia makes it clear to the next "Charlie" (Sebastian) that she wants to see him at 8 o'clock—alone.

On *her* next go-round, Viola has a padlock on her zipper—but Olivia has acquired the key, which she intends to use later.

It is now clear to Viola that Olivia "mistaken seems to dote on me." This time when she reports back to Orson she tells him to give up hope—Olivia will never love him. Orson doesn't believe it, but Viola insists he'll have to accept it, just as a girl in love with Orson would have to believe it if he told her he didn't love her.

Viola pretends that she had a sister who loved greatly.

VIOLA *(sings):*

She never told her love
She never told her love
But let concealment like a worm in the bud
Feed on her damask cheek.

She sat like Patience, like Patience on a monument
Smiling, smiling, smiling at grief. . . . .

ORSON: What happened to your sister?

VIOLA: I don't know yet.

ORSON: Is she anything like you?

VIOLA: Spittin' image.

ORSON: She must be very attractive . . . *(Realizing.)* . . . Charlie! I'll send another letter. No! I don't want to send another letter. Oh hell! . . . . .

Orson is confused and strangely attracted to "Charlie." He questions "Charlie" about his love life, and Viola confesses that she is in love with someone about Orson's age, with Orson's "wonderful qualities." Orson confesses man-to-man that he doesn't understand girls, and Viola offers him a few words of advice in song.

VIOLA *(sings):*
When you love a girl be very gentle
Write her pretty sonnets, give her pretty things
When you love a girl, be very gentle
Whisper in her ear the words she likes to hear. . . . .

Orson rises, crosses to center, pauses, looks back at Viola, confused. He exits. Blackout, except for follow spot on Viola.

WAYNE (SLIDE): That man's falling for that boy!

BOGART (SLIDE): There's your old problem. It's a girl.

WAYNE (SLIDE): Yeh, but he don't know that.

BOGART (SLIDE): Would it change anything if he did?

WAYNE (SLIDE): Sure! It'd be decent.

BOGART (SLIDE): No, just legal.

QUEEN ELIZABETH (SLIDE): I say, "Pair anybody off with anything." The only crime I know is loneliness.

The Shakespeare slide asks "What is love?" in a quoted passage. Viola echoes the question in song, asking herself when she will find love. Then Viola exits. Sebastian comes on singing "Baby, Baby" and knocks on Olivia's door. It is 8 o'clock.

The Apocalypse singers enter upstage. Seeing Sebastian, they order him to join them (they have been looking all over for him). He does join them for a chorus of "Baby, Baby" but when Olivia comes out of her house in response to Sebastian's knock, Sebastian hands her another letter.

Olivia ignores the letter. She pulls out a key, unlocks the padlock on Sebastian's shirt and pulls the zipper part way down. Sebastian's reaction to this signal is far different from Viola's; he whistles and pulls the zipper all the way down. The signals thus exchanged, Olivia exits through the door to her house, closely followed by Sebastian.

Viola comes onstage behind the Apocalypse, who are confused when they turn and see her, because they have just watched "Charlie" disappear in the other direction with Olivia.

Viola questions the Apocalypse about Orson. They tell her that Orson has been wooing Olivia for five years. The Apocalypse's opinion of Orson is voiced by John: "He can't find his bag because it's always over his head." They promise to keep Viola's "secret"—that she is making it with Olivia behind Orson's back.

The stage manager enters, carrying five Hunca Munca costumes for the Apocalypse (the extra one had been ordered for the former Disease). The stage manager is contemptuous of the rock 'n' rollers and calls them "jerks." The Apocalypse consider this word an antique and jeer at the stage manager for using it. As he exits, they all express their defiant new freedom in a number choreographed in the style of modern rock dances.

VIOLA *(sings):*
We're revolting from the age when lines were drawn
To separate the sexes.

ALL:
We're revolting from the age when all the men
Came from the state of Texas

DANNY:
Men and women used to be so far apart in every way
That it's a mother wonder that there's still a mother
Human race today.

Viola and Apocalypse give the stage manager the raspberries, through the door.

. . . . . DANNY *(sings):*
I'm so tightly trussed

MICHAEL:
All this shakin' just

JOHN:
Makes me want to bust

VIOLA:
Right out of my body

. . . . . ALL *(sing):*
Got a feel and the feel is feeling right
Everybody is gonna fly tonight.
Do the things they don't allow
We are the now generation.

Gotta move on in, make the band begin
Waitin' for tonight, gotta look just right

DANNY:
Got the latest gear,

MICHAEL:
Buttons up to here,

JOHN:
Ready to appear,

ALL:
We can't look shoddy.

VIOLA:
Let your hair down and shake out all your curls
What's the difference, the boys all look like girls.

ALL:
Baby you can take a bow, we are the now generation.

When the Apocalypse singers start getting undressed to change into their costumes, Viola, unseen, grabs her costume and modestly moves offstage to change. Sebastian comes on in his underwear and is told to hurry up about getting into his costume. He obeys, as the others finish dressing and exit.

Slide figures debate the morality of changing clothes on the stage.

The scene shifts to Olivia's apartment, where Sebastian and Olivia are discussing his "audition"—she approved. Sebastian tells Olivia how he plans some day to be a geologist. Curiously enough, Olivia once had ambitions to become an archeologist. She spent one summer on four square yards of earth in Libya: "I was given a young Libyan boy to assist me. I spent most of the summer digging him."

Too late, Olivia regrets saying this. Sebastian ignores her comment.

SEBASTIAN *(crossing to Olivia):* You and me'd make a good team. You could dig up the rocks and I could, like, identify them.

OLIVIA: Sounds heaven.

They kiss.

SEBASTIAN: You still haven't told me how you got from your four square yards in Libya to your discotheque off Third Avenue.

OLIVIA: Well, after that summer I went back to Sarah Lawrence.

Sebastian sits on floor.

Did I tell you I had a minor in music? Well, I did. Anyway, Mother wanted me to be a cellist but old Daddy was an account executive at B.B.D. & O. and figured if the cello image wasn't too risky, the position I had to play it in was. So it ended up piano. Well . . .

Lights down. Both follow spots on Sebastian. Olivia crosses to upstage platform and sits, continuing inner monologue.

SEBASTIAN:

This is the air; that is the glorious sun,
This pearl she gave me, I do feel 't and see 't;
And though 'tis wonder that enwraps me thus,
Yet 'tis not madness. What a groovy lady.

I'll be she thinks, "He's a pleasant interlude—for a kid. Nice sense of humor, ambitious—for a kid." Goddamit, I'm nearly twenty. That's old—for a kid. *(Sings.)*

I finally made it! I shook myself free
No more wondering what became of me
I know where I'm going, no crocodile tears
Solved the riddle, I'm in my middle years. . . . .

Olivia asks Sebastian how old he is. Sebastian resents her attempt to classify him with an age number. The stage manager enters with employment forms to be filled out. He hands them to Sebastian and exits.

As Sebastian fills out the forms, Olivia's thoughts appear as slide projections of comic strip balloons.

BALLOON (SLIDE) *(over Olivia's head):* "Why did you have to mention that Libyan boy?"

BALLOON (SLIDE): "Olivia is a dirty old man."

BALLOON (SLIDE) *(superimposed over "man"):* "Lady."

OLIVIA: Right!

BALLOON (SLIDE): "I asked you how old you were" . . . . .

OLIVIA: What you really mean was not, "How old are you, you marvelous, beautiful youth?" but "Olivia, are you too old?" That's the horrible, terrible truth.

SEBASTIAN *(crosses to Olivia, hands her the forms):* Here. This'll tell you how "young" I am.

Exits.

OLIVIA *(sings:)*

He's twenty, I'm thirty, does it matter?
When I'm forty, he'll be thirty, does it matter?
Rules, labels, slots, categories
Lead the way to lonely purgatories,
What does it matter?

. . . . . The nights now are shorter tho' somewhat less gay
No more time to waste, I live each day.
And I happen to like it, so give a few cheers
Tune my fiddle, I'm in my middle years.

Sebastian comes back during Olivia's song. When the song ends, he apologizes for being so sensitive on the age question. So does she. They make a date for that evening.

Sebastion drifts off just as Viola drifts on. The stage manager enters and asks for the forms, to Viola's bewilderment. Olivia hands them to him and he exits.

Viola is bearing a final letter to Olivia from Orson which states (as she reads aloud) that Orson gives Olivia her freedom. He no longer loves her. Viola starts to go, but Olivia takes her hand. Viola pulls her hand away with, "Look Olivia. I'm not what you think I am. I mean, with me this job is going to be strictly business. And if you don't want to play it that way, then I'll quit."

Viola runs off in search of Orson, as Olivia looks after her in puzzlement, then exits.

The scene changes; Orson enters with an armload of books. He is reading from one of them.

ORSON: . . . "It is not uncommon that these latent desires appear, previously suppressed by fear of society's hostility . . ."

Looks around suspiciously, crosses and closes door.

". . . and because the afflicted individual cannot include them in his own concepts of masculine behavior . . ." That's uncool! ". . . behavior which the same society has strictly regulated for him. The sudden appearance of these desires can cause great personality upheaval and mental anguish."

One chord of crash from the orchestra.

I'm glad mother's dead!

Opening another book.

"Throughout history, civilizations have arisen in which the love of one man for another has been an accepted part of the society in which it arose." *(Looks up.)* "So much so that legend has grown up over the devotion of such lovers." *(Double look.)* "Every school child has read of Damon and Pythias, King David and . . ." King David? ". . . and his friend Jonathan." Yes, I read about them in Sunday school. Is that what they were doing?

Sings. During this song, slides are projected over the entire set showing Viola in beguiling poses.

When you're young and in love.
When you're young and in love.
It's a beautiful thing
You're a kid on a swing
You feel higher than high.
When you're young and in love.
When you're young and in love
Everybody's a king
All the world starts to sing
You can float in the sky.

Orson is caught up in a fantasy visualized by slides of historical personages and events, and live silhouette "freezes" of the Apocalypse, Viola and Sebastian. Orson imagines himself and "Charlie" a pair of Roman soldiers dying together. He imagines the Roman and Greek establishment's disapproval of his outlaw form of love. He imagines Goliath calling to King David: "Come out and fight, you big fag!" He imagines a lynching party in the old, rugged West, and he imagines Viola singing "I Never Told My Love" while he urges "Charlie" to escape while there is still time.

Orson snaps out of his fantasy and returns to reality, just as Viola reaches him and calls him "love."

ORSON: You called me "love." Charlie, we've got to play this thing cool.

VIOLA: Orson, I've got something to tell you. I didn't tell you the truth about myself.

ORSON: I'll tell you. I didn't know the truth about myself. But it's okay, Charlie. If that's where it's at, we'll make it work.

VIOLA: I would have told you sooner but at first I was afraid you'd fire me. And then back and forth, back and forth with all those love letters to Olivia . . .

ORSON: That's when I was confused. Charlie, I'm glad you feel the same way.

VIOLA: Call me Viola.

ORSON *(rising):* Charlie, that's not playing this thing very cool.

VIOLA *(rising):* Well, you can't call me Charlie.

ORSON: Give me time, I'm new at this!

VIOLA: New at what?

ORSON: Well, you don't have to believe this if you don't want to, but it's the truth. You're the first boy I ever loved.

VIOLA: What?!!

ORSON: It's the truth. The first boy. I swear on my mother's . . .

VIOLA: But I'm a girl . . .

ORSON: Charlie, it's too soon to talk about role-playing.

VIOLA: You mean you love me because I'm a boy?

ORSON: It was that or nothing. Charlie, you're . . . you're my . . . Him.

VIOLA: Why, you . . . you're a . . .

Orson pleads that there's no problem, this is their thing and they must do it. Viola, hurt because Orson doesn't love her for what she really is, bangs him over the head with a book and stalks off. Orson follows her.

The Apocalypse and Sebastian enter for a number onstage at Olivia's discotheque. The lighting is kaleidoscopic, partly moving in free-form shapes and partly in projection of a series of unrelated photos, the whole intended to create an almost psychedelic effect.

APOCALYPSE AND SEBASTIAN *(sing):*

. . . . . Lights go white to red to blue
Every color ev'ry hue
Silver birds come into view
Me and you
Do the Hunca Munca

DANNY:

Here's one dance that can't be angelic
Here's one dance that can't end up a relic
Furthermore, you'll find the floor
Hypo, micro, psychedelic.

APOCALYPSE AND SEBASTIAN:

Soon you'll get the feeling of
Crazy ceilings up above
Just the dance to turtle dove
Fall in love,
Do the Hunca Munca.

The entire company dances back and forth, miming incidents of love, mistaken identity, and unrelated antics including old movie routines.

Olivia tweaks Viola's cheek, mistaking her for Sebastian. Viola calls her a sex maniac and stalks off indignantly. Sebastian enters, approaches Olivia and gets slapped.

After final episodes of dancing in and out, entangling and door-slamming, the whole company exits except for Sebastian and Olivia, seated at opposite sides of the stage. The icy situation is saved by Buddha, who hands each of them a card reading "Pride and twenty cents get you a ride on the subway." Quickly they warm to each other.

OLIVIA *(sings):*
Don't leave me, don't go away.
Please don't leave me, say that you'll stay.
SEBASTIAN AND OLIVIA:
Believe me, you know it's true.
OLIVIA:
You need me.
SEBASTIAN:
And I need you.
BOTH:
Fill, please fill my heart
Until, until my heart is still
We'll be together.

Orson enters. Believing Sebastian to be his "Charlie," Orson grabs him around the knees imploringly. Sebastian tells his real name (Orson still doesn't believe it) and cries out that Orson "has really freaked out!!" Sebastian frees himself from Orson's grasp and runs off.

Olivia is astonished at Orson's behavior. Viola appears. Orson and Olivia each believe that this is their own Charlie, their lover. Orson and Olivia quarrel over Viola.

VIOLA: I'm not Charlie!
Viola takes off her vest-jacket and shirt and throws them at Orson. She wears only a feminine bra. Sings:
But look at me, look! You can see that I'm real
I'm alive, I'm me!
ORSON: Charlie?!
OLIVIA: Sebastian?!
SEBASTIAN *(enters):* What's the ma . . . Vi!! Boy am I glad to see you!
Sebastian and Viola embrace.
ORSON: One face, one voice, one habit and two persons?

They unravel the situation and establish who belongs to whom—Sebastian to Olivia, Viola to Orson. Orson persuades Viola that he loved her so much for herself alone that he even loved her when he thought she was a boy.

OLIVIA *(to Sebastian):* You don't mind me being older?
SEBASTIAN: It's where I'm at. You don't mind me being younger?
OLIVIA: Listen, it's my bag.
VIOLA *(to Orson):* You don't mind me being a girl?
ORSON: I'll just go with it. You're my thing.
OLIVIA: Sebastian!
SEBASTIAN: Olivia!
VIOLA: Orson!

ORSON: Charlie!

Lights down.

SHAKESPEARE (SLIDE): I had the same trouble with the ending.

The lovers exit. The Apocalypse come on with a final admonition in song to "Do Your Own Thing."

APOCALYPSE *(sing):*

Do your own thing
Pay no attention to people who look down on you
Do your own thing
It makes no difference who turns away and frowns at you
There'll come a day when the world will need you. . . . .

You may change someday
You may find another way
But for now, just for now:
Do your own thing
Find your own dream
Dig your own soul
Or dig your own hole
And die.

The curtain call begins. As each actor bows, his name is projected above him. After the solo bows are completed, a full company Shakespearean tableau is formed, the lights go down, and:

SISTINE GOD (SLIDE) *(with written title):* "Hey boy."

CHRIST (SLIDE) *(with written title):* "Yes father?"

SISTINE GOD (SLIDE) *(with written title):* "When are you going to get a haircut?"

Blackout. Curtain.

A DAY IN THE DEATH OF JOE EGG

A Comedy in Two Acts

BY PETER NICHOLS

Cast and credits appear on page 361

PETER NICHOLS was born in Bristol, England, in 1927, and made early acquaintance with the stage assisting his mother, a contralto, in concert performances. His father was a salesman. Nichols was educated at Bristol Grammar School and performed his military service in the Far East. He studied at the Bristol Old Vic School and worked in repertory in various English cities. While teaching at a London primary school, Nichols wrote a TV play which shared a prize in BBC competition. Thirteen of his TV plays have reached production, including The Hooded Terror, *which was later done in a stage version by the Bristol Old Vic. On the large screen, Nichols is the author of the script for* Catch Us If You Can *and co-author of* Georgy Girl.

Nichols' first West End and Broadway play, A Day in the Death of Joe Egg, *was first produced by the Glasgow Citizens' Theater and was subsequently brought to London where it won an award as the best new play of 1967. Nichols now lives in Bristol with his wife (an art teacher) and their four children—one of whom, like the child in his play, is a handicapped child.*

INTRODUCTION BY THE PLAYWRIGHT

I wonder what strange, snobbish impulse makes people pay too much for theater tickets, travel through the cold and wet, sit in discomfort for two hours and possibly catch a bug. I'd rather see a film: it's cheaper and generally better. But I remember several experiences at theaters during the last few years that couldn't be matched by the cinema. The most notable, Joan Littlewood's *Oh What a Lovely War,* set the 1914 slaughter in the framework of a concert-party. Thus it got the best of both worlds—using the tricks of show biz and, by counteraction, exposing the hollow and reactionary show-biz hilarity, which is always available for unscrupulous persuasion.

Joan Littlewood's show was passionate, angry, informative and continuously entertaining. I have tried timidly to manage something of the same sort with *A Day in the Death of Joe Egg*. Most theater bores me because it's such an easy ride. The seats are uncomfortable but not the events. Seeing a play is like going to a party in that I must enjoy being one of that particular crowd and feel I helped to make it go. Irving Wardle wrote of *Joe Egg* in the London *Times:* "This is not avant-garde writing: it is addressed to the general civic conscience and it endows the random audience with a sense of common bond." Harold Hobson, however, the following Sunday disagreed: "This was not my experience on the first night. Near to me in the audience were people who greeted the jokes with howls and whoops and shrieks appropriate to the Windy Corner in a Fun Fair."

When people speak of audience participation, they generally mean some overt response such as comics used to call for in the pantomimes, when they divided the house for community singing into Boys and Girls. I hated it and was one of the Don't Knows.

One evening during World War II, my father provided the only spontaneous, individual audience participation I've ever seen. A packed Saturday house and a comedian cracking blue gags. I smiled knowingly but they were mostly over my head. All at once, dad, a flamboyant Puritan, began giving the man the slow hand-clap.

"Get off!" he shouted, "Women and children present! No more filth!"

My mother tried to stop him, so did the comedian. I pretended I was with someone else.

"Don't knock your pipe out at me," demanded the entertainer but dad was roused now and loving the attention of the crowd. He kept up his barracking until the poor man cued the band and went into his exit-song. I was about thirteen, shy and short-sighted. I had gone hot under the collar of my utility shirt and decided there and then against audience participation.

Yet some heat under the collar is the whole point, the only justification. By our readiness to assemble in this way, we acknowledge the need for some experience other than we'd get by reading the script at home. I enjoy a play most when I'm alarmed and know the other people are too.

You know the woman who, when the lights go up for the intermission, at once resumes the conversation that was broken mid-sentence by the play's beginning. I should like to make her forget what she was saying.

PETER NICHOLS

Time: The present

Place: Bristol, England

ACT I

SYNOPSIS: A young man in his early 30s comes forward and shouts at the audience, "That's enough!" His name is Bri, short for Brian. He is a schoolteacher controlling his classroom, speaking directly to the audience as though they were his pupils. His discipline is imposed with good nature. Bri is *"hardly ever at rest, acts being maladroit but the act is skillful. Clowning may give way to ineffectual hectoring and then self-piteous gloom."*

Bri is demanding one full minute of absolute silence before dismissing his charges. He leaves them doing this, sitting quietly with hands on heads, while he goes to get his coat.

As Bri exits, the lights come up on the set, which represents Bri and Sheila's living room. The entrance to the hall and front door and stairs is upstage center; to the kitchen and garden through a door at right. The window is at left, in a room which is *"pleasant and comfortable, furnished with a gallant collection of junk-shop bargains"* and paintings with a cowboy motif. There is a birdcage, a fishbowl, plants. The place teems with all kinds of life.

Sheila, wearing trousers and pullover, comes from kitchen with tea on a tray. She is 35, generously built, serious and industrious. When dressed for society, she can be captivating.

Sheila puts down the tray and quickly pushes the kitchen door closed to prevent cats from following her in. At this moment Bri comes home—clowning, typically, with a fake spider confiscated from one of his pupils.

Bri yearns to make love to Sheila at once. That's why he came home early, although he had intended to keep his unruly class after school.

SHEILA: Did you say you would?
BRI: Yes.
SHEILA: To them?
BRI: Yes.
SHEILA: Then why didn't you?
BRI: I kept imagining our room, your legs thrashing about—
SHEILA: When *are* you going to learn?

BRI: My tongue halfway down your throat—

He is at her again.

SHEILA: You must carry out your threats.

BRI: —train screaming into tunnel—

SHEILA: They'll never listen to you if you don't—

BRI: —waves breaking on rocky shore.

She moves out of his reach.

Sheila is amused at Bri's clownish insistence but manages to discourage him. Bri sips his tea. He remembers that, after all, he forgot to dismiss his class: ". . . . . I left them with their hands on heads and went to fetch my coat and suddenly couldn't face them any more, so I never went back. Wonder how long they sat there."

Bri embraces his wife in one more effort to get together, but Sheila holds him off. Their daughter Joe will be home any minute and will have to be cared for. Also, Sheila is going out to an evening of scenery-painting and rehearsal with her amateur theatrical group.

Bri sprawls in the armchair while Sheila briefs him on the evening: his dinner is in the oven; the animals, fish and plants have been fed and watered. Sheila urges Bri to come along with her to the theater meeting, but Bri has had a hard day in class, what with the rising Christmas spirit and all, and he wants to relax.

Sheila suggests that Bri would enjoy the company of her friend Freddie, watching the rehearsal. Bri resents Freddie, and they reach the verge of a quarrel. But they are interrupted by the doorbell—Joe is being brought home.

Bri goes out into the hall to answer the bell. Sheila calls after him that at least she doesn't stay home and wallow in self-pity, she tries to get on with life. She takes the tea things into the kitchen.

Bri has left the hall door open, showing hall and lower part of the stairs. He now comes back wheeling Joe in her invalid chair. Joe is 10, physically normal but for the stiffness of her legs and arms. Her legs, at this stage, are covered with a blanket. She cannot support herself properly and has to be propped wherever she is put; for the most part, she lies supine. In her chair, she sits with the upper part of her body forward on the tray in front of her chair, as though asleep. Her face is pretty but vacant of expression, her voice not strong.

Bri pushes her to the center of the stage. He carries a small grip marked BOAC.

BRI: There we are then, lovely. Home again.

Leaves her, puts down grip, looks at her.

Safe and sound. You been a good girl?

JOE: A-aaah! *(This is her closest approach to speech.)*

BRI: Really good?

JOE: Aaaah!

BRI: The lady in the bus said you'd been good. Sat by the driver, did you?

JOE: Aaaah!

BRI: There's a clever girl!

JOE: Aaaah!

BRI *(as though he understood):* Saw the Christmas trees?

JOE: Aaaah!

BRI: And the shops lit up?

JOE: Aaaah!

BRI: What d'you say? Saw Jesus? Where was he, where was Jesus, you poor softie?

Sheila comes back.

JOE: Aaaah!

BRI: I see.

SHEILA: My great big beautiful darling home at last?

Kneels by her chair.

Got a great big beautiful kiss for Mummy?

Kisses her.

JOE: Aaaah!

SHEILA: I'm lovely, she says.

In the presence of the child, Bri and Sheila instinctively play a game of pretending that she is capable of rational experience. They speak to Joe (it is a means of speaking to each other indirectly) as if she were a normal child, and they invent answers for her. Sometimes their cheerful game is carried to the point of comic absurdity.

Joe sat by the driver today (Bri tells Sheila). She saw the Christmas trees, and Jesus.

SHEILA: Jesus?

BRI: Bathed in light, in the sky.

SHEILA *(aside, to Bri):* She got a screw loose, Dad?

BRI: No, Mum.

SHEILA: Seeing Jesus?

BRI: On top the Electricity Building.

SHEILA *(relieved):* Oh, yes! Thought she was off her chump for a minute, Dad.

BRI: Seeing Jesus in a dump like this? No wonder, Mum. But no, she's doing well, they say.

SHEILA: Daddy's pleased you're trying, love. What with your eleven-plus on the way.

Bri gives a short burst of laughter then resumes.

BRI: You want to get a decent school.

SHEILA: I don't want to be shunted into some secondary modern slum, she says—

Kisses her again.

BRI: Like the one where Daddy works—

SHEILA: Share a room with forty or fifty council-house types and blackies.

BRI: No, I've had enough of them, she says, at the Spastics' Nursery. You want to go on to the Training Center, help to make those ball-point pens.

Rummages in grip.

JOE: Aaaah!

SHEILA: I'm trying my hardest, she says.

From the grip, Bri extracts a note from the Nursery thanking them for a birthday present sent that day to one of Joe's classmates, Colin, a little boy who had meningitis and now cries all the time. Bri reads some of the note aloud: "The physiotherapist lady came and looked at us all today and said Josephine's shoulders show some signs of improvement. She says keep on with the exercises."

But the note disappoints them greatly by adding that Joe suffered a fit that day—the first one in weeks. Sheila caresses Joe while Bri tries to lighten the mood by clowning.

SHEILA: Hullo.

Joe's head has turned slowly from one side to the other. They watch silently. The mouth closes and she undergoes a seizure—not violent but slow and tense, the head turning, one arm stretching out. Sheila takes the note from Bri and reads it.

That's great, that is. Explains it.

BRI: What?

SHEILA: They've run out of anti-convulsant suspension again.

BRI: Again?

SHEILA *(reading):* ". . . excitement over Colin's cake. Or perhaps because we've used up all her yellow medicine."

BRI: Call themselves a day nursery.

SHEILA: How many times is this?

BRI: Why don't they keep a few spare bottles in the 'fridge? Nearly all the kids need it.

SHEILA: The amount they use, they should have it on draught.

The business of fetching Joe's medicine, forcing it down her throat and holding her jaw shut to make her swallow is performed efficiently. But it is still harrowing enough (though they must have done it numberless times) so that Bri is careful to keep joking all through it. Sheila discovers that the child has not been changed at the nursery but has been allowed to "sit like Joe Egg in the damp all day."

Sheila gives Bri instructions about how to change Joe because she herself is in a hurry to get dressed to go out. Bri reminds Sheila that he's "not the new nannie," he's had ten years of this kind of responsibility. He refuses Sheila's offer to call her mother over to sit with Joe so that Bri can join her at rehearsals.

This reminds Bri of Freddie. Bri demands to know what is Freddie's special attraction. Sheila denies emphatically that she and Freddie have ever been lovers. Bri then reminds Sheila of her pre-marital lovers (they told each other everything after they were married), including two Americans and a Canadian.

BRI: You must have enjoyed those fellows at the time.
SHEILA: No!
BRI: One or two.
SHEILA: I've told you.
BRI: Why go on with it then?
SHEILA: Once you get to a certain stage with a man, it's hard to say no.
BRI: Most women manage it. With *me,* at any rate. *Three* out of God knows how many tens of thousands I tried . . .
SHEILA: They didn't know a good thing when they saw it. You were the only one who gave *me* any pleasure.
BRI: When you first told me that I was knocked out. I walked round for days feeling like a phallic symbol. I thought well, perhaps I didn't ring the bell very often but at least I rang it loud.

She smiles.

She'll stick with me, I went on happily, because I've got magic super-zoom with added cold-start.
SHEILA: You have, yes.
BRI: Till Freddie—
SHEILA: O ye Gods—
BRI: Of all people!
SHEILA: He's never been near me.

What it boils down to, Bri declares, is that Sheila prefers to spend the evening with Freddie. Sheila reminds Bri that he encouraged her to take up theatricals, to get away from the house. Bri still wants to know: what is Freddie's specialty? Sheila, unanswering, stalks off to get dressed.

Joe sneezes and bumps herself on the tray. Joe cries weakly and Bri attends her, props her up, talks to her: they'll have a fine evening together: Mummy is upstairs, getting dressed, admiring her naked self in the mirror—"But I'm not running up those stairs three at a time and falling into the bedroom and cringing on the carpet begging her not to go. No fear! I've done all I can without total loss of dignity. I might have known once I got her started on amateur theatricals she'd turn up at every bloody practise. Terrible sense of duty, your mum."

Bri comes forward to speak to the audience, at first as a comic, then as himself, seriously. He tells the audience how well-integrated a person Sheila is, how her whole being reacts and becomes sick when things go wrong. As for himself, Bri confesses, he's "Instant Man. Get one for Christmas, endless fun. I'm made up as I go along from old lengths of string, fag-ends . . . magazine cuttings, film clips . . . all stuck together with wodges of last week's school-dinner. What I mean, she couldn't *pretend* a passion she doesn't feel. Whereas I can't sustain a passion to the end of the sentence. . . . ."

In order to make Sheila happy, Bri goes on, he pretends any emotion he thinks will appeal most deeply to her. As for Joe, "I felt all doomy at first but—well—ten years! I just go through the motions now. . . . ."

Joe comments "Aaaah!" Bri pushes Joe in her chair into the kitchen to see what's for tea, and Sheila enters, changed into a dress and brushing her hair. She too comes downstage and confides in the audience: "He thinks because he throws a tantrum I'm going to stay home comforting him and miss the rehearsal and let them all down. He thinks he's only got to cry to get what he wants. I blame his mother. She gave him the kind of suffocating love that makes him think the world revolved around him but because he's too intelligent to believe it really, he gets into these paddies and depressions. . . . ."

Sheila admits to the audience that it was Bri who made her join the theater group, to "have a rest from Joe." But it's not the child who is a trouble to her, it's the husband. "Watching somebody as limited as Joe over ten years, I've begun to feel she's only one kind of cripple. Everybody's damaged in some way. There's a limit to what we can do. Brian, for instance, he goes so far—and hits the ceiling. Just can't fly any higher. Then he drops to the floor and we get self-pity again . . . despair. . . . ."

Sheila feels that Bri can and should paint, and she hopes he'll spend the time she's out of the house with brushes and canvas. Even if he isn't any good, anything to take his mind off his continuous jealousy of anything Sheila notices—the animals, Joe, even Freddie. She is certain that Bri is jealous of the attention she gives to Joe.

Bri comes back from the kitchen; he's overheard Sheila mentioning Joe to the audience.

BRI *(speaks to the audience):* Sheila's got a theory about Joe's birth. She doesn't blame the doctors. She blames herself.

SHEILA: I don't say that. I say it wasn't *entirely* the doctors.

BRI *(nodding):* It was because she choked it back.

SHEILA: It was partly that.

BRI: Because she'd slept around.

SHEILA: I think it was partly because I'd been promiscuous, yes, and my subconscious was making me shrink or withdraw from motherhood, all right!

Bri and Sheila begin to recall details of their experience of parenthood of this handicapped child, reviewing the problem for the audience's benefit, acting and talking it out with the audience and each other.

The vicar (Bri states) believed the child's handicap was devil's work, but Bri feels simply that "The doctor botched it." It's a million to one against it ever happening to them again.

The baby was on the way when Bri and Sheila were married in a white wedding (they confide to the audience). Six months later the baby arrived in a very long and difficult birth—five days in labor. The doctor kept Sheila sedated, so that she couldn't remember the necessary exercises or speak to tell the doctor to quit doping her so that she would regain enough concentration to give birth.

During the five days, Bri visited his wife occasionally but spent most of the time consoling himself in the local pub. He had perfect faith in the doctor, who kept dropping into the pub to reassure him. Bri had no way of knowing that the birth was being allowed to go on too long. The last day, however, he began to think Sheila was going to die. He resorted to prayer for her safety.

SHEILA: But never mind, your prayer was answered.

BRI: Yes, He heard all right. *(To audience.)* I see Him as a sort of manic depressive rugby-footballer. He looked down and thought to himself, "I'll fix that bastard."

Shakes his fist at roof.

And He did!

SHEILA: By the time the damage was done, they took me to hospital. The next I knew, they handed me this hairless yellow baby with forcep-scars all over her scalp. She was gorgeous. By the time I got her home, the scars and jaundice were gone and she was in working order. You had a cold.

BRI: That's right, yes.

SHEILA: I had to look after you. It was better than having you turn up every day moaning and sniffling.

BRI: More than a cold, 'flu. A delayed action I think it must have been. I was quite poorly.

She smiles, then goes on to audience.

SHEILA: Soon I began to notice these funny turns. We asked our friends who'd had babies but they said it was most likely wind. So in the end we took her to our new G.P.

Bri has fetched a tubular cushion from the set behind them, which is now in semi-darkness. The cushion is the size and shape of a swaddled baby. Sheila nurses it.

Sheila and Bri portray a series of episodes to the audience, with Sheila playing straight and Bri playing the succession of doctors and others as funny men. *"They do it as they might repeat the dialogue from a favorite film. Sometimes they improvise, surprising or corpsing each other"* and there are many asides to the audience.

Bri portrays the first doctor as a cheery muddlehead who doesn't know the time of day. Sheila describes Joe's symptoms—from time to time the child has "Funny turns. Face-making." The doctor shrugs away the symptoms, fumbles in his drawer and comes up with some new kind of medicine he thinks might help because the manufacturers praise it highly.

SHEILA: Doctor—I wish you could *see* one of these turns.

BRI: Oh, I've seen them, dear. Got three great monsters of my own.

SHEILA: I am sorry.

BRI: What?

SHEILA: All your children being—um—

BRI: No, I mean great thriving brutes. Not monsters, no. Your first, is it? First baby?

SHEILA: Yes.

BRI: Well, dear, it's like this. You're throwing an awful lot of gubbins down the old cake-hole there. It's like running in a new car. Till all the tappets and contact breakers get adjusted to the absolute thou, you take it easy, give em a chance. Same with these chaps.

Tickles the cushion. . . . .

Sheila wishes the doctor would wait to observe one of the baby's "funny turns," but the doctor, with a full waiting room, has no time for that. He ushers Sheila out, but she comes back at once to tell the doctor that the medicine did no good, the baby is in a coma.

The doctor shakes the baby, then calls the hospital to prepare them for the baby's arrival, for observation and tests. He sends Sheila off to the hospital on the bus (no ambulance is available) with reassurances about "a starter-motor jammed."

The baby stayed in the hospital for weeks (they inform the audience), during which time Bri caught impetigo and Sheila had to have her breasts treated to draw off the unwanted milk. When they went to get Joe from the hospital they'd "gathered that she wasn't ever going to amount to much." But they are determined to know the worst, so they take the child to a Viennese pediatrician (played by Bri in a stage German accent), who reassures Sheila that they have made every test including a biopsy of brain tissue. They can take Joe home and she will be no trouble at all.

SHEILA: What can she *do?*

BRI: Do? She can't do nozzing at all.

SHEILA: Will she ever?

BRI: Mattam, let me try and tell you vot your daughter iss like. Do you know vot I mean ven I say your daughter vos a wegetable?

Sheila thinks for a moment, gets it, smiles.

SHEILA: Yes! You mean "Your daughter was a vegetable."

BRI: Ach himmel! Still is, still *is,* always ville be! I have trouble vis Englische werbs.

SHEILA: But—when people say to me what kind of cripple is your child, shall I say—she's a wegetable—a vegetable?

BRI: You vant a vord for her? *(Shrugs.)* You can say she iss a spastic vis a damaged cerebral cortex, multiplegic, epileptic, but vis no organic malformation of ze brain.

SHEILA: That *is* a long word.

BRI *(gaily):* Which iss vy I prefer wegetable.

The doctor tells Sheila there are many such children, one born every eight hours. There is nothing to do but take the child home and care for her indefinitely, until she dies of other natural causes. At home, their G.P. checked on Joe once a week. When Sheila finally began to wonder and asked the doctor whose fault it was, the doctor arranged for the vicar to call on Sheila. Bri plays the vicar *"quietly, even seriously, to begin with."*

BRI: It's tragic. Tell me—when you first—knew there was nothing to be done, how did you feel?

SHEILA: Well, of course, you find out gradually, not all at once. But there's a point when you finally accept it. And that's— *(Shakes her head.)* Oh, very nasty. You think "why me?" I don't know about the other mothers but *I* kept saying "Why me, why us?" all day long. Then you get tired of that and you say "Why not me?"

BRI: Indeed. To learn humility. You recognize that we are surely in a vale of tears and you are no exception.

SHEILA: I recognized that I was worse. I'd been promiscuous, you see. All kinds of men. It seemed to me I was responsible for Joe being punished.

BRI: No, no.

SHEILA: No, I don't mean that either. I held the baby back. Out of guilt.

The vicar assures Sheila that this cannot be the cause, it is the Church of England's position that many promiscuous women eventually make excellent mothers. He asks what Bri's reaction has been, and Sheila tells him: "He used to say 'Think of something worse.' And of course that's easy. Joe could have grown older and developed into a real person before it happened. Or she could have been a very in*tell*igent spastic without the use of her limbs. Which is worse, I think, than being a kind of living parsnip."

Bri can live with senseles despair, but Sheila feels a need to know that her suffering means something. Sheila has even been praying, though Bri disapproves. The vicar explains that Joe's sickness doesn't please God, but the devil is always at work—and now and then "some innocent bystander blunders into the crossfire between good and evil."

Sheila protests—she has had enough of "parables" from the doctor. What she wants is magic. The vicar suggests a quiet ceremony of Laying on of Hands in the home (after Bri has been given instruction in sincere prayer). There was one boy who recovered after such a ceremony and went on to win a tap-dancing championship (the incongruity of this achievement sends Bri, in his own character, into a paroxysm of music-hall imitation, dancing and singing).

Sheila and Bri break out of the scene with the vicar. Now Sheila reminds Bri that he refused to permit a Laying on of Hands, though it might have helped. Bri had not wanted to get Sheila's hopes up for anything so ephemeral as a miracle cure. Groping for some sort of silver lining, Bri tells Sheila "Anyway, if the vicar had got her going, she'd only have had one personality. As it is, we've given her dozens down the years."

It's true—they made up dozens of roles for Joe to play in life, imagining her as a concert pianist and other characters. Soon they remember that what they were supposed to be doing was getting Joe's tea, before they became diverted into this grim reminiscence. Bri goes into the kitchen to get the tea.

Sheila, alone, confides to the audience that she indulges Bri in his joking because it makes it easier for him to live with a situation in which he has no faith in the possibility of Joe's improvement. After glancing into the wings to make sure Bri is out of earshot, Sheila confesses that she, on the contrary, is ever hopeful. Once, when Joe was four, it happened: Sheila noticed that a tower of toy bricks which she had built for the child had been knocked down. Sheila built the tower again and witnessed Joe's first "real signs of intention." The child struggled to move her arm—one arm, not both—and managed after ten minutes of effort to touch the tower and knock it down.

Sheila is almost overcome by the poignancy of this memory. Finally she regains her composure and continues her confidences to the audience.

SHEILA: I can't tell you what that was like. But you can imagine, can't you? Several times the hand very nearly touched and got jerked away by spasm . . . and she'd try again. That was the best of it—she had a will, she had a mind of her own. Soon as Bri came home, I told him. I think he said something stupid like—you know—"That's great, put her down for piano lessons." But when he tested her—putting piles of bricks all along the circle of her reach—both arms—and even sometimes out of reach so that she had to stretch to get there—well, of course, he saw it was true. It wasn't *much* to wait for—one arm movement completed—and even that wasn't sure fire. She'd fall asleep, the firelight would distract her, sometimes the effort would bring on a fit. But more often than not she'd manage . . . and a vegetable couldn't have done that. Visitors never believed it. They hadn't the patience to watch so long. And it amazed me—I remember being stunned—when I realized they thought I shouldn't deceive myself. For one thing, it wasn't deception . . . and anyway what else could I do? We got very absorbed in the daily games. Found her colored balls and bells and a Kelly—those clowns that won't lie down. Then she caught some bug and was very sick . . . had fit after fit—the Grand Mal, not the others—what amounted to a complete relapse. When she was over it, we tried the bricks again, but she couldn't even seem to see them. That was when Bri lost interest in her. I still try, though of course I don't bother telling him. I'll tell him when something happens. It seems to me only common sense. If she did it once, she could again. I think while there's life there's hope, don't you?

Looks to wings again.

I wish he'd talk more seriously about her. I wonder if he ever imagines what she'd be like if her brain worked. I do. And Bri's mother always says "Wouldn't she be lovely if she was running about?" which makes Bri hoot with laughter. But I think of it too. Perhaps it's being a woman.

Lights off Sheila. Lights on set upstage, very strong like a continuous lightning flash. Joe skips on, using a rope.

JOE:

Mrs. D, Mrs. I, Mrs. FFI, Mrs. C, Mrs. U, Mrs. LTY

Mrs. D, Mrs. I, Mrs. FFI, Mrs. C, Mrs. U, Mrs. LTY
Stops skipping.
Ladies and gentlemen, there will now be an interval. Afterwards the ordinary play, with which we began the performance, will continue and we shall try to show you what happens when Sheila returns home with their mutual friend, Freddie. Thank you.
She bows and resumes skipping. Blackout. Curtain.

ACT II

The room is in darkness until Sheila opens the hall door and comes in and turns on the lights. There is no sign of Bri or Joe.

Freddie and Pam follow in. He is suited, school-tied, with a hearty barking humorless laugh, same age as Bri but his ample public confidence makes him seem middle-aged.

Pam dresses well, mispronounces her words in an upper class gabble and her postures and manners have been taken from fashionable magazines. She uses this posture to hold her own against Freddie's heartiness. He is hearty, she is blase.

Pam looks around the room and compliments Sheila on what she has done to it, making it "terribly P.L.U." (People Like Us). Apparently Sheila suffered an emotional upset at the rehearsal, bursting into tears. Freddie reassures her it was perfectly understandable, and that she performed well that evening.

Sheila exits upstage, calling upstairs to Bri that she is going to make coffee, shutting the door behind her. Freddie admires the cowboy paintings, which were done by Bri. Pam is bored and didn't want to come here in the first place, but Freddie insisted. He means to help Sheila and Bri, whatever Pam's objections may be: "They need help. We can afford to give it."

Freddie addresses the audience to fill them in on how he persuaded Sheila to take an interest in amateur theatricals, which has helped her but left Bri somewhat jealous and "holding the baby." Freddie is here, he tells Pam, "(A) To tell him there's nothing in it. (B) Get them both to see sense about the poor kiddie. And (C) to give poor Brian back an interest in life."

To begin with, Freddie continues, he will persuade Bri to come see Sheila in the play ("She's not even any *good* in it" is Pam's comment).

Freddie and Bri went to the same school, but Bri was always placed with the backward students—"And there was no need for it, he was brainy enough. Just got in with the wrong crowd. No, that sounds reactionary but you've only got to look at him. Halfway through his life and no degree, no future, not much past . . . coping with the arse-end of a comprehensive school and driving a fifteen-year-old Popular."

Sheila comes in from the kitchen, looking for a missing ginger cat, and exits again, but not before observing that Freddie is scratching his arm and Pam her thigh.

Freddie reminds himself of his own good luck: he merely stepped into his father's business. Pam assures him that he "worked wonders" with it. Freddie admits that he is a success, because of his drive and enthusiasm, not because he is as intelligent or as talented as Bri. Recently Freddie met Bri on a train, and Bri told Freddie all about his life.

FREDDIE: . . . . . Told me all about his poor kiddie and how Sheila was obsessed with her and how keen he was to get her back in the swim.

PAM: Sheila.

FREDDIE *(bewildered):* Yes.

PAM: Not the weirdie.

FREDDIE: The what?

PAM: You know.

Pause.

FREDDIE: Don't call her a weirdie, darling.

PAM: I know, darling, it's absolutely horrid. But she is, though, isn't she?

Pause.

FREDDIE: Try to imagine that one of ours has turned out like that.

PAM *(shocked):* Darling! They're absolutely gorgeous, how could you?

Pause. Freddie gives up, returns to audience.

FREDDIE: I don't want to sound authoritarian or fascist but there's only one useful approach to any human problem and that's a positive one. No use saying: "This is no way to live, in every night with a hopeless cripple." No use at all. Same with problem teenagers. You don't say, "Naughty boy, go stand in the corner." You say "Get ahold of these nails and a hammer!" Then you're in business.

Bri enters from the hall, clowning behind a life-size portrait of a cowboy, shooting off a cap pistol, to Freddie's amusement. Bri is in painting clothes, and he is glad to see the visitors: "Nice having company . . . stuck in here every night like Joe Egg. . . . . My grandma used to say 'Sitting about like Joe Egg' when she meant she had nothing to do."

Bri has been up in the attic painting Wyatt Earp. Freddie compliments Bri on his work. Sheila enters with four cups. She is anxious about Joe, but although Bri hints to her that the problem of Joe this evening was "a bit more than the usual," he refuses to talk about it.

Bri passes around some Spanish cognac. Sheila notices that Bri has forgotten to take off his "teaching shoes" while painting, and they are all spattered.

Freddie tells them that in some ways he envies Bri his life as a teacher. "Instead of a rich and powerful industrialist," Bri remarks, only half-kidding, and Pam assures him they are not rich, merely comfortable.

FREDDIE: Nor powerful! *(Barks.)* You've been watching too much telly. No, hamstrung's nearer the mark. I'm like a last-ditch colonial running things till the natives have got enough know-how to take the reins.

BRI: That's right? *(Tut-tuts at the thought.)* Don't know what the world's coming to.

FREDDIE: How are things on the home front, Bri?

BRI: Oh, much the same, you know.

FREDDIE: Stuck in like Joe Egg?

BRI: Yeah.

FREDDIE: Look—perhaps I'm rushing in where angels fear to tread—

PAM: You always do.

Freddie barks.

FREDDIE: But—why don't you see all the doctors money can buy and tell them you want another baby. To put it bluntly—ask why you're not having one.

SHEILA: Oh, we've had fertility counts. That what you mean?

FREDDIE: You've done that?

BRI: Yes. She was A minus, I was B plus. Must concentrate more.

FREDDIE: Well done. I admire your nerve. Most people wouldn't fancy knowing for sure.

SHEILA: No. 'Specially men. Our doctar had an ex-major who turned really nasty when they told him he was sub-fertile. Wouldn't believe it. He kept saying "But I was in the Normandy landings."

They should try fertility boosters, Freddie urges, and if all else fails he'll pull some strings to speed an adoption. Once they have "a proper working child" who smiles at them and cries and keeps them up at night, they'll be in a position to make the decision Freddie feels they ought to make, to send Joe to a special residential school. "Putting her away" Sheila calls it resentfully. They have tried that. They insist Joe sensed it and didn't like it.

Freddie assures them he is on the board of an excellent place with a devoted staff, a tree-shaded private house where Joe would be cared for and trained if she improves.

FREDDIE: And if she improves she can join their activities—

BRI: Activities?

FREDDIE: Painting . . . wheelchair gardening . . . speech therapy.

BRI: Better not tell *her* that, eh, Mum? She thinks she's very *nicely* spoken. One thing she *does* pride herself on.

SHEILA *(to Freddie):* She wouldn't go to a special school. Not even if you put some ginger under them. We've seen the place she'd go. No private house. No Palladian asylum with acres of graceful parkland.

BRI: Nor Victorian Gothic even.

SHEILA: Army Surplus. Like a transit camp.

BRI: Except they're not going anywhere.

SHEILA: Freddie, thanks for trying but it's too late, honestly. I shall have to look after her till she dies.

BRI: Or until you do.

SHEILA: Yes. Whichever's first.

FREDDIE: Is that possible?

SHEILA: What?

FREDDIE: She could outlive you?

SHEILA: We know one—a man of seventy-six just become a Boy Scout. They said they wouldn't have him any longer in the Cubs.

FREDDIE: These jokes. May I say my piece about these jokes? They've obviously helped you see it through. A useful anesthetic. But. Isn't there a point where the jokes start using *you?*

SHEILA: I thought you were going to speak to Bri about—

FREDDIE: Please. This first. Isn't that the whole fallacy of the sick joke? It kills the pain but leaves the situation just as it was? Look—when we met again—how many?—six months?—ago—you used, I remember, a striking metaphor describing Sheila's state of mind. You said a cataract had closed her eye—like your mother's net curtains, screening off the world outside.

BRI: Did I say that?

FREDDIE: It struck me as so bloody apt.

BRI: So bloody smug.

FREDDIE: But it was true, don't you see? And now—in my opinion—it's all gone arse-over-tip. Sheila's cured and you've caught the cataract. Shoot me down if I'm all to cock, I'm only trying to strip it down to essentials. Thinking aloud.

BRI: I wonder—could you think more quietly?

But Freddie persists: he cannot stand by and watch Sheila and Bri throw their lives away. To Freddie's exasperation, Bri merely tosses him another quip. Pam discloses to Bri that Sheila broke down into a flood of tears that evening at rehearsal, partly because she was upset about Bri's jealousy of Freddie.

Now that the cards are on the table, Freddie takes over and explains to Bri that he has come here to assure him there is nothing between him and Sheila, first because Sheila loves Bri and second because Freddie loves Pam and his family. Pam kisses Freddie gratefully.

BRI: I hardly know how to say this now. After your masterly dismissal of jokes. But—here it is—the whole idea was just another sick fantasy. I know you've never touched her, leave alone shafted her.

PAM: He's a nut.

BRI: I wanted to bring back the magic to our marriage. Stir it up, a kind of emotional aphrodisiac.

PAM: If you ever try that with me, I'll leave you.

FREDDIE: I may be squaresville but I'm not sick.

SHEILA *(to Bri):* You're so round*about.*

BRI: You wouldn't let me near you. All day I'd been running blue movies on the back of my retina—the pair of us romping about the bed shouting with satisfaction. And what did I get?—Your hands are cold.

Pam wants to leave, but Freddie is determined to stay until he has found a way to help (and wonders frankly, to the audience, whether he's wasting his time). Carolers are heard outside, singing "Once in Royal David's City." Sheila suggests bringing Joe down to enjoy the music. Pam panics at the thought of actually seeing the child. Freddie insists they remain.

Sheila starts out to fetch Joe, but Bri stops her by reminding her he hasn't described what happened while Sheila was out. It seems that after Bri had force-fed her a supper of prunes, Joe was whimpering. Bri thought it might perhaps be constipation. He describes in detail the unpleasant physical actions necessary to cause Joe to move her bowels. His efforts were successful.

SHEILA: Oh, good. That was bothering her, poor love.

BRI: No, listen a minute. It was no sooner out than she started all that gulping and lip-smacking, stretching her arms, opening and closing her blind eyes . . . the Grand Mal . . . I thought to myself, that's it, the lot! All you can do. Pain and fits. And not for the first time in ten years I thought: Is it ever worth it?

FREDDIE: It never is.

SHEILA: Worth what?

FREDDIE: The effort.

SHEILA: We've got no choice.

FREDDIE: Of course you have.

BRI: Anyway. When the fit was over I propped her in her chair and stood behind her and put a cushion over her mouth and nose and kept them there while I counted a hundred. There was no struggle or anything. It seemed very—peaceful.

The others are watching him, motionless. Pause.

SHEILA: What? . . .

PAM: God!

BRI: When it was all over I took the cushion away and . . . I said "Nurse, you have seen nothing. We are in this together" . . . I looked up to see the nurse throw off her cape revealing the burly figure of Sergeant Blake, Scotland Yard.

SHEILA *(relieved):* Honestly, Brian!

BRI: You almost believed me, didn't you?

FREDDIE: No almost. I *did.*

Bri challenges Sheila: didn't she feel just a twinge of relief during the split-second when she believed Joe might be dead? Sheila denies it and exits into the hall and up the stairs.

Freddie also denies that he felt relief and reminds Bri that life, even such a life as Joe's, is inviolable. Bri describes Joe's existence as "asphyxiation delayed ten years by drugs." All the animals, fish and plants in the house are symbols of Sheila's defiance of death. That's why this environment teems with life (and now Pam realizes that she has acquired a flea).

Freddie stands firmly behind the commandment "Thou shalt not kill," arguing that exceptions like euthanasia lead to mass-murder like Auschwitz.

Pam comes forward and addresses the audience. Unlike Freddie, she has no instinct for helping the handicapped. "We're none of us perfect . . . I can't stand anything N.P.A. Non Physically Attractive. Old women in bathing-suits—and skin-diseases—and cripples. . . . ." She has a sneaking sympathy for Bri's attitude, and she feels that with hopeless cases kept alive only by modern medicine, "modern medicine should be allowed to do away with them. A committee of doctors and do-gooders, naturally, to make sure there's no funny business and then—if I say gas-chamber that makes it sound horrid —but I do mean put to sleep."

Pam turns from the audience, resolved to depart, but Sheila enters with Joe. The caroling has stopped. Pam and Freddie look at Joe and make polite comments. Sheila has noticed that the child is unusually passive and wonders whether Bri remembered her medicine. Sheila and Bri dance around, singing Joe a carol, but soon Joe goes into a fit and they put her into a chair facing upstage. Sheila is worried—Joe is nearly unconscious.

The doorbell rings. Bri goes to answer it, thinking it is the carolers, but it is Bri's mother Grace.

> *Grace is 65, suburban, fastidious. Wears light-colored suit with frilled decorations: gloves and shoes match handbag. Very short-sighted but refuses to wear spectacles. As well as her bag, she brings a hold-all full of shopping. Her manner is generally bright but gives way to spells of gloom when she tends to sigh a lot. In her presence, Bri is more boyish and struggles to escape her maternal allure.*

Grace is introduced to Pam and Freddie, then she moves downstage center to explain herself to the audience. She has dropped in after a movie, the movies being one of the major adventures remaining in her life nowadays. She manages to fill her hours cheerfully enough with household chores and knitting, but "it *is* very lonely, hour after hour, stuck like Joe Egg with no one to talk to. Why I do so many cardigans, the poor mite dribbles. Not in the way a baby dribbles even, worse than that. It's not nice to talk about, I know, but she can't seem to regulate the flow. Her garments, after a few hours on, they're stiff with saliva."

Grace is "not stopping," she has just come to deliver the finished cardigan. She sits by Joe and measures the sweater—the arms could be half an inch longer, and Grace insists that she must alter them to fit—"Got to do what little we can, haven't we?"

Grace has been Christmas-shopping, and Bri asks his mother if she saw Jesus on the electricity building. But Grace wants to reminisce about taking

Bri to see Santa when he was a child, a subject which makes Sheila laugh too loudly and causes Bri to remember that when they took Joe to see Santa she had a fit right on his lap.

Grace notices that she has acquired a flea—probably from the fleabitten cat known as Beatrice Webb. Grace cautions Sheila against exaggerated fondness of animals. At the same time, Sheila is becoming increasingly alarmed about Joe's worsening condition, which Bri is trying to ignore.

GRACE: I should have it destroyed.

SHEILA: Another dose of medicine.

Goes to kitchen.

GRACE: If it was me.

BRI: What, Mum?

GRACE: I should have whatever-you-call-her put to sleep.

Bri looks at her, having heard only this.

FREDDIE: The cat.

BRI: Oh.

GRACE: Fleas bring disease.

Bri sits by Joe and examines her intently, looking to kitchen anxiously.

Sheila returns from the kitchen holding an empty bottle of medicine, wondering why it is empty. It spilled, Bri tells her.

But Sheila is not satisfied. The medicine is too thick to spill easily out of the bottle, which has been washed clean. Bri declares that he gave Joe a dose from the spilled bottle before washing it, and he argues that Joe has had enough sedation—"I'm turned on, she says."

Sheila insists that Bri go to the store for more medicine. Grace cautions Bri to wrap up warmly.

Bri listens to this, then smiles at them all and goes.

SHEILA *(holding Joe's hand):* What's funny Daddy been up to, eh, my rose?

Pause. Freddie's attention drawn.

FREDDIE: You think he's up to something?

SHEILA: That medicine's thick. You couldn't spill much. The bottle was full, I don't know. He *told* us he'd killed her.

FREDDIE: That wasn't true, so we needn't—

GRACE: Told you what?

SHEILA: He'd killed her. Yes.

GRACE: Oh, no.

FREDDIE: It was an adolescent joke.

GRACE: His jokes, I never listen.

FREDDIE: Showing off to get attention.

GRACE: It *is* showing off.

SHEILA: Like a baby. By saying that, he could take my attention off poor Joe and get it on himself again. And when that palled, he'd make up another

—with himself as the killer or the corpse or—anything—as long as it's the most important part.

GRACE: I can't imagine Brian doing that without provocation.

FREDDIE: Oh, no. The other joke we've had this evening was that Sheila and I are having a love affair. And for that, I assure you, we neither of us gave him the slightest provocation.

GRACE: Perhaps not *you.* I couldn't say.

SHEILA: Hullo?

GRACE: But I shouldn't wonder if Brian thought there was something—going on—

FREDDIE: Why?

GRACE: Perhaps—knowing what he did—he was apt to be oversuspicious.

Grace continues rashly: Bri probably expected that something like this might happen eventually. Sheila wants to know why Grace should make such a supposition. Grace admits that Brian has told his mother all Sheila told him about her past love affairs. Even Pam is shocked by this. Freddie hurries out of the room to "help Brian."

According to Grace, Brian had asked her what to do. Grace told her son he must judge Sheila's past for himself, reach his own conclusions. Sheila accuses Grace of spoiling Brian, doing his thinking for him, wrecking his life.

Freddie and Bri enter—Bri has been sitting in the car, unable or unwilling to start it. Pam offers to go in their car. Bri fumbles around with the prescription for the medicine but finally gives it to Pam, and she goes.

SHEILA *(suddenly, vehemently, to Bri):* Great spoilt baby! Coddled baby!

FREDDIE: Now, Sheila. there's no use—

SHEILA *(to Freddie):* The only way he knows to get what he wants is screaming and stamping his feet, but that's a bit grotesque at his age so he straightaway says Poor Me but nobody listens so he makes some jokes and everybody laughs, which is better than nothing, so he makes more and more jokes and when everyone else has gone I get the "Poor Me," I have to swallow that.

Turns on Grace.

Because *you* spoilt him.

FREDDIE: Now, Sheila, we've had our—

GRACE: I kept the house clean of fleas, I admit that. I spring-cleaned every year instead of once in five. Certainly when he was a tiny mite I used to press his ears back for fear they'd protrude. I boiled a kettle in his room for croup. Made a mustard bath for the cold and kept out the wind. I believe in an insulated house. *(To Bri.)* It's still insulated, Brian, it's still home. You're welcome, I've told you that. Specially since I was left alone. Not so much a home these days as a blooming nunnery. I'm stuck up there day after day like a blooming nun.

SHEILA *(to Freddie):* There you are. "Poor Me!"

Sheila accuses Grace of self-pity and challenges her to move in with her close friend Mrs. Parry if she's indeed lonely. But Grace wants to retain her privacy. Not Sheila—she hates privacy.

Sheila notices that Joe is white, her lips are blue, there is more and more cause to worry. Bri waves Sheila's fears away with "A touch of flatulence . . . . . heartburn." Sheila warns Bri to keep away from Joe. She has decided and is determined to call the doctor.

Grace believes that the child should have been sent to a hospital years ago—"You can't expect a man to take second place to a child like that." After all, the child's handicap isn't Bri's fault, Grace insists. Why not? Because Sheila had a distant relative who once had convulsions as a child (another confidence of Sheila's which Bri has betrayed to his mother). Bri told his mother this after Grace had told Bri that on his side an uncle by marriage had had epilepsy.

The argument has reached a pinnacle of absurdity, and Bri offers to drive his mother home (it seems he can crank up the car, though he didn't make this effort on behalf of Joe's medicine).

SHEILA: What about Joe? You leaving Freddie alone with her?
BRI: Why? You going somewhere?
SHEILA: To phone the doctor.
BRI: I'll do that when I get back. If you really want to bother him.
SHEILA: No we'll do it now. She's unconscious.
BRI: I'll only *be* twenty minutes.
SHEILA: Half an hour, if we're *lucky*. She'll make tea.
BRI: I shan't stop for tea.
GRACE: I've got some Garibaldis, I know you—
BRI: Right, I'll ring from there. *(To Grace.)* Can I do that?
GRACE: Have I ever said no to you?
BRI *(to Sheila):* All right?

No, it's not all right with Sheila, they must call the doctor *now*. Freddie offers to do it, and Bri calls him an "interfering bastard!" Freddie reminds Bri once again "Thou shalt not kill," and Bri retorts, "Except when it shall come to pass that thy trade-routes shall be endangered."

The others are rummaging for a threepenny piece for the public telephone (there is no phone in this house). Freddie reminds Bri that twenty years from now a cure might be found for Joe. Bri wonders what kind of brain she might have then: "A six-weeks-old brain in a thirty-years-old body." No, Freddie suggests, maybe some kind of brain-grafting. In that case, Bri wants to know, "Whose soul will she have?"

Bri finds thruppence in his own pocket. Sheila takes it and hurries Freddie out, though Bri makes an effort to stop him. Grace is preoccupied with her makeup kit and is prattling on about the cold weather, noticing nothing of what is going on around her.

Bri looks up. Grace goes on making up. Bri looks at Joe, then toward front door. He lifts the child and throws her over one shoulder. He goes out the kitchen door with her, closing it behind him.

GRACE: I said "I may be old but I'm not quite ready to go yet." So if you're running me, I should put on something warm because it's not so much the cold as the contrast. *(Looks round, sees he is gone, continues to audience.)* Talking to myself. No, but it's an old car with no heater and drafts from all directions and he's always been susceptible to cold.

Sheila comes back from front door into room.

Well, if it's in your nature, I say it's nothing to be ashamed of.

SHEILA: Where's Joe?

GRACE: Pardon?

SHEILA: Joe's gone.

GRACE: How can she have gone? *(Sees she has.)*

SHEILA: He's taken her. Where?

GRACE: He didn't say.

During this, Bri carries Joe across behind Sheila from back door of house to front door.

Sheila, alarmed, runs upstairs looking for Joe. Grace tells the audience about Brian's late father's concern about Joe. Bri comes back to get his mother but runs into the kitchen when Sheila returns from upstairs. Sheila goes into the kitchen, but now Bri comes in from the hall with his mother's coat. Grace tries to hold Bri in the room, but he escapes by the main door just before Sheila enters from the kitchen.

Sheila is increasingly concerned—it is now snowing—and brushes aside Grace's question about alterations to the cardigan. Sheila has gone to the hall when an explosion is heard in the kitchen, with the sound of breaking glass. Sheila goes to investigate and finds that it was not, as they had feared, the gas but only a minor accident with a ginger beer container.

Freddie and Pam arrive with the bottle of yellow medicine. The doctor has been called, an ambulance has been ordered and is on the way. Sheila tells them that Bri is acting strangely. She guesses "He's running about outside. With Joe."

Bri enters with Joe, puts her on the sofa and tells them, "I think it's all over."

FREDDIE: What's all over?

BRI: You look at her.

Sheila kneels by sofa, takes Joe in her arms, nurses and warms her, wrapping her about, rocking her.

SHEILA: My poor blossom.

FREDDIE *(quiet, authoritative):* What happened?

BRI: I took her outside.

FREDDIE: And did what?

BRI: Nothing. Left her lying on the back seat of the car.

FREDDIE: What for?

SHEILA: —little worm, poor little worm—

BRI: Something Mum said suggested it—

GRACE: Me? I never suggested taking—

BRI: No.

GRACE: On a night like this?

BRI: But you said—

GRACE: Is it likely?

BRI: You said it was bitter cold. I was going to leave her in the garden but I couldn't—

SHEILA: Can anyone do the kiss of life?

FREDDIE: I can't.

BRI: So in the end I put her in the car. I don't know what I wanted—just to stop them saving her again. . . . .

Sheila cannot feel any pulse. Bri is dismayed by the others' attempts to revive the child, and he goes to sit by himself as the tests of a mirror and a feather are applied to the child's breathing—with negative results.

The doorbell rings—the ambulance has arrived. All but Bri exit, with Sheila carrying Joe and Grace remarking to Pam: "Wouldn't she have been lovely if she'd been running about?"

Bri comes downstage to tell the audience what happened next: how they raced to the hospital, and how strenuous efforts were made to revive the child. ". . . . . The sawbones got to work with the oil-can and . . . 'I think there's a chance, nurse . . . all our work may not be wasted.' And the upshot was—finally, the feather fluttered." The child lived. Sheila stayed on at the hospital to be with Joe, and Bri resisted his mother's cloying efforts to take him home with her. He accepted a ride home from Freddie and Pam but was "glad to see the back of him" as they drove away.

BRI: . . . . . Our marriage might have worked as well as most if Joe hadn't happened. I was too young for it, that's true, of course. I always will be. But Sheila might just have dragged me screaming into manhood. 'Stead of which, I was one of the menagerie. She loved me as much as any goldfish or aphelandra. So now it was a question of how to tell her I was leaving her. And when I went into it, I saw it wouldn't only be about Joe, but also my ambitions . . . and the first time I saw Father Christmas and—this backache's worse than yesterday and—the pattern on the ceiling . . . so in the end I better just creep away without a word . . .

Goes into room and begins hurriedly putting various objects into his pockets, putting on coats, etc.

So I've shaved and washed and packed a case . . .

Gets case from hall, stands it nearby.

Haven't decided where I'm going yet. Up the smoke, I suppose, get lost among the Australians. . . . .

Bri looks around the room, fixing it in memory, as he reminds himself never to take a teaching job again.

Bri hears Sheila coming in the front door, but he has nowhere to hide. When she enters the room Bri pretends that he is on his way to the school. Sheila urges him to take a day or two off. Joe is better (Sheila informs Bri), good pulse and breathing well. Sheila had supposed that with Joe in a hospital for a few days she could spend some time at home alone with Bri—she had been looking forward to it. She tries to make Bri take off his coat.

SHEILA: I thought, I'll get home before he's up and make him some bacon and eggs and—fried apple rings—did you have something hot?

BRI: Tea and toast. And I've fed the zoo and tidied up.

She is after him, trying to pull his coat off.

No, come on Sheila, be a sport—

SHEILA: And I'll take them up to him in bed, I thought, and after that I'll climb in with him . . . and have him . . . and look what I find . . . he's fully dressed . . . so I shall have to get all those clothes off him and we'll stay all day with the snow outside. Cold and quiet. And us in there, up to our tricks.

She now embraces him. He has stopped struggling.

And it wasn't only lust. I thought about what you'd tried to do to Joe. And honestly—I don't blame you. Honestly I don't. It was all too much of a good thing. From now on we're going to have her looked after—far more often. Have her taken into hospital odd days, here and there. Even weeks. Then we could go away together. It was my fault you tried that. I've been asking too much. Haven't I darling?

BRI: No. I was round the twist. My mum. Freddie. You know.

SHEILA: Tell me in bed. Darling.

Her hands are all over him. At last.

BRI: I'll go and ring the school.

SHEILA: Run all the way there and back. I can't wait long.

He gets free.

And even though you're only going a few yards, I should wrap up warm.

She buttons his coat again.

BRI: I'll be in the car.

SHEILA: Car? Just to go round there?

BRI: Case it's occupied I'll try another.

SHEILA: Don't go too fast then. It's brilliant sun this morning but treacherous underfoot.

BRI: Right.

He moves towards door.

SHEILA: Back in one piece. And—you will be quick, won't you?

BRI: Bye bye.

Sheila goes into the kitchen. As soon as she disappears, Bri picks up his suitcase and departs by the front door, which is heard to slam. He has left, not just to telephone, but for good.

Sheila comes back into the living room from the kitchen.

SHEILA *(to cats, closing door on them):* Daddy fed you? He *is* good.

Scratches arm, goes to birdcage.

Had some seed? What a daddy!

Goes into hall, shakes her hair loose.

Aren't we lucky?

Goes up the stairs. Curtain.

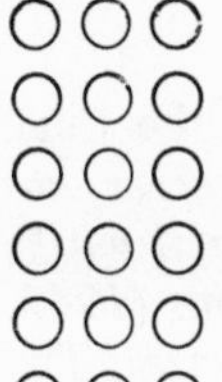

THE PRICE

A Play in One Act

BY ARTHUR MILLER

Cast and credits appear on page 363

ARTHUR MILLER, like the majority (52 per cent) of our established dramatists, was born in New York City, on October 17, 1915. His mother was also a native New Yorker. His father, the owner of a small manufacturing business, came to this country from Austria when he was a child. Miller grew up in New York, attending James Madison and Abraham Lincoln High Schools and then working for two years in an auto parts warehouse before going on to college at the University of Michigan.

At Michigan Miller studied playwriting, wrote a play that won prizes and received his B.A. in 1938. Returning to New York, he worked in the Federal Theater Project and the CBS and NBC radio workshops. A Hollywood studio hired him to tour Army camps to collect background material for Ernie Pyle's The Story of G.I. Joe, *which experience Miller described in the diary report* Situation Normal, *published in 1944. Among Miller's other extra-theatrical works were* Focus *(1945, a novel about anti-Semitism),* The Misfits *(1961, a screen play) and the recently-published volume of short stories,* I Don't Need You Any More.

Miller's first Broadway production was The Man Who Had All the Luck *(1944, 4 performances). His subsequent Broadway playwriting career has been one of the theater's most distinguished. All seven of his original works have been named Best Plays of their seasons, as follows:* All My Sons *(1947, Critics Prize),* Death of a Salesman *(1949, Critics Prize, Pulitzer Prize),* The Crucible *(1953),* A View from the Bridge *(1955, on the same program with* A Memory of Two Mondays), After the Fall *(1964),* Incident at Vichy *(1965) and now* The Price. *Miller also adapted Ibsen's* An Enemy of the People *in 1950.*

Miller now lives in Connecticut with his third wife, Inge Morath, the photographer.

INTRODUCTION BY THE PLAYWRIGHT *

A fine balance of sympathy should be maintained in the playing of the roles of Victor and Walter in *The Price*. The actor playing Walter must not regard his attempts to win back Victor's friendship as mere manipulation. From entrance to exit, Walter is attempting to put into action what he has learned about himself, and sympathy will be evoked for him in proportion to the openness, the depth of need, the intimations of suffering with which the role is played.

This admonition goes beyond the question of theatrics to the theme of the play. As the world now operates, the qualities of both brothers are necessary to it; surely their respective psychologies and moral values conflict at the heart of the social dilemma. The production must therefore withhold judgment in favor of presenting both men in all their humanity and from their own viewpoints. Actually, each has merely proved to the other what the other has known but dared not face. At the end, demanding of one another what was forfeited to time, each is left touching the structure of his life.

The play can be performed with an intermission, as indicated, if circumstances require it. But an unbroken performance is preferable.

ARTHUR MILLER

Time: Today

Place: The attic floor of a Manhattan brownstone

SYNOPSIS: The stage is dark, but soon daylight creeps in through a skylight and a grimy upstage window *"x'd out with new whitewash, as in buildings about to be demolished."*

The light picks out an overstuffed armchair center, beside which is a small table with a radio of the 1920s and a newspaper rack. There are cleaning

* These comments appeared as the author's production note in the script of *The Price*.

materials and instruments near it, and around it is piled *"the chaos of ten rooms of furniture squeezed into this one."* This is the attic of a brownstone, and all the house's furniture has been stored here, including four sofas, numberless bureaus, a harp and sculling oars. In character, the furniture has *"a rich heaviness, something almost Germanic."* It may or may not be of value.

Upstage right is the door to a bedroom. Downstage left is the door to the stairs, through which Victor Franz enters. He is dressed in his uniform of Patrolman of the New York Police Department.

> *Victor halts inside the room, glances about, walks at random a few feet, then comes to a halt. Without expression, yet somehow stilled by some emanation from the room, he lets his gaze move from point to point, piece to piece, absorbing its sphinx-like presence.*

Victor sits on the arm of the chair, then gets up and touches the harp, fidgeting, trying to make time pass while he is waiting. He cranks up an old phonograph and puts on a record: Gallagher and Sheean singing. He takes a newspaper from the rack beside the chair, but it crumbles. He reads the titles of books; he puts on a fencing mask and lunges with the foil, straining his back. He tries putting on another record. It turns out to be a Laughing Record, in which two men, hysterical with laughter, are trying unsuccessfully to speak a sentence. The record induces Victor to start laughing just as his wife Esther enters, looking around, supposing that there's some sort of party going on.

Esther, like Victor, is middle-aged. She is wearing a new suit with a long double strand of artificial pearls. She has been to the doctor for a checkup, and when Victor kisses her he discovers she has also had a drink—against doctor's orders. She protests that one won't hurt her. She examines the furniture, which has been cleaned in preparation for the dealer's visit.

ESTHER: There's something different about it.

VICTOR: No, it's all the way it was.

Indicating one side of the room.

I had my desk on that side and my cot. The rest is the same.

ESTHER: Maybe it's that it always used to seem so pretentious to me and kind of bourgeois. But it does have a certain character . . . I think some of it's in style again. It's surprising.

VICTOR: Well, you want to take anything?

ESTHER *(looking, hesitates):* I don't know if I want it around. *(Looking around.)* It's all so massive . . . where would we put any of it?—that chest is lovely.

Goes to it.

VICTOR: That was mine.

Indicating one across the room.

The one over there was Walter's. They're a pair.

ESTHER *(comparing):* Oh ya! Did you get hold of him?

VICTOR *(as though this had been an issue, he rather glances away):* I called again this morning—he was in consultation.

ESTHER: Was he in the office?

VICTOR: Ya. The nurse went and talked to him for a minute—it doesn't matter. As long as he's notified so I can go ahead.

ESTHER: What about his share?

He turns away.

I don't mean to be a pest, Vic, but there could be some real money here, Vic. You're going to raise that with him, aren't you?

VICTOR: I've changed my mind. I don't really feel he owes me anything. I can't put on an act, he's got a right to his half.

ESTHER: Why don't I meet you somewhere? The whole thing depresses me.

Starts for her purse.

VICTOR: Why?—It won't take long, relax. Come on, sit down—the dealer'll be here any minute.

Victor has bought a couple of tickets to a movie, but Esther refuses to be cheered up. She thinks the harp might be worth something, and Victor promises to drive a hard bargain.

Victor notices his wife's new suit and compliments her on her appearance. Victor has suffered a minor accident with his own suit—that's why he's in uniform. He expects the dry cleaner will have the suit ready in time to wear this evening.

Esther hopes so—she would much prefer that he didn't wear his uniform when they go out.

VICTOR: Well it's only a movie . . .

ESTHER: But we go out so rarely—why must everybody know your salary? I want an evening! I want to sit down in a restaurant without some drunken ex-cop coming over to the table to talk about old times.

VICTOR: It happened twice. After all these years, Esther, it would seem to me . . .

ESTHER: I know it's unimportant—but like that man in the museum, he really did—he thought you were the sculptor.

VICTOR: So I'm a sculptor.

ESTHER *(bridling):* Well, it was nice, that's all! You really do, Vic—you look distinguished in a suit—Why not?

Victor protests that what Esther needs is a job to occupy her time now that their son Richard has grown. But Esther hates the very thought of a job that would take her monotonously to the same place day after day.

Esther returns to the subject of Victor's brother Walter. She is angry at Walter for not coming to the phone. Walter, she believes, owes them "a moral debt" because "he could never have finished medical school if you hadn't taken care of Pop."

KATE REID, ARTHUR KENNEDY, PAT HINGLE
AND DAVID BURNS IN "THE PRICE"

At the very least they should get all of the money from the sale of the furniture, Esther insists. A little nest egg might induce Victor to take his retirement at once; maybe study for a degree, make a whole new career for himself. Victor is a young-looking 50 and has maybe 20 more good years ahead of him. He has been eligible for retirement from the police for three years now.

Esther wishes Vic would persist in getting in touch with his brother, who is an important doctor in an important hospital.

VICTOR: Esther, the man hasn't called me in sixteen years.

ESTHER: But neither have you called him!

He looks at her in surprise.

Well you haven't. That's also a fact.

VICTOR *(as though the idea were new and incredible):* What would I call him for?

ESTHER: Because he's your brother, he's influential, and he could help— Yes, that's how people do, Vic!—Those articles he wrote had a real idealism, there was a genuine human quality . . . I mean people do change, you know.

VICTOR *(turning away):* I'm sorry, I don't need Walter.

ESTHER: I'm not saying you have to approve of him; he's a selfish bastard, but he just might be able to put you on the track of something. I don't see the humiliation.

VICTOR *(pressed, irritated):* I don't understand why it's all such an emergency.

ESTHER: Because I don't know where in hell I am, Victor!

To her own surprise, she has ended nearly screaming. He is silent. She retracts . . .

I'll do anything if I know why, but all these years we've been saying, once we get the pension we're going to start to live . . . it's like pushing against a door for twenty-five years and suddenly it opens . . . and we stand there.—Sometimes I wonder, maybe I misunderstood you, maybe you like the department.

VICTOR: I've hated every minute of it.

But the financial security of a police job meant a lot to him, Esther reminds him, so that she has endured their shabby apartment and other privations. Victor should have quit the police during the war when everyone was making money. She wants money, Esther insists: *"I want money!"*

Victor has started to fill out the retirement forms a couple of times, he admits, but can't bring himself to go through with it. His life is like this attic full of old furniture.

VICTOR: . . . . . I mean you look back, and so many things that seemed so important turn out to be ridiculous.

He looks at the chair, breaks off.

Like that whole way I was with him—it's inconceivable to me now.

ESTHER: Well, you loved him.

VICTOR: I know, but it's all words somehow. What was he?—a busted businessman like thousands of others, and I acted like some kind of a mountain crashed. I don't know—sometimes I wonder maybe I don't sign out because I regret it all more than I realize and I can't face it. Except what's the difference what you do if you don't do the work you love?—It's a luxury, most people never get near it—*(But he loses that reassurance.)* I don't know, I tell you there are days when the whole thing is like a story somebody told me. . . .

To Esther, too, it seemed like a masquerade all those years ago when Victor came home with his first uniform. Victor admits he's stuck, his life seems to have hit a snag, but again he promises to do something about it.

Victor fiddles with an old radio he made himself. Once he was proud of it, he got Tokyo on it. He and Walter had a pretty good little laboratory up here in the attic.

Esther tries to get back into some kind of harmony with Victor, but at the moment his emotions are deadened, he pushes her off, he remarks lamely "We'll get my suit and act rich!" Esther encourages him to show her how he uses the fencing foil, which he does, using Esther as a target.

VICTOR: Don't be afraid.

Snapping the tip.

—It's a beautiful foil, see how alive it is? I beat Princeton with this.

Laughs tiredly and makes a tramping lunge from yards away, the button touching her stomach.

ESTHER *(springs back as the button touches her):* God!—Victor!

VICTOR: What!

ESTHER: You looked beautiful.

He laughs, surprised and half embarrassed—when both of them are turned to the door by a loud, sustained coughing out in the corridor. The coughing increases and . . . enter Gregory Solomon. In brief, a phenomenon; a man nearly 90 but still straight-backed and the air of his massiveness still with him. He has perfected a way of leaning on his cane without appearing weak.

He wears a worn, fur-felt, black fedora, its brim turned down on the right side like Jimmy Walker's—although much dustier—and a shapeless topcoat. His frayed tie has a thick knot, askew under a curled-up collar tab. His vest is wrinkled, his trousers baggy. A large diamond ring is on his left index finger. Tucked under his arm, a wrung-out leather portfolio. He hasn't shaved today.

Solomon sinks into the armchair at stage center, still struggling to catch his breath after the long climb upstairs. Victor puts down his foil. When he can speak, Solomon explains that he is the second-hand furniture dealer, and he is mildly surprised to find that his client is a policeman.

Solomon admires Esther's new suit. Esther leaves to pick up Victor's suit from the cleaner, but not before admonishing Solomon to give them a good price for the furniture. Solomon reassures her: "I'm not sixty-two years in the business by taking advantage."

Solomon is a registered appraiser, and Victor selected him from an ad in the phone book. Victor explains to Solomon that here in the attic is a whole houseful of furniture that once belonged to his family.

VICTOR: . . . . . the old man moved everything up here after the '29 crash. My uncles took over the house and they let him keep this floor.

SOLOMON *(as though to emphasize that he believes it):* I see.

He walks to the harp.

VICTOR: Can you give me an estimate now, or do you have to . . . ?

SOLOMON *(running a hand over the harp frame):* No-no, I'll give you right away, I don't waste a minute, I'm very busy.

He plucks a string, listens. Then bends down and runs a hand over the sounding board.

He passed away, your father?

VICTOR: Oh, long time ago—about sixteen years.

SOLOMON *(standing erect):* It's standing here sixteen years?

VICTOR: Well, we never got around to doing anything about it, but they're tearing the building down, so . . . It was very good stuff, you know—they had quite a little money.

SOLOMON: Very good, yes . . . I can see.

He leaves the harp with an estimating glance.

I was also very good; now I'm not so good. Time, you know, is a terrible thing.

He is a distance from the harp and indicates it.

That sounding board is cracked, you know. But don't worry about it, it's still a nice object.

Goes to the armoire and strokes the veneer.

It's a funny thing—an armoire like this, thirty years ago you couldn't give it away; it was a regular measles. Today all of a sudden, they want it again. Go figure it out.

He goes to one of the chests.

VICTOR *(pleased):* Well, give me a good price and we'll make a deal.

SOLOMON: Definitely. You see, I don't lie to you—

He is pointing to the chest.

For instance, a chiffonier like this I wouldn't have to keep it a week.

Solomon also admires the carved bed which Victor's parents brought back from Europe. But instead of coming straight to the point and naming a price, Solomon prefers to circumambulate, to approach it by degrees—that's his way. He asks Victor about his life, and learns that Victor went to college for a couple of years, and that Victor is now a policeman whose beat is way out in the Siberia of the airports ("I like it better that way," Victor declares).

When Solomon learns that Victor has a brother, he insists on some kind of a paper giving proof of ownership, because "I don't have to tell you the average family they love each other like crazy, but the minute the parents die is all of a sudden a question who is going to get what and you're covered with cats and dogs."

Victor promises Solomon a statement from his brother and tries to bring Solomon to the point of naming a price, but again Solomon launches into an evasion. Some of the furniture is out of style. Maybe Victor would sell a few pieces for a "knockout price," but Victor insists that Solomon must take all or nothing. The building is to be torn down and all the furniture must go.

Solomon notices the Gallagher and Sheean record and informs Victor that he himself was once an acrobat, the bottom man in "The Five Solomons." Victor wants to stick to business, but Solomon insists on showing him his discharge from the British Navy. Victor is amazed to note the date of birth—Solomon is almost 90. "Yes, my boy," Solomon admits, "I left Russia sixty-five years ago, I was twenty-four years old. And I smoked all my life. I drinked, and I loved every woman who would let me. So what do I need to steal from you?"

Again, Victor urges Solomon to name a price. Solomon is unnerved because he cannot seem to reach Victor in any way. He expresses his irritation by making a move toward his portfolio, as though to depart.

SOLOMON: I can't work this way. I'm too old every time I open my mouth you should practically call me a thief.

VICTOR: Who called you a thief?

SOLOMON *(he is moving toward the door):* No—I don't need it. I don't want it in my shop.

Wagging a finger into Victor's face.

And don't forget it—I never gave you a price, and look what you did to me. You see?—I never gave you a price!

VICTOR *(angering):* Well what did you come here for—to do me a favor? What are you talking about?

SOLOMON: Mister, I pity you! What is the matter with you people! You're worse than my daughter!—Nothing in the world you believe, nothing you respect—how can you live? You think that's such a smart thing? That's so hard, what you're doing? Let me give you a piece advice—it's not that you can't believe nothing, that's not so hard—it's that you still got to believe it. *That's* hard. And if you can't do that, my friend—you're a dead man!

He starts toward the door.

VICTOR *(chastened despite himself):* Oh, Solomon, come on, will you?

Solomon puts down his portfolio, takes out a tape measure and becomes all businesslike. One piece is forty inches wide, too wide to get in the door of a modern apartment. The library table is worthless, because apartments no longer have libraries.

Is Solomon trying to tell Victor the furniture is worthless? That would be jumping to conclusions, the dealer informs him. But they will *not* talk money just yet. Solomon presses his fingers into his eyes and declares "It's too much for me."

Solomon confides to Victor that he has long since ceased operating a furniture store. He has sold most of his stock and lives in back of the store. But he loves to work and could not resist Victor's phone call. Victor, resigned, offers to forget the whole deal, but once again Solomon asks "What're you jumping?" He intends to buy the furniture, he's not bargaining with Victor—but he wants him to know that this is the kind of furniture that makes people nervous.

Now Victor is more confused than ever, so Solomon explains: this furniture makes people nervous because it lasts. People like disposable goods, they enjoy shopping. "I'm telling you the truth!—If they would close the stores for six months in this country there would be from coast to coast a regular massacre. With this kind of furniture the shopping is over, it's finished, there's no more possibilities, you *got* it, you see? So you got a problem here."

This time Victor just laughs—Solomon can't fool him any more with that kind of negative talk. Solomon tries to divert Victor's attention by mentioning that he got married when he was 75 and his wife is still living, though they are separated. But Victor will not be diverted; the time for digression is up. So Solomon finally declares himself "I'm going to buy it!" He will take all the furniture and give Victor a good price.

But instead of naming a figure, Solomon takes a hard-boiled egg out of his portfolio, together with a pad of foolscap. Despite Victor's impatience, Solomon eats the egg before beginning his price calculations on the pad. Even now, Solomon hems and haws and digresses: he informs Victor that he has been married three times. He goes over to one of the armoires and opens it, and a lap robe falls out (Victor's family once had a car and chauffeur). Solomon also finds an opera hat in the armoire.

SOLOMON: And from all this he could go so broke?
VICTOR: Why not? Sure. Took five weeks. Less.
SOLOMON: You don't say. And he couldn't make a comeback?
VICTOR: Well some men don't bounce, you know.
SOLOMON *(a grunt):* Hmm! So what did he do?
VICTOR: Nothing. Just sat there. Listened to the radio.
SOLOMON: But what did he do? What . . . ?
VICTOR: Well, now and then he was making change at the Automat. Toward the end he was delivering telegrams.
SOLOMON *(with grief and wonder):* You don't say. And how much he had?
VICTOR: Oh . . . couple of million, I guess.
SOLOMON: My God. What was the matter with him?
VICTOR: —Well, my mother died around the same time—I guess that didn't help. Some men just don't bounce, that's all.

Victor's father believed in the system and blamed himself, not the crash, for his failure—But Victor has had enough of this conversation and brings Solomon back to the furniture. Solomon is running out of evasions but has one more personal confidence to bestow. His daughter committed suicide in 1915, and he never knew why; he never understood how he might have helped to prevent it. Now Solomon remembers that he had four wives, not three. He has spent a lifetime struggling to get his share, and now his whole life seems unreal, the present furniture deal as well as the past memories.

SOLOMON: . . . . . It's like now I'm sitting here talking to you and I tell you it's a dream, it's a dream! You see, you can't imagine it because . . .
VICTOR: I know what you're talking about. But it's not a dream—it's that you've got to make decisions and you can never know what's involved until it's too late. Like I was very good in science, I loved it but I had to drop out to feed the old man. And I figured I'd go on the force temporarily, just to get us through the Depression, then go back to school. But the war came, and then we had the kid, and you turn around and you've got fifteen years racked up on the pension, and it's hard to dump that. Which I don't regret—we brought up a terrific boy, for one thing; nobody's ever going to kid him. But it's like you were saying—it's impossible to know what's important. We always agreed—we stay out of the rat race and live our own life. That was important. But it ends up, she wants, she wants. And I can't really blame her—there's just no respect for anything but money.

SOLOMON: What have you got against money?

VICTOR: Nothing, I just didn't want to lay down my life for it. But I laid it down another way, and I swear to you, I don't know any more what the point was. I look back and all I can see is a long walk in the street. —I guess it's the old story, you can do anything, just be sure you win. Like my brother; years ago I was living up here with the old man, and he used to contribute five dollars a month. A *month;* and a successful doctor. I had to drop out of school to keep the guy from starving to death. Point I'm making though, is that the few times he'd come around, the expression on the old man's face—you'd think God walked in. The respect, you know what I mean? And why not? Why not?

SOLOMON: Well sure, he had the power.

VICTOR: Now you said it—if you got that you got it all—you're even lovable! *(He laughs.)* Well, what do you say? Give me the price.

SOLOMON *(slight pause):* I will give you eleven hundred dollars.

VICTOR *(slight pause):* For everything.

SOLOMON *(in a breathless way):* Everything. . . . .

Victor will never get a better price (Solomon assures him as he takes out a wad of bills). Victor has to split the money with his brother, so Solomon offers to make out the bill of sale for only four hundred dollars if Victor wishes (Victor doesn't).

At first, Victor wants to delay the decision until tomorrow; then, on impulse, he makes the decision: he will accept the eleven hundred. Solomon wants Victor to feel happy about the price. Victor can buy Esther a fur coat with his share. But Victor feels nothing. He merely holds out his hand for the money. Solomon begins counting the money into Victor's hand, reaching seven hundred dollars.

A man appears in the doorway. In his mid-50s, well barbered; hatless, in a camel's hair coat, very healthy complexion. A look of sharp intelligence on his face.

Victor, seeing past Solomon, starts slightly with shock, withdrawing his hand from the next bill which Solomon is about to lay in it.

VICTOR *(he is suddenly flushed, his voice oddly high and boyish):* Walter!

WALTER *(he enters the room, coming to Victor with extended hand, and with a reserve of warmth, but a stiff smile):* How are you, kid?

Solomon has moved out of their line of sight.

VICTOR *(he shifts the money to his left as he shakes):* God, I never expected you.

WALTER *(of the money—half-humorously):* Sorry I'm late. What are you doing?

VICTOR *(fighting a treason to himself, thus taking on a strained humorous air):* I . . . I just sold it.

WALTER: Good! How much?

VICTOR *(as though absolutely certain now he has been had):* Ah . . . eleven hundred.

WALTER *(in a dead voice shorn of comment):* Oh. Well, good.

He turns rather deliberately—but not overly so—to Solomon.

For everything?

SOLOMON *(with an energized voice that braves everything, he comes to Walter, his hand extended):* I'm very happy to meet you, Doctor! My name is Gregory Solomon.

WALTER *(the look on his face is rather amused, but his reserve has possibilities of accusation):* How do you do?

He shakes Solomon's hand. Victor raises his hand to smooth down his hair, a look of near-alarm for himself on his face.

(EDITOR'S NOTE: This is the point at which the author places the first-act curtain, should circumstances require that the play be presented in two parts. But the author's preference is for continuous action in an unbroken performance, as in the original Broadway production.)

Walter turns to face Victor and asks after Esther and their son Richard, who is now at M.I.T. on full scholarship. Walter's daughter Jean (whom Victor has never seen) is a designer, and his sons are in and out of school—Walter no longer worries about them. Walter's wife Dorothy is "all right, I guess."

Now that Walter has shown up in person (Victor says), perhaps they'd better renegotiate the whole furniture deal. But Walter indicates he doesn't want to interfere. Solomon suggests that Walter take anything he wants now, before the deal is closed. Walter doesn't want anything, not even his old oar . . . but the harp has a good deal of sentimental value. Walter is surprised that Victor is not keeping the harp. Solomon protests—the harp is important in the overall package, "with used furniture you cannot be emotional."

Walter wonders what happened to his mother's old dresses. Solomon hands Walter a gold-embroidered gown from the armoire.

WALTER: . . . . . Isn't that beautiful!—Say, I think she wore this at my wedding!

Holds it up.

Sure! You remember this?

VICTOR *(surprised at this emotion):* What do you want with it?

WALTER *(drawing out another gown off the rack):* Look at this one! Isn't that something?!—I thought Jeannie might make something new out of the material, I'd like her to wear something of mother's.

VICTOR *(a new, surprising idea):* Oh! Fine, that's a nice idea.

SOLOMON *(laying a second gown on the couch):* Take, take—they're beautiful.

WALTER *(suddenly glancing about as he lays the gowns across a chair):* . . . What happened to the piano?

VICTOR: Oh we sold that while I was still in school. We lived on it for a long time.

WALTER *(very interestedly):* I never knew that.

VICTOR: Sure. And the silver.

WALTER: Of course! Stupid of me not to remember that.

VICTOR: Why? Why should you?

WALTER: I suppose you know—you've gotten to look a great deal like dad.

VICTOR: *I* do?

WALTER: It's very striking. And your voice is very much like his.

VICTOR: I know; it has that sound to me, sometimes.

Solomon brings them back to business and tries to resume counting the bills into Victor's hand.

VICTOR: That price all right with you?

WALTER: Oh, I don't want to interfere—It's just that I dealt with these fellows when I split up Dorothy's and my stuff last year, and I found . . .

VICTOR *(from an earlier impression):* Your're not divorced, are you?

WALTER *(a nervous shot of laughter):* Yes!

Esther enters on his line; she is carrying a suit in a plastic wrapper.

Walter and Esther exchange greetings and compliments—he should have brought her some of the Bombay bracelets sent him by a grateful patient, who also supplied the expensive-looking coat he is wearing. Walter continues on the subject of his divorce: "It was coming a long time. We're both much better off—we're almost friendly now."

Walter hints that perhaps they can do better on the furniture elsewhere, but Solomon assures them all that he is a past president of the Appraisers Association, he helped write the rules and he has offered the Franz family a fair price. Esther asks about the offer, and Victor is actually embarrassed to tell her: eleven hundred dollars. Esther is quick to comment that this is not enough.

WALTER *(delicately):* Maybe I oughtn't interfere . . .

ESTHER: Why?! *(Of Solomon.)* Don't let him bulldoze you . . .

SOLOMON: My dear girl, you're talking without a basis . . .

ESTHER *(slashing):* I don't like this kind of dealing, Mr. Solomon! I just don't like it!

She is near tears. A pause. She turns back to Walter.

This money is very important to us, Walter.

WALTER *(chastised):* Yes. I . . . I'm sorry, Esther.

He looks about.

Well . . . if it was mine . . .

ESTHER: Why? It's yours as much as Victor's.

WALTER: Oh, no, dear—I wouldn't take anything from this.

A pause.

VICTOR: No, Walter, you get half.

WALTER: I wouldn't think of it, kid. I came by to say hello, that's all.

A pause.

ESTHER *(she is very moved):* That's terrific, Walter. It's . . . Really, I . . .

VICTOR: Well, we'll talk about it.

WALTER: No-no, Vic, you've earned it. It's yours.

VICTOR *(rejecting the implication):* Why have I earned it? You take your share.

Walter suggests they discuss this point later; in the meantime, he admits that he would have thought a fair price would be a minimum of three thousand. Solomon calls this ridiculous. Walter suggests that Victor should have gotten a couple of other estimates, and Victor replies, "I've been calling you all week for just that reason, Walter, and you never came to the phone."

Solomon points out that Walter referred to the furniture as "a lot of junk" when he came in, and Solomon and Walter argue about its quality. Esther ridicules Victor's acceptance of a mere eleven hundred dollars—Victor's self-respect is under attack along with the price. Solomon sees this and protests—Victor drove a good bargain, they should not demean him in this way. To Victor, Solomon declares "you made a very nice deal, you got no right to be ashamed . . ."

Solomon points out that Victor already has money in his hand, it's possible that the deal has been legally concluded. Not without his signature, Walter argues, because he is part owner—not that he's making any claim, of course. Walter suggests that Solomon go into the other room while the family talks the matter over.

Victor tries to give Solomon back the money, but Solomon refuses it; as he does so he sways as though in the beginning of a faint. Walter goes to help him, and he escorts Solomon into the other room. The furniture dealer is not sick, merely a little tired and hungry.

As they go, Victor puts the money on the dining table and weighs it down with the foil. Esther reproaches Victor with not bargaining hard enough; at least he is getting the whole amount, such as it is. But Victor is not certain that he intends to accept Walter's share; after all that's happened in twenty-eight years, including last week when Walter wouldn't even come to the phone, Victor can't suddenly embrace him and accept his largesse as though he were a loving brother.

Victor's doubts about accepting all the money drives Esther to the edge of frantic despair, she is so keenly in favor of accepting it.

Walter comes back into the room, and Esther wonders what he thinks they ought to do.

Slight pause. Walter is trying to modify what he believes is his overpowering force so as not to appear to be taking over. He is faintly smiling toward Victor.

WALTER: There is a way to get a good deal more out of it. I suppose you know that, though.

VICTOR: Look, I'm not married to this guy—if you want to call another dealer we can compare.

WALTER: You don't have to do that; he's a registered appraiser—You see, instead of selling it, you could make it a charitable contribution.

VICTOR: I don't understand.

WALTER: It's perfectly simple. He puts a value on it—let's say twenty-five thousand dollars, and . . .

ESTHER *(fascinated and with a laugh):* Are you kidding?

WALTER: It's done all the time. It's a dream world but it's legal—he estimates its highest retail value; which could be put at some such figure. Then I donate it to the Salvation Army; I'd have to take ownership, you see; because my tax rate is much higher than yours so it would make more sense if I took the deduction. I pay around fifty per cent tax, so if I make a twenty-five-thousand-dollar contribution I'd be saving around twelve thousand in taxes. Which we could split however you wanted to. Let's say we split it in half, I'd give you six thousand dollars.

A pause.

It's really the only sensible way to do it, Vic.

ESTHER *(she glances at Victor, but he remains silent):* Would it be costing you anything?

WALTER: On the contrary—it's found money to me. *(To Victor.)* I mentioned it to him just now.

VICTOR *(as though this had been the question):* What'd he say?

WALTER: It's up to you. We'd pay him an appraisal fee—fifty, sixty bucks.

Victor wants to think over this proposition, and while he does so Walter tells Esther that although he kept all the furniture from his home (his apartment looks much like this attic), he expects never to marry again. He is much too preoccupied with the practise of medicine to be married.

Victor wonders how he could explain such a large sum of money on his own income tax. As a gift, Walter explains. But the idea of a gift from Walter, even a technical one, arouses Victor's resentment.

Walter changes the subject to fencing: their mother used to love to watch Victor fence and presented him with beautiful French gauntlets for Christmas 1929. They find the gauntlets in Victor's old bureau—they are still in fine shape. Esther, too, thinks the gauntlets beautiful. Victor, staring at them, finds that he can remember his mother well—all except for her face.

Solomon comes in and calls Walter into the bedroom to consult with him, leaving Victor and Esther alone.

Esther thinks they should forget the past and take the money—go off on a trip. Victor is still puzzled that his brother would walk in so casually after all these years and behave "as though nothing ever happened."

VICTOR *(with a self-bracing tension):* I'm not going to take this money unless I talk to him.

ESTHER *(frightened):* You can't bear the thought that he's decent.

He looks at her sharply.

That's all it is, dear. I'm sorry, I have to say it.

VICTOR *(without raising his voice):* I can't bear that he's *decent.*

ESTHER: You throw this away you've got to explain it to me. You can't go on blaming everything on him or the system or God knows what else! You're free and you can't make a move, Victor, and that's what's driving me crazy!

He is silent, staring at her.

(Quietly) You take this money! Or I'm washed up. If you're stuck it doesn't mean I have to be.

Movement is heard within the bedroom. She straightens. Victor smoothes down his hair with a slow, preparatory motion of his hand, like one adjusting himself for combat.

Walter comes back. Sensing Victor's hostility, Walter tries to get him to talk about it. Victor admits that he is still disturbed by the way Walter's secretary brushed him off on the telephone, as though Walter had warned her that he considered his brother Victor some sort of pest. Walter is sincerely apologetic. There was nothing personal in this incident, the secretary is often rude and Walter is simply too busy to keep a check on her.

Walter informs Victor that Solomon is willing to make the high appraisal, and Victor can have all the tax saving, the whole amount. Walter understands that Victor is near retirement now and could use the money, and Victor is of course embarrassed by Walter's knowledge and Esther's frank admission of their uncertainty, their need.

Walter touches Victor's knee, as though reaching out to make contact with him, to reassure Victor that he need not be suspicious. Walter has been meaning to get ahold of Victor, to get to know him better. But Walter has been away. He has been sick, hospitalized. Walter has had a nervous breakdown (he tells them to their astonishment) that lasted almost three years.

The breakdown (Walter continues) was a blessing in disguise. Now he lives differently, thinks differently. He used to own and worry about three lucrative nursing homes, but now he concentrates on medicine and spends half his time in city hospitals.

There is so much that Walter wants to tell Victor about his new insights and feelings. For example, Walter has friends now—he never used to have. At first, Walter was merely striving to excel, but soon he began to forget the human element in himself and his patients and became merely "an instrument that cuts money out of people." Power warped him, made him stupid.

WALTER: . . . . . One night I found myself in the middle of my living room, dead drunk with a knife in my hand, getting ready to kill my wife.

ESTHER: Good Lord!

WALTER: Oh ya—and I nearly made it too! *(Laughs nervously.)* But there's one virtue in going nuts—provided you survive, of course. You get to see the terror—not the screaming kind, but the slow, daily fear you call ambition, and cautiousness, and piling up the money. And really, what I wanted to tell you for some time now—is that you helped me to understand that in myself.

VICTOR: Me?

WALTER: Yes. *(Grins warmly; embarrassed.)* Because of what you did. I could never understand it, Vic—after all you *were* the better student. And to stay with a job like that through all those years seemed . . .

He breaks off momentarily with the uncertainty of Victor's reception.

You see, it never dawned on me until I got sick—that you'd made a choice.

VICTOR: A choice, how?

WALTER: You wanted a real life.—And that's an expensive thing; it costs.

He senses that perhaps he has found his theme now; he sees that he has at last touched something in Victor.

I'll be frank with you, Vic—I didn't answer your calls this week because I was afraid—I've struggled so long for a concept of myself and I'm not sure I can make it believable to you. But I'd like to.

He sees his permission to go on in Victor's perplexed eyes. But it is more difficult too.

Walter tells them of his own inner drive to achieve the impossible. He accepted cases which more prudent doctors considered inoperable, taking greater and greater surgical risks until suddenly he lost three patients in a row and lost his own nerve along with them.

WALTER: . . . . . But suddenly I saw something else. And it was terror. In dead center, controlling my brains, my hands, my ambition—for thirty years.

Slight pause.

VICTOR: Terror of what?

A pause.

WALTER *(his gaze is direct on Victor now):* Of it ever happening to me . . .

He glances at the center chair.

. . . as it happened to him. Overnight for no reason, to find yourself degraded and thrown-down. *(With the faintest hint of impatience and a challenge.)* You know what I'm talking about, don't you?

Victor turns away slightly, refusing commitment.

Isn't that why you turned your back on it all? We've both been running from the same thing, Vic. I thought I wanted to be tops, but what it was was untouchable:—I ended in a swamp of success and bankbooks, you in Civil Service. The difference is that you haven't hurt other people to defend yourself. And I've learned to respect that, Vic; you simply tried to make yourself useful.

In this escape, Walter feels a brotherly kinship with Vic for the first time in years. He wants to be better friends. Walter congratulates them on the reality of their life, which has brought them a happy marriage and a well-adjusted son.

Walter also has an idea that Victor with his interest in science—and his beginning knowledge of it—might work into the administrative side of the hospital's new wing. Walter is chairman of the committee and can arrange to get Victor a job. Esther jumps at the opportunity, but Victor is doubtful.

Solomon enters, takes an orange from his portfolio, raises his offer for the harp by fifty dollars, then hurries out again.

Walter and Esther wait for Victor's decision. Victor lets them watch him for a long pause, then tells Walter: "I'm not sure I know what you want." Victor is frankly suspicious; this would be a big step; he cannot suddenly bury his resentment after all that has happened.

Walter sees that he is unlikely to break down Victor's resistance and he gives up, prepares to leave, declares that Victor can get what he can from Solomon for the furniture, Walter doesn't want any part of it.

Esther tries to smooth over the situation, but Victor will not be persuaded that Walter's offer can be taken at face value. In reality (Victor's reality) he doesn't know enough physics and chemistry to work in a research lab, even as an administrator. He would become a mere errand boy, the boss's brother.

What's more, Victor cannot overlook the irony of Walter's remark that it was a pity Victor didn't go on with his study of science, which he had loved so much.

VICTOR *(smiling still, and pointing at the center chair, a new reverberation sounds in his voice):* There used to be a man in that chair, staring into space. Don't you remember that?

WALTER: Very well, yes—I sent him money every month.

VICTOR: You sent him five dollars every month.

WALTER: I could afford five dollars. But what's that got to do with you?

VICTOR: What it's got to do with me!

WALTER: Yes, I don't see that.

VICTOR: Where did you imagine the rest of his living was coming from?

WALTER: Victor, that was your decision, not mine.

VICTOR: My decision!

WALTER: We had a long talk in this room once, Victor.

VICTOR *(not recalling):* What talk?

WALTER *(astonished):* Victor! We came to a complete understanding—just after you moved up here with dad. I told you then that I was going to finish my schooling come hell or high water, and I advised you to do the same. In fact, I warned you not to allow him to strangle your life. *(To Esther.)* And if I'm not mistaken I told you the same at your wedding, Esther.

VICTOR *(with an ironic laugh):* Who the hell was supposed to keep him alive, Walter!

WALTER *(with a strange fear, more than anger):* Why did anybody have to? He wasn't sick. He was perfectly fit to go to work.

VICTOR: Work? In 1936? With no skill, no money . . . ?

WALTER *(outburst):* Then he could have gone on welfare! Who *was* he, some exiled royalty? What did a hundred and fifty million other people do in 1936? He'd have survived, Victor—good God, you must know that by now, don't you?

Slight pause.

VICTOR *(suddenly at the edge of fury, and caught by Walter's voicing his own opinion, he turns to Esther):* I've had enough of this, Esther; it's the same old thing all over again, let's get out of here.

But Walter continues his persuasion: he loved their father too, but he believes Victor was exploited. Victor resents any reflection upon himself as victim. He repeats, he had no choice: "The icebox was empty and the man was sitting there with his mouth open."

Esther believes that Walter has come here in good faith and that his offer of help should be considered in the same light. Victor pretends he is still considering it, but Esther knows that in his innermost thoughts Victor has decided to turn the offer down.

Solomon enters and assures them that he will make the appraisal for charity, if they insist. Solomon thinks the brothers are still haggling over how to dispose of the furniture, and he is alarmed by their hostility. He points out that the Federal government will have the last word, anyway—possibly it will disallow the deduction. Solomon urges them to stop quarreling, then resigns himself to returning to the bedroom. He exits.

Walter is ready to resign himself to an outright sale, and as for the other problems, they can consider them later in a more suitable atmosphere. But Esther sees money slipping away merely because the brothers can't clear the air with a little plain speaking. She brings up the time when Victor asked Walter for a five-hundred-dollar loan to finish his education and Walter refused. Walter admits that he could have afforded the loan. After refusing it, he realized he was behaving badly, and he phoned Victor to offer him the money. Their father answered the phone: "When I called here he told me you'd joined the Force. And I said—he mustn't permit you to do a thing like that; I said—you had a fine mind and with a little luck you could amount to something in science. That it was a terrible waste. Etcetera. And his answer was—'Victor wants to help me. I can't stop him.' "

Victor can hardly believe that this happened—his father never told him. Walter never pressed his offer because he was afraid to interfere with such a warm father-son relationship, which he himself did not share. Victor doesn't see how Walter could have thought that five hundred dollars would have such an effect. No, "You didn't give me the money because you didn't want to."

Walter had no obligation, of course; neither did he have any desire to help Victor (as Victor sees it). And Victor resents the implication in Walter's job offer that Victor needs Walter's rescue now.

VICTOR: . . . . . Why do you have to offer me anything?

Walter is silent, morally checked.

It sounds like I have to be saved, or something.

WALTER: I simply felt that there was work you could do that you'd enjoy and I . . .

VICTOR: Walter, I haven't got the education, what are you talking about? You can't walk in with one splash and wash out twenty-eight years. There's a price people pay. I've paid it, it's all gone, I haven't got it any more. Just like you paid, didn't you?—you've got no wife, you've lost your family, you're rattling around all over the place—can you go home and start all over again from scratch? This is where we are; now, right here, now. . . . .

Still Victor hunts for a hidden meaning in Walter's attitude—is Walter trying to break it to him gently that his sacrifice for his father was unnecessary after all? Walter explains once more: he feels he can be of help to Victor at this time, and he doesn't want to pass up the chance as he did before. If Victor doesn't accept Walter's help, he will be defeating himself again—as he did before.

Victor could have walked out on their father and gone on with his education, Walter insists, without his loan of five hundred dollars. Victor points out bitterly that in this attic they were living on garbage—outside lettuce leaves and rotten grapefruit which they scrounged.

Somehow, it seems to Victor, Esther and Walter are in league to convice him that the problem wasn't real, only a dream. But Victor persists: their need was real and compelling.

VICTOR: . . . . . I could have left him with your five dollars a month? I'm sorry, you can't brainwash me—if you got a hook in your mouth don't try to stick it into mine.

In starts he is moving upstage.

You want to make up for things, you don't come around to make fools out of people—I didn't invent my life. Not altogether. You had a responsibility here and you walked out on it . . . You can go. I'll send you your half.

He crosses to the harp.

WALTER: If you could reach beyond your anger, I'd like to tell you something—Vic—I know I should have said this many years ago. But I did try . . . when you came to me I told you . . . remember I said, "Ask dad for money." I did say that . . . He had money left, after the crash.

VICTOR: What are you talking about?

WALTER: He had nearly four thousand dollars.

ESTHER: When?

WALTER: When they were eating garbage here.

Slight pause.

VICTOR: How did you know that?

WALTER: He'd asked me to invest it for him.

VICTOR: Invest it.

WALTER: Yes. That's why I never sent him more than I did. And if I'd had the strength of my convictions I wouldn't have sent him that!

There is a long pause. Shame is flooding into Victor. He looks at nobody.

VICTOR: He actually had it?—in the bank?

WALTER: Vic, that's what he was living on, basically, till he died. What we gave him wasn't enough; you know that.

VICTOR: But he had those jobs . . .

WALTER: Meant very little.—He lived on his money, believe me.—I told him at the time, if he would send you through I'd contribute properly. But here he's got you running from job to job to feed him—I'm damned if I'd sacrifice when he was holding out on you. You can understand that, can't you?

Victor turns to the center chair, and shaking his head exhales a blow of anger and astonishment.

Walter continues (very gently, fearing an emotional explosion): their father always expected that Victor would walk out some day. They were amazed at his devotion, at such cost to his career. Victor sees the point, but he takes it in silence at first; then he reproaches Walter for not telling him about the four thousand. The hint "ask dad" was not enough. Walter, by his silence, helped his father make a fool of him.

Walter insists that Victor's self-sacrifice was part of a fantasy created by Victor himself. For example, the harp was sitting there, obviously worth enough to get started toward a degree. "It's a fantasy, Victor," Walter repeats, "—your father was penniless and your brother a son of a bitch, and you play no part at all." Walter insists that Victor must have known his father had something left.

VICTOR: You mean, if he had a few dollars left, that . . . ?

ESTHER: What do you mean, a few dollars?

VICTOR *(trying to retract):* I didn't know he . . . had four—

ESTHER: But you knew he had something?

VICTOR *(caught; as though in a dream where nothing is explicable):* . . . I didn't say that.

ESTHER: Then what are you saying? I want to understand what you're saying!! You knew he had money left?

VICTOR: Not four thousand dol . . .

ESTHER: But enough to make out?

VICTOR *(crying out in anger and for release):* I couldn't nail him to the wall, could I? He said he had nothing.

ESTHER: But you knew better!?

VICTOR: I don't know what I knew!

He has called this out, and his voice and words surprise him. He sits staring, cornered by what he senses in himself.

Esther is appalled that they made all the sacrifices, even delayed having children, for "a miserable cheap manipulator." Their whole life and its meaning was a lie—a nightmare.

But that is not the truth either (Victor asserts in a voice which *"comes as though from the center of a calm in a storm"*). The truth (Victor now confesses) is that he *did* ask his father for the money, as Walter suggested. His father answered with a wild laugh which drove Victor out of the house to Bryant Park, where he saw the lawn covered with "busted business men" with shined shoes but no job and no hope of mercy from society. And Victor remembers that his father loved him.

VICTOR *(his voice swelling with sorrow):* He loved me, Esther! He just didn't want to end up on the grass! It's not that you don't love somebody, it's that you've got to survive. We know what that feels like, don't we!?

She can't answer, feeling the barb.

We do what we have to do, Esther.

With a wide gesture including her and Walter and himself.

What else are we talking about here? If he did have something left it was . . .

ESTHER: *"If"* he had . . .

VICTOR: What does that change?—I know I'm talking like a fool, but what does that change?—he couldn't believe in anybody any more, and it was unbearable to me. *(Of Walter.)* He'd kicked him in the face; my mother . . .

He glances toward Walter as he speaks. There is hardly a pause.

the night he told us he was bankrupt, my mother . . . It was right on this couch. She was all dressed up—for some affair, I think. Her hair was piled up, and long earrings? And he had his tuxedo on . . . and made us all sit down; and he told us it was all gone. And she vomited.

Slight pause.

All over his arms. His hands. Just kept on vomiting, like thirty-five years coming up. And he sat there. Stinking like a sewer.—And a look came onto his face. I'd never seen a man look like that. He was sitting there, letting it dry on his hands.

Pause. He turns to Esther.

What's the difference what you know? *(In mourning.)* Do *you* do everything you know?

She avoids his eyes, his charge received.

—Not that I excuse it; it was idiotic, nobody has to tell me that. But you're brought up to believe in one another, you're filled full of that crap—you can't help trying to keep it going, that's all.

Victor has it wrong, Walter argues, they weren't brought up to sustain each other, they were brought up to *succeed.* "Was there ever any love here? When he needed her, she vomited. And when you needed him, he laughed.—What was unbearable is not that it all fell apart, it was that there was never anything here."

Esther doubts that they can face such an emptiness, but Walter continues: there was no love in this house, that is the awful truth which Victor sensed. Walter himself had been troubled with memories until he finally faced the fact that their family relationship was a mere financial convenience; no love lost.

Walter has faced this fact, and now "I don't look high and low for some betrayal any more; my days belong to *me* now. . . . ." Victor, who could never stand the sight of blood, became a policeman, just as Walter, who merely wanted to steep himself in science, began to chase the buck. "We invent ourselves, Vic, to wipe out what we know. You invent a life of self-sacrifice, a life of duty; but what never existed here cannot be upheld."

It is only an illusion of Victor's that Walter betrayed his brother and father, and if only Vic will realize this they can reach each other again, maybe.

But Victor feels lost in this emotional maze; he needs some reality to cling to. Walter asks him: suppose in those old days Walter really *had* wanted to hold Victor back? Would such an admission help him to face reality now?

VICTOR *(as though he sees the opening toward their old confidence in one another):* Is that what you wanted?—Walter, tell me the truth.

WALTER *(in a vise):* I wanted the freedom to do my work. Does that mean I stole your life?

Crying out and standing.

You made those choices, Victor! And that's what you have to face!

VICTOR: But, what do you face? You're not turning me into a walking fifty-year-old mistake—we have to go home when you leave, we have to look at each other. What do *you* face?

WALTER: I have offered you everything I know how to!

VICTOR: I would know if you'd come to give me something! I would know that!

WALTER *(crossing for his coat):* You don't want the truth, you want a monster!

VICTOR: You came for the old handshake, didn't you! The okay!

Walter halts in the doorway.

And you end up with the respect, the career, the money, and the best thing of all, the thing that nobody else can tell you so you can believe it—that you're one hell of a guy and never harmed anybody in your life! Well, you're not going to get it. Not till I get mine.

WALTER: And you? You never had any hatred for me? Never a wish to see me destroyed? To destroy me, to destroy me with this saintly self-sacrifice, this mockery of sacrifice? What will you give me, Victor!

VICTOR: I don't have it to give you. Not any more. And you don't have it to give me. And there's nothing to give—I see that now. I just didn't want him to end up on the grass. And he didn't. That's all it was. I couldn't work with you, Walter. I can't. I don't trust you.

WALTER: Vengeance. Down to the end. He is sacrificing his life to vengeance.

ESTHER: Nothing was sacrificed.

WALTER: To prove with your failure what a treacherous son of a bitch I am—to hang yourself in my doorway. Then and now.

ESTHER *(quietly, not facing either of them):* Leave him, Walter, please. Don't say any more.

WALTER: You lay down and quit, and that's the long and short of all your ideology. It is all envy!

Solomon enters, apprehensive, looks from one to the other.

—And to this moment you haven't the guts to face it! You are a failure. But your failure does not give you moral authority! Not with me! I *worked* for what I made—and there are people walking around today who'd have been dead if I hadn't. Yes.

He points at the center chair.

He was smarter than all of us—he saw what you wanted and he gave it to you! He killed that woman and he killed you. But not me. Not then and not now. He will never kill me.

He is furious. He takes an unplanned step toward the door.

Go ahead, you old mutt—rob them blind, they love it! Love it.

He turns to Victor.

You will never, never again make me ashamed!

A gown lies on the table beside his coat. Suddenly he sweeps it up and rushes at Victor, flinging it at him with an outcry. He exits. Victor starts after him.

VICTOR: Walter!

SOLOMON *(stopping him with his hand):* Let him go. . . . .

Esther admires Solomon for his ability to believe what he sees. Not Esther. She had always thought that if the brothers could get together, somehow the family disaster could be wiped out. She *still* thinks so, she believes in the possibility of salvation no matter how unreal it looks on the surface.

Solomon replies that he remembers his dead daughter clearly every night—but if a miracle occurred and she came back to life, what could he find to say to her?

Solomon returns to business: fifty bucks more for the harp, and the deal is closed. Victor and Esther can still make that movie. Victor tears the plastic wrapper off the suit, but Esther tells him not to bother to change out of his uniform. She accepts her life as it is. She exits.

Solomon is listing each piece on his pad. Victor will return the next day for the suit—and for the foil, mask and gauntlets. Solomon thanks Victor for inspiring him to return to business of buying and selling a load of second-hand furniture. Victor wishes Solomon goodby and good luck and exits.

Left alone, Solomon looks at the pile of furniture apprehensively—it is going to be a big job. He plucks at the harp. He starts the phonograph.

The Laughing Record plays. Hearing the two comedians beginning the routine, his depressed expression gives way to surprise.

Now he smiles. He chuckles, and remembers. Now a laugh escapes, and he nods his head in recollection. He is laughing now, and shakes his head back and forth as though to say, "It still works!" And the laughter both of the record and his own increase. He holds his head, unable to stop laughing, and sits in the center chair. He leans back sprawling in the chair, laughing with tears in his eyes, howling helplessly to the air.

Slow curtain.

PLAZA SUITE

A Program of Three One-Act Plays

BY NEIL SIMON

Cast and credits appear on page 363

NEIL SIMON was born in the Bronx, N.Y., on July 4, 1927. He attended New York University and the University of Denver. His first theatrical work was sketches for camp shows at Tamiment, Pa., in collaboration with his brother Danny. He became a TV writer, supplying a good deal of material to Sid Caesar and Phil Silvers. On Broadway, Simon contributed sketches to Catch a Star *(1955) and* New Faces of 1956. *His first Broadway play was* Come Blow Your Horn *(1961), followed by the book for the musical* Little Me (1962). *His comedy* Barefoot in the Park *(1963) was selected as a Best Play of its season, as was* The Odd Couple *(1965). Neither of these had closed when* Sweet Charity, *a musical for which Simon wrote the book, came along in early 1966; and none of the three had closed when Simon's* The Star-Spangled Girl *opened the following season in December, 1966—so that Simon had four hit shows running at one time on Broadway during the season of 1966-67. When the last of the four closed the following summer, Simon's hits had played a combined total of 3,367 performances over a period of four theater seasons.*

Plaza Suite *is Simon's first program of one-acters, his third Best Play and his fifth hit in a row. Our method of synopsizing it in these pages differs from that used for the other nine Best Plays.* Plaza Suite's *three stories are told mostly in pictures, in order to record the total "look" of a popular Broadway comedy in the 1967-68 season, and of two of its outstanding performances by the* Plaza Suite *stars: George C. Scott and Maureen Stapleton.*

The photographs depict the succession of scenes as produced by Saint-Subber and directed by Mike Nichols as of the play's opening February 14, 1968 at the Plymouth Theater, with scenery by Oliver Smith and costumes by Patricia Zipprodt. Our special thanks are enthusiastically tendered to the producer and his press representatives, Harvey B. Sabinson, Lee Solters and Harry Nigro, for their help in obtaining the excellent photographs by Martha Swope.

Time: The present in three episodes

Place: A suite in the Plaza Hotel, New York City

I. VISITOR FROM MAMARONECK

(A late winter afternoon)

Karen Nash (Maureen Stapleton) and her husband Sam (George C. Scott) have taken a suite at the Plaza while their suburban house is being painted. Karen has chosen the same suite they occupied on their honeymoon 24 years before. She is all set for a warm, sentimental evening and has ordered champagne. But when Sam arrives from the office *(above)* he is tense and preoccupied and fails to respond to Karen's affectionate mood.

All photos by Martha Swope

Below, Sam moves to the suite's bedroom to phone his office, where evidently there are some problems.

Coat off, Sam returns to the living room to study his papers *(above).* Karen tries to coax him into a party mood. *Below,* she suggests that he take her out on the town. But it's no use.

Right, Karen resigns herself to the collapse of her hopes for a special evening. Their temperamental differences come to the surface. Karen is romantic where Sam is practical; easygoing where he is rigidly self-disciplined. She would be happy to relax and spread into middle age. He clings to youth.

Below, Sam's secretary Jean (Claudette Nevins)—28, divorced and pretty—comes to the suite with some papers from the office. There's a problem, it seems. Sam will have to return to the office to confer with "Howard" and he sends Jean on ahead while he prepares to follow her.

In the bedroom as Sam prepares to leave, Karen in her disappointment playfully suggests that Jean is Sam's mistress and in reality Sam has a rendezvous with her. Sam denies this. Karen persists—not so playfully. Finally, to her shocked surprise, Sam admits it. It's true. . . . .

. . . . . Jean *is* his mistress (Sam declares as he crosses to the living room and continues his confession). He has no business appointment, he really is going to meet Jean. It's all part of wanting not to grow old.

Right, Sam pleads that he can't help himself. Karen's first reaction is icy, whereas Sam expects and wants fury.

nally, Karen asks Sam to cancel his ite and stay. Sam cannot. He is de- rmined to meet Jean as planned, ough perhaps after tonight Sam and aren can try again.

Sam leaves the suite. Shortly afterward, the waiter (Jose Ocasio) arrives with the ordered bottle of champagne and two glasses. *Curtain.*

II. VISITOR FROM HOLLYWOOD
(Early afternoon in spring)

Jesse Kiplinger (George C. Scott), Hollywood producer, has invited Muriel Tate, his New Jersey home town sweetheart whom he hasn't seen in years, to join him for the afternoon in New York. Muriel is down in the Plaza lobby, and Jesse is on the phone *(above)* persuading her to come up to his suite.

Muriel (Maureen Stapleton) arrives at Jesse's suite.

He's now a famous personality, the friend and employer of stars. She's a housewife with three children. Naturally, Muriel is a little nervous at first. . . . .

. . . . but he is very hospitable *(left)*. Soon she begins to thaw *(below)*.

Muriel is softening with vodka and glamorous movie-star anecdotes. They exchange confidences. Muriel protests (too much) that hers is an idyllic marriage. Jesse confesses that his several wives were unloving, that Muriel was and is his only chance to know the love of a good woman. Finally, Jesse captures Muriel's rapt attention by telling her all the details of an Academy Award banquet.

As he tells the Academy Award story, Jesse easily leads Muriel to the bedroom, where they can talk more comfortably. . . . .

. . . and Jesse is reeling off a list of famous movie stars' names, as the curtain falls.

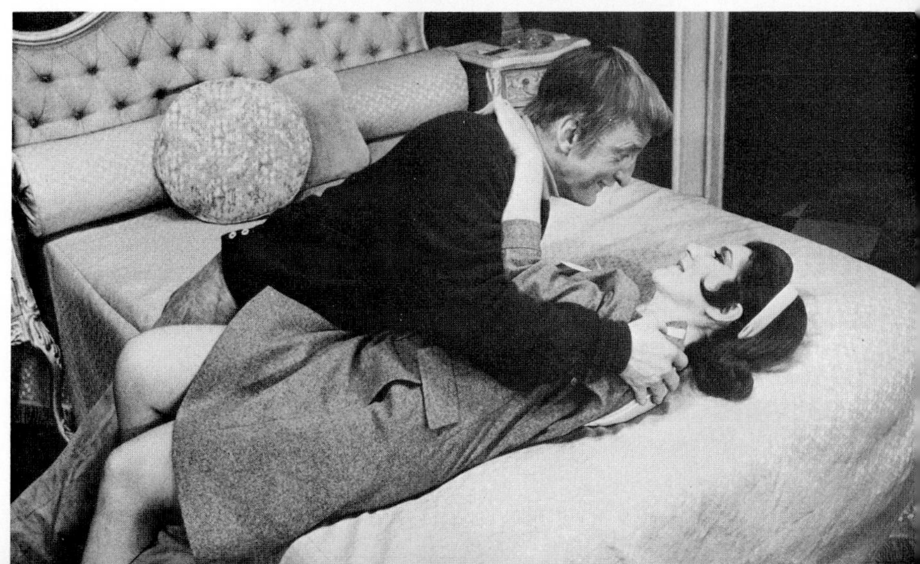

III. VISITOR FROM FOREST HILLS
(A Saturday afternoon in June)

Right, Norma Hubley (Maureen Stapleton) phones downstairs to the ballroom, where the Hubley-Eisler wedding is ready to take place. She urgently requests her husband Roy to come up to the suite. . . . .

. . . . . Roy Hubley (George C. Scott) bursts into the room, where there is a major crisis. The bride, their daughter Mimsey, has locked herself in the bathroom and won't come out, even though the guests are assembled and the "Wedding March" is about to begin.

Roy can't believe anyone could do this to him, with everything hired and ready. But when he orders Mimsey to come out of the bathroom there is no answer. Through the keyhole Roy can see that his daughter is in there, crying.

Above, Roy loses his temper. The result *(below)* is that his rented morning coat is ripped up the back. Now determined to get Mimsey out by any means, he goes out the window and disappears along a narrow ledge, as he tries to reach the bathroom from the outside. . . . .

. . . . . and when he comes back into the suite through the hall door *(right),* he is ready to kill.

As he explains to Norma *(below),* there was a thunder shower while he was out there, and Mimsey had locked the bathroom window. . . . .

. . . . . and he had to climb back in through the window of a strange bedroom.

After Norma again tries to communicate with Mimsey by knocking on the locked door, Mimsey passes a note under the door. *Left,* Norma reads it: "I would rather talk to daddy." Disheveled but touched, Roy goes to the door and is admitted for a conference with his daughter.

After talking with Mimsey, Roy reports *(right)* that she has panicked because she fears what she and her groom, Borden, "may become" in marriage. Norma doubts that she and Roy have set so bad an example of wife and husband. In any case, Mimsey wants to talk to Borden.

Borden (Bob Balaban, *below left*) is sent for. Roy explains the situation to him. Borden crosses and speaks a terse, sensible order through the bathroom door, then turns and leaves the suite, confident that the bride will follow.

Borden was right. Two short words from the groom have accomplished what parental ire and cajolery could not. The bride (Claudette Nevins, *below*) emerges from her seclusion. . . . .

. . . . . and the Hubley-Eisler wedding is ready to take place as planned. *Curtain*.

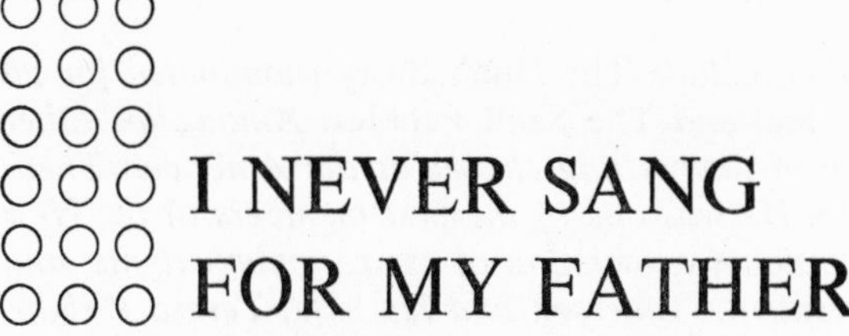

I NEVER SANG FOR MY FATHER

A Play in Two Acts

BY ROBERT ANDERSON

Cast and credits appear on page 359

ROBERT ANDERSON is a native New Yorker born April 28, 1917. At Harvard (B.A. 1939, M.A. 1940, Ph.D. 1942) he wrote, acted in and directed plays, wrote drama criticism and taught drama and writing. In the Navy in World War II he won the National Theater Conference Award for the best play written by a service man overseas. After about 70 radio and television scripts, he made his Broadway debut as the author of Tea and Sympathy, *September 30, 1953.* Tea and Sympathy *ran 712 performances, was named a Best Play of its season and appeared in a movie version for which Anderson wrote the screen play.*

Anderson became a member of the Playwrights Company, an association of leading Broadway playwrights, which produced his next two Broadway scripts: All Summer Long *(1954) and* Silent Night, Lonely Night *(1959). In the season of 1965-66 his play* The Days Between *was chosen by the American Playwrights Theater circuit for production in college and community theaters around the country. Anderson made the Best Plays list last season with* You Know I Can't Hear You When the Water's Running, *so that he is the only two-in-a-row repeater among the Best Play authors in this 1967-68 volume.*

Anderson's screen play credits include The Nun's Story *(nominated for an Academy Award),* Until They Sail *and* The Sand Pebbles. *Among his other achievements was the initiating of playwriting classes at the American Theater Wing and the Actors Studio. He was one of the first members of the New Dramatists Committee, a professional association of aspiring playwrights, and he served for a time as its president. Anderson and his wife, Teresa Wright, live in Connecticut.*

INTRODUCTION BY THE PLAYWRIGHT

Every play has its bizarre and possibly interesting footnotes as to how it was written and how it got produced. *I Never Sang for My Father* is no exception.

Back in 1962 I was momentarily fed up with the theater. Leland Hayward had one of my plays under option (*The Days Between*), and we were running into an absurd series of problems finding a cast and a director. For example, we had an excellent director. We submitted the play to a brilliant actress who liked the play very much and expressed her almost-willingness to do it, but she wouldn't do the play with the director we had. Because I think directors should choose actors, I stayed with my director. Two months later, the director departed. This was just the beginning.

At any rate, I was fed up with the theater. While waiting for some word on the play, I had seen a number of movies which I had liked, among them *A Taste of Honey* and *The Loneliness of the Long Distance Runner.* I decided that I would take a crack at writing my first original movie (I had written a few screen adaptations before). And so I wrote the story of an 80-year-old man and his 40-year-old son and called it *The Tiger.*

The summer of 1962 my wife, Teresa Wright, was starting out with the national tour of *Mary, Mary* on the West Coast. One Sunday night, Fred Zinnemann was with us for dinner, and he told me that his plans for directing *Hawaii* had hit a snag and did I have anything in mind that we might do together in the immediate future? (I had written the screenplay for Zinnemann for *The Nun's Story.*) I had just finished typing *The Tiger,* and I gave the script to him. He was leaving for England the next day, but he said he would read it on the plane.

Two days later, Fred called from London to say that he liked the script and wanted to do it if Spencer Tracy would play the old man.

While we were waiting word from Tracy, I sent the script to a few friends who usually read everything I write soon after it is written. Elia Kazan is one of these friends. He wrote me from Europe to say that he felt *The Tiger* was my best piece of work and if Fred Zinnemann didn't want to go ahead with it, would I consider turning it into a play for Lincoln Center Repertory, plans for which were just getting under way. Robert Whitehead also read the script and concurred in Kazan's feelings.

Spencer Tracy decided he did not want to play the old man, and I told

Kazan and Whitehead that I would hold up on further submissions until they knew their plans. After a number of months, I met with them, and they told me that they had formed their company and they didn't feel they had the actor to play the old man.

John Frankenheimer had asked to see the script if the Zinnemann and Lincoln Center plans fell through. John called me from the desert where he was shooting *Seven Days in May* to say that he was very excited about the script and he had given it to Fredric March and they were definitely going to do it together, with Freddie's wife, Florence Eldridge, playing the mother. This delighted me, and I went on with my other projects, waiting for John to finish *Seven Days in May* and to make some kind of production plans for *The Tiger*.

Months later, I received a letter from John's secretary saying that John had left for Europe to take over the direction of *The Train* and he would be in touch with me on his return. I wrote to John and asked him what plans he had for *The Tiger,* and he wrote that he had just taken on four or five major productions and he didn't feel he could commit for it, and he didn't want to keep me waiting.

Two other well-known directors became enthusiastic, made plans, held conferences, but nothing ever came of it all, and I finally sent the script to Nan Talese, my editor at Random House. She urged me to turn it into a novel. When things have gone badly for me in the theater, I have often thought of writing a novel, but I am afraid that it is not just *writing* that interests me, but it is specifically writing in the dramatic form.

When I had written another screen adaptation and had again earned myself the luxury of writing for the theater, I went back to *The Tiger* and decided to turn it into a play. When it was finished, I changed the title to *I Never Sang for My Father,* because Murray Schisgal had come out with a play called *The Tiger*.

The play was turned down by every producer who read it. Many of them admired it. Some found it "shattering," but felt that a Broadway audience did not want to be "shattered."

While *I Never Sang for My Father* was still being circulated, I wrote *You Know I Can't Hear You When the Water's Running*. This evening of one-act plays also started to make the rounds, and like *I Never Sang for My Father,* it was turned down by every producer who read it. We felt we had exhausted the list of producers who might be interested in either play; and, needless to say, I was very depressed. Then my agent, Audrey Wood, sent *You Know I Can't Hear You* to a television producer who had never produced on Broadway, Jack Farren. He liked the one-acts, and he and his partner, Gilbert Cates, took them on for production.

When *You Know I Can't Hear You* was successful, Gilbert Cates decided he wanted to produce *I Never Sang for My Father*. Alan Schneider, who had directed the one-act plays, said he would like to direct it. I was delighted.

At this exact moment I had a telephone call from an old friend in California, Martin Manulis. I had written some television shows for him years ago, and a film on Dr. Tom Dooley which had never been produced. Manulis told me that CBS had engaged him to produce a television special and he wanted to do *The Tiger,* and that Spencer Tracy now wanted to play the old man and that it was fairly sure that Katharine Hepburn would play the mother! I asked him to give me a few days to think. Gilbert Cates was very understanding about it. No contracts had been signed. I knew he would have trouble casting and raising money for a play like this, and I finally told Manulis he could go ahead and do it on television with Tracy and Hepburn. He also wanted my wife, Teresa Wright, to play the sister (She had originated the part of Annie Sullivan in *The Miracle Worker* when it was done on "Playhouse 90" before it was done on Broadway). He would also try to get Richard Widmark, who had always been interested in playing the middle-aged son. A week later, Manulis called back to say that CBS had turned down the whole project because it was too grim.

And that is how it came about that *I Never Sang for My Father* opened at the Longacre Theater on January 25, 1968, starring Hal Holbrook, Alan Webb, Teresa Wright and Lillian Gish, directed by Alan Schneider.

When young playwrights say to me, "Oh, but you have it easy. You can always get your plays produced," I tell them this story. It seems to comfort them. It does not comfort me. Just re-telling it here makes me wonder about the wisdom of starting a new play.

ROBERT ANDERSON

Time: The present and the past

Place: New York City and a town in Westchester County

ACT I

SYNOPSIS: Gene Garrison, 40, well dressed, has come to Pennsylvania Station, New York City, to meet his mother and father, who are arriving on a train from Florida.

This and other settings are suggested by a fixed, triple-arched architectural shape. The center arch is open to the cylorama, but the side arches are screened to carry symbolic light projections which change as the play's locale changes. The few necessary props come on and off from behind these screens on turntables. *"With a few exceptions, the scenes are intended to cross-fade into one another, the lights going down on one area and coming up immediately on another area. . . . . Lighting is the chief means for setting the stage."*

A porter reassures Gene that he will meet him on the platform, so that Gene is able to relax for a moment. He comes downstage and addresses the audience.

GENE: Death ends a life, but it does not end a relationship, which struggles on in the survivor's mind towards some final resolution, some clear meaning, which it perhaps never finds. . . . . My mother read a great deal, liked to play bridge and chatter and laugh gaily with "the girls" . . . make her eyes sparkle in a way she had and pretend that she had not had two operations for cancer, three heart attacks, and painful arthritis . . . She used to say, "Old age takes courage." She had it. My father, though he had never been in the Service, had the air of a retired brigadier general. He read the newspapers, all editions, presumably to help him make decisions about his investments. He watched Westerns on television and told anyone who would listen the story of his life. I loved my mother . . . I wanted to love my father . . .

The lights come up on another area of the stage, where the Porter is already standing with the wheelchair and baggage cart . . .

Tom Garrison is standing amidst suitcases which have been piled up on the platform . . . He is a handsome man, almost 80 . . . erect in his bearing, neat in his dress. He speaks distinctly, and when he is irritated his voice takes on a hard, harsh edge.

At the moment, he is irritated, slightly bewildered, on the brink of exasperation.

TOM: We had four bags. I don't see any of them. We had one in the compartment with us. That can't have been lost.

He fumes for a moment . . . As Gene watches his father for a moment, we can see in his face something of his feelings of tension. On the surface he shows great kindness and consideration for the old man . . . underneath, there is usually considerable strain.

GENE: Hello, Dad.

Tom's face lights up at the sight of his son (Tom had forgotten Gene was going to meet the train, though Gene had written him about it; Tom forgets things easily nowadays). Tom frets about the bags, but Gene assures his father it will be all right, he has even brought a wheel chair for Mother. Tom has one of his coughing fits, then resumes fussing about the bags (he's looking for his old brown bag, forgetting that Gene gave him a new gray one for this trip).

The porter is amused, Gene annoyed at his father's stubborn anxiety about lost luggage. Gene takes the wheelchair to another part of the stage where his mother, Margaret Garrison, is sitting.

Margaret is waiting patiently. She is 78 . . . still a pretty woman. She has great spirit, and a smile that lights up her whole face. She is a good sport about her problems . . . When she is put out she says "darn" and not "damn" . . . She is devoted to her son, but she is not the possessive and smothering mother. She is wearing a white orchid on her mink stole.

Margaret embraces her son . . . she was so proud of her Easter orchid that she made it last until now so that Gene, who gave it to her, could see how carefully she had kept it.

Margaret is concerned about her husband Tom's health and feels he should see a doctor.

MARGARET: . . . . . He's got me sick with worry. *(She starts to cry.)*

GENE *(comforts her):* I'll get him to a doctor, Mother. Don't you worry.

MARGARET: He makes me so mad. He coughs all night and keeps us both awake. Poor man, he's skin and bone . . . And he's getting so forgetful. This morning he woke up here on the train and he asked me where we were going.

GENE: Well, Mother, he's almost eighty.

MARGARET: Oh, I know and he's a remarkable man. Stands so straight. Everyone down there always comments on how handsome your father is . . . But I've given up. You get him to a doctor.

GENE: I've got a wheel chair for you, Mother. Save you the long walk up the ramp.

MARGARET: Oh, my precious. What would we ever do without you?

GENE *(is always embarrassed by these expressions of love and gratitude):* Oh, you manage pretty well.

Gene helps his mother into the chair and joins Tom, who is still fussing about a missing bag. Gene explains the arrangements he has made to drive his parents home to Westchester in his car. Tom tries to rearrange the plans and give new directions, but Gene gently resists his father's interference. All but Gene exit, with Tom still keeping a suspicious eye on the luggage.

His parents live in a Westchester suburb (Gene explains to the audience) in a mushrooming town of which his father was once the mayor. The Garrisons' house is one of the dowdy survivors of a more gracious era.

Tom and Margaret (now drifting back onstage) are living the experience of homecoming, checking on everything, commenting. Tom expects only the worst, but everything seems to be as they had left it. Margaret, more cheerful, goes to inspect her garden.

TOM *(intense . . . he has been waiting for someone to say this to):* I tell you, the strain has been awful.

GENE: She looks well.

TOM: I know. But you never know when she might get another one of those damned seizures. *(He looks at the ground and shakes his head at the problem of it all.)*

GENE *(pats his father's shoulder):* It's rough. I know.

TOM: Well, we'll manage. She's a good soldier. But you know, she eats too fast. The doctor said she must slow down. But not your mother . . . Incidentally, don't forget she has a birthday coming up.

GENE *(knows it's his mother's birthday, and hates being reminded of it each year):* Yes, I know.

As he has done for years, Tom is planning to buy handkerchiefs as his present to Margaret. Gene takes this opportunity to urge his father to consult the doctor. Tom promises to see the doctor—tomorrow. But he appreciates Gene's concern.

Tom urges Gene to stay for supper because, as he says, Margaret "has missed you a lot." To Tom's delight, Gene is planning to take them out to Schrafft's. Tom brings up the subject of Gene's recent visit to California, and his letters which mentioned a woman Gene had met there.

TOM: You seemed to see a lot of her.

GENE: Yes . . . I did.

TOM: Carol's been dead now . . . what is it?

GENE: About a year.

TOM: And there's no reason why you shouldn't go out with other women . . .

Gene just waits.

I was in California with the Senator . . . and before that. It's a perfectly beautiful place. I can understand your enthusiasm for it. Gorgeous place.

GENE: Yes. I like it a lot.

TOM: But listen, Gene . . . *(He bites his upper lip . . . and his voice is heavy with emotion.)* If you were to go out there, I mean, to live . . . it would kill your mother.

He looks at his son with piercing eyes . . . tears starting . . . This has been in the nature of a plea and an order. Gene says nothing . . . He is angry at this order . . . that his father would say such a thing.

God, you know you're her whole life.

Gene is further embarrassed and troubled by this statement of what he knows to be the truth . . . from his father.

Yes, you are! Oh, she likes your sister. But you . . . are . . . her . . . life!

GENE: Dad, we've always been fond of each other, but—

TOM: Just remember what I said.

Margaret joins them and asks Gene for a big hug and kiss, as though confirming what Tom has just said about her devotion to her son. They move on to Schrafft's, where Tom flirts with the waitress Mary, as is his habit. The men order martinis (Tom commands them six-to-one), and Tom for the nth time shows Gene the diamond ring he inherited from the Senator.

Tom challenges Gene as to who is going to pay for the dinner, but Gene insists: even though he is on sabbatical, and therefore on half salary, this is his treat. Gene coaxes his father to order what he wants without looking at the prices, for once.

Margaret points out a friend at another table whose wife died while they were away in Florida. Tom accuses her of morbidity. But Margaret goes on: she can never invite anyone over to the house because Tom is either watching Westerns or pressing on visitors detailed reminiscences of his life—in which, Tom argues, "they seem to be interested."

It is almost a quarrel. They try to draw Gene into it, but he holds back. Margaret continues: Tom is always telling people the story of his mother's funeral. Tom argues that all Margaret likes to do is gossip and play cards (still Gene refuses to take sides).

Margaret repeats: Tom is always telling people about barring his father from his mother's funeral.

TOM: —He'd run out on us when we were kids, and I told him—

MARGARET: —I'm not saying you were wrong. You're so defensive about it. I'm saying you're wrong to keep bringing it up.

TOM: You brought it up this time.

MARGARET: Well, I'm sorry. Imagine going around telling everyone he shoved his father off the funeral couch.

She is consulting the menu.

TOM: And I'd do it again. I was only ten, but I'd do it again . . . We hadn't seen him in over a year, living, the four of us, in a miserable two-room tenement, and suddenly he shows up weeping and begging, and drunk, as usual. And I shoved him off! *(He almost relives it.)* I never saw him again till some years later when he was dying in Bellevue . . . of drink. *(The hatred and anger are held in, but barely.)*

MARGARET *(has been studying the menu):* What looks good to you?

TOM *(a hard sharp edge to his voice):* I have not finished! I went down to see him, to ask him if he wanted anything. He said he wanted an orange. I sent him in a half dozen oranges. I would have sent more, except I knew he was dying and there was no point in just giving a lot of oranges to the nurses. The next morning he died.

There is a silence for a moment, while Gene and Margaret look at the menu, and Tom grips and ungrips his hand in memory of his hatred for his father.

Mary's arrival with the martinis lightens the situation. Tom snaps out of his mood and flirts again with Mary. But Margaret makes it clear that in her opinion Tom is making a fool of himself with this flirting. Tom is angry and hurt and wants Gene to take his side, but Gene refuses.

The scene moves from Schraffts (where Tom ate only his dessert then rushed home, which is just down the street, to doze in front of his favorite TV Western) to the sidewalk where Gene and his mother stroll, talking.

Margaret reminds Gene that he should be proud of his father, who has devoted his life to his family. "So he didn't dance with me at parties. You took care of that." Only because she was a great dancer, Gene assures his mother. Margaret finally comments: "What a shame that children can't see their parents when they're young and courting, and in love. All they see them being is tolerant, sympathetic, forbearing and devoted. All the qualities that are so unimportant to passionate young people."

Now they are home, and Tom calls for Gene to come watch the Western. But Margaret still has a good deal on her mind and takes Gene to her room. To Gene's acute embarrassment, she reminds her son of the days when they would listen to opera broadcasts together here in this room, and Gene would dress up and act out characters like d'Artagnan.

What Margaret really wants to talk about, though, is California. She has an intuition that Gene loves the woman he wrote to them about, and Gene believes that he does.

MARGARET *(fidgets a moment from embarrassment, then):* I know it's not a mother's place to pry and talk about these things . . . But I've been worried about you, I mean, you're a man . . . and . . . well . . . sex.

GENE *(smiles):* I'm . . . all right.

MARGARET: You mean you've been . . . communicating?

GENE *(broad smile):* Yes . . . I've been . . . communicating.

MARGARET: You don't mind my talking about that, do you?

GENE *(amused and a little embarrassed):* No.

MARGARET: I'll never understand your generation, I guess. I'm glad I didn't have to face all . . . well, all that, in my day. People simply waited. And I'm not so sure we weren't right.

GENE *(not wanting to go into it):* Well . . .

MARGARET: Too late for me to worry about that now. Though sometimes I wish I'd known more . . . understood more.

Stops . . . embarrassed. Gene is sad and uncomfortable that his 78-year-old mother would seem to want to talk to someone at last about her unsatisfactory sex life . . . The moment passes.

Margaret has guessed that Gene wants to marry the girl he met in California—Peggy—and move out there to a new life. Selflessly she urges him to do so. She can see him, or phone him often enough, as in the case of Gene's sister Alice, who lives in Chicago.

Margaret takes Gene's hand to thank him for having been such a devoted son. Gene gave her the companionship she craved when Gene's father "withdrew behind his investments and golf."

MARGARET: . . . . . I tried not to be one of those possessive mothers, Gene. If I did things wrong, I just did the best I knew how.

GENE: You did everything just fine.

He pats his mother's hand before he draws his own away.

MARGARET: And your father has done the best he knew how.

GENE: Yes.

This is her old song. She knows that Gene knows it's probably true, but he gets no satisfaction from the knowledge.

MARGARET: Of course you know your father will object to your going away.

GENE: He already has. He said it would kill you.

MARGARET: How sad. Why can't he say it would kill him. He doesn't think it would hold you or mean anything to you. *(She shakes her head.)* He dotes on your letters down there. Reads them and re-reads them. Tells everyone what a fine relationship he has with you. "My door is always open . . ." ". . . Anything he wants, he can have . . ." ". . . We have always had each other's confidence."

Gene smiles at this, sadly shakes his head . . .

Well, you go to California. Your father and I can take care of each other. I'll remember where he put his checkbook, and he'll make the beds, which is the only thing I'm really not supposed to do. . . . .

Efficiently, Margaret has already picked out her nursing home, so she won't be a burden to her children, no matter what. Margaret offers to break the news about California and Peggy gently to Tom, but Gene wants to tell his father himself in a few days.

They make plans for Margaret's birthday—she begs Gene to buy no more handkerchiefs, whatever Tom says. She wants perfume for a change.

Gene leaves his mother and goes to his father, who is asleep in front of the TV set. Gene wakes up Tom to say goodbye, and Tom reacts at once in the fashion that so irritates Gene: he tries to persuade his son to stay longer.

TOM: . . . . . Why don't you just stay for this show?

GENE *(the anger building):* No, Dad. I've got to run along.

TOM: Well, all right. We see so little of you.

GENE: I'm up at least once a week, Dad.

TOM: Oh, I'm not complaining. *(But he is.)* There just doesn't seem to be any time . . . And when you are here, your mother's doing all the talking . . . The way she interrupts. She just doesn't listen. And I say, "Margaret, please." . . . But she goes right on . . . Well, all's lost, all's spent, when we our desires get without content . . . 'tis better to be that which we destroy, than by destruction dwell with doubtful joy.

Gene is always puzzled by his father's frequent use of this quotation . . . It never is immediately appropriate, but it indicates such unhappiness that it is sad and touching to him.

GENE: We'll get a chance to talk, Dad.

Moves toward porch.

TOM: I can't tell you what a comfort it is knowing you are just down in the city. Don't know what we'd do without you . . . No hat or coat?

Tom directs Gene to dress carefully, and Gene directs Tom to take care of his cough. Tom wants a word about Gene's next visit and harps on Mother's Day and Mother's birthday, as though Mother were the only reason for Gene to come and see them.

Tom urges Gene to drive carefully and gives him directions for returning along a way he has driven for 20 years. "Just trying to be helpful," Tom adds as Gene departs.

Gene faces the audience and comments: "Take your first left and your second right . . . then turn left under the bridge . . . But do not go as far as California . . . because it would kill your mother . . . I hated him for that, for sending up warning flares that if I left, it would not be with his blessing, but with a curse . . . as he had banished my sister Alice, years ago, for marrying a Jew . . . and the scene so terrified me at fourteen, I was sick . . . He knew his man . . . that part of me at least . . . a gentleman who gave way at intersections. . . . ."

Gene's reflections are interrupted by an emergency phone call from his father. Margaret has suffered a heart attack and has been rushed to the hospital.

Gene joins his father at the hospital—for the moment Margaret is sleeping quietly. While he was waiting, Tom saw the doctor about his cough and was given a shot. Tom is half-shaken, half-puzzled by his wife's illness; he worries over *why* it happened—maybe she's been eating too fast—but seems only perfunctorily aware that it *has* happened.

Tom reflects that he wishes he'd spent more time with Margaret during their Florida visit (Margaret was drawn to bridge-playing and ladies' chatter). Then Tom plunges into an incongruous reminiscence about his first love, which was broken up almost before it began.

Gene is touched by this memory—and almost immediately Tom changes the subject, suggesting (to Gene's astonishment under the circumstances) that while Margaret sleeps they should attend the Rotary Club dinner. Gene sees that his father is serious and agrees to go with him.

At the Rotary Club gathering, suggested onstage by tinkle of glasses and hum of voices, Tom introduces Gene to their minister, Dr. Pell, and manages to work into the conversation proudly (to Gene's embarrassment) that Gene was a Marine who "saw the flag go up on Iwo." After complaining to the minister about overcrowding in his church pew, Tom orders his usual, a six-to-one-martini.

Tom slips so easily into the role of hail-fellow-well-met-at-Rotary that he seems almost callously indifferent to Margaret's illness—until a friend asks him the automatic question.

MARVIN: How's Margaret?

Tom goes very dramatic . . . pauses for a moment and bites his lip. Marvin looks at Gene.

GENE: Mother's . . .

TOM: Margaret's in an oxygen tent in the hospital.

MARVIN *(surprised that Tom is here . . . looks at Gene . . . then at Tom):* I'm terribly sorry to hear that, Tom.

TOM: Heart. *(He shakes his head and starts to get emotional.)*

GENE *(embarrassed):* We're just going to grab a bite and get back. Mother's sleeping, and if we were there, she'd want to talk.

MARVIN: I'm sorry to hear that, Tom . . . When did it happen?

TOM *(striving for control . . . his emotion is as much anger that it could happen . . . and self-pity . . . as anything else . . .):* This morning . . . I was in the kitchen, getting something for Margaret, when suddenly I heard her scream . . . "Tom . . . Tom . . ." and I ran upstairs . . . and there she was stretched out on the bedroom floor . . . "Nitro . . . nitro" . . . she said . . . We have nitroglycerine all over the house, you know . . . since her last two attacks . . . So, I get her the nitro and call the doctor . . . and now she's in an oxygen tent in the hospital . . .

The bell starts to ring to call them to table . . .

MARVIN: Well, I hope everything's all right . . . Tom . . .

GENE: Thank you . . .

TOM: What happened to those martinis? . . . We've got to go into dinner and we haven't gotten them yet.

GENE: We can take them to the table with us.

TOM: I have to drink mine before I eat anything . . . It brings up the gas . . . Where the hell are they?

At the hospital a nurse is sitting with Margaret. The oxygen tent has been moved away. Gene and Tom come in, and Gene goes to the bedside to reassure his mother: she is on the mend, and she need not worry about Tom, who has been treated for his cough. It was worrying about Tom (Margaret indicates) that brought on the attack.

Tom approaches the bed, and his attempts to be cheerful and jocular are all too obvious. Margaret gives instructions about bringing some of her things to the hospital. She was rushed here in her slip, without even a nightgown. Gene takes note of her wishes and admires the flowers sent by his sister Alice.

Dr. Mayberry comes into the room and insists on being heartily optimistic; Margaret has had a bad attack, but the worst seems to be over now. The doctor also assures Gene there's nothing seriously wrong with his father—just a cough. Dr. Mayberry suggests that Tom and Gene leave so that Margaret can rest. They say their goodnights with a cheer that is a bit forced, but with a warmth of affection that is not.

They are on their way home when Tom asks Gene, "Do you remember what she asked us to bring her? My mind is like a sieve." While speaking of household matters, Tom indicates that he expects Gene to stay for the night.

GENE: I . . . uh . . . I've got an early appointment at college tomorrow.

TOM: I thought you were on your sabbatical.

GENE: I am . . . But I arranged a meeting with someone there, Dad.

TOM: You could stay and still make it.

GENE: It's very early, Dad.

TOM: We've got an alarm. Alarm clocks all over the house.

GENE: I want to change before the appointment . . . shirt . . .

TOM: I've got plenty of shirts . . . underwear . . . socks . . .

GENE *(more uncomfortable):* I don't wear your sizes, Dad.

TOM: I could get you up earlier, then. I don't sleep beyond five these days.

GENE *(tense):* No, Dad . . . I just . . . No. I'll come by and—

TOM: There may be something good on television . . . Wednesday night. I think there is . . .

GENE: . . . We'll watch a little television, Dad . . . and have some drinks . . . But then I'll have to go.

TOM *(after a moment):* All right, old man.

Gene instinctively reaches out to touch his father's arm, to soften the rejection—They look at each other a moment, then Tom drifts off into the dark, as Gene moves directly downstage . . .

GENE: I sat with my father. Much longer than I meant to . . . Because I knew I should stay the night. But . . . I couldn't . . . We watched television. He slept on and off . . . and I went home . . . The next morning, around nine-thirty, my mother died . . .

Gene turns and walks upstage, as the lights dim. Curtain.

ACT II

Gene is carrying a small overnight case with his mother's things. Dr. Mayberry is advising him that it was not worry over Tom that caused the heart trouble—Margaret had been "living on borrowed time for quite a while." And Dr. Mayberry reassures Gene that Tom will come through this sad experience: "Old people live with death. He's been prepared for this for years. It may in some way be a relief. He's taken wonderful care of her." Dr. Mayberry is glad to hear that Gene has called his sister Alice to come East, because Tom "shouldn't be staying in that house alone."

Gene asks Dr. Mayberry to replace the wedding ring (which he gives to the doctor) on his mother's hand.

At the undertaker's office, Gene joins his father who is attended by a nurse (Tom has been given a sedative). Somewhat to Gene's annoyance in these tragic circumstances, Tom is joking with the nurse about Florida; flirting with her, almost. *"Obviously there is to be no sharing of the experience of the mother's death."*

The nurse departs, and the undertaker, Mr. Scott, enters. He is gentle and considerate throughout the difficult process of making arrangements. Margaret is to be buried in the family plot where Gene's wife was buried the year before *("Tom reaches out and puts his hand on Gene's arm . . . implying that they have something to share. Gene doesn't really want to share his father's kind of emotionalism.")*

There are such details to be decided as open or closed casket and the wording of an obituary notice. But Tom cannot keep his mind on these matters.

TOM: —She was my inspiration. When I met her, the clouds hung low and dark. I was going to night school, studying shorthand and typing and *elocution* . . . and working in a lumber yard in the daytime . , . wearing a cutaway coat, if you please, someone at the church had given me . . . I was making a home for my brother and sister . . . my mother had died, and my father had deserted us . . .

He has gone hard on his father . . . and stops a moment . . .

"He did not know the meaning of the word 'quit'." They said that some years ago when The Schoolboys of Old Harlem gave me an award. You were there, Gene?

GENE: Yes.

TOM: "Obstructions, yes. But go through them or over them, but never around them." Teddy Roosevelt said that, I took it down in shorthand for practise . . . Early in life I developed a will of iron . . .

You can feel the iron the way he says it.

"Any young man in this country, who has a sound mind and a sound body, who will set himself an objective, can achieve anything he wants within reason."

He has said all this firmly, as though lecturing or giving a speech. He now looks at his cigarette.

Ugh . . . Filthy habit. Twenty years ago a doctor told me to give these things up, and I did. But when things pile up . . . Well . . . All's lost, all's spent, when we our desires get without content.

They must face the necessity of choosing a coffin (the many different showroom samples are symbolized by oblong projections of light on the stage floor). Tom and Gene move among them learning about different prices and construction.

A child's coffin brings back to Tom a tearful memory of his mother's funeral—"My mother would have fit in that . . . she was a little bit of a thing"—and barring his own father from the ceremony. Finally Tom faces the bewildering choice, picking a coffin for its moderate price and gray color; then he moves back to the child's coffin and returns to his reverie of the past.

The scene changes to a bar where Gene is blowing off steam with his sister Alice, who has come on from Chicago for the funeral. Gene is irritated because, instead of thinking of Margaret, Tom keeps thinking of himself and his problems "when the clouds hung low and dark"—and friends keep remarking, not that Margaret was a remarkable woman, but that Tom is a remarkable man.

Gene remembers all too well the un-remarkable behavior of his father the night he kicked Alice out of the house for marrying a Jew. Gene remembers the shouting and the tension. Alice comments: "I shouted, and you threw up. That was pretty much the pattern."

GENE *(touches her arm, smiles):* Mother loved your flowers.

ALICE: I've felt guilty about Mother, all the way coming here. I should have seen her more, invited her more often, brought the kids more often. Instead, I sent flowers.

GENE: I guess that's an inevitable feeling when a person dies. I feel the same way.

ALICE: But you were so good to her. You made her life.

GENE *(has always hated that phrase . . . slowly, quietly):* A son is not supposed to make his mother's life . . . Oh, I loved Mother. You know that. But to be depended on to make her life . . . Dad says, he boasts, he never knew the meaning of the word "quit". Well, he quit on her all right. And I . . . I was just there.

Alice looks at this sudden revelation of his feelings, his resentment and that he was left to save his mother from loneliness and unhappiness.

Still, wait till you see him. There's something that comes through . . . the old Tiger. Something that reaches you and makes you want to cry . . . He'll probably be asleep when we get home, in front of television. And you'll see. The Old Man . . . the Father. But then he wakes up and becomes Tom Garrison, and I'm in trouble . . . Last night he asked me to stay with him, and I didn't . . . I couldn't. I'm ashamed of that now.

ALICE *(touched by the complexity of Gene's feelings, looks at him a long moment, then . . .):* Have you called California?

GENE *(frowns . . . a problem):* No.

He takes a drink, wanting to avoid the subject.

They realize that they're going to have a problem with Tom, but for the moment they avoid that subject too.

Gene and Alice return to the Garrison house to find that Tom is indeed a touching Father figure, innocently asleep in front of the TV. They wake him, and it takes him time to return to the world; to remember what has happened, and why Alice is here.

At Margaret's graveside, the family and a few friends gather to hear the service conducted by Dr. Pell. Gene turns away from the ceremony to explain why there are so few people in attendance: most of Margaret's friends are dead.

The ceremony over, the guests and Dr. Pell drift off while Tom examines the family plot. Then, dissatisfied with the way it is being kept up, Tom goes off to register a complaint. Gene and Alice move to another outdoor area with a bench and slowly begin to make plans for the future.

Alice advises Gene to go ahead and marry Peggy and move to California, but she lays her cards on the table: "It would be murder" if Tom came to live with her family in Chicago. Gene agrees "That would never work" but adds: "I can't tell you what it does to me as a man . . . to see someone like that . . . a man who was distinguished, remarkable . . . just become a nuisance."

They discuss the possibility of an old folks' home, or a full-time housekeeper. Alice learns that Gene hasn't yet phoned Peggy in California, even to report his mother's death. Alice fears that Gene is being slowly trapped and urges him to get away. Gene reminds Alice of all their father has done for them over the years, but his plea falls on unsympathetic ears.

ALICE: . . . . . We might as well face it, his mind's going. Sooner or later we'll have to think about powers of attorney, perhaps committing him to an institution.

GENE: God, it's all so ugly.

ALICE *(smiling):* Yes, my gentle Gene . . . a lot of life is.

GENE: Now, look, don't go trying to make me out some softhearted . . . *(He can't find the word.)* I know life is ugly.

ALICE: Yes, I think you know it. You've lived through a great deal of ugliness. But you work like a Trojan to deny it, to make it not so.

After a moment . . . not arguing.

He kicked me out. He said he never wanted to see me again. He broke Mother's heart over that for years. He was mean . . . unloving . . . He beat the hell out of you when you were a kid . . . You've hated and feared him all your adult life . . .

GENE *(cutting in):* Still, he's my father, and a man. And what's happening to him appals me as a man.

ALICE: We have a practical problem here.

GENE: It's not as simple as all that.

ALICE: To me it is. I don't understand this mystical haze you're casting over it. I'm going to talk to him tomorrow, after the session with the lawyer, about a housekeeper.

Gene reacts but says nothing.

Just let me handle it. He can visit us, and we can take turns coming to visit him. Now, I'll do the dirty work. Only when he turns to you, don't give in.

GENE: I can't tell you how ashamed I feel . . . not to say with open arms, "Poppa come live with me . . . I love you, Poppa, and I want to take care of you." . . . I need to love him. I've always wanted to love him.

He drops his arms and wanders off.

Back at the Garrison house, they are sorting out Margaret's things. Tom is answering letters of condolence, and somehow his words instead of being about Margaret turn to a description of his own life and career . . .

Alice and Gene know that the time has come to face the future. Alice's approach to the subject is forthright; Gene is very gentle. Tom intends to keep on living in this house, making do for himself. Alice tells him they are worried about his health, he shouldn't be here alone, he should have a full-time housekeeper. This suggestion angers Tom—first, because it sounds improper, and second, because it demeans him. Angrily he tells his children he's been taking care of himself since he was eight years old, he has hired and fired thousands of people, and he'll run his own household now.

Alice points out to her father that it is dangerous for him to be alone, he has dizzy spells. Tom denies this (rising from his chair and suffering slight dizziness). He'll be all right if only Gene will look in on him from time to time.

TOM: . . . . . I imagine we could have dinner every once in a while, couldn't we, Gene . . . Once a week or so. Take you up to Rotary. Some of the speakers are quite amusing.

Alice looks at Gene to see if he is going to speak up.

GENE: Sure, Dad.

TOM: Give us some time together at last . . . get to know each other.

ALICE *(quietly but firmly):* Gene wants to get married.

GENE: Alice!

TOM: What?

ALICE: Gene wants to move to California and get married.

GENE: Alice, shut up.

ALICE *(almost in tears):* I can't help it. You've never faced up to him. You'd let him ruin your life.

GENE *(angry):* I can take care of my own life.

ALICE: You can't!

TOM *(loud):* Children! . . . Children!

They stop arguing and turn to their father at his command.

(A note of sarcasm.) I have no desire to interfere with either of your lives. I took care of myself at eight. I can take care of myself at eighty. I have never wanted to be a burden to my children.

GENE: I'm going to hang around, Dad.

TOM: There's no need to.

GENE: I'll move in here at least till you're feeling better.

Alice turns away, angry and despairing.

Tom continues in a sarcastic vein—he had always known his only value to the family was as a breadwinner. His anger makes him dizzy but he manages to retain control and assures Alice, icily, that she may go, they will continue to get along without her: "You chose to lead your own life. Well, we won't keep you now."

Tom dares them to call him incompetent and goes off, leaving them together.

Gene accuses Alice of trying to destroy Tom instead of helping him. Alice accuses Gene of cowardice in confronting their father: "You shrank." Gene replies: "I shrank at the ugliness of what was happening."

To Alice, Tom is merely "an unreasonable old man," but Gene's conscience will not allow him to dismiss the problem so easily, nor could he forgive himself if the old man were to die neglected, no matter how coldly Tom seems to reject his children's help.

Alice insists that Tom is not going to ruin *her* life. Gene insists that he knows what he must do.

GENE: . . . . . I never had a father . . . I ran away from him . . . He ran away from me . . . Maybe he's right. Maybe it is time we found each other.

ALICE: I find that sentimental crap! . . . I think this is all rationalization to make tolerable a compulsion you have to stay here. You hate the compulsion, so you've dressed it up to look nice.

GENE: How do you know what you're saying isn't a rationalization to cover up a callousness, a selfishness, a coldness in yourself. To make *it* smell nice?

ALICE: What do you think you'll find?

GENE: I don't know.

ALICE: You hope to find love. Couldn't you tell from what he just said what you're going to find? Don't you understand he's got to hate you? He may not think it in his head or feel it in his heart, but you are his enemy! From the moment you were born a boy, you were a threat to this man and his enemy.

GENE: That sounds like the textbooks, Alice.

ALICE: He wants your balls . . . and he's had them!

Gene . . . . . starts to leave the room.

I'm sorry. I want to shock you. When has he ever regarded you as a man, an equal, a male? When you were a Marine. And that you did for him. Because even back there you were looking for his love. You didn't want to be a Marine. "Now, Poppa, will you love me?" And he did. No, not love. But he was proud and grateful because you gave him an extension of himself he could boast about, with his phony set of values . . . When was he ever proud about the thing *you* do? The things *you* value? When did he ever mention your teaching or your books, except in scorn?

GENE: You don't seem to have felt the absence of a father. But I feel incomplete . . . deprived . . . I just do not want to let my father die a stranger to me.

Alice accuses Gene of looking for soft mother-love in a father, whereas "fathers are hard and rough." She learned this lesson from Tom, and it taught her that the world, too, is a hard place; she's grateful for the lesson (but making this statement leads her to tears).

Alice warns Gene not to lose Peggy, who is coming on from California soon. Gene admits that he's been thinking more of his dead wife Carol lately than of Peggy. Again, Alice warns: "The image . . . of the eternally bereaved husband . . . forgive me . . . the dutiful son . . . They're very appealing and seductive . . . But they're not living."

Alice kisses Gene good night, and then once again dissolves into tears—she misses their mother so.

Some time later, Gene has moved in to the Garrison house and is watching Tom in his pajamas and bathrobe, on his knees, praying, just before going to bed. On the bed is a bureau drawer full of mementos.

The robe is too big for Tom—he has lost a good deal of weight. Tom remembers when he and Gene used to swing Indian clubs. Going over his mementos, he finds a small revolver for which he no longer has a permit (which reminds him that he doesn't have the political pull he once had, a trooper actually gave him a ticket one day before the Florida trip). Among the mementos are several old photographs.

GENE *(very tentatively):* You know, Dad, I've never seen a picture of your father.

Tom looks at him a long time . . . should I really show him . . . then finally, with his hatred showing on his face, he unwraps another tissue and hands over a small picture. Gene looks at it a long moment.

He's just a boy?

TOM: That was taken about the time he was married.

GENE: I'd always thought of him as . . . the way you talked about him . . . as . . .

Gene is obviously touched by the picture.

TOM: Oh, he was a fine looking man before he started to drink. Big, square, high color . . . But he became my mortal enemy . . . Did I ever show you that?

He takes out a small piece of paper.

Careful . . . When I set up a home for my brother and sister . . . one day we were all out, and he came around . . . and ripped up all my sister's clothes and shoes . . . Drunk, of course . . . A few days later he came around to apologize and ask for some money, and I threw him out . . . The next day he left this note . . . "You are welcome to your burden."

GENE: And you kept it?

TOM: Yes. I never saw him again until many years later he was dying . . . in Bellevue . . . and someone got word to me, and I went down and asked him if he wanted anything . . . He said he'd like some fruit . . . so I sent him in a few oranges. He died the next day.

GENE: There must have been something there to love . . . to understand.

TOM: In my father? *(Shakes his head . . . "No.")*

Tom has kept all of Gene's Father's Day cards, and he tells his son how much he appreciated them, and what a comfort Gene is being in Tom's old age. Gene is touched, as Tom continues to inspect the mementos. He finds a Glee Club concert program and remembers how Gene used to sing to his mother's accompaniment.

TOM: . . . . . I remember your mother would sit at the piano, hour after hour, and I'd be up here at my desk, and I'd hear you singing . . .

GENE *(smiles . . . kidding):* You always wanted me to sing "When I Grow Too Old To Dream."

TOM: Did I? . . . I don't remember your ever singing that . . . You always seemed to be just finishing when I came into the room . . .

Looks at Gene.

Did you used to sing that for me?

GENE *(not a joke any more):* No . . . but you always asked me to sing it for you.

TOM: Oh.

Puts the program away.

Well, I enjoyed sitting up here and listening.

Tom finds a picture of his mother in the box of mementos and is brought to tears by his memories. As Gene puts his arm around his father, Tom is now weeping for his own loneliness. Gene comforts him and helps him put the mementos away.

Deeply moved with sympathy for his father, Gene tells Tom of his plans for marrying Peggy and living in California. Gene suggests that his father come to California with them and perhaps find an apartment near them.

Tom smiles at Gene and suggests that Gene and Peggy come to live here in the Garrison house. Gene explains why this is impossible: Peggy is a doctor with a practise in California. Her divorced husband lives there too, and Peggy's children want to be near him for easy visits. Besides, Gene has found it hard to live in the East ever since Carol's death.

Tom casts reflections on Gene's good judgment in deciding to help rear another man's children. He cannot understand that Gene loves Peggy. Did Margaret know about Gene's plans? Yes, and approved of them, Gene tells his father.

Bitterly, Tom bids Gene go and "Send me a Christmas card . . . if you remember." Gene reminds his father that he just now offered companionship from son to father; he asked Tom to go to California with him. Stubbornly, Tom refuses to acknowledge or accept this offered gift of love. Brutally, he tells his son: "Did you want me to make it easy for you the way your mother did? Well, I won't. If you want to go, go!"

Infuriated, Gene confronts his father and tells him "Shut up!"

TOM *(coming at him):* —Don't you—

GENE *(shouting):* —Shut up! I asked you to come with me. What do you want? What the hell do you want? If I lived here the rest of my life, it wouldn't be enough for you. I've tried, God damn it, I've tried to be the dutiful son, to maintain the image of the good son . . . Commanded into your presence on every conceivable occasion . . . Easter, Christmas, birthdays, Thanksgiving . . . Even that Thanksgiving when Carol was dying, and I was staying with her in the hospital. "We miss you so. Our day is nothing without you. Couldn't you come up for an hour or two after you leave Carol?" You had no regard for what was really going on . . . My wife was dying!

TOM: Is it so terrible to want to see your own son?

GENE: It is terrible to want to possess him . . . entirely and completely!

TOM *(coldly . . . after a moment):* There will be some papers to sign for your mother's estate. Be sure you leave an address with my lawyer.

GENE *(cutting in):* Dad!

TOM *(cutting, no self-pity):* From tonight on, you can consider me dead.

Turns on him in a rage of resentment.

I gave you everything. Since I was a snot-nosed kid, I've worked my fingers to the bone. You've had everything and I had nothing. I put a roof over your head, clothes on your back—

GENE: —food on the table.

TOM: —things I never had.

GENE: I know!

TOM: You ungrateful bastard!

GENE *(seizes him, almost as though he would hit him):* What do you want for gratitude? Nothing, nothing would be enough. You have resented everything you ever gave me. The orphan boy in you has resented everything. I'm sorry as hell about your miserable childhood. When I was a kid and you told me those stories, I used to go up to my room at night and cry. But there is nothing I can do about it . . . and it does not excuse everything . . . I *am* grateful to you. I also admire you and respect you, and stand in awe of what you have done with your life. I will never be able to touch it.

Tom looks at him with contempt.

But it does not make me love you. And I wanted to love you.

Tom snorts his disbelief.

You hated your father. I saw what it did to you. I did not want to hate you.

TOM: I don't care what you feel about me.

GENE: I do . . .

He moves away from his father.

I came so close to loving you tonight . . . I'd never felt so open to you. You don't know what it cost me to ask you to come with me . . . when I have never been able to sit in a room alone with you . . . Did you really think your door was always open to me?

TOM: It was not my fault if you never came in.

GENE *(starts to move out):* Goodbye, Dad. I'll arrange for someone to come in.

TOM *(shouting):* I don't want anyone to come in. I can take care of myself. I have always had to take care of myself. Who needs you? Out . . . I have lived each day of my life so that I could look any man in the eye and tell him to GO TO HELL!

This last, wildly at Gene. The lights dim out quickly, except for a lingering light on Gene . . .

GENE *(after a few moments):* That night I left my father's house forever . . . I took the first right and the second left . . . and this time I went as far as California . . . Peggy and I visited him once or twice . . . and then he came to California to visit us, and had a fever and swollen ankles, and we put him in a hospital, and he never left . . . The reason we gave, and which he could accept, for not leaving . . . the swollen ankles. But the real reason . . . the arteries were hardening, and he gradually over several years slipped into complete and speechless senility . . . with all his life centered in his burning eyes.

A Nurse wheels in Tom . . . dressed in a heavy, warm bathrobe

. . . and wearing a white linen golf cap . . . to protect his head from drafts . . . The Nurse withdraws into the shadows.

When I would visit him, and we would sit and look at each other, his eyes would mist over and his nostrils would pinch with emotion . . . But I never could learn what the emotion was . . . anger . . . or love . . . or regret . . . One day, sitting in his wheelchair and staring without comprehension at television . . . he died . . . alone . . . without even an orange in his hand.

The light fades on Tom.

Death ends a life . . . but it does not end a relationship, which struggles on in the survivor's mind . . . toward some resolution, which it never finds. Alice said I would not accept the sadness of the world . . . What did it matter if I never loved him, or if he never loved me? . . . Perhaps she was right . . . But, still, when I hear the word "father" . . .

He cannot express it . . . there is still the longing, the emotion . . . He looks around . . . out . . . as though he would finally be able to express it . . . but he can only say . . .

It matters.

He turns and walks slowly away, into the shadows as the lights dim . . . Curtain.

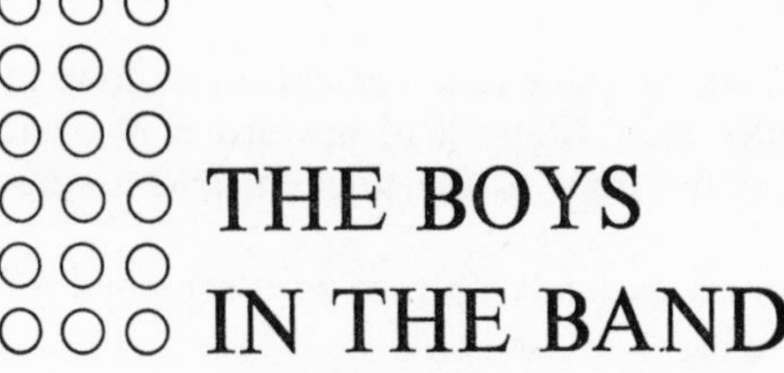

THE BOYS IN THE BAND

A Play in Two Acts

BY MART CROWLEY

Cast and credits appear on page 404

MART CROWLEY was born August 21, 1935 in Vicksburg, Miss., where his father owned a pool hall known as Crowley's Smoke House. He studied at St. Aloysius High School in Vicksburg and at Catholic University of America in Washington, D.C. Crowley has written television shows produced by Martin Manulis, Four Star and others, his major credit being Cassandra at the Wedding. *He is co-author of a new Paramount movie,* Fade-In. *He is a member of Theater 1968's experimental Playwright's Unit.* The Boys in the Band *is his first professionally-produced play.*

Time: The present, one evening

Place: A smartly appointed duplex apartment in the East Fifties, New York City

ACT I

SYNOPSIS: Bossa nova music is playing from the phonograph as Michael *("30, average face, smartly groomed"),* wearing a dressing gown, enters left from the kitchen of his New York apartment carrying liquor bottles to set on the bar at extreme right.

This is a duplex with living room area at right and the entrance door at right. Behind the living room is a library area. Stairs lead upward at the left side of the stage. Behind them at left is the door to the kitchen, and a sideboard is placed against the left wall.

On the upstairs level, a dressing-room area leads upstage to a screened-off bed at left and the bathroom door at right.

Michael goes upstairs and fusses with his hair, using comb and drier. The doorbell rings. Michael goes downstairs, turns off the music and opens the door to admit Donald *("28, medium blond, wholesome American good looks")*. Donald, in khakis and a Lacoste shirt, and carrying a small bag, has arrived sooner than expected (his psychiatrist has canceled an appointment).

Donald heads upstairs, intending to take a shower, as though he owned the place. Apropos, Michael has bought Donald a few things.

MICHAEL *(holds up a cylindrical can)*: . . . . . something called "Control". Notice nowhere is it called hair spray—just simply, "Control". And the words "For Men" are written about thirty-seven times all over the goddam can!

DONALD: It's called butch assurance.

MICHAEL: Well, it's *still* hair spray—no matter if they call it "Balls". It's all going on your very own shelf which is to be labeled: Donald's Saturday Night Douche Kit. By the way, are you spending the night?

DONALD: Nope. I'm driving back. I still get very itchy when I'm in this town too long. I'm not that well yet.

MICHAEL: That's what you say every weekend.

DONALD: Maybe after about ten more years of analysis I'll be able to stay one night.

MICHAEL: Maybe after about ten more years of analysis you'll be able to move back to town permanently.

DONALD: If I live that long.

MICHAEL: You will. If you don't kill yourself on the Long Island Expressway some early Sunday morning. I'll never know how you can tank-up on martinis and make it back to the Hamptons in one piece.

DONALD: Believe me, it's easier than getting here. Ever had an anxiety attack at sixty miles an hour? Well, tonight I was beside myself to get to the doctor—and just as I finally made it, rush in, throw myself on the couch and vomit-out how depressed I am, he says, "Donald, I have to cancel tonight—I'm just too sick."

MICHAEL: Why didn't you tell him you're sicker than he is?

DONALD: He already knows *that.*

Donald goes to bedroom, drops bag.

Donald discusses with Michael the birthday party that is to be given here, this evening, for Michael's friend Harold. Michael complains that it will be "screaming queens singing 'Happy Birthday' ". They will be seven, including Donald, "the same old tired fairies you've seen around since the day one."

Michael fusses with his hair—it is thinning out and receding, he is not getting any younger, it's all a big joke—but in reality Michael's appearance is very important to him. While Donald disappears into the bathroom, Michael takes off his robe and tries on a sweater. He insists that Donald tell him why's he's depressed. Donald appears in the doorway, swallowing some pills, explaining that today he realizes he was trained to be a failure by his "Evelyn and Walt," his mother and father.

Michael tries to cheer Donald up first with a Barbara Stanwyck and then with a Judy Garland imitation (Michael is obsessive about movies and frequently falls into mimicry of their language and attitudes). But Donald fails to cheer.

MICHAEL: Meanwhile—back at the Evelyn and Walt syndrome.

DONALD: America's Square Peg in America's Round Hole.

MICHAEL: Christ, how sick analysts must get of hearing how mommy and daddy made their darlin' into a fairy.

DONALD: It's beyond just that now. Today I finally began to see how some of the other pieces of the puzzle relate to them.—Like why I never finished anything I started in my life . . . my neurotic compulsion to not succeed. I've realized it was always when I failed that Evelyn loved me the most—because it displeased Walt who wanted perfection. And when I fell short of the mark she was only too happy to make up for it with her love. So I began to identify failing with winning my mother's love. And I began to fail on purpose in order to get it. I didn't finish Cornell—I couldn't keep a job in this town. I simply retreated to a room over a garage and scrubbing floors in order to keep alive. Failure is the only thing with which I feel at home. Because it is what I was taught at home.

MICHAEL: Killer whales is what they are. Killer whales. How many whales could a killer whale kill?

DONALD: A lot. Especially if they get them when they were babies.

Pause. Michael suddenly tears off his sweater, throws it in the air, letting it land where it may, whips out another, pulls it on as he starts for the living room. Donald follows.

Neither of the sweaters (one is vicuna) is paid for, Michael admits to Donald. Wearing expensive clothes and running up unpaid bills is Michael's way of life. Michael, needled by Donald, admits that it's childish. Wrapping up a present for Harold, Michael confesses to Donald how unsatisfactory his butterfly life has been.

MICHAEL: . . . . . Bored with Scandinavia, try Greece. Fed up with dark meat, try light. Hate tequila, what about slivovitz? Tired of boys, what about girls—or how about boys and girls mixed and in what combination? And if you're sick of people, what about poppers? Or pot or pills or the hard stuff. And can you think of anything else the bad baby would like to indulge his spoiled-rotten, stupid empty, boring, selfish, self-centered self in? Is that what you think has style, Donald? Huh? Is that what you think you've missed out on—my hysterical escapes from country to country, party to party, bar to bar, bed to bed, hangover to hangover, and all of it, hand to mouth! . . . . .

A beat.

And why? And why?

DONALD: Why, Michael? Why?

MICHAEL: I really don't want to get into it.

DONALD: Then how can we have a conversation in depth?

MICHAEL: Oh, you know it all by heart anyway. Same song, second verse. Because my Evelyn refused to let me grow up. She was determined to keep me a child forever and she did one helluva job of it. And my Walt stood by and let her do it.

A beat.

What you see before you is a thirty-year-old infant. And it was all done in the name of love—what *she* labeled love and I suppose sincerely believed to be love, when what she was really doing was feeding her own need—satisfying her own loneliness.

A beat.

She bathed me in the same tub with her until I grew too big for the two of us to fit and she made me sleep in the same bed with her until I was fourteen years old—until I finally flatly refused to spend one more night there.

Michael's mother still loves him like a baby, which maddens him. But he has "dropped enough dough on the couch" to realize that the dangerous, excessive love of an Evelyn and Walt is only part of the cause; each person is, at last, responsible for his own destiny.

Donald puts an arm around Michael to comfort him. Michael breaks out of the mood of self pity with sudden mimicry of Bette Davis: "I adore cheap sentiment"—and busies himself getting ready for the party, bringing ice and a bowl of cracked crab, while Donald returns to the bathroom.

The phone rings, and Michael picks it up. It is Alan, one of Michael's former roommates at Georgetown. Alan happens to be in town and wants to drop in, but Michael tells him it would be inconvenient because of the party. Alan begins to cry on the other end of the phone conversation. Alarmed, Michael tells Alan to come right over.

When Donald comes downstairs (bathed and changed) and mixes himself a martini, Michael is worrying about his big new problem: his roommate Alan is "straight" and "square city" and is going to land right in the middle of "the freak show we've got booked for dinner."

DONALD: . . . . . Why'd you invite him over?

MICHAEL: I didn't. He invited himself. He said he had to see me tonight. Immediately. He absolutely lost his spring on the phone—started crying.

DONALD: Maybe he's feeling sorry for himself too.

MICHAEL: Great heaves and sobs. Really boo-hoo-hoo-time—and that's not his style at all. I mean he's so pulled-together he wouldn't show any emotion if he were in a plane crash. What am I going to do?

DONALD: What the hell do you care what he thinks?

MICHAEL: Well, I don't really but . . .

DONALD: Or are you suddenly ashamed of your friends?

MICHAEL: Donald, *you* are the only person I know of whom I am truly ashamed. Some people *do* have different standards from yours and mine, you know. And if we don't acknowledge them, we're just as narrow-minded and backward as we think they are.

DONALD: You know what you are, Michael? You're a *real* person.

MICHAEL: Thank you and fuck you.

Michael crosses to take a piece of crab and nibble on it.

Want some?

DONALD: No, thanks. How could you ever have been friends with a bore like that?

MICHAEL: Believe it or not there was a time in my life when I didn't go around *announcing* that I was a faggot.

DONALD: That must have been before speech replaced sign language.

MICHAEL: Don't give me any static on that score. I didn't come out until I left college.

DONALD: It seems to me that the first time we tricked we met in a gay bar on Third Avenue during your junior year.

Donald has noticed that Michael is drinking only soda, with no liquor in it. Michael has been doing this for several weeks and seems much more tranquil, less hostile, as a result. Michael admits he's quit drinking (and smoking) partly on the advice of his analyst. Michael could no longer stand the "icks"—fierce attacks of anxiety and guilt that racked him after each night of drinking. Michael has stepped off the merry-go-round of boozing and hangover cures.

The bell rings, but it isn't Alan, as expected: it's Emory, Larry and Hank, guests arriving for the birthday party. Emory *("33, small, frail, very plain . . . . . in Bermuda shorts and a sweater")* bursts in bearing a casserole dish, shrieking hello, kissing Michael on the cheek, calling Donald an "exotic woman."

Larry *("29 with a starkly simple sense of individual style and color in his clothes. Dark eyes, dark hair, extremely handsome . . .")* comes in quietly, says "Hi" and shakes hands. So does Hank *("32, tall, solid, athletic, attractive"),* who is wearing *a dark Ivy League* suit with vest and *cordovan* shoes. Larry and Hank have brought presents. Emory's will arrive later.

Michael introduces Larry to Donald, but it seems they have met—or at least seen each other—before. There is an air of concealment that arouses Hank's suspicions. Hank and Larry seem to be in a state of hair-trigger jealousy.

Michael informs the others that he wants them to behave when his roommate arrives. They have already met another of Michael's roommates, Justin

Stuart, who is "about as straight as the yellow brick road." But Alan is another roommate, Michael reminds them, a very different person. Alan is not only straight but believes that Michael is straight also. Michael acted straight in college, for the most part; in fact, he even fooled himself.

MICHAEL: . . . . . I was still in the "Christ-Was-I-Drunk-Last-Night Syndrome."

LARRY: The what?

MICHAEL: The "Christ-Was-I-Drunk-Last-Night Syndrome." You know, when you made it with some guy in school and the next day when you had to face each other there was always a lot of shit-kicking crap about, "Man, was I drunk last night! Christ, I don't remember a thing."

Everyone laughs.

DONALD: You were just guilty because you were Catholic, that's all.

MICHAEL: That's not true. The "Christ-Was-I-Drunk-Last-Night Syndrome" knows no religion. It has to do with immaturity. Although I will admit there's a high percentage of it among Mormons.

EMORY: Trollop.

MICHAEL: Somehow we all managed to justify our actions in those days. Why, I later found out that even Justin Stuart, my closest friend . . .

DONALD: Other than Alan McCarthy.

MICHAEL *(a look to Donald):* . . . was doing the same thing. Only he was going to Boston on weekends.

Emory and Larry laugh.

LARRY *(to Hank):* Sound familiar?

MICHAEL: Yes, long before Justin or I or God-only-knows how many others *came out,* we used to get drunk and "horse around" a bit. You see, in the "Christ-Was-I-Drunk-Last-Night Syndrome," you really *are* drunk. That much of it is true. It's just that you *do remember everything.*

General laughter.

Oh God, I used to have to get drunk before I could go into a gay bar!

The bars have lost their appeal, though getting drunk helps some guys to have sex (Larry comments with a meaningful glance at Hank). Donald and Michael met in a bar and got to know each other so quickly that they never really became lovers.

The door buzzer sounds.

MICHAEL: Oh, Jesus, it's Alan! Now, please everybody, do me a favor and cool it for the few minutes he's here.

EMORY: Anything for a sis, Mary.

MICHAEL: That's *exactly* what I'm talking about, Emory. *No camping!*

EMORY: Sorry. *(Deep, deep voice to Donald.)* Think the Giants are gonna win the pennant this year?

DONALD *(deep, deep voice):* Fuckin' A, Mac.

Michael goes to the door, opens it to reveal Bernard (28, Negro, nice-looking) dressed in a shirt and tie and a sports jacket. He carries a birthday gift and two bottles of red wine.

MICHAEL: Hey—Bernard!

EMORY *(big scream):* Oh, it's only another queen!

BERNARD: And it ain't the red one, either.

EMORY: It's the queen of spades!

Bernard enters.

Bernard and Emory needle each other in friendly exchanges of insult. The phone rings. The party hubbub is increasing, so Michael takes the call on the upstairs extension. It's Alan. He's not coming after all.

Meanwhile, Larry uses another line on the downstairs phone to call the bakery about the birthday cake, but he can get no answer.

The conversation turns to the subject of pastimes. Donald reads voluminously. (Michael decides to change to a red sweater and does so.) Emory is planning a trip to the West Coast, where he might do a couple of business errands (he is a decorator), but mostly he wants to relax and spend a week in the Club Baths.

Michael returns downstairs and tells them Alan isn't coming. Hank puts on a record, and Michael and Bernard start dancing. The buzzer rings downstairs. Emory cries: "Oh my God, it's Lilly Law! Everybody three feet apart!" But it's only the delivery boy from the bakery, with the birthday cake.

They start doing a dance they used to do on Fire Island; soon they are in a position somewhat like a chorus line, all but Donald and Hank. The doorbell sounds. No one hears it except Hank, who opens the door, revealing Alan *("30, aristocratic Anglo-Saxon features")* standing there, dressed in a dinner jacket. His dinner party was nearby, and he has decided to drop in for a moment, after all.

The dancers stop dancing; Michael turns off the music abruptly and tries to save the situation. He introduces Alan to his friends (Emory curtsies). Donald goes to get Alan a Scotch. Alan just naturally seems to gravitate to Hank, the pipe-smoking Ivy-League-type member of the group. They make small talk about sports and occupation (Hank is a teacher; Alan a lawyer).

Michael manages to maneuver Emory and Bernard out of the way, into the kitchen to prepare dinner. Donald and Larry both move to the bar for refills, and when their eyes meet they greet each other in friendly fashion. Alan and Hank sit on the couch.

ALAN *(to Hank):* You're married?

Larry hears this, turns to look in the direction of the couch. Michael enters from the kitchen.

HANK: What?

ALAN: I see you're married.

He points to Hank's wedding band.

HANK: Oh.

MICHAEL: Yes. Hank's married.

ALAN: You have any kids?

HANK: Yes. Two. A boy nine and a girl seven. They're great kids. You should see my boy play tennis—really puts his dad to shame.

Hank looks toward Larry and Donald.

DONALD *(avoiding Hank's eyes):* I better get some ice.

He exits, catching sight of Michael, who has been watching on the way out.

ALAN *(to Hank):* I have two kids too. Both girls.

HANK: Great.

Michael asks about Alan's children. Alan dotes on them—he's been married nine years to Fran, a girl Michael used to date in college.

To Alan's embarrassment, Hank explains that he is in the process of divorcing his wife and now lives with Larry, his roommate.

Donald comes in with the ice bucket and mixes a drink for Alan, who is too jittery to mix one for himself. Emory breezes in and out with plates. Michael persuades Alan to get another drink and join him upstairs, where they can talk.

In a cross-current of jealousies, Hank keeps wondering where Larry and Donald knew each other. Then Hank tries to pretend that Larry is jealous of his interest in Alan. Larry replies angrily, "I'm Larry—*you're* jealous" and deliberately engages in close conversation with Donald.

Upstairs, Michael is trying to explain the evening to Alan, who tries to be broad-minded about Michael's friends, even Larry.

ALAN: I liked Donald too. The only one I didn't care too much for was—what's his name—Emory.

MICHAEL: Yes. Emory.

ALAN: I just can't stand that kind of talk. It just grates on me.

MICHAEL: What kind of talk, Alan?

ALAN: Oh, you know. His brand of humor, I suppose.

MICHAEL: He can be really quite funny sometimes.

ALAN: I suppose so. If you find that sort of thing amusing. He just seems like such a goddam little pansy . . . that I . . .

Silence. A pause.

I'm sorry I said that. I didn't mean to say that. That's such an awful thing to say about *anyone*. But you know what I mean, Michael—you must admit he *is* effeminate.

MICHAEL: He is a bit.

ALAN: A bit! *(Laugh.)* He's like a . . . a butterfly in heat! I mean there's no wonder he was trying to teach you all a dance. He *probably* wanted to dance *with* you!

Pause.

Oh, come on, man, you know me—you know how I feel—your private life is your own affair.

MICHAEL *(icy):* No. I *don't* remember that about you.

ALAN: I couldn't care less about what people do—as long as they don't do it in public—or—or try to force their ways on the whole damned world.

Michael tries to discover Alan's reason for crying over the telephone, but Alan now apologizes for the outburst and refuses to discuss it. Alan escapes Michael's questions by going into the bathroom.

Downstairs, Emory is fussing with the table and needling Bernard, who sometimes even plays Uncle Tom for Emory. Michael comes downstairs.

Downstairs, Hank crosses to Larry.

HANK: I thought maybe you were abiding by the agreement.

LARRY: We have no agreement.

HANK: We *did.*

LARRY: *You* did. I never agreed to anything!

Donald looks up, raises a crab claw toward Michael . . .

DONALD: To your health.

MICHAEL: Up yours.

DONALD: Up my health?

BERNARD: Where's the gent?

MICHAEL: In the gents' room. If you can all hang on for five more minutes, he's about to leave.

The door buzzes. Michael crosses to it.

LARRY: Well, at last!

Michael opens the door to reveal a musclebound young man (22, light blond, too pretty) wearing boots, tight levis, a calico neckerchief and a cowboy hat. Around his wrist there is a large card tied with a string.

COWBOY *(singing fast):*

Happy birthday to you,
Happy birthday to you,
Happy birthday, dear Harold,
Happy birthday to you.

And with that, he throws his arms around Michael and gives him a big kiss on the lips. Everyone stands in stunned silence.

MICHAEL: Who the hell are you?

Emory swings in from the kitchen.

EMORY: She's Harold's present from me and she's early! *(Quick to Cowboy.)* And that's not even Harold, you idiot!

COWBOY: You said whoever answered the door.

EMORY: But not until *midnight!* . . . . .

Cowboy explains to them all (gravely, simple-mindedly) that he came early because he hopes to make the bars by midnight—he wants to get to bed early, he has sprained his back doing his exercises. Emory reminds Cowboy that he has been paid for the whole night, as a birthday present to Harold.

Before Michael can protest to Emory, Alan comes downstairs, on his way out.

ALAN *(sees Cowboy):* Are you . . . Harold?

EMORY: No, he's not Harold. He's *for* Harold.

Silence. Alan lets it pass. Turns to Hank.

ALAN: Goodby, Hank. It was nice to meet you.

HANK: Same here.

They shake hands.

ALAN: If . . . if you're ever in Washington—I'd like for you to meet my wife.

LARRY: That'd be fun, wouldn't it, Hank.

EMORY: Yeah, they'd love to meet him—*her.* I have such a problem with pronouns.

ALAN *(quick, to Emory):* How many esses are there in the word "pronoun?"

EMORY: How'd you like to kiss my ass—that's got two or more *essesss in it!*

At this, Alan explodes into an obscene suggestion to Emory, who replies in kind, with a reference to Alan's wife. Now hysterical, Alan calls Emory names—"faggot, fairy, pansy"—and assaults him. Alan knocks Emory down and bloodies his nose before anyone can stop him.

Hank drags Alan off Emory while others come to Emory's aid with ice and a towel. Donald, the observer, warns Cowboy to keep out of the way and watches the others working over Emory.

The doorbell rings, and Donald admits Harold *("32, dark, lean, strong limbs, unusual Semitic face")* who has finally arrived at his own party. Harold, a one-time professional ice skater, is wearing a Nehru suit and beads. His face is pockmarked. In calm appraisal, he surveys the tableau of Emory on the floor and bleeding and Alan being held down.

At this point, Cowboy sings "Happy Birthday" to Harold and kisses him.

Donald turns on the record player. Harold reads the card, begins to laugh. Michael turns to survey the room. Donald watches him.

Slowly, Michael begins to move, stepping over Alan. He slowly walks to the bar . . . pours a glass of gin . . . raises it to his lips . . . downs it all. Donald watches silently as Harold continues to laugh and laugh . . . Curtain.

ACT II

A moment later, Harold is still laughing. Michael downs a drink and turns on Harold in irritation.

MICHAEL: What's so fucking funny?

HAROLD *(unintimidated; quick hand to hip):* Life. Life is a god-damn laff-riot. You remember life.

MICHAEL: *You're stoned.*

LARRY: Happy birthday, Harold.

MICHAEL *(to Harold):* You're stoned and you're late! You were supposed to arrive at this location at approximately eight-thirty dash nine o'clock!

HAROLD: What I *am,* Michael, is a thirty-two-year-old, ugly, pockmarked Jew fairy—and if it takes me a while to pull myself together and if I smoke a little grass before I can get up the nerve to show my face to the world, it's nobody's goddam business but my own. *(Instant switch to chatty tone.)* And how are *you* this evening?

Hank lifts Alan to the couch. Michael turns away from Harold, pours himself another drink. Donald watches.

Harold finds out from Emory what has happened. Harold is very enthusiastic about his birthday present. Alan is still speechless, in shock.

Bernard helps Emory upstairs to get him cleaned up and change his blood-stained sweater. Michael gives Harold a cold bottle of Puilly-Fuisse and apologizes to Harold for having allowed Alan to come in and spoil the celebration. Alan has his hands over his ears, pretending not to hear anything, but soon he feels sick and has to be helped upstairs by Hank. Alan bolts to the bathroom, scaring Emory in passing.

Harold flourishes a cigarette and announces that he's turning on. He invites the others to share the cigarette, but only Cowboy accepts.

Emory has had enough—he wants to leave, but Michael insists that he must stay; this is an order. Harold compliments Emory on his cooking, so Emory decides to go ahead with preparing dinner, with Bernard's assistance.

Contemplating Cowboy, Harold and Michael are led into a discussion of beauty ("Faggots are worse than women about their age," sneers Michael). Harold confesses he would sell his own beautiful soul for "some skin-deep, transitory, meaningless beauty." Harold accuses Michael, a Catholic, of hedging in the matter of God.

Emory enters with the casserole.

HAROLD *(to Michael):* You hang on to that great insurance policy called The Church.

MICHAEL: That's right. I believe in God and if it turns out that there really isn't one, okay. Nothing lost. But if it turns out that there *is*—I'm covered.

Bernard enters carrying a huge salad bowl. He puts it down, lights table candles.

EMORY *(to Michael):* Harriet Hypocrite, that's who you are.

MICHAEL: Right. I'm one of those truly rotten Catholics who gets drunk, sins all night and goes to Mass the next morning.

Goes to bar for more gin.

EMORY: Gilda Guilt. It depends on what you think sin is.

MICHAEL: Would you just shut-up your goddam minty mouth and get back in the goddam kitchen!

EMORY: Say anything you want—*just don't hit me!*

He exits. A beat.

MICHAEL: Actually, I suppose Emory has a point—I only go to confession before I get on a plane.

BERNARD *(arranging table and pouring wine):* You think God's power only exists at thirty thousand feet?

MICHAEL: It must. On the ground I *am* God. In the air, I'm just one more scared son of a bitch.

A beat.

BERNARD: I'm scared on the ground.

COWBOY: Me too.

A beat.

That is, when I'm not high on pot or up on acid.

Hank comes down the stairs.

LARRY *(to Hank):* Well, is it bigger than a breadstick?

HANK *(ignores last remark; to Michael):* He's lying down for a minute.

Larry doesn't miss the opportunity for getting in a couple of cutting remarks about Hank's attentions to Alan. Indeed, as Emory announces dinner and the guests help themselves, hostilities flicker beneath the action like heat lighting. Michael has adopted a sarcastic manner toward all, and Harold is prepared to trade him insult for insult. Donald watches. Cowboy, nettled at being called "a steal" by Emory, argues: "I'm not a steal. I cost twenty dollars."

Michael's growing hostility leads him to criticize Harold for always being late because he spends too much time fussing over his appearance.

MICHAEL: Standing before a bathroom mirror for hours and hours before you can walk out on the street. And looking no different after Christ knows how many applications of Christ knows how many ointments and salves and creams and masks.

HAROLD: I've got bad skin, what can I tell you.

MICHAEL: Who wouldn't after they deliberately take a pair of tweezers and *deliberately* mutilate their pores—no wonder you've got holes in your face after the hack-job you've done on yourself year in and year out!

HAROLD *(coolly but definitely):* You hateful sow.

MICHAEL: Yes, you've got scars on your face—but they're not that bad and if you'd leave yourself alone you wouldn't have any more than you've already awarded yourself.

HAROLD: You'd really like me to compliment you now for being so honest, wouldn't you. For being my best friend who will tell me what even my best friends won't tell me. Swine!

MICHAEL: And the pills! *(Announcement to group.)* Harold has been gathering, saving and storing up barbiturates for the last year like a goddam squirrel. Hundreds of nembutals, hundreds of seconals. All in preparation for and anticipation of the long winter of his death.

Silence. Drinking again at bar.

But I tell you right now, Hallie. When the time comes, you'll never have the guts. It's not always like it happens in plays, not all faggots bump themselves off at the end of the story.

HAROLD: What you say may be true. Time will undoubtedly tell. But, in the meantime, you've left out one detail—the cosmetics and astringents are *paid* for. The bathroom is *paid* for, the tweezers are *paid* for, *and* the pills *are paid for!*

This is the moment which Bernard and Cowboy (who have gone into the kitchen) and Emory (who turns out the lights) choose to bring on the birthday cake. Ceremoniously, Harold blows out the candles while Michael fixes himself another drink.

It's now time to open the presents. Larry's, opened first, is a large-scale pop-art reproduction of a deed to the Boardwalk in a Monopoly game (Larry is a commercial artist). Hank's present is a sweater. Bernard's is a pair of knee pads with sequined initials. Michael's is a picture of himself in a silver frame, with a personal inscription which is not shown to the others.

Bernard puts on a slow recording and dances with Emory. Alan comes down the stairs and makes his way toward the door. But Michael intercepts him.

Turning off the music, Michael announces that they are all going to play a game. He insists on it. He has just made up this game; it's called Affairs of the Heart.

Once more, Alan moves to leave but Michael tells him to stay.

HAROLD: Michael, let him go.

MICHAEL: He really doesn't *want* to. If he did, he'd have left a long time ago—or he wouldn't have come here in the first place.

ALAN *(holding his forehead):* . . . Mickey, I don't *feel* well!

MICHAEL *(low tone but distinctly articulate):* My name is Michael. I am called Michael. You must never call anyone called Michael, Mickey. Those of us who are named Michael get very nervous about it. If you don't believe it—try it.

ALAN: I'm sorry. I can't think.

MICHAEL: You can think. What you can't do—is leave. It's like watching an accident on the highway—you can't look at it and you can't look away.

ALAN: I . . . feel . . . weak . . .

MICHAEL: You are weak. Much weaker than I think you realize.

Alan sits.

Now! Who's going to play with Alan and me? Everyone?

HAROLD: I have no intention of playing.

DONALD: Nor do I.

MICHAEL: Well, not everyone is a participant in life. There are always those who stand on the sidelines and watch.

LARRY: What's the game?

MICHAEL: Simply this: We all have to call on the telephone the *one person* we truly believe we have loved.

HANK: I'm not playing.

LARRY: Oh, yes you are.

HANK: You'd like me to, wouldn't you?

LARRY: You bet I would. I'd like to know who you'd call after all the fancy speeches I've heard lately. Who would you call? Would you call me?

Larry and Hank rasp at each other. Michael explains that Affairs of the Heart is to be scored by a point system: a point for making the call, two points if the person answers, two points for giving your name and five points for declaring your love.

Alan asks Hank to leave with him, as though he and Hank were both strangers in the midst of these events. Michael calls them "the he-men" scornfully.

Hank tells Alan he can't leave with him, and Alan cannot understand why not. Michael elucidates.

MICHAEL: Alan . . . Larry and Hank are lovers. Not just roommates, *bed*-mates. *Lovers.*

ALAN: Michael!

Turns away.

MICHAEL: No man's still got a roommate when he's over thirty years old. If they are not lovers, they're sisters.

Alan sits.

LARRY: Hank is the one who's over thirty.

MICHAEL: Well, you're pushing it!

ALAN: . . . Hank?

A beat.

HANK: Yes, Alan. Larry is my lover.

ALAN: But . . . but . . . you're married.

Michael, Larry, Emory and Cowboy are sent into instant gales of laughter.

HAROLD: I think you said the wrong thing.

MICHAEL: Don't you love that quaint little idea—if a man is married, then he is automatically heterosexual.

A beat.

Alan—Hank swings both ways—with a decided preference.

Now that *that's* settled, the game is to begin. Emory prods Bernard to go first. Bernard admits he's always loved a Detroit boy he knew (Bernard's mother was the boy's family's laundress). Bernard steels himself to call Detroit, but when he gets the boy's mother on the phone he can't carry on the conversation as prescribed in the game. Bernard merely stammers out his good wishes (and his regrets at hearing that her son has been divorced for the third time) and hangs up.

Bernard has scored two points in the game—but the experience has unnerved him, and he broods over it.

Emory is next. Unhesitatingly, he picks up the phone to call one Delbert Botts, whom Emory met in high school and has never forgotten. Emory once asked Botts to be his friend because "I never had a friend who I could talk to and tell everything and trust" (even Cowboy is touched by this revelation). Botts agreed, and Emory was so elated that he bought Botts a cigarette lighter as a present. But Botts told his girl friend all about the incident, the girl told the whole school and Emory became a laughing-stock.

EMORY: . . . . . What they didn't know was that I *loved* him. And that I would go on loving him years after they had all forgotten my funny secret.

Pause.

HAROLD: Well I, for one, need an insulin injection.

MICHAEL: *Call him.*

BERNARD: Don't, Emory.

MICHAEL: Since when are you telling him what to do!

EMORY *(to Bernard):* What do I care—I'm pissed! I'll do anything. Three times.

BERNARD *(kneels):* Don't. *Please.*

MICHAEL: I said call him.

BERNARD: Don't! You'll be sorry. Take my word for it.

EMORY: What have I got to lose?

BERNARD: Your dignity. That's what you've got to lose.

MICHAEL: Well, *that's* a knee-slapper! I love *your* telling *him* about dignity when you allow him to degrade you constantly by Uncle Tom-ing you to death.

BERNARD *(rises): He* can do it, Michael. *I* can do it. But *you can't* do it.

MICHAEL: Isn't that discrimination?

BERNARD: I don't like it from him and I don't like it from me—but I do it to myself and I let him do it. I let him do it because it's the only thing that, to him, makes him my equal. We both got the short end of the stick—but I got a hell of a lot more than he did and he knows it. I let him Uncle Tom me just so he can tell himself he's not a complete loser.

MICHAEL: How very considerate.

BERNARD: It's his defense. You have your defense, Michael. But it's indescribable.

Goes back to steps, sits.

Michael lashes out at Bernard again, embarrassing even Donald. Emory apologizes to Bernard: "I'm sorry, I won't ever say those things to you again." Michael shifts his attack to Emory, who lets the insults roll off him.

Emory gets a busy signal. Larry takes the phone to call someone named Charlie, in a deliberate effort to inflame Hank's jealousy. But Emory insists it's still his turn. He tries Botts again, gets him on the line, tells him a drunken friend is calling. Botts hangs up, preventing Emory from going on. Only three points for Emory.

Hank insists on taking his turn next. While Hank is dialing, Larry is expounding: he is the promiscuous type, he *must* be allowed to play the field (but he can't help being curious about whom Hank is phoning). Hank has reached an answering service. He leaves a message: "The message is for my roommate, Larry. Just say that I called and . . . . . and said . . . I love you."

Larry is speechless, Michael delighted: "Seven points total! Hank, you're ahead, baby." Alan is horrified. Hank informs Alan that he left his wife and family for Larry, but Alan doesn't want to believe it.

ALAN: No! I don't want to hear it. It's disgusting!

A beat.

HANK: Some men do it for another woman.

ALAN: Well, I could understand *that*. That's *normal.*

HANK: It just doesn't always work out that way. No matter how you might want it to. And God knows, nobody ever wanted it more than I did. I really and truly believed I was in love with my wife when I married her. It wasn't altogether my trying to prove something to myself. No, I did love her and she loved me. But . . . there was always that something there . . .

DONALD: You mean your attraction to your own sex.

HANK: Yes.

ALAN: Always?

HANK: I don't know. I suppose so.

EMORY: I've known what I was since I was four years old.

MICHAEL: Everybody's always known it about *you,* Emory.

DONALD: I've always known it about myself too.

HANK: I don't know when it was I started admitting it to myself. For so long I either labeled it something else or denied it completely.

MICHAEL: Christ-I-was-drunk-last-night.

HANK: But there did come a time when I just couldn't lie to myself any more . . . You see, Alan, I thought about it but I never did anything about it—I think the first time I ever really did anything about it was during my wife's last pregnancy. We were living near New Haven—in the country. She and the kids still live there.—Anyway, there was a teacher's meeting here in New York. And my wife didn't feel up to the trip so I said I'd come alone. And that day on the train I started to think about it and think about it and think about it. I didn't think of anything else the whole ride. And within fifteen minutes after I had arrived I picked up a guy in the men's room of Grand Central Station.

ALAN *(quietly):* Jesus.

HANK: It was the first time I'd ever done anything like that in my life and I was scared to death. But he turned out to be a nice fellow. I haven't seen him since, and funny thing is, I can't remember his name any more.

A beat.

After that, it got easier.

A short time later, Hank met Larry and left his wife. Larry's reaction to this story is heated. He resents being characterized as a kind of villain. He is promiscuous—Hank will have to accept that fact if he wants to continue any sort of relationship. He claims to be in the majority, too. Most who pretend fidelity are lying; very few really practise it.

Hank and Larry talk things out in front of everyone, interrupted only occasionally by a needle from Michael or a dumb comment by Cowboy. They have tried a *menage a trois* in an attempted compromise between fidelity and promiscuity, but it didn't prove satisfactory to either of them.

Michael prods Larry into admitting that he and Donald made love together once, anonymously in a chance meeting, and enjoyed the experience.

Larry tells Hank what he wants: "Respect for each other's freedom." He will not flaunt his adventures in Hank's face, but neither will he lie if challenged.

Larry picks up the phone and dials the number of the second, private, line in Michael's apartment. The upstairs phone rings and Larry tells Hank the call is for him. Hank goes upstairs to answer the phone. Downstairs, Larry tells Hank on the phone: "For what it's worth, I love you." In the game, Larry has scored ten points (and on the phone Larry and Hank exchange promises to keep on trying).

Emory declares Larry the winner, but Michael points out that the game isn't over yet. Alan hasn't had his turn, and Michael puts the phone down in front of him. Instead of making a call, Alan apologizes to Emory for assaulting him. To Michael's irritation, Emory accepts the apology. Larry excuses himself and goes upstairs to join Hank behind the partition in the screened-off area. Michael dares Alan to consider what Hank and Larry are doing.

EMORY: Whatever they're doing, they're not hurting anyone.

HAROLD: And they're minding their own business.

MICHAEL: And you mind yours, Harold. I'm warning you!

A beat.

HAROLD *(coolly):* Are you now? Are you warning *me? Me?* I'm Harold. I'm the one person you don't warn, Michael. Because you and I are a match. —And we tread very softly with each other because we both play each other's game too well. Oh, I know this game you're playing. I know it very well. And I *play* it very well.—You play it very well too. But you know what, *I'm* the only one that's better at it than you are. I can beat you at it. So don't push me. I'm warning *you.*

A beat. Michael starts to laugh.

MICHAEL: You're funny, Hallie. A laff-riot. Isn't he funny, Alan? Or, as you might say, isn't he amusing. He's an amusing faggot, isn't he? Or, as you might say, freak.—That's what you called Emory, wasn't it? A freak? A pansy? My, what an antiquated vocabulary you have. I'm surprised you didn't say sodomite or pederast.

Michael suggests to Alan that he is a "closet queen", a secret homosexual, but Alan denies it repeatedly, emphatically and totally. Michael accuses Alan of fondness for their mutual college friend Justin Stuart. Alan admits that he found Justin very attractive, as a friend only. When Michael insists that Justin told him of having sex relations with Alan—many times—Alan brands this as a lie.

ALAN: *Justin . . . lied.* If he told you that, he lied. It is a lie. A vicious lie. He'd say anything about me now to get even. He could never get over the fact that *I* dropped *him.* But I had to. I had to because . . . he told me . . . he told me about himself . . . he told me that he wanted to be my lover. And I . . . I . . . told him . . . he made me sick . . . I told him I pitied him.

Sits on sofa. A beat.

MICHAEL: You ended the friendship, Alan, because you couldn't face the truth about yourself. You could go along, sleeping with Justin as long as he lied to himself and you lied to yourself and you both dated girls and labeled yourselves men and called yourselves just fond friends. But Justin finally had to be honest about the truth, and you couldn't take it. You couldn't take it and so you destroyed the friendship and your friend along with it.

Michael goes to the desk and gets the address book.

ALAN: No!

MICHAEL: Justin could never understand what he'd done wrong to make you drop him.

ALAN: No!

MICHAEL: He blamed himself. He did, that is, until he eventually found out who he was and what he was.

ALAN: No!

Shouting, Michael demands that Alan call Justin to apologize for his behavior years ago. Alan refuses, and Michael starts to dial the number. Alan stops him, takes the phone. Then Alan himself dials.

Alan finishes dialing, lifts the receiver to his ear.

ALAN: . . . Hello?

MICHAEL: One point.

ALAN: . . . It's . . . it's Alan.

MICHAEL: Two points.

ALAN: . . . Yes, yes, it's *me.*

MICHAEL: Is it Justin?

ALAN: . . . You sound surprised.

MICHAEL: I should hope to think he would be—after twelve years! Two more points.

ALAN: No . . . I . . . I'm in New York. Yes. I . . . I won't explain now . . . I . . . I just called to tell you . . .

MICHAEL: THAT I LOVE YOU, GOD DAMN IT! *I LOVE YOU!*

ALAN: I love you.

MICHAEL: Five points bonus. TEN POINTS TOTAL! JACKPOT!

COWBOY *(very softly):* He said it.

ALAN: I love you and I beg you to forgive me.

MICHAEL: Give me that telephone.

He snatches the phone from Alan.

Justin! Did you hear what that son of a bitch said!

A beat. Michael is speechless for a moment.

. . . Fran.

A beat.

Well, of course I knew it was you! . . .

A beat.

How are you? Fine. Me too. Yes . . . he told me all about it. Oh, don't thank *me.* Please . . .

A beat.

Look, I'll . . . I'll put him back on the line . . .

A beat.

Give my love to the kids . . .

He hands the phone back to Alan and begins to wander weakly across the room.

ALAN *(takes phone):* . . . Darling? I'll catch the first plane I can get.—Yes. I'm sorry too . . . I love you very much.

He hangs up, stands up, crosses to the door, stops. He turns around, surveys Michael.

Thank you, Michael.

He looks at the group. He opens the door and exits. Silence. Pause.

COWBOY: Who won?

DONALD: It was a tie.

Harold crosses to Michael.

HAROLD *(calmly, coldly, clinically):* Now it is my turn. And ready or not, Michael, here goes.

A beat.

You are a sad and pathetic man. You're a homosexual and you don't want to be. But there is nothing you can do to change it.—Not all your prayers to your God, not all the analysis you can buy in the years you've got left to live. You may very well one day be able to know a heterosexual life if you want it desperately enough—if you pursue it with the fervor with which you annihilate—but you will always be homosexual as well. Always, Michael. Always. Until the day you die.

This final series of blows leaves Michael paralized, unseeing, unhearing, while his guests take their leave. Harold leaves with his present, Cowboy, thanking Michael "for the laughs," but Michael doesn't answer. Emory leaves, half-dragging the drunken Bernard.

Donald closes the door on the departing guests.

Silence. Michael slowly collapses on the floor. A beat. Then . . . slowly . . . he begins a low moan that increases in volume—almost like a siren. Suddenly, he slams his open hands to his ears.

MICHAEL *(in desperate panic):* Donald! Donald! DONALD! *DONALD!*

Donald puts down his drink, rushes to Michael. Michael is now white with fear, and tears are bursting from his eyes. He begins to gasp his words.

Oh, no! No! What have I done! Oh my God, what have I done!

Michael starts to writhe. Donald grabs him, cradles him in his arms.

DONALD: Michael! Michael!

MICHAEL *(tears pouring forth):* Oh, no! NO! It's beginning! The anxiety! Oh, NO! No! I feel it! I know it's going to happen. Donald!! Donald! Don't leave. Please! Please! Oh, my God, what have I done! Oh Jesus, I can't handle it. I won't make it!

DONALD *(physically subduing him):* Michael! Michael! Stop it! Stop it! I'll give you a Valium—I've got some in my pocket!

MICHAEL *(hysterical):* No! No! Pills and alcohol—I'll die!

DONALD: I'm not going to give you the whole bottle! Come on, let go of me!

MICHAEL *(clutching him): NO!*

DONALD: Let go of me long enough for me to get my hand in my pocket!

Donald manages to get loose long enough to get at the bottle of tranquilizers and fetch a glass of water. After swallowing the pill, Michael collapses into Donald's arms, and Donald rocks and comforts him while he calms down.

Self-hatred has brought on this paroxysm, but Michael used to be in even worse condition than this (Donald reassures him). With continued treatment and effort, perhaps they both can cut themselves loose from despair.

Michael has recovered enough to rise and comment on the party wreckage in the apartment. Donald wonders why Alan stayed at the party so long and took so much abuse. Who was telling the truth—Alan or Justin?

Michael cannot answer, he doesn't know. Now calm, he puts on a raincoat and moves to the door. His bedroom is occupied, he might just as well go out for a while and walk off the alcohol.

MICHAEL: . . . . . And . . . and . . . there's a midnight mass at St. Malachy's that all the show people go to. I think I'll walk over there and catch it.

DONALD *(raises his glass):* Well, pray for me.

MICHAEL *(indicates bedroom):* Maybe they'll be gone when I get back.

DONALD: Well, *I* will be—just as soon as I knock off that bottle of brandy.

Goes to bar.

MICHAEL: Will I see you next weekend?

DONALD: Unless you have other plans.

Michael turns to go.

Michael?

Michael stops, turns back.

Did he ever tell you why he was crying on the phone—what it was he *had* to tell you?

MICHAEL: No. It must have been that he'd left Fran—Or maybe it was something else and he changed his mind.

DONALD: Maybe so.

A beat.

I wonder why he left her.

A pause.

MICHAEL: . . . As my father said to me when he died in my arms, "I don't understand any of it. I never did."

A beat. Donald goes to his stack of books, selects one, sits.

Turn out the lights when you leave, will you?

Donald nods. Michael looks at him for a long silent moment, then opens the door and exits. Curtain.

A GRAPHIC GLANCE

JOEL GREY AS GEORGE M. COHAN IN "GEORGE M!"

MARLENE DIETRICH IN HER ONE-WOMAN PROGRAM OF SONGS

FLORENCE HENDERSON AND GIORGIO TOZZI IN THE REVIVAL OF "SOUTH PACIFIC" AT THE MUSIC THEATER OF LINCOLN CENTER

ROBERT GOULET SURROUNDED BY (CLOCKWISE) MIKE RUPERT, JULIE GREGG, GEORGE S. IRVING, JUNE SQUIBB, JEANNE ARNOLD, CHARLES DURNING AND DAVID WAYNE (LOWER RIGHT) IN "THE HAPPY TIME"

GEROME RAGNI (TOP OF THE HEAP) AND JAMES RADO (CORPORAL AT LOWER LEFT) IN "HAIR"

MELVYN DOUGLAS AND
ERT KELTON IN "SPOFFORD"

DONALD MOFFAT, NANCY WALKER AND UTA HAGEN
IN THE APA-PHOENIX REVIVAL OF "THE CHERRY ORCHARD"

JOHN COLICOS AS WINSTON CHURCHILL IN "SOLDIERS"

KEIR DULLEA AND BURL IVES
IN "DR. COOK'S GARDEN"

MAUREEN O'SULLIVAN AND PATRICK MAGEE
IN "KEEP IT IN THE FAMILY"

EDWARD ALBEE

IAN MCSHANE, EILEEN ATKINS AND IAN MCKELLEN IN "THE PROMISE"

SANDY DENNIS IN
"DAPHNE IN COTTAGE D"

HERMIONE BADDELEY IN
"I ONLY WANT AN ANSWER"

PLAYS PRODUCED IN THE UNITED STATES

PLAYS PRODUCED ON BROADWAY

Figures in parentheses following a play's title indicate number of performances. Plays marked with an asterisk (*) were still running on June 1, 1968, and their number of performances is figured from opening night through May 31, 1968, not including extra non-profit performances. In a listing of a show's numbers—dances, sketches, musical scenes, etc.—the titles of songs are identified by their appearance in quotation marks (").

HOLDOVERS FROM PREVIOUS SEASONS

Plays which were running on June 1, 1967 are listed below. More detailed information about them is to be found in previous *Best Plays* volumes of appropriate years. Important cast changes are recorded in a section of this volume.

Barefoot in the Park (1,530). By Neil Simon. Opened October 23, 1963. (Closed June 25, 1967)

* **Hello, Dolly!** (1,824). Musical suggested by Thornton Wilder's *The Matchmaker;* book by Michael Stewart; music and lyrics by Jerry Herman. Opened January 16, 1964.

Funny Girl (1,348). Musical with book by Isobel Lennart; music by Jule Styne; lyrics by Bob Merrill. Opened March 26, 1964. (Closed July 1, 1967)

* **Fiddler on the Roof** (1,540). Musical based on Sholom Aleichem's stories; book by Joseph Stein; music by Jerry Bock; lyrics by Sheldon Harnick. Opened September 22, 1964.

The Odd Couple (964). By Neil Simon. Opened March 10, 1965. (Closed July 2, 1967)

* **Man of La Mancha** (1,052). Musical suggested by the life and works of Miguel de Cervantes y Saavedra; book by Dale Wasserman; music by Mitch Leigh; lyrics by Joe Darion. Opened November 22, 1965.

* **Cactus Flower** (1,033). By Abe Burrows; based on a play by Pierre Barillet and Jean-Pierre Gredy. Opened December 8, 1965.

Sweet Charity (608). Musical based on the screenplay *Nights of Cabiria* by Federico Fellini, Tullio Pinelli and Ennio Flaiano; book by Neil Simon; music by Cy Coleman; lyrics by Dorothy Fields. Opened January 29, 1966. (Closed July 15, 1967)

* **Mame** (846). Musical based on the novel *Auntie Mame* by Patrick Dennis and the play by Jerome Lawrence and Robert E. Lee; book by Jerome Lawrence and Robert E. Lee; music and lyrics by Jerry Herman. Opened May 24, 1966.

The Apple Tree (463). Musical based on *The Diary of Adam and Eve* by Mark Twain, *The Lady or the Tiger?* by Frank R. Stockton and *Passionella* by Jules Feiffer; book by Sheldon Harnick and Jerry Bock; additional book material by Jerome Coopersmith; music by Jerry Bock; lyrics by Sheldon Harnick. Opened October 18, 1966. (Closed November 25, 1967)

Don't Drink the Water (598). By Woody Allen. Opened November 17, 1966. (Closed April 20, 1968)

* **Cabaret** (639). Musical based on John van Druten's play *I Am a Camera* and stories by Christopher Isherwood; book by Joe Masteroff; music by John Kander; lyrics by Fred Ebb. Opened November 20, 1966.

* **I Do! I Do!** (543). Musical based on Jan de Hartog's play *The Fourposter;* book and lyrics by Tom Jones; music by Harvey Schmidt. Opened December 5, 1966.

The Star-Spangled Girl (261). By Neil Simon. Opened December 21, 1966. (Closed August 5, 1967)

The Homecoming (324). By Harold Pinter. Opened January 5, 1967. (Closed October 14, 1967)

The Association of Producing Artists (APA) Repertory Company. Two of six-play repertory (see entry in 1966-67 *Best Plays* volume) continuing runs were: **The Wild Duck** (45), revival of the play by Henrik Ibsen; translated by Eva Le Gallienne; opened January 11, 1967, and **War and Peace** (56), adaptation of Leo Tolstoy's novel by Alfred Neumann, Erwin Piscator and Guntram Prufer; English version by Robert David MacDonald; opened March 21, 1967. Repertory opened November 21, 1966. (Closed June 17, 1967)

Black Comedy and **White Lies** (337). By Peter Shaffer. Opened February 12, 1967. (Closed December 2, 1967)

* **You Know I Can't Hear You When the Water's Running** (510). By Robert Anderson. Opened March 13, 1967.

Illya Darling (318). Musical based on the movie *Never on Sunday;* book by Jules Dassin; music by Manos Hadjidakis; lyrics by Joe Darion. Opened April 11, 1967. (Closed January 13, 1968)

The Repertory Theater of Lincoln Center. Season of four plays (see entry in 1966-67 *Best Plays* volume) concluded with **Galileo** (76). Revival of the play by Bertolt Brecht; adapted by Charles Laughton. Opened April 13, 1967. (Closed June 17, 1967)

Hallelujah, Baby! (293). Musical with book by Arthur Laurents; music by Jule Styne; lyrics by Betty Comden and Adolph Green. Opened April 26, 1967. (Closed January 13, 1968)

The New York City Center Light Opera Company. Spring season of three musical revivals (see entry in 1966-67 *Best Plays* volume) concluded with **Wonderful Town** (23). Book by Joseph Fields and Jerome Chodorov; music by Leonard Bernstein; lyrics by Betty Comden and Adolph Green. Opened May 17, 1967. (Closed June 4, 1967)

PLAYS PRODUCED JUNE 1, 1967—MAY 31, 1968

Sing Israel Sing (8). Reopening of the Yiddish musical in an English translation based on texts and music by Asaf Halevi, Moishe Broderson, M.M. Warshavsky, Wolf Younin, M. Neu, Shlomo Weisfisch, Joel Chayes, E. Kishon, H. Kon; special material by M. Nudelman. Produced by Ben Bonus at the Brooks Atkinson Theater (see note). Opened June 7, 1967. (Closed June 11, 1967)

NOTE: The Yiddish-language version opened 5/11/67 and suspended 5/21/67 after 14 performances, for translation into English. For cast and other production credits, see entry in 1966-67 *Best Plays* volume.

South Pacific (104). Musical revival based on James A. Michener's *Tales of the South Pacific;* book by Oscar Hammerstein II and Joshua Logan; music by Richard Rodgers; lyrics by Oscar Hammerstein II. Produced by Music Theater of Lincoln Center, Richard Rodgers president and producing director, at the New York State Theater of Lincoln Center. Opened June 12, 1967. (Closed September 9, 1967)

Ngana ....Dana Shimizu
Jerome ....Keenan Shimizu
Henry ....Robert Ito
Ensign Nellie Forbush ..Florence Henderson
Emile de Becque ....Giorgio Tozzi
Bloody Mary ....Irene Byatt
Abner ....Judd Jones
Stewpot ....Brad Sullivan
Luther Billis ....David Doyle
Professor ....Mickey Karm
Lt. Joseph Cable, U.S.M.C. ....Justin McDonough
Capt. George Brackett, U.S.N. ..Lyle Talbot
Cmdr. William Harbison, U.S.N. ....Bob Monroe
Yeoman Herbert Quale ....Ted Story
Sgt. Kenneth Johnson ....William Lutz
Seabee Richard West ....Frank Scannelli
Seabee Morton Wise ......Alexander Orfaly
Pvt. Tom O'Brien ....James O'Sullivan
Radio Operator ....Roger Brown
Marine Cpl. Hamilton Steves...Dick Ensslen
Seabee Thomas Hassinger ....Phil Lucas
Seabee James Jerome .....Joseph della Sorte
Pvt. Sven Larsen ....Don Dolan
Pvt. Jack Walters ....Bob Barbieri
Pvt. Dick Sederholm ....Jess E. Richards
Seabee Roger Pitt ....Marvin Camillo
Seabee Keith Moore ....Laried Montgomery
Lt. Genevieve Marshall ....Jane Coleman
Ensign Lisa Manelli ....Lisa Damon
Ensign Connie Walewska ...Martha Danielle
Ensign Janet McGregor ....Susan Campbell
Ensign Bessie Noonan ....Joyce Maret
Ensign Pamela Whitmore ....Patti Davis
Ensign Rita Adams ....Anne Nathan
Ensign Sue Yaeger ....Judy Case
Ensign Cora MacRae ....Lynn Dovel
Ensign Dinah Murphy ....Bobbi Baird
Liat ....Eleanor Calbes
Lt. Buzz Adams ....Jack Knight

Standby: Emile de Becque—Gene Hollmann. Principal understudies: Miss Henderson—Bobbi Baird; Miss Byatt—Jane Coleman; Mr. Doyle—Brad Sullivan; Mr. McDonough—David Jarratt; Mr. Talbot—Howard Fischer; Miss Shimizu—Nancy Asai.

Directed by Joe Layton; musical director, Jonathan Anderson; scenery and costumes, Fred Voelpel; lighting, Jules Fisher; orchestrations, Robert Russell Bennett; production stage manager, Harry Young; stage managers, Howard Fischer, Phil King; press, Frank Goodman, Martin Shwartz.

Time: During World War II. Place: Two islands in the South Pacific.

South Pacific was first produced April 7, 1949, by Richard Rodgers, Oscar Hammerstein II, Leland Hayward and Joshua Logan at the Majestic Theater for 1,925 performances. It was revived at New York City Center May 4, 1955, for 15 performances; April 24, 1957, for 23 performances; April 26, 1961, for 23 performances, and June 2, 1965, for 15 performances.

ACT I

"Dites-moi Pourquoi" ....Ngana, Jerome
"A Cockeyed Optimist" ....Nellie
"Twin Soliloquies" ....Nellie, Emile

"Some Enchanted Evening" .... Emile
"Dites-moi Pourquoi" (Reprise) .... Ngana, Jerome, Emile
"Bloody Mary Is the Girl I Love" .... Sailors, Seabees, Marines
"There Is Nothin' Like a Dame" .... Billis, Stewpot, Professor, Sailors, Seabees, Marines
"Bali Ha'i" .... Bloody Mary
"Bali Ha'i" (Reprise) .... Lt. Cable
"I'm Gonna Wash That Man Right Outa My Hair" .... Nellie, Nurses
"Some Enchanted Evening" (Reprise) .... Nellie, Emile
"I'm in Love With a Wonderful Guy" .... Nellie, Nurses
"Younger Than Springtime" .... Lt. Cable
"Bali Ha'i" (Reprise) .... Liat
Finale .... Nellie, Emile

ACT II

Opening .... Nellie, Nurses, Sailor, Seabees, Marines
"Happy Talk" .... Bloody Mary, Liat
"Younger Than Springtime" (Reprise) .... Lt. Cable
"Honey Bun" .... Nellie, Billis, Nurses, Sailors, Seabees, Marines
"You've Got To Be Carefully Taught" .... Lt. Cable
"This Nearly Was Mine" .... Emile
"Some Enchanted Evening" (Reprise) .... Nellie
"Honey Bun" (Reprise) .... Nurses, Sailors, Marines, Seabees
Finale .... Nellie, Emile, Ngana, Jerome

The Unknown Soldier and His Wife (148). By Peter Ustinov. Produced by Alexander H. Cohen at the Vivian Beaumont Theater of Lincoln Center. Opened July 6, 1967. (Closed November 12, 1967)

Sergeant .... W. B. Brydon
35914 .... Don Scardino
General .... Brian Bedford
Rebel .... Marco St. John
Wife .... Melissa C. Murphy
Archbishop .... Howard Da Silva
14768 .... Andrew Johns
71696 .... William Dolive
Unknown Soldier .... Christopher Walken
94343 .... James Storm
Enemy Leader .... Alan Mixon
Inventor .... Bob Dishy
Woman .... M'el Dowd
Reinforcements .... Andrew R. Amic-Angelo, Gary Barton, B. J. DeSimone, Larry Swanson

Musicians: Robert Rogers, conductor, organ; Bernard Berger, reeds; William Kirby, trumpet; Irwin Farberman, percussion.

Understudies: Mr. Bedford—Larry Swanson; Mr. Walken—James Storm; Misses Murphy, Dowd—Kathleen Dabney; Mr. Mixon—B. J. DeSimone; Mr. Dishy—William Dolive.

Directed by John Dexter; music, David Shire; scenery and costumes, Motley; lighting, Jules Fisher; associate producer, Hildy Parks; production supervisor, Jerry Adler; production stage manager, Ben Janney; stage manager, Robert L. Borod; press, James D. Proctor.

The play is divided into "two acts of war", as the Unknown Soldier goes off to die in battle again and again in various places, for 2,000 years from Roman times to the present—until, finally, he turns and refuses to go to war another time. A foreign (English) play which had its world premiere in this production.

The Unknown Soldier and His Wife moved from Lincoln Center 9/18/67, after 84 performances, to the George Abbott Theater, where it played an additional 64 performances.

Zale Kessler replaced Bob Dishy 9/18/67.

Judy Garland at Home at the Palace (24). Musical revue. Produced by Sid Luft in A Group V Ltd. Production at the Palace Theater. Opened July 31, 1967. (Closed August 26, 1967)

Francis Brunn
John Bubbles
Judy Garland
Lorna Luft
Joey Luft
Jackie Vernon

Directed by Richard Barstow; musical director, Bobby Cole; costumes, Bill Smith Travilla; lighting, Ralph Alswang; stage manager, Paul Phillips; press, Bill Doll & Co.

ACT I: Francis Brunn, John Bubbles, Jackie Vernon. ACT II: Judy Garland. During her performance Miss Garland introduced Lorna and Joey Luft, her children. Miss Garland had previously appeared at the Palace October 16, 1951 and September 26, 1956. Her song numbers in this engagement included "You Made Me Love You," "For Me and My Gal," "I Feel a Song Coming On," "Me and My Shadow," "Together," "Rockabye Baby," "I Loved Him, He Didn't Love Me," "The Trolley Song," "That's Entertainment" and "Over the Rainbow."

Eddie Fisher-Buddy Hackett at the Palace (42). Two-man revue. Produced by Hackett Productions and Fisher Productions at the Palace Theater. Opened August 28, 1967. (Closed October 7, 1967)

Musical director, Colin Romoff; production stage manager, Bunny Fisher; press, Frank Goodman, Martin Shwartz, Fred Weterick. Divided into two parts, one of Eddie Fisher doing song numbers including "Let Me Entertain You," "The Impossible Dream," "If She Walked Into My Life," "Mame," "People Like You" and "Do, Re, Mi," and one of Buddy Hackett comedy monologue, with the two performers combining for a finale.

Dr. Cook's Garden (8). By Ira Levin. Produced by Saint-Subber at the Belasco Theater. Opened September 25, 1967. (Closed September 30, 1967)

Dr. Jim Tennyson .... Keir Dullea
Bea Schmidt .... Bette Henritze
Dora Ludlow .... Lee Sanders
Elias Hart .... Bob Berger
Dr. Leonard Cook .... Burl Ives

Understudies: Messrs. Ives, Gerger—Seymour Penzner; Mr. Dullea—Peter Haig; Misses Henritze, Sanders—Jen Jones.

Directed by Ira Levin; scenery and lighting, David Hays; costumes, Noel Taylor; associate producers, Frank Prince, Manuel Seff; production stage manager, Mortimer Halpern; press, Harvey B. Sabinson, Lee Solters.

Time: A Friday in the fall of 1966. Place: The home and office of Dr. Leonard Cook, in the village of Greenfield Center, Vermont. Act I: Late afternoon. Act II: Ten minutes later. Act III: Half an hour later.

A young doctor discovers a kindly old Vermont doctor's secret—that he has been poisoning unwanted human beings to improve the character of his community.

Keep It In The Family (5). By Bill Naughton. Produced by David Merrick by arrangement with Allan Davis, Ltd. and Michael Medwin at the Plymouth Theater. Opened September 27, 1967. (Closed September 30, 1967)

Daisy Brady .... Maureen O'Sullivan
Florence Brady .... Marian Hailey
Betsy Jane .... Sudie Bond
Billy Brady .... Jeff Siggins
Michael Brady .... Burt Brinckerhoff
Hilda Brady .... Karen Black
Frank Brady .... Patrick Magee
Arthur .... Tom Atkins

Standby: Misses O'Sullivan, Bond—Elizabeth Parrish. Understudies: Mr. Magee—William Chambers; Messrs. Brinckerhoff, Atkins—Ed Garrabrandt; Misses Hailey, Black—Louise Shaffer; Mr. Siggins—Edmund Gaynes.

Directed by Allan Davis; scenery, Lloyd Burlingame; costumes, Mary McKinley; associate producer, Samuel Liff; production stage manager, Gerald O'Brien; stage manager, William Chambers; press, Harvey B. Sabinson, Lee Solters, Leo Stern.

Time: Autumn almost 20 years ago. Place: The Brady home in a town in Massachusetts. Act I: Friday. Act II, Scene 1: Sunday. Scene 2: Monday.

A stern parent enforces his will on his wife and children for their own good, but he presses too hard and causes his family to revolt against him. A foreign play previously produced in London as *Spring and Port Wine,* with a Yorkshire setting which was adapted to Boston for this production.

Song of the Grasshopper (4). By Alfonso Paso; adapted from the Spanish by William Layton and Agustin Penon. Produced by Gene Dingenary, Miranda d'Ancona and Nancy Levering at the ANTA Theater. Opened September 28, 1967. (Closed September 30, 1967)

Bisbiana .... Diana Davila
Euphemia .... Robin Ponterio
Aristobulo .... Alfred Drake
Alfredo .... Ben Piazza
Elena .... Jan Farrand
Pepe .... Michael Enserro

Directed by Charles Bowden; scenery, Oliver Smith; lighting, Martin Aronstein; costumes, Noel Taylor; production stage manager, Tom Sawyer; associate producer, Eugenie Snell; stage manager, Gene Nye; press, Ben Kornzweig, Reginald Denenholz.

Time: The present. Place: The house of Aristobulo Rivas on the outskirts of Madrid. Act I: Morning. Act II: Evening a week later.

Comedy about an amiable idler whose relaxed standards of living and loving come into conflict with middle-class achievement and snobbery. A foreign play previously produced in Spain.

The Birthday Party (126). By Harold Pinter. Produced by Haila Stoddard, Mark Wright and Leonard S. Field at the Booth Theater. Opened October 3, 1967. (Closed January 20, 1968)

Petey .... Henderson Forsythe
Meg .... Ruth White
Stanley .... James Patterson
Lulu .... Alexandra Berlin
Goldberg .... Ed Flanders
McCann .... Edward Winter

Standbys: Mr. Forsythe—James Karen; Misses White, Berlin—Marilyn Chris; Messrs. Patterson, Winter—Jordan Charney; Mr. Flanders—Jack Hollander.

Directed by Alan Schneider; scenery and costumes, William Ritman; lighting, Tharon Musser; associate producer, Duane Wilder; production stage manager, John Drew Devereaux; press, David Rothenberg.

Time: The present. Place: The living room of a house in a seaside town, in England. Act I: A morning in summer. Act II: Evening of the same day. Act III: The next morning.

Two take-charge types thrust themselves into a sleazy boarding house to organize a violent birthday party for the seedy young boarder, then dress him in his best clothes and take him away with them. A foreign play previously produced in London and elsewhere.

Jordan Charney replaced James Patterson 1/15/68.

A Minor Adjustment (3). By Eric Nicol. Produced by E. & R. Mirvish at the Brooks Atkinson Theater. Opened October 6, 1967. (Closed October 7, 1967)

Ron Webster .... William Redfield
Cameron Clark .... Austin Willis
Mary Clark .... Margaret Draper
Cam Clark Jr. .... Paul Collins
Gilian Walsh .... Joan Darling

Standby: Mr. Redfield—Carleton Carpenter; Mr. Willis—Casey Walters; Miss Darling—Arleen Lawrence; Miss Draper—Evelyn Paeper; Mr. Collins—Kenneth Carr.

Directed by Henry Kaplan; scenery, Leo B. Meyer; costumes, Saul Bolasni; lighting, Jules Fisher; production stage manager, Murray Gitlin; press, Frank Goodman, Martin Shwartz.

Time: The present, May. Place: The library-den of the Clark home in a suburb of Vancouver, British Columbia. Act I, Scene 1: Early evening. Scene 2: Late afternoon, Saturday, about a week later. Scene 3: Late that evening. Act II, Scene 1: Sunday morning. Scene 2: The following Thursday, late afternoon; Scene 3: The following Saturday morning.

Comedy about a father who deals with his rebellious son by assigning the mistress of his firm's press agent to seduce the young man. A foreign play previously produced in Vancouver and Toronto.

Johnny No-Trump (1). By Mary Mercier. Produced by Theater 1968 (Richard Barr, Clinton Wilder, Charles Woodward Jr.) at the Cort Theater. Opened and closed at the evening performance October 8, 1967.

Harry Armstrong .... Pat Hingle
Mrs. Franklin .... Barbara Lester
John Edwards .... Don Scardino
Florence Edwards .... Sada Thompson
Alexander Edwards .... James Broderick
Bettina .... Bernadette Peters

Directed by Joseph Hardy; scenery, lighting, costumes, William Ritman; stage manager, D. W. Koehler; press, Howard Atlee.

Time: The present, February. Place: The Armstrong home on Long Island. Act I, Scene 1: A rainy Saturday morning. Scene 2: Forty-five minutes later. Act II: A cold sunny Sunday afternoon.

Restless teen-ager, a would-be poet, wrestles with two father-figures (his father and his uncle) and reconciles himself to them just before his mother is accidentally killed.

After The Rain (64). By John Bowen. Produced by Helen Jacobson by arrangement with John Roberts at the John Golden Theater. Opened October 9, 1967. (Closed December 2, 1967)

The Lecturer .... Paul Sparer
His Assistants .... Edward J. Moore, Alan Rachins
Captain Hunter .... Anthony Oliver
Arthur Henderson .... Alec McCowen
Gertrude Forbes-Cooper .... Nancy Marchand
Tony Batch .... Bill Burns
Wesley Otterdale .... John Carpenter
Muriel Otterdale .... Maureen Pryor
Harold Banner .... Alan MacNaughtan
Alan Armitage .... John Colenback
Sonya Banks .... Gretchen Corbett

Understudies: Messrs. McCowen, Oliver, Carpenter—Colgate Salsbury; Misses Marchand, Pryor—Joyce Reed; Messrs. Sparer, MacNaughtan—John Carpenter.

Directed by Vivian Matalon; scenery designed by Brian Currah, executed by Paul Morrison; lighting, Tharon Musser; costumes, Domingo A. Rodriguez; production stage manager, Ben Janney; stage manager, Nelle Nugent; press, Sol Jacobson, Lewis Harmon.

Time: Two hundred years after The Rain of 1969. Place: A university lecture hall. The play is divided into two parts.

A lecturer describes the second Flood, acted out as he talks: a handful of survivors is dominated by a self-appointed leader who has to be killed when he sets himself up as a cruel god, but who leaves an authoritarian form of society which persists after he has gone. A foreign play adapted by Bowen from his novel of the same title and previously produced in London.

A Best Play; see page 131

Marlene Dietrich (48). One-woman program of songs performed by Marlene Dietrich. Produced by Alexander H. Cohen in A Nine O'Clock Theater Production at the Lunt-Fontanne Theater. Opened October 9, 1967. (Closed November 18, 1967)

Arrangements and orchestra conducted by Bert Bacharach; lighting, Joe Davis; production stage manager, Tony Chardet; stage manager, Daniel Broun; press, John Springer Associates, Louise Weiner.

Miss Dietrich's program was presented without intermission. Song numbers were "I Can't Give You Anything But Love, Baby," "You're the Cream in My Coffee," "My Blue Heaven,"

"See What the Boys in the Back Room Will Have," "The Laziest Girl in Town," "When the World Was Young," "Jonny," "Go Away from My Window," "I Wish You Love," "The War's Over, Seems We Won, Hooray," "Boomerang Baby," "Naughty Lola," "Don't Ask Me Why," "Everyone's Gone to the Moon," "Marie, Marie," "Lili Marlene," "Where Have All the Flowers Gone," "Honeysuckle Rose," "Falling in Love Again," "La Vie en Rose," "Shir Hatan."

By George (13). One-man program of material from the non-theatrical works of George Bernard Shaw, performed by Max Adrian. Devised by Michael Voysey. Produced by Arthur Cantor and Nicholas Vanoff, Ltd. at the Lyceum Theater. Opened October 12, 1967. (Closed October 22, 1967)

Produced in association with Santa Fe Productions, Inc.; production stage manager, Paul A. Foley; press, Artie Solomon.

Act I: The search. Act II: The arrival. Act III: The eminence. Max Adrian impersonates Shaw in various stages of his life from age 38 to age 93 in material from Shaw's letters, essays, reviews, etc. A foreign play previously produced in Edinburgh and London.

Daphne in Cottage D (49). By Stephen Levi. Produced by Robert Leder and Michael Productions at the Longacre Theater. Opened October 15, 1967. (Closed November 26, 1967)

Daphne .... Sandy Dennis
Joseph .... William Daniels

Standbys: Miss Dennis—Rose Gregorio; Mr. Daniels—John P. Ryan.

Directed by Martin Fried; scenery and lighting, Jo Mielziner; costumes, Theoni V. Aldredge; associate producer, Porter van Zandt; production stage manager, Philip Mandelker; stage manager, John Actman; press, Harvey B. Sabinson, Lee Solters, Robert Larkin.

Time: The present. Place: The living room of a cottage in a resort hotel on the New England coast on a summer night. The play was divided into three parts in the first few performances of its run, and subsequently into two parts.

Two neurotics meet at a resort hotel and spend the evening drinking, sparring and finally confessing their innermost fears and longings to each other.

* **Rosencrantz and Guildenstern Are Dead** (262). By Tom Stoppard. Produced by David Merrick Arts Foundation by arrangement with The National Theater of Great Britain at the Alvin Theater. Opened October 16, 1967.

Rosencrantz .... Brian Murray
Guildenstern .... John Wood
The Player .... Paul Hecht
Tragedians
  Alfred .... Douglas Norwick
  The King .... Roger Kemp
  The Poisoner .... Dino Laudicina
  The Spies .... B. J. DeSimone, Roy Lozano
Hamlet .... Noel Craig
Ophelia .... Patricia McAneny
Claudius .... Roger Hamilton
Gertrude .... Anne Meacham
Polonius .... Ralph Drischell
Soldier .... Alexander Courtney
Ambassador .... Carl Jacobs
Horatio .... Michael Holmes

Courtiers, Ambassadors, Soldiers, Attendants: Walter Beery, Stephen Bernstein, Gaetano Bongiovanni, Margaret Braidwood, Esther Buffler, Elizabeth Eis, Elizabeth Franz, William Grannell, John Handy, Mary Hara, Edward Marshall, Ted Pezzulo. Musicians: Bruce Levine, Bernard Karl, Jack Knitzer, Don Arol.

Standbys: Mr. Murray—Jonathan Reynolds; Mr. Wood—Garnett Smith.

Directed by Derek Goldby; scenery and costumes, Desmond Heeley; lighting, Richard Pilbrow; music, Marc Wilkinson; associate producer, Samuel Liff; production stage manager, Mitchell Erickson; stage manager, Andre St. Jean; press, Harvey B. Sabinson, Lee Solters, Robert Larkin.

Time and place: Within and around the action of Shakespeare's *Hamlet*. The play is divided into three parts.

The action of *Hamlet* is treated as dark comedy as seen from the point of view of Rosencrantz and Guildenstern, a couple of born losers who are being pushed to their deaths by forces and motivations which they are unable to perceive or comprehend. A foreign play previously produced in Oxford, Edinburgh and London.

A Best Play; see page 171

* **There's a Girl in My Soup** (260). By Terence Frisby. Produced by Saint-Subber and Michael Codron in association with Columbia Pictures Corp. at the Music Box. Opened October 18, 1967.

Robert Danvers .... Gig Young
Clare .... Rita Gam
Andrew .... Jon Pertwee
Porter .... George Hall
Paola .... Erica Fitz
Marion .... Barbara Ferris
Jimmy .... Gawn Grainger

Standbys: Miss Ferris—Marie Masters; Miss Gam—Judith Searle; Messrs. Pertwee, Hall—Steven Scott; Mr. Grainger—Wisner Washam.

Directed by Robert Chetwyn; original production design, Hutchinson Scott; costumes, Stanley Simmons; lighting, Lloyd Burlingame; production stage manager, Harvey Medlinsky; stage manager, Wisner Washam; press, Harvey B. Sabinson, Lee Solters, Harry Nigro.

Time: The present. Place: Robert Danvers' flat in London. Act I: An evening in late summer. Act II: The next morning. Act III: Two weeks later.

Comedy about the romantic adventures of a middle-aged gourmet who becomes entangled with a pretty young mod. A foreign play previously produced in London.

Amanda Reis replaced Barbara Ferris 4/22/68. Lawrence Hugo replaced Gig Young 5/13/68.

The Jewish State Theater of Poland. Repertory of two plays in the Yiddish language. **Mirele Efros** (42). By Jacob Gordin; adapted by Ida Kaminska. Opened October 19, 1967. **Mother Courage and Her Children** (11). By Bertolt Brecht; translated and adapted by Ida Kaminska. Opened November 16, 1967. Produced by Harold Leventhal and Marie Desmarais at the Billy Rose Theater. (Repertory closed December 17, 1967)

PERFORMER	"MIRELE EFROS"	"MOTHER COURAGE AND HER CHILDREN"
Juliusz Berger	Josele	Szwejcerkez
Mieczyslaw Bram		Escorting Soldier
Seweryn Dalecki		Cook
Izaak Dogim		Copyist; Peasant
Dina Fijalkowska	Oksana	Ivette
Maria Fridman	Machle	Peasant's Wife
Harry Gold	Szlojmele	
Henryk Grynberg	Jurke	Young Artisan
Ida Kaminska	Mirele Efros	Mother Courage
Ruth Kaminska	Szejndele	Katrin
Ruth Kowalska	Chane Dwojre	Artisan's Mother
Karol Latowicz	Donie	Eilif
Herman Lercher		Sergeant Major; Elder Soldier; Soldier 2
Marian Melman	Reb-Szalmen	Chaplain
Josef Retik		Peasant's Son; Man with Eye Patch

PERFORMER	"MIRELE EFROS"	"MOTHER COURAGE AND HER CHILDREN"
Samuel Rettig		Feldfebel; Drunken Soldier
Abraham Rozenbaum		Soldier; Standard Bearer
Marian Rudenski	Cantor	Armorer; Younger Soldier
Szymon Szurmiej		Commander; Soldier 1
Michael Szwejlich	Nuchemtse	Recruiting Soldier; Colonel

Both plays: artistic director, Ida Kaminska; director, Ida Kaminska; stage manager, Mieczyslaw Bram; press, Ben Kornzweig, Reginald Denenholz, Benjamin Rothman.

MIRELE EFROS scenery, Marian Stanczak; lighting consultant, Charles Elson; accompanying English translation, Raphael Rothstein.

Time: The second half of the 19th century. Place: Poland. Act I: In Sluck. Act II: In Grodno, three years later. Act III: In Grodno. Act IV: In Grodno, ten years later.

A Yiddish stage classic in which a matriarch is victimized by her unfeeling children, somewhat in the manner of King Lear. A foreign play previously presented in Poland and elsewhere.

MOTHER COURAGE AND HER CHILDREN scenery, Zenobius Strzelecki; music, Paul Dessau.

Time: 1624. Place: Europe. The play is divided into two acts and eleven scenes.

This chronicle play of the Thirty Years' War was first produced in New York March 28, 1963 by Cheryl Crawford and Jerome Robbins at the Martin Beck Theater for 52 performances. It was named a Best Play of its season.

The City Center Drama Company. Schedule of two revivals. **Life With Father** (22). By Howard Lindsay and Russel Crouse; based on the book by Clarence Day. Opened October 19, 1967. (Closed November 5, 1967). **The Tenth Man** (23). By Paddy Chayefsky. Opened November 8, 1967. (Closed November 26, 1967). Produced by The City Center Drama Company, Jean Dalrymple director, at New York City Center.

LIFE WITH FATHER

Vinnie ....Dorothy Stickney
Annie ....Emily Peden
Clarence ....Rusty Thacker
John ....Gary Enck
Whitney ....Jeff Stuart
Harlan ....Jimmie Grubman
Father ....Leon Ames
Margaret ....Abby Lewis
Cousin Cora ....Jean Sincere
Mary Skinner ....Sandy Duncan
The Rev. Dr. Lloyd .....William LeMassena
Delia ....Ann Freeman
Nora ....Toni Darnay
Dr. Humphreys ....Alexander Clark
Dr. Sommers ....John D. Seymour
Maggie ....Marta Heflin

Standby: Miss Stickney—Muriel Kirkland. Understudies: Mr. Ames—Alexander Clark; Messrs. Thacker, Enck—George Coleman; Masters Grubman, Stuart—Mark Kearney.

Directed by Gus Schirmer; scenery, Stewart Chaney; costumes, Edith Lutyens Bel Geddes; production stage manager, Herman Shapiro; stage mangers, Forrest Carter, Jeff Chambers. Press, Homer Poupart, John Clugstone.

Time: The 1880s. Place: The morning room of the Day house on Madison Avenue in New York.

Life With Father was first produced November 8, 1939 by Oscar Serlin at the Empire Theater, with Miss Stickney and Mr. Lindsay as Vinnie and Father. It ran for 3,224 performances—Broadway's longest run—and was named a Best Play of its season. This is its first professional New York revival.

THE TENTH MAN

Hirschman ....Muni Seroff
Sexton ....Jon Silo
Schlissel ....Lou Polan
Zitorsky ....Joseph Mell
Alper ....Boris Tumarin
Foreman ....Michael Gorrin
Evelyn Foreman ....Pamela Kingsley
Arthur Landau ....John Kerr
Harris ....Sam Nudell
Rabbi ....Gene Gross
Kessler Boys ....Sol Serlin, Haig Chobanian
Policeman ....Daniel P. Hannafin

Standby: Mr. Kerr—Donald Buka. Understudy: Miss Kingsley—Linda Washburn.

Directed by Arthur Cantor; scenery and lighting, David Hays; costumes, Frank Thompson; assistant to Mr. Cantor, Donald Buka; production stage manager, Herman Shapiro; stage manager, William Chambers.

Time: The present. Place: An Orthodox Synagogue in Mineola, Long Island.

The Tenth Man was first produced November 5, 1959 by Saint-Subber and Arthur Cantor at the Booth Theater for 623 performances. It was named a Best Play of its season. This is its first professional New York revival.

What Did We Do Wrong? (48). By Henry Denker. Produced by Michael Myerberg and Donald Flamm at the Helen Hayes Theater. Opened Ocotber 22, 1967. (Closed December 2, 1967)

Norma Davis ....Philippa Bevans
Walter Davis ....Paul Ford
Walter Davis Jr. ....Russell Horton
Scott ....Gregory Rozakis
Cindy ....Heidi Vaughn
Woody ....Roy Providence
Clarence Cahill ....Hugh Franklin
Charlotte Cahill ....Enid Markey

Understudies: Mr. Ford—Hugh Franklin; Messrs. Horton, Rozakis—Christopher Strater.

Directed by Sherwood Arthur; scenery, Albert Johnson; costumes, Jack Edwards; lighting, Leo B. Meyer; music, Paul Martin; executive producer, Paul Jacobson; production stage manager, Herman Magidson; press, Bill Doll & Co.

Time: The present. Place: The Davis living room, White Plains, N.Y. Act I, Scene 1: A spring evening. Scene 2: Early the next morning. Act II, Scene 1: Several hours later. Scene 2: Later that afternoon.

Comedy about a businessman who turns himself into a hippie in an effort to out-freak his wayward son.

Henry, Sweet Henry (80). Musical based on the novel *The World of Henry Orient* by Nora Johnson; book by Nunnally Johnson; music and lyrics by Bob Merrill. Produced by Edward Specter Productions and Norman Twain at the Palace Theater. Opened October 23, 1967. (Closed December 31, 1967)

Kafritz ....Alice Playten
Valerie Boyd ....Robin Wilson
Miss Cooney ....Barbara Beck
Marian Gilbert ....Neva Small
Henry Orient ....Don Ameche
Stella ....Louise Lasser
Mrs. Gilbert ....Trudy Wallace
Usherette ....Julie Sargant
Mrs. Boyd ....Carol Bruce
Russ ....John Mineo
Captain Kenneth ....George NeJame
Hal ....Robert Iscove
Policeman ....Gerard Brentte
Mr. Boyd ....Milo Boulton
Policeman ....Charles Rule
Big Val ....................K.C. Townsend

Norton School Students: Chris Bocchino, Lori Cesar, Terry Forman, Joyce James, Baayork Lee, Gina Page, Ilene Schatz, Rebecca Urich, Pia Zadora. Knickerbocker Greys: Paul Charles, Robert Iscove, Joe Mazzello, Kim Milford, John Mineo, George NeJame, Craig Wineline.

Adult Ensemble: Robert Avian, Barbara Beck, Gerard Brentte, Gene Castle, Robert Fitch, Marvin Goodis, Neil Jones, Mary Ann Kerrick, Priscilla Lopez, Lee Lund, Laried Montgomery, Charles Rule, Julie Sargant, Mary Ann Snow, Trudy Wallace.

Standbys: Mr. Ameche—Joseph Leon; Miss Lasser—Leila Martin. Understudies: Miss Bruce—Mary Ann Snow; Miss Wilson—Rebecca Urich; Miss Small—Pia Zadora; Miss Playten—Lori Cesar.

Directed by George Roy Hill; choreography, Michael Bennett; musical direction and vocal arrangements, Shepard Coleman; scenery and lighting, Robert Randolph; costumes, Alvin Colt; orchestrations, Eddie Sauter; dance music, William Goldenberg, Marvin Hamlisch; production stage manager, William Dodds; stage manager, Harry Clark; press, Harvey B. Sabinson, Lee Solters, David Powers.

Time: The present. Place: New York City.

Lonesome teen-ager, neglected by her globe-trotting parents, idealizes and chases after a handsome and sportive bachelor. Nora Johnson's novel *The World of Henry Orient* was previously dramatized as a screen play by her father, Nunnally Johnson, the librettist of *Henry, Sweet Henry*.

ACT I

Scene 1: A street in New York City
"Academic Fugue" .... Company
Scene 2: Locker room
"In Some Little World" .... Val
Scene 3: Central Park Zoo
"Pillar to Post" .... Orient, Stella
Scene 4: Two bedrooms
"Here I Am" .... Val
Scene 5: Concert hall
Scene 6: Val's bedroom
"Whereas" .... Val, Gil
Scene 7: Telephone booths
Scene 8: Luncheonette
"I Wonder How It Is To Dance With a Boy" .... Gil, Girls
Scene 9: Street telephone booth
"Nobody Steps on Kafritz" .... Kafritz
Scene 10: Orient's apartment—exterior and interior
"Henry, Sweet Henry" .... Val, Gil
"Woman in Love" .... Val, Gil
"The People Watchers" .... Company

ACT II

Scene 1: Boyd's living room
Scene 2: Washington Square
"Weary Near to Dyin'" .... Val, Hippies
Scene 3: Orient's apartment
Scene 4: Boyd's living room
Scene 5: Exterior school and locker room
"Poor Little Person" .... Kafritz, Girls, Knickerbocker Greys
"I'm Blue Too" .... Val, Gil
Scene 6: Cocktail bar
"To Be Artistic" .... Orient, Mrs. Boyd
Scene 7: Exterior Orient's apartment
Scene 8: Boyd's living room
Scene 9: Orient's bedroom
"Forever" .... Orient
Scene 10: Val's bedroom
"Do You Ever Go To Boston" .... Val
Finale: Knickerbocker Grey Happening
"Here I Am" (Reprise) .... Val

* **The Repertory Theater of Lincoln Center.** Schedule of four revivals. **The Little Foxes** (100; see note). By Lillian Hellman. A special invitational production under the supervision of Saint-Subber. Opened October 26, 1967. (Closed at Lincoln Center December 16, 1967; see note) **Saint Joan** (44). By George Bernard Shaw. Opened January 4, 1968. (Closed February 10, 1968). **Tiger at the Gates** (44). By Jean Giraudoux; adapted by Christopher Fry. Opened February 29, 1968. (Closed April 6, 1968). * **Cyrano de Bergerac** (42). By Edmond Rostand; new English version by James Forsyth. Opened April 25, 1968. Produced by The Repertory Theater of Lincoln Center, under the direction of Jules Irving, at the Vivian Beaumont Theater.

THE LITTLE FOXES

Addie .... Beah Richards
Cal .... Andre Womble
Birdie Hubbard .... Margaret Leighton
Oscar Hubbard .... E. G. Marshall
Leo Hubbard .... Austin Pendleton
Regina Giddens .... Anne Bancroft
William Marshall .... William Prince
Benjamin Hubbard .... George C. Scott
Alexandra Giddens .... Maria Tucci
Horace Giddens .... Richard A. Dysart

Standby: Misses Bancroft, Leighton—Elizabeth Wilson. Understudies: Mr. Scott—Robert Symonds; Messrs. Marshall, Prince—John Braden; Miss Tucci—Kathleen Eric; Mr. Dysart—Ray Fry; Mr. Pendleton—Frank Bayer; Mr. Womble—George Carter; Miss Richards—Ruth Attaway.

Directed by Mike Nichols; scenery and lighting, Howard Bay; costumes, Patricia Zipprodt; production stage manager, Tom Porter; stage managers, Frank Bayer, Brent Sutton; press, Harvey B. Sabinson, Lee Solters, Harry Nigro.

Time: The spring of 1900. Place: The living room of the Giddens house in a small town in the South.

The Little Foxes was first produced February 15, 1939 by Herman Shumlin for 410 performances, with Tallulah Bankhead as Regina and Charles Dingle as Ben. It was named a Best Play of its season. It reached the screen with Bette Davis as Regina in 1941 and formed the basis for the Marc Blitzstein opera *Regina* produced October 31, 1949 at the Forty-sixth Street Theater for 53 performances. This is its first professional New York revival.

NOTE: This production of *The Little Foxes* ran for 60 performances at the Vivian Beaumont Theater, through 12/16/67. On 12/19/67 it moved to the Ethel Barrymore and continued its run for 40 more performances through 1/20/68.

On 12/19/67 Margaret Leighton replaced Anne Bancroft; Felicia Monteliagre replaced Miss Leighton; Geraldine Chaplin replaced Maria Tucci; E. G. Marshall replaced George C. Scott; Scott McKay replaced E. G. Marshall; Liam Sullivan replaced William Prince.

SAINT JOAN

Bertrand de Poulengy ....John Braden
Steward ....Nicholas Kepros
Joan ....Diana Sands
Robert de Beaudricourt; an English Soldier..........Ted D'Arms
The Archbishop of Rheims ....Roger De Koven
Monseigneur de la Tremouille ....Ronald Bishop
Court Page ....Tom Fuccello
Gilles de Rais; a Gentleman of 1920 .....Richard Clarke
Captain La Hire ....Earle Hyman
The Dauphin (later Charles VII) ....Edward Zang
Duchess de la Tremouille ....Shirley Jac Wagner
Dunois, Bastard of Orleans ....Philip Bosco
Dunois' Page ....Northern Calloway
Richard de Beauchamp, Earl of Warwick ....William Hutt
Chaplain de Stogumber .....Robert Symonds
Peter Cauchon, Bishop of Beauvais ......Tony van Bridge
Warwick's Page ....Ryan Listman
The Inquisitor ....John Heffernan
D'Estivet ....Earl Montgomery
De Courcelles ....Ray Fry
Brother Martin Ladvenu .....Stephen Joyce
The Executioner ....Ronald Weyand

Members of the French Court: Charles Burks, Roberta Callahan, Jane Karel, Stephen Lemberg, Barbara Thurston, William Walsh.

English Soldiers: John Dorrin, Robert Haswell, Robert Phalen, Edmond Varrato. French Soldiers: Christopher Bernau, John Felton, Jon Froscher, Chris Kelly, Michael Maurer, Fred Seagraves.

Standby: Miss Sands—Rae Allen. Understudies: Mr. Zang—Nicholas Kepros; Mr. Bosco—John Braden; Mr. Hutt—Richard Clark; Mr. van Bridge—Ronald Bishop.

Directed by John Hirsch; scenery, David Hays; costumes, Michael Annals; lighting, John Gleason; music, Stanley Silverman; production stage manager, Brent Sutton; stage manager, Ronald Schaeffer; press, Susan Bloch.

Time 1429 to 1456. Place: France. Part I, Scene 1: A fine spring morning on the river Meuse, between Lorraine and Champagne, in the year 1429 in the castle of Vaucouleurs. Scene 2: Late afternoon, March 8, 1429. The castle of the Dauphin at Chinon, in Touraine. Scene 3: Evening, April 29, 1429. The bank of the river Loire, near Orleans. Scene 4: A tent in the English camp. Part II, Scene 5: The ambulatory in the cathedral of Rheims. Scene 6: Morning, May 30, 1431. The great hall of the castle at Rouen. Epilogue: A night in June, 1456. The bedroom in King Charles' chateau.

Saint Joan was first produced on Broadway by the Theater Guild on December 28, 1923 at the Garrick Theater for 195 performances. Its most recent New York revival was its production in repertory by the Old Vic on February 20, 1962 at New York City Center, with Barbara Jefford as Joan. Its most recent American production was off Broadway by the Phoenix Theater on September 11, 1956 for 77 performances, with Siobhan McKenna as Joan.

TIGER AT THE GATES

Cassandra ....Diana Sands
Andromache ....M'el Dowd
Laundress ....Diane Kagan
Hector ....Philip Bosco
Attendant ....Northern Calloway
Paris ....Dennis Cooney
Abneos ....Edgar Daniels
Anchises ....Al Corbin
Priam ....Roger De Koven
Demokos ....Howard St. John
Hecuba ....Aline MacMahon
(Polyxene) ....Eileen Dolphin, Rebecca Symonds
Mathematician ....Ray Fry
Maids-in-Waiting ....Janet League, Sandy Rochelle
Helen ....Jennifer West
Oneah ....Lloyd Hollar
Minos ....Robert Phalen
Troilus ....Bruce Davison
Old Man ....Robert Haswell
Busiris ....Richard Clarke
Priests ....Earle Montgomery, Charles Burks
Ajax ....Ronald Weyand
Ulysses ....Tony van Bridge
Topman ....John Braden
Olpides ....Ted D'Arms

(Parentheses indicate role in which the actors alternate)

Trojans: Charles Burks, Christopher Kelly, Ryan Listman, Fred Seagraves, Daniel Sullivan, Shirley Jac Wagner.

Understudies: Mr. Bosco—John Braden; Misses Sands, MacMahon—Shirley Jac Wagner; Miss Dowd—Winifred Mann; Mr. Cooney—Richard Clarke.

Directed by Anthony Quayle; scenery, David Hays; costumes, Fred Voelpel; lighting, John Gleason; music, Stanley Silverman; production stage manager, James Kershaw; stage manager, Barbara-Mae Phillips.

Time: Just before the Trojan War. Place: Troy.

This Christopher Fry adaptation of Giraudoux' *The Trojan War Will Not Take Place* was presented on Broadway October 3, 1955 at the Plymouth Theater for 217 performances with Michael Redgrave as Hector and was named a Best Play of its season.

CYRANO DE BERGERAC

Jodelet; Spanish Officer ....Roger De Koven
Orange Girl ....Sasha von Scherler
Porter ....Robert Haswell
Citizen ....Earl Montgomery
(His Son) ....Donnie Melvin, Kim Michaels
Musketeer ....Ted D'Arms
Cavalier ....Robert Benson
Pickpocket ....Robert Levine
Cutpurse; Lute Player ....John Danelle
Apprentice Thief ....Gary Barton
(Appentice Thief) ....Eileen Dolphin, Gail Honig
Drunkard ....Robert Phalen
Cuigy ....Richard Buck
Brissaile ....Leon Russom
Marquis de Tremblay ....Richard Clarke
Fop ....Larry Pine
Bald Fop ....David Vilner
Christian de Neuvillette .....Dennis Cooney
Ligniere; Capuchin ....Ray Fry
Barthenoide ....Shirley Jac Wagner
Urimedonte ....Janet League
Cassandace ....Maeve McGuire
Felixerie; Lise ....Winifred Mann
Roxane ....Suzanne Grossmann
Duenna (later, Sister Claire) ....Nancy Marchand
Comte de Guiche ....Philip Bosco
Valvert ....Albert Cavens
Le Bret ....John Braden
Ragueneau ....Joseph Palmieri
Montfleury ....Edgar Daniels
Cyrano de Bergerac ....Robert Symonds
(Children) ...Donnie Melvin, Kim Michaels, Eileen Dolphin, Gail Honig
Carbon de Castel-Jaloux ....Ronald Weyand
Sister Marthe ....Blythe Danner
Mother Marguerite ....Aline MacMahon
Musicians ......Karl Kraber, James Pedrick

(Parentheses indicate roles in which the actors alternated)

Pages, Footmen, Tradesmen, Lightsmen, Whores, Jodelet's Troupe, Bakers, Apprentices, Scullions, Poets, Cadets, Spanish Soldiers, Nuns: Tom Atkins, Gary Barton, Robert Benson, Richard Buck, Roberta Callahan, Dorothy Chace, James Cook, Thomas Costello, John Danelle, Ted D'Arms, Pamela Fife, Howard Green, Robert Haswell, Lloyd Hollar, Christopher Kelly, Janet League, Robert Levine, Ryan Listman, Bryan Marks, Jerry Mayer, Maeve McGuire, Earl Montgomery, Robert Phelan, Barbara-Mae Phillips, Sandy Rochelle, Leon Russom, Jack Ryland, Brent Sutton, David Vilner, Shirley Jac Wagner, Ronald Weyand.

Understudies: Mr. Symonds—Jack Ryland; Miss Grossmann—Maeve McGuire; Mr. Cooney—Leon Russom; Mr. Bosco—Richard Clarke.

Directed by Carl Weber; scenery, David Hays; costumes, James Hart Stearns; lighting, John

Gleason; music, William Bolcom; swordplay, Albert Cavens; production stage manager, Timothy Ward.

Time: 17th century. Place: France. Act I, Scene 1: Paris, 1640, winter. Scene 2: The same, the next day. Act II: Paris, 1640, May. Act III, Scene 1: The siege of Arras, 1640, late summer. Scene 2: Paris, 1655, fall.

Rostand's *Cyrano de Bergerac* was first produced in New York in 1898 (the year following its debut in Paris) with Richard Mansfield as Cyrano and Margaret Anglin as Roxane. Other Cyranos in New York included Walter Hampden (1923-1936), Ralph Richardson (with the 1946 Old Vic) and José Ferrer (1946). It was last revived on Broadway at New York City Center in 1953 with José Ferrer and Arlene Dahl.

More Stately Mansions (142). By Eugene O'Neill. Produced by Elliot Martin at the Broadhurst Theater. Opened October 31, 1967. (Closed March 2, 1968)

Jamie Cregan ....Barry Macollum
Mickey Maloy ....Vincent Dowling
Nora Melody ....Helen Craig
Sara ....Colleen Dewhurst
Simon Harford ....Arthur Hill
Cato ....John Marriott
Deborah ....Ingrid Bergman
Nicholas Gadsby ....Fred Stewart
Joel Harford ....Lawrence Linville
Benjamin Tenard ....Kermit Murdock

Standby: Misses Bergman, Dewhurst—Jacqueline Brookes. Understudies: Mr. Hill—Lawrence Linville; Messrs. Linville, Macollum—William Goodwin; Messrs. Stewart, Dowling—Alfred Hinckley; Benjamin—Vincent Dowling.

Directed by José Quintero; scenery, Ben Edwards; costumes, Jane Greenwood; lighting, John Harvey; production associate, Marjorie Martin; production stage manager, William Weaver; stage manager, Alfred Hinckley; press, Nat & Irvin Dorfman.

Time: 1832-1841. Place: Massachusetts. Act I, Scene 1: Dining room of Melody's Tavern, an inn in a Massachusetts village near a city; night in October, 1832. Scene 2: A cabin on the shore of a small lake near the village, the following afternoon. Scene 3: Deborah's garden, Henry Harford's home in the city; night in summer, 1836. Scene 4: Sitting room of Sara Harford's home in a neighboring textile mill town, the following night. Act II, Scene 5: Simon Harford's office at Harford in the city, a morning in fall, 1840. Scene 6: Deborah's garden, the Harford home in the city, afternoon of the same day. Scene 7: Parlor of the Harford home; night of the same day. Scene 8: Simon Harford's office again; morning in summer, 1841. Scene 9: Deborah's garden; evening of the same day.

More Stately Mansions follows Eugene O'Neill's *A Touch of the Poet* chronologically. Sara Melody (Con's daughter) has married Simon Harford whose mother, Deborah, disapproves of the marriage and contends with the wife for possession and domination of Simon. Previously produced in Stockholm and Salzburg. The script was cut and edited by José Quintero from the playwright's notes for its American premiere in this production, which opened in Los Angeles 9/12/67.

The Trial of Lee Harvey Oswald (9). By Amram Ducovny and Leon Friedman; based on an idea by Harold Steinberg and Amram Ducovny. Produced by Gene Persson at the ANTA Theater. Opened November 5, 1967. (Closed November 11, 1967)

Lee Harvey Oswald ....Peter Masterson
Hammond Morton (Judge) ......Dan Priest
Lawrence Phelps
(Prosecuting Attorney) ....Clifton James
Henry Rogers
(Defense Counsel) ....Ralph Waite
Witnesses for the prosecution:
Jesse Bellknapp; George Robinson;
Elbert Briggs ....John Gerstad
Daniel Gibbon;
Dr. Paul Dettering ....Glenn Kezer
Carl Turner;
Capt. Frank McQueen ...Douglas Stark
Gov. John B. Connally;
Abner Finchlea ....Barton Stone
Lincoln King;
Harry Stevens ....Garrett Saunders
Sanford Alexander ......Charles Randall
Steve Barton;
Norman Astor ....William Leach
Mrs. Sally Newfield .....Anne Shropshire
Witnesses for the defense:
Elizabeth Rote ....Anne Shropshire
Philip Markfield ....Barton Stone
Clyde Landers;
Sanford Alexander ....Charles Randall
Harrison Edwards ....John Gerstad
Alice Williams ....Louise Stubbs
Harold Lane ....Garrett Saunders
Bruce Currie ....Douglas Stark
Dr. Ray Jones ....William Leach
Rebuttal witness:
Victoria Mavis ....Louise Stubbs

Understudies: Mr. Masterson—William Leach; Messrs. Waite, Stone, Randall—Michael Miller; Messrs. Stark, Leach, Saunders—Will Gregory.

Directed by Tunc Yalman; scenery, Robin Wagner; costumes, Theoni V. Aldredge; lighting, Jules Fisher; associate producer, Jay Fuchs; production stage manager, Del Hughes; stage manager, Fred Reinglas; press, Max Eisen, Jeanne Gibson Merrick, Carl Samrock.

Time: The present. Place: A courtroom. The play is divided into two parts.

Imaginary trial of Lee Harvey Oswald for the assassination of President Kennedy. The case against him is presented in the first part; in the second he testifies that he was merely the dupe of a well-organized conspiracy. Testimony offered by prosecution and defense witnesses is based on actual evidence.

The Ninety-Day Mistress (24). By J. J. Coyle. Produced by Philip Rose, David Wilde and Nederlander-Steinbrenner Productions at the Biltmore Theater. Opened November 6, 1967. (Closed November 25, 1967)

Leona Hastings ....Dyan Cannon
Danny Liken ....Martin Milner
Phyllis ....Doris Belack
Alan ....Nicolas Coster
Judith Hastings ....Ruth Ford
Bill Hastings ....Walter Abel
Rudy Avarian ....Tony Lo Bianco

Standbys: Miss Cannon—Beverly Ballard; Mr. Milner—Joe Ponazecki; Miss Ford—Mary Cooper; Mr. Abel—John Wardwell; Miss Belack—Rose Arrick; Messrs. Coster, Lo Bianco—Gregory Sierra.

Directed by Philip Rose; scenery, Leon Munier; costumes, Pearl Somner; lighting, Clarke Dunham; associate producer, Selma Leichtling; production stage manager, Leonard Auerbach; stage manager, Norman Shelly; press, Merle Debuskey, Violet Welles, Faith Geer.

Time: The present. Place: The apartment of Leona Hastings on the East Side of Manhattan. Act I, Scene 1: Late Friday night. Scene 2: The next morning. Act II, Scene 1: Friday evening, six weeks later. Scene 2: The following Wednesday afternoon. Scene 3: Ten days later, late Saturday night.

A 25-year-old girl, who has been warned against lasting attachments, limits her love affairs, of which there are several, to 90 days' duration.

Halfway up the Tree (64). By Peter Ustinov. Produced by Alexander H. Cohen at the Brooks Atkinson Theater. Opened November 7, 1967. (Closed December 31, 1967)

Lady Fitzbuttress ....Eileen Herlie
Helga ....Hanne Bork
General Sir Mallalieu Fitzbuttress ....Anthony Quayle
Robert ....Sam Waterston
Lesley ...."Lesley"
Judy ....Margaret Linn
Tiny Gilliatt-Brown ....William Larsen
Basil Utterwood ....John Tillinger
The Vicar ....Graham Jarvis

Understudies: Messrs. Quayle, Larsen, Jarvis—Rufus Smith; Miss Herlie—June Prud'homme; Misses Bork, Linn—Kristin Helmore, Barbara Blaire; Messrs. Waterston, Tillinger—Franklin Kiser.

Directed by Peter Ustinov; scenery and lighting, Ralph Alswang; costumes, James Hart Stearns; associate producer, Hildy Parks; production supervisor, Jerry Adler; production stage manager, Jake Hamilton; stage manager, Charles Austin; press, James D. Proctor, David Roggensack, Ruth Cage.

Time: More or less now. Place: A cottage in Hampshire, England. The play is divided into three parts.

Comedy about the generation gap in England, as a retired general tries to understand his dropout children and turns himself into a bearded, guitar-playing hippie living in a tree. A foreign (English) play previously produced in Germany and Paris; subsequently produced in London.

The Promise (23). By Aleksei Arbuzov; translated by Ariadne Nicolaeff. Produced by Helen Bonfils, Morton Gottlieb and Peter Bridge at Henry Miller's Theater. Opened November 14, 1967. (Closed December 2, 1967)

Lika ....Eileen Atkins
Marat (Marik) ....Ian McShane
Leonidik ....Ian McKellen

Standbys: Miss Atkins—Nancy Acly; Mr. McShane—Leon Russom; Mr. McKellen—DeVeren Bookwalter.

Directed by Frank Hauser; scenery, William Ritman; lighting, Tharon Musser; production stage manager, Warren Crane; stage manager, Wayne Carson; press, Dorothy Ross.

Time: 1942 to 1959. Place: A room in a Leningrad apartment. Act I: 1942. Act II: 1946. Act III: 1959.

Two young men and a girl meet in bombed-out Leningrad during the siege and form attachments which develop over the years into a triangular design for living. A foreign play previously produced in 66 theaters throughout the Soviet Union and in Tokyo, Warsaw, Paris, Athens, Tel Aviv and London.

Something Different (103). By Carl Reiner. Produced by King/Hyman/Wolsk/Azenberg at the Cort Theater. Opened November 28, 1967. (Closed February 24, 1968)

Sheldon "Bud" Nemerov ....Bob Dishy
Beth Nemerov ....Linda Lavin
Phil Caponetti ....Gabriel Dell
Kevin & Bevin .....Messrs. Starkman, Battle
Mrs. Kupferman ....Victoria Zussin
Rose Keller ....Helena Carroll
Ida Schwartz ....Maureen Arthur
Sarah Goldfine ....Claudia McNeil
The Players ....Messrs. Jones, Mansfield

Standby: Messrs. Dishy, Dell—Richard Schaal. Understudies: Misses Lavin, Arthur—Zina Jasper; Miss McNeil—Helen Martin; Misses Zussin, Carroll—Mina Kolb.

Directed by Carl Reiner; scenery and lighting, Will Steven Armstrong; costumes, Ann Roth; associate producers, Jack Edreich, Doris Kuller, Jane Cohen; production supervisor, Jose Vega; stage manager, Charles Gray; press, Mike Merrick Co., Barry Kobrin.

Time: The present. Place: The den of the Nemerovs' suburban home. Act I, Scene 1: Late one night. Scene 2: The following morning. Act II, Scene 1: The following morning. Scene 2: The following morning.

Comedy about a playwright trying to repeat a past success by recreating the conditions under which he wrote the play while he was still unmarried and living with his mother.

Everything in the Garden (84). By Edward Albee; based on the play by Giles Cooper. Produced by Theater 1968 (Richard Barr and Clinton Wilder) at the Plymouth Theater. Opened November 29, 1967. (Closed February 10, 1968)

Jenny ....Barbara Bel Geddes
Richard ....Barry Nelson
Jack ....Robert Moore
Mrs. Toothe ....Beatrice Straight
Roger ....Richard Thomas
Beryl ....Mary K. Wells
Chuck ....Whitfield Connor
Louise ....M'el Dowd
Gilbert ....Tom Aldredge
Perry ....Charles Baxter
Cynthia ....Augusta Dabney

Standby: Mr. Nelson—Mark O'Daniels. Understudies: Mr. Thomas—Steve Skiles; Misses Wells, Dowd, Dabney—Delphi Harrington.

Directed by Peter Glenville; scenery and costumes, William Ritman; lighting, Tharon Musser; production stage manager, Gerald O'Brien; stage manager, Joseph Cali; press, David Rothenberg.

Time: The present. Place: Suburbia. The play is divided into two parts.

The country club set's craving for luxuries like a second car or a greenhouse is satisfied after the wives find they can earn wads of money in a few spare hours a week at a big city brothel.

* **Association of Producing Artists (APA) Repertory Company.** Repertory of four plays. * **Pantagleize** (50). By Michel de Ghelderode; translated by George Hauger. Opened November 30, 1967. * **The Show-Off** (69). Revival of the play by George Kelly. Opened December 5, 1967. * **Exit the King** (45). By Eugene Ionesco; translated by Donald Watson. Opened January 9, 1968. **The Cherry Orchard** (38). Revival of the play by Anton Chekhov; translated by Eva Le Gallienne. Opened March 19, 1968. Produced by APA-Phoenix (a project of Theater Incorporated), T. Edward Hambleton managing director, at the Lyceum Theater.

PERFORMER	"PANTAGLEIZE"	"THE SHOW-OFF"	"EXIT THE KING"	"THE CHERRY ORCHARD"
George Addis	Bank Mgr.			
Joseph Bird	Gen. MacBoom	Mr. Fisher		
Kermit Brown	Bank Mgr.			Station Master; Servant
Patricia Conolly	Rachel		Queen Marie	Dunyasha
Clayton Corzatte		Aubrey		Firs
Keene Curtis	Anarchist			Epidohov
Gwyda Donhowe		Clara		
Michael Durrell				Clerk
Richard Easton	Policeman		King Berenger	Trofimov
Alan Fudge	Officer	Frank		Tramp; Visitor
Gordon Gould	Generalissimo	Mr. Rodgers		
James Greene		Mr. Gill		
Harley Hackett				Visitor; Servant
Uta Hagen				Mme. Ranevskaya
Jennifer Harmon				Maid
Helen Hayes		Mrs. Fisher		
Nikos Kafkalis				Visitor
Eva Le Gallienne			Queen Marguerite	
Nicholas Martin	Poet		Guard	
Betty Miller				Varya
Donald Moffat				Lopahin
Etain O'Malley				Visitor
Pamela Payton-Wright		Amy	Juliette	Anya
George Pentecost	1st Soldier	Joe		Yasha
Ellis Rabb	Pantagleize			
Nat Simmons	Bamboola			
Nancy Walker				Charlotta
Sydney Walker	Innocenti			Semyonov
James Whittle	2d Soldier			Visitor
Richard Woods	Counsel		Doctor	Gaev

Soldiers, Waiters, Jurymen in *Pantagleize:* George Addis, Dan Bly, Kermit Brown, Alan Fudge, Reuben Green, Gil Michaels, Gastone Rossilli.

All plays: Artistic director, Ellis Rabb; costumes, Nancy Potts; scenery and lighting (except *Exit the King* scenery), James Tilton; press, Ben Kornzweig, Reginald Denenholz.

PANTAGLEIZE directed by John Houseman and Ellis Rabb; assistant director, Jack O'Brien; music, Bob James; incidental lyrics, Jack O'Brien; stage managers, George Darveris, Nikos Kafkalis.

Time: On the eve of one war and the morrow of another. Place: A city. The play is presented in two parts.

Comedy about an innocent who unknowingly gives the signal for a bloody revolution which destroys him. A foreign play (1927) previously produced in Belgium and elsewhere including the United States. This is its first professional New York production.

THE SHOW-OFF directed by Stephen Porter; stage managers, R. Derek Swire, Harley Hackett.

Time: 1924. Place: The home of the Fisher family in North Philadelphia.

The Show-Off was first produced on Broadway Feb. 5. 1924 for 571 performances and was named a Best Play of its season. It was revived on Broadway Dec. 12, 1932 for 119 performances; on March 5, 1937 by the Negro Theater; and on May 31, 1950 in the round at the Arena. Film versions under various titles appeared in 1926, 1929, 1934 and 1947.

EXIT THE KING directed by Ellis Rabb; scenery, Rouben Ter-Arutunian; music, Conrad Susa; stage managers, R. Derek Swire, Harley Hackett.

The script designates no time or place and the performance was presented without intermission.

The dying king of a crumbling kingdom cries out against his own predicted end and the mortality of all things; but despite his protests his disintegration and death take place inexorably, on schedule. A foreign play previously produced in Paris (in 1963), London and elsewhere. This is its first professional New York production.

THE CHERRY ORCHARD directed by Eva Le Gallienne; assistant director, Jack O'Brien; music supervision, Conrad Susa; stage managers, George Darveris, Dan Bly, Harley Hackett.

Time: 1904. Place: The estate of Madame Ranevskaya.

The Cherry Orchard was first produced on Broadway by the Moscow Art Theater in January and February 1923 at the 59th Street Theater. It was most recently presented here, in the Russian language, by the Moscow Art Theater at New York City Center February 9, 1965 for 11 performances. It was last presented in English off Broadway by David Ross at Theater Four, Nov. 14, 1962 for 61 performances; and on Broadway at the City Center by Carly Wharton and Margaret Webster January 1, 1945 for 8 performances.

* **How Now, Dow Jones** (201). Musical based on an original idea by Carolyn Leigh; book by Max Shulman; music by Elmer Bernstein; lyrics by Carolyn Leigh. Produced by David Merrick by arrangement with Edwin H. Morris & Co., Inc. at the Lunt-Fontanne Theater. Opened December 7, 1967.

Cynthia ....Brenda Vaccaro
Herbert ....James Congdon
Broker ....Joe McGrath
Kate ....Marlyn Mason
Wingate ....Hiram Sherman
Nichols ....Bob Gorman
Judy Evans ....Patti Davis
Wally ....Alexander Orfaly
Charley ....Anthony Roberts
Sue Ellen ....Jennifer Darling
Bradbury ....Rex Everhart
Waiter ....Tommy Tune
Senator McFetridge ....Barnard Hughes
Dow ....Stanley Simmonds
Jones ....Martin Ambrose
Tycoons ....Frank DeSal, Bob Gorman, John Joy, Alex Orfaly
Lion ....Ron Schwinn
Customers' Men ....Bob Gorman, Frank DeSal, John Joy, Doug Spingler
Dr. Gilman ....Sammy Smith
Mrs. Ragosa ....Francesca Smith
Mrs. Klein ....Fran Stevens
Mrs. Harris ....Sally DeMay
Mrs. Callahan ....Lucie Lancaster
Mrs. Millhauser ....Charlotte Jones
A.K. ....Arthur Hughes

Dancers: Oscar Anthony, Linnea Chandler, Joel Conrad, Patricia Cope, Frank DeSal, Lois Etelman, Cyndi Howard, Yanco Inone, Eileen Lawlor, Debra Lyman, Diana Quijano, Sally Ransone, George Ramos, Ron Schwinn, Doug Spingler, Ron L. Steinbeck, Pat Trott.

Singers: Martin Ambrose, Leigh Curran, Patti Davis, Bill Gibbens, Bob Gorman, Maria Hero, John Joy, Joe McGrath, Jack Murray, Alexander Orfaly, Anna Pagan, Dixie Stewart, Mara Worth.

Standby: Mr. Roberts—Lester James. Understudies: Miss Mason—Maria Hero; Miss Vaccaro—Leigh Curran; Miss Darling—Patricia Cope; Mr. Sherman—Alexander Orfaly.

Directed by George Abbott; dances and musical numbers staged by Gillian Lynne; musical direction and dance and vocal arrangements, Peter Howard; scenery, Oliver Smith; costumes, Robert Mackintosh; lighting, Martin Aronstein; orchestrations, Philip J. Lang; associate producer, Samuel Liff; production stage manager, Charles Blackwell; stage manager, Henry Velez; press, Lee Solters, Harvey B. Sabinson, David Powers.

Time: The present. Place: New York City.

Comedy about the Wall Street stock market and its bulls, bears, lions and pussy cats, as the Dow Jones girl throws the financial world into a tizzy by falsely reporting that the average has hit 1,000 because her fiance has promised to marry her when that happens.

Barnard Hughes replaced Hiram Sherman, Ted Tiller replaced Barnard Hughes and Barney Martin replaced Rex Everhart 3/4/68.

ACT I

Scene 1: Financial District
"A-B-C" ....Cynthia, Tourists, Wall Streeters
Scene 2: Childs Restaurant
"They Don't Make 'em Like That Anymore" ....Kate, Cynthia
"Live a Little" ....Charley, Kate, New Yorkers
Crazy Night Ballet
"The Pleasure's About To Be Mine" ....Charley, Kate
Scene 3: Wingate's private office
"A Little Investigation" ....Wingate, McFetridge, Dow, Jones, Tycoons
Scene 4: Kate's apartment
"Walk Away" ....Kate

Scene 5: Wall Street—early a.m.
Scene 6: Wingate & Co., brokers
"Goodbye, Failure, Goodbye" .... Charley, Customers' Men, Brokers
Scene 7: Mrs. Millhauser's living room
"Step to the Rear" .... Charley, Mrs. Millhauser, Widows, Ensemble
Scene 8: Kate's apartment
"Shakespeare Lied" .... Kate, Cynthia, Gilman
Scene 9: Wingate's private office
Scene 10: Wall Street
Scene 11: Dow Jones office
"Big Trouble" .... Kate

ACT II

Scene 1: New York City
"Credo" .... Gilman, Mrs. Klein, Widows, New Yorkers
"One of Those Moments" .... Kate
Scene 2: Wingate's private office
"Big Trouble" (Reprise) .... Wingate, Tycoons
Scene 3: Mrs. Millhauser's living room
Scene 4: Cynthia's apartment
"He's Here!" .... Cynthia
Scene 5: Financial District
"Panic" .... Entire Cast
Scene 6: Kate's apartment
"Touch and Go" .... Charley, Kate
Scene 7: Wingate & Co., brokers
"That's Good Enough For Me" .... Entire Cast

Brigadoon (23). Musical revival with book and lyrics by Alan Jay Lerner; music by Frederick Loewe. Produced by The City Center Light Opera Company, Jean Dalrymple director, at New York City Center. Opened December 13, 1967. (Closed December 31, 1967)

Tommy Albright .... Bill Hayes
Jeff Douglas .... Russell Nype
Sandy Dean .... Henry Lawrence
Meg Brockie .... Karen Morrow
Archie Beaton .... Earl McDonald
Harry Beaton .... Edward Villella
(Harry Beaton) .... Frank Andre
Andrew MacLaren .... Alexander Clark
Jean MacLaren .... Sarah Jane Smith
Fiona MacLaren .... Margot Moser
Angus McGuffie .... Gordon Cook
Charlie Dalrymple .... Evan Thomas
Maggie Anderson .... Leslie Franzos
Sword Dancers .... Dennis Cole, Wilfred Schuman
Mr. Lundi .... William LeMassena
Bagpiper .... Maurice Eisenstadt
Frank .... Paul Adams
Jane Ashton .... Jeanne Murray Vanderbilt

(Parentheses indicate role in which the actor alternated)

Townsfolk of Brigadoon: Chris Callen, Phyllis Bash, Jane Coleman, Peggy Cooper, Mona Elson, Marta Heflin, Oksana Iweszczenko, Mina Jo King, Barbara Miller, Roberta Vatske, Paul Adams, Donald Brassington, Edward Becker, Peter Clark, Gordon Cook, Henry Lawrence, Ken Richards, Robert Monteil, Don Wonder.

Dancers: Anita Arnell, Joanna Crosson, Chele Graham, Jane Jaffe, Nicole Karol, Karen Kristin, Lucia Lambert, Toodie Wittmer, Marget Wyeth, Paul Berne, Scott Hunter, J. David Kirby, William Koch, Dick Korthaze, Wilfred Schuman, Bud Spencer, Ron Tassone, Duane Taylor.

Standby: Miss Vanderbilt—Betty Hyatt Linton. Understudies: Mr. Hayes—Gordon Cook; Mr. Nype—Paul Adams; Mr. McDonald—Ed Becker; Mr. Clark—Henry Lawrence.

Directed by Gus Schirmer; original dances and musical numbers by Agnes de Mille; restaged for this production by Gemze de Lappe and Dennis Cole; musical director, Jonathan Anderson; scenery, Oliver Smith; lighting, Peggy Clark; costumes, Stanley Simmons; production stage manager, Herman Shapiro; stage managers, Forrest Carter, Paul Philips; press, Homer Poupart, John Clugstone.

Time: May of last year. Place: Brigadoon.

Brigadoon was first produced by Cheryl Crawford March 13, 1947 at the Ziegfeld Theater for 581 performances. It won the Critics Award for best musical and was named a Best Play of its season. It has been revived five times previously at New York City Center, most recently on December 23, 1964 for 17 performances.

The list of musical numbers in *Brigadoon* appears on pages 301 and 302 of the 1961-62 *Best Plays* volume.

* **Spofford** (192). By Herman Shumlin; based on Peter DeVries' novel *Reuben, Reuben.* Produced by Zev Bufman in association with James Riley at the ANTA Theater. Opened December 14, 1967.

Spofford	Melvyn Douglas	Pycraft	Wallace Rooney
George	Alan North	Mrs. Springer	Audra Lindley
Mare	Tresa Hughes	Gromier	Joseph Boland
First Customer	Carole Ann Lewis	Hopwood	Ian Martin
Mrs. Punck	Pert Kelton	Gowan McGland	Jerome Dempsey
Mrs. Beausigneur	Barbara Britton	Maid	Jan DeVries
Geneva	Penelope Windust	Mrs. Crane	Joen Arliss
Tad	Jeffrey Weiss	Committee Members	Ian Martin, Charles Maggiore
Second Customer	Oceana Briggs		

Understudies: Mr. Douglas—Wallace Rooney; Miss Kelton—Oceana Briggs; Mr. Weiss—Robert Tananis.

Directed by Herman Shumlin; scenery and lighting, Donald Oenslager; costumes, Winn Morton; production stage manager, Edward Julien; stage manager, Lola Shumlin; press, Bill Doll & Co.

Time: The present. Place: A town in Connecticut. The play is divided into two parts.

Comedy about a retired chicken farmer who sees his rustic community invaded by commuters and sets out to make a study of their habits and customs.

Brief Lives (16). One-man performance by Roy Dotrice as John Aubrey. By Patrick Garland; adapted from the works of John Aubrey. Produced by David Susskind and Daniel Melnick at the John Golden Theater. Opened December 18, 1967. (Closed December 30, 1967)

Directed by Patrick Garland; designed by Julia Trevelyan Oman; lighting design and set supervision, Lloyd Burlingame; production stage manager, Porter Van Zandt; stage manager, Lynn Montgomery; press, Frank Goodman, Martin Schwartz.

Time: 1697, the year of Aubrey's death. Place: Mistress Byerley's lodgings in Dirty Lane, Bloomsbury. The play is divided into two acts.

The 17th century biographer John Aubrey (portrayed by Mr. Dotrice) in his old age remembers many of the people and events he has seen (in his own written words). A foreign play previously produced at the Hampstead Theater Club, England.

How To Be a Jewish Mother (21). Play with music based on the book by Dan Greenburg; conceived by Seymour Vall; music by Michael Leonard; lyrics by Herbert Martin. Produced by Jon-Lee and Seymour Vall at the Hudson Theater. Opened December 28, 1967. (Closed January 13, 1968)

Godfrey Cambridge — Molly Picon

Standby: Mr. Cambridge—Tiger Haynes. Understudy: Miss Picon—Naomi Riseman.

Directed by Avery Schreiber; musical staging, Doug Rogers; musical direction and arrangements, Julian Stein; scenery, Robert Randolph; costumes, Michael Travis; lighting, John J. Moore; associate producers, Rick Mandell, Margaret Aldrich; production stage manager, William Krot; stage manager, John Glennon; press, Seymour Krawitz, Ruth Cage.

Time: the present. The play is divided into two acts.

Series of comedy sketches, with music, about the typical Jewish mother, with Miss Picon as the mother and Mr. Cambridge as various other characters.

Musical Numbers—ACT I: "Once the Man You Laughed At," "Laugh a Little." ACT II: "Since the Time We Met," "The Wedding Song," "Child You Are."

Staircase (61). By Charles Dyer. Produced by Bill Freedman and Charles Kasher at the Biltmore Theater. Opened January 10, 1968. (Closed March 3, 1968)

Charles Dyer .... Eli Wallach
Harry C. Leeds .... Milo O'Shea

Directed by Barry Morse; scenery and costumes, Michael Annals; lighting, Gil Wechsler; production stage manager, Thomas Bohdanetzky; stage manager, Wayne Carson; press, Mike Merrick Co., Barry Kobrin.

Time: the present. Place: a barber's shop in a suburb of London. The play is divided into two acts.

Two lonely male homosexuals, "hair stylists," cling to their last hope for companionship and affection in their friendship, despite its somewhat ludicrous tensions and the conflicts of their differing natures. A foreign play previously produced in London by the Royal Shakespeare Company.

A Best Play; see page 192

Before You Go (29). By Lawrence Holofcener. Produced by Peregrine Productions, Inc. at Henry Miller's Theater. Opened January 11, 1968. (Closed February 3, 1968)

Man .... Gene Troobnick
Woman .... Marian Seldes
Dog .... L.P.

Directed by Mark Gordon; scenery, Ed Wittstein; costumes, Theoni V. Aldredge; lighting, Jules Fisher; produced by Peter Moreau; associate producer, S. Walter Epstein; production stage manager, Stephen Gardner; stage manager, Gill Dennis; press, Merle Debuskey, Violet Welles, Faith Geer.

Time: the present. Place: the Greenwich Village apartment of Stanley Fish. Act I: Around 6 o'clock on a summer afternoon. Act II, Scene 1: A few minutes later. Scene 2: A half hour later.

The determined seduction of an aspiring actress by a would-be sculptor in his Greenwich Village pad, where the actress and her dog have taken refuge from a thunderstorm.

* **The Prime of Miss Jean Brodie** (157). By Jay Allen; adapted from the novel by Muriel Spark. Produced by Robert Whitehead in association with Robert W. Dowling at the Helen Hayes Theater. Opened January 16, 1968.

Sister Helena .... Denise Huot
Mr. Perry .... Douglas Watson
Jean Brodie .... Zoe Caldwell
Sandy .... Amy Taubin
Jenny .... Diana Davila
Monica .... Catherine Burns
Mary MacGregor .... Kathryn Baumann
Miss MacKay .... Lennox Milne
Gordon Lowther .... Joseph Maher
Teddy Lloyd .... Roy Cooper
McCready .... Brooks Morton
Miss Campbell .... Sheila Coonan

Citizens, Girl Guides, Schoolgirls, etc.: Roberta Maxwell, Celia Watson, Nora Heflin, Mady Heflin, Jane Actman, Doreen Miller, Donna Conforti, Stephanie Sheppard, Jami Fields, Jim Oyster, Brooks Morton, Janice Mars, Jack Knight.

Understudies: Miss Caldwell—Denise Huot; Miss Milne—Sheila Coonan; Misses Huot, Taubin—Roberta Maxwell.

Directed by Michael Langham; scenery and lighting, Jo Mielziner; costumes, Jane Greenwood; incidental music composed and arranged by John Cook; production stage manager, Harry Young; stage manager, William Webster; press, Seymour Krawitz, Ruth Cage.

Time: Now, and from 1931 to 1936. Place: Edinburgh, Scotland. Act I: Now and from 1931 to 1933. Act II: The action continues from 1933 to 1936.

A willful but devoted Scottish school teacher, in her "prime" of early and overly-romantic middle age, teaches her girl pupils to live passionately; but she is finally "assassinated" from her beloved teaching job by a favorite pupil who discloses Miss Brodie's romantic admiration of fascism. An American play which had its world premiere in London.

* **The Happy Time** (150). Musical based on the play by Samuel Taylor and the book by Robert L. Fontaine; book by N. Richard Nash; music by John Kander;

lyrics by Fred Ebb. Produced by David Merrick at the Broadway Theater. Opened January 18, 1968.

Jacques Bonnard ....Robert Goulet	The Six Angels
Suzanne Bonnard ....Jeanne Arnold	Lizette ....Jacki Garland
Philippe Bonnard ....George S. Irving	Dorine ....Mary Gail Laverenz
Bibi Bonnard ....Mike Rupert	Sylvie ....Tammie Fillhart
Louis Bonnard ....Charles Durning	Monique ....Mary Ann O'Reilly
Annabelle Bonnard ....Kim Freund	Bella ....Vicki Powers
Gillie Bonnard ....Julane Stites	Grace ....Susan Sigrist
Nanette Bonnard ....Connie Simmons	Laurie Mannon ....Julie Gregg
Felice Bonnard ....June Squibb	Foufie ....Jeffrey Golkin
Grandpere Bonnard ....David Wayne	Ganache ....Dallas Johann

Students of St. Pierre Boys' School: Dancers—Ron Abshire, Jovanni Anthony, Quinn Baird, Andy Bew, Blake Brown, Leonard Crofoot, Ron Crofoot, Wayne Dugger, Joe Giamalva, Dallas Johann, Gene Law, Steve Reinhart, John Simonson, Michael Stearns; Swing Dancer—Sammy Williams; Singers—Marc Anthony, Alan Blight, George Connolly, Tom De Mastri, Paul Dwyer, Scott Gandert, Eric Hamilton, Gary Hamilton, Jeffrey Hamilton, Kevin Hamilton, Mark Lonergan, Brian Shyer, Brandy Wayne, Teddy Williams, Marc Winters.

Standbys: Messrs. Goulet, Irving—John Gabriel; Messrs. Wayne, Durning—Ben Kapen; Misses Arnold, Squibb—Iva Withers. Understudies: Miss Gregg—Vicki Powers; Mr. Rupert—Leonard Crofoot.

Directed, filmed and choreographed by Gower Champion; musical direction and vocal arrangements, Oscar Kosarin; scenery, Peter Wexler; costumes, Freddy Wittop; lighting, Jean Rosenthal; film sequences created by Christopher Chapman; film technical direction, Barry O. Gordon; orchestrations, Don Walker; associate choreographer, Kevin Carlisle; dance and incidental music arrangements, Marvin Laird; production manager, Michael Thoma; stage managers, Bob Bernard, Jeff Chambers; press, Harvey B. Sabinson, Lee Solters, David Powers.

Time: The past. Place: Jacques Bonnard's studio and his home in a small town in Canada.

Using film projections to set the mood for live action, the musical dramatizes a magazine photographer's memory of a visit to his home and family in a small Canadian town. Samuel Taylor's straight-play version of *The Happy Time* was previously produced on Broadway by Rodgers & Hammerstein at the Plymouth Theater January 24, 1950 for 614 performances. It was named a Best Play of its season.

ACT I

"The Happy Time" ....Jacques and Family
"He's Back" ....The Family
"Catch My Garter" ....The Six Angels
"Tomorrow Morning" ....Jacques, Grandpere, Bibi, The Six Angels
"Please Stay" ....Bibi, Jacques
"I Don't Remember You" ....Jacques
"St. Pierre" ....The Glee Club
"I Don't Remember You" (Reprise) ....Laurie, Jacques
"Without Me" ....Bibi, Schoolmates
"The Happy Time" (Reprise) ....Jacques

ACT II

"Among My Yesterdays" ....Jacques
"The Life of the Party" ....Grandpere, The Six Angels, Schoolboys
"Seeing Things" ....Jacques, Laurie
Ballet ....Bibi, Gillie, Annabelle, Nanette, Schoolboys
"A Certain Girl" ....Grandpere, Jacques, Bibi
"Being Alive" ....Jacques
"The Happy Time" (Reprise) ....Jacques, Entire Company

I Never Sang for My Father (124). By Robert Anderson. Produced by Gilbert Cates in association with Doris Vidor at the Longacre Theater. Opened January 25, 1968. (Closed May 11, 1968)

Gene Garrison .... Hal Holbrook
Porter .... Earl Sydnor
Tom Garrison .... Alan Webb
Margaret Garrison .... Lillian Gish
Mary .... Sloane Shelton
Nurse .... Laurinda Barrett
Reverend Pell .... Allan Frank
Marvin Scott .... Matt Crowley
Waiter .... James A. Spearman
Dr. Mayberry .... Daniel Keyes
Alice .... Teresa Wright

Standbys: Mr. Holbrook—Thomas Coley; Miss Gish—Lois Wilson. Understudies: Mr. Webb—Daniel Keyes; Miss Wright—Laurinda Barrett; Messrs. Frank, Keyes, Crowley—William Callan; Miss Barrett—Sloane Shelton.

Directed by Alan Schneider; scenery and lighting, Jo Mielziner; costumes, Theoni V. Aldredge; production stage manager, Paul A. Foley; stage manager, William Callan; press, Lee Solters, Harvey B. Sabinson, Harry Nigro.

Time: The present and the past. Place: New York City and a town in Westchester County. The play is divided into two acts.

A middle-aged son strives to create an affectionate relationship with his father, who is approaching his dotage.

A Best Play; see page 277

Darling of the Day (33). Musical based on Arnold Bennett's *Buried Alive;* music by Jule Styne; lyrics by E.Y. Harburg; book authorship, see note. Produced by The Theater Guild and Joel Schenker at the George Abbott Theater. Opened January 27, 1968. (Closed February 24, 1968)

Oxford .... Peter Woodthorpe
Priam Farll .... Vincent Price
Henry Leek .... Charles Welch
Old Gentleman .... Carl Nicholas
Lady Vale .... Brenda Forbes
Cabby .... Ross Miles
Doctor; Judge .... Leo Leyden
Alice Challice .... Patricia Routledge
Daphne .... Joy Nichols
Alf .... Teddy Green
Bert .... Marc Jordan
Rosalind .... Beth Howland
Sydney .... Reid Klein
Attendant .... Larry Brucker
Frame Maker .... Paul Eichel
Duncan .... Mitchell Jason
Equerry; Constable .... John Aman
The King .... Charles Gerald
Mrs. Leek .... Camila Ashland
Curates .... Herb Wilson, Fred Siretta
Pennington .... Michael Lewis

Singers: Marian Haraldson, Kay Oslin, Jeannette Seibert, Maggie Task, Maggie Worth, John Aman, Larry Brucker, Paul Eichel, Reid Klein, Carl Nicholas, Albert Zimmerman.

Dancers: Bonnie Ano, Reby Howells, Beth Howland, Georgianne Thon, Phyllis Wallach, Denise Winston, Christopher Chadman, George Lee, Jim May, Ross Miles, Fred Siretta, Herb Wilson.

Standbys: Mr. Price—Mitchell Jason; Miss Routledge—Joy Nichols. Understudies: Miss Forbes—Jeannette Seibert; Mr. Woodthorpe—Michael Lewis; Mr. Green—Ross Miles; Doctor—Zale Kessler.

Directed by Noel Willman; choreography, Lee Theodore; musical director and vocal arrangements, Buster Davis; scenery, Oliver Smith; costumes, Raoul Pène du Bois; lighting, Peggy Clark; dance music, Trude Rittman; orchestrations, Ralph Burns; assistant to director, Fred Hebert; production stage manager, Phil Friedman; stage managers, Michael Sinclair, Phil King; press, Arthur Cantor, Artie Solomon.

Time: 1905. Place: London and environs. Act I, Scene 1: Oxford's Art Gallery—London. Scene 2: Farll's London house. Scene 3: The pub in Putney. Scene 4: Farll's London house. Scene 5: London street. Scene 6: Paradise Villa, Putney. Scene 7: Oxford's salon. Scene 8: The Thames River bank. Scene 9: Paradise Villa. Act II, Scene 1: Oxford's salon. Scene 2: Paradise Villa garden. Scene 3: Putney High Street. Scene 4: The pub. Scene 5: The courtroom.

A famous painter chooses to assume the identity—and marry the widow—of his dead valet.

NOTE: Authorship of the book was credited to Nunnally Johnson at the show's out-of-town tryout opening, but the credit was withdrawn for the Broadway presentation and no other credit substituted.

ACT I

"Mad For Art" .... Art Lovers
"He's A Genius" .... Oxford, Priam, Henry
"To Get Out Of This World Alive" .... Priam
"It's Enough To Make A Lady Fall In Love" .... Alice, Alf, Bert, Putney Friends
"A Gentleman's Gentleman" .... Alice, Alf, Bert, Priam, Duncan, Bystanders
"Double Soliloquy" .... Priam, Alice
"Let's See What Happens" .... Alice, Priam
"Panache" .... Oxford, Lady Vale
"I've Got A Rainbow Working For Me" .... Priam, Putney Friends
"Money, Money, Money—" .... Alf, Bert, Sydney
"That Something Extra Special" .... Alice
"Money, Money, Money—" (Reprise) .... Alf, Bert, Sydney

ACT II

"What Makes a Marriage Merry" .... Alice, Priam, Alf, Bert, Daphne, Rosalind
"He's A Genius" (Reprise) .... Oxford, Assistants
"Not On Your Nellie" .... Alice, Alf, Bert, Putney Friends
"Sunset Tree" .... Priam, Alice
"Butler In The Abbey" .... Priam, Courtroom
"Not On Your Nellie" (Reprise) .... Entire Company

Avanti! (21). By Samuel Taylor. Produced by Morris Jacobs and Jerome Whyte in association with Richard Rodgers at the Booth Theater. Opened January 31, 1968. (Closed February 17, 1968)

John Wesley .... Rik Pierce
Alexander Ben Claiborne .... Robert Reed
A Waiter .... Frank Nastasi
Baldassare Pantaleone .... Keith Baxter
Alison Ames .... Jennifer Hilary
A Porter .... Loreto Caringi
Helen Claiborne .... Betsy von Furstenberg

Standbys: Misses Hilary, von Furstenberg—Susan Sullivan; Mr. Reed—Vince Carroll; Mr. Baxter—Loreto Caringi; Mr. Pierce—Steven Meyer.

Directed by Nigel Patrick; scenery and lighting, Donald Oenslager; costumes, Winn Morton; stage manager, Randall Brooks; press, Betty Lee Hunt.

Time: Spring. Place: Rome, the sitting room of an apartment in a hotel. Act I, Scene 1: A morning in May. Scene 2: Late that night. Act II, Scene 1: Two days later. Scene 2: A few hours later.

Comedy about a young American business man, an English girl and an Italian fixer all wound round in Roman red tape and each other's sex life.

* **A Day in the Death of Joe Egg** (137). By Peter Nichols. Produced by Joseph Cates and Henry Fownes, Michael Medwin (for Memorial Ltd.) at the Brooks Atkinson Theater. Opened February 1, 1968.

Bri .... Albert Finney
Sheila .... Zena Walker
Joe .... Susan Alpern
Pam .... Elizabeth Hubbard
Freddie .... John Carson
Grace .... Joan Hickson

Understudies: Misses Walker, Hubbard—Jo Henderson; Miss Alpern—Moni Ferguson.

Directed by Michael Blakemore; design, Robin Pidcock; music, Andy Park; lighting design and set supervision, Lloyd Burlingame; production stage manager, Ben Janney; stage manager, Nelle Nugent; press, Max Eisen, Carl Samrock, Jeanne Gibson Merrick.

Time: The present. Place: Bristol, in England. The play is divided into two acts.

Comedy about the parents of a severely handicapped child who are trying laughter as a last resort to ease the pain of their affliction. A foreign play previously produced by The Glasgow Citizens' Theater and in London.

Donal Donnelly replaced Albert Finney 4/16/68.

A Best Play; see page 226

* **Golden Rainbow** (135). Musical based on a play by Arnold Schulman; book by

Ernest Kinoy; music and lyrics by Walter Marks. Produced by Joseph P. Harris and Ira Bernstein at the Sam S. Shubert Theater. Opened February 4, 1968.

Mr. Novotny ....Alan Kass	Gordon; Nebuchadnezzar ......John Anania
Ally ....Scott Jacoby	Mr. Korngold ....Sam Kressen
Mr. Hausknecht ....Howard Mann	2d Reporter; Victor ....Lanier Davis
Eloise; Persian Girl ....Linda Jorgens	Lead Dancer; Virgin ....Diana Saunders
Laundryman; 1st Reporter; Stage Manager ....Charles Karel	Judy Harris ....Eydie Gorme
Henry ....Will Hussung	Georgia ....Carol Conte
Mr. Diamond ....Sid Raymond	Stripper ....Thelma Sherr
Larry Davis ....Steve Lawrence	Sam ....Frank Pietri
Mrs. Magruder ....Fay Sappington	Umbawa ....Larry Merritt
Lou Garrity ....Joseph Sirola	Cat-Girl ....Carole Bishop
Jerome Stone ....Gene Foote	Hero ....Antony De Vecchi
Rosemary Garrity ....Marilyn Cooper	Gambler ....Michael Vita

Dancers: Carole Bishop, Carol Conte, Susan Donovan, Antony De Vecchi, Tina Faye, Alice Glenn, Linda Jorgens, Maralyn Miles, Jean Preece, Wayne Boyd, Gene Foote, Blair Hammond, Larry Merritt, Frank Pietri, Tom Rolla, Michael Shawn, Michael Vita.

Showgirls: Betty Jo Alvies, Bernadette Brookes, Rae Samuels, Thelma Sherr.

Standbys: Mr. Lawrence—Mace Barrett; Miss Gorme—Marilyn Cooper. Understudies: Mr. Kass—Gene Foote; Mr. Jacoby—Dewey Golkin.

Directed by Arthur Storch; choreography, Tom Panko; musical direction, vocal arrangements, additional scoring, Elliot Lawrence; scenery and lighting, Robert Randolph; costumes, Alvin Colt; orchestrations, Pat Williams, Jack Andrews; dance music arrangements, Marvin Hamlisch, Luther Henderson; associate choreographer, Martin Allen; production stage manager, Terence Little; stage manager, George Thorn; press, Mike Merrick Co., Karl Bernstein, Barry Kobrin.

Time: The present. Place: Las Vegas. Act I, Scene 1: The Strip—Las Vegas. Scene 2: Golden Rainbow lobby. Scene 3: The airport. Scene 4: Golden Rainbow lobby. Scene 5: The Algeria Patio Restaurant. Scene 6: Golden Rainbow pantry. Scene 7: Golden Rainbow lobby. Act II, Scene 1: Babylon Nightclub. Scene 2: Backstage. Scene 3: The desert. Scene 4: Golden Rainbow lobby. Scene 5: Babylon Casino. Scene 6: The Golden Rainbow.

Book is based on Arnold Schulman's play *A Hole in the Head* about a widower allowing his beloved son to grow up too fast and with too little discipline, in a run-down resort hotel (locale switched from Florida, in the original play, to Las Vegas in this musical).

ACT I

"Golden Rainbow" ....Las Vegans
"We Got Us" ....Larry, Ally
"He Needs Me Now" ....Judy
"Kid" ....Larry
"For Once in Your Life" ....Judy, Larry, The Boys
"Taking Care of You" ....Judy, Ally, Friends
"I've Got To Be Me" ....Larry

ACT II

"The Fall of Babylon" ....Babylonians
"Taste" ....Lou, Friends
"Desert Moon" ....Larry, Judy
"All in Fun" ....Larry, Judy
"It's You Again" ....Judy
"I've Got To Be Me" (Reprise) ....Larry
"How Could I Be So Wrong" ....Judy
"We Got Us" (Reprise) ....Larry, Judy, Ally
Finale ....Entire Company

The Grand Music Hall of Israel (64). Vaudeville revue in the Hebrew, Yiddish and English languages. Produced by Lee Guber and Shelly Gross by arrangement with Bruno Coquatrix at the Palace Theater. Opened February 6, 1968. (Closed March 31, 1968)

PART I: (Introductions by Alice); Israeli Rhapsody with the Karmon Histadruth Ballet; "Songs of Youth" with Ilan and Ilanit; Dance of the Fisherman with Karmon Histadruth Ballet; Oriental Rhythms with Boaz and Nechemia; The New Sound of Israel's Hit Parade with The Carmelim, Michal, Ruty, David, Shiman and Hannan; Hassidic with the Karmon Histadruth Ballet.

PART II: Desert Rhythms (On the Seaside of the Mediterranean) with the Karmon Histadruth Ballet; "The Story of the Israeli People in Song" with Helena Hendel; A Day Like Every Day in a Kibbutz on the Border with Yona and the Karmon Histadruth Ballet; Music in a Novel Manner with Nishri; "The New Spirit" with The High Willows, Geula Gill, David, Igal; The Feasts of the Kibbutz with the Karmon Histadruth Ballet; Shalom from the Grand Music Hall of Israel (including "Jerusalem of Gold") with the Entire Company.

Directed and choreographed by Jonathan Karmon; musical direction and arrangements, Itzchak Graziani; costumes, Hovav Kruvi; costumes executed by Bertha Kwartz; lighting, Jules Fisher; assistant director, Gavri Levi; assistant conductor, Ami Gilad; production stage manager, John Actman; press, Saul Richman.

A collection of songs, dances and novelty acts presented by a young Israeli troupe. A foreign play previously produced in Israel, Paris and elsewhere.

* **The Price** (131). By Arthur Miller. Produced by Robert Whitehead in association with Robert W. Dowling at the Morosco Theater. Opened February 7, 1968.

Victor Franz ....Pat Hingle
Esther Franz ....Kate Reid
Gregory Solomon ....Harold Gary
Walter Franz ....Arthur Kennedy

Standbys: Miss Reid—Joan Copeland; Mr. Hingle—Eugene Roche; Mr. Kennedy—Paul Sparer.

Directed by Ulu Grosbard; scenery and costumes, Boris Aronson; lighting, Paul Morrison; production stage manager, Del Hughes; stage manager, Howard Fischer; press, James D. Proctor, David Roggensack.

Time: Today. Place: The attic floor of a Manhattan brownstone. The play was presented without intermission.

Two brothers, one a police patrolman and one a successful doctor, prepare to sell an atticful of unwanted family furniture, an abrasive process which exposes each to the other's judgment of lives spent and sacrifices made to attain widely divergent goals.

David Burns created the role of Gregory Solomon on pre-Broadway tour but was replaced, owing to illness, by Harold Gary on 2/2/68, in New York previews.

A Best Play; see page 251

* **Plaza Suite** (123). Program of three one-act plays by Neil Simon: *Visitor from Mamaroneck, Visitor from Hollywood* and *Visitor from Forest Hills.* Produced by Saint-Subber at the Plymouth Theater. Opened February 14, 1968.

VISITOR FROM MAMARONECK

Bellhop ....Bob Balaban
Karen Nash ....Maureen Stapleton
Sam Nash ....George C. Scott
Waiter ....Jose Ocasio
Jean McCormack ....Claudette Nevins

VISITOR FROM HOLLYWOOD

Waiter ....Jose Ocasio
Jesse Kiplinger ....George C. Scott
Muriel Tate ....Maureen Stapleton

VISITOR FROM FOREST HILLS

Norma Hubley ....Maureen Stapleton
Roy Hubley ....George C. Scott
Bordon Eisler ....Bob Balaban
Mimsey Hubley ....Claudette Nevins

Standbys: Miss Stapleton—Elizabeth Wilson; Mr. Scott—Alfred Sandor; Miss Nevins—Judith Barcroft; Messrs. Balaban, Ocasio—Wisner Washam.

Directed by Mike Nichols; scenery, Oliver Smith; lighting, Jean Rosenthal; costumes, Patricia Zipprodt; production stage manager, Harvey Medlinsky; stage manager, Wisner Washam; press, Harvey B. Sabinson, Lee Solters, Harry Nigro.

Time: The present—*Visitor from Mamaroneck,* a late winter afternoon; *Visitor from Hollywood,* early afternoon in spring; *Visitor from Forest Hills,* a Saturday afternoon in June. Place: A suite in the Plaza Hotel, New York City.

Three comedies with different characters in the same Plaza Hotel setting. *Mamaroneck* is about a wife and husband whose marriage has lost its excitement in middle age. *Hollywood* is about a Hollywood producer who invites his childhood New Jersey sweetheart to town for an afternoon of sexual sport. *Forest Hills* is the farcical treatment of a wedding day, with the bride locking herself in the bathroom of her frantic parents' suite just before the ceremony.

Nicol Williamson replaced George C. Scott 5/27/68.

A Best Play; see page 275

Les Ballets Africains (55). Return engagement of the dance and musical show in the French language by the National Ensemble of the Republic of Guinea. Produced by Joseph Cates and Henry Fownes at the Mark Hellinger Theater. Opened February 20, 1968. (Closed April 6, 1968)

Mademoiselles
Sadio Bah
Mariama Barry
Moussouroura Camara
Nalo Camara
Manana Cisse
Eintou Diabate
Marie Dialio
Saran Diawara
Malene Fofana
Fanta Kaba
Jeanne Macauley
Goundo Square
Marie Sylla
Aissatou Toure

Messieurs
Fauly Camara
Ibrahima Camara
Moriba Camara
Damany Conde
Noumba Conde
Sekou Conde I
Sekou Conde II
Ibrahima Conte
Koca Sale Diabate
Almany Dioubate
Karamoko Fofana
Vomo Gbamou
Bakary Keita
Famoudou Konate
Moussa Kone
Mamandi Kourouma
Mamadi Mansare
Bakary Mara
Guila Traore
Arafan Toure
Jules Zambo

Impresario for the American tour, Bill Levine; general manager, Sekou Sakho; assistant general manager, Mamadou Limine Sane; administrator, Mohamed Lamine Camara; stage manager, Salifou Bangoura; artistic managers, Hamidou Bangoura, Italo Zambo; press, Max Eisen, Jeanne Gibson Merrick.

Collection of folk dances, songs and legends, with native instrumental music, last presented on Broadway November 16, 1966 at the Ethel Barrymore Theater for 85 performances. A foreign show previously produced in the Republic of Guinea and on a 20-year world tour.

List of scenes and musical numbers of *Les Ballets Africains* appears on page 369 of the 1966-67 *Best Plays* volume.

Carry Me Back to Morningside Heights (7). By Robert Alan Aurthur. Produced by Saint-Subber in association with Harold Loeb at the John Golden Theater. Opened February 27, 1968. (Closed March 2, 1968)

Willie Nurse ....Louis Gossett
Seymour Levin ....David Steinberg
Henry Hardy ....Johnny Brown
Myrna Jessup ....Cicely Tyson
Alma Sue Bates ....Diane Ladd

Standbys: Mr. Gossett—Spencer Holden; Mr. Steinberg—Richard Blair; Miss Tyson—Beverly Todd; Miss Ladd—Marilyn Madderom; Mr. Brown—Douglas Johnson.

Directed by Sidney Poitier; designed by Kurt Lundell; production stage manager, Victor Straus; press, Harvey B. Sabinson, Lee Solters, Robert Ullman.

Comedy about a white Jewish youth's insistence on becoming a slave to a Negro law student, as a kind of personal penance for historical wrong.

Portrait of a Queen (61). By William Francis. Produced by H. Clay Blaney, Albert W. Selden and Hal James at Henry Miller's Theater. Opened February 28, 1968. (Closed April 20, 1968)

Balladsinger ....Nicholas Smith
King Leopold of the Belgians;
Viscount Palmerston .....Richard Waring
Victoria ....Dorothy Tutin
Lord Melbourne and
other Ministers ....Michael Barrington
Bishop of Durham; Gentleman
of the Press ....Frederic Warriner
1st Lady in Waiting ....Nancy Acly
2d Lady in Waiting ....Holly Brooke
Archbishop of Canterbury; Editor
of the *Times* ....Thomas Barbour
Prince Albert ....Derek Waring
Gentleman of the Press;
Footman ....Michael Bradshaw
Benjamin Disraeli ....Dennis King
William Gladstone ....James Cossins
Footmen ....Christopher Flavell,
John Milligan, Harlan Cary Poe,
Bernard Taylor

Directed by Val May; scenery and lighting, Marvin Reiss; costumes, Theoni V. Aldredge; ballad selection and arrangement, William Francis, Charles Chilton; production stage manager, James Gelb; press, Merle Debuskey, Violet Welles, Faith Geer.

Time: Between 1837 and 1900. Place: London and elsewhere. The play is divided into three parts.

Queen Victoria's comments on her own life in diaries and letters, and comments written or spoken by other historical personages, have been edited and arranged by the author into an informal stage biography of the queen. A foreign play previously produced in Bristol and London.

Here's Where I Belong (1). Musical based on the novel *East of Eden* by John Steinbeck; book by Alex Gordon; music by Robert Waldman; lyrics by Alfred Uhry. Produced by Mitch Miller at the Billy Rose Theater. Opened and closed at the evening performance March 3, 1968.

Adam Trask ....Paul Rogers
Caleb Trask ....Walter McGinn
Aron Trask ....Ken Kercheval
Lee ....James Coco
Will Hamilton ....Casper Roos
Mrs. Bacon ....Betty Henritze
Mrs. Tripp ....Dena Dietrich
Mrs. Heink ....Patricia Kelly
Abra Bacon ....Heather MacRae
School Children .....Lee Wilson, Tod Miller
Miss Ida ....Barbara Webb
Rabbit Holman ....Scott Jarvis
Faith ....Graciela Daniele
Eva ....Aniko Morgan
Della ....Dorothy Lister
Kate ....Nancy Wickwire
Joe ....Joseph Nelson
Juana ....Joetta Cherry
Newspaper Man ....Taylor Reed
British Purchasing Agent .....Darrell Askey

Townspeople, Mexican Field Workers, Denizens of Castroville Street: Darrell Askey, Joetta Cherry, Graciela Daniele, Elisa DeMarko, Larry Devon, John Dickerson, Bud Fleming, John William Gardner, Gene Gavin, John Johann, Ray Kirchner, Jane Laughlin, Dorothy Lister, Andy Love, Richard Marr, David McCorkle, Joyce McDonald, Tod Miller, Aniko Morgan, Joan Nelson, Joseph Nelson, Donald Norris, Taylor Reed, Clifford Scott, Joy Serio, Michele Simmons, David Thomas, Barbara Webb, Lee Wilson.

Directed by Michael Kahn; dances and musical staging, Tony Mordente; musical direction and vocal arrangements, Theodore Saidenberg; scenery, Ming Cho Lee; costumes, Ruth Morley; lighting, Jules Fisher; dance music, Arnold Goland; orchestrations, Glenn Osser, Norman Leyden, Jonathan Tunick; production stage manager, William Dodds; stage manager, D.W. Koehler; press, Frank Goodman, Martin Shwartz.

Time: 1915-1917. Place: Salinas, Calif.

The father-son relationship in *East of Eden* was the focus of the book in the Broadway musical version.

ACT I

Prologue: The Trask house, Salinas, Calif., 1915
"We Are What We Are" .... Adam, Cal, Lee Aron
"Cal Gets By" .... Cal
Scene 1: Castroville Street, two years later
"Raising Cain" .... Cal, Ensemble
Scene 2: The Trask house, later that day
"Soft Is the Sparrow" .... Aron
Scene 3: Kate's place, immediately following
Scene 4: The streets of Salinas, immediately following
"Where Have I Been" .... Adam, Lee, Townspeople
Scene 5: The ice house, several weeks later
"No Time" .... Cal, Aron
"Progress" .... Male Ensemble
"Good Boy" .... Cal
Scene 6: The lettuce fields, six weeks later
Ballet .... Cal, Juana, Abra, Dancing Ensemble
Scene 7: Near the depot, the same day
"Act Like a Lady" .... Abra
Scene 8: The train depot, immediately following
"The Send-Off" .... Townspeople
Scene 9: The Trask house, three days later
"Top of the Train" .... Adam, Cal
Scene 10: The willow tree, early the next morning
"Waking Up Sun" .... Abra, Cal

ACT II

Scene 1: Salinas, downtown. Two months later
"Pulverize the Kaiser" .... Mrs. Bacon, Mrs. Tripp, Mrs. Heink, Townspeople
"Where Have I Been" (Reprise) .... Adam
Scene 2: The Salinas Bank, two weeks later
"Good Boy" (Reprise) .... Cal
Scene 3: Kate's place, the same day
"You're Momma's" .... Kate
Scene 4: The willow tree, the next day
"Here's Where I Belong" .... Cal, Abra
Scene 5: The Trask house, Thanksgiving dinner
"We're a Home" .... Adam, Lee, Aron, Abra, Cal
Scene 6: Outside Kate's immediately following
Scene 7: The Trask house, a few hours later

The Guide (5). By Harvey Breit and Patricia Rinehart; based on the novel by R.K. Narayan. Produced by Noel Weiss at the Hudson Theater. Opened March 6, 1968. (Closed March 9, 1968)

Raju .... Zia Mohyeddin
Bhabani .... Titos Vandis
Velan .... Michael Kermoyan
Devi .... Madhur Jaffrey
Boy .... Jerry Ram
Chandra .... Peter De Anda
Muthu .... Richard Dmitri
Soma .... Martin Meyers
Ramu .... Vikas
Shopkeeper .... Ian Edward
Villagers .... Vincente Elias, John Patrick Hart, Shireen Subramanya, Osceola Archer, Angela D'Ambrosia
Police Officer .... John Branon

Understudies: Mr. Mohyeddin—Peter De Anda; Mr. Vandis—Martin Meyers; Mr. Kermoyan—Ian Edward.

Directed by George L. Sherman; music supervision, Ravi Shankar; Temple Dance staged by Matteo; production design, William Pitkin; lighting, Martin Aronstein; production stage manager, Roger Johnson Jr.; stage manager, Donald King; press, Harvey B. Sabinson, Lee Solters, Jay Russell.

Time: The present. Place: South India, a neglected temple on the bank of a river. Act I: Midday. Act II: Ten months later. Act III: Five days later.

Story of the play is based on R.K. Narayan's novel about a tour director posing as a holy man in an Indian village.

Weekend (21). By Gore Vidal. Produced by Saint-Subber and Lester Osterman at the Broadhurst Theater. Opened March 13, 1968. (Closed March 30, 1968)

Roger ....John Marriott
Miss Wilson ....Kim Hunter
Norris Blotner ....Gene Blakely
Senator MacGruder ....John Forsythe
Senator Andrews ....Staats Cotsworth
Mrs. Andrews ....Eleanor Wilson
Estelle MacGruder ......Rosemary Murphy
Beany MacGruder ....Marco St. John
Louise Hampton ....Carol Cole
Mrs. Hampton ....Zaida Coles
Dr. Hampton ....Graham Brown
1st Photographer ....John Newton
2d Photographer ....Robert Lawson
Reporter ....Norma Darden

Standbys: Mr. Forsythe—Gene Blakely; Misses Murphy, Hunter, Wilson—Virginia Robinson; Miss Cole—Norma Darden; Miss Coles—Javotte Sutton Greene; Messrs. Marriott, Brown—Stanley Greene.

Directed by Joseph Anthony; scenery, Oliver Smith; costumes, Theoni V. Aldredge; lighting, Jean Rosenthal; associate producer, Simon L. Saltzman; production stage manager, William Ross; stage manager, Bernard Pollock; press, Harvey B. Sabinson, Lee Solters.

Time: An election year. Place: The library of Senator MacGruder's house in Washington, D.C. The play is divided into two parts.

Comedy about a Presidential candidate who turns a potential political embarrassment into an asset when his son brings home a Negro mistress.

Loot (22). By Joe Orton. Produced by Losal Productions Inc. by arrangement with Oscar Lewenstein and Michael White at the Biltmore Theater. Opened March 18, 1968. (Closed April 6, 1968)

McLeavy ....Liam Redmond
Fay ....Carole Shelley
Hal ....Kenneth Cranham
Dennis ....James Hunter
Truscott ....George Rose
Meadows ....Norman Barrs
A Policeman ....William McAdam

Standbys: Messrs. Rose, Redmond—Norman Barrs; Miss Shelley—Joan Bassie; Mr. Cranham—William MacAdam; Dennis—John Horn.

Directed by Derek Goldby; scenery and lighting, William Ritman; costumes, Patton Campbell; production stage manager, Warren Crane; stage manager, William MacAdam; press, Sol Jacobson, Lewis Harmon.

Time: The present, afternoon. Place: A room in McLeavy's house. The play is presented in two parts.

Murder, bank robbery, corpse kidnaping and a whole calendar of lesser crimes, including the successful bribery of a Scotland Yard detective, are treated in the grotesque stage style which has come to be known as black comedy. A foreign play previously produced in Cambridge and London.

The Vienna Burgtheater. Repertory of four plays in the German language. **Professor Bernhardi** (6). By Arthur Schnitzler. Opened March 19, 1968. **Das Konzert** (*The Concert*) (6). By Hermann Bahr. Opened March 23, 1968. **Maria Stuart** (6). By Friedrich von Schiller. Opened March 26, 1968. **Einen Jux Will Er Sich Machen** (*He Wants To Have a Good Time*) (6). By Johann Nestroy; music by Adolf Müller and Alexander Steinbrecher. Opened April 2, 1968. Produced by The Association for International Theatrical Exchange, Gert von Gontard president, and The City Center of Music and Drama, Inc. at New York City Center. (Repertory closed April 7, 1968)

PERFORMER	"PROFESSOR BERNHARDI"	"DAS KONZERT"	"MARIA STUART"	"EINEN JUX WILL ER SICH MACHEN"
Trude Ackermann		Miss Wehner		Philippine
Ewald Balser			Talbot	
Achim Benning	Dr. Schreimann		Davison	
Hans Brand	Servant		Burgoyn	2d Waiter
Ernst Deutsch	Prof. Bernhardi			
Lona Dubois	Ludmilla	Mrs. Mell	Margareta	
Heinz Ehrenfreund			Okelly	Sonders
Heinrich Eis	Dr. Bernhardi		Guard	
Richard Eybner	Dr. Tugendvetter			
Sebastian Fischer			Dudley	
Wolfgang Gasser	Rev. Reder		Melvil	Watchman
Walter Gerhardt				Brunninger
Adrienne Gessner				Miss Blumenblatt
Hugo Gottschlich		Pollinger		Melchior
Paul Hoffmann			Cecil	
Paul Hörbiger	Dr. Cyprian			
Manfred Inger	Dr. Goldenthal			
Michael Janisch	Hochroitzpointner			Rab
Eva Kerbler		Eva Gerndl		
Otto Kerry	Dr. Feuermann			
Inge Konradi				Christopherl
Hilde Krahl			Elisabeth the Queen	
Lotte Ledl		Mrs. Kann		Mrs. von Fischer
Fritz Lehmann	Dr. Löwenstein			Hupfer
Fred Liewehr	Prof. Flint			Zangler
Sylvia Lukan		Miss Meier	Lady-in-Waiting	Marie
Johanna Matz		Delfine		
Josef Meinrad	Dr. Winkler			Weinberl
Kurt Meisel	Dr. Ebenwald			
Heinz Moog	Prof. Pflugfelder		Paulet	
Susi Nicoletti		Marie Heink		
Max Pfeiler	Servant	Johann		1st Waiter
Aglaja Schmid			Maria Stuart	
Peter Schratt	Dr. Wenger		Kent	
Edd Stavjanik	Dr. Adler			Kraps
Lilly Stepanek				Gertrude
Walter Stumvoll	Manservant		Drury	Superintendant
Curth A. Tichy	Dr. Pflugfelder		Bellievre	Coachman
Franziska Tilden		Miss Garden	Lady-in-Waiting	Lisette
Jane Tilden		Mrs. Floderer		Miss Knorr
Axel von Ambesser		Gustav Heink		
Hilde Wagener			Hanna	
Peter Weck		Dr. Jura		
Andreas Wolf	Dr. Filitz		Aubespine	
Gusti Wolf		Mrs. Pollinger		
Klaus Jürgen Wussow			Mortimer	

ALL PLAYS: Ernst Haeusserman, managing director; scenery, Lois Egg; producer, Gert von Gontard; narrators of English translation, Iris Merlis, Maria Pelikan, Eva Schulz; stage managers, Doris Einstein Siegel, Adalbert Jezel; press, Nat and Irvin Dorfman.

PROFESSOR BERNHARDI directed by Kurt Meisel; costumes, Maxi Tschunko. Time: Circa 1910. Place: Vienna. A problem drama about a physician who follows his conscience in a matter of religion and suffers for it.

DAS KONZERT directed by Josef Meinrad; costumes, Ernie Kniepert. Time: Circa 1910. Place: In and near Vienna. Comedy about a philandering piano teacher and his willing students.

MARIA STUART directed by Rudolf Steinböck; costumes, Ronny Reiter; technical direction and lighting, Sepp Nordegg. Time: 1587. Place: London and Fotheringhay. The epic drama of Mary Queen of Scots.

EINEN JUX WILL ER SICH MACHEN directed by Axel von Ambesser; musical direction, Alexander Steinbrecher; costumes, Ernie Kniepert. Time: 1830. Place: In and near Vienna. Folk play with music on which Thornton Wilder based his play *The Matchmaker,* which in turn provided the basis for *Hello, Dolly!*

The Seven Descents of Myrtle (29). By Tennessee Williams. Produced by David Merrick at the Ethel Barrymore Theater. Opened March 27, 1968. (Closed April 20, 1968)

Chicken .... Harry Guardino
Myrtle .... Estelle Parsons
Lot .... Brian Bedford

Standby: Miss Parsons—Marilyn Chris. Understudies: Mr. Bedford—Michael Stoddard; Mr. Guardino—Don Barnett.

Directed by José Quintero; scenery and lighting, Jo Mielziner; costumes, Jane Greenwood; associate producer, Samuel Liff; stage manager, Charles Blackwell; press, Lee Solters, Harvey B. Sabinson, Robert Larkin.

Time: The present. Place: A farm in the South. The play is divided into two acts.

An effete, dying mother's-boy marries a faded blossom and brings her home to spite his swarthy, earthy half-brother who works but does not own the family farm.

The Education of H*Y*M*A*N K*A*P*L*A*N (28). Musical based on the stories by Leo Rosten; book by Benjamin Bernard Zavin; music and lyrics by Paul Nassau and Oscar Brand. Produced by André Goulston/Jack Farren and Stephen Mellow at the Alvin Theater. Opened April 4, 1968. (Closed April 27, 1968)

Jimmy .... Stephen Bolster
Pushcart Vendor .... Dick Ensslen
Old Clothes Man .... Cyril Murkin
Kathy McKenna .... Donna McKechnie
Sam Pinsky .... Nathaniel Frey
Reuben Plonsky .... David Gold
Giovanni Pastora .... Dick Latessa
Mrs. Moskowitz .... Honey Sanders
Sarah Moskowitz .... Susan Camber
Mr. Parkhill .... Gary Krawford
Fanny Gidwitz .... Maggie Task
Rose Mitnick .... Barbara Minkus
Hyman Kaplan .... Tom Bosley
Eileen Higby .... Dorothy Emmerson
Marie Vitale .... Beryl Towbin
Mrs. Mitnick .... Mimi Sloan
Officer Callahan .... Wally Engelhardt
Yissel Fishbein .... Hal Linden
Guard .... David Ellin
Judge Mahon .... Rufus Smith

Dancers: Pamela Barlow, Mickie Bier, Susan Camber, Joanne DiVito, Andrea Duda, Lee Lund, Kuniko Narai, Eileen Woliner, Takeshi Hamagaki, Yanco Inone, Pat Matera, Barry Preston, George Ramos, Steven Ross.

Singers: Alice Cannon, Martha Danielle, Trudy Wallace, Edward Becker, David Ellin, Jack Fletcher.

Understudies: Mr. Bosley—Hal Linden; Miss Minkus—Alice Cannon; Messrs. Linden, Frey—David Ellin; Misses Sloan, Sanders—Maggie Task.

Directed by George Abbott; dances and musical staging, Jaime Rogers; musical direction and vocal arrangements, Julian Stein; scenery, William and Jean Eckart; costumes, Winn Morton; lighting, Martin Aronstein; orchestrations, Larry Wilcox; dance music arrangements, Lee Holdridge; production stage manager, Edward Preston; associate producer, David W. Sampliner; assistant to choreographer, Yanco Inone; stage manager, Edward Julien; press, Harvey B. Sabinson, Lee Solters, Leo Stern.

Time: 1919-1920. Place: New York City, the Lower East Side.

As in the Rosten stories, a group of immigrants studies to become Americans, reciting their lessons and their dreams in fractured English, none more flamboyantly and ambitiously than the little man whose tailor-shop sign reads H*Y*M*A*N K*A*P*L*A*N.

ACT I

"Strange New World" .... Parkhill
"OOOO-EEEE" .... Kaplan, Rose, Parkhill, Students

"A Dedicated Teacher" .... Higby, Miss Vitale, Parkhill
"Lieben Dich" .... Kaplan
"Loving You" .... Rose
"The Day I Met Your Father" .... Mrs. Mitnick
"Anything Is Possible" .... Kaplan, Students, Dancers, Singers
"Spring in the City" .... Kathy, Pastora, Plonsky, Pinsky, Mrs. Moskowitz, Fanny, Dancers, Singers

ACT II

"Old Fashioned Husband" .... Fishbein
"Julius Caesar" .... Kaplan
"I Never Felt Better in My Life" .... Kaplan, Dancers, Singers
"When Will I Learn" .... Rose
"All American" .... Pinsky, Students

* **George M!** (60). Musical with book by Michael Stewart and John and Fran Pascal; music and lyrics by George M. Cohan; lyric and musical revisions by Mary Cohan; musical supervision by Laurence Rosenthal. Produced by David Black, Konrad Matthaei and Lorin E. Price at the Palace Theater. Opened April 10, 1968.

Dog Trainer; 2d Pianist; Rose .... Loni Ackerman
Living Statue; Secretary .... Jonelle Allen
Fay Templeton; Draper's Asst.; Wardrobe Lady .... Jacqueline Alloway
Living Statue; Pushcart Girl .... Karin Baker
1st Little Girl; Mrs. Red Deer; Sharpshooter's Asst.; Little Girl in Tempelton scene .... Susan Batson
Acrobat; Pushcart Boy .... Bill Brandon
Dr. Webb; E.F. Albee; Living Statue; Ben; Mayor .... Roger Braun
Louis Behman; Bell Ringer; Vendor; Templeton Mgr. .... Danny Carroll
Willie; Sharpshooter; Stage Mgr. .... Gene Castle
Jerry Cohan .... Jerry Dodge
Ethel Levey .... Jamie Donnelly
Stagehand; Dog Trainer; Louie; Congressman; Actor .... James Dybas
Sam Harris; Violinist; Bell Ringer .... Harvey Evans
George M. Cohan .... Joel Grey
Nellie Cohan .... Betty Ann Grove
2d Little Girl; Acrobat ...... Patti Mariano
Ventriloquist; Ma Templeton .... Angela Martin
Drummer; Draper; Dockhand; Judge; 1st Policeman; Man on Street .... John Mineo
Agnes Nolan .... Jill O'Hara
Josie Cohan .... Bernadette Peters
1st Pianist; Acrobat; Bell Ringer; Piano Player .... Scotty Salmon
Living Statue; Pushcart Girl .... Kathie Savage
Mme. Grimaldi; Mrs. Baker; Flamethrower's Asst. .... Janie Sell
Buck and Winger; Designer's Asst.; Sailor; Frankie .... Alan Weeks
Saxophonist; Flamethrower; Bell Ringer; Captain; Alderman; Accordionist; Director .... Ronald Young

Understudies: Mr. Grey—Jerry Dodge; Miss Peters—Patti Mariano; Mr. Dodge—Danny Carroll; Misses Grove, O'Hara—Karin Baker.

Direction and choreography, Joe Layton; musical direction and vocal arrangements, Jay Blackton; scenery, Tom John; costumes, Freddy Wittop; lighting, Martin Aronstein; orchestrations, Philip J. Lang; production supervisor, José Vega; stage manager, Tony Manzi; press, Frank Goodman, Martin Shwartz.

Time: 1878 to 1937. Place: The environment of show business on the road and in New York.

The book tells of the life and career of the popular musical comedy star George M. Cohan; the music is Cohan's own.

ACT I

Scene 1: Prologue
Scene 2: Providence, Rhode Island, 1878
Scene 3: Onstage, Columbia Theater, Cedar Rapids
"Musical Moon" .... Jerry and Nellie

"Oh, You Wonderful Boy" .... Josie
"All Aboard for Broadway" .... George, then Four Cohans
Scene 4: Street in Cedar Rapids
"Musical Comedy Man" .... Four Cohans, Full Company
Scene 5: Madame Grimaldi's boarding house
Scene 6: En route to New York
"All Aboard for Broadway" (Reprise) .... Four Cohans, Full Company
Scene 7: Adams Street Theater, various other theaters, New York, 1901-1903
"I Was Born in Virginia" .... Ethel
"Twentieth Century Love" .... Four Cohans, Ethel
Scene 8: General area, New York, then in front of Savoy Theater
"My Town" .... George
Scene 9: Stage of Liberty Theater, New York
"Billie" .... Agnes
"Push Me Along in My Pushcart" .... Ethel, Pushcart Girls
"Ring to the Name of Rose" .... Josie, Bell Ringers
"Popularity" .... Willie, Full Company
"Give My Regards to Broadway" .... George, Full Company

ACT II

Scene 1: Office of Cohan and Harris, Fay Templeton's apartment
"Forty-five Minutes from Broadway" .... George, then Rose
"So Long, Mary" .... George, Sam, then Rose, Freddie, Ma Templeton
"Down by the Erie" .... Secretary, Politicians, Little Girl, then Full Company
Scene 2: Onstage, New Amsterdam Theater
"Mary" .... Fay Templeton
Scene 3: Rector's Restaurant, Jan. 1, 1907
"All Our Friends" .... Sam, Full Company
Scene 4: Street outside Rector's, next morning
Scene 5: The years till 1919
"Yankee Doodle Dandy," "Nellie Kelly I Love You," "Harrigan," "Over There,"
"You're a Grand Old Flag" .... George, Full Company
Scene 6: The years till 1937
"The City" .... Full Company
Scene 7: Midtown New York, February 1937
Scene 8: Stage of the Alvin Theater
"I'd Rather Be Right" .... George, Company
"Give My Regards to Broadway" (Reprise) .... George
Scene 9: Epilogue
"Dancing Our Worries Away," "The Great Easter Sunday Parade," "Hannah's a Hummer," "Barnum and Bailey Rag," "The Belle of the Barber's Ball," "The American Ragtime," "All in the Wearing," "I Want To Hear a Yankee Doodle Tune" .... Full Company
Voice in recording .... George M. Cohan

Mike Downstairs (4). By George Panetta. Produced by Zev Bufman, Abe Margolies and Edward A. Franck at the Hudson Theater. Opened April 18, 1968. (Closed April 20, 1968)

Mike .... Dane Clark
Lupo .... William Daprato
Joe .... Leonardo Cimino
1st Authority .... John Tormey
2d Authority .... Alan Peterson
Donna Maria .... Loretta Fury
Paul .... Tom Pedi
Minnie Picarella .... Eleni Kiamos
Patsy .... Arnold Soboloff
Sam .... Richard Castellano
Josie Spero .... Kay Michaels
Big Authority .... Russell Baker
Priest .... David Ellis
Uncle .... Lloyd Harris
1st Soldier .... Johnny Evans
2d Soldier .... Edmond Varrato

Citizens: Barbara Beckley, John Bentley, Louise Clay, Michael Enserro, Roxee Graziano, Antonia Rey, Helen G. Ross.

Understudies: Mr. Clark—Arnold Soboloff; Messrs. Daprato, Pedi, Soboloff, Baker—John Bentley.

Directed by Donald Driver; scenery, Edward Burbridge; lighting, Thomas Skelton; costumes, Hal George; music arrangement, Peter Matz; associate producer, Philip Turk; assistant to Mr. Driver, Rudy Tronto; production stage manager, William Krot; stage manager, Carol Raymont; press, Betty Lee Hunt, Henry Luhrman.

Time: The present. Place: The Little Italy section of Manhattan. The action is presented in two parts.

Comedy about a Mulberry Street resident who does all he can to help his neighbors amid the complexities of the modern world.

I'm Solomon (7). Musical based on the play *King Solomon and the Cobbler* by Sammy Gronemann (American adaptation in collaboration with Zvi Kolitz); book by Anne Croswell and Dan Almagor; music by Ernest Gold; lyrics by Anne Croswell. Produced by Zvi Kolitz, Solomon Sagall and Abe Margolies at the Mark Hellinger Theater. Opened April 23, 1968. (Closed April 27, 1968)

Meir .... Meir Alon
Ali .... Al DeSio
Issac .... John Dorrin
Tavern Dancer .... Sally Neal
Yoni; Solomon .... Dick Shawn
Na'Ama .... Karen Morrow
Yoel .... Kenneth Scott
Mago .... Johnny La Motta
Lemech .... Ed Ericksen
Aviva .... Alice Evans
Bruria .... Lynn Archer
Officer .... Gordon Cook
Ben-Hesed .... Paul Reed
Princess Nofrit .... Barbara Webb
F'htar .... Mary Barnett
Bathsheba .... Carmen Mathews
Ambassador .... Nat Horne
Ranor .... Fred Pinkard
Aide to Ranor .... Garrett Morris
Rachel, One of Solomon's Wives .... Caryl Tenney
Makedah .... Salome Jens

Solomon's Concubines, Other Wives, People of Jerusalem, Courtiers, Guards, Slaves, Children, Ethiopians, etc.: Clifford Allen, Meir Alon, Lynn Archer, Jeri Barto, Connie Burnett, Chris Callan, Al Cohen, Gordon Cook, Nikolas Dante, Jaque Dean, Esteban De Leon, Al DeSio, John Dorrin, Miriam Ehrenberg, Ed Eriksen, Alice Evans, Carol Flemming, Stokeley Gray, Rodney Griffin, Jerry Grimes, Marsha Hastings, Nat Horne, Mary Jane Houdina, Jason Howard, Nina Janik, Sherry Lambert, Johnny La Motta, Carol Manning, Garrett Morris, Sally Neal, Keith Perry, Martha Pollak, Ken Richards, Renee Rose, Jeffrey Shawn, Clay Taliaferro, Joan Tannen, Caryl Tenney, Nina Trasoff, Kyle Weaver, Bruce Wells, Myrna White.

Standby: Mr. Shawn—Alfred Toigo. Understudies: Miss Morrow—Alice Evans; Miss Mathews—Lynn Archer; Mr. Pinkard—Nat Horne; Misses Webb, Jens—Carol Flemming.

Directed by Michael Benthall; dances and musical numbers staged by Donald McKayle; musical direction and vocal arrangements, Gershon Kingsley; scenery, Rouben Ter-Arutunian; costumes, Jane Greenwood; lighting, Martin Aronstein; orchestrations, Hershy Kay; special material, David Finkle, Bill Weeden; dance arrangements, Dorothea Freitag; associate producers, Philip Turk, Kalman Ginzburg; production stage manager, Mortimer Halpern; stage managers, Norman Shelly, Bert Wood; press, Max Eisen, Cheryl Sue Dolby.

Time: About 100 B.C., from the morning of one day to noon of the next. Place: Various locales in and around Jerusalem.

Cobbler who resembles King Solomon is king for a day, taking Solomon's place while the King goes among his people.

ACT I

"David & Bathsheba" .... Yoni, People of Jerusalem
"Hail the Son of David" .... Solomon, Courtiers, Wives
"Preposterous" .... Solomon
"Have You Heard?" .... People of Jerusalem
"The Citation" .... Ben-Hesed
"In Love with a Fool" .... Na'Ama
"Someone Like Me" .... Solomon
"In Someone Else's Sandals" .... Yoni, Bathsheba, Slaves, Concubines
"The Three Riddles" .... Ranor, Ben-Hesed, Solomon, People of Jerusalem
(Lyrics by Erich Segal)

ACT II

"Once in 2.7 Years" .... Solomon's Wives
"Have You Ever Been Alone with a King Before?" .... Yoni, Na'Ama
(Music by Bill Weeden, lyrics by David Finkle)
"Lord I Am But a Little Child" .... Solomon
"I Am What I Am" .... Solomon
"Something in His Eyes" .... Na'Ama
"That Guilty Feeling" .... Yoni
(Music by Bill Weeden, lyrics by David Finkle)
"Time To Let Go" .... Bathsheba
"With Your Hand in My Hand" .... Yoni, Na'Ama, Bathsheba, People of Jerusalem
"Lord I Am But a Little Child" (Reprise) .... Entire Company

The Exercise (5). By Lewis John Carlino. Produced by Lyn Austin, Oliver Smith, Jay J. Cohen and Leslie J. Stark at the John Golden Theater. Opened April 24, 1968. (Closed April 27, 1968)

The Actor .... Stephen Joyce
The Actress .... Anne Jackson

Standbys: Miss Jackson—Peggy Feury; Mr. Joyce—Tony Lo Bianco.

Directed by Alfred Ryder; scenery, Oliver Smith; lighting, Jean Rosenthal; sound, Teiji Ito; associate producer, Ann McIntosh; production stage manager, Wayne Carson; press, Samuel Lurie, Stanley F. Kaminsky.

Time: The present. Place: A bare stage. Act I—Incubus. Act II—Redemption.

An actor and actress "rehearsing" on a bare stage "improvise" expressions of their own emotional traumas as a test of their art.

City Center Gilbert & Sullivan Company. Repertory of five operetta revivals with book and lyrics by W.S. Gilbert, music by Arthur Sullivan. **The Pirates of Penzance** (7). Opened April 25, 1968. **H.M.S. Pinafore** (8). Opened April 27, 1968. **The Mikado** (8). Opened May 1, 1968. **The Yeomen of the Guard** (3). Opened May 8, 1968. **Patience** (3). Opened May 15, 1968. Produced by The City Center of Music and Drama, Inc. at New York City Center. (Repertory closed May 19, 1968)

THE PIRATES OF PENZANCE

(Maj.-Gen. Stanley) .... Douglas Watson, Emile Renan
Pirate King .... William Chapman
(Samuel) .... William Ledbetter, Will Roy
(Frederic) .... Frank Porretta, John Harger Stewart
(Sgt. of Police) .... Jack Bittner, Richard Wentworth
Maj.-Gen. Stanley's Wards:
(Mabel) .... Patricia Wise, Margot Moser
Edith .... Ellen Shade
(Kate) .... Janet Winburn, Helen Guile
Isabel .... Diana Kehrig
Ruth .... Muriel Greenspon

(Parentheses indicate roles in which the actors alternated)

Directed by Allen Fletcher; conductors, Felix Popper, David Effron; scenery, Lloyd Evans; costumes, Patton Campbell; lighting, Hans Sondheimer.

H.M.S. PINAFORE

(Sir Joseph Porter, K.C.B.) .... Raymond Allen, Robert Trehy
(Capt. Corcoran) .... Richard Fredricks, William Chapman
(Ralph Rackstraw) .... Enrico DiGiuseppe, Evan Thomas, Frank Porretta
(Dick Deadeye) .... Don Yule, Paul Ukena
Bill Bobstay .... Robert Hale
(Bob Becket) .... Will Roy, Don Yule
(Josephine) .... Joy Clements, Barbara Blanchard
(Cousin Hebe) .... Janet Winburn, Ellen Shade, Helen Guile
(Little Buttercup) .... Joan Caplan, Muriel Greenspon

(Parentheses indicate roles in which the actors alternated)

Directed by Allen Fletcher; conductors, Thomas P. Martin, David Effron; scenery and costumes, Patton Campbell; lighting, Hans Sondheimer.

THE MIKADO

(Mikado) .....Paul Ukena, Edward Pierson
(Nanki-Poo) ....Frank Porretta, Enrico DiGiuseppe
(Ko-Ko) ....John Lankston, Raymond Allen
(Pooh-Bah) ....Richard Wentworth, Vern Shinall
(Pish-Tush) ....William Ledbetter, Robert Hale
(Yum-Yum) ....Carol Bergey, Joy Clements, Barbara Blanchard
(Pitti-Sing) ......Mary Burgess, Ellen Shade
(Peep-Bo) .....Janet Winburn, Helen Guile
(Katisha) ...Muriel Greenspon, Joan Caplan
Solo Dancer ....Miyoko Watanabe
Koken ....John Henry-Thomas

(Parentheses indicate roles in which the actors alternated)

Directed by Jack and Virginia Frymire; conductor, Byron Dean Ryan; scenery, Donald Oenslager; costumes, Patton Campbell.

THE YEOMEN OF THE GUARD

Sir Richard Cholmondeley .....Robert Hale
(Col. Fairfax) ....Frank Porretta, John Harger Stewart
Sgt. Meryll ....Paul Ukena
Leonard Meryll ....John Lankston
Jack Point ....Robert Trehy
Wilfred Shadbolt ....Jack Bittner
1st Yeoman ....Evan Thomas
2d Yeoman ....David Hicks
1st Citizen ....Harris Davis
2d Citizen ....Don Henderson
(Elsie Maynard) ....Margot Moser, Patricia Wise
Phoebe Meryll ....Mary Burgess
Dame Carruthers ....Ellen Alexander
Kate ....Fredreika Wisehart

(Parentheses indicate roles in which the actors alternated)

Directed by Allen Fletcher; conductor, Felix Popper; scenery, Stephen O. Saxe; costumes, Alvin Colt; lighting, Hans Sondheimer.

PATIENCE

Col. Calverley ....William Chapman
Maj. Murgatroyd ....Nico Castel
Duke of Dunstable ....John Lankston
Reginald Bunthorne ....Emile Renan
Archibald Grosvenor ......William Metcalf
Mr. Bunthorne's Solicitor ....John Henry-Thomas
Lady Angela ....Mary Burgess
Lady Saphir ....Helen Guile
Lady Ella ....Fredreika Wisehart
Lady Jane ....Claramae Turner
(Patience) ......Joy Clements, Carol Bergey

(Parentheses indicate role in which the actors alternated)

Directed by Leon Major; conductor, Felix Popper; scenery and costumes, Motley; lighting, Hans Sondheimer.

Ensemble (for all plays): Arlene Adler, Ronald Bentley, Don Carlo, Anthony Darius, Harris Davis, Joseph Galiano, Nino Garcia, Pearle Goldsmith, Marilyn Armstrong, Harriet Greene, Don Henderson, Lila Herbert, Douglas Hunnikin, Suzy Hunter, Diana Kehrig, Karl Patrick Krause, Donna Owen, Hanna Owen, Raymond Papay, Richard Park, Leo Postrel, Joaquin Romaguera, Stefanya Weicker, Maria West, Marie Young, John Henry-Thomas.

ALL PLAYS—General director, Felix Popper; associate director, John S. White; artistic coordinator, Ruth M. Hider; music administrator, Daniel R. Rule; stage manager, Dan Butt; press, Nat and Irvin Dorfman.

The last Broadway revival of Gilbert & Sullivan operettas was November 15, 1966 for 32 performances of five programs by the D'Oyly Carte Opera Company. Five operettas were revived off Broadway this season by the American Savoyards (see their entry in the Plays Produced Off Broadway section of this volume).

* **Hair** (38; see note). Musical with book and lyrics by Gerome Ragni and James Rado; music by Galt MacDermot. Produced by Michael Butler in the Natoma Production at the Biltmore Theater. Opened April 29, 1968.

Claude ....James Rado
Ron ....Ronald Dyson
Berger ....Gerome Ragni
Woof ....Steve Curry
Hud ....Lamont Washington
Sheila ....Lynn Kellogg
Jeannie ....Sally Eaton
Dionne ....Melba Moore
Crissy ....Shelley Plimpton
Mother ......Sally Eaton, Jonathan Kramer, Paul Jabara
Father ....Robert I. Rubinsky, Suzannah Norstrand, Lamont Washington
Principal .....Robert I. Rubinsky, Suzannah Norstrand, Lamont Washington
Tourist Couple ....Jonathan Kramer, Robert I. Rubinsky
Waitress ....Diane Keaton
Young Recruit ....Jonathan Kramer
General Grant ....Paul Jabara
Abraham Lincoln ....Lorri Davis
Sergeant ....Donnie Burks
Parents ...Diane Keaton, Robert I. Rubinsky

The Tribe: Donnie Burks, Lorri Davis, Leata Galloway, Steve Gamet, Walter Harris, Diane Keaton, Hiram Keller, Marjorie LiPari, Emmaretta Marks, Natalie Mosco, Suzannah Norstrand, Robert I. Rubinsky.

Standby: Mr. Rado—Seth Allen.

Directed by Tom O'Horgan; dance director, Julie Arenal; musical director, Galt MacDermot; scenery, Robin Wagner; costumes, Nancy Potts; lighting, Jules Fisher; sound, Robert Kiernan; executive producer, Bertrand Castelli; production stage manager, Fred Reinglas; stage manager, Michael Maurer; press, Robert Ganshaw, Michael F. Goldstein Inc.

Time: The present.

Rock 'n' roll musical about the lives and loves of hippies, one of whom must decide whether to burn his draft card or go to Vietnam (he decides the latter).

NOTE: *Hair* was first produced off Broadway where it played 94 performances before moving to Broadway (see its entry in the off-Broadway section of this volume).

ACT I

"Aquarius" ....Ron, Company
"Donna" ....Berger, Company
"Hashish" ....Company
"Sodomy" ....Woof, Company
"Colored Spade" ....Hud, Company
"Manchester" ....Claude, Company
"Ain't Got No" ....Woof, Hud, Dionne, Company
"I Believe in Love" ....Sheila
"Air" ....Jeanie, Crissy, Dionne, Company
"Initials" ....Company
"I Got Life" ....Claude, Company
"Going Down" ....Berger, Company
"Hair" ....Claude, Berger, Company
"My Conviction" ....Tourist Lady, Company
"Easy To Be Hard" ....Sheila
"Hung" ....Berger, Woof, Claude, Sheila, Jeanie, Company
"Don't Put It Down" ....Berger, Steve, Woof
"Frank Mills" ....Crissy
"Hare Krishna" ....Company
"Where Do I Go" ....Claude, Company

ACT II

"Electric Blues" ....Suzannah, Leata, Steve, Paul
"Black Boys" ....Diane, Suzannah, Natalie
"White Boys" ....Dionne, Lorri, Emmaretta
"Walking in Space" ....Company
"Abie Baby" ....Hud, Ron, Donnie, Lorri
"Prisoners in Niggertown" ....Company
"What a Piece of Work Is Man" ....Ronald, Walter
"Good Morning Starshine" ....Sheila, Dionne, Company
"The Bed" ....Company
"The Flesh Failures" ....Claude, Sheila, Dionne, Company

Soldiers (22). By Rolf Hochhuth; translated by Robert D. MacDonald. Produced by Herman Shumlin, Zev Bufman and Raphael Silver by arrangement with Kenneth Tynan at the Billy Rose Theater. Opened May 1, 1968. (Closed May 19, 1968)

Dorland	Colin Fox	Lord Cherwell	Joseph Shaw
The Sculptor	Muni Seroff	Gen. Sir Alan Brooke	Basil Langton
Dorland's Son	Richard Monette	Gen. Sikorski	Eric House
An Actor (Kocjan)	James Luisi	Group Capt. Clark	Michael Lewis
Helen MacDonald	Patricia Wheel	Messenger	David Thomas
Churchill	John Colicos	Bell, Bishop of Chichester	Tony Church

Understudies: Mr. Shaw—Michael Lewis; Messrs. Langton, Fox, Lewis—Leslie Redford; Messrs. Monette, Luisi, Thomas—Edmund Williams; Miss Wheel—Catherine Ellis.

Directed by Clifford Williams; design, Ralph Koltai; scenery supervision, James Riley; costume supervision, Richard Anderson; production stage manager, Daniel Broun; press, Joe Wolhandler, Marianne Mackay.

Prologue and Epilogue—Time: The 100th Anniversary of the Geneva Convention. Place: St. Michael's Cathedral, Coventry, England. The Play—Time: 1943. Place: England. Act I: The ship; North Sea, early in 1943. Act II: The bed; London, June 1943. Act III: The garden; Chequers, July 1943.

A play is "rehearsed" at Coventry for production in honor of the Geneva Convention's 100th anniversary. The "play" alleges that Winston Churchill backed the mass bombing of German cities in 1943 (and condoned the murder of Poland's General Sikorski) in order to satisfy Stalin's demands for support. A foreign play previously produced in Berlin and Toronto.

* **Leonard Sillman's New Faces of 1968** (34). Musical revue conceived by Leonard Sillman. Produced by Jack Rollins at The Booth Theater. Opened May 2, 1968.

Michael K. Allen	Madeline Kahn
Suzanne Astor	Robert Klein
Rod Barry	Joe Kyle
Gloria Bleezarde	Robert Lone
Trudy Carson	Brandon Maggart
Marilyn Child	George Ormiston
Dottie Frank	Rod Perry
Elaine Giftos	Nancie Phillips

Standbys: For the ladies—Kelly Britt; for the gentlemen—F. David Halpert.

Entire production staged by Leonard Sillman; choreographed and directed by Frank Wagner; musical direction, Ted Simons; scenery and costumes, Winn Morton; lighting, Paul Sullivan; orchestrations, Lanny Meyers; production stage manager, Jack Timmers; production coordinator, Jacqueline Adams; stage manager, Paul Sullivan; press, Sol Jacobson, Lewis Harmon.

ACT I

Illustrated Overture
Definitions by Random House
Girl .... Gloria Bleezarde
Boy .... Rod Barry
Welcome
Producer .... Leonard Sillman
"Opening" .... Entire Company
(Music and lyrics by Ronny Graham)
Audition (by Robert Klein)
The Auditioner .... Robert Klein
"By the Sea" .... Brandon Maggart
(Music and lyrics by Clark Gesner)
"Where Is the Waltz?" .... Michael K. Allen
Dance .... Dottie Frank, Elaine Giftos, Trudy Carson
(Music and orchestration by Alonzo Levister, lyrics by Paul Nassau)

"A New Waltz" .... Marilyn Child
Dance .... Robert Lone, Joe Kyle
(Music by Fred Hellerman, lyrics by Fran Minkoff)
Happy Landings (by Jack Sharkey)
Airline Stewardess .... Madeline Kahn
"The Girl in the Mirror" .... Rod Perry
(Music by Fred Hellerman, lyrics by Fran Minkoff)
Isolation .... Kyle, Miss Bleezarde
The American Hamburger League (by Norman Kline)
Introduction .... Barry
Beth .... Miss Kahn
Helene .... Miss Child
Rex .... Maggart
Dexter .... George Ormiston
Wayne .... Klein
Isolation .... Miss Carson, Barry
Love Songs
Introduction .... Sillman
"Something Big" .... Ormiston, Miss Giftos
(Music by Sam Pottle, lyrics by David Axelrod)
"Love in a New Tempo" .... Klein
(Music and lyrics by Ronny Graham)
"Hungry" .... Suzanne Astor, Barry
(Music and lyrics by Murray Grand)
"Luncheon Ballad" .... Misses Astor, Child, Kahn, Nancie Phillips
(Music by Jerry Powell, lyrics by Michael McWhinney)
The Underachiever (by Peter De Vries)
Introduction .... Miss Bleezarde
Freshman .... Klein
His Wife .... Miss Kahn
"You're the One I'm For" .... Maggart
(Music and lyrics by Clark Gesner)
"Where Is Me?" .... Miss Child
(Music by Arthur Siegel, lyrics by June Carroll)
Isolation—"Right About Here" .... Allen
(Music and lyrics by Arthur Siegel)
Gospel According to Jack (by William F. Brown)
Performers .... Misses Astor, Carson, Child, Frank, Kahn; Messrs. Barry, Klein, Lone, Maggart, Perry
Isolation .... Klein, Miss Giftos
Mama Doll (by Charles Tobias and Nat Simon, conception by George Ormiston and Nancie Phillips)
Doll .... Miss Phillips
Little Boy .... Ormiston
"Toyland" (dialogue, music and lyrics by Gene P. Bissell)
Production Singer .... Miss Kahn
Compere .... Klein

and Company

ACT II

Introduction .... Sillman, Miss Bleezarde
"Hullabaloo at Thebes" (music and lyrics by Ronny Graham)
Introduction .... Sillman
Oedipus .... Klein
Jocasta .... Miss Astor
Antigone .... Miss Carson
Ismene .... Miss Giftos
"#X9RL220" .... Miss Bleezarde
(Music by Jerry Powell, lyrics by Michael McWhinney)
"You Are" .... Maggart
(Music and lyrics by Clark Gesner)

"Evil" .... Allen
(Music and lyrics by Sydney Shaw)
The Refund (by Peter De Vries)
Introduction and Clarification .... Ormiston
Fred Abernathy .... Klein
Ben Abernathy .... Maggart
Sarah Cobleigh .... Miss Frank
"Prisms" .... Miss Child
(Music by Carl Friberg, lyrics by Hal Hackady)
"Tango" (music by Sam Pottle, lyrics by David Axelrod)
Introduction .... Sillman
Performed by .... The Company
Isolation—"Cymbals & Tambourines" .... Miss Bleezarde, Lone
(Music and lyrics by Arthur Siegel)
"Philosophy" .... Perry
Dance .... Miss Frank, Giftos, Mr. Kyle
(Music by Carl Friberg, lyrics by Hal Hackady)
The Pile-Up .... Maggart
"Das Chicago Song" .... Miss Kahn
(Music by Michael Cohen, lyrics by Tony Geiss)
"Missed America" (dialogue, music and lyrics by Kenny Solms and Gail Parent, additional dialogue by Ronny Graham)
Emcee .... Ormiston
Miss Alabama .... Miss Phillips
Miss Minnesota .... Miss Frank
Miss Connecticut .... Miss Astor
"Die Zusammenfugung" (music by Sam Pottle, lyrics by David Axelrod)
Introduction .... Miss Bleezarde
Scheiss .... Maggart
Pfeffer .... Klein
Heidi .... Miss Kahn
The Connection .... Ormiston
"Opening" (Reprise)
Introduction .... Sillman
"The Girl of the Minute" .... Entire Company
(Music by David Shire, lyrics by Richard Maltby Jr.)

Happiness Is Just a Little Thing Called a Rolls Royce (1). By Arthur Alsberg and Robert Fisher. Produced by Anamark Productions at the Ethel Barrymore Theater. Opened and closed at the evening performance, May 11, 1968.

Myra Bagley .... Hildy Brooks
Walter Bagley .... Pat Harrington
Chuck Kinsey .... Marvin Lichterman
Karen Kinsey .... Phoebe Dorin
Andrew McIntire .... John McGiver
Jerry Ramsey .... Ray Fulmer
Sanford Rutchik .... Shimen Ruskin
Phil Gorshin .... Lee Bergere
Andrea Clithero .... Alexandra Berlin

Directed by David Alexander; scenery, Larry Reehling; costumes, Ann Roth; lighting, John Harvey; production stage manager, Don Doherty; stage manager, Joe Calvan; press, Bernard Simon, Gary Stevens.

Time: The past, the present and the future. Place: New York. The play was presented in two acts.

Comedy about a diffident lawyer being pushed by his ambitious wife.

* **The Only Game in Town** (14). By Frank D. Gilroy. Produced by Edgar Lansbury at the Broadhurst Theater. Opened May 20, 1968.

Fran Walker .... Tammy Grimes
Joe Grady .... Barry Nelson
Thomas Lockwood .... Leo Genn

Standby: Messrs. Nelson, Genn—James Karen.

Directed by Barry Nelson; scenery, George Jenkins; costumes, Theoni V. Aldredge; lighting, Jules Fisher; production stage manager, Ben D. Kranz; press, Samuel J. Friedman, Jane Friedman.

Place: Fran Walker's second-floor garden apartment just off the Strip in Las Vegas, Nevada. Act I: Seven scenes of which the first six take place two years ago within a period of 36 hours. The final scene occurs three months later. Act II: Two scenes that happen tonight.

Lonely Las Vegas dancer and piano player embark upon a no-strings-attached affair, only to find themselves caught up in "The only game in town"—love and marriage.

A production of *The Only Game in Town* was mounted earlier in the season under Daniel Petrie's direction, with Carolan Daniels (Fran), Richard Mulligan (Joe) and Albert Paulsen (Lockwood) and went on tryout tour, opening in Baltimore 1/16/68, New Haven 2/5/68 and Boston 2/12/68, ending its run 2/24/68.

* **The King and I** (10). Musical revival based on the novel *Anna and the King of Siam* by Margaret Landon; book and lyrics by Oscar Hammerstein II; music by Richard Rodgers. Produced by The City Center Light Opera Company, Jean Dalrymple director, at New York City Center. Opened May 23, 1968.

Captain Orton ....Sam Kirkham
Louis Leonowens ....Eric Hamilton
Anna Leonowens ....Constance Towers
The Interpreter ....Paul Flores
The Kralahome ....Ted Beniades
The King ....Michael Kermoyan
Phra Alack ....Robert Lenn
Lun Tha ....Stanley Grover
Tuptim ....Eleanor Calbes
Lady Thiang ....Anita Darian
Prince Chululongkorn ....Michael Thom
Princess Ying Yoalwalk ......Dana Shimizu
Sir Edward Ramsey .....Christopher Hewett

Princes and Princesses: Caryn Chow, Sonja Furiya, Dana Shimizu, Rachel Ticotin, Nancy Ticotin, Russell Chow, Lewis Gerardo, Lawrence Kikuchi, Jaime Roque, Jason Rosen, Keenan Shimizu, Marcus Ticotin.

The Royal Dancers: Diane Adler, Paula Chin, Carol Fried, Linda Gumiela, Joann Ogawa, Margot Parsons, Kathleen Pierini, Susan Platt, Juanita Londono, Wonci Lui, Stephanie Satie, Britt Swanson, Margot Travers, Jaclynn Villamil, Rebecca West, Lazar Dano, Gary Dutton, Vito Durante, Rodger Gerhardstein, Tim Ramirez.

The Singers (Wives, Priests, Amazons, Slaves): Joan diDonato, Lee Hooper, Charlotte Marcheret, Betsy Norden, Barbara Reisman, Rebecca West, Maggie Worth, Larry Devon, Beno Foster, Richard Kie Wye Khan.

Standbys: Miss Towers—Virginia Vestoff; Mr. Kermoyan—Ted Beniades; Mr. Beniades—Paul Flores.

Directed by John Fearnley; choreography, Jerome Robbins, reproduced by Yuriko; musical director, Jonathan Anderson; scenery, Paul McGuire; costumes, Irene Sharaff, supervised by Frank Thompson; lighting, Feder; orchestrations, Robert Russell Bennett; production stage manager, Herman Shapiro; stage managers, Sean S. Cunningham, James Struthers; press, Homer Poupart, John Clugstone.

Time: The 1860s. Place: In and around the King's palace, Bangkok, Siam.

The King and I was first produced by Rodgers and Hammerstein at the St. James Theater, March 29, 1951, for 1,246 performances. It was last revived on Broadway by the Music Theater of Lincoln Center, Richard Rodgers president and producing director, at the New York State Theater, July 6, 1964 for 40 performances.

The list of musical numbers in *The King and I* appears on page 361 of the 1950-51 *Best Plays* volume.

* **The Venetian Twins (I Due Gemelli Veneziani)** (5). Revival of the play in the Italian language by Carlo Goldoni. Produced by Arthur Cantor and Zenon R. Mocarski, Inc. in The Theater of Genoa *(Teatro Stabile di Genova)* production at Henry Miller's Theater. Opened May 28, 1968.

Dr. Balanzoni ....Mario Bardella
Rosaura ....Silvia Monelli
Pancrazio ....Camillo Milli
Zanetto; Tonino
(The Twins) ....Alberto Lionello
Lelio ....Eros Pagni
Beatrice ....Lucilla Morlacchi
Florino ....Giovanni De Lellis
Brighella ....Omero Antonutti
Colombina ....Margherita Guzzinati
Arlecchino ....Giancarlo Zanetti
Tiburzio ....Luigi Carubbi
Chief Constable ....Enrico Ardizzone
Constables ....Marcello Aste,
Vittorio Melloni
Porter ....Gianni Fenzi
Footman ....Marcello Aste

Directed by Luigi Squarzina; artistic directors, Ivo Chiesa, Luigi Squarzina; scenery and costumes, Gianfranco Padovani; music, Giancarlo Chiaramello; production associate, Henry Popkin; production stage manager, William Chambers; stage manager, Giorgio Catani; press, Arthur Solomon.

Time: 1754. Place: Verona. The play was presented in three acts.

Improbably complicated comic plot about a mixup of two twins, one bright and courageous and the other dull and cowardly, stressing the flexibility of ethics.

PLAYS WHICH CLOSED PRIOR TO BROADWAY OPENING

Productions which were organized in New York for Broadway presentation, but which closed during their tryout performances out of town or in New York previews, are listed below.

The Freaking Out of Stephanie Blake. By Richard Chandler. Produced by Cheryl Crawford and Carl Schaeffer in preview performances at the Eugene O'Neill Theater. Opened October 30, 1967. (Closed November 1, 1967)

Directed by Michael Kahn; scenery, Ben Edwards; costumes, Jean Button; lighting, Jean Rosenthal; music and lyrics, Jeff Barry; special projections, Bruce W. Stark; press, Betty Lee Hunt. With Jean Arthur, Sidney Lanier, Jan Miner, Alberta Grant, Steve Curry, Franklin Cover, Ellen O'Mara, James Fouratt, Joy Bang.

Time: The present. Place: The East Village. A mid-Western lady succumbs to the pleasures of the hippie life.

Mata Hari. Musical with book by Jerome Coopersmith; music by Edward Thomas; lyrics by Martin Charnin. Produced by David Merrick in a pre-Broadway tryout at the National Theater in Washington, D.C. Opened November 18, 1967. (Closed December 9, 1967)

The Young Soldier .... Jake Holmes
Lt. Boulet .... Mark Dempsey
Capt. Henry LaFarge ...... Pernell Roberts
Lt. Devries .... Joseph Corby
The Dancing Girls
Christiana .... Kuniko Narai
Carlotta .... Reiko Sato
Midge .... Myrna White
Mata Hari .... Marisa Mell
Vaudeville Man .... George Marcy
Vaudeville Woman .... Sandy Ellen
Vaudeville Child .... Ellen Kravitz
Paulette LaFarge .... Martha Schlamme
Flower Vendor; Mr. Dupre ..... Paul Glaser
Philipe .... Seymour Penzner
Claudine .... Nadine Lewis
Pierre .... Ryan Harrison
Michele .... Blythe Danner
Mrs. Dupre .... Helen G. Ross
Maurice .... Dominic Chianese
Innkeeper .... Lewis Pierce
1st German .... Robert Kelly
2d German; Stage Manager .... Gordon Voorhees
Lt. Grant .... Bill Reilly
Major Bonnard .... W.B. Brydon
Landlady .... Jacque Dean

Officers, Diplomats, Vendors, Musicians, Soldiers, Gendarmes, Parisians, etc.: Bobbi Baird, Baruch Blum, Eileen Casey, Joseph Corby, Peter Costanza, Jacque Dean, Anthony Devecchi, Judith Dunford, Carolyn Dyer, Sandy Ellen, Jack Fletcher, Garold Gardiner, Luigi Gasparinetti, Joanne Geahry, Altovise Gore, Peggy Hagen, Robert Kelly, Betty Kent, Ellen Kravitz, Tracy Moore, Ray Morgan, Lewis Pierce, Jeff Phillips, Bill Reilly, Skiles Ricketts, Don Stoms-Vik, Francine Storey, Caryl Tenney, Marshall Thomas, Nina Trasoff, Martha Velez, Gordon Voorhees, Masha Wolfson.

Directed by Vincente Minnelli; dances and musical numbers staged by Jack Cole; musical direction and vocal arrangements, Colin Romoff; scenery and lighting, Jo Mielziner; costumes, Irene Sharaff; orchestrations, Robert Russell Bennett; dance music arrangements, Roger Adams; associate producer, Samuel Liff; production stage manager, Pat Tolson; general stage manager, George Rondo; stage manager, Henry Sutton; press, Harvey B. Sabinson, Lee Solters, Robert Ullman.

Time: World War I. Place: Paris and elsewhere in Europe.

Musical play based on the career of Mata Hari, the famous World War I *femme fatale,* dancer and spy.

ACT I

Scene 1: The Deuxieme Bureau, Paris; a day in World War I
"Is This Fact?" .... LaFarge, Devries, Boulet, Officers
Scene 2: A salon in a wealthy home, that night
Mata Hari's Dance .... Mata Hari, Dancing Girls
"Everyone Has Something to Hide" .... Mata Hari, Ensemble
Scene 3: A taxi cab, later that night
"How Young You Were Tonight" .... LaFarge, Paulette
Scene 4: The flower market, later that day
"I'm Saving Myself for a Soldier" .... Vaudevillians, Ensemble
"I'm Saving Myself for a Soldier" (reprise) .... Vaudevillians, Ensemble
Scene 5: LaFarge's private office, immediately following
Scene 6: Montage of war on two fronts throughout the next two weeks
"Maman" .... The Young Soldier
"The Choice Is Yours" .... Mata Hari, LaFarge
Scene 7: LaFarge's home, night
"Sextet" .... Paulette, LaFarge, Claudine, Mr. Dupre, Mrs. Dupre, Philipe, Michele, Maurice, Pierre
Scene 8: A Left Bank hotel, the next evening
"Not Now, Not Here" .... Mata Hari
"Is This Fact?" (Reprise) .... LaFarge

ACT II

Scene 1: A field in France, several weeks later
"Hello, Yank!" .... The Young Soldier, French and American Soldiers
Scene 2: Mata Hari's bedroom, morning
Scene 3: A cafe in Madrid
"In Madrid" .... Ensemble
Dance at the Cafe del Toro .... Mata Hari, Dancers
Scene 4: A street near LaFarge's house, several weeks later
"I Don't See Him Very Much Anymore" .... Paulette
Scene 5: The Deuxieme Bureau, at dawn
"You Have No Idea" .... Mata Hari, LaFarge, Boulet, Officers
Scene 6: Backstage at the Theatre de Paris, that night
Scene 7: Exterior, St. Lazare Prison
"The Arrest" .... Ensemble
Scene 8: Interrogation
Ballet .... Mata Hari, Major Bonnard, Dancers
Scene 9: A street near LaFarge's house, several weeks later
"Sextet" (Reprise) .... Paulette, Relatives, People on the Street
"There Is No You" .... LaFarge
Scene 10: A visiting room, St. Lazare Prison, immediately following
"There Will Be Love Again" .... Mata Hari
Scene 11: A chalet in Switzerland, a day in late summer
Scene 12: A wooded area, a day in late summer

Leda Had a Little Swan. By Bamber Gascoigne. Produced by Claire Nichtern in preview performances at the Cort Theater. Opened March 29, 1968. (Closed following final preview April 10, 1968)

Harry ....Severn Darden
Virginia ....Joan Darling
Sir George ....Fred Stewart
Harry as a Boy; Noah ....John Pleshette
Lady Fitch; Doctor;
Aunt Mildred ....Cavada Humphrey
Headmaster;
Hodgkinson ....Michael J. Pollard
Herbert; Matt ....Paul Benedict
Matron; Mary Wollen ......Maxine Greene
Rebecca ....Margaret Ladd
Granger ....Merwin Goldsmith
Beggar; Robinson Minor ....Seth Allen

Directed by Andre Gregory; scenery, Wolfgang Roth; costumes, Carrie Fishbein; lighting, Jean Rosenthal; visual projection effects, DesPro Studios, Inc.; music, Teiji Ito; companions, Bil Baird; production manager, Charles Maryan; stage manager, Richard Nelson; press, Ben Kornzweig, Reginald Denenholz.

Time: 1968 to 1985. Place: London. Act I: Saturday, June 1968 to Friday, October 1985. Act II: Saturday, October 1985.

Comedy about hippies' children, who make love to animals. A foreign (English) play in its first production.

PLAYS PRODUCED OFF BROADWAY

Figures in parentheses following a play's title indicate number of performances. Plays marked with an asterisk (*) were still running on June 1, 1968, and their number of performances is figured from opening night through May 31, 1968, not including extra non-profit performances. In a listing of a show's numbers—dances, sketches, musical scenes etc.—the titles of songs are identified by their appearance in quotation marks (").

HOLDOVERS FROM PREVIOUS SEASONS

Plays which were running on June 1, 1967 are listed below. More detailed information about them appears in previous *Best Plays* volumes of appropriate years. Important cast changes are recorded in a section of this volume.

* **The Fantasticks** (3,378). Musical suggested by the play *Les Romantiques* by Edmond Rostand; book and lyrics by Tom Jones; music by Harvey Schmidt. Opened May 3, 1960.

The Pocket Watch (725). By Alvin Aronson. Opened January 5, 1966. (Closed December 27, 1968)

The Mad Show (871). Musical revue based on *Mad Magazine;* book by Larry Siegel and Stan Hart; lyrics by Marshall Barer, Larry Siegel and Steven Vinaver; music by Mary Rodgers. Opened January 9, 1966. (Closed September 10, 1967)

Mixed Doubles (428). Cabaret revue by Rod Warren. Opened October 19, 1966. (Closed July 1, 1967)

America Hurrah (634). Program of three one-act plays by Jean-Claude van Itallie. Opened November 6, 1966. (Closed May 5, 1968)

Man With a Load of Mischief (241). Musical adapted from the play by Ashley Dukes; book by Ben Tarver; music by John Clifton; lyrics by John Clifton and Ben Tarver. Opened November 6, 1966. (Closed June 4, 1967)

Bil and Cora Baird's Marionette Theater. Repertory of two marionette shows. **People Is the Thing That the World Is Fullest Of** (117), marionette revue conceived by Bil Baird, and **Davy Jones' Locker** (18), revival of the marionette musical based on a story by Bil Baird; with book by Arthur Birnkrant and Waldo Salt; music and lyrics by Mary Rodgers. Repertory opened February 20, 1967. (Closed June 25, 1967)

MacBird! (386). By Barbara Garson. Opened February 22, 1967. (Closed January 21, 1968)

Fortune and Men's Eyes (382). By John Herbert. Opened February 23, 1967. (Closed January 21, 1968)

* **You're a Good Man Charlie Brown** (542). Musical based on the comic strip "Peanuts" by Charles M. Schulz; book music and lyrics by Clark Gesner. Opened March 7, 1967.

Hamp (101). By John Wilson; based on an episode from the novel by J.L. Hodson. Opened March 9, 1967. (Closed June 4, 1967)

Gorilla Queen (64). By Ronald Tavel. Opened April 24, 1967. (Closed June 18, 1967)

The Coach with the Six Insides (72). Revival of the play by Jean Erdman, inspired by James Joyce's *Finnegans Wake*. Opened May 11, 1967. (Closed June 25, 1967)

Drums in the Night (69). By Bertolt Brecht; adapted by Frank Jones. Opened May 17, 1967. (Closed July 16, 1967)

Absolutely Free (208). Musical revue with music and lyrics by Frank Zappa. Opened May 24, 1967. (Closed September 4, 1967)

A Time for the Gentle People (12). By Tom Coble. Opened May 25, 1967. (Closed June 4, 1967)

PLAYS PRODUCED JUNE 1, 1967—MAY 31, 1968

In the Nick of Time (22). Revue with Barbara Fried, Charles Appel, Herb Suffrin, Leni Stern, Sue Lawless and Ted Pugh. Produced by David Hedges and William B. Allen in association with Richard Herd at Stage 73. Opened June 1, 1967. (Closed June 18, 1967)

Sue Lawless
Ted Pugh
Andrew Orestes Lesko

Directed by Earl Durham; lighting, Jene Yoult; technical director, Donald Martin; production stage manager, Charles Miller; press, Betty Lee Hunt, Fred Weterick.

Topical revue of songs and skits performed by Miss Lawless and Mr. Pugh, with Mr. Lesko providing musical accompaniment.

Arms and the Man (189). Revival of the play by George Bernard Shaw. Produced by Edgar Lansbury, Stuart Duncan, Dina and Alexander E. Racolin at the Sheridan Square Playhouse. Opened June 22, 1967. (Closed December 3, 1967)

Catherine Petkoff ....Audrey Ward
Raina ....Pamela Burrell
Louka ....Jenny O'Hara
Captain Bluntschli (The Man) ....John Heffernan
Russian Officer ....Dennis Longwell
Nicola ....Sy Travers
Major Petkoff ....Daniel Keyes
Major Sergius Saranoff ....Humbert A. Astrado

Directed by Philip Minor; scenery and costumes, Lloyd Burlingame; lighting, Fred Allison; stage manager, Don Judge; press, Max Eisen, Carl Samrock.

Time: November, 1885. Place: Bulgaria, in a small town near the Dragoman Pass.

Arms and the Man was first produced in London April 21, 1894 and in New York September 17, 1894 (the first Shaw play done in America). Its last professional New York revival was off Broadway April 27, 1964 at East End Theater for 23 performances.

A Midsummer Night's Dream (28). Revival of the play by William Shakespeare. The Circle in the Square production produced by Theodore Mann and Paul Libin at the Theater de Lys. Opened June 29, 1967. (Closed July 23, 1967)

Theseus; Oberon .... Alvin Epstein
Hippolyta; Titania .... Gloria Foster
Philostrate; Puck .... Barton Heyman
Egeus; Snug .... Henry Oliver
Hermia .... Susan Anspach
Demetrius; Flute .... Stephen Wyman
Lysander .... David Tress
Helena .... Robert Benson
Peter Quince .... Marshall Efron
Nick Bottom .... Alan Manson
Robin Starveling .... Mark Charlot
Tom Snout .... Wayne Grace
First Fairy .... Katie Heflin
Peaseblossom .... Carol Anshein
Cobweb .... Anna Stanovitch
Moth .... Amy Vane
Mustardseed .... Catherine Cleaves
Indian Girl .... Nitza Sue

Directed by John Hancock; designed by Robert LaVigne after drawings by Jim Dine; lighting, Al Jutzi; associate director, Kenneth Kitch; presented by special arrangement with Lucille Lortel Productions, Inc.; stage manager, Jan Moerel; press, Merle Debuskey, Violet Welles, Faith Geer.

Black comedy camp version of Shakespeare's play, previously produced at the San Francisco Workshop and the Pittsburgh Playhouse.

The Poker Session (16). By Hugh Leonard. Produced by Richard H. R. Smithies and Maura Cavanagh at the Martinique Theater. Opened September 19, 1967. (Closed October 3, 1967)

Billy Beavis .... Al Settimio
Mrs. Beavis .... Eugenia Rawls
Irene .... Holland Taylor
Kevin .... Tom Keena
Fran .... Eileen Mitchell
Teddy .... Ron Leibman

Directed by Richard H. R. Smithies; designed by C. Murawski; production stage manager, Martha Knight; press, David Rothenberg, Larry Schneider.

Time: A summer evening. Place: The Beavis home.

A young man, released from a mental hospital, comes home and tries to find out why he was sent there. A foreign play previously produced in Dublin and London.

Jonah! (22). By T. J. Spencer. Produced by Hal Thompson at Stage 73. Opened September 21, 1967. (Closed October 8, 1967)

Bos'n .... Colin Craig
Samuel .... Lawrence Barrett
Nicholas .... John Valentine
Zorgo .... Arthur French
Seamen .... Jack Shearer, Charles Murphy
Ezra .... Jay Gerber
Captain .... Russell Baker
Agent .... W. P. Dremak
Jonah .... Laurens Moore
Ulysses .... Joseph Warren
Thersites .... Bradley Bolke

Directed by Hal Thompson; lighting, Peter Russell; costumes, Eileen MacHardy; music, Morris Mamorsky; press, Nat and Irvin Dorfman.

Comedy about the beginning of the age of the God of Mercy, with the Lord's decision to spare the sinful city of Nineveh.

Stephen D (56). By Hugh Leonard; adapted from James Joyce's *A Portrait of the Artist as a Young Man* and *Stephen Hero.* Produced by Lyn Austin and Oliver Smith and Philip Mathias by arrangement with Peter Bridge at the East 74th Street Theater. Opened September 24, 1967. (Closed November 12, 1967)

Stephen Dedalus ....Stephen Joyce
Mrs. Dedalus ....Joan White
Dante ....Betty Garde
Stephen (as a boy) ....Chad Roche
Fleming ....Jamie Roche
Wells ....Geoffrey Martin
Athy ....Sean Roche
Brother Michael; Johnny Cashman;
Father Moran ....Drew Eliot
Mr. Dedalus ....Brendan Fay
Mr. Casey; Confessor ....Niel Fitzgerald
Uncle Charles; President of
University ....Edward J. McPhillips
Father Arnall; Preacher ....Peter Bosche
Father Dolan; Director of
College ....Ian Edward
Stephen (as a youth) ....John McGurran
Woman ....Jean Hickey
Maurice ....Douglas Richardson
Cranley ....Roy R. Scheider
Davin ....Dermot McNamara
McCann ....Paul Jenkins
Dixon ....Thomas McCready
Temple ....John Luce
Emma ....Flora Elkins
Flower Seller ....Patricia Fay
Isobel ....Joan E. Spalding
Girl ....Valerie Romig

Directed by James D. Waring; scenery and lighting, Jack Brown; stage manager, Charles Atkin; press, Samuel Lurie & Associates.

Time: Between the years 1882 and 1902. Place: Dublin and other parts of Ireland.

James Joyce's life from childhood through his university years and departure from Ireland. A foreign play previously produced in Dublin and London.

Now Is the Time for All Good Men (112). Musical with book and lyrics by Gretchen Cryer; music by Nancy Ford. Produced by David Cryer and Albert Poland at the Theater de Lys. Opened September 26, 1967. (Closed December 31, 1967)

Sarah Larkin ....Sally Niven
Eugenie Seldin ....Judy Frank
Mike Butler ....David Cryer
Tooney ....Donna Curtis
Albert McKinley ....David Sabin
Betty Brown ....Margot Hanson
Esther Mason ....Regina Lynn
Herbert Heller ....Art Wallace
Bill Miller ....John Bennett Perry
Jasper Wilkins ....Murray Olson
Ramona ....Anne Kaye
Tommy ....Steve Skiles

Directed by Word Baker; musical direction, Stephen Lawrence; musical arrangements, Stephen Lawrence and Nancy Ford; scenery, Holly Haas; costumes, Jeanne Button; lighting, Carol Rubinstein; stage manager, David Shanstrom; press, Public Relations Corporation of America.

Time: Now. Place: Bloomdale, Indiana.

Young teacher, popular with his students in a small Indiana town, preaches peace and resistance to the draft. He is abandoned and destroyed when the townspeople discover he's served time in prison for refusal to fight in Vietnam.

ACT I

"We Shall Meet in the Great Hereafter" ....The Company
"Quittin' Time" ....Tooney, Betty, Esther
"What's in the Air" ....Mike
"Keep 'em Busy, Keep 'em Quiet" ....Miller, Albert, Esther, Mike, Betty, Sarah, Jasper, Herbert
"Tea in the Rain" ....Sarah
"What's a Guy Like You Doin' in a Place Like This?" ....Eugenie
"Halloween Hayride" ....Betty, Tooney, Esther, Miller, Jasper, Tommy, Ramona
"Campfire Songs" ....Betty, Miller, Esther, Jasper, Tooney, Tommy, Ramona
"See Everything New" ....Mike and Sarah
"All Alone" ....Mike
"He Could Show Me" ....Sarah
"Washed Away" ....Tooney, Esther, Albert, Sarah, Herbert, Jasper, Miller, Tommy, Ramona

"Stuck-Up"	Eugenie
"My Holiday"	Sarah and Mike
"On My Own"	Tommy and Ramona
"On My Own" (Reprise)	Tommy and Mike

ACT II

"It Was Good Enough for Grandpa"	The Company
"A Simple Life"	Albert and Sarah
"A Star on the Monument"	Herbert, Miller, Jasper, Tommy
"Rain Your Love on Me"	Mike and Sarah
"Stuck-Up" (Reprise)	Eugenie
"There's Goin' To Be a Wedding"	Herbert, Tooney, Tommy, Ramona, Betty, Miller, Esther, Jasper
"On My Own" (Reprise)	Tommy, Ramona, Mike, Herbert

The Niggerlovers (25). By George Tabori. Produced by Lyn Austin, Oliver Smith and Hale Matthews at the Orpheum Theater. Opened October 1, 1967. (Closed October 22, 1967)

THE DEMONSTRATION

Creampuff	Morgan Freeman	August	Stacy Keach
Freckles	James Spruill	Angela	Viveca Lindfors

MAN AND DOG

The God	Viveca Lindfors	Freckles	James Spruill
The Man	Stacy Keach	Creampuff	Morgan Freeman

Directed by Gene Frankel; scenery and lighting, Jack Brown; costumes, Jeanne Button; music, Richard Peaslee; lyrics, George Tabori; production stage manager, James Dwyer; press, Samuel Lurie, Stanley Kaminsky.

Time: Today. Place: New York City.

Two short plays with a common theme about the racial problem and the motives and ambivalence of white liberals in racial prejudice.

Fragments (24). Program of two one-act plays by Murray Schisgal: *The Basement* and *Fragments.* Produced by Edgar Lansbury and Marc Merson at the Cherry Lane Theater. Opened Ocotber 2, 1967. (Closed October 22, 1967)

THE BASEMENT

Zach	Gene Hackman	Leo	James Coco
Minna	Sylvia Gassell		

FRAGMENTS

Jax	Humbert Allen Astredo	Max	James Coco
Baxter	Gene Hackman	Ann	Tresa Hughes

Directed by Larry Arrick; scenery, Kert Lundell; costumes, Liz Dominick; production stage manager, Gigi Cascio; press, Max Eisen, Jeanne Gibson Merrick, Carl Samrock.

THE BASEMENT—Time: The present. Place: The basement of an old one family house. Phony would-be scientist sacrifices everything for his work.

FRAGMENTS—Time: The present. Place: A furnished room. Three men inhabiting one room turn out to be "fragments" of one man.

Beyond Desire (7). By Constance Loux; based on the life of Felix Mendelssohn; adapted from the novel by Pierre La Mure. Produced by Jean Dalrymple at Theater Four. Opened October 10, 1967. (Closed October 15, 1967)

Directed by Jean Dalrymple; scenery and lighting, Feder; costumes, Pat Stuart; music arranged by Max Marlin; associate producer, Homer Poupart; stage manager, Rachel Meltzer;

press, Homer Poupart. With Jay Barney, Samuel Behar, Mary Bell, Norman Budd, Jo Flores Chase, Richard Kuss, Michael Pedersen, Andre Plamondon, Jane Marla Robbins, John Scanlon, Ethel Smith, Richard Sterne, Deidre Sullivan, Franchot Tone, Jay Velie, Betsy von Furstenberg, Ben Yaffee.

A biographical play about composer Felix Mendelssohn.

* **Scuba Duba** (265). By Bruce Jay Friedman. Produced by Ivor David Balding in association with Alvin Ferleger and Gordon Crowe at the New Theater. Opened October 10, 1967.

Harold Wonder	Jerry Orbach	Dr. Schoenfeld	Ken Olfson
Miss Janus	Brenda Smiley	Cheyenne	Christine Norden
Tourist	Conrad Bain	Jean Wonder	Jennifer Warren
Landlady	Rita Karin	Foxtrot	Cleavon Little
Thief	Judd Hirsch	Reddington	Rudy Challenger
Gendarme	Bernard Poulain	Voice of Harold's Mother	Stella Longo

Standby: Mr. Ohrbach—Judd Hirsch.

Directed by Jacques Levy; scenery, Peter Larkin; costumes, Willa Kim; lighting, Jules Fisher; incidental music, Stanley Walden; stage manager, Ed Powers; press, Michael Alpert.

Time: The present. Place: A chateau in the south of France.

A "tense comedy" (the author's own billing) about a frantic tourist whose wife has run off with a Negro skin diver.

A Best Play; see page 153

The American Savoyards. Repertory of five Gilbert & Sullivan operetta revivals. **Patience** (20). Opened October 12, 1967. **H.M.S. Pinafore** (16). Opened October 17, 1967. **The Gondoliers** (16). Opened October 18, 1967. **The Mikado** (18). Opened October 24, 1967. **Iolanthe** (18). Opened October 31, 1967. Produced by the American Gilbert & Sullivan Presentations, Inc., Dorothy Raedler executive director, at the Jan Hus Playhouse. (Repertory closed December 31, 1967)

PERFORMER	"PATIENCE"	"H.M.S. PINAFORE"	"THE MIKADO"	"IOLANTHE"
Helene Andreu		Tom Tucker	Peep-Bo	Fleta
John Carle	Bunthorne	Sir Joseph	Ko-Ko	Chancellor
Bill Collins		Bob Becket		
Cliff Cunningham	Solicitor			
Sandra Darling	Patience	Josephine		Celia
Richard Duncan	Murgatroyd	Capt. Corcoran	Pish-Tush	Strephon
William Fleck	Calverley	Dick Deadeye	Mikado	Pvt. Willis
Carol Grant	Lady Saphir			Leila
Kate Hurney	Lady Ella		Yum-Yum	Phyllis
Marilyn Jewett	Lady Jane	Buttercup	Katisha	Fairy Queen
Ruth Ray	Lady Angela	Hebe	Pitti-Sing	Iolanthe
William Tost	Grosvenor	Bill Bobstay	Pooh-Bah	Mountararat
James Wilson	Dunstable	Rackstraw	Nanki-Poo	Tolloller

THE GONDOLIERS

Duke of Plaza-Toro	John Carle	Casilda	Kate Hurney
Luiz	Robert Trombetta	Contadine:	
Don Alhambra	William Fleck	Gianetta	Sandra Darling
Venetian Gondoliers:		Tessa	Ruth Ray
Marco Palmieri	James Wilson	Fiametta	Irma Rogers
Giuseppe Palmieri	Richard Duncan	Vittoria	Lana Caradimas
Antonio	William Tost	Giulia	Brenda Gardner
Francesco	Don Derrow	Inez	Mina Jo King
Giorgio	Bill Collins	Solo Cachucha Dancers	Helene Andreu, Dennis Carpenter
Annibale	Dennis Carpenter		
Duchess of Plaza-Toro	Marilyn Jewett		

Others in all operettas: Elliott Mann, Craig Palmer, Laura Thomas, Nick Titakis.

Directed by Dorothy Raedler; musical direction, Lucille Burnham; scenery, Michael Hotopp; lighting, Kip Newland; assistant musical director, Margaret Singer; production stage manager, Bob Fahey; press, Ben Kornzweig, Reginald Denenholz.

The Beard (100). By Michael McClure. Produced by James Walsh and Queen of Spades, Inc. at the Evergreen Theater. Opened October 24, 1967. (Closed January 14, 1968)

Harlow	Billie Dixon	Billy the Kid	Richard Bright

Directed by Rip Torn; costumes, Ann Roth; lighting, C. Murawski; design and Media Mix Prologue, USCO; production stage manager, Paul john Austin; press, David Rothenberg.

A movie sex goddess and a favorite outlaw meet in eternity in a relationship of hostile sexuality, culminating in a sex act.

Where People Gather (7). By Peter Copani. Produced by The W.P.G. Company at the Gramercy Arts Theater. Opened October 25, 1967. (Closed October 29, 1967)

Directed and designed by James Nisbet Clark; stage manager, Joan Lebowitz; press, Bernard Simon. With R. C. Cobb, Elek Hartman, Holly Hill, Michael Kapec, June Miller, Andy Milligan, Ruth Ann Norris, Dan Tyra and Janis Young.

About people's secret acquiescence in brutal violence.

* **New York Shakespeare Festival Public Theater.** Indoor schedule of four plays. **Hair** (94; see note). Musical with book and lyrics by Gerome Ragni and James Rado; music by Galt MacDermot. Opened October 29, 1967 (Closed December 10, 1967; see note). **Hamlet** (56). Revival of the play by William Shakespeare. Opened December 26, 1967. (Closed February 11, 1968). **Ergo** (49). By Jakov Lind; based on his novel. Opened March 3, 1968. (Closed April 14, 1968). * **The Memorandum** (31). By Vaclav Havel; translated by Vera Blackwell. Opened May 5, 1968. Produced by Joseph Papp (Gerald Freedman artistic director, Bernard Gersten associate producer) at New York Shakespeare Festival Public Theater.

HAIR

Dionne	Jonelle Allen	Linda	Linda Compton
Dad	Ed Crowley	Suzannah	Suzannah Evans
Claude	Walker Daniels	Lynda	Lynda Gudde
Woof	Steve Dean	Louise	Jane Levin
Jeannie	Sally Eaton	Alma	Alma Robinson
Mom	Marijane Maricle	Charlie	Warren Burton
Sheila	Jill O'Hara	Thommie	Thommie Bush
Crissy	Shelley Plimpton	Bill	William Herter
Berger	Gerome Ragni	Paul	Paul Jabara
Hud	Arnold Wilkerson	Bob	Bob Johnson
Susan	Susan Batson	Jim	Edward Murphy, Jr.

Directed by Gerald Freedman; musical director, John Morris; scenery, Ming Cho Lee; costumes, Theoni V. Aldredge; lighting, Martin Aronstein; production stage manager, Russell McGrath; stage manager, Michael Chambers; press, Merle Debuskey.

Rock 'n' roll musical about the lives and loves of hippies, one of whom must decide whether to burn his draft card or go to Vietnam (he decides the latter).

NOTE: *Hair* played 49 performances at the Public Theater, 10/29/67-12/10/67; then moved to Cheetah, where it played 45 additional performances, 12/22/67-1/28/68. It then opened on Broadway 4/29/68 at the Biltmore Theater (see its entry in the "Plays Produced on Broadway" section of this volume).

Steve Curry replaced Gerome Ragni 12/22/67-1/28/68.

ACT I

"Red, Blue and White" .... Mom, Dad
"Ain't Got No" .... Claude, Berger, Woof, Hud, The Company
"I Got Life" .... Claude, Mom
"Air" .... Jeannie, Crissy, Dionne
"Going Down" .... Berger, The Company
"Hair" .... Claude, Berger, The Company
"Dead End" .... Sheila, The Company
"Frank Mills" .... Crissy
"Where Do I Go" .... Claude, The Company

ACT II

"Electric Blues" .... Suzannah, Linda, Paul
"Easy to be Hard" .... Suzannah, Linda, Paul, The Company
"Manchester" .... Claude
"White Boys" .... Dionne, Susan, Alma
"Black Boys" .... Linda, Crissy, Suzannah
"Walking in Space" .... The Company
"Aquarius" .... The Company
"Good Morning Starshine" .... Sheila, The Company
"Exanaplanetooch" .... Claude, Sheila
"Climax" .... Sheila

HAMLET

Hamlet .... Martin Sheen
Horatio .... Michael Heit
Claudius .... Ralph Waite
Osric .... Albert Quinton
Laertes .... Jeff David
Polonius .... John Call
Gertrude .... Anita Dangler
Ghost .... Fred Warriner
Ophelia .... April Shawhan
Rossencraft .... Merwin Goldsmith
Guilderstone .... James J. Sloyan
Norwegian Captain .... Jared Martin

Guards: Paul Benjamin, Gerry Black, Paul M. Glaser, Jared Martin, Tom McCready, Paul Speyser, Lisle Wilson.

Directed by Joseph Papp; scenery, David Mitchell; costumes, Theoni V. Aldredge; lighting, Martin Aronstein; music, Galt MacDermot; musical director, John Morris; Ophelia's Act choreographed by George and Ethel Martin; assistant director, Ted Cornell; production stage manager, Russell McGrath; stage manager, Gage Andretta.

A 90-minute version of *Hamlet* highly stylized in an antic production.

ERGO

Wondra .... Tony Capodilupo
Bunzig; Commentator .... Frank Groseclose
Wacholder .... Jack Hollander
Rita .... Maxine Greene
Wurz .... Tom Aldredge
Arnulf .... Cliff Gorman
Arnold .... Irwin Pearl
Leo .... Robert Stattel
Asian .... Sam Waterston
Dr. Gertrude Bockling .... Miriam Lehmann-Haupt
Journalist .... Steven Shaw

Citizens: Hope Arthur, Peter Burnell, Dutch Miller, C. Leonard Williams, Joel Wolfe.

Directed by Gerald Freedman; scenery, Ming Cho Lee; costumes, Theoni V. Aldredge; lighting, Martin Aronstein; original music and sound score, John Morris; assistant director, Amy Saltz; production stage manager, Russell McGrath; stage manager, Michael Chambers.

Time: Now. Place: Vienna and everywhere else.

Act I, Scene 1: A street. Scene 2: Wurz' place (Melchior Street). Scene 3: Wacholder's place (The Customshed). Scenes 4,5,6,7: From Wurz' to Wacholder's. Act II, Scene 1: Wacholder's place. Scene 2: Wurz' place. Scene 3: A hotel room (the Congress). Scene 4: Wurz' place. Scene 5: Wacholder's place. Scene 6: Outside Wacholder's place.

Absurdist exaggeration of the Germanic character in various manifestations from gemütlich to obsessively organized, with many overtones of political symbolism. A foreign (English) play making its debut in this production.

THE MEMORANDUM

Josef Gross	Paul Stevens	Helena	Olympia Dukakis
Jan Ballas	John Heffernan	Maria	Mari Gorman
Hana	Sudie Bond	George, Staff Watcher	Brad Sullivan
Mark Lear	Robert Ronan	Ferdinand Pillar; Column	George Bartenieff
Peter Thumb	William Duell	Clerks	Raul Julia, Lisa Maria
Otto Stroll	William Kiehl		
Alex Savant	Fred Burrell		

Directed by Joseph Papp; scenery, Douglas W. Schmidt; costumes, Theoni V. Aldredge; lighting, Martin Aronstein; music, John Morris; associate to Miss Aldredge, Milo Morrow; assistant to the director, Lynne Gould; stage manager, Gage Andretta.

Time: The present. Place: Prague, Czechoslovakia. Act I, Scene 1: The Director's office. Scene 2: The Ptydepe classroom. Scene 3: The secretariat of the translation center. Scene 4: The Director's office. Scene 5: The Ptydepe classroom. Scene 6: The secretariat of the translation center. Act II, Scene 1: The Director's office. Scene 2: The Ptydepe classroom. Scene 3: The secretariat of the translation center. Scene 4: The Director's office. Scene 5: The Ptydepe classroom. Scene 6: The secretariat of the translation center.

A complicated bureaucracy is further dehumanized by the introduction of an absurdly complicated artificial language called Ptydepe into office use. A foreign play previously produced in Prague (in 1965) and elsewhere.

The American Place Theater. Schedule of four programs. **Father Uxbridge Wants To Marry** (11). By Frank Gagliano. Opened October 28, 1967. (Closed November 7, 1967). **The Ceremony of Innocence** (14). By Ronald Ribman. Opened January 1, 1968. (Closed January 13, 1968) * **The Electronic Nigger and Others** (86; see note). Program of three one-act plays by Ed Bullins: *A Son, Come Home, The Electronic Nigger* and *Clara's Ole Man.* Opened March 6, 1968. (Closed March 16, 1968; see note) **Endecott and the Red Cross** (15). By Robert Lowell. Opened May 7, 1968. (Closed May 18, 1968) Produced by The American Place Theater, Wynn Handman director, at The American Place Theater, St. Clements Church of the Episcopal Diocese of New York.

FATHER UXBRIDGE WANTS TO MARRY

Mrs. Bethnal-Green; The Mother; Stepney Green; Debden	Olympia Dukakis	Father Uxbridge	John Coe
Morden	Gene Roche	Angel	Carol Carpenter
		Father Ongar	Ken Kercheval

Directed by Melvin Bernhardt; design, Douglas Schmidt; lighting, John Gleason; special sound and music, James Reichert; Bach arias sung by Sandra Gagliano; words and music for *Ballad of Great Fall Hill* and *Mother's Lullaby,* Frank Gagliano; production stage manager, Peter Galambos; press, John Springer Associates, Louise Weiner.

Time: The present. The action takes place without intermission.

An elevator and its operator are symbols of the human condition; the operator is soon to be replaced by automation and reflects on his past troubles when the machine breaks down.

THE CEREMONY OF INNOCENCE

First Monk	Robert Shattuck	Alfreda	Nancy R. Pollock
Sussex	Dolph Sweet	Emma	Olive Deering
Kent	William Devane	Thulja	Sandy Duncan
Bishop	Ralph Clanton	Sweyn	Ernest Graves
Abbott	Peter Bosche	Edmund	David Birney
Ethelred	Donald Madden	Thorkill	Howard Green

Monks, Servants: Oliver Lewis Bachelle, Lee J. Caldwell, Anthony T. Casco, Jr., Edward Gallardo, Davidson Lloyd, Lou Prudenti, Jeffrey A. Rasi, Ronn Ridgeley, James Robiscoe, Walter Skolnik.

Directed by Arthur A. Seidelman; scenery, Kurt Lundell; costumes, Willa Kim; lighting, Roger Morgan.

Time: 1013. Place: England. Act I: A monastery on the Isle of Wight, Christmas Day, and the castle of King Ethelred the previous winter. Act II: King Ethelred's Castle, late summer, and then the Isle of Wight, Christmas evening.

Chronicle play about King Ethelred's attempt to establish peace and prosperity in his realm.

A SON, COME HOME

Mother ....Estelle Evans
Son ....Wayne Grice
Girl ....Kelly-Marie Berry
Boy ....Gary Bolling

THE ELECTRONIC NIGGER

Mr. Jones ....Wayne Grice
Lenard ....Warren Pincus
Miss Moskowitz ....Jeanne Kaplan
Mr. Carpenter ....L. Errol Jaye
Bill ....Roscoe Orman
Sue ....Hedy Sontag
Martha ....Helen Ellis
Students ....Roland A. Hirsch, Maie Mottus

CLARA'S OLE MAN

Clara ....Kelly-Marie Berry
Big Girl ....Carolyn Y. Cardwell
Jack ....Roscoe Orman
Baby Girl ....Helen Ellis
Miss Famie ....Estelle Evans
Stoogie ....Kris Keiser
Bama ....George Miles
Hoss ....Gary Bolling
C.C. ....L. Errol Jaye

ALL PLAYS in *The Electronic Nigger and Others* directed by Robert Macbeth; scenery, John Jay Moore; lighting, Roger Morgan. Music for *A Son, Come Home* composed by Gordon Watkins.

A SON, COME HOME—Time: The present and the past. Place: South Philadelphia and the mind. A poet comes home for a visit with his impoverished, superstitious mother. THE ELECTRONIC NIGGER—Time: The present. Place: A Southern California community college. Comedy about an eccentric who breaks up a writing class with his obsessive comments about such scientific matters as computers, wire-tapping and research analysis. CLARA'S OLE MAN—Time: Mid-1950s. Place: South Philadelphia. Gentleman caller visits a pretty girl while her "Ole Man" is supposedly out; but the "Ole Man" turns out to be a woman in this sorded and deprived household.

NOTE: *The Electronic Nigger and Others* played 12 performances at The American Place Theater; then moved to the Martinique Theater 3/28/68 to continue its run. Following its opening at the Martinique its title was changed to *Three Plays by Ed Bullins.*

ENDECOTT AND THE RED CROSS

Assawamset ....Gregory Sierra
Thomas Morton ....John Harkins
Daughter of Assawamset ....Yolande Skeete
Mr. Blackstone ....Nick Kepros
Indian Whore ....Roberta Shubert
Edith ....Frances Hession
Edward ....Spalding Gray
Sergeant ....Dan Morgan
Private ....Stephen Wyman
Governor Endecott ....Kenneth Haigh
Palfrey ....Ralph Clanton

Directed by John Hancock; scenery, John Wulp; costumes, Robert LaVigne; lighting, Roger Morgan; music, Richard Peaslee, Robert Dennis.

Time: 1630. Place Merry Mount, Mass. The action takes place without intermission.

Derived from two stories by Nathaniel Hawthorne—*Endecott and the Red Cross* and *The Maypole at Merry Mount*—the play is about an early American governor's suppression of a hedonistic community, symbolizing the conflict between the Puritan and the non-conforming spirits in American life.

No Exit, revival of the play by Jean Paul Sartre, adapted from the French by Paul Bowles, and **The Little Private World of Arthur Fenwick** by John A. Topa (8). Program of two one-act plays. Produced by the Gree-Moo Production Company at the Bouwerie Lane Theater. Opened October 30, 1967. (Closed November 5, 1967)

NO EXIT directed by Chester Moody; scenery and lighting, Gregory Martin; stage manager, Ed Dougherty; press, David Lipsky, Marian Graham. With Raul Julia, Carolyn Y.

Cardwell, Susan McMullen, Michael D. Moore. First produced on Broadway at the Biltmore Theater November 26, 1946 for 31 performances. THE LITTLE PRIVATE WORLD OF ARTHUR FENWICK directed by John A. Topa. With John A. Topa, Susan McMullen. Study of a pyschotic who cannot face reality.

In Circles (222). By Gertrude Stein; music by Al Carmines. The Judson Poets Theater Production produced by Franklin de Boer at the Cherry Lane Theater. Opened November 5, 1967. (Closed May 12, 1968)

Cousins	Theo Barnes	Sylvia	Arlene Rothlein
Mildred	Jacque Lynn Colton	Dole	Al Carmines
Mable	Elaine Summers	Ollie	David Vaughan
Jessie	Lee Guilliatt	The Citizen	Arthur Williams
George	George McGrath	Lucy Armitage	Nancy Zala

Directed by Lawrence Kornfeld; scenery, Roland Turner and Johnnie Jones; lighting, Eric Gertner; stage manager, Roland Turner; press, Samuel J. Friedman, Jane Friedman.

Time and place: The present. A complex arrangement of word, song and dance effects, each one conceived as describing its own circle, without conventional story or subject line in the production as a whole.

The Trials of Brother Jero and **The Strong Breed** (115). Program of two one-act plays by Wole Soyinka. Produced by Farris-Belgrave Productions in association with Afolabi Ajayi at the Greenwich Mews Theater. Opened November 9, 1967. (Closed February 18, 1968)

THE TRIALS OF BROTHER JERO

Brother Jero	Harold Scott	Girl Who Passes By	Lauren Jones
Old Prophet	Dennis Tate	Drummer Boy	Edward Luis Espinosa
Chume	Afolabi Ajayi	Penitent	Yvonne Warden
Amope	Cynthia Belgrave	Member of Parliament	Roger Robinson
A Trader Woman	Peggy Kirkpatrick		

THE STRONG BREED

Eman	Harold Scott	Eman's Father	Robertearl Jones
Sunma	Mary Alice	Attendant	Willie Woods
Ifada	Edward Luis Espinosa	Omae	Lauren Jones
A Sick Girl	Yvette Hawkins	Young Eman	G. Tito Shaw
Jaguna	James Spruill	Tutor	Vernon Washington
Orage	Dennis Tate	Priest	Roger Robinson
From Eman's Past:			

Neighbors, Villagers, Worshippers in *The Trials of Brother Jero:* Yvette Hawkins, G. Tito Shaw, Mary Alice, Vernon Washington, James Spruill. Attandant Stalwarts and Villagers in *The Strong Breed:* Peggy Kirkpatrick, Afolabi Ajayi, Yvonne Warden, Tom Hawkins, Austin Briggs Hall Jr.

Directed by Cynthia Belgrave; scenery and lighting, Jack Blackman; music composed and arranged by Pat Patrick; original Nigerian costumes, Edward Wolrond; stage manager, Bernard Ward; press, David Lipsky, Marian Graham.

THE TRIALS OF BROTHER JERO—Scene 1: Jero's hut, morning. Scene 2: The beach (Jero's church), later that morning. Scene 3: Jero's hut, that evening. Scene 4: The beach, that night. A bogus African prophet keys up his believing congregation with a series of "do nots."

THE STRONG BREED—Time: Late evening until midnight. Scene 1: Eman's hut. Scene 2: A passageway between huts. Scene 3: From Eman's past; his father's village. Scene 4: A village street, the present. Scene 5: From Eman's past; near his father's village. Scene 6: Before Eman's hut, the present. Scene 7: From Eman's past; Omae's grave. Scene 8: A village street, the present. Scene 9: The same village street; Eman's vision. Scene 10: In front of Eman's hut, the present. A teacher is ritually sacrificed to symbolize all his village's evils in the course of a year.

Foreign (Nigerian) plays previously produced in Africa and in London.

Chuck Gordone replaced Harold Scott as Jero and Vernon Washington replaced Dennis Tate as Old Prophet and Harold Scott as Eman on 11/12/67.

* **The Repertory Theater of Lincoln Center.** Schedule of two programs. **Walking to Waldheim** and **Happiness** (42). Two one-act plays by Mayo Simon. Opened November 10, 1967. (Closed December 16, 1967) * **Summertree** (101). By Ron Cowen. Opened March 3, 1968. Produced by The Repertory Theater of Lincoln Center at the Forum Theater.

WALKING TO WALDHEIM

H. Goldblatt ....Roger De Koven
Mina ....Aline MacMahon
Ralph ....George Bartenieff
Eddie Bromberg ....Jacob Ben-Ami
Yetta Sher ....Sylvie Straus
Zelda ....Mari Gorman

HAPPINESS

Old Lady ....Lili Darvas
Old Man ....Jacob Ben-Ami

Directed by George L. Sherman; scenery, Peter Harvey; lighting, John Gleason; costumes, Melly Eigsti; production stage manager, James Kershaw; press, Susan Bloch.

WALKING TO WALDHEIM—Five relatives accompanying a Jewish widower to his wife's funeral leave one by one to die. HAPPINESS—A widow and widower discuss the future, in a vignette of lonely old age.

SUMMERTREE

Young Man ....David Birney
Little Boy ....Barry Symonds or Donnie Melvin
Mother ....Priscilla Pointer
Father ....Philip Sterling
Girl ....Blythe Danner
Soldier ....Tom Fuccello

Directed by David Pressman; scenery and costumes, James A. Taylor; lighting, John Gleason; production stage manager, Ronald Schaeffer.

A dramatic study, free in its movement back and forth in place and time, of a young Vietnam war casualty—his youthful dreams, his schoolboy romance, the attitudes of his middle-class parents.

I Must Be Talking to My Friends (27). One-man performance by Micheal MacLiammoir. Produced by St. John Terrell and Krone-Olim Productions at the Orpheum Theater. Opened November 16, 1967. (Closed December 10, 1967)

Directed and designed by Hilton Edwards; manager and stage director, Brian Tobin; press, Max Eisen, Carl Samrock.

A recapitulation by Mr. MacLiammoir of Irish literature from pre-Christian times to the present, in quotations from the dramatists, poets, wits and revolutionaries of Ireland. A foreign presentation previously produced in Dublin and elsewhere.

Iphigenia in Aulis (232). Revival of the play by Euripides; English version by Minos Volanakis. Produced by Circle in the Square, Inc., Theodore Mann artistic director, Paul Libin managing director, Gillian Walker associate director, at Circle in the Square. Opened November 21, 1967. (Closed May 26, 1968)

Agamemnon ....Mitchell Ryan
Old Man ....Tom Klunis
Menelaus ....Alan Mixon
Messenger ....Robert Stattell
Clytemnestra ....Irene Papas
The Child ....John Marks
Iphigenia ....Jenny Leigh
Achilles ....Frank Langella
Chorus Leader ....Erin Martin

Chorus: Kathleen Adams, Patricia Bower, Margaret Cathell, Karen Cross, Shirley Luban, Lynda Myles, Linda Simon, Valerie Von Volz. Soldiers: John Garber, Nick Cantrell.

Directed by Michael Cacoyannis; music, Martin David Levy; scenery and costumes, Michael

Annals; lighting, Jules Fisher; stage manager, Jan Moerel; press, Merle Debuskey, Violet Welles, Faith Geer.

Euripides's drama about Agamemnon's need to sacrifice his daughter Iphigenia in order to sail to war on Troy was last revived in New York by the Oratorio Society April 17, 1921 at Manhattan Opera House.

Jane White replaced Irene Papas 3/12/68. Gretchen Corbett replaced Jenny Leigh 5/8/68.

* **Curley McDimple** (234). Musical with book by Mary Boylan and Robert Dahdah; music and lyrics by Mr. Dahdah. Produced by The Curley Company at the Bert Wheeler Theater. Opened November 22, 1967.

Jimmy	Paul Cahill	Bill	George Hillman
Sarah	Helon Blount	Miss Hamilton	Norma Bigtree
Alice	Joyce Nolen	Mr. Gillingwater	Gene Galvin
Curley McDimple	Bayn Johnson		

Directed by Robert Dahdah; musical numbers staged by Larry Stevens; musical arrangements and direction, Keith McClelland; dance arrangements, Bob Atwood; scenery, Richard Jackson; costumes, John Hirsch; lighting, Barry Arnold; conductor, Bob Atwood; production stage manager, Jack Saunders; press, Max Eisen, Jeanne Gibson Merrick, Carl Samrock.

Time: 1934. Place: Sarah's boarding house in New York City. Act I: Morning. Act II: One hour later.

Spoof of the Shirley Temple song-and-dance films of the 1930's.

ACT I

"A Cup of Coffee"	Jimmy
"I Try"	Jimmy, Alice
"Curley McDimple"	Curley, Jimmy, Sarah, Alice, Bill
"Love is the Loveliest Love Song"	Alice
"Are There Any More Rosie O'Gradys?"	Sarah, Jimmy, Alice, Curley, Bill
"Dancing in the Rain"	Curley, Bill, Company
"At the Playland Jamberee"	Curley, Company
"I've Got a Little Secret"	Jimmy, Curley

ACT II

"Stars and Lovers"	Alice, Jimmy, Company
"The Meanest Man in Town"	Alice, Jimmy, Company
"I Try" (Reprise)	Jimmy, Alice
"Something Nice is Going to Happen"	Curley
"Swing-a-Ding-a-Ling"	Curley
"Hi de hi de hi, Hi de hi de ho"	Sarah, Alice, Jimmy, Bill, Mr. Gillingwater, Miss Hamilton
"Dwarfs' Song"	Sarah, Alice, Jimmy, Bill, Mr. Gillingwater, Miss Hamilton
"Swing-a-Ding-a-Ling" (Reprise)	Curley, Company
"Something Nice is Going to Happen" (Reprise)	Miss Hamilton
"Love is the Loveliest Long Song" (Reprise)	Jimmy, Company

Take It From the Top (15). One-woman program of songs and scenes performed by Ethel Colt. Produced by Duane Camp at the Gramercy Arts Theater. Opened November 22, 1967. (Closed December 3, 1967)

Directed by Maurice Edwards; scenery and lighting, Duane Camp; piano accompaniment, Rolf Barnes; press, Bernard Simon.

A parade of numbers and scenes from the American musical theater, 1787 to the present.

Winnie the Pooh (185). Bil and Cora Baird's marionettes in a show conceived by Bil Baird; adapted by A.J. Russell from the book by A.A. Milne; music by Jack Brooks; lyrics by A.A. Milne and Jack Brooks. Produced by The American Puppet Arts Council, Arthur Cantor executive producer, at the Bil Baird Theater. Opened November 23, 1967. (Closed May 19, 1968)

Winnie the Pooh	Franz Fazakas	Christopher Robin	Phyllis Nierendorf
Piglet	Jerry Nelson	Rabbit	Frank Sullivan
Eeyore	Bil Baird	Tigger	Byron Whiting
Kanga	Fania Sullivan	Mice	The Simon Sisters
Roo	Byron Whiting	Owl	Frank Sullivan

Directed by Fania Sullivan; executive director, Cora Baird; press, Artie Solomon.

Place: In and around the 100 Aker wood. The Winnie the Pooh story of Christopher Robin and his friendly animals was followed on this program by Act II—A Pageant of Puppet Variety, in which the puppeteers demonstrated techniques and revealed some of their secrets.

Performances of other shows in the Baird repertory during the season were as follows: *People Is the Thing That the World Is Of* (6) and *Davy Jones' Locker* (5).

The Peddler and **The Dodo Bird** (29). Program of two one-act plays by Emanuel Fried. Produced by Lily Turner at the Martinique Theater. Opened December 8, 1967. (Closed December 31, 1967)

THE PEDDLER

Pete Taylor	Thomas Anderson	Frank Nowak	Philip Sterling
Art Sternmiller	John Randolph		

THE DODO BIRD

Bull Blatter	Walter Flanagan	The Dodo Bird	Leonardo Cimino
Nick	Thomas Anderson	Russ Nowark	John Randolph

Directed by Sidney Walters; scenery, Helen Pond and Herbert Senn; lighting, James Nisbet Clark; costumes, Sonia Lowenstein; stage manager, Leonard Ross; press, Bernard Simon and Avivah Simon.

THE PEDDLER—Time: The present. Place: The second floor of Sternmiller's Repossessed Furniture Store. Wheeler-dealer bests a nice guy in a business deal. THE DODO BIRD—Time: The present. Place: A bar across from a foundry in a western New York industrial town. Study of an alcoholic laborer who has been defeated by life because he hasn't been allowed to do the job he knows and likes best at the foundry.

A Certain Young Man (8). By Thomas deWitt Walsh. Produced by Marjorie and Sherman Ewing in association with Oliver Smith at Stage 73. Opened December 26, 1967. (Closed December 31, 1967)

Directed by Sherman Ewing; scenery, Robin Wagner; lighting, Jene Youtt; production stage manager, Will Richter; press, Fred Weterick. With Jay Barney, R. C. Cobb, Alan Howard, Charles Hull, Richard Kronold, Elizabeth Lawrence, Jody Locker, Constance Meng, Roger Omar Serbagi.

Young man's mystical experience, a vision of the Crucifixion, alters the lives of his family and friends.

The Negro Ensemble Company. Schedule of four plays. **Song of the Lusitanian Bogey** (40). By Peter Weiss; translated from the German by Lee Baxandall. Opened January 2, 1968. (Closed February 4, 1968) **Summer of the 17th Doll** (40). Revival of the play by Ray Lawler. Opened February 20, 1968. (Closed March 24, 1968) **Kongi's Harvest** (33). By Wole Soyinka. Opened April 14, 1968. (Closed May 12, 1968). To be followed by *Daddy Goodness* by Louis Sapin, translated and adapted by Richard Wright, opening June 4, 1968. Produced by The Negro Ensemble Company, Douglas Turner Ward artistic director, Robert Hooks executive director, Gerald S. Krone administrative director, at St. Marks Playhouse.

SONG OF THE LUSITANIAN BOGEY

Rosalind Cash	Judyann Jonsson
David Downing	Denise Nichols
Arthur French	Hattie Winston
Moses Gunn	Allie Woods
William Jay	

Directed by Michael A. Schultz; dance direction, Louis Johnson; scenery, Edward Burbridge; costumes, Bernard Johnson; lighting, Marshall Williams; music, Coleridge-Taylor Perkinson; production stage manager, Edmund Cambridge; press, Howard Atlee, Margie Clay.

Drama set in Africa, condemning Portugal's domination and exploitation of its colonies, with insinuation that the U.S. tacitly approves. The play is divided into two acts. A foreign (German) play previously produced in Stockholm.

SUMMER OF THE 17TH DOLL

Pearl Cunningham .... Esther Rolle
Bubba Ryan .... Hattie Winston
Olive Leech .... Frances Foster
Barney Ibbot .... Norman Bush
Emma Leech .... Clarice Taylor
Roo Webber .... Moses Gunn
Johnnie Dowd .... William Jay

Directed by Edmund Cambridge; scenery, Edward Burbridge; costumes, Gertha Brock; lighting, Shirley Prendergast.

Summer of the 17th Doll was first produced on Broadway on January 22, 1958 for 29 performances. The locale was changed from Australia to Louisiana for this revival.

KONGI'S HARVEST

Oba Danlola .... Douglas Turner
Sarumi .... Clarice Taylor
(Ogbo Aweri) .... Frances Foster, Rosalind Cash
Wuraola .... Roberta Raysor
Dende .... Richard Mason
Superintendent .... Judyann Jonsson
Praise Singer .... Denise Nicholas
Praise Singer .... Hattie Winston
1st Aweri .... David Downing
2d Aweri .... Norman Bush
3d Aweri .... Allie Woods
4th Aweri .... Carl Gordon
5th Aweri .... William Jay
6th Aweri .... Tom Brimm II
Organizing Secretary .... Arthur French
Daoudu .... Robert Hooks
(Segi) .... Rosalind Cash Frances Foster
Kongi .... Moses Gunn
Right Ear of State ...... Charles Greene Jr.
Left Ear of State .... Ozzie Waite
Photographer .... Bernard Marsh
Capt. of Carpenters; Segi's Entertainer .... Afolabi Ajayi

(Parentheses indicate roles in which the actresses alternated)

Carpenter's Brigade: Ken Davis, Carl Gordon, Charles Greene Jr., Bernard Marsh, Ozzie Waite. Night Club Habituees and Dancers: Maxine Griffith, Roberta Raysor, Gloria Schultz, Joyce Walker, Ken Davis, Ed Dougherty, Charles Greene Jr., Bernard Marsh, Ozzie Waite. Danlola's Ceremonial Corps: Youmi-Youmi, Sonny Morgan, Babafemi Akinlana, Richard Pablo Landrum.

Directed by Michael A. Schultz; choreography, Louis Johnson; scenery, Edward Burbridge; costumes, Jeanne Button; lighting, Jules Fisher; music, Pat Patrick.

Time: The eve and day of the national celebration of Isma. Place: Africa. Part I: A penal detention camp; thereafter alternation between Kongi's mountain retreat and Segi's tavern. Part II: Danlola's palace; thereafter at Kongi Square.

Today's modern African state is contrasted with the rituals and emotionalism of yesterday. A foreign (Nigerian) play previously produced in Africa.

Love and Let Love (14). Musical based on *Twelfth Night* by William Shakespeare; adapted by John Lollos; music by Stanley Jay Gelber; lyrics by John Lollos and Don Christopher. Produced by the L. & L.L. Co. at Sheridan Square Playhouse. Opened January 3, 1968. (Closed January 14, 1968)

Directed by John Lollos; musical direction, Daniel Paget; orchestrations and musical supervision, Arthur Rubinstein; musical staging, Rhoda Levine; scenery, Barbara Miller; costumes,

Ynes; lighting, Fred Allison; stage manager, George Callahan; press, Frank Goodman, Martin Shwartz. With Roy Clary, John Cunningham, Michael Hawkins, Tony Hendra, Tom Lacy, Don Moran, Michael O'Sullivan, Marcia Rodd, Joseph R. Sicari, Nic Ullett, Virginia Vestoff, Susan Willis.

Have I Got One For You (1). Musical with music by Jerry Blatt; book and lyrics by Jerry Blatt and Lonnie Burstein. Produced by Harlan P. Kleiman at Theater Four. Opened and closed at the evening performance January 7, 1968.

Directed by Roberta Sklar; musical supervision, George Taros; musical direction and arrangements, Alan Marlowe; scenery and costumes, John Conklin; lighting by Peter Hunt; stage manager, Martin Herzer; press, Saul Richman. With Gloria De Haven, Ted Pugh, Dick O'Neill, Anne Kaye, John Michael King.

Musical fairy tale of romance among toads, moles, princes and princesses.

* **Your Own Thing** (158). Musical with book by Donald Driver; suggested by William Shakespeare's *Twelfth Night;* music and lyrics by Hal Hester and Danny Apolinar. Produced by Zev Bufman and Dorothy Love at the Orpheum Theater. Opened January 13, 1968.

Apocalypse singing group:
Danny .... Danny Apolinar
John .... John Kuhner
Michael .... Michael Valenti
Orson .... Tom Ligon
Olivia .... Marcia Rodd
Viola .... Leland Palmer
Sebastian .... Rusty Thacker
Purser; Stage Manager .... Igors Gavon
Nurse .... Imogene Bliss

Directed by Donald Driver; musical direction and dance arrangements, Charles Schneider; scenery, Robert Guerra; costumes, Albert Wolsky; lighting, Tom Skelton; orchestrations, Hayward Morris; technical direction, Richard Thayer; associate producer, Walter Gidaly; slide sequences designed by Michael W. Lunstead; slide photography, Frank Derbas; motion picture sequences, Michael Morse; press, Robert Ganshaw, Michael F. Goldstein Inc.

Rock musical in which a twin brother and sister (Sebastian and Viola) are shipwrecked on Manhattan Island and, because they are dressed alike, create sexual confusion in their meetings with others. The action takes place without intermission and includes frequent asides with slides and film footage.

A Best Play; see page 209

MUSICAL NUMBERS

"No One's Perfect, Dear" .... Sebastian, Viola
"The Flowers" .... Viola
"I'm Me! (I'm Not Afraid)" .... Apocalypse
"Baby! Baby!" .... Apocalypse, Viola
"Come Away, Death" .... Sebastian
"I'm On My Way to the Top" .... Sebastian
"She Never Told Her Love" .... Viola
"Be Gentle" .... Viola, Orson
"What Do I Know?" .... Viola
"Baby! Baby!" (Reprise) .... Apocalypse, Sebastian, Viola
"The Now Generation" .... Apocalypse, Viola
"The Middle Years" .... Sebastian
"The Middle Years" (Reprise) .... Olivia
"When You're Young and in Love" .... Orson
"Hunca Munca" .... Apocalypse, Company
"Don't Leave Me" .... Olivia, Sebastian, Orson
"Do Your Own Thing" .... Company

* **The Indian Wants the Bronx** and **It's Called the Sugar Plum** (154). Program of two one-act plays by Israel Horovitz. Produced by Ruth Newton Productions in association with Diana Mathews at the Astor Place Theater. Opened January 17, 1968.

THE INDIAN WANTS THE BRONX

Gupta ....John Cazale
Murph ....Al Pacino
Joey ....Matthew Cowles

IT'S CALLED THE SUGAR PLUM

Wallace Zuckerman ....John Pleshette
Joanna Dibble ....Marsha Mason

Directed by James Hammerstein; designed by Fred Voelpel; production stage manager, Patrick Horrigan; press, Howard Atlee.

THE INDIAN WANTS THE BRONX—Time: A chilly September night. Place: A bus stop on upper Fifth Avenue in New York City. Helpless East Indian waiting for a Bronx bus attracts the attention of two toughs who tease him and then beat him up, just for kicks. IT'S CALLED THE SUGAR PLUM—Time: Late afternoon, the present. Place: A cramped, one-room flat in Cambridge, Massachusetts. Harvard man seduces a co-ed after he has accidentally run over her fiance.

Jill Clayburgh replaced Marsha Mason and John Leskowitz replaced John Pleshette 3/5/68.

* **Jacques Brel Is Alive and Well and Living in Paris** (144). Cabaret revue with music by Jacques Brel; production conception, English lyrics, additional material by Eric Blau and Mort Shuman; based on lyrics and commentary by Jacques Brel. Produced by 3 W Productions, Inc. at the Village Gate. Opened January 22, 1968.

Shawn Elliott
Mort Shuman
Elly Stone
Alice Whitfield

Directed by Moni Yakim; musical direction, Mort Shuman; consultant to producers, Nat Shapiro; music arranged and conducted by Wolfgang Knittel; scenery, Henry E. Scott III; costumes, Ilka Suarez; lighting, James Nisbet Clark; production supervised by Eric Blau; production stage manager, James Nisbet Clark; press, Ivan Black.

An evening of songs with music by the Belgian composer Jacques Brel and with lyrics and dialogue translated into English from Brel's lyrics or from his published comments.

June Gable replaced Alice Whitfield 5/7/68. Robert Guillaume replaced Mort Shuman 5/31/68.

ACT I: "Marathon"—The Company; "Alone"—Elliott; "Madeleine"—The Company; "I Loved"—Miss Stone; "Mathilde"—Shuman; "Bachelor's Dance"—Elliott; "Timid Frieda"—Miss Whitfield; "My Death"—Miss Stone; "Girls & Dogs"—Shuman, Elliott; "Jackie"—Shuman; "The Statue"—Elliott; "Desperate Ones"—The Company; "Sons Of"—Miss Stone; "Amsterdam"—Shuman.

ACT II: "The Bulls"—Elliott; "Old Folks" and "Marieke"—Miss Stone; "Brussels"—The Company; "Fannette"—Elliott; "Funeral Tango"—Shuman; "The Middle Class"—Shuman, Elliott; "You're Not Alone"—Miss Stone; "Next"—Shuman; "Carousel"—Miss Stone; "If We Only Have Love"—The Company.

House of Flowers (57). Revival of the musical by Truman Capote and Harold Arlen. Produced by Saint-Subber at Theater de Lys. Opened January 28, 1968. (Closed March 17, 1968)

Drummer ....Daniel Barrajanos
The Houngan ....Charles Moore
Ottilie ....Yolande Bavan
Mamselle Tulip ....Hope Clarke
Mamselle Pansy ....Thelma Oliver
Madame Fleur ....Josephine Premice
Madame Tango ....Novella Nelson
Senorita Maria ....Carla Pinza
Lord Jamison ....Tom Helmore
The Champion ....Bob Broadway
Royal ....Robert Jackson
Old Bonaparte ....Josephine Premice
Woman ....Trina Parks
Man ....Walter Raines

Directed by Joseph Hardy; musical direction and arrangements, Joseph Raposo; choreography, Talley Beatty; scenery, Kert Lundell; costumes, Richard Casler; lighting, Tharon Musser; associate producer, Charles Weiss; presented by special arrangement with Lucille Lortel Productions, Inc.; production stage manager, Charles Kindl; press, Dorothy Ross, Ruth D. Smuckler.

Place: An island in the Caribbean. *House of Flowers* was first produced on Broadway

December 30, 1954 at the Alvin Theater for 165 performance. Five new songs were added to the score for this revival.

ACT I

"Two Ladies in de Shade of the Banana Tree" ....Pansy, Tulip
"A Sleepin' Bee" ....Ottilie, Pansy, Tulip
"Somethin' Cold to Drink" ....Madame Fleur
"Smellin' of Vanilla" ....Pansy, Tulip, Madame Tango, Company
"House of Flowers" ....Royal, Ottilie
"Don't Like Goodbyes" ....Ottilie
"Jump de Broom" ....Houngan, Company

ACT II

"Waitin' " ....Pansy, Tulip
"I Never Has Seen Snow" ....Ottilie
"Walk to de Grave" ....Houngan, Mourners
"Woman Never Understan' " ....Royal
"Madame Tango's Particular Tango" ....Madame Tango, Maria, Tulip, Pansy
"What is a Friend For?" ....Lord Jamison, Madame Fleur
"A Sleepin' Bee" and "I Never Has Seen Snow" (Reprise) ....Royal, Ottilie
"Two Ladies in de Shade of the Banana Tree" (Reprise) ....Madame Fleur, Tulip, Pansy, Company

Who's Who, Baby? (16). Musical with book by Gerald Frank; music and lyrics by Johnny Brandon. Produced by Edmund J. Ferdinand and Charlotte Schiff by arrangement with George Wiener at the Players Theater. Opened January 29, 1968. (Closed February 11, 1968)

Carol Winslow ....Jacqueline Mayro
Daisy ....Marcia Lewis
Smitty ....Danny Guerrero
Benny Hare ....Frank Andre
Sabine ....Glory Van Scott
Frankie ....Gloria Kaye
Al ....Tommy Breslin
Louis ....Tom Eatman
Jean ....Ural Wilson
Sir Peveril Ballantyne ....Humphrey Davis
Toby (Lord MacLaren) ....Erik Howell

Directed and choreographed by Marvin Gordon; scenery and costumes, Alan Kimmel; lighting, John Beaumont; musical direction and dance music, Leslie Harnley; orchestrations and dance music, Clark McClellan; production stage manager, Gail Bell; press, Bernard Simon, Avivah Simon.

Time: The present. Place: Here, there and everywhere on the island of Manuella.

A mix-up in the cradle is discovered and corrected, but it turns out that the original mix-up worked better than the new change-back. An early version of the book was based on *Who's Who,* a comedy by Guy Bolton and P.G. Wodehouse produced in London in 1934.

ACT I

"Island of Happiness" ....Sir Peveril, Jean, Louis, Carol, Benny, Sabine, Frankie, Daisy, Al, Smitty
"That'll be the Day" ....Toby, Carol
"Come-Along-a-Me, Babe" ....Benny, Al, Smitty, Frankie
"Nothin's Gonna Change" ....Benny, Frankie
"There Aren't Many Ladies in the Mile End Road" ....Daisy
"Syncopatin' " ....Carol, Louis, Jean, Smitty, Benny, Daisy, Al, Frankie, Toby
"Syncopatin' " (Reprise) ....Louis, Jean, Smitty, Al, Frankie, Sir Peveril
"Voodoo" ....Sabine, Louis, Jean
"How Do You Stop Loving Someone?" ....Frankie, Toby, Carol, Benny
"That'll be the Day" (Reprise) ....Benny

ACT II

"Come-Along-a Me, Babe" (Reprise) ....Toby
"Drums" ....Frankie, Al, Smitty, Toby

"Feminine-inity" .... Daisy, Carol, Frankie, Sabine
"That's What's Happening, Baby" .... Benny, Sabine, Louis, Frankie, Toby, Smitty, Al, Carol, Daisy
"Me" .... Benny
"Syncopatin'" (Reprise) .... Benny, Toby, Sir Peveril, Daisy, Jean, Louis, Al, Smitty
"Island of Happiness" (Reprise) .... Sabine, Jean, Louis
"Nobody To Cry To" .... Carol
"Feminine-inity" (Reprise) .... Daisy, Sir Peveril

The Theater Institute of the University of Chile (ITUCH). Schedule of two programs in the Spanish language. **La Remolienda** (*Bawdy Party*) (6). By Alejandro Sieveking. **ITUCH Anthology** (2). Fifteen scenes from ITUCH repertory. Produced by Theater of Latin America (TOLA) at the Barbizon Plaza Theater. Schedule opened February 2, 1968. (Closed February 9, 1968)

LA REMOLIENDA

Doña Nicolasa .... Bélgica Castro
Nicolás .... Mario Lorca
Graciano .... Tomás Vidiella
Gilberto .... Franklin Caicedo
Yola .... Kerry Keller
Isaura .... Claudia Paz
Chepa .... Sonia Mena
Doña Rebeca .... Carmen Bunster
Renato Sepúlveda .... Tennyson Ferrada
Mirta .... María Cánepa
Mauro .... Sergio Aguirre
Telmo .... Ruben Sotoconi
Baudilio .... Jorge Boudon

Directed by Victor Jara; scenery and costumes, Bruna Contreras; lighting, Sergio Zapata; music, Victor Jara; press, Sol Jacobson, Lewis Harmon.

Act I, Scene 1: A road. Scene 2: Out of doors restaurant. Act II, Scene 1: Out of doors restaurant. Scene 2: The same road as Act I. Comedy about a peasant woman and her three sons who are traveling and stop by mistake at a brothel.

ITUCH ANTHOLOGY included scenes from *Who's Afraid of Virginia Woolf?* by Edward Albee, *Death of a Salesman* by Arthur Miller, *Macbeth* by William Shakespeare, *Long Day's Journey Into Night* by Eugene O'Neill, *Marat/Sade* by Peter Weiss and *The Threepenny Opera* by Bertolt Brecht, as well as scenes from plays by Fernando de Rojas, Lope de Vega, Luco Cruchaga, José Pineda, Antonio Acevedo Hernández, Calderón, Pablo Neruda and Fernando Debesa.

I Only Want an Answer (8). English translation by Basil Ashmore of the one-character German play *Langusten* by Fred Denger. Produced by Margaret Hewes and Rick Hobard at Stage 73. Opened February 5, 1968. (Closed February 11, 1968)

Directed by Tony Tanner; production designed by Stewart Chaney; lighting, Roger Morgan; music, Dolphe Martin; production stage manager, John Glennon; press, Fred Weterick. With Hermione Baddeley.

A day in the life of a garrulous old British charwoman. A foreign play previously produced in Berlin, Zurich, Frankfurt and Vienna.

Oh, Say Can You See L.A. and **The Other Man** (14). Program of two one-act plays by John Allen. Produced by Richard Lerner, Frances Drucker and Gilberto Zaldivar at the Actors Playhouse. Opened February 8, 1968. (Closed February 18, 1968)

Directed by John Allen; designed by Boyd Dumrose; choreography, Vernon Lusby; production stage manager, Robert Buzzell; press, David Lipsky, Marian Graham. With Glenn Kezer, Alan Manson, George Voskovec, George Welbes.

OH, SAY CAN YOU SEE L.A.—Four vaudeville troupers symbolize the decadence of modern life. THE OTHER MAN—Jewish survivors of the Nazi death camps find a war criminal being held prisoner and tortured for revenge in Buenos Aires.

Saturday Night (66). By Jerome Kass. Produced by Dwubba Productions, Inc. at the Sheridan Square Playhouse. Opened February 25, 1968. (Closed April 21, 1968)

Mr. Harris	Shimen Ruskin	Ellie	Gina Collens
Rochelle	Zina Jasper	Iggy	Marvin Lichterman
Gabe	Lee Wallace	Policeman	Wendell Phillips Jr.

Directed by Burt Brinckerhoff; scenery, Jack H. Cornwell; lighting, Roger Morgan; costumes, Joe Aulisi; executive producer, Davis Weinstock; production stage manager, David Shanstrom; press, Reuben Rabinovitch.

Time: Saturday night. Place: A Bronx apartment. Act I: Early evening. Act II: Later that evening.

Unhappy Bronx librarian creates a dream world in which she lives an imaginary life of high culture.

Goa (30). By Asif Currimbhoy. Produced by Dhiandil Productions at the Martinique Theater. Opened February 22, 1967. (Closed March 17, 1967)

Rose	Jody Locker	Portuguese Vicar	Elek Hartman
Administrator	Jay Barney	Goan Hindu	Tazewell Thompson
Goan Nationalist	Jose Perez	Smuggler	Dennis Tate
Chico	Elliot Paul	Senhora Miranda	Sylvia Gassell
Old Woman	Mildred Chandler	Krishna	Cal Bellini
Old Man	James Cook	Alfonso	Erik Silju

Villagers: Hortensia Colorado, Harriet Karr, Carrie Ann Kessler, Linda Taverna, Nancy Volkman.

Directed by Patricia Newhall; scenery and lighting, C. Murawski; costumes, Robert Pusilo; sound, Terry Ross; incidental music, Ali Akbar Kahn; production stage manager, Lewis S. Rosen; press, David Rothenberg.

Place: A patio in Goa. About India taking over the enclave of Goa from Portugal in 1961. A foreign (Indian) play making its debut in this production.

The Bench (1). By N.R. Teitel. Produced by LBG Productions and Esther Prince in association with David Morgan at the Gramercy Arts Theater. Opened and closed at the evening performance, March 4, 1968.

Directed by Val Bisoglio; scenery, Robert U. Taylor; costumes, Jeanne Button; lighting, Michael Davidson; music, Teiji Ito; production stage manager, Larry Catusi; press, Howard Atlee. With Fayne Blackburn, Gretchen Corbett, Thayer David, Richard Hamilton, Joseph Leon, David Nillo, Michael O'Sullivan, Carol Teitel.

A group of "bohemians" expounds upon life, love and art.

The Victims (6). Program of three one-act plays: *On the Hazards of Smoking Tobacco* by Anton Chekhov, translated by Charles Fischer; *Victims of Duty* by Eugene Ionesco, translated by Donald Watson; *Escurial* by Michel de Ghelderode, translated by George Hauger. Produced by Yon Enterprises, Inc. at the East 74th Street Theater. Opened March 5, 1968. (Closed March 10, 1968)

Artistic director, Charles Fischer; costumes, Cynthia Penn; lighting, Jene E. Youtt; stage manager, Will Richter; press, Fred Weterick. With Charles Fischer, Kaye Kingston, Charles Lutz, Edward McPhillips, Robert R. Ruth.

Three plays chosen to show man as Everyman beleaguered by life, death and himself.

Fun City (31). Revue with sketches by David Rogers; special material by Fred Silver, Nelson Garringer, Jay Jeffries, Franklin Underwood and Norman Martin; title song by David Rogers and James Reed Lawlor. Produced by Jack Irving at Jan Hus Playhouse. Opened March 6, 1968. (Closed March 31, 1968)

Lynne Carter
Mel Edwards
Dee Robinson

Directed by David Rogers; musical direction and orchestrations, James Reed Lawlor; scenery, Sal Tinnerello, Richard Burnside; costumes, Frank Page, Michael Landi; lighting, David Anderson; press, Dorothy Ross, Ruth D. Smuckler.

Program built around female impersonations by Lynne Carter.

ACT I: "Fun City" (Mel 'n' Dee), A Voice That Will Ring Forever (Ethel Merman), Have Piano and Hanky . . . Will Travel (Hildegarde), A Tragic Queen (Hermione Gingold), Cover Girl (Phyllis Diller), Where the Elite Meet—Carnegie Hall, Manners, Goodness Had Nothing To Do With It (Mae West). ACT II: Sudden Beauty (Marlene Dietrich), Going Highbrow (Bette Davis), A Bunny's Mother, Dear John—Help! (Tallulah Bankhead), Make Me a Match (Pearl Bailey), "Fun City" (Entire Company).

Scarlet Lullaby (7). By Elliott Taubenslag. Produced by Myrnel Productions at the Masque Theater. Opened March 10, 1968. (Closed March 17, 1968)

Directed by Elliott Taubenslag; scenery, Donald Cotter; costumes, H.N. Hinkle; lighting, Paul Inverso; stage manager, Leo Stella; press, David Lipsky, Marian Graham. With Ann Rollins, Kathleen Scarlett, Dolly Vasta, Aurelia De Felice, Joseph Vasta, Owen Hollander, Bob E. Lloyd, Richard Graham, Earl George, Mel Boyd and Lori Shelle.

Prostitute is reformed by association with her orphaned 10-year-old niece.

Winter Journey (15). Revival of *The Country Girl* by Clifford Odets. Produced by Herbert S. Alpert and Mitchell Nestor at the Greenwich Mews Theater. Opened March 12, 1968. (Closed March 24, 1968)

Directed by Mitchell Nestor; scenery and lighting, Richard Kerry; costumes, Jan; music and sound effects, John Batiste; production stage manager, Carmine Pontilena; press, Max Eisen. With Walter Allen, Patrick Baldauff, John Batiste, Jean Fowler, Will Hare, Barbara Loden, Delos V. Smith Jr., Robert Viharo.

The Country Girl is billed here under Odets' second title for the play—*Winter Journey*. Some of its references were updated for this production.

The Four Seasons (6). By Arnold Wesker. Produced by Bruce W. Stark in association with Savage-Friedman at the Theater Four. Opened March 14, 1968. (Closed March 17, 1968)

Directed by Arthur A. Seidelman; scenery and lighting, C. Murawski; costumes, Jeanne Button; music, Frangipane and Dante; production manager, Vincent Lynne; press, David Rothenberg. With Barbara Hayes, Paul Roebling.

Two lovers meet, love, then drift apart, in an abandoned house. A foreign play previously produced in London.

Two Camps by Koutoukas (18). Program of two one-act plays by H.M. Koutoukas. Produced by Barbara Wise Productions, Inc. at the Actors Playhouse. Opened March 18, 1968. (Closed April 2, 1968)

THE LAST TRIANGLE

Noel Cowel ....Eddie McCarty
Virginia Wolfgang ....Margaret Wright
Lottie Lemming ....Gretel Cummings
The Hawk ....Aileen Passloff

ONLY A COUNTESS MAY DANCE WHEN SHE'S CRAZY

Countess Olie Sandowitch ...Gretel Cummings

Directed by H. M. Koutoukas; incidental music, Robert Cosmos Savage; costumes, Maria Irene Fornes; lighting, Johnny Dodd; choreography, Aileen Passloff; musical director and pianist, Benji Heywood; production stage manager, Yon Koski; press, Howard Atlee.

THE LAST TRIANGLE—Time: No longer. Place: The ruins of Newswanstein. About the last three survivors of a nuclear disaster. ONLY A COUNTESS MAY DANCE WHEN

SHE'S CRAZY—Place: The tower of Dr. Tills' laboratory, mid-Atlantic. Monologue of a peeress who is a receptionist for a mad scientist whose mistake has caused the big blow-up.

* **Tom Paine** (75). By Paul Foster. Produced by William Dorr in association with Michael White as conceived for the La Mama Troupe at Stage 73. Opened March 25, 1968.

Tom Paine's Reputation; Dodger ....John Bakos
1st Deaf Woman; Amer. Committee of Secret Correspondence; A Greedy; Woman in Red Cloak; Marguerite Bonville ....Mari-Claire Charba
Major Domo; Roger ....Peter Craig
Sergeant; Captain; General; Quartermaster; George III; Sentry; Edmund Burke ....Jerry Cunliffe
Bishop; de Beaumarchais; Capt. Lambesc ....Jay Fletcher
Gin Seller; 2d Deaf Woman; A Greedy; Gouverneur Morris; Mary Wollstonecraft; Old Man; Registrar ....Sally Kirkland
Tom Paine ....Kevin O'Connor
Pvt. of England; Mate Drummer; Silas Deane; Cromwell's Shadow; Sentry; Lord Justice ....Victor Lipari
Buleah; de Vergennes; Simonne; Registrar II; A Greedy ....Beth Porter
Marie; John Jay; A Greedy; Marie Antoinette; Marie ....Marilyn Roberts
Governor; Black Dick; Altar Boy; Quaker; Old Man; Louis XVI; Blake ....Bob Thirkield

Directed by Tom O'Horgan; lighting, Johnny Dodd; costumes, Michael Warren Powell; stage manager, Steve Whitson; press, David Rothenberg, Larry Schneider.

Time: 1809. Place: A bear pit, Lower Manhattan. Part I, Scene 1: Improvisational. Scene 2: Presentation of the cast. Scene 3: The Sergeant and the Private. Scene 4: Consecration of the house. Scene 5: The great crossing. Scene 6: Paine prays to God. Scene 7: Paine and the Quaker. Scene 8: Improvisational. Scene 9: The Governor, the General, the Bishop. Scene 10: The fit and the rite of exorcism. Scene 11: Black Dick. Scene 12: The Rat Pack's intrigue. Scene 13: Investiture of the King. Part II, Scene 1: Improvisational. Scene 2: Blake receives Paine at the Coast. Scene 3: The Royal Gluttons. Scene 4: Captain Lambesc and the Old Man. Scene 5: The termites of Paris march to the bread and cake Queen. Scene 6: Blake's suspicion. Scene 7: Paine's trial. Scene 8: Paine pleads for the life of the King. Scene 9: Luxembourg dungeon. Scene 10: Welcome home. Scene 11: Improvisational.

Series of sketches about the life of Tom Paine, who is presented as a flawed but humane character. An American play previously produced by the La Mama Troupe in Edinburgh and London.

Rate of Exchange (1). By Milo Thomas. Produced by Monroe Productions at the Players Theater. Opened and closed at the evening performance April 1, 1968.

Directed by Dorothy Chernuck; scenery and costumes, Peter Wingate; lighting, Robert L. Benson; production stage manager, Frank S. Torok; press, Warren Pincus. With Esther Benson, Lydia Bruce, Walter Flanagan, Jill Harmon, Kevin Hanily, Nick Lewis, George Renschler, Garrett Saunders, Jerry Strickler, Donald Symington, Strat Walling.

Drama with a theme of anti-war, including Vietnam.

* **The Boys in the Band** (53). By Mart Crowley. Produced by Richard Barr and Charles Woodward Jr. at Theater Four. Opened April 15, 1968.

Michael ....Kenneth Nelson
Donald ....Frederick Combs
Emory ....Cliff Gorman
Larry ....Keith Prentice
Hank ....Laurence Luckinbill
Bernard ....Reuben Greene
Cowboy ....Robert La Tourneaux
Alan ....Peter White
Harold ....Leonard Frey

Directed by Robert Moore; design, Peter Harvey; stage manager, Charles Kindl; press, David Rothenberg, Larry Schneider.

Time: The present, one evening. Place: A smartly appointed duplex apartment in the East Fifties, New York City. The play is presented in two acts.

Personal frictions among a group of homosexuals giving a birthday party for one of their number.

A Best Play; see page 299

Le Tréteau de Paris. Repertory of two revivals in the French language. **Le Tartuffe** (29). By Molière. Opened April 16, 1968. **En Attendant Godot** (*Waiting for Godot*) (11). By Samuel Beckett. Opened April 22, 1968. Produced by Jacques Courtines and Seff Associates Ltd. by special arrangement with Jean de Rigault at the Barbizon-Plaza Theater. (Repertory closed May 14, 1968)

LE TARTUFFE

Madame Pernelle ....Janine Souchon
Orgon ....Gilles Léger
Elmire ....Giselle Touret
Damis ....Guy Michel
Mariane ....Francine Walter
Valere ....Pierre Coustères
Cleante ....Michel Favory
Tartuffe ....Yves Gasc
Dorine ....Marcelle Ranson
Monsieur Loyal ....Philippe Laudenbach
Un exempt ....Michel Hervé
Flipote ....Geneviève Léomy

Directed by Yves Gasc; scenery, Yves Gasc; costumes, Jacques Mornas.

Tartuffe was last produced in New York by the Repertory Theater of Lincoln Center in Richard Wilbur's English verse translation at the ANTA-Washington Square Theater, January 14, 1965, for 74 performances.

EN ATTENDANT GODOT

Estragon ....Jean Rodien
Vladimir ....Rene Lesage
Pozzo ....Raoul Marco
Lucky ....Charles Schmitt
Un Garcon ....Vincent Ridard

Directed by Rene Lesage; scenery, Bernard Floriet.

Waiting for Godot was first produced by Michael Myerberg at the John Golden Theater, April 19, 1956, for 49 performances. It was named a Best Play of its season. It was revived the following season by Mr. Myerberg for 6 performances at the Ethel Barrymore Theater.

BOTH PLAYS: Produced by Jean de Rigault and presented under the sponsorship of the Government of the French Republic and with the patronage of Edward Morot-Sir, Cultural Counselor to the French Embassy; production stage manager, Erwen Kerné; press, Arthur Cantor, Arthur Solomon.

The Hawk (15). By Murray Mednick and Tony Barsha. Produced by James Walsh and Dina and Alexander E. Racolin at the Actors Playhouse. Opened April 17, 1968. (Closed April 28, 1968)

Directed by Tony Barsha; music, Eddie Hicks; lighting, Barbara Nollman; stage manager, Joel Walker; press, David Rothenberg, Larry Schneider. With Barbara Eda-Young, Walter Hadler, O-Lan Johnson, Scarlett Johnson, Lee Kissman, Sommer Sally, Tony Serchio and Ching Yeh.

Drama of a drug pusher and his victims.

* **Muzeeka** by John Guare and **Red Cross** by Sam Shepard (36). Program of two one-act plays. Produced by Warren Lyons and Betty Ann Besch at the Provincetown Playhouse. Opened April 28, 1968.

MUZEEKA

Jack Argue ....Burt Brinckerhoff
His Wife ....Marcia Jean Kurtz
Evelyn Landis ....Peggy Pope
Number Two ....Sandy Baron
Stagehands Number One, Three and Four ....Kevin Bryan Conway, John Lawlor, Frank Prendergast

Directed by Melvin Bernhardt stage movement, Ralf Harmer.

Young musician seeks to revitalize the vapid music mass-produced by a taping firm (symbolic of American inertia and conformity). Previously produced at the Eugene O'Neill Memorial Theater, Waterford, Conn. and Mark Taper Forum, Los Angeles.

RED CROSS

Carol ....Marcia Jean Kurtz
Jim ....Sam Waterston
The Maid ....Florence Tarlow

Directed by Jacques Levy.

Place: A cabin in the forest. An absurdist study of three lice-infested characters—a husband, wife and maid. Previously produced at Judson Poets Theater.

BOTH PLAYS: Design, Peter Harvey; sound, James Reichert; lighting, Johnny Dodd; production stage manager, Patrick Horrigan; stage manager, Frank Prendergast; press, David Rothenberg.

Carving a Statue (12). By Graham Greene. Produced by Dina and Alexander E. Racolin and Berenice Weiler at the Gramercy Arts Theater. Opened April 30, 1968. (Closed May 12, 1968)

Directed by Margaret Webster; design, John Braden; music, John Duffy; production stage manager, Martin Herzer; press, Samuel J. Friedman, Jane Friedman. With Judy Allen, Tony Capodilupo, Saylor Creswell, Fran Myers.

A sculptor is obsessed by the ambition to carve a statue of God. A British play previously produced in London.

* **Collision Course** (27). Program of 11 one-act plays (for titles and authors see list below). Produced by Lyn Austin, Hale Matthews and Oliver Smith at the Cafe Au Go Go. Opened May 8, 1968.

WANDERING by Lanford Wilson

He ....Tom Rosqui
She ....Susan Browning
Him ....Scott Glenn

Generation-gap play about lack of communication between a young boy on the one hand and a man and woman on the other.

STARS AND STRIPES by Leonard Melfi

Henry James ....Tom Rosqui
Amy Lowell ....Meg Myles
Walt Whitman ....Sam Groom
Herman Melville ....Scott Glenn
Emily Dickinson ....Susan Browning
Edna St. Vincent Millay ....Leora Dana

Imaginary conversation of literary figures (note character names).

CHUCK by Jack Larson

Mrs. Wilcox ....Susan Browning
Chuck ....Sam Groom

An argument for the written word in communication, as opposed to radio and TV.

SKYWRITING by Rosalyn Drexler

Woman ....Leora Dana
Man ....Tom Rosqui

Absurdist husband-wife sketch about non-communication between the sexes.

JEW! by Harvey Perr

Patti ....Susan Browning
Hattie ....Meg Myles
Curley ....Sam Groom
Red ....Scott Glenn

An exercise in prejudice and name-calling.

THOUGHTS ON THE INSTANT OF GREETING A FRIEND ON THE STREET
by Jean-Claude van Itallie and Sharon Thie

Woman ....Meg Myles
Man ....Sam Groom

See title—friends, meeting, speak their thoughts aloud in two monologues.

TOUR by Terrence McNally

Mrs. Wilson ....Leora Dana
Mr. Wilson ....Tom Rosqui
Driver ....Scott Glenn
Monks ....Members of the Company

An American tourist couple's failure to understand other societies (including Vietnam).

CAMERA OBSCURA by Robert Patrick

Male Announcer ....Sam Groom
Female Announcer ....Julia Curry
He ....Tom Rosqui
She ....Susan Browning

Futuristic fantasy about a couple courting by remote electronic control.

METAPHORS by Martin Duberman

Interviewer ....Sam Groom
Paul ....Scott Glenn

A Yale admissions officer interviews a homosexual seeking entrance to the college as a student.

THE UNEXPURGATED MEMOIRS OF BERNARD MERGENDEILER by Jules Feiffer

Bernard ....Sam Groom
Naomi ....Meg Myles

Boy-girl dialogue about sex.

RATS by Israel Horovitz

Jebbie ....Tom Rosqui
Bobbie ....Scott Glenn
Baby ....Tom Scott

Modern life as seen through the eyes of rodents.

Standbys: Julia Curry, Mylo Quam.
Directed by Edward Parone; design, Michael Davidson; costumes, Diedre Cartier; production stage manager, M.M. Streicher; press, Samuel Lurie & Associates, Stanley F. Kaminsky.

* **The Believers** (26). Musical with book by Josephine Jackson and Joseph A. Walker; music by Benjamin Carter, Dorothy Dinroe, Josephine Jackson, Anje Ray and Ron Steward. Lyrics by Benjamin Carter, Dorothy Dinroe, Josephine Jackson, Anje Ray, Ron Steward and Joseph A. Walker. Produced by Jesse DeVore and Harold L. Oram in association with Gustav Heningburg at the Garrick Theater. Opened May 9, 1968.

Members of Voices Inc.:

Benjamin Carter
Jesse DeVore
Dorothy Dinroe
Barry Hemphill
Josephine Jackson
Sylvia Jackson
Shirley McKie
Don Oliver
Anje Ray
Veronica Redd
Ron Steward
James Wright
Joseph A. Walker (narrator)

Directed by Barbara Ann Teer; musical direction and vocal dimensions, Brooks Alexander; scenery, Joseph A. Walker; costumes, Robert Pusilo; lighting, R. Robert Lussier, J.D. Regan; assistant to director, Louis Johnson; African drums, Ladji Camara; American drums, Andre Strobert; production stage manager, J. Pat Regan; press, David Rothenberg.
Act I: The gone years. Act II: The then and now years.
Negro history from pre-slavery days to the present is related to song, dance and dramatized numbers performed by Voices Inc.

Private Lives (9). Revival of the play by Noel Coward. Produced by Haila Stoddard, Mark Wright and Duane Wilder at the Theater de Lys. Opened May 19, 1968. (Closed May 26, 1968)

Directed by Richard Barr; scenery, Herbert Senn, Helen Pond; lighting, David F. Segal; Mr. Coward's music arranged and performed by Don Elliott; press, David Rothenberg, Warren Pincus, Lawrence Schneider. With Howard Erskine, Russell Nype, Anita Palacine, Elaine Stritch, Betsy von Furstenberg.

Private Lives was last revived by John C. Wilson, starring Tallulah Bankhead, at the Plymouth Theater, October 4, 1948, for 248 performances.

Some Additional Productions

This selected listing of off-off-Broadway and experimental productions was compiled by R.J. Schroeder (see his article on 1967-68 off off Broadway in "The Season in New York" section of this volume). Leading groups are identified in alphabetical order and examples of their outstanding 1967-68 work are noted. Performances and opening dates are given when available, but in many cases there was no premiere or engagement of record.

ANTA Matinee Theater Series. The Greater New York Chapter of the American National Theater and Academy's series, under the direction of Lucille Lortel, of 5 productions on Monday evenings and Tuesday afternoons at the Theater de Lys.

TWO NEW AMERICAN PLAYS (2). Program of two one-act plays. December 4, 1967. *The Club Bedroom* by Louis Auchincloss; directed by Robert Moss; with Carolyn Coates, Jessie Royce Landis, Dorothy Sands. *Postcards* by James Prideaux; directed by Jean Dalrymple; with Hugh Marlowe, Paula Trueman.

DOUBLE PLAY (2). Program of two one-act plays: *Limb of Snow* and *The Meeting* by Anna Marie Barlow. December 11, 1967. Directed by Joel Friedman; with Mary Doyle, Don Fellows, Leonard Hicks, Salome Jens, Robert Walden.

LET THEM DOWN, GENTLY (2). Program of two one-act plays: *Our Man in Madras* and *On Vacation* by Gert Hofmann. January 29, 1968. Directed by Charles Maryan; with Stan Hart, John Kendrick, Courteen Landis, Simm Landres, Patrick McVey, Sarah Sanders.

A MADRIGAL OF SHAKESPEARE (2). Program of excerpts from William Shakespeare's works. February 12, 1968. Directed by Joan White; with Ethel Barrymore Colt, Peggy Wood; piano, John Ranck.

MR. AND MRS. LYMAN (2). By Joel Friedman. March 4, 1968. Directed by Alfred Christie; with Sylvia Gassels, Alan Mixon.

The Anthony Mannino Repertory Club. A facility for the presentation of plays "packaged" by playwrights or directors. Each bill ran several weekends at the Mannino Theater.

I REMEMBER FOXTROT. By Tom Sydorick. Directed by Jack Spencer; with Diane Ellis, Kevin Sullivan.

MODERN STATUARY. By Donald Kvares. Directed by Jack Spencer; with Barbara Goll, Dorothy Opalach, Stanley Seidman.

The Blackfriars' Guild. Two new plays produced by the Blackfriars' Guild (Rev. Thomas F. Carey, Moderator) at the Blackfriars' Guild.

GUIMPES AND SADDLES. By Rev. Edward A. Molloy, C. SS. R. Directed by Walter Cool; double cast included Evelyn Denon, William Houston, Angela Kochera, Dorothy Ott, Ted Rado.

BABES DON'T CRY ANYMORE. By Michael Kallesser. Directed by Walter Cool; double cast included Kathleen Beal, Dawn Eman, James Gaughan, Dylan Stephen de Guzman, Debbie Howard, Kathleen Madden, Thomas O'Callaghan, Frances Panzella, Marilyn Tass.

Caffe Cino. Founded and operated by the late Joe Cino, and one of the earliest and most influential of the off-off-Broadway theaters, the Caffe Cino closed during the 1967-68 season, after a number of Cino's friends had tried unsuccessfully to keep the cafe open in the period after his untimely death. One of the typical and better-known productions at the Cino is listed below.

VINYL. By Ronald Tavel; with music by John Harrill. Directed by Harvey Tavel; choreography, Ron Pratt; with Raymond Edwards, John Harrill, Sterling Houston, Norman Thomas Marshall, Mike St. Shaw, Mary Woronov.

Classic Stage Company. Christopher Martin's company performing at Rutgers Church. An annual repertory of classics or near-classics was staged throughout the theater season. Two are listed below.

THE CAVERN. By Jean Anouilh; translated by Lucienne Hill. Directed by Christopher Martin; with Lance Brilliantine, Barbara Gambel, Robert Gatto, F. Richard Holland, Harriet Mason, Mary McLain, Paul J. Pfadenhauer.

MAN AND SUPERMAN. By George Bernard Shaw. Directed by Christopher Martin; associate director, Harris Laskawy; with Andrew Arnold, Lance Brilliantine, Jeanne Chaffee, Jeffrey Kramer, Christopher Martin, Roger Mason, Kathryn Wyman.

The Cooper Square Arts Theater. Ed Wode maintains facilities available to playwrights and directors who "package" shows for presentation at one or another (or at several) of the off off Broadway theaters. The Cooper Square Arts Theater generally offered productions in two-weekend runs. Productions this season included:

THE PENALTY FOR BEING SLOW. By Burton Snyder. Directed by David Leary; with Veronica Castang, Tony Tonuta.

CHRISTMAS TURKEY. Written and directed by Ed Wode. With Darryl Edwards, Barry Granick, Patrick Whitaker, M. Whitehead, Wilford Winnis.

The Dove Company. Harold Herbstman's unit performed new and old scripts, usually directed by a "house" director, at St. Peters Church. Productions ran two to four weekends, and often reappeared in a sort of repertory. This season's work included:

I CAN'T SLEEP. By Clifford Odets. Directed by Harold Herbstman; with Michael Fischetti, Bill Maloney.

ANNAJANSKA, THE BOLSHEVIK EMPRESS. By George Bernard Shaw. Directed by Harold Herbstman; with Jerold Broudy, Michael Fischetti, Bill Maloney, Andy Milligan, Natalie Rogers.

THE TINKER'S WEDDING. By John Millington Synge. Directed by Andy Milligan; with John Borske, Michael Fischetti, Miriam Levenson, Margaret Miller.

D.M.Z. Cabaret. Isaiah Sheffer and Eric Bentley have opened this political cabaret theater, which gave performances nightly Tuesdays through Sundays at Forlini's Restaurant near Columbia University. A typical program was:

D.M.Z. REVUE. Musical revue with skits and lyrics by Eric Bentley, Albert Bermel, Wolf Biermann, Jules Feiffer, Anthony Harrison, Robert Lowell and Adrian Mitchell; music by Arnold Black, Bruce Kirle, Wolf Biermann, Irma Jurist and Richard Peaslee. Directed by Isaiah Sheffer; with James Antonio, Tony Harrison, Josephine Lemmo; piano, Bruce Kirle.

Equity Theater. The following plays were produced by Equity Theater at the Master Theater.

BABES IN ARMS (15). Musical with book by George Oppenheimer; lyrics by Lorenz Hart; music by Richard Rodgers. October 20, 1967. Directed by Leland Ball; dances and musical numbers staged by Jim Hoskins; with Jerry Clark, Jamie Donnelly, Erik Howell, John Kuhner, Sally Stark, Jacquie Ullendorf.

HE WHO GETS SLAPPED (9). By Leonid Andreyev; translated by Gregory Zilboorg. November 17, 1967. Directed by Joseph della Sorte; with Clement Fowler, Lois Grandi, Richard Mansfield, Adriana Mejiaf, Anthony Ponzini, Joel Wolfe.

UNDER THE GASLIGHT (9). By Augustin Daly. December 8, 1967. Directed by Allan Lokos; new music and lyrics by Norman Dean; musical numbers staged and choreographed by Bill Bradley; with Raymond Allen, Laurie Hutchinson, Clay Johns, Jan La Prade, Bob Riehl, Rose Roffman.

REDHEAD (15). Musical with book by Herbert and Dorothy Fields, Sidney Sheldon, and David Shaw; lyrics by Dorothy Fields; music by Albert Hague. January 12, 1968. Directed and choreographed by Noel Schwartz; with Chip Carle, Cherry Davis, Georgia Dell, George Emch, Danna Hansen, Jim Ray-James.

AN ENEMY OF THE PEOPLE (9). By Henrik Ibsen; adapted by Arthur Miller. February 9, 1968. Directed by Joseph France; with Herman O. Arbeit, Terry Beasor, Donald Bishop, Patrick McCullough, Jan Owen, Dan Tyra.

NEXT TIME I'LL SING TO YOU (9). By James Saunders. March 1, 1968. Directed by Albert Lipton; with Margo Ann Berdeshevsky, Bob Berger, Bayne Ellis, James Heath, Harvey Solin.

LOST IN THE STARS (15). By Maxwell Anderson; music by Kurt Weill. March 22, 1968. Directed by Ella Gerber; musical director and conductor, William Mount-Burke; with Hazel J. Bryant, Chet Doherty, Woodie King, Robert Mosley, Freda Payne, Millard Williams.

THE VISIT (9). By Friedrich Duerrenmatt; adapted by Maurice Valency. April 19, 1968. Directed by Paul John Austin; with John Saunders Branon, Parke Godwin, Renata Mannhardt, Chris Manor, Reuben Shafer, Jack Somack.

YES, MY DARLING DAUGHTER (9). By Mark Reed. May 10, 1968. Directed by Joseph Hamer; with Alice Arden, Scotty Bloch, Mark Foley, Anita Keal, William Martel, David Lynn Selby.

Equity Theater Informals. The following shows were presented by Equity Theater for three early evening or matinee performances at the Library and Museum of the Performing Arts at Lincoln Center:

POP POEMS POP OUT (3). Adapted by Cliff Frazier from the book by Ronald Gross; music by Phil Gaberman. October 9, 1967. Directed by Cliff Frazier; with Suzanne Granfield, Woodie King Jr., Anne Lynn, Gary Maxwell, Cele McLaughlin, Angel Pineda, Leslie Rivers.

THE FAMILY REUNION (3). By T. S. Eliot. November 20, 1967. A reading directed by Alfred Christie; with Madeleine Clive, Nancy Coleman, Marie Donnet, Virginia Downing, Ronnie Claire Edwards, Mary Fogarty, John Leighton, John Vari.

THE WAVES (3). Adapted from the novel by Virginia Woolf by Joyce Whitcomb and Gail Bell. February 26, 1968. Directed by Gail Bell; with Wally Androchuk, James Cook, Tom De Wolfe, Jamie Donnelly, Mary Lynn Hanley, Erik Howell, Jacqueline Mayro.

THE WORLD OF CARL SANDBURG (3). Adapted by Norman Corwin. March 21, 1968. Directed by Lee Foley; with Barbara Berjer, Garry Hearne, Alex Reed.

AMERICAN MIME THEATER (3). Lecture-demonstration by Paul Curtis, director of American Mime Theater, assisted by a company of nine. May 2, 1968.

The Extension. Walter Leyden Brown's activity presents both new and older playwrights, usually supervised by "house" directors. Plays ran Wednesdays through Sundays for two to three weeks, at the Extension Theater. Recent productions included:

MANDRAGOLA. By Niccolo Machiavelli. Directed by Peter Wilson Strader; with Virginia Anton, Jon Carlson, Ashley Carr, Charlie Frost, Jessica Rains, Charles Regan, John Welsh.

THE BREASTS OF TIRESIAS. By Guillaume Apollinaire, in a new translation by James Clancy. Directed by Walter Leyden Brown; with Stephen Barnett, Louis Brodesser, Walter Leyden Brown, Jon Carlson, Ashley Carr, Minnie Gordon Gaster, Douglas Travis.

SHOWER. By Ronald Tavel; music by Harold Prucha and John Harrill. Directed by Harvey Tavel; with Joey London, Ondine, Zeph.

Der Grüne Kakadu. Founded by S. J. Vogel, and now run by David Gale, this cafe eschews new plays in order to concentrate upon classics or near-classics that have only rarely been performed in New York. Productions supervised by its own associates ran three to four weekends. Presentations this season included:

THE MAN WHO MARRIED A DUMB WIFE. By Anatole France. Adapted and directed by David Gale; incidental music by Carol Miller. With Christopher Downing, Ada McAllister, Judie Messier, Harry Orzello, Michael Starr, Mel Weinberg, Noel Young.

DER GRÜNE KAKADU. By Arthur Schnizler; translated and adapted by S. J. Vogel. Directed by S. J. Vogel and Judie Messier; with Bob Beardsley, Tom Everett, Bob Hart, Ada McAllister, Kathleen McGee, Judie Messier, Ed Rosenthal, M. A. Whiteside.

SALOME. By Oscar Wilde. Directed by S. J. Vogel; with Bob Beardsley, Peter Bumstead, Randy Jay, Ada McAllister, M. A. Whiteside.

Institute for Advanced Studies in the Theater Arts (IASTA). John and Miriam Mitchell's project brings foreign directors to New York, on an irregular schedule, to train American actors in the performance of plays from the visiting directors' repertory. This season there was one production at the IASTA Theater.

KANJINCHO. By Namiki Gohei, as adapted by James R. Brandon and Tamako Niwa. February 14, 1968. Directed by Matsumoto Koshiro VIII and Nakamura Matagoro II; assisted by Miyoko Watanabe; chorus directed by Raymond Hargrave and Seiko Koshiro; with Zeke Berlin, June Compton, Miguel Flores, Joan de Marrais, Tom Matsusaka, Patricia Peardon.

The Judson Poets Theater. Under the direction of Al Carmines, this activity at Judson Memorial Church produces mostly new plays, frequently with original music by Al Carmines, and usually directed by one of a few "house" directors. Productions generally ran several weekends. This year's presentations included:

UNTITLED PLAY. By Lanford Wilson; music by Al Carmines. Directed by Marshall W. Mason; musical numbers staged by Remy Charlip and Aileen Passloff; with Joy Bang, Claris Erickson, David Groh, Michael McClanathan, Michael Warren Powell, Rob Thirkield.

THE SAYINGS OF MAO TSE-TUNG. An "opera", with words by Chairman Mao; music by Al Carmines. Movement staged by Remy Charlip; with Reathel Bean, David Berk, Al Carmines, Christopher Carrick, Julie Kurniz, Florence Tarlow, Margaret Wright.

THE LINE OF LEAST EXISTENCE. By Rosalyn Drexler; music by Al Carmines. Directed by Lawrence Kornfeld; with George Bartenieff, Crystal Field, Eugene Heller, Katherine Litz, and Louis Waldon; music performed by The Feds.

La Mama Experimental Theater Club. Ellen Stewart, impressario of La Mama, maintains facilities which are made available to playwrights and directors who "package" shows, often rehearsed elsewhere. These shows may play for only a couple of nights, or as long as ten days to two weeks. The stage is rarely dark, year around. There was an unprecedented dark period in the spring and summer of 1968, while La Mama made a foundation-grant-financed move to a new and larger La Mama Theater. Two of the most impressive productions this season were:

THE MOON DREAMERS. Written, produced, and directed by Julie Bovasso. Associate director and choreographer, Buzz Miller; with Julie Bovasso, Jean David, Ted Henning, Buzz Miller, Don Signore, Jeanne Wrubel.

LINE. By Israel Horovitz. Directed by James Hammerstein; with John Cazale, Paul Haller, Israel Horovitz, Michael del Medico, Ann Wedgeworth.

The Loft. Lyn Austin's theater for occasional showcase presentations. Length of the runs at the Loft Theater varied. Recent productions included:

FATAL BEAUTY. Program of one-act plays: *The Treatment* and *Soap Opera* by John Gruen. Directed by Gaby Rodgers; with Emory Bass, Mary Laslo, Katherine Litz, Michael Vale.

The Mannhardt Theater Foundation, Inc. This is the production unit of the Renata Mannhardt theater school. New and old American and European plays are performed, usually under "house" direction, at the Mannhardt Theater. Productions usually ran weekends for four to five weeks. Recent productions included:

MUSHROOMS. By Donald Kvares; music by John Herbert McDowell. Directed by John Chace; with Jane Macleod, Etain O'Malley, Bob Sonderskov, Margaret Steele, Stephen Mark Weyte, Frank Wilson.

POINT OF DEPARTURE. By Jean Anouilh. Directed by Renata Mannhardt; with William Dancy, Mary Gilbert, Donald Kvares, Etain O'Malley, Thurman Scott, Charles Stradella.

The New Theater Workshop. Monday Night Play Series of productions at the New Theater.

GOD BLESS US, EVERY ONE (3). By Charles L. Mee Jr. November 13, 1967. Directed by Stephen Aaron; with Robert Cosenza, John Fink, Brenda Lesley, Michael McGuire, Albert M. Ottenheimer, David Tress.

BIG NOSE MARY IS DEAD (3). By Barry Pritchard. December 11, 1967. Directed by Richard Smithies; with Joseph Keyes, John H. Lawlor, and Al Settimio.

CONFESSION OF AN IGNORANT (3). Written and directed by Paul john Austin. Feb. 19, 1968. With W. B. Brydon, Susan Dorlen, Ernesto Gonzalez, David Hixon, Anthony Ponzini, Jack Somack, M. Emmet Walsh.

A MESSAGE FROM COUGAR and SEX AND THE SINGLE DOG (3). By Jean Raymond Maljean. March 4, 1968. Directed by MacIntyre Dixon; with Jay Devlin, Alix Elias, Marvin Peisner, Leonard Phipps, Toni Romer.

AS HAPPY AS KINGS (3). By Jack Richardson. March 11, 1968. Directed by C. K. Alexander; with Francine Beers, William Bush, Angus Cairns, Lon Clark, Donald Marye, Elizabeth Morgan.

SKIN TIGHT (3). By Frank Cucci. March 25, 1968. Directed by Colgate Salsbury; with Don Blakely, Janet Lee Parker, Robert Shea.

Playbox Studio. Robert S. Weinstein maintains facilities available to playwrights and directors who "package" shows for presentation at one or another (or at several) of the off-off-Broadway theaters. The Playbox Studio generally offered two-week runs, Wednesdays through Sundays. Productions this season included:

WOYZECK. By Georg Büchner; translated by Susan Shantl; adapted by Louis Simmon. Directed by Robert Volin; with Louis Simmon, Shelly Slater.

Play-House of the Ridiculous. John Vaccaro's vehicle for his far-out productions of original scripts. Played this season at the Bouwerie Lane Theater, offering an extended albeit intermittent run of a single production:

CONQUEST OF THE UNIVERSE. By Charles Ludlam; music by John Vaccaro. Directed by John Vaccaro; with Beverly Grant, Taylor Mead, Ondine, John Vaccaro, Ultra Violet, and Mary Woronov; music performed by The Third Eye.

Playwrights' Workshop. 'Ntoni Bastiano maintains this facility for productions "packaged" by directors or playwrights. Productions generally ran two weekends at the Playwrights' Workshop Theater. Recent presentations included:

NOVEMBER 22ND. By Tom Eyen. Directed by Tom Eyen; with Kay Michaels, Monty Montgomery, Bob Mooty.

The Rising Sun Theater. Produced new and classic plays at Christ Church Presbyterian, usually supervised by "house" directors, presented on weekends for three to five weeks. Recent productions included:

THE CELEBRATION. By Anton Chekhov. Directed by Dana Bate; with Melissa Churchill, Kirk London, Bennett Oberstein, Rehn Scofield, Rebecca Young.

Roundabout Theater. An off-off-Broadway repertory company directed by Gene Feist. Played Wednesdays through Sundays, at times doing several plays in repertory, and at other times engaging in lengthy "runs". Recent productions at the Roundabout Theater included:

THE BOND. By August Strindberg. Directed by Gene Feist; with Herschell Burton, Josephine Duffy, Lynne Garmston, Sterling Jensen, Elizabeth Owens, Winston May.

WAITING FOR LEFTY. By Clifford Odets. Directed by Gene Feist; with Joe Abramski, John Byrd, Ann D'Andrea, Robert A. Guinan, Elizabeth Owens, Hector J. Troy.

Theater Genesis. Ralph Cook produced and frequently directed a series of new plays and new musicals at Theater Genesis in St. Marks-in-the-Bowery Church. "Showcase" productions played from one to five nights, and "regular" productions played from two to four weekends. Interesting productions this season included:

WILLIE THE GERM. By Murray Mednick. Directed by Ralph Cook; with Michele Collison, Pat Cook, Delia Duck, Gene Elman, Victor Eschbach, Tom Lillard, Jerry Lipani.

FORENSIC AND THE NAVIGATORS. By Sam Shepard. Directed by Ralph Cook; with Beeson Carroll, Walter Hadler, Lee Kissman, O'Lan Johnson, Robert Schlee; music performed by The Moray Eels.

The Theater of The Riverside Church. Plays by established American and European writers were presented under the supervision of John Young. Plays ran Thursdays through Sundays, for one or two weeks, in a theater wing of The Riverside Church. This season's productions included:

SILENT NIGHT, LONELY NIGHT. By Robert Anderson. Directed by Kent Paul; with Alice Cannon, Devan Carter, Frank Geraci, Anne Lynn, Dolly Mallon, Richard Morse.

HIATUS. An "American adaptation" by Paul Giovanni of Jean Giraudoux' *Intermezzo.* Directed by Paul Giovanni; with Beth Bowden, Bruce Brighton, Joseph Daly, Spalding Gray, Richard Mazza, P.L. Pfeiffer.

Thresholds. An experimental theater group led by Donna Carlson and John Parkinson. While an occasional "package" production is brought in, this group generally gives new playwrights, or foreign playwrights not generally known in the United States, productions under either Miss Carlson's or Parkinson's supervision. Performances ran for four to five weekends, at the Thresholds Theater. Presentations this season included:

OUT AT SEA. By Slawomir Mrozek. Directed by John Parkinson; with Morris Mark Alpern, Cloice Fannin, Sam Kilman, Joseph D. Rosevich, William Tulley.

FREEDOM FOR CLEMENS. By Tankred Dorst. Directed by John Parkinson; with David Alan, Cloice Fannin, Carol Steiner.

NOW YOU SEE IT. By Kenneth Patchen. Directed by Don Signore; with Jean David, Cloice Fannin, Ted Henning, Richard Nettum, Joseph D. Rosevich, Mary Tiffany, Alice Worth.

Troupe Repertory Theater Club. Christopher St. John's establishment for productions "packaged" by playwrights, directors and sometimes himself. Plays ran several weekends at the Troupe Theater. Recent productions included:

TENNIS ANYONE? One of six related one-act plays by F. V. Hunt (group title is *The Park*). Directed by Christopher St. John; with Jacqueline Britt, Robert Shea.

CAST REPLACEMENTS AND TOURING COMPANIES

The following is a listing of some of the more important cast replacements in productions which opened in previous years, but which were still playing in New York during a substantial part of the 1967-68 season; or were still on a national tour; or opened in 1967-68 and cast a touring company in that same season. The name of the character is listed in italics beneath the title of the play in the first column, and in the second column appears the name of the actor who created the role and, immediately beneath, his subsequent replacements. The third column gives information about first-class touring companies of these shows (produced under the auspices of their original Broadway managements). Where there is more than one roadshow company (not including bus-truck troupes), #1, #2, and #3 appear before the name of the performer who created the role in those companies. Their subsequent replacements, if any, are listed beneath. A note on bus-truck tours appears at the end of this section.

	NEW YORK COMPANY	TOURING COMPANIES
THE APPLE TREE		
Eve, Barbára, Passionella	Barbara Harris 10/18/66 Phyllis Newman (matinees only) 11/23/66 (all perfs) 7/10/67 Barbara Harris (evenings only) 7/31/67 Carmen Alvarez (matinees only) 8/9/67 Sue Ann Langdon (evenings only) 11/1/67	
Adam, Sanjar, Flip	Alan Alda 10/18/66 Ken Kercheval 3/27/67 Hal Holbrook 4/6/67 Alan Alda 7/3/67	
BLACK COMEDY		
Brindsley Miller	Michael Crawford 2/12/67 Jordan Christopher 6/26/67	Jeremy Clyde 11/4/67
Carol Melkett	Lynn Redgrave 2/12/67 Jennifer Tilston 4/10/67	Jennifer Tilston 11/4/67

	NEW YORK COMPANY	TOURING COMPANIES
CABARET		
Emcee	Joel Grey 11/20/66 Martin Ross 1/1/68	#1 Robert Salvio 12/26/67 #2 Barry Dennen 2/28/68
Clifford Bradshaw	Bert Convy 11/20/66	#1 Gene Rupert 12/26/67 #2 Kevin Colson 2/28/68
Fraulein Schneider	Lotte Lenya 11/20/66 Peg Murray 3/6/67 Lotte Lenya 3/18/67	#1 Signe Hasso 12/26/67 #2 Lila Kedrova 2/28/68
Sally Bowles	Jill Haworth 11/20/66	#1 Melissa Hart 12/26/67 #2 Judi Dench 2/28/68
CACTUS FLOWER		
Stephanie	Lauren Bacall 12/8/65 Betsy Palmer 10/17/66 Lauren Bacall 10/24/66 Betsy Palmer 11/20/67	Elizabeth Allen 7/31/67
Julian	Barry Nelson 12/8/65 Kevin McCarthy 5/8/67 Barry Nelson 5/29/67 Lloyd Bridges 10/16/67	Hugh O'Brien 7/31/67
DON'T DRINK THE WATER		
Kilroy	Anthony Roberts 11/17/66 Len Cotchman 7/31/67	
Walter Hollander	Lou Jacobi 11/17/66	
Marion Hollander	Kay Medford 11/17/66 Peggy Cass 6/19/67	
THE FANTASTICKS		
The Narrator	Jerry Ohrbach 5/3/60 Gene Rupert Bert Convy John Cunningham Don Stewart David Cryer Keith Charles John Boni 1/13/65 Jack Mette 9/14/65 George Ogee Keith Charles John Boni	
The Girl	Rita Gardner 5/3/60 Carla Huston Liza Stuart Eileen Fulton Alice Cannon Royce Lenelle B.J. Ward 12/1/64 Leta Anderson 7/13/65 Carol Deems 12/5/66 Anne Kaye 5/28/68	
The Boy	Kenneth Nelson 5/3/60 Gino Conforti Jack Blackton Paul Giovanni Ty McConnell Richard Rothbard Gary Krawford Bob Spencer 9/5/64 Erik Howell Gary Krawford 12/12/67 Steve Skiles 2/6/68	

	NEW YORK COMPANY	TOURING COMPANIES
FIDDLER ON THE ROOF		
Tevye	Zero Mostel 9/22/64 Luther Adler 8/15/65 Herschel Bernardi 11/8/65 Harry Goz 8/14/67 Herschel Bernardi 9/18/67 Harry Goz 11/6/67	Luther Adler 4/11/66 Paul Lipsom (matinees only) 9/20/67 (all perfs.) 10/9/67 Theodore Bikel 12/28/67
Golde	Maria Karnilova 9/22/64 Helen Verbit 6/26/67 Maria Karnilova 7/17/67 Martha Schlamme 4/9/68	Dolores Wilson 4/11/68
FORTUNE AND MEN'S EYES		
Smitty	Terry Kiser 2/23/67	Peter Beiger 10/19/67
Queenie	Bill Moor 2/23/67	Bill Moor 10/19/67
GOLDEN BOY		
Joe Wellington	Sammy Davis Jr. 10/20/64	Sammy Davis Jr. 4/23/68
Lorna Moon	Paula Wayne 10/20/64	Gloria De Haven 4/23/68
HALLELUJAH, BABY!		
Georgina	Leslie Uggams 4/26/67	
Momma	Lillian Hayman 4/26/67	
Clem	Robert Hooks 4/26/67 Billy Dee Williams 6/26/67 Robert Hooks 10/23/67	
HELLO, DOLLY!		
Mrs. Dolly Gallagher Levi	Carol Channing 1/16/64 Ginger Rogers 8/9/65 Martha Raye 2/27/67 Betty Grable 6/12/67 Bibi Osterwald 11/6/67 Pearl Bailey 11/12/67	#1 Mary Martin 4/17/65 Dora Bryan 5/14/66 #2 Carol Channing 9/6/65 #3 Betty Grable 11/3/65 #4 Ginger Rogers 4/19/67 Dorothy Lamour (alternate) 8/23/67 Ginger Rogers 10/20/67 #5 Pearl Bailey 10/11/67
Horace Vandergelder	David Burns 1/16/64 Max Showalter 3/13/67 Cab Calloway 11/12/67	#1 Loring Smith 4/17/65 Replaced 5/14/66 #2 Horace McMahon 9/6/65 Milo Boulton #3 Max Showalter 11/3/65 #4 David Burns 4/19/67 Max Showalter 8/23/67 #5 Cab Calloway 10/11/67
THE HOMECOMING		
Max	Paul Rogers 1/5/67 William Roerick 10/16/67	William Roerick 10/16/67
Ruth	Vivien Merchant 1/5/67 Lynn Farleigh 4/24/67 Patricia Roe 6/26/67 Carolyn Jones 10/12/67	Carolyn Jones 10/16/67
Lenny	Ian Holm 1/5/67 Michael Jayston 4/24/67 Lloyd Battista 6/26/67 John Church 7/31/67	John Church 10/16/67

	NEW YORK COMPANY	TOURING COMPANIES
I DO! I DO!		
She (Agnes)	Mary Martin 12/5/66 Carol Lawrence (matinees only) 10/18/67 (all perfs.) 12/4/67	Mary Martin 4/8/68
He (Michael)	Robert Preston 12/5/66 Gordon MacRae (matinees only) 10/18/67 (all perfs.) 12/4/67	Robert Preston 4/8/68
THE IMPOSSIBLE YEARS		
Dr. Jack Kingsley	Alan King 10/13/65 Ed McMahon 1/17/66 Alan King 1/24/66 Sam Levene 8/22/66	Sam Levene 10/23/67
THE KILLING OF SISTER GEORGE		
June Buckridge	Beryl Reid 10/5/66	Claire Trevor 12/29/67 Hermione Baddeley 4/15/68
Alice "Childie" McNaught	Eileen Atkins 10/5/66	Natalie Schafer 12/29/67 Sylvia O'Brien 4/15/68
THE LITTLE FOXES (Revival)		
Regina Giddens	Anne Bancroft 10/26/67 Margaret Leighton 12/19/67	Margaret Leighton 1/22/68 Geraldine Page 3/18/68
Birdie Hubbard	Margaret Leighton 10/26/67 Felicia Monteliagre 12/19/67	Felicia Monteliagre 1/22/68 Betty Field 3/18/68
Alexandra Giddens	Maria Tucci 10/26/67 Geraldine Chaplin 12/19/67	Geraldine Chaplin 1/22/68 Maria Tucci 3/18/68
Benjamin Hubbard	George C. Scott 10/26/67 E.G. Marshall 12/19/67	E.G. Marshall 1/22/68 Richard Dysart 3/18/68
Oscar Hubbard	E.G. Marshall 10/26/67 Scott McKay 12/19/67	Scott McKay 1/22/68
William Marshall	William Prince 10/26/67 Liam Sullivan 12/19/67	Liam Sullivan 1/22/68 Jack Manning 3/18/68
Leo Hubbard	Austin Pendleton 10/26/67	Austin Pendleton 1/22/68 Franklin Kaiser 3/18/68
MAME		
Mame	Angela Lansbury 5/24/66 Sheila Smith 2/13/67 Angela Lansbury 2/27/67 Celeste Holm 8/14/67 Angela Lansbury 8/28/67 Janis Paige 4/1/68	#1 Celeste Holm 9/28/67 #2 Angela Lansbury 5/30/68
Vera Charles	Beatrice Arthur 5/24/66 Sheila Smith 3/27/67 Beatrice Arthur 4/10/67 Anne Francine 7/10/67 Audrey Christie 4/1/68	#1 Vicki Cummings 9/28/67 #2 Anne Francine 5/30/68
Young Patrick	Frankie Michaels 5/24/66 Stuart Getz 5/8/67 David Manning 4/1/68	#1 Shawn McGill 9/28/67 #2 Stuart Getz 5/30/68
MAN OF LA MANCHA		
Quixote (Cervantes)	Richard Kiley 11/22/65 José Ferrer 5/28/66 John Cullum 2/24/67	#1 José Ferrer 9/24/66 Richard Kiley 4/11/67 José Ferrer 7/17/67

	NEW YORK COMPANY	TOURING COMPANIES
	José Ferrer 4/11/67 David Atkinson 7/14/67	Richard Kiley 8/7/67 Keith Andes 12/4/67 #2 Keith Michell 4/24/68
Aldonza	Joan Diener 11/22/65 Marion Marlowe 1/17/67 Maura K. Wedge 4/11/67 Bernice Massi 7/25/67 Carolyn Maye (matinees only) 3/20/68	#1 Maura K. Wedge 9/24/66 Joan Diener 4/11/67 Marion Marlowe 7/31/67 Carolyn Maye 11/7/68 Natalie Costa 3/18/68 #2 Joan Diener 4/24/68

MACBIRD!

MacBird	Stacy Keach 2/22/67 Wayne Tippit 9/29/67	

THE STAR-SPANGLED GIRL

Andy Hobart	Anthony Perkins 12/21/66	
Norman Cornell	Richard Benjamin 12/21/66 Paul Sand 7/3/67	
Sophie Rauschmeyer	Connie Stevens 12/21/66 Sheila Wells 6/5/67	

SWEET CHARITY

Charity	Gwen Verdon 1/29/66 Helen Gallagher 7/11/66 Gwen Verdon 7/25/66 Helen Gallagher 7/1/67	#1 Juliet Prowse 12/29/66 Gretchen Wyler 4/29/68 #2 Chita Rivera 9/11/67

WAIT A MINIM!

Revue Cast	Sarah Atkinson 3/7/66 Kendrew Lascelles Michel Martel April Olrich Nigel Pegram Andrew Tracey Paul Tracey Dana Valery	Sarah Atkinson 4/18/67 Kendrew Lascelles Michel Martel April Olrich Nigel Pegram Andrew Tracey Paul Tracey Dana Valery

YOU KNOW I CAN'T HEAR YOU WHEN THE WATER'S RUNNING

Pawling, George, Chuck	Martin Balsam 3/13/67 Larry Blyden 2/27/68	Eddie Bracken 10/16/67
Harriet, Edith, Muriel	Eileen Heckart 3/13/67 Irene Dailey 2/27/68	Ruth Manning 10/16/67
Jack, Salesman, Herbert	George Grizzard 3/13/67 William Redfield 2/27/68	Robert Elson 10/16/67

YOU'RE A GOOD MAN CHARLIE BROWN

Charlie Brown	Gary Burghoff 3/7/67 Sean Simpson 3/4/68	#1 Wendell Burton 6/1/67 #2 David Rhys Anderson 10/18/67 #3 Jim Ricketts 12/19/67 #4 Gary Burghoff 3/12/68 #5 Alan Lofft 5/30/68
Lucy	Reva Rose 3/7/67	#1 Janell Pulis 6/1/67 #2 Bonnie Anten 10/18/67 #3 Ann Gibbs 12/19/67 #4 Judy Kaye 3/12/68 #5 Cathy Wallace 5/30/68

	NEW YORK COMPANY	TOURING COMPANIES
Snoopy	Bill Hinnant 3/7/67	#1 Austin O'Toole 6/1/67 #2 Don Potter 10/18/67 #3 Bob Becker 12/19/67 #4 Robert Towers 3/12/68 #5 Grant Cowan 5/30/68

BUS-TRUCK TOURS: These are touring productions designed for maximum mobility and ease of handling in one-night and split-week stands (with occasional engagements of a week or more). Among Broadway shows on tour in the season of 1967-68 were the following: *Wait Until Dark* with Phyllis Kirk, 47 cities 9/22/67-11/30/67; *The Impossible Years* with Tom Ewell, 56 cities 10/2/67-12/16/67, 38 cities 2/13/68-3/30/68; *On a Clear Day You Can See Forever* with John Raitt/Howard Keel/Bill Hayes and Carla Alberghetti, 71 cities 12/31/67-5/26/68; *Stop the World I Want to Get Off* with Jackie Warner, 104 cities 9/25/67-11/30/67, 1/23/68-3/31/68; *The Lion in Winter* with Walter Slezak and Margaret Phillips, 75 cities 1/17/68-5/5/68; *Hello, Dolly!* with Dorothy Lamour, 93 cities 11/14/67-5/26/68 (continuing); *The Roar of the Greasepaint, the Smell of the Crowd* with Edward Earle and David Jones, 106 cities 9/21/67-4/6/68.

FACTS AND FIGURES

LONG RUNS ON BROADWAY

(500 or more performances. Where there are title similarities, the production is identified as follows: (p) straight play version, (m) musical version, (r) revival)

THROUGH MAY 31, 1968

(PLAYS MARKED WITH ASTERISK WERE STILL PLAYING JUNE 1, 1968)

Plays	*Number Performances*
Life with Father	3,224
Tobacco Road	3,182
My Fair Lady	2,717
Abie's Irish Rose	2,327
Oklahoma!	2,212
*Hello, Dolly!	1,824
Harvey	1,775
South Pacific	1,694
Born Yesterday	1,642
Mary, Mary	1,572
The Voice of the Turtle	1,557
*Fiddler on the Roof	1,540
Barefoot in the Park	1,530
Arsenic and Old Lace	1,444
The Sound of Music	1,443
How To Succeed in Business Without Really Trying	1,417
Hellzapoppin	1,404
The Music Man	1,375
Funny Girl	1,348
Angel Street	1,295
Lightnin'	1,291
The King and I	1,246
Guys and Dolls	1,200
Mister Roberts	1,157
Annie Get Your Gun	1,147
The Seven Year Itch	1,141
Pins and Needles	1,108
Kiss Me, Kate	1,070
Pajama Game	1,063
*Man of La Mancha	1,052
*Cactus Flower	1,033
The Teahouse of the August Moon	1,027
Damn Yankees	1,019
Never Too Late	1,007
Any Wednesday	982
A Funny Thing Happened on the Way to the Forum	964
The Odd Couple	964
Anna Lucasta	957
Kiss and Tell	957
The Moon Is Blue	924
Bells Are Ringing	924
Luv	901
Can-Can	892
Carousel	890
Hats Off to Ice	889
Fanny	888
Follow the Girls	882
Camelot	873
The Bat	867
My Sister Eileen	865
White Cargo	864
Song of Norway	860
A Streetcar Named Desire	855
Comedy in Music	849
*Mame (m)	846

Plays	Number Performances
You Can't Take It With You	837
La Plume de Ma Tante	835
Three Men on a Horse	835
The Subject Was Roses	832
Inherit the Wind	806
No Time for Sergeants	796
Fiorello!	795
Where's Charley?	792
The Ladder	789
Oliver	774
State of the Union	765
The First Year	760
Two for the Seesaw	750
Death of a Salesman	742
Sons o' Fun	742
Gentlemen Prefer Blondes	740
The Man Who Came to Dinner	739
Call Me Mister	734
West Side Story	732
High Button Shoes	727
Finian's Rainbow	725
Claudia	722
The Gold Diggers	720
Carnival	719
The Diary of Anne Frank	717
I Remember Mama	714
Tea and Sympathy	712
Junior Miss	710
Seventh Heaven	704
Gypsy (m)	702
The Miracle Worker	700
Cat on a Hot Tin Roof	694
Li'l Abner	693
Peg o' My Heart	692
The Children's Hour	691
Dead End	687
The Lion and the Mouse	686
Dear Ruth	683
East Is West	680
Come Blow Your Horn	677
The Most Happy Fella	676
The Doughgirls	671
The Impossible Years	670
Irene	670
Boy Meets Girl	669
Beyond the Fringe	667
Who's Afraid of Virginia Woolf?	664
Blithe Spirit	657

Plays	Number Performances
The Women	657
A Trip to Chinatown	657
Bloomer Girl	654
The Fifth Season	654
Rain	648
Witness for the Prosecution	645
Call Me Madam	644
Janie	642
The Green Pastures	640
Auntie Mame (p)	639
*Cabaret	639
A Man for All Seasons	637
The Fourposter	632
The Tenth Man	623
Is Zat So?	618
Anniversary Waltz	615
The Happy Time (p)	614
Separate Rooms	613
Affairs of State	610
Star and Garter	609
The Student Prince	608
Sweet Charity	608
Bye Bye Birdie	607
Broadway	603
Adonis	603
Street Scene	601
Kiki	600
Flower Drum Song	600
Don't Drink the Water	598
Wish You Were Here	598
A Society Circus	596
Blossom Time	592
The Two Mrs. Carrols	585
Kismet	583
Detective Story	581
Brigadoon	581
No Strings	580
Brother Rat	577
Show Boat	572
The Show-Off	571
Sally	570
Golden Boy (m)	568
One Touch of Venus	567
Happy Birthday	564
Look Homeward, Angel	564
The Glass Menagerie	561
Wonderful Town	559
Rose Marie	557

Plays	Number Performances
Strictly Dishonorable	557
A Majority of One	556
Toys in the Attic	556
Sunrise at Campobello	556
Jamaica	555
Stop the World—I Want to Get Off	555
Ziegfeld Follies	553
Floradora	553
Dial "M" for Murder	552
Good News	551
Let's Face It	547
*I Do! I Do!	543
Milk and Honey	543
Within the Law	541
The Music Master	540
Pal Joey	540
What Makes Sammy Run?	540
What a Life	538
The Unsinkable Molly Brown	532
The Red Mill (r)	531
A Raisin in the Sun	530
The Solid Gold Cadillac	526
Irma La Douce	524
The Boomerang	522
Rosalinda	521
The Best Man	520
Chauve Souris	520
Blackbirds	518
Sunny	517
Victoria Regina	517
Half a Sixpence	511
The Vagabond King	511
*You Know I Can't Hear You When the Water's Running	510
The New Moon	509
The World of Suzie Wong	508
Shuffle Along	504
Up in Central Park	504
Carmen Jones	503
The Member of the Wedding	501
Panama Hattie	501
Personal Appearance	501
Bird in Hand	500
Room Service	500
Sailor, Beware!	500
Tomorrow the World	500

LONG RUNS OFF BROADWAY

Plays	Number Performances
*The Fantasticks	3,378
The Threepenny Opera	2,611
The Blacks	1,408
Little Mary Sunshine	1,143
Leave It to Jane (r)	928
The Mad Show	871
A View From the Bridge (r)	780
The Boy Friend (r)	763
The Pocket Watch	725
The Connection	722
The Knack	685
The Balcony	672
America Hurrah	634
Hogan's Goat	607
The Trojan Women (r)	600
Krapp's Last Tape and The Zoo Story	582
The Dumbwaiter and The Collection	578
The Crucible (r)	571
The Iceman Cometh (r)	565
The Hostage (r)	545
*You're a Good Man Charlie Brown	542
Six Characters in Search of an Author (r)	529
Happy Ending and Day of Absence	504
The Boys From Syracuse (r)	500

DRAMA CRITICS CIRCLE VOTING 1967-68

The New York Drama Critics Circle voted *Rosencrantz and Guildenstern Are Dead* the best play of the season regardless of origin by a majority of 13 first-choice votes out of 20 on the first ballot, so that no second point-system ballot was necessary to determine the award, as in the past two seasons. Other first-choice votes for best play were distributed as follows: *A Day in the Death of Joe Egg,* 4; *I Never Sang for My Father,* 1; *Plaza Suite,* 1; *The Price,* 1.

The critics voted *Your Own Thing* the best musical of the season by a majority of 9 first-choice votes out of 16 (there were 4 abstentions in this category). Other first-choice votes for best musical were distributed as follows: *George M!,* 2; *Hair,* 2; *The Happy Time,* 2; *In Circles,* 1.

Since the critics' best play citation went to a British script, there was a ballot of first choices in the category of best American play, with the votes distributed as follows: *The Price,* 7; *Plaza Suite,* 3; *The Prime of Miss Jean Brodie,* 3; *I Never Sang for My Father,* 2; *The Beard,* 1; *More Stately Mansions,* 1; *Saturday Night,* 1; *Summertree,* 1; Abstained, 1. No play received a majority of first-choice votes out of the 19 cast (with one abstention), and it was then voted to give no award for a best American play, instead of proceeding to a second point-system ballot in this category.

Here's the way the individual members of the New York Drama Critics Circle voted:

FIRST BALLOTS IN CRITICS VOTING

Critic	*Best Play*	*Best Musical*	*Best American Play*
Clive Barnes *Times*	Rosencrantz and Guildenstern Are Dead	Your Own Thing	The Price
Whitney Bolton *Morning Telegraph*	I Never Sang for My Father	Your Own Thing	I Never Sang
John Chapman *Daily News*	R & G	George M!	The Price
Harold Clurman *The Nation*	The Price	(Abstain)	The Price
Ethel Colby *Journal of Commerce*	R & G	The Happy Time	Plaza Suite
Richard Cooke *Wall St. Journal*	R & G	Your Own Thing	The Price
Jack Gaver UPI	R & G	George M!	The Price
Brendan Gill *New Yorker*	A Day in the Death of Joe Egg	Your Own Thing	Summertree
William H. Glover AP	Joe Egg	Your Own Thing	The Price
Martin Gottfried *Women's Wear Daily*	R & G	(Abstain)	Saturday Night
Henry Hewes *Saturday Review*	R & G	Hair	More Stately Mansions
Edward Sothern Hipp *Newark News*	R & G	(Abstain)	I Never Sang
Ted Kalem *Time*	R & G	(Abstain)	(Abstain)

Critic	*Best Play*	*Best Musical*	*Best American Play*
Walter Kerr *Times*	Joe Egg	Your Own Thing	The Prime of Miss Jean Brodie
Jack Kroll *Newsweek*	R & G	Hair	The Beard
Emory Lewis *Cue*	Joe Egg	In Circles	Jean Brodie
Hobe Morrison *Variety*	Plaza Suite	The Happy Time	Plaza Suite
George Oppenheimer *Newsday*	R & G	Your Own Thing	The Price
William Raidy Newhouse Papers	R & G	Your Own Thing	Jean Brodie
Richard Watts Jr. *Post*	R & G	Your Own Thing	Plaza Suite

Choices of some other critics:

Critic	*Best Play*	*Best Musical*
Judith Crist "Today"	R & G	Your Own Thing
Edwin Newman WNBC-TV	Joe Egg	(Abstain)
Allan Jefferys WABC-TV	I Never Sang	The Happy Time
Theodore Hoffman Westinghouse Broadcasting	Scuba Duba	Hair
Stanley Kauffmann *Die Zeit*	Joe Egg	In Circles
Norman Nadel Scripps-Howard	R & G	(Abstain)
Leo Lerman *Mademoiselle*	Joe Egg	Your Own Thing
Tom Prideaux *Life*	R & G	Your Own Thing

NEW YORK DRAMA CRITICS CIRCLE AWARDS

Listed below are the New York Drama Critics Circle Awards, classified as follows: (1) Best American Play, (2) Best Foreign Play, (3) Best Musical, (4) Best, regardless of category.

1935-36—(1) Winterset
1936-37—(1) High Tor
1937-38—(1) Of Mice and Men, (2) Shadow and Substance
1938-39—(1) No award, (2) The White Steed
1939-40—(1) The Time of Your Life
1940-41—(1) Watch on the Rhine, (2) The Corn Is Green
1941-42—(1) No award, (2) Blithe Spirit
1942-43—(1) The Patriots
1943-44—(1) No award, (2) Jacobowsky and the Colonel
1944-45—(1) The Glass Menagerie
1945-46—(1) No award, (2) No Award, (3) Carousel
1946-47—(1) All My Sons, (2) No Exit, (3) Brigadoon
1947-48—(1) A Streetcar Named Desire, (2) The Winslow Boy

1948-49—(1) Death of a Salesman, (2) The Madwoman of Chaillot, (3) South Pacific
1949-50—(1) The Member of the Wedding, (2) The Cocktail Party, (3) The Consul
1950-51—(1) Darkness at Noon, (2) The Lady's Not for Burning, (3) Guys and Dolls
1951-52—(1) I Am a Camera, (2) Venus Observed, (3) Pal Joey (Special citation to Don Juan in Hell)
1952-53—(1) Picnic, (2) The Love of Four Colonels, (3) Wonderful Town
1953-54—(1) The Teahouse of the August Moon, (2) Ondine, (3) The Golden Apple
1954-55—(1) Cat on a Hot Tin Roof, (2) Witness for the Prosecution, (3) The Saint of Bleecker Street
1955-56—(1) The Diary of Anne Frank, (2) Tiger at the Gates, (3) My Fair Lady
1956-57—(1) Long Day's Journey Into Night, (2) Waltz of the Torreadors, (3) The Most Happy Fella
1957-58—(1) Look Homeward, Angel, (2) Look Back in Anger, (3) The Music Man
1958-59—(1) A Raisin in the Sun, (2) The Visit, (3) La Plume de Ma Tante
1959-60—(1) Toys in the Attic, (2) Five Finger Exercise, (3) Fiorello!
1960-61—(1) All the Way Home, (2) A Taste of Honey, (3) Carnival
1961-62—(1) The Night of the Iguana, (2) A Man for All Seasons, (3) How To Succeed in Business Without Really Trying
1962-63—(4) Who's Afraid of Virginia Woolf? (Special citation to Beyond the Fringe)
1963-64—(4) Luther, (3) Hello, Dolly! (Special citation to The Trojan Women)
1964-65—(4) The Subject Was Roses, (3) Fiddler on the Roof
1965-66—(4) The Persecution and Assassination of Marat as Performed by the Inmates of the Asylum of Charenton Under the Direction of the Marquis de Sade, (3) Man of La Mancha
1966-67—(4) The Homecoming, (3) Cabaret
1967-68—(4) Rosencrantz and Guildenstern Are Dead, (3) Your Own Thing (1) No award

PULITZER PRIZE WINNERS

1917-18—Why Marry?, by Jesse Lynch Williams
1918-19—No award
1919-20—Beyond the Horizon, by Eugene O'Neill
1920-21—Miss Lulu Bett, by Zona Gale
1921-22—Anna Christie, by Eugene O'Neill
1922-23—Icebound, by Owen Davis
1923-24—Hell-bent for Heaven, by Hatcher Hughes
1924-25—They Knew What They Wanted, by Sidney Howard
1925-26—Craig's Wife, by George Kelly
1926-27—In Abraham's Bosom, by Paul Green
1927-28—Strange Interlude, by Eugene O'Neill
1928-29—Street Scene, by Elmer Rice
1929-30—The Green Pastures, by Marc Connelly
1930-31—Alison's House, by Susan Glaspell
1931-32—Of Thee I Sing, by George S. Kaufman, Morrie Ryskind, Ira and George Gershwin
1932-33—Both Your Houses, by Maxwell Anderson
1933-34—Men in White, by Sidney Kingsley
1934-35—The Old Maid, by Zoë Akins
1935-36—Idiot's Delight, by Robert E. Sherwood
1936-37—You Can't Take It with You, by Moss Hart and George S. Kaufman
1937-38—Our Town, by Thornton Wilder
1938-39—Abe Lincoln in Illinois, by Robert E. Sherwood
1939-40—The Time of Your Life, by William Saroyan
1940-41—There Shall Be No Night, by Robert E. Sherwood
1941-42—No award
1942-43—The Skin of Our Teeth, by Thornton Wilder
1943-44—No award
1944-45—Harvey, by Mary Chase
1945-46—State of the Union, by Howard Lindsay and Russel Crouse
1946-47—No award.
1947-48—A Streetcar Named Desire, by Tennessee Williams
1948-49—Death of a Salesman, by Arthur Miller
1949-50—South Pacific, by Richard Rodgers, Oscar Hammerstein II and Joshua Logan

1950-51—No award
1951-52—The Shrike, by Joseph Kramm
1952-53—Picnic, by William Inge
1953-54—The Teahouse of the August Moon, by John Patrick
1954-55—Cat on a Hot Tin Roof, by Tennessee Williams
1955-56—The Diary of Anne Frank, by Frances Goodrich and Albert Hackett
1956-57—Long Day's Journey into Night, by Eugene O'Neill
1957-58—Look Homeward, Angel, by Ketti Frings
1958-59—J. B., by Archibald MacLeish
1959-60—Fiorello!, by Jerome Weidman, George Abbott, Sheldon Harnick and Jerry Bock
1960-61—All the Way Home, by Tad Mosel
1961-62—How to Succeed in Business Without Really Trying, by Abe Burrows, Willie Gilbert, Jack Weinstock and Frank Loesser
1962-63—No award
1963-64—No award
1964-65—The Subject Was Roses, by Frank D. Gilroy
1965-66—No award
1966-67—A Delicate Balance, by Edward Albee
1967-68—No award

ADDITIONAL PRIZES AND AWARDS, 1967-1968

The following is a list of major prizes and awards for theatrical achievement. In all cases the names of winners—persons, productions or organizations—appear in **bold face type.**

MARGO JONES AWARDS. **Paul Baker,** managing director of Dallas Theater Center, for daring and continuous new play production. **George C. White** and the **Eugene O'Neill Memorial Theater** for their work in developing new playwrights.

KELCEY ALLEN AWARD. **Brooks Atkinson** in recognition of his lifelong devotion to the theater as reviewer, critic, author and humanist.

CLARENCE DERWENT AWARDS (for best non-featured performances). **Catherine Burns** as Monica in *The Prime of Miss Jean Brodie.* **David Birney** as Young Man in *Summertree.*

DRAMA DESK-VERNON RICE AWARDS (for outstanding contribution to off-Broadway theater). Playwrights: **Ron Cowen** (*Summertree*), **Israel Horovitz** (*The Indian Wants the Bronx*), **Bruce Jay Friedman** (*Scuba Duba*), **Ed Bullins** (*Three Plays by Ed Bullins*). Directors: **Donald Driver** (*Your Own Thing*), **Tom O'Horgan** (*Tom Paine*), **Robert Moore** (*The Boys in the Band*). Composers: **Al Carmines** (*In Circles*), **Galt MacDermot** (*Hair*). Organizations: **The New York Shakespeare Festival Public Theater, The Negro Ensemble Company.**

DRAMA DESK AWARD (for the best performance in a repertory company). **Helen Hayes** as Mrs. Fisher in *The Show-Off.*

JOSEPH MAHARAM FOUNDATION AWARDS (for design). Straight play scene design, **Ming Cho Lee** for *Ergo.* Musical scene design, **Peter Wexler** for *The Happy Time.* Costumes, **Nancy Potts** for *The Show-Off, Pantagleize, Exit the King, The Cherry Orchard.*

SAM S. SHUBERT AWARD. **Neil Simon,** in recognition of his outstanding contribution to the American theater.

VILLAGE VOICE OFF-BROADWAY (OBIE) AWARDS (for off-Broadway achievement). Best actress, **Billie Dixon** as Harlow in *The Beard.* Best actor, **Al Pacino** as Murph in *The Indian Wants the Bronx.* Best director, **Michael A. Schultz** for *Song of the Lusitanian Bogey.* Best musical, ***In Circles*** by Gertrude Stein and Al Carmines. Best foreign play, ***The Memorandum*** by Vaclav Havel. Best design, **Robert LaVigne** for *A Midsummer Night's Dream* and *Endecott and the Red Cross.* Distinguished direction, **John Hancock** (*A Midsummer Night's Dream*), **Rip Torn** (*The Beard*). Distinguished playwriting, **Israel Horovitz** (*The Indian Wants the Bronx*), **John Guare** (*Muzeeka*), **Sam Shepard** (*Forensic and the Navigators* and *Melodrama Play*). Distinguished performances, **John Cazale** (*Line* and *The Indian Wants the Bronx*), **James Coco** (*Fragments*), **Jean David** (*Istanbul*), **Cliff Gorman** (*The Boys in the Band*), **Mari Gorman** (*The Memorandum* and *Walking to Waldheim*), **Moses**

Gunn (The Negro Ensemble Company repertory), **Peggy Pope** (*Muzeeka*), **Roy R. Scheider** (*Stephen D*). Special citations to: **El Teatro Campesino** for creating a workers' theater to demonstrate the politics of survival; **The Fortune Society** for expanding public awareness of the problems of the ex-convict and the prison system in America; **The Negro Ensemble Company** for sustained excellence in repertory theater and the development of new theatrical talent; **San Francisco Mime Troupe** for uniting theater and revolution and grooving in the park.

OUTER CIRCLE AWARDS (voted by critics who cover New York Theater for out-of-town periodicals). Outstanding performances: **Pearl Bailey** as Dolly Gallagher Levi and **Cab Calloway** as Horace Vandergelder in *Hello, Dolly!*, **Harold Gary** as Gregory Solomon in *The Price*, **Joel Grey** as George M. Cohan in *George M!*, **Helen Hayes** as Mrs. Fisher in *The Show-Off*, **Zena Jasper** as Rochelle in *Saturday Night*. Outstanding productions: ***Rosencrantz and Guildenstern Are Dead, George M!, The Price.*** **Herman Shumlin** for his career as a director and for his playwriting debut with *Spofford*, which he also directed. **Mike Nichols** for direction of *Plaza Suite*. Citations to **The Forum Theater** of The Repertory Theater of Lincoln Center and **The New York Shakespeare Festival Public Theater** as important new forces in the American theater.

GEORGE JEAN NATHAN AWARD (for drama criticism). **Elizabeth Hardwick,** New York *Review of Books.*

THE TONY AWARDS

The Antoinette Perry (Tony) Awards are voted by members of The League of New York Theaters, the governing bodies of The Dramatists Guild, Actors Equity and the Society of Stage Directors and Choreographers, and members of the official first and second night press lists, from a list of four nominees in each category prepared by a committe of critics. Here are the 1967-68 Tony nominees selected by a committee composed of Harold Clurman, William Glover, Otis L. Guernsey Jr., Allan Jefferys, Leo Lerman, George Oppenheimer and Tom Prideaux, with the winners in the final voting listed in **bold face type:**

BEST PLAY (award goes to both producer and author). *A Day in the Death of Joe Egg* by Peter Nichols, produced by Joseph Cates and Henry Fownes; *Plaza Suite* by Neil Simon, produced by Saint-Subber; ***Rosencrantz and Guildenstern Are Dead*** by **Tom Stoppard,** produced by **David Merrick Arts Foundation;** *The Price* by Arthur Miller, produced by Robert Whitehead.

BEST MUSICAL PLAY (award goes to both producer and author). ***Hallelujah, Baby!*** by Arthur Laurents, produced by Albert Selden, Hal James, Jane Nusbaum, Harry Rigby; *The Happy Time* by N. Richard Nash, produced by David Merrick; *How Now, Dow Jones* by Max Shulman, produced by David Merrick; *Illya Darling* by Jules Dassin, produced by Kermit Bloomgarden.

ACTOR—Dramatic star. **Martin Balsam** in *You Know I Can't Hear You When the Water's Running;* Albert Finney in *A Day in the Death of Joe Egg;* Milo O'Shea in *Staircase;* Alan Webb in *I Never Sang for My Father.*

ACTRESS—Dramatic star. **Zoe Caldwell** in *The Prime of Miss Jean Brodie;* Colleen Dewhurst in *More Stately Mansions;* Maureen Stapleton in *Plaza Suite;* Dorothy Tutin in *Portrait of a Queen.*

ACTOR—Musical star. **Robert Goulet** in *The Happy Time;* Robert Hooks in *Hallelujah, Baby!;* Anthony Roberts in *How Now, Dow Jones;* David Wayne in *The Happy Time.*

ACTRESS—Musical star. Melina Mercouri in *Illya Darling;* **Patricia Routledge** in *Darling of the Day;* (tie for first place) **Leslie Uggams** in *Hallelujah, Baby!*; Brenda Vaccaro in *How Now, Dow Jones.*

ACTOR—Dramatic featured or supporting. Paul Hecht, Brian Murray and John Wood in *Rosencrantz and Guildenstern Are Dead;* **James Patterson** in *The Birthday Party.*

ACTRESS—Dramatic featured or supporting. Pert Kelton in *Spofford;* **Zena Walker** in *A Day in the Death of Joe Egg;* Ruth White in *The Birthday Party;* Eleanor Wilson in *Weekend.*

ACTOR—Musical featured or supporting. Scott Jacoby in *Golden Rainbow;* Nikos Kourkoulos in *Illya Darling;* Mike Rupert in *The Happy Time;* **Hiram Sherman** in *How Now, Dow Jones.*

ACTRESS—Musical featured or supporting. Geula Gill in *Grand Music Hall of Israel;* Julie Gregg in *The Happy Time;* **Lillian Hayman** in *Hallelujah, Baby!;* Alice Playten in *Henry, Sweet Henry.*

DIRECTOR—Play. Michael Blakemore for *Joe Egg;* Derek Goldby for *Rosencrantz and Guildenstern Are Dead;* **Mike Nichols** for *Plaza Suite;* Alan Schneider for *You Know I Can't Hear You When the Water's Running.*

DIRECTOR—Musical play. George Abbott for *How Now, Dow Jones;* **Gower Champion** for *The Happy Time;* Jules Dassin for *Illya Darling;* Burt Shevelove for *Hallelujah, Baby!*

COMPOSER AND LYRICIST. Elmer Bernstein and Carolyn Leigh for *How Now, Dow Jones;* Manos Hadjidakis and Joe Darion for *Illya Darling;* John Kander and Fred Ebb for *The Happy Time;* **Jule Styne, Betty Comden** and **Adolph Green** for *Hallelujah, Baby!*

SCENIC DESIGNER. Boris Aronson for *The Price;* **Desmond Heeley** for *Rosencrantz and Guildenstern Are Dead;* Robert Randolph for *Golden Rainbow;* Peter Wexler for *The Happy Time.*

COSTUME DESIGNER. Jane Greenwood for *More Stately Mansions;* **Desmond Heeley** for *Rosencrantz and Guildenstern Are Dead;* Irene Sharaff for *Hallelujah, Baby!;* Freddy Wittop for *The Happy Time.*

CHOREOGRAPHER. Michael Bennett for *Henry, Sweet Henry;* Kevin Carlisle for *Hallelujah, Baby!;* **Gower Champion** for *The Happy Time;* Onna White for *Illya Darling.*

SPECIAL AWARDS. **Audrey Hepburn, Carol Channing, Pearl Bailey, David Merrick, Maurice Chevalier, APA-Phoenix** (accepted by Helen Hayes), **Marlene Dietrich.**

VARIETY'S POLL OF NEW YORK DRAMA CRITICS

Each year, representative New York drama critics are polled by *Variety* to learn their choices for bests in categories other than best play or musical. Eighteen critics participated in the balloting on the 1967-68 season: Clive Barnes, Ethel Colby, Richard Cooke, Martin Gottfried, Walter Kerr, Harold Clurman, Henry Hewes, Ted Kalem, Emory Lewis, Tom Prideaux, Leonard Harris, Allan Jefferys, Edwin Newman, David Goldman, Alvin Klein, Peggy Stockton, Jack Gaver, Norman Nadel. The names of those cited in the various categories appear below, together with the number of critics' votes received. The winner in each category is listed in **bold face type.**

MALE LEAD—Straight play. **Albert Finney** (5) in *A Day in the Death of Joe Egg,* John Colicos (4) in *Soldiers,* George C. Scott (2) in *Plaza Suite,* Melvyn Douglas (1) in *Spofford,* Ellis Rabb (1) in *Pantagleize,* George Rose (1) in *Loot,* Roy Dotrice (1) in *Brief Lives,* Alan Webb (1) in *I Never Sang for My Father,* No choice (2).

FEMALE LEAD—Straight play. **Zoe Caldwell** (9) in *The Prime of Miss Jean Brodie.* Maureen Stapleton (5) in *Plaza Suite,* Marian Seldes (2) in *Before You Go,* Zena Walker (2) in *Joe Egg.*

MALE LEAD—Musical. Joel Grey (5) in *George M!,* Robert Goulet (4) in *The Happy Time,* Anthony Roberts (2) in *How Now, Dow Jones,* Walter McGinn (1) in *Here's Where I Belong,* **No choice** (6).

FEMALE LEAD—Musical. **Patricia Routledge** (12) in *Darling of the Day,* Shelley Plimpton (2) in *Hair,* No choice (4).

ACTOR SUPPORTING ROLE. **Harold Gary** (8) in *The Price,* Paul Hecht (4) in *R & G,* James Patterson (3) and Ed Flanders (2) in *The Birthday Party,* Sydney Walker (1) in *Pantagleize.*

ACTRESS SUPPORTING ROLE. **Pert Kelton** (4) in *Spofford.* (tie) **Zena Walker** (4) in *Joe Egg,* Rosemary Murphy (2) in *Weekend,* Joan Hickson (1) in *Joe Egg,* Margaret Leighton (1) in *The Little Foxes,* Alice Playten (1) in *Henry, Sweet Henry,* Kate Reid (1) in *The Price,* Carole Shelley (1) in *Loot,* Sada Thompson (1) in *Johnny No-Trump,* Brenda Vaccaro (1) in *How Now, Dow Jones,* Ruth White (1) in *The Birthday Party.*

MOST PROMISING NEW BROADWAY ACTOR. Mike Rupert (3) in *The Happy Time,* Milo O'Shea (2) in *Staircase,* Roy Cooper (1) in *Jean Brodie,* Ed Flanders (1) in *The Birthday Party,* Paul Hecht (1) and John Wood (1) in *R & G,* Ian McKellen (1) and Ian McShane (1) in *The Promise,* **No choice** (7).

MOST PROMISING NEW BROADWAY ACTRESS. **Zena Walker** (6) in *Joe Egg,* Barbara Ferris (2) in *There's a Girl in My Soup,* Carol Cole (1) in *Weekend,* Geraldine Chaplin (1) in *The Little Foxes,* Madeline Kahn (1) in *Leonard Sillman's New Faces of 1968,* Bernadette Peters (1) in *Johnny No-Trump,* Shelley Plimpton (1) in *Hair,* No choice (5).

BEST DIRECTOR. **Derek Goldby** (8) for *R & G* and *Loot,* Tom O'Horgan (6) for *Hair,* Joe Layton (1) for *George M!,* Mike Nichols (1) for *Plaza Suite,* Stephen Porter (1) for *The Show-Off,* José Quintero (1) for *The Seven Descents of Myrtle.*

BEST SCENIC DESIGNER. **Desmond Heeley** (5) for *R & G,* Peter Wexler (3) for *The Happy Time,* Boris Aronson (2) for *The Price,* Ming Cho Lee (2) for *Here's Where I Belong,* Julia Trevelyan Oman (2) for *Brief Lives,* Edward Burbridge (1) for *Mike Downstairs,* William Ritman (1) for *The Birthday Party,* Jo Mielziner (1) for *The Seven Descents,* No choice (1).

BEST COSTUME DESIGNER. **Desmond Heeley** (7) for *R & G,* Nancy Potts (3) for APA-Phoenix productions, Jane Greenwood (2) for *More Stately Mansions* and *Jean Brodie,* Raoul Pène du Bois (2) for *Darling of the Day,* Freddy Wittop (1) for *George M!,* No choice (3).

BEST COMPOSER. **Galt MacDermot** (8) for *Hair,* Elmer Bernstein (2) for *How Now, Dow Jones,* John Kander (2) for *The Happy Time,* Jule Styne (2) for *Darling of the Day,* George M. Cohan (1) for *George M!,* No choice (3).

BEST LYRICIST. **Gerome Ragni** and **James Rado** (7) for *Hair,* E.Y. Harburg (6) for *Darling of the Day,* Fred Ebb (2) for *The Happy Time,* Carolyn Leigh (1) for *How Now, Dow Jones,* No choice (2).

MOST PROMISING PLAYWRIGHT. **Tom Stoppard** (14) for *R & G,* Stephen Levi (1) for *Daphne in Cottage D,* Mary Mercier (1) for *Johnny No-Trump,* Peter Nichols (1) for *Joe Egg,* No choice (1).

ORIGINAL CAST ALBUMS OF NEW YORK SHOWS

The following albums were issued during the 1967-68 season. The first number appearing after each title is the number of the monaural version, the second the number of the stereo version. If there was only one version it is indicated in parentheses by (M) monaural or (S) stereo.

Darling of the Day. RCA Victor. LOC-1149; LSC-1149.
George M! Columbia. (S) KOS-3200.
Golden Rainbow. Columbia. (S) 1001.
Hair. RCA Victor. LOC-1143; LSO-1143.
The Happy Time. RCA Victor. LOC-1144; LSO-1144.
Hello, Dolly! (German Cast). Columbia. OL-6710; OS-3110.
Hello, Dolly! (New Broadway Cast). RCA Victor. LOC-1147; LOS-1147.
Henry, Sweet Henry. ABC. (S) OC-4.
How Now, Dow Jones. RCA Victor. LOC-1142; LSO-1142.
In Circles. Avant-Garde. m-108; s-108.
Jacques Brel is Alive and Well and Living in Paris. Columbia. (S) D2S-779.
Now Is the Time for All Good Men. Columbia. OL-6730; OS-3130.
South Pacific (Lincoln Center revival). Columbia. OL-6700; OS-3100.
Your Own Thing. RCA Victor. LOC-1148; LSO-1148.

1967-68 PUBLICATION OF RECENTLY-PRODUCED PLAYS

After The Rain. John Bowen. Random House.
America Hurrah. Jean-Claude van Itallie. Coward-McCann.
Black Comedy. Peter Shaffer. Stein and Day.
Brief Lives. Patrick Garland. Faber and Faber.
A Day in the Death of Joe Egg. Peter Nichols. Grove Press.
Don't Drink the Water. Woody Allen. Random House.
Everything in the Garden. Edward Albee's adaptation of the play by Giles Cooper. Atheneum.
Fortune and Men's Eyes. John Herbert. Grove Press.
Halfway up the Tree. Peter Ustinov. Random House.
Harpers Ferry. Barrie Stavis. A.S. Barnes.
In the Matter of J. Robert Oppenheimer. Heinar Kipphardt; translated by Ruth Speirs. Methuen.
The Latent Heterosexual. Paddy Chayefsky. Random House.
La Turista. Sam Shepard. Bobbs Merrill.
Loot. Joe Orton. Grove Press.
Lovers: Winners and Losers. Brian Friel. Farrar Straus.
The Memorandum. Vaclav Havel; translated by Vera Blackwell. Grove Press.
The Price. Arthur Miller. Viking Press.
The Promise. Aleksei Arbuzov; translated by Ariadne Nicolaeff. Oxford.
Rosencrantz and Guildenstern Are Dead. Tom Stoppard. Grove Press.
Scuba Duba. Bruce Jay Friedman. Simon & Schuster.
Soldiers. Rolf Hochhuth; translated by Robert David MacDonald. Grove Press.
The Sorrows of Frederick. Romulus Linney. Harcourt, Brace.
Staircase. Charles Dyer. Grove Press.
The Star-Spangled Girl. Neil Simon. Random House.
That Summer—That Fall and *Far Rockaway*. Frank D. Gilroy. Random House.

Tom Paine. Paul Foster. Grove Press.
The Unknown Soldier and His Wife. Peter Ustinov. Random House.
You Know I Can't Hear You When the Water's Running. Robert Anderson. Random House.
You're a Good Man Charlie Brown. (Musical) Based on the comic strip by Charles Schulz; book, music and lyrics by Clark Gesner. Random House.

A SELECTED LIST OF OTHER PLAYS PUBLISHED IN 1967–1968

And People All Around. George Sklar. Random House.
Armstrong's Last Goodnight. John Arden. Grove Press.
The Bald Soprano. Eugene Ionesco; translated by Donald M. Allen. Grove Press.
Belcher's Luck. David Mercer. Hill and Wang.
Best Plays of the Early American Theater: The Contrast by Royall Tyler; *Superstition* by James N. Barker; *Fashion* by Anna Cora Mowatt; *The Octoroon* by Dion Boucicault; *Secret Service* by William Gillette; *The Great Divide* by William Vaughn Moody; *Charles the Second* by John Payne and Washington Irving; *The New York Idea* by Langdon Mitchell; *The Truth* by Clyde Fitch; *The Witching Hour* by Augustus Thomas; *The Scarecrow* by Percy MacKaye; *The Mouse-Trap* by William Dean Howells; *Uncle Tom's Cabin* by George L. Aiken; *The Easiest Way* by Eugene Walter; *The Count of Monte Cristo* by Charles Fechter; *Salvation Nell* by Edward Sheldon; edited by John Gassner. Crown.
A Bond Honoured. Adaptation by John Osborne from the Lope de Vega play. Faber and Faber.
Caesar at the Rubicon. Theodore H. White. Atheneum.
The Caucasian Chalk Circle. Bertolt Brecht; revised by Eric Bentley. Grove Press.
The Collection and *The Lover.* Harold Pinter. Methuen.
Come and Go. Samuel Beckett. Calder & Boyars.
Crimes of Passion: The Erpingham Camp and *The Ruffian on the Stair.* Joe Orton. Methuen.
The Deep Blue Sea and Other Plays. Terence Rattigan. Includes *Harlequinade, Adventure Story* and *The Browning Version.* Pan Books.
The Devil's Disciple. George Bernard Shaw. Illustrated by Leonard Everett Fisher. Franklin Watts.
Exit the King. Eugene Ionesco; translated by Donald Watson. Grove Press.
Five Plays: Chicago; Icarus's Mother; Red Cross; Melodrama Play; Fourteen Hundred Thousand. Sam Shepard. Bobbs Merrill.
Flesh and Blood. William Hanley. Random House.
Four Plays: Flood; Mister, Mister; Only Ten Minutes to Buffalo; The Wicked Cooks. Gunter Grass. Harcourt, Brace.
Futz and What Came After: Futz; The String Game; Beclch; Istanbul; Homo. Rochelle Owens. Random House.
Geography and Plays. Gertrude Stein. Something Else Press.
The Lion and the Jewel. Wole Soyinka. Oxford Press.
Mark Twain Tonight! Hal Holbrook. Pyramid.
Moving Out and *A Garden Party.* Brendan Behan. Proscenium Press.
The New Underground Theater: Eight off-off-Broadway plays. Promenade by Maria Irene Fornes; *I'm Really Here* by Jean-Claude van Itallie; *The Golden Screw* by Tom Sankey; *Red Cross* by Sam Shepard; *Sand* by Murray Mednick; *Fruit Salad* by Grant Duay; *Istanbul* by Rochelle Owens; *The Life of Lady Godiva* by Ronald Tavel. Edited by R.J. Schroeder. Bantam.
One for the Grave. Louis Macneice. Faber and Faber.
Plays of Our Time: The Iceman Cometh; Death of a Salesman; Come Back, Little Sheba; A Raisin in the Sun; Luv; A Streetcar Named Desire; Mister Roberts; Look Back in Anger; A Man for All Seasons. Edited by Bennett Cerf. Random House.
The Rimers of Eldritch and Other Plays: Days Ahead; The Madness of Lady Bright; Wandering; This Is the Rill Speaking. Lanford Wilson. Hill and Wang.
The Room and *The Dumbwaiter.* Harold Pinter. Methuen.
Sappho. Lawrence Durrell. Faber & Faber.
The Waltz Invention. Vladimir Nabokov. Phaedra.
The Winslow Boy and Other Plays. Terence Rattigan. Includes *Flare Path* and *French Without Tears.* Pan Books.
The Workhouse Donkey. John Arden. Grove Press.

THE BEST PLAYS, 1894-1967

Listed in alphabetical order below are all those works selected as Best Plays in previous volumes in the *Best Plays* series. Opposite each title is given the volume in which the play appears, its opening date and its total number of performances. Those plays marked with an asterisk (*) were still playing on June 1, 1968 and their number of performances was figured through May 31, 1968. Adaptors and translators are indicated by (ad) and (tr), and the symbols (b), (m) and (1) stand for the author of the book, music and lyrics in the case of musicals.

PLAY	VOLUME	OPENED	PERFS.
Abe Lincoln in Illinois—Robert E. Sherwood	38-39	Oct. 15, 1938	472
Abraham Lincoln—John Drinkwater	19-20	Dec. 15, 1919	193
Accent on Youth—Samson Raphaelson	34-35	Dec. 25, 1934	229
Adam and Eva—Guy Bolton, George Middleton	19-20	Sept. 13, 1919	312
Affairs of State—Louis Verneuil	50-51	Sept. 25, 1950	610
After the Fall—Arthur Miller	63-64	Jan. 23, 1964	208
Ah, Wilderness!—Eugene O'Neill	33-34	Oct. 2, 1933	289
Alien Corn—Sidney Howard	32-33	Feb. 20, 1933	98
Alison's House—Susan Glaspell	30-31	Dec. 1, 1930	41
All My Sons—Arthur Miller	46-47	Jan. 29, 1947	328
All the Way Home—Tad Mosel, based on James Agee's novel *A Death in the Family*	60-61	Nov. 30, 1960	334
Allegro—(b, 1) Oscar Hammerstein, II, (m) Richard Rodgers	47-48	Oct. 10, 1947	315
Ambush—Arthur Richman	21-22	Oct. 10, 1921	98
America Hurrah—Jean-Claude van Itallie	66-67	Nov. 6, 1966	634
American Way, The—George S. Kaufman, Moss Hart	38-39	Jan. 21, 1939	164
Amphitryon 38—Jean Giraudoux, (ad) S. N. Behrman	37-38	Nov. 1, 1937	153
Andersonville Trial, The—Saul Levitt	59-60	Dec. 29, 1959	179
Andorra—Max Frisch, (ad) George Tabori	62-63	Feb. 9, 1963	9
Angel Street—Patrick Hamilton	41-42	Dec. 5, 1941	1,295
Animal Kingdom, The—Philip Barry	31-32	Jan. 12, 1932	183
Anna Christie—Eugene O'Neill	21-22	Nov. 2, 1921	177
Anna Lucasta—Philip Yordan	44-45	Aug. 30, 1944	957
Anne of the Thousand Days—Maxwell Anderson	48-49	Dec. 8, 1948	286
Another Language—Rose Franken	31-32	Apr. 25, 1932	344
Another Part of the Forest—Lillian Hellman	46-47	Nov. 20, 1946	182
Antigone—Jean Anouilh, (ad) Lewis Galantière	45-46	Feb. 18, 1946	64
Apple Tree, The—(b), (1) Sheldon Harnick, (b), (m) Jerry Bock, add'l (b) Jerome Coopersmith, based on stories by Mark Twain, Frank R. Stockton and Jules Feiffer	66-67	Oct. 18, 1966	463
Arsenic and Old Lace—Joseph Kesselring	40-41	Jan. 10, 1941	1,444
As Husbands Go—Rachel Crothers	30-31	Mar. 5, 1931	148
Autumn Garden, The—Lillian Hellman	50-51	Mar. 7, 1951	101
Awake and Sing—Clifford Odets	34-35	Feb. 19, 1935	209
Bad Man, The—Porter Emerson Browne	20-21	Aug. 30, 1920	350
Bad Seed—Maxwell Anderson, adapted from William March's novel	54-55	Dec. 8, 1954	332
Barbara Frietchie—Clyde Fitch	99-09	Oct. 23, 1899	83
Barefoot in Athens—Maxwell Anderson	51-52	Oct. 31, 1951	30
Barefoot in the Park—Neil Simon	63-64	Oct. 23, 1963	1,530
Barretts of Wimpole Street, The—Rudolf Besier	30-31	Feb. 9, 1931	370
Becket—Jean Anouilh, (tr) Lucienne Hill	60-61	Oct. 5, 1960	193

PLAY	VOLUME	OPENED	PERFS.
Beggar on Horseback—George S. Kaufman, Marc Connelly	23-24	Feb. 12, 1924	224
Behold the Bridegroom—George Kelly	27-28	Dec. 26, 1927	88
Bell, Book and Candle—John van Druten	50-51	Nov. 14, 1950	233
Bell for Adano, A—Paul Osborn, based on John Hersey's novel	44-45	Dec. 6, 1944	304
Berkeley Square—John L. Balderston	29-30	Nov. 4, 1929	229
Bernardine—Mary Coyle Chase	52-53	Oct. 16, 1952	157
Best Man, The—Gore Vidal	59-60	Mar. 31, 1960	520
Beyond the Horizon—Eugene O'Neill	19-20	Feb. 2, 1920	160
Big Fish, Little Fish—Hugh Wheeler	60-61	Mar. 15, 1961	101
Bill of Divorcement, A—Clemence Dane	21-22	Oct. 10, 1921	173
Billy Budd—Louis O. Coxe, Robert Chapman, based on Herman Melville's novel	50-51	Feb. 10, 1951	105
Biography—S. N. Behrman	32-33	Dec. 12, 1932	267
Black Comedy—Peter Shaffer	66-67	Feb. 12, 1967	337
Blithe Spirit—Noel Coward	41-42	Nov. 5, 1941	657
Born Yesterday—Garson Kanin	45-46	Feb. 4, 1946	1,642
Both Your Houses—Maxwell Anderson	32-33	Mar. 6, 1933	104
Boy Meets Girl—Bella and Sam Spewack	35-36	Nov. 27, 1935	669
Boy Friend, The—(b, l, m) Sandy Wilson	54-55	Sept. 30, 1954	485
Bride of the Lamb, The—William Hurlbut	25-26	Mar. 30, 1926	109
Brief Moment—S. N. Behrman	31-32	Nov. 9, 1931	129
Brigadoon—(b, l) Alan Jay Lerner, (m) Frederick Loewe	46-47	Mar. 13, 1947	581
Broadway—Philip Dunning, George Abbott	26-27	Sept. 16, 1926	322
Burlesque—George Manker Watters, Arthur Hopkins	27-28	Sept. 1, 1927	372
Bus Stop—William Inge	54-55	Mar. 2, 1955	478
Butter and Egg Man, The—George S. Kaufman	25-26	Sept. 23, 1925	243
*Cabaret—(b) Joe Masteroff, (m) John Kander, (l) Fred Ebb, based on John van Druten's play *I Am a Camera* and stories by Christopher Isherwood	66-67	Nov. 20, 1966	639
*Cactus Flower—Abe Burrows, based on a play by Pierre Barillet and Jean-Pierre Gredy	65-66	Dec. 8, 1965	1,033
Caine Mutiny Court-Martial, The—Herman Wouk, based on his novel	53-54	Jan. 20, 1954	415
Caligula—Albert Camus, (ad) Justin O'Brien	59-60	Feb. 19, 1960	38
Call It a Day—Dodie Smith	35-36	Jan. 28, 1936	194
Candide—(b) Lillian Hellman, based on Voltaire's satire (l) Richard Wilbur, John Latouche, Dorothy Parker, (m) Leonard Bernstein	56-57	Dec. 1, 1956	73
Candle in the Wind—Maxwell Anderson	41-42	Oct. 22, 1941	95
Caretaker, The—Harold Pinter	61-62	Oct. 4, 1961	165
Case of Rebellious Susan—Henry Arthur Jones	94-99	Dec. 29, 1894	80
Cat on a Hot Tin Roof—Tennessee Williams	54-55	Mar. 24, 1955	694
Chalk Garden, The—Enid Bagnold	55-56	Oct. 26, 1955	182
Changelings, The—Lee Wilson Dodd	23-24	Sept. 17, 1923	128
Chicago—Maurine Watkins	26-27	Dec. 30, 1926	172
Chicken Feed—Guy Bolton	23-24	Sept. 24, 1923	144
Children's Hour, The—Lillian Hellman	34-35	Nov. 20, 1934	691
Chips With Everything—Arnold Wesker	63-64	Oct. 1, 1963	149
Christopher Blake—Moss Hart	46-47	Nov. 30, 1946	114
Circle, The—W. Somerset Maugham	21-22	Sept. 12, 1921	175
Clarence—Booth Tarkington	19-20	Sept. 20, 1919	306
Claudia—Rose Franken	40-41	Feb. 12, 1941	722
Clearing in the Woods, A—Arthur Laurents	56-57	Jan. 10, 1957	36
Climate of Eden, The—Moss Hart, based on Edgar Mittelholzer's novel *Shadows Move Among Them*	52-53	Nov. 13, 1952	20
Climbers, The—Clyde Fitch	99-09	Jan. 21, 1901	163
Clutterbuck—Benn W. Levy	49-50	Dec. 3, 1949	218
Cocktail Party, The—T. S. Eliot	49-50	Jan. 21, 1950	409
Cold Wind and the Warm, The—S. N. Behrman	58-59	Dec. 8, 1958	120
Collection, The—Harold Pinter	62-63	Nov. 26, 1962	578

PLAY	VOLUME	OPENED	PERFS.
Come Back, Little Sheba—William Inge	49-50	Feb. 15, 1950	191
Command Decision—William Wister Haines	47-48	Oct. 1, 1947	408
Complaisant Lover, The—Graham Greene	61-62	Nov. 1, 1961	101
Confidential Clerk, The—T. S. Eliot	53-54	Feb. 11, 1954	117
Constant Wife, The—William Somerset Maugham	26-27	Nov. 29, 1926	233
Connection, The—Jack Gelber (Not picked as one of Ten Best, but included as a supplementary play)	60-61	Feb. 22, 1961	722
Coquette—George Abbott, Ann Preston Bridgers	27-28	Nov. 8, 1927	366
Corn Is Green, The—Emlyn Williams	40-41	Nov. 26, 1940	477
Country Girl, The—Clifford Odets	50-51	Nov. 10, 1950	235
County Chairman, The—George Ade	99-09	Nov. 24, 1903	222
Cradle Song, The—Gregorio & Maria Martinez Sierra, (tr) John Garrett Underhill	26-27	Nov. 2, 1926	108
Craig's Wife—George Kelly	25-26	Oct. 12, 1925	360
Criminal Code, The—Martin Flavin	29-30	Oct. 2, 1929	173
Crucible, The—Arthur Miller	52-53	Jan. 22, 1953	197
Cynara—H. M. Harwood, R. F. Gore-Browne	31-32	Nov. 2, 1931	210
Daisy Mayme—George Kelly	26-27	Oct. 25, 1926	112
Damask Cheek, The—John van Druten, Lloyd Morris	42-43	Oct. 22, 1942	93
Dancing Mothers—Edgar Selwyn, Ermund Goulding	24-25	Aug. 11, 1924	312
Dark at the Top of the Stairs, The—William Inge	57-58	Dec. 5, 1957	468
Dark Is Light Enough, The—Christopher Fry	54-55	Feb. 23, 1955	69
Darkness At Noon—Sidney Kingsley, based on Arthur Koestler's novel	50-51	Jan. 13, 1951	186
Darling of the Gods, The—David Belasco, John Luther Long	99-09	Dec. 3, 1902	182
Daughters of Atreus—Robert Turney	36-37	Oct. 14, 1936	13
Dead End—Sidney Kingsley	35-36	Oct. 28, 1935	687
Deadly Game, The—James Yaffe, based on Friedrich Duerrenmatt's novel	59-60	Feb. 2, 1960	39
Dear Ruth—Norman Krasna	44-45	Dec. 13, 1944	683
Death of a Salesman—Arthur Miller	48-49	Feb. 10, 1949	742
Death Takes a Holiday—Alberto Casella, (ad) Walter Ferris	29-30	Dec. 26, 1929	180
Deburau—Sacha Guitry, (ad) H. Granville-Barker	20-21	Dec. 23, 1920	189
Decision—Edward Chodorov	43-44	Feb. 2, 1944	160
Déclassée—Zoë Akins	19-20	Oct. 6, 1919	257
Deep Are the Roots—Arnaud d'Usseau, James Gow	45-46	Sept. 26, 1945	477
Delicate Balance, A—Edward Albee	66-67	Sept. 22, 1966	132
Deputy, The—Rolf Hochhuth	63-64	Feb. 26, 1964	109
Design for Living—Noel Coward	32-33	Jan. 24, 1933	135
Desire Under the Elms—Eugene O'Neill	24-25	Nov. 11, 1924	208
Desperate Hours, The—Joseph Hayes, based on his novel	54-55	Feb. 10, 1955	212
Detective Story—Sidney Kingsley	48-49	Mar. 23, 1949	581
Devil Passes, The—Benn W. Levy	31-32	Jan. 4, 1932	96
Devil's Advocate, The—Dore Schary, based on Morris L. West's novel	60-61	Mar. 9, 1961	116
Dial "M" for Murder—Frederick Knott	52-53	Oct. 29, 1952	552
Diary of Anne Frank, The—Frances Goodrich, Albert Hackett, based on Anne Frank's *The Diary of a Young Girl*	55-56	Oct. 5, 1955	717
Dinner at Eight—George S. Kaufman, Edna Ferber	32-33	Oct. 22, 1932	232
Disenchanted, The—Budd Schullberg, Harvey Breit, based on Mr. Schulberg's novel	58-59	Dec. 3, 1958	189
Disraeli—Louis N. Parker	09-19	Sept. 18, 1911	280
Distaff Side, The—John van Druten	34-35	Sept. 25, 1934	177
Dodsworth—Sidney Howard, based on Sinclair Lewis's novel	33-34	Feb. 24, 1934	315
Doughgirls, The—Joseph Fields	42-43	Dec. 30, 1942	671
Dover Road, The—A. A. Milne	21-22	Dec. 23, 1921	324
Dream Girl—Elmer Rice	45-46	Dec. 14, 1945	348
Duel of Angels—Jean Giraudoux's "Pour Lucrèce," (ad) Christopher Fry	59-60	Apr. 19, 1960	51
Dulcy—George S. Kaufman, Marc Connelly	21-22	Aug. 13, 1921	246

PLAY	VOLUME	OPENED	PERFS.
DYBBUK, THE—S. Ansky, (ad) Henry G. Alsberg	25-26	Dec. 15, 1925	120
DYLAN—Sidney Michaels	63-64	Jan. 18, 1964	153
EASIEST WAY, THE—Eugene Walter	09-19	Jan. 19, 1909	157
EASTWARD IN EDEN—Dorothy Gardner	47-48	Nov. 18, 1947	15
EDWARD, MY SON—Robert Morley, Noel Langley	48-49	Sept. 30, 1948	260
EGG, THE—Felicien Marceau, (ad) Robert Schlitt	61-62	Jan. 8, 1962	8
ELIZABETH THE QUEEN—Maxwell Anderson	30-31	Nov. 3, 1930	147
EMPEROR'S CLOTHES, THE—George Tabori	52-53	Feb. 9, 1953	16
EMPEROR JONES, THE—Eugene O'Neill	20-21	Nov. 1, 1920	204
ENCHANTED, THE—Maurice Valency, adapted from Jean Giraudoux's play "Intermezzo"	49-50	Jan. 18, 1950	45
END OF SUMMER—S. N. Behrman	35-36	Feb. 17, 1936	153
ENEMY, THE—Channing Pollock	25-26	Oct. 20, 1925	203
ENTER MADAME—Gilda Varesi, Dolly Byrne	20-21	Aug. 16, 1920	350
ENTERTAINER, THE—John Osborne	57-58	Feb. 12, 1958	97
EPITAPH FOR GEORGE DILLON—John Osborne, Anthony Creighton	58-59	Nov. 4, 1958	23
ESCAPE—John Galsworthy	27-28	Oct. 26, 1927	173
ETHAN FROME—Owen and Donald Davis, based on Edith Wharton's novel	35-36	Jan. 21, 1936	120
EVE OF ST. MARK, THE—Maxwell Anderson	42-43	Oct. 7, 1942	307
EXCURSION—Victor Wolfson	36-37	Apr. 9, 1937	116
FALL GUY, THE—James Gleason, George Abbott	24-25	Mar. 10, 1925	176
FAMILY PORTRAIT—Lenore Coffee, William Joyce Cowen	38-39	May 8, 1939	111
FAMOUS MRS. FAIR, THE—James Forbes	19-29	Dec. 22, 1919	344
FAR COUNTRY, A—Henry Denker	60-61	Apr. 4, 1961	271
FARMER TAKES A WIFE, THE—Frank B. Elser, Marc Connelly, based on Walter Edmonds' novel *Rome Haul*	34-35	Oct. 30, 1934	104
FATAL WEAKNESS, THE—George Kelly	46-47	Nov. 19, 1946	119
*FIDDLER ON THE ROOF—(b) Joseph Stein, (l) Sheldon Harnick, (m) Jerry Bock, based on Sholom Aleichem's stories	64-65	Sept. 22, 1964	1,540
FIORELLO!—(b) Jerome Weidman, George Abbott, (l) Sheldon Harnick, (m) Jerry Bock	59-60	Nov. 23, 1959	795
FIREBRAND, THE—Edwin Justus Mayer	24-25	Oct. 15, 1924	269
FIRST LADY—Katharine Dayton, George S. Kaufman	35-36	Nov. 26, 1935	246
FIRST MRS. FRASER, THE—St. John Ervine	29-30	Dec. 28, 1929	352
FIRST YEAR, THE—Frank Craven	20-21	Oct. 20, 1920	760
FIVE FINGER EXERCISE—Peter Shaffer	59-60	Dec. 2, 1959	337
FIVE-STAR FINAL—Louis Weitzenkorn	30-31	Dec. 30, 1930	175
FLIGHT TO THE WEST—Elmer Rice	40-41	Dec. 30, 1940	136
FLOWERING PEACH, THE—Clifford Odets	54-55	Dec. 28, 1954	135
FOOL, THE—Channing Pollock	22-23	Oct. 23, 1922	373
FOOLISH NOTION—Philip Barry	44-45	Mar. 3, 1945	104
FOURPOSTER, THE—Jan de Hartog	51-52	Oct. 24, 1951	632
FRONT PAGE, THE—Ben Hecht, Charles MacArthur	28-29	Aug. 14, 1928	276
GENERATION—William Goodhart	65-66	Oct. 6, 1965	299
GEORGE WASHINGTON SLEPT HERE—George S. Kaufman, Moss Hart	40-41	Oct. 18, 1940	173
GIDEON—Paddy Chayefsky	61-62	Nov. 9, 1961	234
GIGI—Anita Loos, based on Colette's novel	51-52	Nov. 24, 1951	219
GIRL ON THE VIA FLAMINIA, THE—Alfred Hayes, based on his novel	53-54	Feb. 9, 1954	111
GLASS MENAGERIE, THE—Tennessee Williams	44-45	Mar. 31, 1945	561
GOLDEN APPLE, THE—(b, l), John Latouche, (m) Jerome Moross	53-54	Apr. 20, 1954	125
GOLDEN BOY—Clifford Odets	37-38	Nov. 4, 1937	250
GOOD GRACIOUS ANNABELLE—Clare Kummer	09-19	Oct. 31, 1916	111
GOOSE HANGS HIGH, THE—Lewis Beach	23-24	Jan. 29, 1924	183

PLAY	VOLUME	OPENED	PERFS.
Goodbye, My Fancy—Fay Kanin	48-49	Nov. 17, 1948	446
Grand Hotel—Vicki Baum, (ad) W. A. Drake	30-31	Nov. 13, 1930	459
Great Divide, The—William Vaughn Moody	99-09	Oct. 3, 1906	238
Great God Brown, The—Eugene O'Neill	25-26	Jan. 23, 1926	271
Green Bay Tree, The—Mordaunt Shairp	33-34	Oct. 20, 1933	166
Green Goddess, The—William Archer	20-21	Jan. 18, 1921	440
Green Grow the Lilacs—Lynn Riggs	30-31	Jan. 26, 1931	64
Green Hat, The—Michael Arlen	25-26	Sept. 15, 1925	231
Green Pastures, The—Marc Connelly, adapted from Roark Bradford's *Ol Man Adam and His Chillun*	29-30	Feb. 26, 1930	640
Guys and Dolls—(b) Jo Swerling, Abe Burrows, based on a story and characters by Damon Runyon, (1, m) Frank Loesser	50-51	Nov. 24, 1950	1,200
Gypsy—Maxwell Anderson	28-29	Jan. 14, 1929	64
Hamp—John Wilson; based on an episode from a novel by J.L. Hodson	66-67	Mar. 9, 1967	101
Happy Time, The—Samuel Taylor, based on Robert Fontaine's book	49-50	Jan. 24, 1950	614
Harriet—Florence Ryerson, Colin Clements	42-43	Mar. 3, 1943	377
Harvey—Mary Coyle Chase	44-45	Nov. 1, 1944	1,775
Hasty Heart, The—John Patrick	44-45	Jan. 3, 1945	207
He Who Gets Slapped—Leonid Andreyev, (ad) Gregory Zilboorg	21-22	Jan. 9, 1922	308
Heart of Maryland, The—David Belasco	94-99	Oct. 22, 1895	240
Heiress, The—Ruth & Augustus Goetz, suggested by Henry James' novel *Washington Square*	47-48	Sept. 29, 1947	410
Hell-Bent fer Heaven—Hatcher Hughes	23-24	Jan. 4, 1924	122
* Hello Dolly!—(b) Michael Stewart, (1) (m) Jerry Herman, based on Thornton Wilder's *The Matchmaker*	63-64	Jan. 16, 1964	1,824
Her Master's Voice—Clare Kummer	33-34	Oct. 23, 1933	224
Here Come the Clowns—Philip Barry	38-39	Dec. 7, 1938	88
Hero, The—Gilbert Emery	21-22	Sept. 5, 1921	80
High Tor—Maxwell Anderson	36-37	Jan. 9, 1937	171
Hogan's Goat—William Alfred	65-66	Nov. 11, 1965	607
Holiday—Philip Barry	28-29	Nov. 26, 1928	229
Homecoming, The—Harold Pinter	66-67	Jan. 5, 1967	324
Home of the Brave—Arthur Laurents	45-46	Dec. 27, 1945	69
Hope for a Harvest—Sophie Treadwell	41-42	Nov. 26, 1941	38
Hostage, The—Brendan Behan	60-61	Sept. 20, 1960	127
House of Connelly, The—Paul Green	31-32	Sept. 28, 1931	91
How To Succeed in Business Without Really Trying—(b) Abe Burrows, Jack Weinstock, Willie Gilbert, based on Shepherd Mead's novel, (1, m) Frank Loesser	61-62	Oct. 14, 1961	1,417
I Am a Camera—John van Druten, based on Christopher Isherwood's Berlin stories	51-52	Nov. 28, 1951	214
If I Were King—Justin Huntly McCarthy	99-09	Oct. 14, 1901	56
I Know My Love—S. N. Behrman, adapted from Marcel Achard's *Auprès de Ma Blonde*	49-50	Nov. 2, 1949	246
I Remember Mama—John van Druten, based on Kathryn Forbes's book *Mama's Bank Account*	44-45	Oct. 19, 1944	714
Icebound—Owen Davis	22-23	Feb. 10, 1923	171
Iceman Cometh, The—Eugene O'Neill	46-47	Oct. 9, 1946	136
Idiot's Delight—Robert E. Sherwood	35-36	Mar. 24, 1936	300
Immoralist, The—Ruth and Augustus Goetz, based on André Gide's novel	53-54	Feb. 8, 1954	96
In Abraham's Bosom—Paul Green	26-27	Dec. 30, 1926	116
In the Summer House—Jane Bowles	53-54	Dec. 29, 1953	55
In Time to Come—Howard Koch, John Huston	41-42	Dec. 28, 1941	40
Inadmissible Evidence—John Osborne	65-66	Nov. 30, 1965	166
Incident at Vichy—Arthur Miller	64-65	Dec. 3, 1964	99
Inherit the Wind—Jerome Lawrence, Robert E. Lee	54-55	Apr. 21, 1955	806

PLAY	VOLUME	OPENED	PERFS.
Innocents, The—William Archibald, based on Henry James' *The Turn of the Screw*	49-50	Feb. 1, 1950	141
Innocent Voyage, The—Paul Osborn, based on Richard Hughes's novel *High Wind in Jamaica*	43-44	Nov. 15, 1943	40
Inspector Calls, An—J. B. Priestley	47-48	Oct. 21, 1947	95
"It's a Bird It's a Plane It's SUPERMAN"—(b) David Newman and Robert Benton, (l) Lee Adams, (m) Charles Strouse, based on the comic strip "Superman"	65-66	Mar. 29, 1966	129
J. B.—Archibald MacLeish	58-59	Dec. 11, 1958	364
Jacobowsky and the Colonel—S. N. Behrman, based on Franz Werfel's play	43-44	Mar 14, 1944	417
Jane—S. N. Behrman, suggested by W. Somerset Maugham's story	51-52	Feb. 1, 1952	100
Jane Clegg—St. John Ervine	19-20	Feb. 23, 1920	158
Jason—Samson Raphaelson	41-42	Jan. 21, 1942	125
Jest, The—Sem Benelli, (ad) Edward Sheldon	19-20	Sept. 19, 1919	197
Joan of Lorraine—Maxwell Anderson	46-47	Nov. 18, 1946	199
John Ferguson—St. John Ervine	09-19	May 13, 1919	177
John Loves Mary—Norman Krasna	46-47	Feb. 4, 1947	423
Johnny Johnson—(b, l) Paul Green, (m) Kurt Weill	36-37	Nov. 19, 1936	68
Journey's End—R. C. Sherriff	28-29	Mar. 22, 1929	485
June Moon—Ring W. Lardner, George S. Kaufman	29-30	Oct. 9, 1929	273
Junior Miss—Jerome Chodorov, Joseph Fields	41-42	Nov. 18, 1941	710
Kataki—Shimon Wincelberg	58-59	Apr. 9, 1959	20
Key Largo—Maxwell Anderson	39-40	Nov. 27, 1939	105
Killing of Sister George, The—Frank Marcus	66-67	Oct. 5, 1966	205
Kingdom of God, The—G. Martinez Sierra, (ad) Helen and Harley Granville-Barker	28-29	Dec. 20, 1928	92
Kiss and Tell—F. Hugh Herbert	42-43	Mar. 17, 1943	957
Kiss the Boys Good-bye—Clare Boothe	38-39	Sept. 28, 1938	286
Lady in the Dark—(b) Moss Hart, (l) Ira Gershwin, (m) Kurt Weill	40-41	Jan. 23, 1941	162
Lark, The—Jean Anouilh, (ad) Lillian Hellman	55-56	Nov. 17, 1955	229
Last Mile, The—John Wexley	29-30	Feb. 13, 1930	289
Last of Mrs. Cheyney, The—Frederick Lonsdale	25-26	Nov. 9, 1925	385
Late Christopher Bean, The—(ad) Sidney Howard from the French of René Fauchois	32-33	Oct. 31, 1932	244
Late George Apley, The—John P. Marquand, George S. Kaufman, based on Mr. Marquand's book	44-45	Nov. 23, 1944	385
Leah Kleschna—C. M. S. McLellan	99-09	Dec. 12, 1904	131
Left Bank, The—Elmer Rice	31-32	Oct. 5, 1931	242
Let Us Be Gay—Rachel Crothers	28-29	Feb. 19, 1929	132
Letters to Lucerne—Fritz Rotter, Allen Vincent	41-42	Dec. 23, 1941	23
Life with Father—Howard Lindsay, Russel Crouse, based on Clarence Day's book	39-40	Nov. 8, 1939	3,224
Life with Mother—Howard Lindsay, Russel Crouse, based on Clarence Day's book	48-49	Oct. 20, 1948	265
Light Up the Sky—Moss Hart	48-49	Nov. 18, 1948	216
Liliom—Ferenc Molnar, (ad) Benjamin Glazer	20-21	Apr. 20, 1921	300
Lion in Winter, The—James Goldman	65-66	Mar. 3, 1966	92
Little Accident—Floyd Dell, Thomas Mitchell	28-29	Oct. 9, 1928	289
Little Foxes, The—Lillian Hellman	38-39	Feb. 15, 1939	410
Little Minister, The—James M. Barrie	94-99	Sept. 27, 1897	300
Living Room, The—Graham Greene	54-55	Nov. 17, 1954	22
Long Day's Journey into Night—Eugene O'Neill	56-57	Nov. 7, 1956	390
Look Back in Anger—John Osborne	57-58	Oct. 1, 1957	407
Look Homeward, Angel—Ketti Frings, based on Thomas Wolfe's novel	57-58	Nov. 28, 1957	564

PLAY	VOLUME	OPENED	PERFS.
LOST HORIZONS—Harry Segall, revised by John Hayden	34-35	Oct. 15, 1934	56
LOST IN THE STARS—(b, l) Maxwell Anderson, based on Alan Paton's novel *Cry, The Beloved Country,* (m) Kurt Weill	49-50	Oct. 30, 1949	273
LOVE OF FOUR COLONELS, THE—Peter Ustinov	52-53	Jan. 15, 1953	141
LOYALTIES—John Galsworthy	22-23	Sept. 27, 1922	220
LUTE SONG—(b) Sidney Howard, Will Irwin, from the Chinese classic *Pi-Pa-Ki,* (l) Bernard Hanighen, (m) Raymond Scott	44-45	Nov. 23, 1944	385
LUTHER—John Osborne	63-64	Sept. 25, 1963	211
LUV—Murray Schisgal	64-65	Nov. 11, 1964	901
MACHINAL—Sophie Treadwell	28-29	Sept. 7, 1928	91
MADWOMAN OF CHAILLOT, THE—Jean Giraudoux, (ad) Maurice Valency	48-49	Dec. 27, 1948	368
MAGIC AND THE LOSS, THE—Julian Funt	53-54	Apr. 9, 1954	27
MAGNIFICENT YANKEE, THE—Emmet Lavery	45-46	Jan. 22, 1946	160
MALE ANIMAL, THE—James Thurber, Elliott Nugent	39-40	Jan. 9, 1940	243
MAMMA'S AFFAIR—Rachel Barton Butler	19-20	Jan. 19, 1920	98
MAN FOR ALL SEASONS, A—Robert Bolt	61-62	Nov. 22, 1961	637
MAN FROM HOME, THE—Booth Tarkington, Harry Leon Wilson	99-09	Aug. 17, 1908	406
*MAN OF LA MANCHA—(b) Dale Wasserman, suggested by the life and works of Miguel de Cervantes y Saavedra, (l) Joe Darion, (m) Mitch Leigh	65-66	Nov. 22, 1965	1,052
MAN WHO CAME TO DINNER, THE—George S. Kaufman, Moss Hart	39-40	Oct. 16, 1939	739
MARGIN FOR ERROR—Clare Boothe	39-40	Nov. 3, 1939	264
MARY, MARY—Jean Kerr	60-61	Mar. 8, 1961	1,572
MARY OF SCOTLAND—Maxwell Anderson	33-34	Nov. 27, 1933	248
MARY ROSE—James M. Barrie	20-21	Dec. 22, 1920	127
MARY THE 3RD—Rachel Crothers	22-23	Feb. 5, 1923	162
MATCHMAKER, THE—Thornton Wilder, based on Johann Nestroy's *Einen Jux will es sich Machen,* based on John Oxenford's *A Day Well Spent*	55-56	Dec. 5, 1955	486
ME AND MOLLY—Gertrude Berg	47-48	Feb. 26, 1948	156
MEMBER OF THE WEDDING, THE—Carson McCullers, adapted from her novel	49-50	Jan. 5, 1950	501
MEN IN WHITE—Sidney Kingsley	33-34	Sept. 26, 1933	351
MERRILY WE ROLL ALONG—George S. Kaufman, Moss Hart	34-35	Sept. 29, 1934	155
MERTON OF THE MOVIES—George S. Kaufman, Marc Connelly, based on Harry Leon Wilson's novel	22-23	Nov. 13, 1922	381
MICHAEL AND MARY—A. A. Milne	29-30	Dec. 10, 1929	246
MILK TRAIN DOESN'T STOP HERE ANYMORE, THE—Tennessee Williams	62-63	Jan. 16, 1963	69
MINICK—George S. Kaufman, Edna Ferber	24-25	Sept. 24, 1924	141
MISTER ROBERTS—Thomas Heggen, Joshua Logan, based on Thomas Heggen's novel	47-48	Feb. 18, 1948	1,157
MOON FOR THE MISBEGOTTEN, A—Eugene O'Neill	56-57	May 2, 1957	68
MOON IS DOWN, THE—John Steinbeck	41-42	Apr. 7, 1942	71
MORNING'S AT SEVEN—Paul Osborn	39-40	Nov. 30, 1939	44
MOTHER COURAGE AND HER CHILDREN—Bertolt Brecht, (ad) Eric Bentley	62-63	Mar. 28, 1963	52
MOURNING BECOMES ELECTRA—Eugene O'Neill	31-32	Oct. 26, 1931	150
MR. AND MRS. NORTH—Owen Davis, based on Frances and Richard Lockridge's stories	40-41	Jan. 12, 1941	163
MRS. BUMSTEAD-LEIGH—Harry James Smith	09-19	Apr. 3, 1911	64
MRS. MCTHING—Mary Coyle Chase	51-52	Feb. 20, 1952	350
MRS. PARTRIDGE PRESENTS—Mary Kennedy, Ruth Hawthorne	24-25	Jan. 5, 1925	144
MY FAIR LADY—(b, l) Alan Jay Lerner, based on Bernard Shaw's *Pygmalion,* (m) Frederick Loewe	55-56	Mar. 15, 1956	2,717
MY SISTER EILEEN—Joseph A. Fields, Jerome Chodorov, based on Ruth McKenney's stories	40-41	Dec. 26, 1940	865

PLAY	VOLUME	OPENED	PERFS.
My 3 Angels—Sam and Bella Spewack, based on Albert Husson's play *La Cuisine des Anges*	52-53	Mar. 11, 1953	341
Native Son—Paul Green, Richard Wright, based on Mr. Wright's novel	40-41	Mar. 24, 1941	114
Nest, The—Paul Geraldy, Grace George	21-22	Jan. 28, 1922	152
Next Time I'll Sing to You—James Saunders	63-64	Nov. 27, 1963	23
Nice People—Rachel Crothers	20-21	Mar. 2, 1921	247
Night of the Iguana, The—Tennessee Williams	61-62	Dec. 28, 1961	319
No More Ladies—A. E. Thomas	33-34	Jan. 23, 1934	162
No Time for Comedy—S. N. Behrman	38-39	Apr. 17, 1939	185
No Time for Sergeants—Ira Levin, adapted from Mac Hyman's novel	55-56	Oct. 20, 1955	796
O Mistress Mine—Terence Rattigan	45-46	Jan. 23, 1946	452
Odd Couple, The—Neil Simon	64-65	Mar. 10, 1965	964
Of Mice and Men—John Steinbeck	37-38	Nov. 23, 1937	207
Of Thee I Sing—(b) George S. Kaufman, Morrie Ryskind, (l) Ira Gershwin, (m) George Gershwin	31-32	Dec. 26, 1931	441
Oh Dad, Poor Dad, Mamma's Hung You in the Closet and I'm Feelin' So Sad—Arthur L. Kopit	61-62	Feb. 26, 1962	454
Oklahoma!—(b, l) Oscar Hammerstein II, based on Lynn Riggs's play *Green Grow the Lilacs,* (m) Richard Rodgers	42-43	Mar. 31, 1943	2,212
Old Maid, The—Zoë Akins, based on Edith Wharton's novel	34-35	Jan. 7, 1935	305
Old Soak, The—Don Marquis	22-23	Aug. 22, 1922	423
On Borrowed Time—Paul Osborn, based on Lawrence Edward Watkin's novel	37-38	Feb. 3, 1938	321
On Trial—Elmer Rice	09-19	Aug. 19, 1914	365
Once in a Lifetime—George S. Kaufman, Moss Hart	63-64	Feb. 11, 1964	15
One Sunday Afternoon—James Hagen	30-31	Sept. 24, 1930	406
Orpheus Descending—Tennessee Williams	32-33	Feb. 15, 1933	322
Outrageous Fortune—Rose Franken	56-57	Mar. 21, 1957	68
Our Town—Thornton Wilder	43-44	Nov. 3, 1943	77
Outward Bound—Sutton Vane	37-38	Feb. 4, 1938	336
Over 21—Ruth Gordon	23-24	Jan. 7, 1924	144
Overture—William Bolitho	43-44	Jan. 3, 1944	221
	30-31	Dec. 5, 1930	41
P.S. 193—David Rayfiel			
Paris Bound—Philip Barry	62-63	Oct. 30, 1962	48
Passion of Joseph D, The—Paddy Chayefsky	27-28	Dec. 27, 1927	234
Patriots, The—Sidney Kingsley	42-43	Jan. 29, 1943	173
Period of Adjustment—Tennessee Williams	60-61	Nov. 10, 1960	132
Persecution and Assassination of Marat as Performed by the Inmates of the Asylum of Charenton Under the Direction of the Marquis de Sade, The—Peter Weiss, English version by Geoffrey Skelton, verse (ad) Adrian Mitchell	65-66	Dec. 27, 1965	144
Petrified Forest, The—Robert E. Sherwood	34-35	Jan. 7, 1935	197
Philadelphia Story, The—Philip Barry	38-39	Mar. 28, 1939	417
Philadelphia, Here I Come!—Brian Friel	65-66	Feb. 16, 1966	326
Physicists, The—Friedrich Duerrenmatt, (ad) James Kirkup	64-65	Oct. 13, 1964	55
Pick-Up Girl—Elsa Shelley	43-44	May 3, 1944	198
Picnic—William Inge	52-53	Feb. 19, 1953	477
Pigeons and People—George M. Cohan	32-33	Jan. 16, 1933	70
Play's the Thing, The—Ferenc Molnar, (ad) P. G. Wodehouse	26-27	Nov. 3, 1926	260
Pleasure of His Company, The—Samuel Taylor, Cornelia Otis Skinner	58-59	Oct. 22, 1958	474
Plough and the Stars, The—Sean O'Casey	27-28	Nov. 28, 1927	32
Point of No Return—Paul Osborn, based on John P. Marquand's novel	51-52	Dec. 13, 1951	364
Ponder Heart, The—Joseph Fields, Jerome Chodorov, adapted from Eudora Welty's story	55-56	Feb. 16, 1956	149

PLAY	VOLUME	OPENED	PERFS.
POOR BITOS—Jean Anouilh, (tr) Lucienne Hill	64-65	Nov. 14, 1964	14
PORGY—DuBose Heyward	27-28	Oct. 10, 1927	217
POTTING SHED, THE—Graham Greene	56-57	Jan. 29, 1957	143
PRIDE AND PREJUDICE—Helen Jerome, based on Jane Austen's novel	35-36	Nov. 5, 1935	219
PROLOGUE TO GLORY—E. P. Conkle	37-38	Mar. 17, 1938	70
R.U.R.—Karel Capek	22-23	Oct. 9, 1922	184
RACKET, THE—Bartlett Cormack	27-28	Nov. 22, 1927	119
RAIN—John Colton, Clemence Randolph, based on the story by W. Somerset Maughm	22-23	Nov. 7, 1922	648
RAISIN IN THE SUN, A—Lorraine Hansberry	58-59	Mar. 11, 1959	530
RATTLE OF A SIMPLE MAN—Charles Dyer	62-63	Apr. 17, 1963	94
REBOUND—Donald Ogden Stewart	29-30	Feb. 3, 1930	114
REHEARSAL, THE—Jean Anouilh, (ad) Pamela Hansford Johnson and Kitty Black	63-64	Sept. 23, 1963	110
REMAINS TO BE SEEN—Howard Lindsay, Russel Crouse	51-52	Oct. 3, 1951	199
REQUIEM FOR A NUN—Ruth Ford, William Faulkner, adapted from Mr. Faulkner's novel	58-59	Jan. 30, 1959	43
REUNION IN VIENNA—Robert E. Sherwood	31-32	Nov. 16, 1931	264
RHINOCEROS—Eugene Ionesco, (tr) Derek Prouse	60-61	Jan. 9, 1961	240
ROAD TO ROME, THE—Robert E. Sherwood	26-27	Jan. 31, 1927	392
ROCKET TO THE MOON—Clifford Odets	38-39	Nov. 24, 1938	131
ROMANCE—Edward Sheldon	09-19	Feb. 10, 1913	160
ROPE DANCERS, THE—Morton Wishengrad	57-58	Nov. 20, 1957	189
ROSE TATTOO, THE—Tennessee Williams	50-51	Feb. 3, 1951	306
ROYAL FAMILY, THE—George S. Kaufman, Edna Ferber	27-28	Dec. 28, 1927	345
ROYAL HUNT OF THE SUN, THE—Peter Shaffer	65-66	Oct. 26, 1965	261
RUGGED PATH, THE—Robert E. Sherwood	45-46	Nov. 10, 1945	81
ST. HELENA—R. C. Sheriff, Jean de Casalis	36-37	Oct. 6, 1936	63
SATURDAY'S CHILDREN—Maxwell Anderson	26-27	Jan. 26, 1927	315
SEARCHING WIND, THE—Lillian Hellman	43-44	Apr. 12, 1944	318
SEASON IN THE SUN—Wolcott Gibbs	50-51	Sept. 28, 1950	367
SECOND THRESHOLD—Philip Barry	50-51	Jan. 2, 1951	126
SECRET SERVICE—William Gillette	94-99	Oct. 5, 1896	176
SEPARATE TABLES—Terence Rattigan	56-57	Oct. 25, 1956	332
SEVEN KEYS TO BALDPATE—George M. Cohan	09-19	Sept. 22, 1913	320
SHADOW AND SUBSTANCE—Paul Vincent Carroll	37-38	Jan. 26, 1938	274
SHADOW OF HEROES—Robert Ardrey, also called *Stone and Star*	61-62	Dec. 5, 1961	20
SHE LOVES ME—(b) Joe Masteroff, based on Miklos Laszlo's play *Parfumerie,* (l) Sheldon Harnick, (m) Jerry Bock	62-63	Apr. 23, 1963	302
SHINING HOUR, THE—Keith Winter	33-34	Feb. 13, 1934	121
SHOW-OFF, THE—George Kelly	23-24	Feb. 5, 1924	571
SHRIKE, THE—Joseph Kramm	51-52	Jan. 15, 1952	161
SILVER CORD, THE—Sidney Howard	26-27	Dec. 20, 1926	112
SILVER WHISTLE, THE—Robert E. McEnroe	48-49	Nov. 24, 1948	219
SIX CYLINDER LOVE—William Anthony McGuire	21-22	Aug. 25, 1921	430
SKIN GAME, THE—John Galsworthy	20-21	Oct. 20, 1920	176
SKIN OF OUR TEETH, THE—Thornton Wilder	42-43	Nov. 18, 1942	359
SKIPPER NEXT TO GOD—Jan de Hartog	47-48	Jan. 4, 1948	69
SKYLARK—Samson Raphaelson	39-40	Oct. 11, 1939	256
SLOW DANCE ON THE KILLING GROUND—William Hanley	64-65	Nov. 30, 1964	88
SOLDIER'S WIFE—Rose Franken	44-45	Oct. 4, 1944	253
SQUAW MAN, THE—Edwin Milton Royle	99-09	Oct. 23, 1905	222
STAGE DOOR—George S. Kaufman, Edna Ferber	36-37	Oct. 22, 1936	169
STAR-WAGON, THE—Maxwell Anderson	37-38	Sept. 29, 1937	223
STATE OF THE UNION—Howard Lindsay, Russel Crouse	45-46	Nov. 14, 1945	765
STONE AND STAR—Robert Ardrey, also called *Shadow of Heroes*	61-62	Dec. 5, 1961	20

PLAY	VOLUME	OPENED	PERFS.
Stop the World—I Want to Get Off—(b, l, m) Leslie Bricusse, Anthony Newley	62-63	Oct. 3, 1962	555
Storm Operation—Maxwell Anderson	43-44	Jan. 11, 1944	23
Story of Mary Surratt, The—John Patrick	46-47	Feb. 8, 1947	11
Strange Interlude—Eugene O'Neill	27-28	Jan. 30, 1928	426
Street Scene—Elmer Rice	28-29	Jan. 10, 1929	601
Streetcar Named Desire, A—Tennessee Williams	47-48	Dec. 3, 1947	855
Strictly Dishonorable—Preston Sturges	29-30	Sept. 18, 1929	557
Subject Was Roses, The—Frank D. Gilroy	64-65	May 25, 1964	832
Summer of the 17th Doll—Ray Lawler	57-58	Jan. 22, 1958	29
Sunrise at Campobello—Dore Schary	57-58	Jan. 30, 1958	556
Sun-Up—Lula Vollmer	22-23	May 25, 1923	356
Susan and God—Rachel Crothers	37-38	Oct. 7, 1937	288
Swan, The—Ferenc Molnar, (tr) Melville Baker	23-24	Oct. 23, 1923	255
Sweet Bird of Youth—Tennessee Williams	58-59	Mar. 10, 1959	375
Take a Giant Step—Louis Peterson	53-54	Sept. 24, 1953	76
Tarnish—Gilbert Emery	23-24	Oct. 1, 1923	248
Taste of Honey, A—Shelagh Delaney	60-61	Oct. 4, 1960	334
Tchin-Tchin—Sidney Michaels, based on François Billetdoux's play	62-63	Oct. 25, 1962	222
Tea and Sympathy—Robert Anderson	53-54	Sept. 30, 1953	712
Teahouse of the August Moon—John Patrick, based on Vern Sneider's novel	53-54	Oct. 15, 1953	1,027
Tenth Man, The—Paddy Chayefsky	59-60	Nov. 5, 1959	623
There Shall Be No Night—Robert E. Sherwood	39-40	Apr. 29, 1940	181
They Knew What They Wanted—Sidney Howard	24-25	Nov. 24, 1924	414
They Shall Not Die—John Wexley	33-34	Feb. 21, 1934	62
Thousand Clowns, A—Herb Gardner	61-62	Apr. 5, 1962	428
Thurber Carnival, A—James Thurber	59-60	Feb. 26, 1960	127
Tiger at the Gates—Jean Giraudoux's *La Guerre de Troie n'aura pas lieu,* (tr) Christopher Fry	55-56	Oct. 3, 1955	217
Time of the Cuckoo, The—Arthur Laurents	52-53	Oct. 15, 1952	263
Time Of Your Life, The—William Saroyan	39-40	Oct. 25, 1939	185
Time Remembered—Jean Anouilh's *Léocadia,* (ad) Patricia Moyes	57-58	Nov. 12, 1957	248
Tiny Alice—Edward Albee	64-65	Dec. 29, 1964	167
Toilet, The—LeRoi Jones	64-65	Dec. 16, 1964	151
Tomorrow and Tomorrow—Philip Barry	30-31	Jan. 13, 1931	206
Tomorrow the World—James Gow, Arnaud d'Usseau	42-43	Apr. 14, 1943	500
Touch of the Poet, A—Eugene O'Neill	58-59	Oct. 2, 1958	284
Tovarich—Jacques Deval, (tr) Robert E. Sherwood	36-37	Oct. 15, 1936	356
Toys in the Attic—Lillian Hellman	59-60	Feb. 25, 1960	556
Trelawny of the Wells—Eugene W. Presbrey	94-99	Nov. 22, 1898	131
Two Blind Mice—Samuel Spewack	48-49	Mar. 2, 1949	163
Unchastened Woman, The—Louis Kaufman Anspacher	09-19	Oct. 9, 1915	193
Uncle Harry—Thomas Job	41-42	May 20, 1942	430
Under Milk Wood—Dylan Thomas	57-58	Oct. 15, 1957	39
Valley Forge—Maxwell Anderson	34-35	Dec. 10, 1934	58
Venus Observed—Christopher Fry	51-52	Feb. 13, 1952	86
Very Special Baby, A—Robert Alan Aurthur	56-57	Nov. 14, 1956	5
Victoria Regina—Laurence Housman	35-36	Dec. 26, 1935	203
View From the Bridge, A—Arthur Miller	55-56	Sept. 29, 1955	149
Visit, The—Friedrich Duerrenmatt, (ad) Maurice Valency	57-58	May 5, 1958	189
Visit to a Small Planet—Gore Vidal	56-57	Feb. 7, 1957	388
Voice of the Turtle, The—John van Druten	43-44	Dec. 8, 1943	1,557
Waiting for Godot—Samuel Beckett	55-56	Apr. 19, 1956	59
Waltz of the Toreadors, The—Jean Anouilh, (tr) Lucienne Hill	56-57	Jan. 17, 1957	132

PLAY	VOLUME	OPENED	PERFS.
Watch on the Rhine—Lillian Hellman	40-41	Apr. 1, 1941	378
We, the People—Elmer Rice	32-33	Jan. 21, 1933	49
Wedding Bells—Salisbury Field	19-20	Nov. 12, 1919	168
Wednesday's Child—Leopold Atlas	33-34	Jan. 16, 1934	56
What a Life—Clifford Goldsmith	37-38	Apr. 13, 1938	538
What Price Glory?—Maxwell Anderson, Laurence Stallings	24-25	Sept. 5, 1924	433
When Ladies Meet—Rachel Crothers	32-33	Oct. 6, 1932	191
White Steed, The—Paul Vincent Carroll	38-39	Jan. 10, 1939	136
Who's Afraid of Virginia Woolf?—Edward Albee	62-63	Oct. 13, 1962	664
Why Marry?—Jesse Lynch Williams	09-19	Dec. 25, 1917	120
Why Not?—Jesse Lynch Williams	22-23	Dec. 25, 1922	120
Witching Hour, The—Augustus Thomas	99-09	Nov. 18, 1907	212
Wild Birds—Dan Totheroh	24-25	Apr. 9, 1925	44
Winged Victory—(b) Moss Hart, (m) Sgt. David Rose	43-44	Nov. 20, 1943	212
Winslow Boy, The—Terence Rattigan	47-48	Oct. 29, 1947	215
Wings Over Europe—Robert Nichols, Maurice Browne	28-29	Dec. 10, 1928	90
Winterset—Maxwell Anderson	35-36	Sept. 25, 1935	195
Winter Soldiers—Daniel Lewis James	42-43	Nov. 29, 1942	25
Wisdom Tooth, The—Marc Connelly	25-26	Feb. 15, 1926	160
Wisteria Trees, The—Joshua Logan, based on Anton Chekhov's *The Cherry Orchard*	49-50	Mar. 29, 1950	165
Witness for the Prosecution—Agatha Christie	54-55	Dec. 16, 1954	645
Women, The—Clare Boothe	36-37	Dec. 26, 1936	657
Wonderful Town—(b) Joseph Fields, Jerome Chodorov, based on their play *My Sister Eileen* and Ruth McKenney's stories, (l) Betty Comden, Adolph Green, (m) Leonard Bernstein	52-53	Feb. 25, 1953	559
World We Make, The—Sidney Kingsley, based on Millen Brand's novel	39-40	Nov. 20, 1939	80
Years Ago—Ruth Gordon	46-47	Dec. 3, 1946	206
Yes, My Darling Daughter—Mark Reed	36-37	Feb. 9, 1937	405
You and I—Philip Barry	22-23	Feb. 19, 1923	178
You Can't Take It With You—Moss Hart, George S. Kaufman	36-37	Dec. 14, 1936	837
*You Know I Can't Hear You When the Water's Running—Robert Anderson	66-67	Mar. 13, 1967	510
Young Woodley—John van Druten	25-26	Nov. 2, 1925	260
Youngest, The—Philip Barry	24-25	Dec. 22, 1924	104
*You're a Good Man Charlie Brown—(b), (m), (l) Clark Gesner, based on the comic strip "Peanuts" by Charles M. Schulz	66-67	Mar. 7, 1967	542

NECROLOGY

JUNE 1, 1967—MAY 31, 1968

PERFORMERS

Nick Adams (36)—May 31, 1968
Lois Alexander (77)—May 3, 1968
Lois Andrews (44)—April 4, 1968
Phil Arnold (55)—May 9, 1968
June Astor (49)—August 22, 1967
Fay Bainter (76)—April 16, 1968
Cora Baird (54)—December 7, 1967
Oliver Barbour (63)—April 11, 1968
Richard Bartell (69)—July 22, 1967
Guy Bates (92)—January 16, 1968
Lucien Baroux (79)—May 21, 1968
Ida Barr (85)—December 17, 1967
Jeanne Barr (35)—August 10, 1967
St. Clair Bayfield (91)—May 19, 1967
Don Beck (31)—June 18, 1967
Scotty Beckett (38)—May 10, 1968
Raikin Ben-Ari (64)—January 2, 1968
Wilda Bennett (73)—December 20, 1967
Phillippa Bevans (55)—May 10, 1968
Charles Bickford (77)—November 9, 1967
Gus Bing (74)—August 4, 1967
Robert Bottomley (83)—March 11, 1968
James Burke—May 23, 1968
Frances Cleveland Bush (78)—November 21, 1967
Arthur Bushnell (50)—November 8, 1967
Jean Cadell (83)—September 26, 1967
Orville Caldwell—September 24, 1967
Annette Carell—October 20, 1967
Jack Carter (65)—November 9, 1967
Ralph Chambers (76)—March 16, 1968
Charles S. Chaplin Jr. (42)—March 20, 1968
Johnny Clark—July 3, 1967
Una Clayton (Fanny Pearl Keyes) (92)—April 3, 1968
June Cochrane (64)—December 31, 1967
June Collyer (61)—March 16, 1968
Clyde Courtright (82)—October 6, 1967
Edward Crandall (64)—May 9, 1968
Ruth Cumming (63)—August 11, 1967
Zamah Cunningham (74)—June 2, 1967
Finlay Currie (90)—May 9, 1968
Jane Darwell (87)—August 13, 1967
Frances Mack Davidoff (60)—September 26, 1967
Albert Dekker (62)—May 5, 1968
Reginald Denny (75)—June 16, 1967
Frank De Silva (78)—March 20, 1968
Charlotte Dieterle (72)—May 19, 1968
Cliff Dixon (79)—March 25, 1968
Ludwig Donath (67)—September 29, 1967
Sam Downing (82)—August 16, 1967
Ethel M. Dudley (76)—February 19, 1968
James Dunn (61)—September 3, 1967
Stuart Erwin (64)—December 21, 1967
Douglas Evans (64)—March 25, 1968
Barbara Everest (77)—February 9, 1968
Eric Feldary (48)—February 26, 1968
Michael T. Fitzmaurice (59)—August 31, 1967
Helen Flint (69)—September 9, 1967
Franklyn Fox (73)—November 2, 1967
Leo W. Franks (62)—February 3, 1968
Howard Freeman (65)—December 8, 1967
Lionel Gamlin (64)—October 16, 1967
Jimmy Gold (87)—October 7, 1967
Louise Goodwin (86)—January 30, 1968
Hal Hackett (44)—December 4, 1967
Matti Haim (56)—July 30, 1967
Juanita Hall (66)—February 28, 1968
John F. Hamilton (73)—July 11, 1967
George Hayes (78)—July 13, 1967
Al Herman (84)—July 2, 1967
Helen Oursler Hill—May 11, 1968
John F. Howes (54)—May 11, 1968
Benita Hume (60)—November 1, 1967
Herman Hyatt (62)—January 24, 1968
Herman Hyde (69)—August 3, 1967
John Irvine (55)—February 15, 1968
Thomas Jackson (81)—September 8, 1967
Katherine E. Kay (Mrs. Jack E. Leonard) (44)—November 21, 1957
Eva Kirkwood-Hackett (91)—February 8, 1968
Lee Krieger (48)—December 22, 1967
Bert Lahr (72)—December 3, 1967
Jewel LaKota (60)—May 10, 1968
Vivien Leigh (53)—July 8, 1967
Miguel Ligero (71)—February 20, 1968
Olga Lindo (69)—May 7, 1968
Doris Lloyd—May 21, 1968
Marion Lorne (82)—May 9, 1968
Joseph MacCaulay (76)—October 6, 1967
Gertrude MacFadden (67)—June 3, 1967
Bruce MacFarlane (62)—November 25, 1967
Norman MacKaye (62)—April 24, 1968
Douglas Maclean (77)—July 9, 1967
Nathaniel J. Madison (72)—January 29, 1968
Jayne Mansfield (34)—June 29, 1967
Theodore Marcuse (47)—November 29, 1967
Mae Marsh (72)—February 13, 1968
Boris Marshalov (65)—October 16, 1967
Viola Martinelli—August 23, 1967
Virginia Maskell (31)—January 25, 1968

Owen McGiveney (83)—July 31, 1967
Frank Merlin (76)—March 1, 1968
Jackie Miles (54)—April 24, 1968
Lorena A. Adee Morris (83)—July 19, 1967
Doretta Morrow (41)—February 28, 1968
Maitland Moss (66)—August 19, 1967
Walter C. Moulder (34)—July 1, 1967
Paul Muni (71)—August 25, 1967
Gladys Murray (65)—July 14, 1967
Bobby Naidoo (40)—July 6, 1967
Tommy Noonan (46)—April 24, 1968
Mary O'Farrell (75)—February 10, 1968
Derek Oldham (75)—March 20, 1968
Nat Pendleton (72)—October 12, 1967
Howard A. Petrie (61)—March 26, 1968
Addison Pitt (91)—January 22, 1968
Lewis Prentiss (62)—June 26, 1967
Cameron Prud'homme (75)—November 27, 1967
Basil Rathbone (75)—July 21, 1967
Anna Ratner (75)—July 2, 1967
Cora Redd (about 70)—March 21, 1968
Florence Reed (84)—November 21, 1967
Bill Rhodes (72)—July 24, 1967
Don Richard (22)—December 25, 1967
John Ridgely (59)—January 18, 1968
Cyril Ring (74)—July 17, 1967
Diana Rodrigues (25)—February 17, 1968
Marion Castleray Savery (62)—July 22, 1967
Vivian Curtis Schubert (75)—June 26, 1967
Montague Shaw (85)—February 6, 1968
Henry Sherwood (83)—June 8, 1967
Otto Simanek (66)—October 15, 1967
Howard I. Smith (73)—January 10, 1968
Elza K. Splane (63)—February 16, 1968
Jack Stanford (67)—April 29, 1968
Basil Sydney (73)—January 10, 1968
Susan Conroy Torrey (61)—April 15, 1968
Spencer Tracy (67)—June 10, 1967
William Tracy (48)—June 18, 1967
Gus Van (80)—March 13, 1968
Harry Vejar (78)—March 1, 1968
Anton Walbrook (66)—August 9, 1967
Patricia Wheeler Walters—December 31, 1967
Elizabeth Watts (79)—July 27, 1967
Billy Wehle (73)—March 6, 1968
Bert Wheeler (73)—January 18, 1968
Olive Willey (80)—March 24, 1968
Annabelle Rucker Williams (63)—December 26, 1967
Molly Williams—October 20, 1967
Barbara Winchester (70s)—April 20, 1968
Donald Wolfit (65)—February 17, 1968
Amanda Wright (78)—March 17, 1968

PLAYWRIGHTS

Marcel Ayme (65)—October 14, 1967
Margaret A. Barnes (81)—October 25, 1967
Jonathan Bates (42)—July 27, 1967
Harvey Breit (58)—April 9, 1968
George E. Brewer Jr.—February 20, 1968
Mercedes de Acosta (75)—May 9, 1968
Charles Stafford Dickens (71)—October 12, 1967
Ross Evans (51)—August 21, 1967
Edna Ferber (80)—April 16, 1968
Francis Field (59)—November 9, 1967
Edith Fitzgerald (75)—February 4, 1968
Martin Flavin (84)—December 27, 1967
Lili Hatvany (77)—November 12, 1967
Vyvyan Holland (80)—October 10, 1967
Kenneth Hume (41)—June 25, 1967
Peter Jerome (74)—July 9, 1967
Patrick Kavanagh (62)—November 30, 1967
Margaret Kennedy (70s)—July 31, 1967
Joseph Kesselring (65)—November 5, 1967
Harry Kurnitz—March 18, 1968
Reginald Lawrence (67)—November 20, 1967
David Liebovitz (76)—February 4, 1968
Howard Lindsay (76)—February 11, 1968
Joan Lowell (67)—November 7, 1967 (Helen Trask)
Donagh MacDonagh (55)—January 1, 1968
Carson McCullers (50)—September 29, 1967
Frank Merlin—March 1, 1968
George Middleton (87)—December 23, 1967
John Moore (50)—July 30, 1967
George Munro (66)—April 15, 1968
Edwin O'Connor—March 23, 1968
Joe Orton (34)—August 9, 1967
Dorothy Parker (73)—June 7, 1967
Edward Percy (77)—May 28, 1968
Raoul Praxy (75)—July 28, 1967
Kenneth S. Reddin (72)—August 19, 1967
Maurice Rostand (76)—February 21, 1968
Robert St. Clair (57)—June 17, 1967
Paul Gerard Smith (73)—April 4, 1968
Laurence Stallings (73)—February 28, 1968
Justin Sturm (68)—August 6, 1967
Randall Swingler (58)—June 19, 1967
Iris Tree—April 13, 1968

COMPOSERS AND LYRICISTS

Irving Actman (60)—September 24, 1967
Burke Bivens (64)—November 6, 1967
George Bowles (78)—March 29, 1968
Monte Carlo (83)—June 9, 1967
James Cavanaugh (75)—August 19, 1967
Norman Demuth (69)—April 21, 1968
Richard F. Fenno (40)—July 2, 1967
Woody Guthrie (55)—October 2, 1967
Lawrence William Hansen—March 23, 1968
Harold A. Levey (73)—June 18, 1967
George F. Marion Jr. (68)—February 25, 1968
Bernard Rogers (75)—May 24, 1968
Charles Sansone (63)—January 17, 1968
Serge Saxe (67)—July 12, 1967
Harry Seymour (77)—November 11, 1967
Beasley Smith (67)—May 14, 1968
George Steiner (67)—June 21, 1967
Walter C. Stockhoff (91)—April 2, 1968
Healey Willan (87)—February 16, 1968

PRODUCERS, DIRECTORS AND CHOREOGRAPHERS

Reginald Burston—April 22, 1968
William Cox-Ife—March 24, 1968
Edward Duryea Dowling (63)—December 18, 1967
Eugene Endrey (76)—June 26, 1967
William B. Friedlander (83)—January 1, 1968
Henry W. Gerber (85)—November 12, 1967
Will J. Harris (73)—December 14, 1967
Charles Henry (77)—February 28, 1968
John Holden—July 11, 1967
Stella Holt (50)—August 28, 1967
Andree Howard (57)—April 18, 1968
Harold Huth (75)—October 26, 1967
Claud Jenkins (88)—December 12, 1967
Stephen Joseph (46)—October 5, 1967
Sammy Lee (78)—March 30, 1968
Sidney Potts (62)—March 13, 1968
Albertina Rasch (76)—October 2, 1967
Fred Seymour (68)—April 3, 1968
Henry Sherek (67)—September 23, 1967
Jay Stanwyck (58)—September 16, 1967
Buddy Thomas (55)—August 3, 1967

CONDUCTORS

Arturo Basile (54)—May 21, 1968
Walter Fleischer (85)—March 27, 1968
Henry W. Gerber (85)—November 12, 1967
Garry C. Joachim (70)—April 8, 1968
Franco Patane (60)—May 13, 1968
Henry Russell (54)—April 14, 1968

DESIGNERS

Albert C. Hamilton (57)—January 25, 1968
Albert Johnson (57)—December 21, 1967
Ernie Nordli (55)—April 20, 1968
Ruth Sobotka (42)—June 17, 1967

CRITICS

Howard Barnes (64)—March 12, 1968
Alton F. Cook (62)—August 15, 1967
David Jay Culver (65)—March 22, 1968
George Freedley (63)—September 11, 1967
Patterson Greene (69)—January 27, 1968
John G. Keating (50)—January 29, 1968
Virgil Miers (42)—November 28, 1967
Allan Morrison (51)—May 22, 1968
Lee Patterson (49)—July 24, 1967
Sidney B. Pfeifer (73)—June 5, 1967
Sam Shaw (50)—May 12, 1968
Warner Twyford (57)—April 17, 1968

OTHERS

Morton Baum (62)—February 7, 1968
Attorney for N. Y. City Center
Dave Beehler (87)—February 18, 1968
Vaudeville franchise agent, theater operator
Joseph H. Belford (70)—January 12, 1968
Managing director of Roseland Ballroom
Herbert L. Berger—April 21, 1968
Managing director of School of Performing Arts at International University, San Diego
Hal Bongard (61)—September 13, 1967
Executive of American Guild of Variety Artists
George W. Brayfield—February 17, 1968
Secretary-treasurer of IATSE District 5
Captain Billy Bryant (79)—January 26, 1968
Last master of showboats up and down Mississippi and Ohio Rivers
David L. Cantor (68)—April 7, 1968
Publicist
Maud Carpenter—June 16, 1967
50 years with Liverpool Playhouse Repertory
Max Cohen—January 6, 1968
N.Y. theater manager
Edward Ray Downes (63)—March 13, 1968
Stage manager
Leo William Fitzgerald (78)—February 14, 1968
Vaudeville and legitimate agent
Melvin J. Fox (53)—April 1, 1968
Theater owner
Zac Freedman (61)—April 25, 1968
Publicist
Isabel Costa Gallagher—June 23, 1967
Executive secretary, ASCAP membership committee
Martin Goldblatt (43)—April 1, 1968
Publicist
William Goldhardt (72)—August 15, 1967
Treasurer of Shubert Theater
Lawrence William Hansen—March 23, 1968
Music publisher
Ben Irving (48)—February 7, 1968
Assistant executive secretary, Actors Equity
William K. Jenkins (77)—January 21, 1968
Pioneer theater executive
E. H. Johnson (62)—March 10, 1968
Treasurer, Radio City Music Hall
Cloris W. Leachman (66)—December 8, 1967
Pioneer in little theater
Cal Lowell (45)—October 24, 1967
Stage manager
Fred Lynch (59)—January 10, 1968
Publicist, Radio City Music Hall
Maybelle Manning (74)—January 1, 1968
Costumer
Stanley McCandless (70)—August 4, 1967
Lighting expert
Max Michaels (70)—January 11, 1968
Manager of Wilbur Theater, Boston
Lillian Moore (55)—July 28, 1967
Dance historian and teacher
David T. Nederlander (81)—October 14, 1967
President, Nederlander Theatrical Corp.
Joseph J. Newman (80)—November 21, 1967
N.Y. ticket broker

James F. Reilly (80)—August 4, 1967
Former executive director, League of N.Y. Theaters

George Ronkin (59)—November 28, 1967
Operator of George M. Cohan Music Corp.

Dick Ruedebusch (42)—May 5, 1968
Milwaukee jazzman

Sam Saltzman (80)—March 21, 1968
Founder of Masque Sound & Recording Co.

Jules Saranoff (80)—November 25, 1967
Oldest member of Friars

Arthur Scott (66)—April 16, 1968
General secretary, Variety Artists' Benevolent Fund

Edward Serlin (56)—February 6, 1968
Publicist, Radio City Music Hall

May Davenport Seymour (83)—October 5, 1967
Founder of theater and music collection, Museum of City of N.Y.

Arthur R. Singer (66)—September 5, 1967
Manager of Lyceum and Ambassador Theaters

Winifred Smith (88)—October 28, 1967
Founder of Vassar College drama dept.

Sam Stratton (80)—December 29, 1967
Publicist for Ringling Bros.

Les Thomas (71)—June 23, 1967
Business manager

Eugene A. Walton (76)—November 2, 1967
Theatrical hauler

David Barry Whalen (58)—August 20, 1967
Publicist

Winfield H. White Jr.—January 29, 1968
Business agent of IATSE

Douglass Whitehead (93)—April 9, 1968
Drama instructor

INDEX

Bold face page numbers refer to pages where Cast of Characters may be found.